SCHLESINGER

SCHLESINGER
THE IMPERIAL HISTORIAN

RICHARD ALDOUS

W. W. NORTON & COMPANY
Independent Publishers Since 1923
NEW YORK | LONDON

For information about permission to reproduce selections from this book,
write to Permissions, W. W. Norton & Company, Inc., 500 Fifth Avenue,
New York, NY 10110

For information about special discounts for bulk purchases, please contact
W. W. Norton Special Sales at specialsales@wwnorton.com or 800-233-4830

Manufacturing by Quad Graphics Fairfield
Book design by Fearn Cutler de Vicq
Production manager: Julia Druskin

Library of Congress Cataloging-in-Publication Data

Names: Aldous, Richard, author.
Title: Schlesinger : the imperial historian / Richard Aldous.
Description: First edition. | New York : W.W. NORTON & COMPANY, 2017. |
Includes bibliographical references and index.
Identifiers: LCCN 2017019909 | ISBN 9780393244700 (hardcover)
Subjects: LCSH: Schlesinger, Arthur M., Jr. (Arthur Meier), 1917-2007. |
Historians—United States—Biography.
Classification: LCC E175.5.S38 A43 2017 | DDC 973.07202 [B]—dc23
LC record available at https://lccn.loc.gov/2017019909

W. W. Norton & Company, Inc., 500 Fifth Avenue, New York, N.Y. 10110
www.wwnorton.com
W. W. Norton & Company Ltd., 15 Carlisle Street, London W1D 3BS

1 2 3 4 5 6 7 8 9 0

For Elizabeth

Contents

Schlesinger

WHERE HE WAS

W*hite House. Friday, November 22, 1963.* "What kind of a country is this?" Schlesinger demanded as he burst into the West Wing.

With the president away in Dallas, he had been in the New York offices of *Newsweek* with its proprietor Katharine Graham, who also happened to own the *Washington Post*. While they were drinking prelunch martinis, a staffer entered the room nervously, the urgency of the moment signaled by the fact that he approached Graham in just his shirtsleeves.

"I think you should know," he reported, "that the president has been shot in the head in Texas."

Schlesinger immediately bolted for Washington, returning first to the White House and then heading out to Andrews Field to meet the plane returning with Kennedy's remains. "Everyone is stunned," he recorded. "I still cannot believe that this splendid man, this man of such intelligence and gaiety and strength, is dead. The wages of hate are fearful."

While the body was taken to Bethesda Naval Hospital for an autopsy, Schlesinger busied himself with practicalities, "trying to fight off the appalling reality." Jacqueline Kennedy wanted her husband's lying in state in the East Room to look like President Lincoln's. Schlesinger phoned the Library of Congress, telling Lincoln scholar Roy Basler to get details immediately. A sketch was found in *Harper's* showing Lincoln's catafalque. Bill Walton, the artist and Kennedy confidant, took charge, but Schlesinger did his bit, tacking black crepe to the mantels, all the while stopping to write notes and observations on his index cards.

The coffin arrived at the White House just after four in the morning of November 23. When the family withdrew from the East Room, Kennedy's brother Bobby pulled Schlesinger aside. Would he and the White House social secretary, Nancy Tuckerman, look at the body to see whether the casket should be closed?

"And so I went in, with the candles fitfully burning, three priests on their knees praying in the background," Schlesinger recorded, "and took a last look at my beloved president." For a moment, he was "shattered." Then reality took hold. Everything was "too waxen, too made up." The body "did not look like him." Perhaps it never could have "with half his head blasted away."

Schlesinger returned to the waiting Bobby. "It's appalling," he reported. Others went in to look. When Robert McNamara, secretary of defense, gently protested that it was inappropriate for the coffin of a head of state to be closed, Schlesinger intervened, assuring them that a strong precedent existed. FDR's coffin had not been open, he advised. Robert Kennedy considered for a moment and then said, "Close it."

As the Kennedys retired to the family quarters, White House staff began to drift away for a few hours' rest. Schlesinger offered to drive McNamara home. In the corridor on his way out, he saw his friend Dick Goodwin and invited him back to Georgetown for a drink. They drove in separate cars, and by the time Goodwin arrived his friend was already home. He was shown up to the study, where he discovered Schlesinger primed and in a familiar pose.

"He was seated in front of his typewriter," Goodwin vividly remembered.

It was a first principle for Arthur Schlesinger: he was always ready to write. His entire life had prepared him for this moment. Harvard historian, Pulitzer Prize–winning author, presidential speechwriter, with millions of words already published: Schlesinger was going to write the story of John F. Kennedy for posterity. In the process, he would use the gifts of perhaps the most famous historian of his time to honor Kennedy's legacy. But this choice would raise as many questions as it answered. Was he a great and important historian, a model of how academics and public service can mix? Or was he a popularizer and court historian held captive to the Establishment that nurtured his career? Among his contemporaries—historians like Richard Hofstadter and Edmund Morgan—most hewed closely to their craft. Schlesinger in contrast chose to make history as well as recording it. He was never quite sure whether his loyalties lay mostly with his profession or with the people whose lives he chronicled. He knew that "to act" was "to give hostages—to parties, to policies, to persons." But Schlesinger's life and work would put a simple idea to the test: whether, in his own words in 1963, "to smell the dust and sweat of battle, is surely to stimulate and amplify the historical imagination."[1]

CHAPTER ONE

BECOMING
ARTHUR SCHLESINGER JR.

I n the mocking words of Vice President Lyndon Johnson, they were "the Harvards." That group comprised the dozens of Cambridge professors who occupied the White House in January 1961. Not without cause, wags began calling Harvard the fourth branch of government. And within that group, Arthur Schlesinger Jr. stood out. Journalists dubbed him Kennedy's in-house intellectual and "bridge to the intellectual community." Certainly Schlesinger, with his bow tie, "egghead" and two-generation faculty professorship, epitomized the Cambridge type. So it often came as a surprise to many that Schlesinger was not a New Englander at all but was in fact a midwesterner from Ohio. Even professional colleagues who came from the Midwest were taken by surprise. "In the conversations I had with Arthur, there was no mention of the Midwest," Walter LaFeber, the Cornell historian, recalls. "I always thought of him as an East Coast kind of person."[1]

If this New England intellectual was not, in fact, from New England, neither did he start life with the name that would eventually adorn his many books. For it was Arthur Bancroft Schlesinger, not Arthur Meier Schlesinger Jr., who was born at Grant Hospital in Columbus, Ohio, on October 15, 1917, at 1:55 in the morning. The baby's two given names balanced traditions from both parents. Arthur was his father's given name; Bancroft his mother's maiden name. Later on, the child would recalibrate that relationship by changing Bancroft to Meier, thus adopting his father's full name and adding "Junior," effectively exiling his mother from his public persona.*

Elizabeth Bancroft, like her son, had been born in Columbus, Ohio, in 1886. Her family did in fact have some New England connections, certainly enough for them to claim a relationship to George Bancroft, the famous nineteenth-century historian of Worcester, Massachusetts. Elizabeth's childhood was not a happy one. Her parents, unusually for the time, divorced when she was young, leaving the girl at the mercy of her imperious mother. "Grandmother Bancroft retained an awful desire to dominate my mother and a capacity to wound her," Arthur later recalled. "Telephone calls with her could reduce my emotional mother to tears."

At her best, Elizabeth was a free spirit and well read, with a creative, artistic sensibility. She often brimmed with fervor about ideas and the arts, and consciously sought to impart that same spirit in her son. To make the point to him, she gave Arthur a note written in her father's hand. "Enthusiasm is the genius of sincerity," read the quote from Samuel Taylor Coleridge, "and truth accomplishes no victory without it."

But on her bad days, of which there were many, Elizabeth could be unpredictable and overwrought. "His mother was kind of a pain in the neck," Marian Cannon, later Arthur's first wife, remembers. "But she was one of these people that was made to be a pain in the neck."[2]

Perhaps recognizing her own highly strung nature, Elizabeth sought out her temperamental opposite when it came to love. She met Arthur Meier Schlesinger in 1908 when both were studying at Ohio State University (OSU). Elizabeth had returned there after earning enough money to cover tuition by teaching for two years in a one-room country school. Two years older than Schlesinger, she was in many ways more sophisticated and progressive than he. In particular, she pushed him to reconsider his views about the role of women in politics, not least in having the vote. Schlesinger grudgingly conceded the point. "I don't object to you being a

*For clarity, Arthur Schlesinger (Sr.) is referred to in this childhood chapter as "Schlesinger" or colloquially as "Arthur Sr." Arthur Schlesinger Jr. is referred to as "Arthur"; contemporaries often referred to him as "Young Arthur" or, less kindly, "Little Arthur."

suffragette, as long as you aren't too militant," he told her. But he couldn't really see the sense of it all. "I don't anticipate any better political conditions from a feminine addition to the vote than we have under the present regime," he judged. "Obviously," Arthur, their son, wrote dryly years afterwards, "his consciousness needed raising."[3]

Yet Schlesinger's stodgy nature came with other advantages for Elizabeth, not least that he was a calm, stable figure. A second-generation immigrant, he combined an ability to stand up for himself with a certain knack for fitting in wherever he went. His father, Bernhard, had come from East Prussia, making the journey to the United States as a teenager in 1860. He made knapsacks for Union soldiers during the Civil War before moving out west to Xenia, Ohio. It was there he met Katharine Feurle, whose parents had immigrated in the 1850s from the Tyrol in Austria. The couple married in 1873. Because he was Jewish and she was Roman Catholic, they chose to get around any religious difficulty by emphasizing their shared Germanic heritage and marrying in the German Reformed Church.[4] How Bernhard felt about leaving the faith of his fathers is unknown. What is clear, however, is his sense of pride in the New World. He insisted that his children speak English at home and threw himself into civic life, serving for almost forty years on the local school board. When his son was bullied because his father was European-born, he advised, "You tell them your father came because he wanted to—because he thought the United States the best country on earth." It was a lesson his son never forgot: "Not a chosen people but what seemed better: a choosing people."[5]

Arthur Sr. also inherited something of his father's calm authority. Although the taciturn Bernhard spoke little, the entire household understood that when he resorted to the German instruction *"Genung!"* it really did mean enough. That sense of equilibrium appealed to Elizabeth. The college couple stayed together even when Schlesinger went off to Columbia University for graduate school. When Elizabeth's mother, who worked at the Pension Bureau, transferred to Washington, DC, taking her daughter with her, Arthur Schlesinger finally took the plunge. Elizabeth Bancroft and Arthur Schlesinger married in September 1914, settling in Columbus,

Ohio where Arthur took up an OSU instructorship in history, soon converted to an assistant professorship paying fifteen hundred dollars a year. "Now indeed we felt we were in clover," Schlesinger recorded happily.[6]

It did not last long. Exactly a year after the couple's wedding, Elizabeth gave birth to a daughter, Katharine Bancroft Schlesinger, who died just ten months later of intestinal complications. Arthur Schlesinger, not unusually for his generation, always found it next to impossible to speak of his grief. Even more than four decades later, when shown a letter of condolence from 1916, he "looked blank" before saying tersely, "I've driven all of that out of my mind." His son Arthur, however, would name his own daughter Katharine Bancroft Schlesinger in memory of the sister he never knew.[7]

Within a few months of the loss, Elizabeth was pregnant again. Schlesinger was concerned enough about her welfare, and perhaps his own, that with the United States having recently entered World War I, he requested in his draft registration in June 1917 an exemption from service on the grounds of "Wife support (pregnant)."

For whatever reason, Schlesinger was not called up, which meant he was in the city of Columbus on October 15 when Arthur Bancroft Schlesinger was born at Grant Hospital—an event, Schlesinger recalled, "made all the more welcome" after the "sadness [of] the loss of our first child."[8]

For nervous parents who had already lost a child in infancy, the first eighteen months of Arthur's life came at a worryingly dangerous time. As fall turned to winter, a global "Spanish" flu pandemic began that would last well into 1919. Mortality was so high that estimates of how many people died worldwide are anywhere between 30 and 50 million. In the United States, an estimated 675,000 died from the disease, and by September 1918, Ohio was in the throes of the epidemic. As Arthur celebrated his first birthday, the state reported 1,541 deaths per week. In Columbus itself, public schools and libraries closed down for ten weeks. Young adults were particularly at risk, so classes at the university where his father taught were temporarily suspended, as lecture halls became makeshift infirmary wards. Various ordinances and quarantines were put in place throughout the city, with stern warnings given about the vulnerability of infants. At least with the authorities extolling the benefits of fresh air, Elizabeth and Arthur Sr. were able to stroll together with their baby son in his pram in the one hundred acres of Franklin Park.[9]

Arthur survived the great flu pandemic. Examining him at the Schlesinger home, 398 W. 9th Avenue, on the edge of the OSU campus in 1918, the visiting Children's Bureau nurse had found him to be "healthy, strong and normal." By the time the boy turned four, the nurse was somewhat less enthusiastic that "Arthur is about 2 ½ lbs. heavier than the average child of his height." A school physical two years later also judged him "overweight," with the next year's report noting specifically that he was "6% overweight." Thus began a battle with his waistline that Arthur would fight for the rest of his life.[10]

By the time Arthur was piling on the pounds, his family had moved from Columbus, Ohio, to Iowa City, Iowa, more than five hundred miles away. In the spring of 1919, a dean from the University of Iowa had sought advice from George Wells Knight, Ohio State's imperious professor of American history, on the delicate question of finding a new head for Iowa's warring History Department. Knight suggested the diplomatic Schlesinger, who went to Iowa City to meet Walter A. Jessup, the school's charismatic president. Schlesinger had his doubts about moving so far away from home—not so much from Columbus, but from his home town of Xenia, where the family still spent most of their spare time. His reluctance turned out to be a good negotiating tactic. Jessup made him an offer not to be refused, including a pay raise of one thousand dollars per annum and the freedom to teach whatever courses and graduate students he liked. Although the Schlesingers were sorry to leave Ohio, they recognized "that this was the cost inherent in so nomadic a profession."[11]

Later on, young Arthur would have only the vaguest recollection of Iowa City, where he lived until the summer of 1924. Decades afterwards, finding himself at the Herbert Hoover Library in West Branch, Iowa, he drove over to nearby Iowa City for the first time since childhood. There were thoughts about Max, the family dog, "run over by a careless motorist," and the time Arthur, having bitten through his own tongue, "was rushed to the hospital where the tongue was efficiently sewn up with, I was told, kangaroo fiber." No wonder he always preferred Xenia.[12]

Arthur's parents enrolled him at a preschool on the University of Iowa campus, which, as it turned out, was at the center of one of the most important experiments in modern American education. The Iowa Child Welfare Research Station, established in 1917, argued that if you could have a research institute for agriculture, why not one for child welfare? The Station is usually cited as the first research institute in the world whose sole mission was to conduct original research on the development of "normal children." Most experts at the time believed that nature, not nurture, was the determining factor in the development of children. The Iowa scientists set out to determine whether early environment was as significant as hereditary factors in a child's IQ. Investigators habitually monitored pupils from an observation area behind a wire mesh. Tests were not just educational but also dietary and anthropometric. Whatever may be said about environment at a young age, the school's ties to a Christian temperance union did not seem to leave any lasting effect on the boy, who grew up to be a daily drinker. Nevertheless, Arthur was present for the invention of academic child development research. "I survived," he later wryly noted.[13]

While Arthur survived, his father was positively thriving. In the same month that his first son was born, October 1917, Schlesinger had finished his first book, *The Colonial Merchants and the American Revolution*, published the next year by Columbia University Press. He followed this up in 1922 with *New Viewpoints in American History*, published by Macmillan. Taken together, the two books established him as an important new voice in American history.

At Columbia, Schlesinger had come under the influence of two historians, both controversial in their different ways. Charles A. Beard had been the enfant terrible of the historical profession, having scandalized and exhilarated public and professional opinion alike with his best-selling *Economic Interpretation of the Constitution*. Beard argued that the Founding Fathers were driven more by economic self-interest than thoughts about "the people." Schlesinger admired the book and Beard's analytic approach. Beard in turn took an interest in the younger man, reading his draft chapters and even suggesting the title for *The Colonial Merchants and the American Revolution.* "Don't say a word in title or text about 'economic interpretation,'" he warned, "just gives the mob a chance to yell and kill you." When *The Colonial Merchants* appeared in print, Beard, in a generous bit of logrolling, called it "the most significant contribution that has ever been made to the history of the American Revolution."

Less famous, but just as influential on Schlesinger, was Columbia historian James Harvey Robinson. His lectures at the university, and his seminal book *The New History*, were formative in Schlesinger's thinking about the breadth of historical enquiry. Robinson argued that to write the "new history," practitioners had to draw widely on other disciplines such as sociology, anthropology, economics, and political science, and must use those "allies" to write about aspects of history that lay beyond the traditional political sphere. By the time Schlesinger went back to Ohio State in 1912, he was a convert. He introduced elements of the New History into his teaching, and once at Iowa, offered a new course in "The Social and Cultural History of the United States," often said to be the first of its kind in any university.

Schlesinger's second book, *New Viewpoints in American History*, put the New History into action. In a series of interpretative essays written for a broad audience, he ranged across American history, drawing particular attention to scholarship in social, cultural, intellectual, and particularly economic history that would not be well known outside the academy. His aim, he said, was "to bring together and summarize, in non-technical language" the state of the discipline for the general reader and "to show [its] importance to a proper understanding of American history."

Almost seventy years later, on rereading *New Viewpoints*, Arthur would be struck by the extent to which his father in this book had shaped his own preoccupations as a historian. "I was surprised to find how much my father had anticipated my own historical excursions," he said in a lecture in 1988, "or, to put it more accurately, how much I unconsciously absorbed from his." Not the least of these direct influences was the essay "The Significance of Jacksonian Democracy," which emphasized the important East Coast influences on the frontier experience. Arthur would take up that idea in *The Age of Jackson*. Another gift he inherited was his father's polished literary style, which, said one reviewer of *New Viewpoints*, "flows easily, smoothly, with here and there a refreshing eddy of humor."

Schlesinger wrote *New Viewpoints* for a broad audience of interested readers, but it also made an impact in the profession. "This is no doctrinaire history," praised R. W. Kelsey in the *American Historical Review*. "He has come through the fires of economic determinism [i.e., Beard] with even temper. He can discern some good in both conservatives and radicals—and some bad. He seems to be progressive with one foot on the brake-pedal."[14]

Those qualities appealed to Samuel Eliot Morison, a rising star at Harvard who was a year older than Schlesinger. The two men could hardly have been more different in background. Morison was the personification of Boston Brahmin. He would spend most of his life in the gracious Brimmer Street house that his grandfather built on the "flat of Beacon Hill" and from where he would still ride on horseback to Harvard, the last faculty historian to do so. ("Ours was the horsey end of town," he wrote later.) After his death, he would be honored among the Boston great and the good with a statue on the Commonwealth Avenue Mall near Exeter Street.

Morison was known for a certain coldness of manner and asperity of tongue, once humiliating a colleague who dared visit his house one morning with the putdown, "Don't you know that a gentleman does not call on another gentleman before noon?" But Morison was also a disciplined and enterprising historian, as passionate about studying maritime history as sailing his own boats, and committed to the writing of history as a sacred trust which, in the famous dictum of Leopold von Ranke, required the past to be presented "as it actually was." He often complained that historians would produce better work if they were subject to an equivalent of the Hippocratic oath. And he was scathing about what he called the "chain reaction of dullness" in academic life: professors of "dull, solid, valuable monographs" who trained graduate students to write dull, solid monographs.[15]

Many years later, a friend sent Arthur a copy of his father's *New Viewpoints* picked up in a second-hand bookshop. Pasted inside was a bookplate with the image of a clipper sailing ship and the words "Ex Libris Samuel Eliot Morison." Annotations abounded throughout. Next to one passage on conservatives and radicals, where Schlesinger had written that "the two schools have more in common than either would admit," Morison had drawn a heavy black line in the margin and written "Très bien." It turned out to be the most important judgment of Schlesinger's career.[16]

Morison, as it happened, was to spend another year at Oxford, where he was the inaugural holder of the Harmsworth chair in American history. While he was away in England, Morison suggested, why not appoint Schlesinger as a visitor at Harvard for the academic year 1924–1925? Frederick Jackson Turner, the university's senior American historian (and, as author of the "frontier thesis" that the American West forged American democracy, its most famous), warmly supported the idea. Turner admired *The Colonial Merchants and the American Revolution*; perhaps as significantly, he was grateful to Schlesinger for having introduced him to Charles Beard at an American Historical Association conference. "When I myself advanced in the profession and was in turn sought out," Schlesinger would later write, "I discovered that the benefit did not lie only in the one direction, for acquaintance with younger men kept me informed of the interests of the oncoming generation." At this earlier stage in his career, however, it was the younger generation making the most of an eminent acquaintance. A certain entrepreneurial ruthlessness in the game of academic politics was another quality that Arthur would inherit from his quietly ambitious father. With Turner about to retire, it was clear to everyone that Arthur Schlesinger was being given a tryout.[17]

———

THE SCHLESINGERS LEFT for Harvard in the summer of 1924, just before Arthur turned seven. Surprisingly, given that he had lived in Iowa City since the age of two, Arthur seemed to leave without so much as a backward glance. In part, he assumed he would be away only for the year; perhaps more importantly, it had always been Xenia, not Iowa City, that felt like the family's real home and where they celebrated important holidays. "What fun July 4 was for small boys seventy five years ago!" he later remembered happily.[18]

Those small boys now included Thomas Bancroft Schlesinger, a brother for Arthur born in 1922. The two would have a complicated relationship even in childhood, with the more fun-loving Tom often irritating his straitlaced older brother. "We were nearly five years apart in age," Arthur later wrote, "and no doubt, like too many older brothers, I had moments of exasperation."[19]

The Cambridge that the Schlesinger boys and their parents were moving to was twelve hundred miles and a whole world away from the midwestern one in which they had all grown up. On their leaving Iowa City, the local Lions Club had thrown a farewell lunch for Schlesinger, inviting locals to "come out and hear Art roar." The contrast with Cambridge was marked. Tales of the snobbishness at Harvard towards midwesterners had already reached Iowa City. Even the esteemed Turner was said to have been deeply unhappy at Harvard, where, according to reports Schlesinger heard, "his testy Yankee colleague" Edward Channing had "made life so miserable for this son of a newer and rawer part of the United States that he had ever since regretted leaving Wisconsin." Turner would later reassure Schlesinger this was not the case, but the new midwestern professor anticipated that he could "expect no different treatment."[20]

There was another reason besides class and region that may have left the senior Schlesinger nervous about the move. Harvard in the 1920s was in the middle of a nasty public row about anti-Semitism. In 1922 the college president, Abbott Lawrence Lowell, had expressed concern about the rise of Jewish enrolment since 1900 from 7 to 21.5 percent. The university announced it was looking into "limitation of enrolment." An uproar ensued. The New York Times ran the story on its front page. The Boston City Council passed a resolution condemning the university. A member of the Massachusetts Legislature moved to have Harvard investigated. Rather than retract, Lowell doubled down, suggesting that every college in America should take only "a limited proportion of Jews." This proposal drew a stinging rebuke from W. E. B. Du Bois, Harvard's first African American to be awarded a PhD, who condemned the "renewal of the Anglo-Saxon cult; the worship of the Nordic totem: the disenfranchisement of Negro, Jew, Irishman, Italian, Hungarian, Asiatic, South Sea islander—the world rule of Nordic white through brute force." As Alfred A Benesch, a Jewish alumnus of the college, wrote to Lowell in a letter published in the *New York Times*: "Carrying your suggestion to its logical conclusion would inevitably mean that a complete prohibition against Jewish students in the colleges would solve the problem of anti-Semitism." By 1928 the share of Jewish freshmen at Harvard would drop to 16 percent, a result of Lowell's vile restriction on "men who do not mingle indistinguishably with the general stream."[21]

Whether Professor Schlesinger would "mingle indistinguishably" as a faculty member at Harvard was an open question. Institutional anti-Semitism was swirling around the university throughout the 1920s and 1930s for faculty as well as students. "Eyebrows went up," for example, when the Economics Department wanted to appoint the Jewish labor economist Leo Wolman; an offer was eventually made, but Wolman decided against taking the position. Similarly, Paul Samuelson, elected to Harvard's distinguished Society of Fellows, was barred from teaching Economics I, the major course for undergraduates, and sent instead to teach "Jewish courses" in statistics and accounting. He eventually left for MIT, where he wrote the book, *Foundations of Economic Analysis*, that marked out a mathematical revolution in the discipline.[22]

The Schlesingers had a loose association with the Unitarian Church. On arriving at Cambridge, Elizabeth would briefly teach at the local Unitarian Sunday school, but the family stopped going "after a fair trial" following protests from Arthur Jr., who by high school had ceased to believe in God. But Schlesinger Sr. was culturally Jewish on his father's side and would have been perceived as such by contemporaries. His approach to the issue, one that was later followed by his son, was simply to ignore the matter. In his memoirs, Lowell's intervention merits just one sentence: "As a Boston Brahmin he had, shortly before my going to Harvard, vainly sought to induce the faculty to restrict the admission of Jewish students." The linking of "Boston Brahmin" with reflexive anti-Semitism is itself revealing, but whatever hostility or resentment lay beneath the surface, it remained unspoken.[23]

In Arthur Jr.'s memoirs, the question of his Jewish heritage would only come up in the context of Bernhard Schlesinger's changing religion when he married Katharine Feurle. Many years later, in an undated letter probably from the 1950s, Arthur would vigorously reject any suggestion that he was Jewish. When the *Jewish Daily Forward* newspaper wrote asking to include him in a series about leading Jewish figures, Arthur wrongly asserted that his "paternal grandfather, when he came to this country in the 1850s, was a Lutheran," and went on to outline the family's Congregationalist and Unitarian denominational affiliations. "This branch of the Schlesinger family has identified itself more or less unquestionably with the Protestant community over the last century or so," he informed the paper. Then came a revealing, slightly awkward coda: "I write this with some embarrassment, because the tragedy of recent years has given this kind of question an understandable tension, and no one likes to seem to be running out of a situation or seeming to be what they are not. I can only report the facts and feeling in my own case, which I can hardly alter." For all that the context and circumstances had been irrevocably changed by the Holocaust, this disposition was essentially one that Arthur had learned many years earlier watching his father navigate anti-Semitism at Harvard in the 1920s. Like Bernhard Schlesinger before them, Arthurs Sr. and Jr. both combined pragmatism, liberalism, and personal ambition. If getting ahead required some self-reinvention, so be it. But it would be Arthur Jr. who was left to answer the question of whether he cut the cloth of his liberal values to suit his ambitions.[24]

Schlesinger Sr. initially struggled socially in his new Cambridge environment. "It proved slower to form close personal ties at Harvard," he reflected, as "the professors guarded their privacy for research and writing." He would not be the first or last midwesterner to find the Northeast emotionally chilly in comparison to home; the later song from *Wonderful Town*—"Why, Oh why, Oh why, Oh, Why did I ever leave Ohio?" might almost have been written for him. Whether or not it was a coincidence, his first real friend on the faculty was Jewish—the law professor and later Supreme Court justice Felix Frankfurter. By skill or luck, he could not have made a better choice. Frankfurter, while not a practicing Jew, was unapologetic about his background. Before returning to Harvard as a faculty member after a brilliant undergraduate career, Frankfurter had taken a job at the waspy New York law firm of Hornblower, Byrne, Miller and Potter. "I'd heard they had never taken a Jew and wouldn't take a Jew," he would tell friends like Schlesinger, so "I decided that was the office I wanted to get into." Frankfurter's mother had told him early on to "Hold yourself dear!" That was a lesson that Schlesinger soon absorbed from his new friend.[25]

Whatever social difficulties Schlesinger may have encountered, academically he remained in high demand. "We were not put off by the subterfuge of a 'temporary appointment'" recalled Edward C. Kirkland, a graduate student who later taught at Bowdoin College. "We expected that the 'new boy' had been chosen to bring a message from the Olympus of Trans-Appalachia, whence Turner had come." However, in the fall of 1924, just a few weeks after his arrival, Schlesinger received a tenured job offer not from Harvard but from Columbia University, where he would replace James Harvey Robinson—the leading light of New History. The position seemed a perfect fit. Schlesinger had enjoyed his graduate studies, was honored as a disciple of Robinson to be asked to replace him, and, with *New Viewpoints*, had already made an outstanding contribution to the New History. As important, Columbia was offering him a generous salary of $6,000 a year. Running into a Harvard colleague, Frederick Merk, at a football game, Schlesinger, politically or not, shared the exciting news. Two days later President Lowell made him a matching offer at Harvard. Soon afterwards, President Jessup traveled in person from Iowa City to Cambridge to make him an even higher offer.[26]

The History Department at Harvard was on the cusp of becoming one of the strongest programs of study in the university and one of the best in the country, with new faculty appointments including Morison, Merk, William Langer, Crane Brinton, and Paul Buck (the latter also from Columbus, Ohio). But in 1924 Columbia had a reputation as an institution challenging disciplinary boundaries, including a dynamic history faculty; Young Turks Parker Moon and Carlton Hayes had arrived to replace luminaries such as Beard, Robinson, and E. R. A. Seligman.[27]

In 1910, as a graduate student, Schlesinger had picked Columbia over Harvard. Now in 1924 he went the other way. He sounded out Frederick Jackson Turner, who "flatly and convincingly denied" that he had regretted leaving the Midwest. As he was the father of young children, Cambridge seemed "a better place to raise a family" than Manhattan. Promises were made that he would have freedom to develop social and cultural history. ("Social history?" students complained. "The history of laundry slips and ticket stubs.") There was the pull of working in "a cradle of American liberty as well as of American literature." And perhaps somewhere in the back of Schlesinger's mind there lurked reservations about the shabby way that Columbia had treated his mentor, Charles Beard, who had resigned warning that the university's efforts to "humiliate or terrorize every man who held progressive, liberal, or controversial views" had made his continued presence "impossible." A progressive such as Schlesinger did not take those words lightly. Too ambitious to return to Iowa, in the end he picked Harvard over Columbia, a decision he never came to regret. Schlesinger would spend the rest of his career in Cambridge.[28]

The family had been living in an apartment on Hilliard Street, near Harvard Square. Now their possessions made the thousand-mile journey east to join them, where they furnished rented houses in Avon Street and at 32 Avon Hill Street (the latter where Arthur and Tom would sled perilously in winter, dicing with the steep incline and new-fangled automobile traffic). Elegant though these colonial style houses were, they were also cold and drafty. When the Schlesingers looked for a house to buy near the university, most within their price range were lacking anything much in the way of modern conveniences. "In one unforgettable case," Schlesinger recalled, "the daughter of a family having no electric lighting was engaged to a son of Thomas A. Edison, its famed inventor." These eccentric ways of the Cambridge upper-middle classes, who often turned their noses up at vulgar displays of wealth or even comfort, were not for the Schlesingers. Instead they purchased a lot on a new estate, Gray Gardens, near the Botanical Gardens—a twenty-minute walk across the Common to Schlesinger's office at Widener Library. The land cost $6,000—a year's salary.[29]

The colonial revival brick house the Schlesingers built for a cost of $20,000 at 19 Gray Gardens East would be the family home until shortly before Elizabeth's death in 1977. The estate, with its narrow streets and neat little gardens divided by privet hedges, lacked the grandeur of Brattle Street and traditional "Tory Row" Cambridge, but it compensated with the suburban charms of a warm, comfortable modern home in a friendly neighborhood with space in which Arthur and Tom could run and play. Christina Schlesinger, Arthur's daughter, later recalled that the garden in particular gave her grandparents real pleasure, not least "the tomatoes in the backyard that grandpa was so proud of." Still struggling to make close friendships at the university, the Schlesingers compensated by inviting students to the house every Sunday for tea—a tradition they maintained until Schlesinger's retirement in 1954. "When I became a professor myself," Arthur would note wearily, "I marveled at my parents' readiness thus to surrender every Sunday afternoon—I could never have done it."[30]

In his own memoirs, Arthur says not a single word about how he felt when his parents told him that the temporary move to Cambridge had now become permanent. "Liberal Boston and liberal Cambridge offered an environment into which my parents happily fitted and from which they drew continuing sustenance," he wrote of their decision to move east. It was a sentiment that would hold true for Arthur during most of his childhood and young adult life too. His earliest letters show a cheerful, opinionated boy with a sense of humor and, surprisingly, a love of sports. Aged seven, recently arrived in Cambridge, he set out his ambition for life, one shared with boys throughout the country. "When I am a man I wish to be a fast-ball player," he declared earnestly. "I would like to be a fastball player because I am interested in fast-ball, because it is a good sport and because it is fun." Besides Harvard football and baseball games, his father took him to Fenway Park to watch the Red Sox, the team still recovering from the loss of Babe Ruth to the Yankees. That interest would soon develop into a passion for keeping intricate books of statistics and listening to games on the radio with scorebook and pencil in hand.[31]

Attending games and talking about baseball was one of the ways that father and son began to develop their close relationship. Books were another. All the time, Arthur was reading, reading: *20,000 Leagues Under the Sea*, *Moby Dick*, *The Diaries of Adam and Eve*, and heroic tales about Sir Francis Drake defeating the Spanish Armada. In the division of labor in the Schlesinger house, each parent seems to have taken primary responsibility for one child, with Arthur going to his namesake. Perhaps that was because, in the older brother's words in 1926, "Tommy [was] a little bit to [*sic*] frisky. He has become the 'terror' of the house." When Elizabeth went back to Ohio for the summer that year, she took Tommy with her, while Arthur stayed behind with his father. The two ate out at the "Cheerful Chap" as much as they stayed at home. They took sightseeing trips and went out to the beach in the family's first car, not always with successful results. "In driving out past Revere Beach, all my precautions of giving Arthur a soda mint pill in advance and having him chew gum proved of no avail," Schlesinger wrote to Elizabeth of their queasy son. "Therefore we stopped along a street, and while a group of young fellows yelled 'Attaboy!' Arthur surrendered his dinner."[32]

Arthur seems to have been as happy outside the home as in it. Neighborhood boys came round to play to "Detectives and Smugglers." At the parties he attended he would win not just "the prize in hunting for peanuts" but was also "the fastest runner." When he went to summer camp in 1927, the camp director recorded that "Arthur is proving to be a good camper and his counselor reports him as a real boy. He is entering into things here with a very fine spirit." In fact, his all-round good spirits and cheerfulness gave his father at least momentary pause that perhaps Arthur was not quite serious enough. While Arthur wrote a letter to his mother excitedly telling her about taking his father to see his "ten things hanging up" at the school Exhibition Day, Schlesinger added his own rather less enthusiastic account. "Arthur took me on a tour of all the rooms," he reported, adding wryly that "In going through his grade I was humiliated to see on the board the caption 'History' and under it the names of Albert Maguire [one of the "detectives and smugglers"] and Arthur in that order. I haven't dared to ask my son about it!"[33]

The Schlesingers had sent Arthur "as a matter of course" to the local public elementary school, Peabody, just five minutes' walk around the corner from Gray Gardens East on Linnaean Street. "To Middle Westerners popular education was an article of faith," Schlesinger wrote, "a necessary training ground in democratic ideas and associations." But Schlesinger still wanted his son to get ahead, and that meant pushing him hard. And then pushing him harder. Arthur skipped second grade, and then fourth grade, leaving Peabody in 1929 at age 11 instead of 13.[34]

Before he started at his new school, Arthur's mother took him on his first trip to New York and Washington, DC (while her husband, with Harvard commitments, stayed home with Tom). Arthur's excitement as they set sail for New York from Boston's India Wharf, traveling down the Cape Cod canal, was palpable. "SO FAR, SO GOOD," he wrote excitedly in his diary, "Tomorrow New York!!!!!" There is a certain poignancy to him recording that "We walked up Wall Street," with the cataclysm of the 1929 crash just months away. The highlight in New York was going to the top of the Woolworth Building, Cass Gilbert's "Cathedral of Commerce" on Broadway, which at 792 feet and 1 inch was the tallest building in the world. "The only thing I am regretting," Elizabeth wrote home, "is that you are not here to enjoy the revelation and appreciation of Arthur. He really is a joy and as he confided to me on the elevator in the Woolworth Building, 'This is one of the things I've dreamed about doing.'" Around Washington, there were traditional tourist visits to Mt. Vernon, the Lincoln Memorial, and the Washington Monument. Perhaps most telling of all, Arthur made his first visit to the White House, where, he proudly reported, "I met Dr. Joel Boone, Hoover's physician" (and a war hero to boot). Even at eleven, Arthur had a knack for meeting important people.[35]

In the fall of 1929 Arthur started at the Cambridge High and Latin School on Broadway and Trowbridge Street. Although the two children did not know each other there, Arthur's future wife, Marian Cannon, who attended the same institution, left a vivid picture. "It was a true melting pot of a school in those days," she recalls; "from East Cambridge came first-generation Italian and Portuguese and Greek kids; there were bright Jewish boys and girls with heavy Yiddish accents, 'lace curtain' Irish from North Cambridge [where the Schlesingers lived] and Cambridge-port, a few blacks, and the sons and daughters of Protestant yankees." Both Arthur and Marian were "part of a small contingent of academic off-spring, most of our contemporaries having been hustled off to the 'safety' of private day or boarding schools." All told, Cannon recollects, "it was a jolly mix. . . . We were all outsiders thrown together higgledy-piggledy and the rich melange of personality and cultures was an education in itself."[36]

For Arthur that education was a difficult one. In the intelligence tests he took before entering the school, he demonstrated an IQ of 151 and the mental age of eighteen years and one month. The headmaster, L. L. Cleve-land, reported that only one child scored higher "by the narrow margin of a single point." Yet in terms of maturity Arthur was far from eighteen. Plunged into the "higgledy-piggledy" world of the High and Latin, he struggled both personally and academically. At the end of the first term, Cleveland wrote to Schlesinger to tell him that Arthur, while "pretty good" considering that other boys in the class were older, was in fact failing.[37]

Arthur's parents may have had sound reasons for accelerating his progress through the grades, but once he got to the High and Latin that decision began to take its toll. From being a sociable, sporty, outgoing boy in first grade at elementary school, Arthur had been transformed into the class "runt," too small to excel in sports and too emotionally immature to be an equal among his cohort. He was already physically short for his age and, to make matters worse for him, he now wore glasses for myopia and astigmatism. "I was a 'four-eyes' in the school slang of the period," he recalled. In those more rarefied school environments attended by many fashionable Harvard faculty children, such as Shady Hill or Boston Latin, this may not have mattered. In the rough and tumble world of the High and Latin, it made him inward-looking and, in the words of a camp coun-selor at the end of his first year, "a little highly strung." Acceleration had transformed Arthur into a nerd. That could mean "taunts, threats, occa-sionally being surrounded or chased, once or twice even hit." He found it difficult to make friends and fit in. "It is always a problem to get adjusted to new conditions, to learn new ways and make new friends," his father advised him that summer. "You are going through that process now. It is an important part of life, and you will have to do it over and over again in the future."[38]

Schlesinger concluded his letter to Arthur with the rallying cry, "*I am betting on you.*" In truth, he was not. It's easy to imagine the anxiety Arthur's emotional disintegration caused in the Schlesinger household. But what to do? Public education was, after all, an "article of faith, a necessary training ground" for these midwestern parents. To a large degree they had brought the problem on themselves by accelerating his progress through the system. The High and Latin was a first-rate public school that produced alumni around this time such as the poet E. E. Cummings, the Marxist historian and mathematician D. D. Kosambi, and sculptor Korczak Ziolkowski. Later its successor school, Cambridge Rindge and Latin School, would find Hollywood celebrity status as the alma mater of Ben Affleck and Matt Damon. Yet in 1929 it was a very big school for such a little boy, a place, Cannon wrote, that was "challenging and exhilarating" but where "it was easy" to get lost in "the crowd."

After two unhappy years, the Schlesingers made the decision to pull him out. Family legend would say that the turning point came when Arthur, taught by blockheads, returned home saying the inhabitants of Albania were albinos. In reality, the Schlesingers surely concocted the story to help cover their embarrassment over the abandonment of their principles. They had raised a bright but precious child too young to be in the environment in which he found himself. Phillips Exeter Academy, where Schlesinger knew one of the senior masters, Corning Benton, might provide a more sheltered setting. The school had recently been given a hefty endowment by the oil magnate Edward Harkness to encourage a Socratic seminar style of teaching. Schlesinger hoped it might provide a climate in which his son would flourish rather than getting lost in the crowd. "This sacrifice of principle did not come easily," he wrote, "but appeared unavoidable if [Arthur was] to have proper intellectual advantages." And, as the pragmatic and ambitious Schlesinger Sr. knew, the switch put his son into an elite WASP environment that took him one further step away from his Jewish background.[39]

For Arthur the social problems created by acceleration were not easily overcome. In September 1931 he made the journey forty miles north to Exeter, New Hampshire, to start life as a boarder. "I cannot truthfully say that my two years at Exeter were the happiest of my life," he admitted later. The essential problem was his now perennial one. "I was two years younger than the rest of my class," he noted in a sad self-portrait, "shy, stammering, bespectacled and with a case of acne that . . . was demoralizing, especially when I was in the company of girls." Letters home to his parents show him to be lonely, overworked, and often ill. "Of course it's silly that I should send you a postcard each day," he told his mother. To his father, he reported that "I have to wear my glasses all the time now for when I take them off my eyes are awfully strained. I don't know whether it's because I don't get enough sleep. . . . You can see from this that I feel rotten." Even the food was terrible. "In getting over 100 in the infirmary," he reported home, "we beat the record set . . . a couple of weeks ago when they served putrefied chicken and got 71 with ptomaine poisoning." No wonder he would later conclude, "adolescence is an unhappy time."[40]

Sending Arthur to boarding school had been hard enough for his parents. "We said goodbyes," his mother wrote after dropping him off, "and you walked to the window . . . never turning and we drove silently away. It was a wrench for the three of us." Yet they must have despaired on realizing that their son had failed to make a fresh start at his new school, especially when his initial grades were poor. "I just learned my marks," Arthur told them mournfully. "They are awful. I am sure I will do better next term. I will not tell you them as you will hear them too soon." His parents must have tried to relieve the pressure somewhat, as in reply Arthur confirmed that "Yes, it said in the *Exonian* [school paper] that marks are usually very poor in the first month."[41]

The fact that he was much less wealthy than his classmates did not help. That detail affected not just his social standing but also everyday decisions. "I'd like to go out for football," he complained to his parents, "but you have to buy shoes, football uniform, etc, so I think I shall go out for track, probably the cheapest sport." He asked them to send his sweat-shirt from home and to buy him a pair of running shoes. "I shall need more money, too," he pleaded. The contrast to Adolph Coors III, classmate and heir to the Coors beer empire, was stark.[42]

There was no doubt that Arthur in the 1931–1932 academic year was at a personal crossroads. It is easy to see how, being unhappy, strapped for cash, and struggling academically, he might have slipped through the cracks. That he did not is a testament to his own determination to make the most of himself. It was not that he suddenly changed personal-ity, becoming the school wit, jock, or lothario; his social pleasures were restricted to reading the newspaper in the library, listening to baseball, and, in what would become an enduring enthusiasm, watching movies. No, it was that Arthur Schlesinger, looking around for something at which to excel, turned to the closest example on offer to him and decided that academic study was his only viable option. It was an obvious and entirely logical choice. He loved and admired his father. Schlesinger was proof that you didn't need to be physically intimidating or have a loud, showy personality in order to succeed. From modest beginnings, Schlesinger had become a distinguished professor at the most famous university in the United States. That was the model to which Arthur now fully subscribed, increasingly from this time onwards identifying himself to the world as Professor Arthur Schlesinger's son.

Sitting at his desk, Arthur wrote out in his own hand and kept "How to be a student," by John Brewer, director of vocational guidance at Harvard, which included the following stern injunctions:

Learn to do well in each subject; develop pride in doing work in
   each subject.
Learn how to fit new ideas into other activities by applying what
   is learned into other activities at home, at play, in health,
   in religion.
Learn promptness, regularity, initiative, thoroughness, and other
   desirable qualities.
Learn to speak clearly and effectively before class.

Learn to work toward definite goals such as examinations, promotions and life work.

Secure the necessary preparation to handle wisely important decisions.

Learn to solve new and difficult problems: 1. First days in strange places. 2. Work under pressure of noise, headache, injustice or anger.

Learn to use important tools, typewriting, encyclopedias, abstracts, and briefs.

Learn to think of school as an opportunity for future advancement.[43]

Looking back, Arthur's discovery of Brewer's vocational guidance seems revelatory. This manual of self-instruction amounted to a commitment to a life of the mind, but it also applied to the world outside the classroom. Everything pointed towards the primacy of thought. From the material conditions in which it could be conducted, the emotional and physical distress that he would need to overcome, the process of writing and thinking itself, refining his ability to communicate ideas both orally and on the page, and perhaps most imaginatively of all, the conscious application of ideas into all realms of everyday life. In short, this was a blueprint for the self-invention of Arthur not just as an intellectual in the model of his father, but with a pathway for the action-intellectual to come.

In one way, Exeter helped Arthur in his progress. As his father had hoped, the new Harkness method of teaching through seminar discussion gave the boy room to develop both his ideas and his confidence. The Harkness money brought with it new masters and better facilities. "Most of the new classrooms are great with conference tables," Arthur reported enthusiastically to his parents. Now committed to his academic studies, Arthur's performance and grades began to improve dramatically. By the end of his second and final year at the school in 1933, he had caught up and overtaken the older boys. "Last Friday night was Prize Night," he wrote home in a letter to which his mother added, "This was your last letter from Exeter." Arthur proudly reported that he "won two prizes" in Latin, including one for "the exam on the political career of Cicero." To cap off a fine night, he had then watched "*Scarface*, a gang picture."[44]

The contrast with the timid boy who had entered the school in 1931 could hardly have been sharper. Writing a final reference, Exeter headmaster, Lewis Perry, found Arthur to be "a boy with a face illumined by intelligence and adolescent joys." Although he was only fifteen, "his scholastic standing has been very high, and throughout his two years of attendance steadily improving." He was a member of Cum Laude, "excels in everything," ranked in the top quarter of his class of 229 boys, and was particularly outstanding in Latin, history, and English. Perhaps most pertinently of all, Perry found him "earnest and devoted to his studies, with genuine intellectual interests going beyond the limits of the classroom." It had been a remarkable turnaround. Arthur Schlesinger at the age of fifteen had transformed into the person that he himself had found in "How to be a student." Arthur's reward for his hard work followed shortly afterwards. On July 17, 1933, his father received an informal note from the Harvard Entrance Board. "The young man has a handsome record," the letter said, "and I am glad to tell you that he will be sent a certificate of admission a little later in the week."[45]

Arthur's application to Harvard had, naturally enough, been an enthusiastic endorsement of the university's own sense of itself as more *primus* than *inter pares* among American colleges. "I think that I can get a better education at Harvard than elsewhere," he crooned. "The educational facilities at Harvard seem to surpass those of any other college, and I am sure that a Harvard education will help me whatever career I follow." In many ways, the choice had been an obvious one. Harvard was an excellent school. He already knew many of the faculty, staff, and students. After previous difficult experiences in unfamiliar and large environments, there would inevitably have been a risk in once again being among the youngest students in a new situation. Certainly Arthur's parents were acutely conscious of this latter point, which is why they encouraged him to take a year off before he enrolled at Harvard. Thus Arthur would join the class of 1938 rather than 1937. And yet it also says something about the boy at fifteen that he never seriously considered going anywhere else. For sure, legacy and connections, not meritocracy, remained the easiest way to get into Harvard and most other Ivy League universities in the early 1930s. (Henry Chauncey's reform of the Harvard entrance system arrived a few years later.) But Exeter gave Arthur an excellent reference. He scored A grades in his "college boards" (691 in the verbal section and 762 in the mathematical section). Unquestionably other prestigious institutions would have given him a look. Within the small world of the Ivy League and other similar colleges, the name of Harvard professor Arthur Schlesinger would surely have helped smooth the way, especially as Arthur Jr. planned to be a history major. So it tells us something important that he did not want to spread his wings. For Arthur was a homing bird, happy living in his father's intellectual coop.[46]

At Exeter two years earlier, Arthur had identified his father as his model to emulate in order to escape the misery of his adolescent life. In 1933 he took that emulation to the next level by literally becoming his father, or at least the junior version of him. Needing a passport for foreign travel, Arthur decided to petition to change his name from Arthur Bancroft Schlesinger to Arthur Meier Schlesinger Jr. That was a decisive realignment toward his father and away from his mother. In part it reflected the balance of power in the Schlesinger household. "Mrs. Schlesinger was a very intelligent woman," Marian Cannon recalls, "but she was always being put down by people in the family. I was really quite shocked by the way she was treated." But it was also a conscious embrace of being identified as his father's son. It would be easy to overanalyze a teenager's decision, yet this much is clear: aged fifteen, Arthur took two decisions—opting for Harvard and becoming "Junior"—that inevitably saw him cast as the sorcerer's apprentice. Doubtless he would have been known as "Young Arthur" or the more dismissive "Little Arthur" whether he was Arthur B. Schlesinger or Arthur M. Schlesinger Jr., but neither would have been as acute at another institution. He even enrolled in his own father's classes.

These decisions mark the beginning of a period when Arthur consciously set out to become a Harvard historian. He thus leveraged every advantage that his filial relationship could offer him. It was a bargain that Schlesinger Sr. happily entered into with his son. "His father directed him," says Cannon, who first got to know Arthur while he was at Harvard. Sometimes that direction would be taken to extraordinary lengths, confirming every prejudice about the advantages of the insider within a meritocratic system. For by the time Arthur left Exeter, both father and son seemed determined that the boy would be an academic star.[47]

Aware that Arthur needed more maturity and worldly experience, the Schlesingers decided to "redshirt" him by taking him on, literally, a "Cook's tour" of the world. Schlesinger had been invited to give a series of lectures at University College London and the University of Edinburgh in February and March the following year. As Arthur would later note, his parents had previously never left the United States, so it was "a triumphant burst of imagination [when] they decided to travel westward around the world to London, taking Tom and me with them." They would be away for a year, leaving on September 1, 1933, and returning on August 29, 1934. Throughout that time Arthur would keep a diary, so that as well as growing up before our eyes, he now began to develop the lapidary style that would eventually become his hallmark.[48]

Leaving Cambridge on the first morning of September 1933, Arthur was still quite obviously a boy, albeit a precocious one. As on those earlier car trips with his father, he still suffered from travel sickness, although these days he usually managed not to throw up. It is not difficult to imagine him in the railway carriage: blazer and gray flannels, bespectacled, the chin held slightly high to compensate for his lack of height, and with that slightly superior manner of one who, looking around, "found the people in our car were generally unexceptional." It was an attitude that would often get him into trouble during the trip. In Beijing for his birthday, he told a fellow hotel guest who had expressed wonder at the Forbidden City that he did not think much of the place. "She did not speak to me the rest of the time," Arthur recorded, "and made dirty remarks about brains, prodigies and normal children."

It was not just adults who often found his manner grating. After he won a dance with a girl on New Year's Eve on the way to Cairo, she afterwards "avoided me as if I had leprosy." For the adolescent Arthur, girls seemed "very strange," although with bravado he dismissed the whole affair as "merely entertainment." It was the one aspect of life that would not change much throughout the tour. Even by the following July, Arthur was bemoaning his luck. "The day before I left, I met a very pretty girl in the queue of the Gaiety Theatre," he complained. "Why did I not meet her a week or three days earlier? Such, I suppose is life . . ."[49]

Whatever his failures with the opposite sex, other worlds did open up to Arthur during his trip. He visited many of the ancient and modern wonders of the world, including the Great Wall of China and the pyramids of Egypt. As the tour went on, he began to develop his own tastes and, as his startled dinner companion in Beijing discovered, he was unafraid about expressing his own opinions, for example being unimpressed with the famous Taj Mahal. Above all, the vibrancy of Asian life was a revelation. "In Bangkok one realizes completely the color and luxury of the East, which the West cannot approach," he noted, adding his own little contribution to orientalism that "I suppose the Easterners are more naive and can thus let their imaginations and emotions run riot. The Westerners, more restrained, could never do anything like this." Even the terrain was a source of wonderment. "The jungle is remarkable to me," he wrote of French Indo-China, "chiefly because it does not look like a jungle." That was not the last time Arthur and his generation would be left baffled by the jungles of what became Vietnam.[50]

Other elements of the Far East Arthur found more disturbing. "No sane person should travel in China amidst the dirt and filth and human misery," he recorded. "The one thing to do is shut one's eyes toward the conditions of the poor Chinese, try to see the color and picturesqueness in the river life, the alley life and the mud hut life." Sometimes shutting one's eyes was impossible. On the journey to the Great Wall, his train was stopped when a man scrabbling for coal was struck and killed. Passengers took up a collection for the "screaming and sobbing" family, but "then came what was the most pitiful thing: an old hag who had made herself the boss of the affair pulled out the mourning daughters and made them bow to the passengers." It was, Arthur concluded, "too cruel." Later when he was on the wall he could reflect but that "an achievement like the Great Wall could only have been done at the sacrifice of thousands of human lives."[51]

On occasion Arthur found the poverty and desperation of the people a challenge to the progressive ideals that had been drummed into him from a young age. In Banaras, one of India's holiest cities, he found himself "rapidly being stripped of my racial tolerance." At home, he continued, "I never had any objection to negroes: up to India my objection, if any, was tempered with pity. Now in Banares even pity is gone. I felt no pity at all for the dead body at the Burning Ghat [Indian funeral pyre on the Ganges river]. When I see these crippled and deformed beggars approaching, I feel a great desire to kick them instead of pity." His father attempted to reassure him that "this feeling may be caused by the (even in the East) abnormal filth of Banares." Yet it was a deeply unsettling moment for a boy and his liberal sensibility. "I hope he is right," Arthur noted pensively, recognizing that sometimes he could be a jerk. "I do not like to feel this way."[52]

There were other concerns as well. Everywhere there were portents of war. Arthur saw "more soldiers in two weeks in Japan than I have seen in fifteen years in America." In China he "saw more soldiers in two days in China than in two days in Japan." When Schlesinger took his son along to meet an old classmate, the Chinese politician Y. C. Ma, he predicted a war "with Japan on one side and Russia, USA and possibly England on the other." Later, in Germany, the Schlesingers would have their first experience of Nazism, arriving in July two weeks after the infamous Night of the Long Knives. Although their experience was benign, the military undertones lurked. When in Munich, father and son passed a monument guarded by "heavily armed soldiers without raising our hands as, we observed later, everyone else, male and female, did. We were not beaten or clubbed into sensibility." Indeed by the end of his stay in Germany, Arthur concluded that his "illusions about the Hitler regime have been dispelled," not least in the way that ordinary Germans freely "spoke of Hitler with a lack of reverence which rather shocked me." Indeed his greatest surprise was the confounding of the idea that German women did not smoke. (The Nazi regime, including Hitler personally, was strongly anti-tobacco after German scientists linked smoking to cancer.) "In the restaurant where we had dinner," Arthur noted, "several girls smoked just as in any country." Under such laid-back circumstances, it would have seemed extraordinary to him that a decade later he would return to Germany as part of an American army of occupation.[53]

For all the drama and vividness Arthur experienced in Asia and continental Europe, nothing matched his excitement at visiting Britain. "I looked forward to seeing England more than any other country," he wrote after being driven through London for the first time, "since I have read and heard about it so much." Later, he would recall how "Conan Doyle had prepared me for London" with its pea-soup mists and fogs resulting from the burning of soft coal. But soon he was working his way through the works of Anthony Trollope and waxing lyrical about the "feeling of majesty and dignity which gets me" whenever he entered any of the great English cathedrals. It cemented a deep affinity with all things English that would last a lifetime.[54]

Arthur's round-the-world trip was a genuine voyage of discovery for him, but part of what made it important in his development was that he recorded the experience. Reading his diary now, we start to see many of his later traits as a writer emerging as he sets down the sights and sounds of his adventures abroad. He begins to reflect on political questions, asking in the manner of a fledgling op-ed columnist, for example, "Whither India?" and suggesting that "the only way India can ever be ruled" is by a strong hand. "Have the Indians, as a mass, gained anything from the West?" he wonders, before answering, "I think not." He also begins honing a skill for the telling anecdotes that would become a hallmark of his writing. So on the *Quai President Wilson* in Paris, at the home of the League of Nations, he notes that "in front is a statue to [Woodrow] Wilson; (in small letters) '*President de Etats-Unis*'; (in large letters) '*Fondateur de la Société des Nations*.'" Then he asks tartly, "Will posterity view matters in that proportion?" It is the perfect putdown to the self-important hollowness of that hapless organization.[55]

Writing the journal gave Arthur increasing confidence in expressing his own views, allowing him to test opinions and develop aphorisms ("A *pension* is a place with all the bad points and none of the good points of a hotel"). But it also provided him with a sense of the mechanics of writing that laid the groundwork for his later prodigious output. "I find the more I write the more freely I place my most inward thoughts in writing," he noted in January. "I always had a horror of doing so compromising a thing as putting thought which I desire no one else to know in writing; this horror is slowly vanishing." Whereas early in the trip it had taken "a great deal of mental sweating to immortalize my feelings," he now discovered that "sentences about them pop out unexpectedly."

This development had two complementary effects. First it began a commitment to writing a diary that would produce thousands of pages of entries, many of which were published after his death. Although those later diaries are less immediately personal than these childhood versions ("This shyness of mine is very foolish and damned uncomfortable"), they are nevertheless part of an important and continuing narrative as Arthur set down his thoughts on the world around him. And second, writing the diary was a further commitment to that life of the mind he had identified at Exeter in "How to be a student." For like a virtuoso who knows that it takes practice, not just talent, to play Carnegie Hall, so too Arthur seems to have realized, gently prodded by his father, that the best way to become a writer is to write. The growing fluency of style and the "slowly vanishing" barriers to setting down his thoughts that he developed now would turn out to be a major factor in his success both as historian and speechwriter. When drafting his Pulitzer Prize–winning *The Age of Jackson* (1945), he could, bewilderingly, write four to five thousand words each day. Working for Adlai Stevenson's presidential campaigns in the 1950s, his friend and fellow Harvard professor, John Kenneth Galbraith, would marvel that "alone among all I've observed in this craft, he could remove his coat, address his typewriter, and without resort to reference books, documents, or pause for thought, produce an entire speech in one sitting." That ability to make writing as natural as speaking was a skill he started honing while traveling the world in 1933 and 1934.[56]

Arthur's parents had hoped this family adventure would help him grow up. The boy returned home in August 1934—at sixteen not quite a man but having seen much of the world—more confident in his own views and abilities, and a crucial year older. Harvard now beckoned. As Arthur noted in his final diary entry of the tour, "The party's over."[57]

CHAPTER TWO

A Pilgrim's Progress

Harvard in the 1930s had more snob appeal than prestige and inevitability. When James Laughlin IV, class of '36 and future publisher of *New Directions*, picked Harvard ahead of Princeton, his father wept with disappointment on hearing the news. Laughlin soon saw his father's point, complaining that "this dump" was "plum awful." The poet Robert Lowell, class of '39, only bothered to stay two years before leaving to work with John Crowe Ransom at Kenyon College, Ohio. Isaiah Berlin, the historian of ideas visiting in 1940, found simply no comparison between Harvard and Oxford. "Harvard is a desert," he complained to his parents. Students were "sceptical about opinions and naive about facts which they swallow uncritically," which, as he pointed out, "is the wrong way round." And they would "shout *so* much & always the same, & always as if one were intellectually & even physically deaf." He was "glad I don't have to teach them." To many at the time, it was not Harvard but Yale that seemed the more dynamic institution.[1]

Harvard president James Bryant Conant recognized this troubling state of affairs on taking office in 1933. He immediately instructed one of his deans, Henry Chauncey, to shake up the system by promoting greater meritocracy. A glimmer of this shift was already apparent when Arthur arrived the following year. His contemporary Theodore H. White would divide their class members into "white men, gray men and meatballs." Of the elite "white men," the class of '38 still had its fair share of pedigree and/or money, with members from conspicuous families. These included

Roosevelts, Saltonstalls, Strauses, Kennedys, Hearsts, and Marshall Fields, with Rockefellers, Morgans, and more Roosevelts in the years above them. "Students of such names," White wrote, "had automobiles; they went to Boston deb parties, football games, the June crew race against Yale; they belonged to clubs."

In contrast, the "gray" men were those "sturdy sons of America's middle class" who ran for class committees and manned the *Crimson* newspaper or the satirical *Lampoon*. They included the likes of Caspar Weinberger, later President Reagan's secretary of defense, and John King, future governor of New Hampshire. At the bottom came the "meatballs," usually scholarship students, among whom White counted himself. "We were at Harvard not to enjoy the games, the girls, the burlesque shows of the Old Howard, the companionship, the elms, the turning leaves of the fall, the grassy banks of the Charles," he wrote. "We had come to get the Harvard badge." Within this threefold hierarchy, Arthur Schlesinger Jr. "defied categorization." He was someone who had the ability to talk to anyone, apparently happy to socialize with "both white men *and* meatballs." White found him to be a boy of "extraordinary sweetness and generosity." But what really set Arthur apart for White was that he was a rival as "the most brilliant member of the class."[2]

Part of what made Arthur hard to categorize was that he was a faculty child who, while lacking the wealth or elite social status of the "white men," nevertheless had his own kind of inside track that set him apart from the "gray men" and "meatballs." From the moment he walked into Harvard Yard as a freshman, Arthur was already marked out as someone of whom great things were expected and to whom doors were always quietly opened. "He is a boy of originality who thinks for himself," the diplomatic historian James Phinney Baxter, later deputy director of OSS, wrote in Arthur's Harvard reference, "and will, I am sure, become intellectually one of the outstanding members of the class." Naturally, when it came time to admit Arthur to a "house" after freshman year, Baxter welcomed him to Adams, where he was head of house and where Arthur's father was also a fellow.[3]

But intimacy also brought limitations. Arthur never experienced, for example, that moment of wonder on entering a new world that White and many of his other contemporaries enjoyed. He walked precisely one mile from Gray Gardens East to his freshman dorm at Thayer Hall, and did so without ever really leaving home. White may only have traveled into Cambridge from Boston, but his journey from the "ghetto" of Erie Street to Harvard Yard was a shift from one world to another. White recalled that he had emerged "from the subway exit in the Square and faced an old red-brick wall behind which stretched, to my fond eye, what remains still the most beautiful campus in America, the Harvard Yard. If there is a place in all America that mirrors better all American history, I do not know of it." Arthur, in contrast, admitted ennui to his grandmother, Clara Bancroft, telling her in his first week that he had been "in no way anxious to return to America" from his travels abroad, and that the only real advantage of being back in Cambridge was "to have all one's possessions in reach." Unlike most undergraduates in their new environment, Arthur announced the day before classes had even begun that he already had "a sense of being settled."[4]

Sometimes that familiarity manifested itself as the "extraordinary sweetness and generosity" that Teddy White would remember. He was, after all, the gracious host making newcomers feel at home. At other times, however, he could seem a little too comfortable. Gardner Jackson, a former student of Arthur's father, was so astonished by the boy's high-handed sense of entitlement that he felt compelled to take Schlesinger Sr. to one side to warn him. "I talked with his father about this a good deal," he recalled. "His father had been very frank with me about his distress over manifestations of arrogance." It was not a characteristic that Harvard was ever likely to subdue, although Schlesinger's friend Felix Frankfurter tried, writing gently to Arthur to remind him "how persuasive understatement and impersonality in argument are."[5]

Like most Harvard freshmen, Arthur took residence in a dorm on Harvard Yard for his first year. His roommate was a Midwest scholarship student from Chicago, Edward T. James, who would later edit three volumes of *Notable American Women: A Biographical Dictionary*. They lived in rooms in Thayer 7, one of the larger and cheaper dorms, across from the statue of John Harvard and convenient to the Widener Library, Harvard Square, and the subway to Boston. "My roommate and I have two rooms," Arthur reported to his grandmother, "a bedroom and a study between us. The study is much larger than needful; indeed the whole building wastes space in the best Victorian manner and resembles more than anything else a barn." First-years took meals in the elegant setting of the McKim, Mead & White Harvard Union building at the southeast corner of Harvard Yard. With its 14-foot-high fireplaces and the antler chandeliers reportedly donated by Teddy Roosevelt, it had by the 1930s become a rather grand freshman dining room. "The food seems quite good," Arthur judged, apparently somewhat surprised. After the culinary disasters and poisonings of Exeter, it was a not unimportant comfort of his new student life.[6]

After his freshman year, Arthur would spend the next three years at Adams House, again rooming with Ed James. He chose Adams primarily because his father was a fellow, although it was also the only house with a swimming pool. More resonantly, its B staircase included the rooms where the current president, Franklin D. Roosevelt, had lived during his time at Harvard. The collegiate "house" system, established only a few years earlier, was based on the Oxbridge model of residential colleges with associated faculty as fellows. Adams was one of the physically darker, more sombre houses, but Arthur and his roommate overcame this deficit by occupying "an airy suite on the top floor of C" staircase. Although Adams was not as smart as houses such as Eliot, it had other advantages, including its proximity to Harvard Yard and its own kitchen, although the pool ensured it quickly became known as a "jocks" house.[7]

Not surprisingly, Arthur's extracurricular activities at Harvard were less those of the athlete than the aesthete. More surprising given his later interests, politics, whether on campus or nationally, did not much interest him. He did turn out to cheer FDR when the president came to speak at the Harvard Tercentenary in 1936. And he joined the Harvard Chapter of the American Student Union. The chapter was Communist-controlled but run under the banner of the Popular Front, which purported to bring together anti-Fascists of all stripes, uniting the hard Left and New Dealers. Schlesinger was put off by the strident tone and constant "name call-ing," but he did make a lifelong friend in James Wechsler—then a Young Communist and later to join him at the forefront of the non-Communist Left. Instead Arthur's inclinations were mostly cultural, with tastes that ranged from excitement at watching Stravinsky conduct his own works with the Boston Symphony Orchestra to seeing the original Broadway cast in *As Thousands Cheer*, by Irving Berlin and Moss Hart. The obsession with movies continued, with every film religiously detailed and reviewed in a movie logbook. These ranged from A-graded "Grand Hotel" ("Greta [Garbo] wins [against Joan Crawford and John Barrymore] in one of the greatest acting contests!") to E-grades for "Alexander Hamilton" starring George Arliss ("history mauled") and "Huckleberry Finn" with Jackie Coogan ("The book is butchered and what's left isn't worth it").[8]

It was Arthur's enthusiasm for movies that helped him find a niche as a reviewer at the *Harvard Advocate*, the literary magazine founded in 1866, which had included the likes of T. S. Eliot and Wallace Stevens among its contributors. Later, Norman Mailer, who arrived at Harvard in 1939, would complain about the "bunch of snobs" who ran the magazine (although the story he published there, "The Greatest Thing," launched his career). For Schlesinger's cohort, those "snobs" were represented in the person of James "J." Laughlin, the heir to a steel fortune, who was the personification of airy undergraduate *sprezzatura*. Already a protégé of Ezra Pound, Laughlin provoked a scandal with the September 1935 edition of the *Advocate*, which included a bawdy story by Henry Miller. Cambridge police confiscated the edition for being "obscene and degrad-ing." In response, Laughlin's forward-looking father signed over to him on his twenty-first birthday securities worth around $100,000 (roughly $2 million today) so J. could start publishing literary modernism himself; the first volume of *New Directions* came out the following year. Arthur had mixed feelings about Laughlin, who, he noted in his journal, was "utterly charming and utterly unreliable; both adjectives are inescapable." It was his first serious introduction to a patrician type: the "shrewd politician who has devoted most of his great diplomatic talent to one end—obtaining what he wants."[9]

These diplomatic and entrepreneurial skills were ones that Arthur—the smug, precocious boy who had so irritated fellow guests a few years before while on his world trip—soon began to cultivate for himself. Felix Frankfurter had quietly nudged him towards "persuasive understatement"; now in Laughlin he had an exemplar of how to achieve ends by deploying a ruthless charm. Laughlin had been able to talk himself out of trouble in September 1935. When Arthur wrote an article for the *Advocate* the following year that predicted the end of the Harvard "finals" clubs ("I forgot the power of snobbery," he later reflected ruefully), he aroused fierce resistance from the Editorial Board, most of whose members were themselves entrenched clubmen. "And what did I do?" Arthur noted gleefully in his journal. "I turned on the charm and polish; and, without retracting or qualifying a statement in the article, I restored myself to their good graces with all the ease of an accomplished double-dealer. I seem to hunt with the hounds and run with the hares without any strain of conscience or intellect." These same qualities helped get Arthur elected to the prestigious Signet Society, which, unlike the finals clubs, prided itself on admission through talent, particularly wit, rather than social standing—another example of "insider" merit. The society, with its own building at 46 Dunster Street, had a reputation for providing the best lunches in town, during one of which Arthur found himself seated next to a disconcertingly taciturn H. G. Wells. There were other eminent disappointments too. Gertrude Stein was "most of the time incomprehensible." Sean O'Casey made "such an ass of himself... [with] dirty personal remarks." Even so, there was more than a touch of entitlement to his complaint about "very little of much interest going on here." Presumably Wells, Stein, and Casey would not have been regular visitors to Iowa City.[10]

For all his other activities, Arthur never forgot he was at Harvard to study. His letters are peppered with the constant refrain of the pressure of work. "As I remarked before," he complained to his grandmother in Washington, DC, "I have been having to work all the time," telling her at the end of the first semester that "the first night of the vacation I was so tired that I went to bed at eight." Much of that work in Arthur's freshman year was taken up with a broad swathe of courses and the fulfillment of requirements. "I am finding philosophy and economics the most interesting, and also the hardest courses," he reported. "The history course I am taking is simply the assimilation of facts and interpretations discovered by other people and is not hard to understand. Biology, at present writing, interests me not at all." The struggle with the science requirement showed up in his disappointing B grade for biology, a rare blemish in an otherwise perfect record of freshman A grades.[11]

Arthur's dismissal of History I as a class that was nothing more than "facts and interpretations discovered by other people" was an example of the lassitude that often overcame him at Harvard. The class professor, R. B. Merriman, a historian of Britain and Spain, satisfied one of the first obligations of any teacher when confronted with a roomful of undergraduates, many of whom were simply fulfilling a requirement. He kept them amused: "Merriman could entertain a hall of six hundred students and hold them spellbound," recalled Teddy White, who sat in the same class with Arthur. "He paced the platform from end to end, roaring, wheedling, stage-whispering, occasionally screeching in falsetto and earning fairly his [Frisky] nickname." That Arthur was less than charmed made no difference to his grade: he won the LeBaron Russell Briggs prize awarded annually to the freshman whose History I exam best combined historical analysis with literary style. "Schlesinger," the *Harvard Crimson* noted, perhaps mischievously, "is the son of Arthur M. Schlesinger, professor of history."[12]

To keep an eye on Arthur's studies, Schlesinger had arranged for one of his PhD students, Paul Buck, also from Ohio, to act as the boy's formal advisor. Buck, a rising man in the discipline, would soon join the Harvard faculty and win the 1938 Pulitzer Prize for a book based on his doctoral thesis, *The Road to Reunion, 1865–1900.* Despite Buck's gentle manner, Arthur Jr. recalled him as an advisor of "subtle and steely intelligence and a strong will." He was also shrewd about Arthur's ambition. Writing his freshman advisor's report, Buck counseled any future tutor to give Arthur some rope but not enough to hang himself. The key, Buck judged, would be to remind him of the need to have "a sound grounding in fundamentals, and at the same time capitalize upon the boy's eagerness for professional advance."[13]

For his major, Arthur picked American History and Literature, part of the oldest field of concentration at Harvard, although, as he reassured his family, "the bulk of my courses will be in history." Over the period of his four years at Harvard, he would take nine history classes, including one with his father on social and intellectual history, and four literature courses. He achieved A grades in all but one of his history and lit classes, winning a John Harvard scholarship and numerous prizes. It would be satisfying to report that Arthur's single B grade in history came from his father; but in fact, it came from Samuel Eliot Morison, whose early dislike of "smart-alecky" Arthur would harden as the years went on.[14]

Another historian who got on Morison's nerves was the historian of ideas, Perry Miller, with whom he would later have a very public spat about Cotton Mather. So doubtless it did not improve Arthur's relationship with Morison when he became Miller's advisee. Miller was the perfect foil to Arthur's father as a mentor. Where Schlesinger Sr. was quiet and ascetic, the brilliant Miller was a boozy, macho figure. He was a magnet for precocious students such as the young Schlesinger or Edmund S. Morgan (a year ahead of Arthur and like him with a father on the faculty), who relished his terrorizing. "Luckily," a terrified Arthur noted in his undergraduate diary, "my memory of Perry Miller's onslaught on me in our first tutorial conference last October is revived every time I see him, and makes for excessive intellectual humility." Looking back years afterwards, he judged that it was Miller who "taught me that glibness was not enough, a valuable lesson."[15]

Miller was often criticized for the severe complexity of his prose. "His work is written in a style that puzzles and even angers some readers," Robert Middlekauff points out in an essay on Miller. "Much of the bewilderment and anger arise from a feeling that he is making history too difficult for understanding." That Arthur did not fall into the same trap was due in no small part to another important Harvard influence. He had known the maverick Bernard DeVoto since childhood. The author of a delightful paean to the martini, *The Hour: A Cocktail Manifesto*, DeVoto provided alcohol sourced in Canada for so many of the parties held at 19 Gray Gardens East during Prohibition that Arthur as a boy had for some considerable time assumed he was the local bootlegger.[16]

DeVoto taught as a part-time instructor at Harvard, where he was viewed warily by many, including President James Conant, who saw his creative writing courses as somewhat beneath the dignity of the university. For Arthur, the class was an important corrective to Miller's "style that puzzles." DeVoto instructed his students to "write for the reader, never for yourself." He was dismissive of Arthur's early baroque efforts. "Your principal trouble," he judged, "remains the vague phrase accepted without scrutiny." Arthur did not take the criticism kindly, but he admitted the "seismic" influence that DeVoto had on him. By the end of the course, somewhat rueful at having been forced to abandon his more florid style, Arthur conceded that DeVoto had "improved (or at least changed) my style about 100%."[17]

At the end of his sophomore year, Arthur attended the last Harvard lecture given by Alfred North Whitehead, the eminent mathematician and philosopher. "Civilizations die of boredom," Whitehead said as his parting shot. He may as well have been talking directly to Arthur, who was bored with life in general and the college in particular. "I have exhausted after two years most of what Harvard has to give me at this time," he complained, adding soon afterwards that "the range of experience here in Cambridge is too confined to increase my knowledge much . . . I need a different life."[18]

But what kind of life? That was the dilemma with which Arthur wrestled that spring. Part of the answer was provided by another Cambridge academic child, Marian Cannon. Arthur still lacked confidence with girls. His small stature, pebble glasses, and already thinning hair made him self-conscious when competing with the Harvard athletes or the Byronic aesthetes. And his relative youth—he was still only twenty when he graduated after four years—reinforced his schoolboy looks with emotional immaturity. "It is," he admitted in his journal, "exceedingly dispiriting."

Perhaps it was inevitable that success in the end would come from within the Cambridge academic family. Marian Cannon was the daughter of Walter Bradford Cannon, the Higginson professor and chairman of the Physiology Department at Harvard Medical School. He was in many ways a most un-Schlesinger-like academic. With a flamboyant touch in his work, coining the famous phrase "fight or flight," Cannon matched his fine intellect with a physical adventurism that saw him become the first person to climb what is now Mount Cannon in Canada's Glacier National Park. Alfred Whitehead described him as "a rugged, ruddy Midwesterner with a hearty voice, simple, direct and no nonsense" who was "freighted with honors which he wears invisibly." Even his committed Unitarianism was more muscular. Aside from the Harvard and Midwest connections, not much else seemed likely to draw Marian and Arthur together, not least because, born in September 1912, she was five years older than he. But she hadn't had much luck in love either. Like Arthur, she had traveled overseas but had stayed in Cambridge for her degree. When Arthur happened by the Cannon house on Frisbie Place, the Radcliffe graduate thought him "the brightest male I had ever come across" and "the kind of man I would like to marry." For Arthur, too, it was *coup de foudre*. "If ever I fell in love at first sight," he wrote excitedly in his journal in May 1937, "it was with Marian Cannon last week."[19]

"Her charm and her beauty" entranced Arthur, but even more so did her "wisdom" about life in Cambridge. A week or so after their first meeting, the two went to the cinema to see Busby Berkeley's *The Go-Getter* ("abominable"). Afterwards they sat talking, listening to Benny Goodman, during which Arthur, perhaps for the first time, poured out his frustrations with Cambridge life. He felt "rather like a machine, all polished and charged and ready to go: but without a destination." He had "not yet turned the corner" or "grown." His "sense of discontent" had been "slowly working its way up from my subconscious and slowing finding formulation." Yet at the same time he was apprehensive about the prospect of graduating the following year, as "I have been believing also that college life was ideally adapted to me." Marian broke open the dam. Their conversation, Arthur proclaimed, "resulted in the complete destruction of [that] notion." The "monumentally important" talk ranked as "one of the two or three significant evenings" of his life.

Looking back, it is clear that this was the moment when Arthur first began to conceive of a life, in Theodore Roosevelt's phrase, as "a man in the arena." He went home that evening to write a long journal entry that was in effect the cri de coeur of a public intellectual. "For a long time I have been feeling with increasing strength that knowledge and experience should be intimately related," he wrote. "The only knowledge worth anything is grounded in experience."

Marian, the professor's daughter, had given, "without malice or special purposes, a very scornful account of universities." The ivory tower, Arthur now began to see, was "a pretty adequate metaphor," because "a college professor is rather well insulated from most of the currents that electrify vital life." But how to address the paradox of his life and ambition, "the problem of my future," as it now stood? That seemed an insuperable riddle. "The only possible career," he despaired, "is the study of American civilization: I cannot doubt my absorption in this, and the question of divorce from experience does not enter in at all." But the only institutions that "would pay me to study American civilization are the colleges; and in sealing myself in them, I am cutting myself off from the only way of life that would give my work any particular depth, any philosophical significance." It was, Arthur admitted, an analysis that "sounds very stupidly intellectual," but no one should doubt that "the underlying emotions are very real.[20]

Ironically, given that it was a rejection of college life in favor of real world experience, Arthur's crisis of direction had the effect of shaking him from his torpor and jump-starting his rewarding final year at Harvard. Perry Miller had been on leave in England during Arthur's junior year. His replacement, F. O. Matthiessen, provided a first serious introduction to Marxism but was not much help when it came to choosing a potential senior thesis topic. In the end, Arthur's father took the boy in hand. The New York Times published a story during the 1937 summer vacation about a vandalized bust portraying a heavily bearded man that had been found at the foot of a pedestal next to the Hudson on Riverside Drive on New York's Upper West Side. The inscription on the plinth declared this to be "Brownson, 1803–1876, Publicist, Philosopher, Patriot."

The difficulty was that no one seemed to know who "Brownson" was, with local police and officials pronouncing themselves baffled. Eventually the New York Public Library had helped identify the nineteenth-century intellectual and minister, Orestes Brownson, but it also admitted that of the nineteen volumes that the library held of his work, none was in circulation. Such, opined the *Times* wisely, is "the instability of fame." But an important figure who has slipped into obscurity is often grist to the historian's mill. Schlesinger gave his son a gentle nudge and "suggested that I look at the article on Brownson in the *Dictionary of American Biography.*" Whether or not Schlesinger was aware of his son's current thinking, the prompt was expertly judged. Here was exactly the kind of intellectual, activist, and controversialist to capture the restless Arthur's imagination.

He wrote immediately to Miller, who warmly approved Brownson as a topic. This was the genesis of *Orestes A. Brownson: A Pilgrim's Progress*, which was published in book form in 1939. For all the importance of Marian's disruptive innovation in Arthur's life, here was another example of his father deftly restoring him to the academic track at the right moment. "A tutorial with a man like Perry Miller and love with a girl like Marian," Arthur wrote brightly, "could do a great deal to enlarge my experience."[21]

Revivified, Arthur completed his final year at Harvard trailing the long predicted clouds of glory. Working with Miller again was a delight, not just because he was "one of the greatest teachers of history," but further because "underneath the bluntness and irascibility he was also in unexpected ways a sweet and considerate man." Researching the thesis among the elegant surroundings and capacious holdings of the Widener Library offered Arthur the excitement of writing his first extended piece of work. "Immersion in Brownson," he wrote, "became immersion in the theology, philosophy, politics and intellectual ferment of the nineteenth century in America."[22]

Arthur's study of "this stormy pilgrim" laid the foundations for his career to come in a number of important ways. Rather than focus on a particular phase of Brownson's career, he chose to examine the life itself, locating it in a broader political and intellectual context, and then pulling the two threads together to make conclusions about nineteenth-century northeastern society. He would go on to use a similar method in chronicling various "ages" framed by the lives of American presidents. The undergraduate thesis also pinpointed the stock market crash of 1837 as revealing to Brownson, and to Arthur, how business interests worked against those of ordinary people. The question was as much ethical as financial. "As the Panic of 1837 deepened into a way of life," Arthur wrote, "he [Brownson] gradually began to see that the complicated financial system had somehow burst the bonds of a personal morality." This youthful take on a business elite he judged venal and antidemocratic provided a jumping-off point for later works on Jackson and FDR. But perhaps the most intriguing aspect of "Orestes Brownson" was the way in which Arthur unapologetically inserted himself into the analysis. "The measure of what is historically important is set by the generation that writes the history, not by the one that makes it," he boldly declared in his opening sentence, continuing, "No historian can entirely escape from judging by the standards of his day. In some sense he must always superimpose one set of values on another." That premise would frame Arthur's entire career as a professional historian.[23]

The self-discipline that dissipated during Arthur's junior year had returned at full throttle. The day after his twentieth birthday, he admonished himself to guard against the personal sentiment in affairs of the heart that "has worked its way into my nervous system—which means that I shall be on my mettle as far as work is concerned." That self-willed enterprise paid off. On a fine June day, with the novelist John Buchan as commencement speaker, Arthur's parents watched proudly as their son graduated with highest honors summa cum laude, winning a Bowdoin Prize, one of Harvard's oldest and most prestigious student awards. His reputation and prospects on leaving Harvard could not have been stronger. As his advisor, Paul Buck, wrote shortly afterwards, "Mr. Arthur M. Schlesinger, Jr., is the most promising historian that I have met. This is a considered and unqualified statement."[24]

Arthur's classmate Theodore White remarked of his own family and summa cum laude, "That was what they had expected" since his schooldays. The same might easily have been said of Arthur's parents, who had been working toward this moment since at least the time when they had pulled the unhappy boy out of public school and sent him to Exeter. Now Schlesinger went into overdrive to facilitate the next stage of his son's career, beginning with converting an undergraduate thesis into a book. He turned to his old friend, Bernard DeVoto, for a favor, asking him to send Arthur's thesis to his publisher, Little, Brown. The publishers dutifully gave the book to readers, but remained lukewarm. "All thought favorably of it intrinsically," Schlesinger reported to his son, "but questioned whether the company could get out of the book what they put into it. . . . They will lose money on the venture." The company would be interested in whatever Arthur did next, so the exercise of making a useful contact had not been a wasted one.[25]

Schlesinger Sr. would not be brushed off so lightly. He called DeVoto back into the fray, even though, as Schlesinger admitted to his son, "he has never seen the manuscript." In the end, the company gave in, recognizing that it was a project that had to be accepted as a courtesy to a favored author. "He took an active part in urging them to take the book on," Schlesinger Sr. reported to Arthur, pointing out the debt that was owed. Royalties were almost nonexistent, but there was no subvention to be paid. "Personally," wrote the head of Team Schlesinger, "I think we are very much to be congratulated."[26]

The deal was a piece of academic "logrolling" quite on a par with another example of paternal string-pulling in that period. For the other notable Harvard thesis to be published around this time was that of John F. Kennedy—the same age as Arthur, but two years behind him in the class of 1940—whose thesis, "Appeasement at Munich: the inevitable result of the slowness of conversion of the British democracy from a disarmament to a rearmament policy," was subsequently published under the snappier title, "Why England Slept." As well as using his contacts to help get the book published, Kennedy's father ensured it became a bestseller, placing multiple orders for boxloads of the book, most of which were found years afterwards piled up in the basement at the family's com-pound in Hyannisport, Massachusetts.[27]

Schlesinger could not buy his son onto the bestseller list, but he had advantages to deploy, not least his experience in how to bring a book to publication. The timeline was tight, with the book due to appear in the spring of 1939. "The plan," Schlesinger wrote the previous October after the contract had been settled, "will be to send you the galley proof but not the page proof. . . . I will make the necessary corrections in the page proof." He would also supervise the compiling of the index.[28]

Schlesinger's strongly directional approach to what was after all his son's, not his own, book was in many ways only a practical response to Arthur's changed circumstances. Towards the end of his final under-graduate year, Arthur had been awarded a prestigious Henry Fellowship, which allowed Harvard students to study in England for a year. Arthur was accepted at Cambridge, so by the time his father wrote to him with the plan for the book, he was already in residence at Peterhouse, the univer-sity's oldest college. Yet there was a doubt gnawing away about the extent of the professor's dominance. "It began when Arthur went away to Cam-bridge for that year and suddenly was exposed to this completely new experience," Marian Cannon recalled. "He discovered there were all sorts of other worlds out there, because, you know, I think Mr. Schlesinger had a very strong control over him."[29]

Arthur's romance with Marian helped prompt thoughts of indepen-dence, but it was in many ways switching one controlling relationship for another. That segue prompted deep feelings of insecurity in Arthur. Inev-itably the relationship was a tempestuous on-off affair. The summer before Arthur left for Peterhouse was one of raging arguments and emotional reconciliations. The couple split up midway through the summer. "She is no longer in love with me," Arthur wrote at the beginning of August. "This is due in part to my strong pride which leads me into petty and self-ish cruelties as a way of compensating for my own feeling of insecurity." Marian left immediately for the family summer home in Franklin, New Hampshire, from where she wrote that "perhaps you're right, darling, per-haps in an unspoken way we recognize that it must be the end." Overcome with remorse, Arthur made an emotional dash to Franklin, where the two were reconciled. "I'm really awfully glad you came last week, dearest," Marian wrote to him afterwards, "for in spite of our usual temperamental fluctuations, I, for one, had great pleasure in having you here: it's wonderful to discover in reality you are not the devouring ogre which superficially you appear to be but in reality a sweet, reasonable and loveable pie." Marian still believed that Arthur was "deserving of immensely better out of life than I seem to be able to give." But when he left Boston for New York on September 1 to take the boat to Europe, Marian saw him off. "I love Marian so very much and want her so much and shall miss her so much—the prospect of not seeing her for ten months . . . fills me with horror," he wrote once on board his ship. "She is the sweetest, loveliest, finest girl imaginable." Within days, however, he was already scouting out a coed from Illinois called Ruth. "I could not bear to leave so fetching a girl alone," he recorded, wondering whether thinking of anyone else but Marian was "blasphemous."[30]

Reading Arthur's journal, it is hard to avoid the obvious conclusion that as he set sail he remained a boy, not a man. Leaving Boston, his parents had come "to the station to say goodbye [and] it was a distinct wrench to part from them." Arthur was leaving home on his own for the first time. "We have appreciated knowing you these twenty one years," his parents telegraphed to him on board the *Niuw Amsterdam*, "and now look forward eagerly to watching our pilgrim's progress for another year until he returns to our wicket." Although Arthur had spent two unhappy years at Exeter, he had still spent regular weekends at a home that was only forty miles south of the boarding school campus. The traditional rite of passage, leaving for university, for him had involved just a fifteen-minute walk to a college where his own father worked. Now in the summer of 1938, it was as if he were setting out for a university for the first time, with all the challenges and excitements that offered. At least he got off to a good start. On arrival in London he went through a traditional induction into manhood. "In the morning," he dutifully recorded in his diary, "I went to Selfridges and actually bought myself some socks."[31]

CHAPTER THREE

ANOTHER CAMBRIDGE

S chlesinger arrived in London in September 1938 at a politically charged time. Coming out of the theater on his very first night in town, he discovered newspaper boys shouting out the late, breaking news. "People were clutching at newspapers that moment all through the West End," he wrote in his diary. "Agreement has been reached at Munich— and this was the news, for the moment heartening and cause for rejoicing, but on reflection chilling cause for indignation." Munich was a turning point in global affairs—the agreement between Hitler and Chamberlain to allow Germany to annex the "Sudetenland" in Czechoslovakia—and Arthur, in contrast to most, recognized the folly, not in retrospect, but at the time. The following day he wrote a blistering account in his journal that condemned the agreement as "disgraceful morally and highly questionable strategically." The deal was nothing more than a "temporary peace" rooted "above everything," he judged, in Chamberlain's fear of the Soviet Union, whose Communism was "the main threat to the power of his own class."[1]

In the midst of these dramatic events, Arthur made his way to King's Cross station, where he took the train to Bletchley (the center for signals intelligence during World War II precisely because it was the intersection for Oxbridge and London), and from there boarded the "Varsity Line" eastbound to Cambridge.

In many ways Cambridge in the 1930s was a surprising choice. It was more detached both geographically and in spirit from affairs of the world. "It is difficult to grasp," the Marxist Eric Hobsbawm recalled in his memoirs, "just how isolated and parochial the place was in the 1930s." Schlesinger's Henry Fellowship contemporaries, by contrast, all headed to Oxford, which most thought of as an altogether more worldly environment. Certainly when Arthur arrived in Cambridge he felt an immediate culture clash when confronted with a porter at Peterhouse every bit as truculent as Skullion, the Head Porter in Tom Sharpe's comic novel *Porterhouse Blue*.[2]

Arthur, it seems, had arrived a day early. Informed of this fact, he immediately lost his temper (never a good idea with the college porters) and did so with all the sense of entitlement of one who had wandered in and out of Harvard at will since childhood. "The business drew me into an instant rage," he reported, not least as he was informed there would be a fine for the offense. "It had never occurred to one," he spluttered, "that a penalty attached to arriving too early—too late, yes—but too early . . ."

Eventually the porter showed him to his rooms at 16 Fitzwilliam Street, where he found waiting "a pleasant looking chap" who seemed to have had no difficulty coming up early. "This turned out to be one Charles Wintour," Arthur wrote in his diary. This housemate was the first good thing that had happened since he'd arrived. In many ways it was an unlikely friendship. Wintour, the son of a major general, was a boy, unlike Arthur, of exceptional height and somewhat cool manner (later his nickname on Fleet Street was "Chilly Charlie"). Yet he was studying history and literature, as was Arthur, was ferociously clever (he graduated with a First), and was the editor of *Granta*—the Cambridge equivalent of *The Advocate* and *Lampoon* combined. There would be moments of exasperation—"Your standards are too high for comfort, Arthur, too high both for my comfort and your own," he fulminated on one occasion that year—but it was a deep friendship that would last six decades until Wintour's death in 1999.[3]

After the staleness and sense of ennui at Harvard, Arthur now threw himself into university life at Cambridge almost as if a first-year student. "My God, how time goes!" he wrote at the end of his first month. But whereas in the past such a comment might have applied to the labor of academic work, now it was a result of the pleasures of student life. He wrote for *Granta*—"a neutral territory," observed Eric Hobsbawm, "for friends of different politics, such as the young Arthur Schlesinger Jr., whom I met there, then as later a consistent anti-Communist New Dealer." The rest of the time he spent with members of the Amateur Dramatic Club (ADC) for whom, to his surprise, he ended up directing Frank Sladen-Smith's one-act play *St. Simeon Stylites*. "I have had to learn to direct as I went along," Arthur wrote, nervous but exhilarated. "It is fun whenever I catch myself up into the dramatic aspects of being a director, but I have some bad moments of rather unromantic despair."[4]

And then there was love. The Harvard years had been difficult. Now older, more confident and with the exoticism of being a Yank, Arthur unexpectedly found himself in demand. "I don't think I've ever known so many attractive girls as well as I do this year," he enthused. Poor Yvonne was dumped because she was "just too dumb," as was Doris, who failed to make the cut because "there's no particular point in coming to England to play around with her type." Anne, on the other hand, was "an extremely pretty blonde, a rather amusing and faintly sensitive girl." But another Anne, the daughter of a Liberal politician, Sir Frederick Whyte, was something else. It was Charles Wintour who introduced him to "one of the most prominent undergraduates." By the end of his first term, Arthur believed "the foundation is about ready for passes to be made" and thought Anne "more suited to me than any girl I've met save Marian, and in some ways more suited." There followed over the next few months "a good deal of *sturm und drang*," but by May week, amid the rounds of balls and drinks parties, Arthur reported that he had enjoyed "one of the happiest and one of the fullest weeks of my life.... Anne is a darling, and at present writing we are getting along beautifully."[5]

Perhaps it was intimations of that burgeoning relationship that brought Marian hurrying across the Atlantic. Throughout the course of the academic year, the pair had exchanged anguished letters of varying degrees of devotion and reproach. Friends in the United States reported that Marian "feels you are losing interest in her and is preparing for the inevitable subsidence of the relationship." In March, she wrote to Arthur to say she no longer loved him. He replied, "OK, we're finished." She immediately wrote back to say she had changed her mind. When Marian eventually made the trip across the Atlantic in June, the couple stayed with Arthur's Cambridge friend Charles Wintour, who was horrified at the relationship. "She does seem considerably older than you in her behaviour," he observed, reminding Arthur that "you said that 'The strain is telling.'" Wintour's advice to his friend "without any politenesses" could hardly have been any clearer. "It seems damn priggish advice to tell anyone that they are not old enough to marry," he wrote, "but perhaps it's not so bad if I say that I do not think you're old enough to marry Marian."[6]

While Arthur fretted about his love life, others were more concerned about his academic prospects. Theater, occasional debates at the Union, writing for *Granta*, and an enthusiastic love life had not left him much space for work, and for the first time in his life, Arthur had neglected his academic studies. He did attend lectures by high profile academics such as I. A. Richards ("a very nice man" who "wasted a sharp and original intelligence"), F. R. Leavis ("at once engrossing and distasteful"), and G. E. Moore ("gentle reasonableness"). But it took him over a month even to make an appearance in the University Library, leading one friend to quip, "For the first time Arthur looked out of his element." It was easy to see how it all happened, as on the typical occasion when "all plans for intensive studies were destroyed" by a request, acceded to "with considerable reluctance and under strong pressure," to direct a production of *The Infernal Machine*. If Jean Cocteau's version of the Oedipus myth prompted any thoughts of "castration anxiety" in Arthur, they may have been heightened by his father, at home in the other Cambridge and seeing Junior's book to publication, rebuking him for a lack of industry. When the proofs he had sent to England for his son to correct were not returned, he fired off a note of distress tinged with sarcasm: "Two days ago I received your note of contrition in regard to the footnotes, etc.," he wrote, exasperated, in February, "but I judge that the proof did not make the same boat since it has not arrived. I do not know how much longer I can hold on to the page proof." Perhaps it was symbolic that during that term, Arthur was a teller for the "ayes" at the Cambridge Union for a debate on the motion, which carried, that "This house despairs of books." That Arthur's book was published on time two months later had more to do with Arthur Sr. than his son, but as Perry Miller, writing to congratulate the new author, conceded to him, "I suppose all this is to the good, because it shows you are a human being as well as a scholar."[7]

Schlesinger and Miller had been active on Arthur's behalf to secure a prestigious berth for him at Harvard. The Society of Fellows had been established in 1933, with twenty-four junior fellows who were given the opportunity to spend three years working on any project they liked for a handsome stipend and privileges at Eliot House. Pushing back against the tyranny of the PhD and its attendant professionalization of academia, the Society forbade its junior fellows from taking formal courses and discouraged teaching. The objective, wrote Samuel Eliot Morison, was "to enable each to contribute his peculiar gifts to the cause of learning when still young and vigorous."[8]

Some at Harvard expressed concern about whether Arthur might even be *too* young for the Society. "I, of course, have tried to meet that objection in advance," Schlesinger informed Arthur, but inevitably there would be "a very keen competition and the Senior Fellows may feel that you should wait another year." There was also the difficulty that "it has been the usual practice of the Senior Fellows not to elect a Junior Fellow without a personal interview," but again Schlesinger was able to intercede, drawing from the senior fellow, Arthur Nock, the Frothingham Professor of the History of Religion, the reluctant admission that there had been "exceptions to this rule."[9]

While Schlesinger worked behind the scenes, Perry Miller was the public face of the campaign. Asked to speak on Arthur's behalf before the Society, Miller "gathered very quickly that your election was a foregone conclusion." However, "we went patiently through all the conventional motions and all did what was expected. . . . The questions were lengthy and my answers were longer, but in general I said Yes and they seemed to have agreed."[10]

Harvard sent the formal letter on April 24, 1939, the day after the *New York Times* published Columbia historian Henry Steele Commager's glowing review of *Orestes Brownson*. "Mr. Schlesinger's study of Brownson is a masterly one," Commager wrote. "It has technical brilliance—a sure control of materials, an affective handling of background, a skillful use of colors and a certain bravura of execution. It has, in addition, sincerity and integrity, sympathetic understanding, and an astonishing maturity."

These were intoxicating times for Arthur, but Perry Miller, his former tutor, urged him to guard against complacency. Think hard about "whether or not the Society will be a good thing for you," Miller advised. Most fellows would "consider their three years a brilliant success" if they produced a book out of them. But he had already jumped that particular hurdle and "the act may lose something of its charm for you." For Arthur, then, "the chief problem you will now have to face will be . . . keeping yourself going for three years on your own steam." The year in England, now drawing to a close, had been a waste of time. "I suppose it is all education," Miller wrote dourly; "nevertheless, I [hope] you will be spending time more profitably and enjoyably in Cambridge, Massachusetts."[11]

Arthur himself had a more nuanced view. He wrote from England to A. C. Hanford, the dean at Harvard, that the year had been "a most happy and profitable one." Half a century later, writing to another beneficiary of the Henry Fellowship, Jacob Neusner, Arthur told him, "I look back on my years as a Henry Fellow as a time that started so many things in my life." As he pointed out when proposing the toast before a dinner of the Harvard Club of Cambridge in May 1939, "The change from one Cambridge to another is deeper than mere names imply."[12]

There were many reasons why the Henry Fellowship "started so many things" in Arthur's life. Not the least of these was that it got him physically out of the orbit of his ambitious father, who could be at best directive, at worst suffocatingly controlling. Cambridge and Peterhouse gave Arthur a new kind of independence and confidence, but also helped him learn to take himself just that little bit less seriously, even to be silly and frivolous. But if 1938–1939 was a year of discovery and optimism, it was also "the twilight year" for Arthur and his generation. Throughout 1938 and most of 1939 he had been a firm isolationist, telling his parents in March 1939, after Germany invaded all of Czechoslovakia, that he remained "very suspicious" of the view that "America's frontier is on the

Rhine."[13] But reviewing the whole experience the following year, 1940, in his journal, he wrote:

> The central fact of the year is the war, which has changed our world for us—particularly for Charles ... and Anne. The invasion of Holland and Belgium finally awoke me to Nazism. Hitler is no mere imperialist conqueror, somewhat nastier and gaudier than the Kaiser. . . . His [is] not a war for markets and colonies. It is a revolution and a crusade. The analogy is not the first world war. It is the spread of Mohammedanism. Hitler will not be controlled by the motives which controlled Cecil Rhodes, say, or even Napoleon. He is the prophet of a new religion, and like all prophets who believe their faith with sufficient intensity, he is out to convert or destroy.[14]

Arthur took the boat home in the middle of August, arriving back in Cambridge, Massachusetts just in time to hear the news on the radio in 19 Gray Gardens East that Britain was at war. "It is democracy or Nazism," he wrote grimly, "a world divided." That Manichean struggle would eventually take him back to England in 1944, not as a scholar, but as a soldier and a spy.

"MANY THANKS FOR YOURS, stating that the 'European situation grows darker every day,'" Charles Wintour wrote in September 1939.[15] "I always said (or will in future) that much of your reputation for intelligence came from putting the obvious just a little more forcefully than your neighbours." It was a stinging example of what Arthur called that English "suave raillery which trips neatly and wittily along and leaves the younger country aghast."[16]

Yet if Arthur was aghast by the fall of 1939, it was not due to his friend's caustic wit, but more to that sense of being on the periphery when his friends were in the eye of the gathering storm. While Arthur resumed his Harvard routine, Wintour, now in uniform with the Royal Norfolk Regiment, was writing frankly that "It'll be a bloody miracle if I'm around for long after the invasion starts" and, with his "taste for self-dramatisation," wondering whether he would be able "to find some suitable exit line, some satisfactory attitude which would help to compensate for being shot off unexpectedly." When Arthur tried to weigh in with his own thoughts on the war, they often drew a sharp response. "Hitler may be on a crusade, but that's no reason for your adopting the rhetoric of a Fifth Day Adventist," Wintour mocked. "I am terrified at indications of loss of mental balance."[17]

Arthur's life had slotted back into its all too familiar groove on his return to Massachusetts, with apparently diminishing returns. There were, of course, the advantages of free board and lodgings, an annual stipend beginning at $1,250, and use of all the university's facilities. Once again, he took up residence in Adams House, occupying a pleasant suite of rooms handily placed near the swimming pool. Each Monday, he would troop over to Eliot House, home of the Society, for a formal dinner of senior and junior fellows. At the first one, the new intake had been primly reminded of the need to be "courteous to their elders and helpful to their juniors." There was also lunch twice a week just for the junior fellows. Orville T. Bailey, a neurologist who overlapped with Arthur, recalled that at these lunches there was "more license given to the direct shock of interests and personalities" than at the formal dinners. Arthur demurred. In comparison to his British friends preparing for war, the whole experience seemed tame in the extreme. It was telling that he abandoned writing his journal for the entirety of this first academic year. There seemed nothing to write.[18]

Instead Arthur's year began with work on an essay about Richard Hildreth, the author of a neglected six-volume history of the United States published in the 1850s. In many ways it was a strange choice of subject. Hildreth, as Arthur admitted in the resulting essay in *The New England Quarterly* in 1940, was "one of the more enigmatic figures in American intellectual history," someone who was "much more confusing than convincing." Moreover, he was the opposite of the prototype that Arthur had outlined in his undergraduate cri de coeur about the life of the intellectual. In 1937 Arthur had expressed his fear that academic life was too "insulated from most of the currents that electrify vital life" and that "the problem of my future" was how to reconcile "the study of American civilization" with the avoidance of "cutting myself off from the only way of life that would give my work any particular depth, any philosophical significance." Now in 1940, he picked as his subject a historian whose life seemed to exemplify the sterility of history that was disengaged from the experience of life.[19]

Hildreth, Arthur wrote, "moved little with the great of his day. He does not appear in their autobiographies and receives only the most casual mention in their letters and journals. . . . Pictures remain of him working silently at the Athenaeum in Boston, a tall, austere lonely man. . . . When he went to New York, he made no indelible impression there." Even his own city behaved "in Boston's usual way—by forgetting him." In contrast stood Arthur's distant relative, George Bancroft, whose rival *History of the United States of America* was a critical and popular success, making him money and winning him fame. Poor Hildreth became "increasingly bitter" as repeated frustrations "made life harder and more disappointing," leaving him helpless to do other than "watch the applause going to [Bancroft]."

Yet this contest was about more than fame and personal rivalry. Instead it was the encapsulation for Arthur of a troubling philosophical question about exactly what kind of historian he wanted to be. In "The Problem of Richard Hildreth," Arthur identified what he did not respect in the work of one professional historian, and in the process was able to develop his own philosophy of history based on the ideals he prized most. The fact that Hildreth, like Arthur (and Bancroft), was an Exeter and Harvard man made the "problem" even more autobiographical. Much of the question turned on genuineness, what Arthur identified as "the essential insincerity of Hildreth's writings." The *History* was characterized by its "infrequently-relieved dryness and the almost Olympian remoteness." Yet in personality, Hildreth was far from the remote or detached figure his historical works would suggest. He was a disputatious and vehement character, whose political pamphlets and newspaper articles often drew angry responses. "The subdued, cold tone of the History, then, is to be explained by Hildreth's suppression of his normal emotions for the sake of complete impartiality," Arthur wrote. The "emotion" of his pamphlets and journalism "drew forth all his gifts of irony, epithet and vigorous statement." But in the *History* "all emotion and viewpoint were specifically banned, and his writing instantly lost the artistic merits that go with them." The result was "dull, bald, commonplace, humdrum in rhythms, and starved in imagination."

"How," Arthur asked, getting to the heart of the matter, "could a man with so generally philosophic a cast of mind write such pedestrian and annalistic history?" The answer was that Hildreth's work was "almost entirely lacking in either flow that comes from a consistency of emotion or the unity that comes from a consistency of viewpoint." Thought and feeling were expelled, so that "Hildreth gained a kind of objectivity, but it was at the cost of readableness and of historical significance."And so finally Arthur drew the inevitable moral from the "problem" of Hildreth:

> He suppressed his thoughts as successfully as he did his feelings, a procedure which made most of his work a dry chronicle. It would have been no better (in fact, much worse) had he written his *History* to illustrate a preconceived theory; but if he had allowed a scheme of organization to rise—so far as he was aware—simply from the study of the facts themselves, he might well have written a work of much more enduring importance.

It was as much a manifesto for Arthur Schlesinger Jr. as a judgment on Richard Hildreth.[20]

Work on Hildreth had been meant as a prelude to something bigger for Arthur: a biography of George Bancroft. His distant relative represented almost everything that he now wanted to achieve as a historian, although if the boy born Arthur *Bancroft* Schlesinger now regretted abandoning his own middle name for that of his father, he did not speak of it. (However, by 1968, with his father having passed away, Schlesinger would admit, "in retrospect, I sometimes wish I had stuck to 'Bancroft' since I do feel a sort of intellectual and political kinship with old George." [21])

Not only was George Bancroft, like Arthur Jr. and Hildreth, another Exeter and Harvard man, he was also someone who had managed to combine consequence as a historian with engagement in public life. In 1845 he served as secretary of the navy under President James K. Polk. He established the US Naval Academy at Annapolis and was instrumental in the acquisition of California during the buildup to the Mexican-American War. His stints abroad included success as US minister in Berlin, where he was cultivated by Bismarck, whom he considered to be Europe's George Washington. Bancroft was "the first consequential American historian," Arthur later reflected. "He was also a Democratic politician, a presidential ghostwriter, a cabinet officer and a diplomat, all of which I dreamily aspired to be." Yet throughout it all, Bancroft "worked steadily away at his monumental *History*" and "kept on dividing his life between politics and history." [22]

Bancroft offered Arthur a model in how to live the life of an action-intellectual. He was "one of the last of America's universal men," whose dramatic, democratic style offered his young adherent a lesson in writing for the broadest possible audience. The contrast with Richard Hildreth, the "cold, subdued" historian who wrote without the sincerity of a viewpoint, was pronounced. Yet having decided that he wanted to be like Bancroft and write like him, Arthur, over the course of doing early research and writing his essay for the *New England Quarterly*, came to the conclusion that the best way to achieve those ends was not to write *about* Bancroft. "As I labored away at the Massachusetts Historical Society," he wrote, "the biography of Bancroft began imperceptibly to give way to an exploration of broader Jacksonian terrain." The proposed biography of the nineteenth-century historian was set aside for a project about the ideas that animated one of the most disruptive eras in American democracy. As it dawned on Arthur that Bancroft had his own stake in that transformation, he began to articulate what many later would judge the most important and far-reaching research question of his career: "whether Jacksonian democracy did not have an eastern and intellectual dimension that had not been fully recognized."

Schlesinger now began to reorient Jacksonianism away from the western frontier and instead to emphasize its national character, including among urban workers, small farmers, and intellectuals in the Northeast. "More can be understood about Jacksonian Democracy if it is regarded as a problem not of sections but of classes," he argued in what would become his book's single most famous line. The Jacksonian movement sought to harness "the power of the capitalistic groups, mainly Eastern, for the benefit of non-capitalist groups, farmers and laboring men, East, West, and South." In doing so, Schlesinger would present Jacksonianism as a forerunner of the Progressive Era and the New Deal in attempting to "restrain the power of the business community." It was a landmark moment for him. In challenging the notion put most famously in Frederick Jackson Turner's "frontier thesis" that American democracy was forged in the West, Arthur Schlesinger Jr. had the makings of a Big Idea.[23]

AS THE FIRST OF HIS three academic years in residence at Harvard's Society of Fellows drew to its close, Arthur was able to report "a fairly successful year" with "lots of work done [and] a new and mildly important book on Jacksonian democracy well under way." And if he had found his feet professionally, the return to Cambridge brought clarity in other ways too. By the spring of 1940, as the war intensified in Europe, Arthur abandoned any ambivalence about whether the United States should keep out of the war. There was, he wrote to friends, no choice but to "fight fire with fire." Convinced that "this war is not a war, it's a revolution," Arthur now believed that "what we must do, of course, is to arm." It was, Charles Wintour noted sardonically, "the end of Arthurian isolationism."[24]

The growing possibility of American involvement in the war also helped bring clarity, or at least resolution, to Arthur's tortured personal life. The previous summer he had admitted to wishing for an altercation with Marian "climactic enough to destroy this miserable affair, which has dragged on in a manic depressive way." Yet much as their bond made him "physically sick," he admitted in his diary that "in any number of ways I need her and cannot get along without her." Things calmed down in a "fairly comforting" way when the two were back in Cambridge together, although Arthur, already recognized on campus as a rising star, coyly admitted to "plenty of female attention on the side." Friends confessed themselves baffled by the stormy nature of the relationship, which saw letters arriving one week to say "it is all finally over" and the next proclaiming "everything is swell." No wonder that when Arthur finally asked Marian to marry him, Wintour, on hearing the news, made no effort to hide his skepticism. "I am absolutely delighted to hear you and Marian may get married," he wrote that spring. "In fact as delighted as I was the last time I heard it."[25]

In fact this time the couple did tie the knot. A Unitarian minister married Arthur and Marian on August 10, 1940, on the grounds of the bride's family home in Franklin, New Hampshire. To Arthur the choice of denomination was coincidental, as Marian's family were regular Unitarian churchgoers. For their honeymoon, the newlyweds went to Cape Breton Island in Nova Scotia. "I'm sorry not to have written earlier," Arthur wrote to his parents a week later, adding with unnecessary gaucheness that "we have been having such a good time while doing so little that can be written about that I have not had the energy to get off a letter." He admitted to the "shock when anyone calls Marian 'Mrs. Schlesinger,'" but was pleased to report "that we are very happy, which will surprise no one." By the end of the month, after "an awfully good time," Arthur was ready to head back to Cambridge to "get settled and get to work again."[26]

After three years of storm and stress, Arthur's life now settled into a period of stability, even tranquility. The newlyweds moved into an apartment in a pretty federal-style house at 341 Harvard Street, where they started giving regular parties, "serving," Marian recalled, "what we thought were sophisticated drinks of canned grapefruit juice and gin and inviting such grand figures as Samuel Eliot Morison, who arrived resplendent in his riding clothes, crop in hand, for cocktails."[27]

Perry Miller had warned of inevitable "soggy moments" and the "problem of keeping yourself going for three years on your own steam, inspired simply by your own urge to get something done." Yet armed with an ambitious new topic and a big idea, and having resolved his personal issues, Arthur now embarked on a conscientious spell of archival research on

Andrew Jackson and his contemporaries. Much of the work was done in the familiar surroundings of Harvard's Widener Library, but there were also extended trips to New York and Washington, DC, in 1941. These visits had the added advantage of giving Arthur and Marian time together away from Cambridge. There were a few awkward duties to be performed, including a visit to Arthur's grandmother in Washington, DC, "evenings [that] were very difficult, and left us both nervously exhausted." But for the most part, still only in his early twenties, Arthur cheerfully burnt the candle at both ends on these research trips. Long hours "in the manuscript room . . . from nine to five every day," he told his parents, were followed (he did not report) by long evenings of drinking and socializing. Watching *Citizen Kane* in New York after "too many old fashioneds at dinner," Arthur admitted, "I had only an imperfect idea of what was going on and had to have crucial details explained to me afterward." Prudently he told his folks the confusion was "because we sat so far from the screen."[28]

Fueled by bourbon and ambition, Arthur began to accumulate shoebox after shoebox of research notes, all carefully cross-indexed on four-by-six cards. He was under no obligation to teach, but to gain experience he tested some of his early ideas on the women undergraduates at Radcliffe College; despite his outward confidence, he was often so affected by nerves that he regularly threw up before lectures began. As his stint at the Society of Fellows began to draw to its close, he drew up an outline for a book in fifty-eight chapters, tentatively entitled "Jackson and the American Democratic Tradition." It showed strong links with the work of Arthur Sr., whose work emphasized the role of labor in the American Revolution. Arthur sat down to lay out the broad thrust of his argument. The new study would redress "the balance of emphasis that represented Jacksonian democracy as essentially the product of the western frontier." More could be understood about it by "a class analysis than by a sectional analysis." By examining "the ideas, theories, and preconceptions which the non-business groups of the day used in their attempt to adjust and moderate a nation increasingly dominated by business," it might be possible to write a new "intellectual history of Jacksonian democracy."[29]

No one could doubt the scale of Arthur's ambition. Indeed, such was the impact of the book that would finally emerge that his success now looks like the academic equivalent of a slam dunk. That's not how it felt to Arthur at the time. As he entered the final year of his fellowship, it began to dawn on him and his supporters that he may actually have fallen down the pecking order of his contemporaries. When in 1939, away in England, he had published *Orestes Brownson* with Little, Brown to warm reviews, there was little doubt that he was a star of the Harvard academic farm system. The junior fellowship at the Society of Fellows was another glittering prize. Yet Arthur had stepped off the traditional academic track for four years. By 1941–1942, as he prepared to enter the job market, it was clear that others had caught up and in some respects overtaken him. Arthur had the advantage of a book already published, but it was one clearly based on undergraduate research. His return to Harvard had seen him hard at work on research for the next book, but he had nothing physical to show for his effort except a slim journal article on Richard Hildreth in the *New England Quarterly*. Meanwhile, most of those with whom he was competing for academic positions had followed a more conventional path at graduate school. But conventional by its definition meant understood and accepted. And in a field that was becoming increasingly professionalized, Arthur's lack of a PhD now suddenly began to look at best eccentric, at worst lackadaisical. The gentlemanly scholar of Harvard's Society of Fellows was suddenly in danger of looking like an amateur and a dabbler.

The growing realization that Arthur had taken a misstep had to be addressed. As usual, it was Arthur Sr. who stepped into the breach to take control. In 1942, Arthur Schlesinger registered Arthur Jr. as his PhD student. In many ways it was an extraordinary step, confirming the younger man's place as "Little Arthur." It also pushed the boundaries of academic propriety or even common sense to the breaking point. Just as in 1933 a bright boy at Exeter whose father taught at Harvard might have thought to apply to a different Ivy League university, there was no shortage of options available to him for a PhD supervisor almost a decade later. Frederick Merk and Paul Buck, the latter a Pulitzer Prize winner, were, after all, both trusted family friends as well as nineteenth-century historians well able to advise Arthur's dissertation. Yet in the end, for Schlesinger, nobody else would do for his son. In part this was pure practicality. Arthur needed a PhD in a hurry. On his registration form with the Harvard Appointment Office, Arthur wrote that his thesis, entitled "Conflict of Ideas in Jacksonian Democracy," was expected in "1942 fall." No one would be better able to push the administrative and examination process along faster than Schlesinger himself, a man who, his friend Bernard DeVoto noted at this time, "dominates every committee he gets on."[30]

But there was something deeper at work too. As Marian remarked of her husband's relationship with his father, "Mr. Schlesinger had a very strong control over him." More than that, he had a vision for his career. DeVoto, no enemy, astutely noted how "the meek and mild Arthur Schlesinger has a tremendous drive for power." He had formidable political skills to match that drive. "He's been on the History committee for four years now," DeVoto observed admiringly, "score: [jobs to] two pupils of Arthur's." Manipulation, maneuver, and jockeying for position—these were skills that Schlesinger routinely applied with masterly deftness in the game of Harvard academic politics. It was inconceivable that he would not pull the same levers for his own son.[31]

Arthur was not keeping his personal journal at this point, so his private thoughts on the subject went unrecorded. Marian recognized that her husband had "an ambivalent attitude towards Harvard that was probably connected with the fact that he felt under his father's pressure." But at the same time, like an academic homing pigeon, whenever Arthur had been given the opportunity to fly off to new horizons, he always came back to the Harvard coop. At moments of extremity, whether suffering a crisis of identity at the end of his junior year, struggling with his book proofs in England, or facing an uncertain future after the Society of Fellows, it was always to Schlesinger Sr. that he turned. For all the intellectual exuberance of the early years and the scope of the Jacksonian project, he was now transformed into a registered PhD student without an academic appointment or higher qualification, struggling with a manuscript that was already too long, and reliant on the good offices of his father and the Society of Fellows, the latter of which now offered to extend his fellowship by an extra year.

In the end, Arthur's ambivalence about Harvard was reconciled not by academic considerations but by life. Not only did he have a child on the way (twins as it turned out), but the world was transformed during his third year at the Society of Fellows. He had tuned in to listen to a Sunday afternoon concert given by the New York Philharmonic Orchestra on December 7, when "the radio suddenly blared out the unbelievable news" that Japanese forces had attacked Pearl Harbor. "An era came to an end," he wrote later.

That was true for many in what Tom Brokaw later called the "Greatest Generation," who would now face perhaps the bloodiest war in history. But for Arthur it also meant leaving home for the second time. In 1942, with his academic prospects sketchy, Arthur applied for a job in a newly created government agency, the Office of War Information (OWI). At the end of August, a week after twins Stephen and Katharine were born, Arthur received an offer. "We can [give] you a place here as a writer-researcher at $3200," Henry Pringle, the chief of the OWI's Bureau of Publications, wrote, "to start at your earliest convenience." The Schlesingers were going to Washington.[32]

CHAPTER FOUR

A KNEE-PANTS GENIUS

Wﾒﾒith an executive order in June 1942, six months after the United States entered World War II, Franklin Roosevelt established the Office of War Information (OWI). The agency would soon become, even by the standards of Washington, DC, a snakepit of intrigue, competing interests, and sharp practice. The problem was a simple but perennial one for any democratic nation at war: how much can you propagandize your own citizens in the search for victory? The agency would provide Arthur Schlesinger Jr. with his first difficult lesson in the conflict between idealism and the hard realities of politics.

Schlesinger arrived in Washington in September 1942, leaving Marian and the newborn twins behind while he looked for a place to live. In the meantime, he stayed with Marian's sister, Wilma, who was married to John King Fairbank, the "dean" of modern Chinese studies in the United States. Although Fairbank was ten years older than Schlesinger, the two men enjoyed a reasonably cordial relationship. Later they worked together in organizing the "non-Communist Left," and Schlesinger would help when his brother-in-law was named in front of the Senate Internal Security Subcommittee (SISS). "Fairbank greatly admired my father and the sentiment was very much reciprocated," Arthur's son Stephen later recalled. "I never saw anything in their relationship other than respect." Even so, there was a slight condescension in Fairbank's attitude, particularly after Arthur became famous. In Fairbank's 1982 memoir, he wrote that Teddy White, in the same class as Arthur, was the "most exciting" student he came across in Cambridge. Teaching White was "like Fourth of July fireworks," even if he had arrived at Harvard "without presenting letters of introduction, being au courant with the theater and books of the moment, having made the grand tour of major European capitals, and the other superficial frills." The sideswipe at his brother-in-law, who in 1934 had returned to Harvard from his world tour replete with letters of recommendation, was obvious enough.[1]

By the end of October, Schlesinger had found a place for his family at 5353 Broad Branch Road, near Chevy Chase village in northwest Washington. The neighborhood resembled the familiar suburban surroundings of 19 Gray Gardens East in Cambridge. Schlesinger "rushed back" to Massachusetts to collect his family before returning with them to Washington's Union Station, where the twins were pushed along the crowded platform by a porter cheerfully shouting "Make way for two of a kind!"[2]

At the OWI, Schlesinger joined the Writers Division, occupying the desk recently vacated by McGeorge Bundy, with whom his Harvard and his political careers would later become so entwined. There he ghosted speeches, memoranda, and letters, including those for presidential signature, quickly discovering that he was "deplorably adept at a ghostwriter's duplicity." He worked long hours, often late into the night, six days a week, but was sustained by the palpable esprit de corps among the tight knit group of writers. The Pulitzer Prize–winning historian Henry Pringle inspired reverence among his high-strung cohort of journalists and academics. "The spirit is extremely good," Schlesinger reported home, with "all devoted to Pringle."[3]

Pringle and the writers saw themselves not just as ghostwriters but as educators for a public they believed did not understand that the United States was "not yet more than ankle deep in this war." To sharpen national awareness of the war, they published solemn pamphlets such as "Divide and Conquer," which profiled Hitler's plans, as well as those like "How to Raise $16 Billion," which drew attention to the required sacrifices on the home front. Many of these pamphlets gave rise to public criticism, not least from a hostile Congress, which often saw them as propaganda, not for the United States but for FDR's New Deal. It was not surprising, then, that Schlesinger's first proper assignment should immediately have thrown him headfirst into the middle of an ongoing political row. Reports of public drunkenness among US soldiers had prompted demands for a ban on sales of liquor near military camps. Some even called for a return to Prohibition, inspired by World War I and repealed less than a decade earlier. Galvanized by this threat to the flourishing drinking culture of the OWI Writers Division, Pringle dispatched his young researchers around the country to investigate the graphic stories of intoxication and debauchery to see if they were true.[4]

Schlesinger traveled south on a sixteen-day tour of alcoholic duty, starting at Fort Bragg in North Carolina before heading down to Fort Benning in Georgia and Keesler Field in Mississippi, and then turning west to Fort Riley in Kansas, Fort Crowder in Missouri, and Fort Knox in Kentucky. "Our mission, we discovered not without pleasure, required frequent stops at local bars and night spots," Schlesinger recalled afterwards. His notes at the time record visits to "crowded juke box joint[s] with a lot of soldiers dancing with a lot of cheap tarts." "You bum!" his wife chided him after receiving his first letter home. "You sound as if you were suffering *no* hardships!"[5]

Reporting back to Pringle at the end of the trip, Schlesinger told him that "It is my judgement that the situation at present is thoroughly under control, and that the enactment of prohibition would enormously complicate the problems of the existing enforcement agencies." Certainly many new recruits drank out of a combination of loneliness, ennui, and anxiety about the coming fight, but public concerns about poor conduct seemed to be mainly connected with rowdy train rides shared with soldiers at the start or end of their furlough. There were no recommendations to be made, because essentially there was no problem. "No American Army in all history has been so orderly," Schlesinger and the other writers concluded in their "Coast to Coast Survey of Drinking Conditions in and around Army Camps."[6]

Schlesinger needed a stiff whisky all the same. Although he had been dispatched to investigate the drinking culture in and around army bases, in fact, he reported to Pringle, "people would show no interest in the drunkenness question and say, 'If you really want to investigate something, you ought to investigate the race question.'" Thus while Marian had been writing to him of "your beautiful children . . . now peacefully sleeping in their little beds . . . tucked up to the chin with warm blankets and completely surrounded by soft animals," Schlesinger confronted for the first time in his life the brutal reality of what race relations meant in the southern United States.[7]

In a long memo to Pringle, Schlesinger embarked on a *tour d'horizon* on "the Negro question." It was as revealing of its author as of race relations in the South. "You would always expect," he started off, "to find bitter anti-Negro feeling among poor whites" who took out "their own frustrations and insecurities" on their African American neighbors. What had changed recently, however, was the relationship between "a majority of the southern ruling class and a majority of the Negro population." Previously "they have understood each other, and this sense of mutual confidence has made a very real kind of feudal and paternalistic relation possible between the races." Now, "so far as I could see, the whole white South is feeling toward the Negro the way that formerly just the poor white felt."

Why the transformation? For Schlesinger, "the basic cause of this change seems to be the steady and unremitting aspiration of the Negro." Increased economic opportunity as a result of a shortfall in manpower aggravated by the draft had "increased the confidence and the intransigence of the Negro." The labor shortage had resulted "not only in higher wages, but in increased impertinence on the part of the servants, and considerable (and unapologetic) absenteeism."

And what to do? "The tragedy of the situation," Schlesinger concluded jarringly in his memorandum, "is that no improvement would be made by giving more power to the Negro. The southern Negro would abuse power even more than the reactionary southern white. . . . The only hope in the situation lies in activity by the southern liberals, and this hope is scant. It is very difficult in the war situation to see any steps which might be taken without antagonizing either the conservative whites or the radical Negroes. The situation just looks bad."[8]

In his 2000 memoir, *A Life in the 20th Century: Innocent Beginnings,*

1917–1950, Schlesinger made much of how "the true horror of the black predicament had not burst upon me until I crossed the Mason-Dixon Line," where "I felt that I had never imagined such misery and wretchedness in America."[9] There can be no doubting his shock at what he heard and saw, which were both far removed from the subtle forms of institutional and personal racism that he would have encountered growing up in the Midwest and in Cambridge, Massachusetts.

Schlesinger would later admit that "my conclusion was grim and contained statements I would soon renounce." Yet subtle differences remain between what he wrote at the time and the vulpine eliding of detail he presented more than half a century later. Some of this difference amounted to no more than a shift away from anachronistic language. More significant were the subtle fakes and feints as he shifted from broad identification with the white population to empathy with embattled African Americans. So, for example, where in 1942 Schlesinger reports how "a charming southern lady of Fayetteville, wife of the local Episcopalian minister, presumably relatively enlightened, told of a brush with her maid over lynching," in 2000 the story becomes that of "a charming southern gentlewoman—*charming, at least, till she launched into a hysterical tirade on race* [my italics]"—the "charming at least" artfully recalibrating the balance of sympathy within the whole experience. Similarly, in 1942, southern whites feared that "their physical security is essentially imperilled, along with the purity of their womanhood and the lives of their children. These fears," Schlesinger judged baldly, "are probably justified." In 2000, he added, "so long, that is, as the white south maintained its rigid belief in white supremacy."[10]

In such ways, the older Schlesinger parsed the casual racism of his 1940s self, carefully re-presenting his views in line with those he held later on racial equality and thereby carefully protecting his progressive reputation in the process. His views on race were not untypical even among progressives. Certainly Franklin Roosevelt, in the words of his aide Tommy Corcoran, "ain't gonna lose votes for it." Instead it was the First Lady, Eleanor Roosevelt, who set the liberal bar with a series of important symbolic gestures such as rising to get a glass of water for a black speaker at

Bethune-Cookman College or resigning from the Daughters of the American Revolution when they barred world-renowned singer Marian Anderson from performing.[11]

Schlesinger did warn Pringle that the South would see "a shocking explosion one of these days," but once he was back at the OWI, the writers were too concerned about bureaucratic disputes to worry about what they had seen. In the fall of 1942, when Schlesinger was on his field trip in the South, the OWI was coming under increasing fire from Congress. Prominent Republican figures such as Senator Henry Cabot Lodge Jr. of Massachusetts denounced its publications as propaganda for the New Deal. Some of the antagonism was procedural; pamphlets such as "Battle Stations for All" on inflation weighed in on policy topics that were under active review in Congress. The rest was fury that OWI often looked like a committee to reelect the president. The first issue of the OWI's *Victory* magazine featured an article on Roosevelt, "President, Champion of Liberty, United States Leader in the War to Win Lasting and Worldwide Peace." Under a huge color photo, it portrayed FDR as a saintly figure whose political philosophy contrasted with "the toryism of the conservative reactionary." John Taber, a Republican congressman from New York, denounced the magazine as "outlandish, ridiculous, expensive." OWI protested that it was meant for overseas, not home consumption. But a groundswell of opinion quickly developed on both sides of the aisle in Congress that OWI was actually doing more to hinder the war effort than help it. It was no surprise when Harry F. Byrd, senator from Virginia, announced that his Joint Committee for the Reduction of Nonessential Federal Expenses would soon be investigating "government propaganda ventures."[12]

Responding to the spiraling political situation, OWI in early 1943 embarked on an internal reorganization, with new figures brought in from advertising and business to help shape the message of its reports. That outraged Schlesinger and most of his fellow writers. "The issue is whether you can sell the war the way you sell cigarettes," Schlesinger wrote to his old tutor, Bernard DeVoto. "There are two kinds of propaganda," he went on, "one makes people think, and the other does their thinking for them;

and OWI is presumably to do the second." The new people were nothing more than "advertising prostitutes." In truth it was an old-fashioned clash of cultures and politics. The OWI had started life as the Office of Facts and Figures, committed to a "strategy of truth" and staffed by the likes of the Pulitzer Prize–winning Pringle. The more recent recruits, often brash, business-savvy ad men, were a poor fit for the left-leaning, intellectually scornful, high-end journalists and academics who made up the Writers Division of the OWI. "The new order," Schlesinger raged, "contemplated a glorified advertising agency, with a cage of copy writers to leap around as the idea men directed."[13]

Schlesinger joined a delegation that "presented very forcibly our opinions" to the administration on these issues, but the "internecine difficulties" continued. When Pringle was dismissed and publicly accused of incompetence, Schlesinger and fourteen other writers resigned in protest. On the day he went, April 14, 1943, Schlesinger had expressed his fury in person to the director of OWI, Elmer Davis, but on every point found his "terribly sad" boss able to provide nothing more than "unhappy and, to my mind, evasive answers." Schlesinger "came out feeling very lousy." Writing his letter of resignation to Davis that same day, he repeated his condemnation of the changes that had put the work of the Writers Division "into the hands of men for whom putting out the truth is a secondary consideration."[14]

Schlesinger and the fourteen other departing writers also issued a statement to the press. "There is only one issue," it said plainly, "the deep and fundamental one of the honest presentation of war information. We are leaving because of our conviction that it is impossible for us, under those who now control our output, to tell the full truth." Predictably, the statement created a stir. The *Washington Daily News* reported, "concerning that OWI upheaval, it was facts vs. ballyhoo and the fact boys walked out." The *Washington Post* columnist, Ernest K. Lindley, weighed in portentously that the "row within OWI again poses [a] perennial question: What is Truth?"[15]

Back at OWI, Davis was so angry with the public embarrassment that he had all the writers struck off the payroll with immediate effect. He rejected their offers to finish work in progress. When Chester Kerr, chief of the OWI book department and later author of the influential "Report on American University Presses," slyly tried to recruit Schlesinger to his own department, Davis informed him in abrupt terms that the rebels would never work for OWI again. "When people jump out of a ten story building," the director observed, "they ought to consider such things in advance."[16]

Davis had a point. There had been a naïveté in Schlesinger's stand—the wartime context had muddied the waters for OWI in ways that he seemed unwilling even to consider—but he had stood his ground on a point of principle and had acted honorably. But neither of those qualities put food on the family table. For all that Schlesinger had found the whole thing "a valuable and enlightening experience," he was at the end of the day unemployed. Clearly that prospect gave him pause before resigning. It was true "that there was no future for me in OWI," he told DeVoto glumly, but "two babies make one hesitate before indulging in romantic gestures."[17]

The odd timing of the government querying his loyalty to the state gave fuel to the fires of conspiracy theorists. That spring, Schlesinger was hauled in front of the Civil Service Commission, which judged the suitability of candidates for employment at agencies such as OWI, to answer questions about his political past. "The examiner would say, 'Information has reached the Civil Service Commission that one Arthur M. Schlesinger . . .' and then the charge would follow," he wrote home to his parents. It soon became clear that "actually I had inherited Dad's dossier, so that I could answer in every case that I was not the person involved." (Later, when Arthur was vetted for the Kennedy administration, investigators found that Schlesinger Sr. had "unwittingly associated with communist front groups in [the] 1930s and early 1940s"—notably in campaigns supporting the Republican side in the Spanish Civil War.) Stony-faced questioners in 1943 charged Schlesinger Jr. with being a "commie," but he was unable to ferret out "how seriously" any of them took their accusations. All told, "it was rather a silly business," but, unspoken, also an unsettling one that anticipated future "red scare" tactics that would also ensnare Schlesinger.[18]

Schlesinger's discomfort at government questions after his leaving OWI in controversial circumstances was intensified by his inability to join the military—an obvious step in 1943 for a man of his age needing employment. When he took soundings about a naval commission, he was firmly rebuffed. In part, his bad eyesight counted against him. But that was hardly an insuperable problem, as the navy was unlikely to have used him to command a ship (or even a boat). Certainly poor vision had not barred McGeorge Bundy from joining the army; this Society of Fellows confrère simply memorized the eyesight test chart beforehand. No, what seemed more important was whether the navy believed Schlesinger would be a security liability. Later in 1943 he would test that security question with a formal application to become a naval officer. For now, however, he concluded that he must "reluctantly accept" the situation on "the naval commission business."[19]

Unemployed, shunned by the navy, and feeling vaguely threatened by the government, Schlesinger might have been concerned about his future. But he had been brought up since childhood as a Harvard man and, now in straitened circumstances, he reverted to type by asking another for help. For most of Schlesinger's life, he had pressed Harvard friends and colleagues of his father into action at crucial moments. Applying to the university in 1933, James Phinney Baxter III, the head of Adams House, the very house that Schlesinger himself joined as an undergraduate and where his father was a fellow, served as Schlesinger's referee. By 1943, Baxter had taken wartime leave from Harvard to join the Office of Strategic Services (OSS), where he headed the Research and Analysis Branch. Come and work for me, Baxter now told him when he became aware of Schlesinger's predicament. "His proposition did not appeal to me particularly," Schlesinger admitted to his parents, but short of returning to Cambridge with his tail between his legs, he had no other option.[20]

OSS began in June 1942 as a successor to the Office of the Coordinator of Information (COI) set up the previous year. The agencies were part of an attempt to harmonize US intelligence efforts and were forerunners of the modern Central Intelligence Agency (CIA). William "Wild Bill" J. Donovan, a charismatic, fearless Irish-American war hero from Buffalo, headed both ventures. Donovan had married into money and had the good luck to be a classmate of FDR's at Columbia Law School. He inspired fierce loyalty among those who worked for him, although not, as it turned out, Arthur Schlesinger. "He is simply an amiable fool," the new recruit wrote home sourly after a few weeks on the job. The cultural historian Louis Menand would later go so far as to say that the visceral Donovan was the "human opposite" of the cerebral Schlesinger.[21]

Schlesinger's scathing judgment on Donovan reflected a broader sense of disappointment that he felt on joining OSS. He had not wanted to work there in the first place, so the frustration became a self-fulfilling prophecy. "The job is very disappointing," he complained, adding, "please do not spread this; I don't want it to get back to OSS until I am ready to leave." Part of the problem was the culture of OSS itself. In *Cloak and Gown: Scholars in the Secret War*, Schlesinger's friend Robin Winks would describe, in a way that cannot entirely have amused Arthur, how Secret Intelligence (SI) and Counterintelligence (X-2) were "the coaches, the clever men, the quarterbacks," while Special Operations (SO) "housed the rest of the jocks." Research and Analysis (R&A) on the other hand, where Schlesinger was billeted, "gave refuge to the weenies and wimps, the glassy-eye students on campus who came out to cheer the team on and who burrowed in the libraries." For Schlesinger, it was unhappily like being back at Phillips Exeter Academy.[22]

R&A was charged to find Axis strengths and weaknesses using open sources such as books, newspapers, and government publications. "R&A," notes Winks, "could, with a good library at its back and scholars skilled in drawing secrets from a library, get at most of the material of the operational branch of OSS, and equally important, of the Army and Navy, State or Treasury, needed." There was even a card index retrieval system that mirrored a great library such as the Widener. But as more recent historians of R&A have pointed out, "it could not always answer the 'so what?' question posed by decision-makers." Information for its own sake was not enough: it needed to serve a strategic or tactical purpose. Both of those characteristics were part of the problem for Schlesinger. There was no question whether he could do the work; rather, the job simply bored him. "Everyone just does research and writes reports which, except for the content, might be carried on in any library, and has about that atmosphere," he griped. But R&A was too much of a back office experience for Schlesinger. He missed the esprit de corps of the OWI writers. And he missed their influence. "It is a tremendous anti-climax after the OWI job," he wrote to Cambridge. "OSS is terrifically remote from the politics of the capital. For all the deathly secrecy of much of the material, there is a kind of ivory-tower serenity about the place; no one seems to care very much about what is happening in Congress or [the War Production Board]." The contrast with his past life in OWI was almost unbearable. "I had some sense of effectiveness," he groaned. "Someone would give a speech or issue a statement which I wrote; but here the effort seems to me largely wasted." As an undergraduate in 1937 he had expressed his great cri de coeur as one who must not become "insulated from most of the currents that electrify vital life." Now those fears of irrelevance seemed to have come true in, of all places, the nation's capital.[23]

At R&A Schlesinger edited an in-house classified journal on psychological warfare called PW Weekly. Right from the beginning, he loathed it. After his first few editions, he wrote a memorandum making the point that the whole premise was flawed. Hard information, such as the movement of ships or trains, the availability of raw materials, the placement of bridges, harbors, beaches: this was the information and research that was essential for military action. But psychoanalysis of Nazi propaganda, he argued, was a waste of time. How could R&A know the extent to which the German Propaganda Ministry was inside the loop? Certainly if it was anything like the OWI, then it would be "in the dark" about military intentions. And propaganda by its nature was unreliable. "Can we escape from the fact," Schlesinger warned, "that Nazi propaganda, in making a point, may choose to make that point directly, or to make the diametrically opposite point, or to make any number of points in between?"

Instead, Schlesinger attempted to push PW Weekly in a more political direction, writing another position paper entitled "The need for intellectual guidance in psychological warfare research." Here Schlesinger argued that R&A needed "a greater degree of intellectual unity." The material that came into his office from the various regional desks was often contradictory. "Scandinavia [desk] disapproves of Danish sabotage, while Central Europe is delighted by it and urges it on," he cited as an example. But no one took "steps towards reconciliation." Yet surely, he urged, only by enforcing "agreement upon itself can R&A hope to bring much influence to bear on people outside." Sherman Kent, often called the "father of intelligence analysis," took the paper sufficiently seriously to put structures in place within his own Europe-Africa Division to ensure a more consolidated approach.[24]

For the most part, however, Schlesinger was on the outside. R&A was nicknamed "the campus" after the nine hundred or so intellectuals and academics who filled its corridors. Specialists like the historians Felix Gilbert and Hajo Holborn would convene weekly evening seminars to debate issues and drink into the early hours. It was an environment in which Schlesinger in other circumstances might have felt at home. But for all his scholarly credentials, within this campus environment he was "staff," not "faculty." While the analysts composed their hundred-page reports, Schlesinger's job was "boiling down and editing" those documents for short articles in *PW Weekly*. The R&A official history would later praise the "peppy style and all-consuming appetite" of his editorship, but at the time it did not bring him much prestige with his colleagues. When they engaged with him at all, it was mostly to complain that he had butchered their precious work.[25]

No doubt Schlesinger was personally unhappy during his stint at *PW Weekly*. "It is like going into retirement," he grouched, adding that "I have a mounting suspicion that the whole thing is a gigantic boondoggle." "Very rarely in this process is anything outside OSS affected by anything happening inside it," he lamented. History would judge that was not the case, but to Schlesinger, stuck with editing the in-house magazine, it felt like a job, he grandly informed his parents, that "will be in no sense a developing experience."[26]

Schlesinger in a position paper that summer had staked out his belief that R&A analysis could not be an "altogether neutral" process. "Fact, judgment and value," he argued, "are inextricably entangled." What he had not anticipated was that the judgments and values of some in R&A might be, to introduce a later controversial term, un-American. That realization not only dragged him into an office row every bit as nasty as the one at OWI; it shaped his worldview in ways that would have profound consequences for his actions during the "red scare" of the postwar years.[27]

Maurice Halperin, born in 1906, was a generation older than Schlesinger, but the two men shared a Boston childhood, a Harvard education, and a European Jewish background that formed a minimal part of their identities. When the war broke out, Halperin was teaching Latin American studies at the University of Oklahoma at a time the discipline was in its infancy. In the summer of 1941, William Langer recruited him to OSS, where he soon became head of the Latin American desk. Unfortunately for Langer, Halperin was also almost certainly a Soviet spy. Towards the end of the war, American and British military code breakers would crack high-grade Soviet communications from Washington, which they codenamed "Venona." By 1953, that information, combined with information from the one-time Soviet spy Elizabeth Bentley, led to an FBI investigation and a subpoena to Halperin to appear before the Senate Internal Security Subcommittee (SISS). He fled, eventually finding his way to Moscow (where he constantly complained about the food) and then to Cuba, until finally he took up residence at Simon Fraser University near Vancouver, British Columbia. Halperin died in 1995, still denying that he was a spy. The weight of recent scholarship and archival releases shows that denial to have been a lie. Even his friend Don Kirschner, who wrote a scholarly book on the case, concluded that Halperin was guilty as charged.[28]

While he was procuring OSS secret files and passing them to the Soviets, Halperin's tactic, like that of the British spy Guy Burgess, was to hide in plain sight. "He used to have copies of the *Daily Worker* [published by the CPUSA and not known for its Latin American coverage] on his desk," Schlesinger later recounted for the OSS Oral History Project. "He took a straight party line."[29]

Things blew up between the two men over the unlikely question of Bolivia. Just before Christmas 1943, members of the Nationalist Revolutionary Movement (MNR) overthrew Bolivian president Enrique

Peñaranda. Given that Peñaranda had supported the US war effort, his overthrow caused concern in Washington. At a press conference immediately afterwards, US Secretary of State Cordell Hull pointed out that leaders of the revolution had visited Argentina ten weeks earlier to confer with Nazi sympathizers. "Included in the relevant considerations," Hull said when asked whether the United States would recognize the new regime, "is the question of whether outside influence unfriendly to the allied cause played any part."[30]

That was the context for Halperin's report for *PW Weekly* on the takeover. "Maybe two months before Peñaranda was overthrown he was in Washington at a big reception," Halperin recalled. "This was official red carpet treatment. And there's no question about it: he was 100% pro-U.S. So this man was overthrown, and you had to look at it very carefully to see what you were getting in return: . . . a combination of populist reformers, anti-imperialists and out-and-out Nazis and anti-Semites. The anti-imperialism was anti-American . . . and accordingly we submitted in our weekly report an analysis of the situation that the new government was hostile to the United States."[31]

Schlesinger saw matters quite differently. Noticing that Halperin's line was almost identical to that of the Communist *Daily Worker*, which condemned the coup as pro-Nazi, he spoke to Laurence Duggan in the Latin American Division of the State Department and Ernesto Galarza at the Pan-American Union (later the Organization of American States). Then he reversed Halperin's line and wrote up the coup as resistance to "the domination of the country by the tin interests, the inefficiency and corruption of the Peñaranda Government, the food shortages and the uncontrolled inflation." An incongruous alliance of mine owners and local Communists spread rumors that the coup was Nazi-inspired. The United States "must await more conclusive evidence of pro-Nazi leanings than tales from sources close to the mine owners or from Communist organizations."[32]

There was little question that Halperin's reports consistently breached the guidelines the State Department laid down for R&A that it should never "suggest, recommend or in any way determine the strategy or the tactical decisions of the war." The rules had been put in place specifically to neutralize what was seen as the infiltration of R&A staff by Communists and the hard Left. Officials in OSS generally turned a blind eye, as did their counterparts in other spheres of government. Sometimes, as when questions were raised about whether Robert Oppenheimer and scientists at the Manhattan Project were spying for the Soviets, the bigger picture prevailed. At other times, domestic political considerations became a factor. Roosevelt knew that American Communists, who supported his war aim of "unconditional surrender" as well as some elements of the New Deal, would vote for the Democratic Party in 1944. The president routinely disavowed Communist support, but as his Republican opponent Thomas A. Dewey pointed out, it was a "soft disclaimer." Either way, the battle lines for postwar debates about fellow travelers and Communism were already being drawn.[33]

The fact that Halperin was working for the Soviets confirms that fears about infiltration were not misplaced. But Schlesinger's judgment on the question was flawed too. He undermined his own case by using information, complete with Spanish mistranslations, that Halperin showed was plagiarized from political tracts by Italian socialist refugees. Then there was the later discovery that Schlesinger's own source, Laurence Duggan, was also a Soviet agent who abused his access to Sumner Welles, undersecretary of state and FDR's most trusted advisor on Latin American affairs. In short, the whole affair was a tangle of confusion and betrayal, exacerbated by a clash of academic egos.[34]

Halperin reacted furiously to the next edition of *PW Weekly*. Storming into the office of William Langer, now head of R&A, Halperin demanded to know who this "pasty face boy" was. "Maybe you don't need a Latin America Division," he sneered, "if you have one man who can handle this, maybe you don't need us." Langer reassured him that was not the case. To prove it, he called Schlesinger in for a dressing-down, telling him to "use the reports from the Latin America desk or nothing."[35]

Accounts differ on what happened next. Both protagonists agree that Schlesinger presented himself in Halperin's office in an agitated state. Halperin remembered Schlesinger being "literally in a rage, like a young child in a tantrum . . . yelling at the top of his voice." When Arthur kept yelling, the dyspeptic Halperin rose from his chair, advanced on the smaller man, "and, as I recall it, I grabbed him by the collar of his coat, turned him around, and shoved him out." Schlesinger remembered the verbal exchange but not the ejection. "I am sure I would have recalled physical assault," he said when Halperin's biographer questioned him on the matter. Either way, Schlesinger certainly came off worse from the incident and his reputation at R&A suffered. For his annual OSS efficiency rating report, he received just "adequate" for "cooperativeness." This came so soon after his acrimonious exit from OWI that Schlesinger was cementing a reputation as a difficult colleague. He was, in Halperin's derisive phrase, too much of "a knee-pants genius."[36]

Schlesinger had not wanted to join OSS in the first place; now he was being censured by his boss, shouting in other people's offices and being physically intimidated by colleagues. It was time to depart. On December 29, his boss and current intelligence chief, another Harvard historian, S. Everett Gleason, told Langer that "AS Jr. wants to go to London." The OSS station there was looking for someone to pep up their R&A weekly summaries. Schlesinger seemed qualified for the task.[37]

Three days later, to help facilitate the move, Schlesinger formally executed an application for a commission in the navy (which would then transfer him back to OSS). In a case of déjà vu, his naval interview turned out to be an uncomfortable affair. A Division of Navy Records summary reflected continuing suspicion that Schlesinger's father was "a member of numerous organizations and movements," some of which were "alleged Communist front groups." The summary also indicated that "the applicant's associates and references had been connected with various radical and front movements." As Schlesinger wrote to his wife years afterwards when his file was opened, "It does not look as if the Navy confused me with my father [as had happened earlier]; rather that the investigators felt that the son was carrying on the dirty work of the father."

In 1948, the FBI, which investigated Schlesinger when he assisted Averell Harriman under the Marshall Plan, found that "all persons interviewed in connection with this investigation described Schlesinger as a violently anti-communist liberal; no one alleged that he was or ever had been a communist or communist sympathizer." The FBI would find that Arthur Sr. had "unwittingly associated with communist front groups in 1930s." In 1944, however, these suspicions kept Schlesinger out of the navy. His "defective vision" provided sufficient excuse to turn him down. On February 19, 1944, the navy advised Schlesinger that after "a complete examination of your qualifications in relation to the overall demands of the service, the Bureau regrets that it is impractical to approve your application. In addition to the foregoing, you do not meet the approved standards of physical qualifications for the appointment as an officer in the US Naval Reserve."[38]

The rejection was yet another blow in a tumultuous twelve months. Fortunately Harvard once again came to the rescue. On February 22, three days after the brush-off from the navy, Crane Brinton, R&A chief in London and another colleague of Arthur Schlesinger Sr., wrote to William Langer saying that he wanted Arthur Jr. anyway. "In order to remedy some of the recognized weaknesses of the present coverage," he recommended "that Arthur Schlesinger be assigned to London at the earliest possible date and that he be entrusted here with the composition of the weekly summary or summaries."[39]

Langer agreed, but matters were complicated when the story of the navy rejecting Schlesinger became public. Drew Pearson, the author of a syndicated muckraking political column, broadcast a story on March 12 on his weekly NBC radio show *Drew Pearson Comments* that the navy had turned Schlesinger down for overtly political reasons. Arthur later noted that Pearson had "picked up the story somewhere," which formulation hides one Phillips Exeter Academy alum telling his story to another. Now the story was sufficiently embarrassing for the navy that Admiral Louis Denfeld asked to see Schlesinger's file. But the memorandum that came back could not have been clearer: "that the report of investigation had been unsatisfactory and that the applicant was not physically qualified." The admiral was in no mood to relent. The navy issued a terse press release saying they had rejected Schlesinger because he was physically unfit for duty. "I have a complete sense of being tried and condemned without a chance to defend myself," Arthur complained to his father.[40]

Despite the setback, Schlesinger continued to agitate for a move to London even while Langer continued to demur. His friends in London continued to call for his presence. "Mr. Schlesinger," wrote Harold Deutsch, the chief of political research and another Harvard-educated historian, would fill "one of the most important posts in the R&A Branch, being that of Chief Editor and, in many cases, direct the composition of projects, which will be directly concerned with the servicing of psychological warfare operations during the anticipated invasion."[41]

Schlesinger, in fact, would miss D-Day on June 6, but in the end Langer relented. On June 27, 1944, Arthur Schlesinger Jr. departed for England aboard the RMS *Queen Elizabeth* to join the Research and Analysis team in London. The previous day, having bid an emotional farewell to the twenty-month-old twins in Washington, he spent a night in New York with Marian. At the Onyx Club on West 52nd Street they heard Billie Holiday, her voice "filled with heartbreak," Schlesinger recalled, "as she sang the song that lingered in my ears for the rest of the war: "I'll be seeing you, In all the old familiar places."

"Darling, I love you so much," he wrote to Marian from the ship. "Kiss the babies and remind them of their father occasionally."[42]

CHAPTER FIVE

THE REAL EDUCATION OF ARTHUR SCHLESINGER JR.

Almost exactly a month after D-Day, Schlesinger arrived in London, where at first he was happy to be back. "Life in London is thus quite pleasant," he reported brightly to his wife Marian, "except for such minor annoyances as the absence of you." But as the weeks wore on, it seemed gradually to dawn on him just how much he missed his American life and family.[1]

The previous year, Schlesinger had bragged to Bernard DeVoto about having a "lovely girl, whom you will meet when you come down" on the side in DC. Now, even when meeting Anne Whyte, his English paramour from his Peterhouse days, he admitted to "developing into a sedate married man, because I promptly showed her the picture" of Marian and the twins. Expressions of love in letters home moved from the generic to the increasingly heartfelt, as Schlesinger came to realize "how god damned lucky I have been to get some one whom I can love as much and trust as much and feel as utterly *sympathique* with as I do with you."

This state of affairs prompted a certain bafflement. "I am fed up to the teeth with being separated," he complained to Marian by September. "All this is very astonishing to me." Theirs would never be an easy relationship, and there were still unhappy moments when "your semi-psychotic" behavior "reminded me of the old days" and he wondered about being married to such a "nasty and beautiful girl." But throughout those summer months, Arthur's sense of what he already had intensified, as "in my general weariness and depression the thought that I am married to you, and have K&S [the twins Katharine and Stephen], and will return to all of you before too long, is the most compelling and wonderful of all thoughts." His English friends provided an insight into what Marian had to put up with. "In some ways he's very immature," Anne Whyte complained to Charles Wintour, "in spite of his enormous brain."[2]

Life in wartime London, so different from the happy time he had spent there in 1938–1939, did not lift his spirits. Schlesinger arrived in London just two weeks after the first V-1 rockets had fallen. "The tense period comes when the motor stops," he wrote home to his parents somewhat thoughtlessly. "You get five to fifty seconds of silence; then comes the explosion. It is not nice." Only belatedly did he reassure them he would "take every precaution" and was getting "a full night's sleep every night; so should you." Danger, however, would heighten from September onwards when the V-1 rockets were supplemented with the much more powerful V-2 ballistic missile, about which he told them, "you never know it is coming until it goes off." Schlesinger witnessed many attacks at first hand. In addition to his regular job, he was required to "stand fireguard" most days, and "occasionally" bombs or rockets would come near ("but you get used to it all").

Schlesinger had the "harrowing" experience of watching as "a good friend of ours suddenly appeared in acute stage of nervous breakdown." His own condition often seemed fragile too. Certainly he enjoyed the gallows humor that the situation prompted, often reporting good one-liners home. ("I am not worried about one of those bombs having my name on it," a colleague laconically observed while they shared fire guard duty. "The one I'm worried about is labeled 'To whom it may concern.'") His brother Tom was posted to England that July, and although the two were never particularly close, Schlesinger enjoyed his visits to see him at his base in Winchester. New friendships helped as well, including the historian Walter Lord, with whom he shared rooms. Even better, he renewed old ones. Whenever Wintour was home on leave from France, the two would meet at the fashionable Savoy Grill and then drink late into the night. They particularly enjoyed the cognac that Charles had brought back from France "marked everywhere 'reserved for the Wehrmacht'" and generally "had a good sodden time." But such nights were the exception. Wintour worried about Arthur's mental and emotional state; his wife Nonie already believed their friend to be "violently and actively" depressed. As Arthur explained to Marian, he was "tired as hell, oversmoked and generally on the downgrade." At such times, the best he could do was look forward to a time when once again he might have "the joys of being surrounded by bourbon, steaks, babies and you."[3]

Facing a job much like his unsatisfactory OSS experience only added to Schlesinger's plight. His principal task was editing R&A's weekly *European Political Report*—essentially the same role that had bored him in Washington, DC. Only the location had changed. "My own job is exhausting, time consuming and not altogether satisfactory," he wrote on August 17. "I am going stale on the matter of putting out a weekly magazine, which I have now done for about 75 weeks without much vacation; I feel, as each weekly rat race recommences, like the Chinese prisoner tortured by the implacable drop of water."[4]

If the work was boring, the office politics were almost too lively. R&A London was engaged that chaotic summer in what historian Nelson McPherson points out was "a desperate, if largely futile, struggle to secure a meaningful role." Its R&A superiors in Washington constantly harassed the London branch. Relationships with British intelligence, the Supreme Headquarters Allied Expeditionary Force (SHAEF), and even other OSS branches in London were at best tenuous, at worst deeply mistrustful. Personnel changed constantly, as different OSS factions maneuvered for influence and authority. "I have for some time felt myself rudderless in a swelling sea," Schlesinger's R&A colleague, the art collector Richard Brown Baker, wrote on July 14. "Despite the lack of a clear sense of direction, we are constantly badgered by ridiculous administrative orders. We are supposed to be an assemblage of scholars and political analysts but in fact we are a herd of baffled people under a barrage of ambitious egotists. My time and the government's money are frequently put to bad use." As Schlesinger himself noted, with the buzz bombs constantly flying overhead, "all this stretched nerves and irascibilities"—not least his own.[5]

Six weeks after arriving in London, Schlesinger was already looking to escape. Luckily, Harvard again came to the rescue. As part of the constant reorganization within OSS, William J. Casey, the head of the Secret Intelligence branch in Europe (and a future director of the CIA under President Reagan), formed a new Secret Intelligence/Research and Analysis Reports Board, based in newly liberated Paris, to centralize the process of dissemination. Philip Horton, the curator of poetry at Harvard's Widener Library and "an old neighbor of ours on Harvard Street," became its chief. In late August, encouraged by Walter Lord, his assistant, Horton asked Schlesinger to become his deputy. "The Paris job will be evidently a pretty good administrative job," Schlesinger wrote to Marian optimistically, "with no weekly responsibilities of the kind which have been demoralizing me here. It is just what I want to round up my career in the government."[6]

Not until the middle of October did the new appointment grind its way through the OSS administrative system, and the intervening lull gave Schlesinger "a little time for thinking, something which I ordinarily can't slow down to do these days." As he pondered, old doubts about academic life began to resurface. In part this was a reaction to putting his next book, *The Age of Jackson*, through the proof stages. Schlesinger found it painful to reduce the original draft at 333,000 words by a third. ("As I go over the damn thing," he told Bernard DeVoto, "I am constantly shocked to see how badly I can write on occasion.") Correcting the Little, Brown page proofs and galleys from thousands of miles away with all the stresses of wartime postal delays strained nerves on both sides of the Atlantic. "I called up your father yesterday about my idea of his working on the master proofs," Marian reported, "but he was highly unenthusiastic so I quickly withdrew my suggestion." Even Arthur Sr. had his limits, although tellingly, Marian also related that "I'll be transferring your father's editorial marks onto the master galleys." But short-term frustrations with Team Schlesinger did not alone account for Junior's uncertainties. For much of his life, his "vision was academic." Now as he began to contemplate life in the postwar world, he found himself "wondering what in hell I will do." Writing for serious magazines seemed more attractive than teaching, "although I don't know how long this mood will last." But whatever opportunities awaited him, Schlesinger was increasingly "impatient to get started on the postwar thing" and keen to resolve his professional future. "You know how uncertainty affects one," he explained to Marian.[7]

On October 19, four days after celebrating his twenty-seventh birthday, Schlesinger finally left London for Paris, arriving, he told his parents, "as the skies cleared and we had a wonderful view of the city as we circled over it: bomb craters near the railroad yards, the Eiffel Tower and the Arc de Triomphe, and everything else." As a civilian with a rank equivalent to a junior officer's (complete with faux military uniform), Arthur was billeted at a hotel on the Rue François 1er between the Champs-Élysées and the Avenue George V, and ate daily in the Officers' Mess, "where the food is simple and good." Life in the wartorn city was not without its discomforts. "There is no heat anywhere, and practically no hot water," he reported. "Hotels have hot water every two or three weeks, which means a long time between baths." Long woolen underwear purchased in London and experience with northeastern winters helped with the cold.[8]

His work, however, was something of an improvement on London. The SIRA project remained chaotic and ill-defined, with the R&A element quickly sidelined by the Secret Intelligence branch. R&A as a unit again proved hopeless at bureaucratic politics and too sniffy about the chore of processing data to give Schlesinger any real chance of being the one to coordinate intelligence on order-of-battle, troop movements, and weaponry. "Everything is in a state of huge uncertainty," Schlesinger wrote days after his arrival, but he added, "it all ought to be fun for a time." Part of the reason for the cheerfulness was that Schlesinger liked working for Philip Horton and enjoyed the renewed company of Horton's assistant, Walter Lord. Even the other deputy chief (military intelligence), Harold Jefferson Coolidge, a direct descendant of the third president of the United States, was a Harvard graduate, "so everything has a distinctly Cantabridgian atmosphere." Together on World War I Armistice Day, November 11, 1944, they stood at "a window over the Champs Elysees in ebullient spirits to watch Churchill and De Gaulle . . . in an open car surrounded by a hollow square of grenadiers on horseback—it was most picturesque and the crowd went wild."[9]

The high spirits of Armistice Day in Paris were quickly dissipated when the United States Army intervened. As the war had developed, eyesight requirements were reduced. "In 1940 minimum visual acuity for general service was set at 20/100 in each eye without glasses, if correctable to 20/40 bilaterally," the US Army Office of Medical History reports. "This was the second most important cause for rejection, and these requirements were progressively lowered. The lowest visual acuity requirements were reached in April 1944, when 20/200 in each eye, or 20/100 in one eye and 20/400 in the second eye (if correctable to 20/40 in each eye, 20/30 in the right and 20/70 in the left, or 20/20 in the right and 20/400 in the left), was sufficient for general service." Even Schlesinger met these new requirements, so the Cambridge Draft Board wrote that fall, ordering him to report for induction into the army. By the time the letter arrived in Paris, he was already "delinquent."[10]

"I am feeling somewhat low at the moment," he wrote to Marian. "The ax has fallen." He would likely be seconded back to OSS in some capacity, but "OSS enlisted men are miserably treated; most of them sleep in the office, in preference to the barracks; they do not eat as well as I have been eating, and so on. I also have misgivings over whether it will be possible for me to carry on my present job dressed as a private." Even his salary would be substantially reduced—more than just a technicality for a man supporting a wife and two small children in Washington.[11]

Certainly Arthur had no desire to become a soldier engaged in active combat. That disposition caused at least some self-reproach. His brother Tom was serving in the Ardennes as a forward observer for the artillery in December when the Battle of the Bulge got under way. Churchill later called it "undoubtedly the greatest American battle of the war." Tom's cheerful note saying, "Doubt like Hell if I'll get to Paris, meet you in Berlin though," provoked "guilty feelings" in his older brother. "I was in comparative safety in Paris, and Tom was at the fighting front," Arthur recalled. "I do not find much virtue in guilt, but this was one point in life when guilt was inescapable." Still, he did not attempt to assuage it by telling the army he wanted to fight.[12]

A brief hiatus followed while the cumbersome army bureaucracy tried to work out how to induct Schlesinger in Paris rather than bringing him back to Cambridge. During that time he busied himself with queries about page proofs and the vexing question of a title for the new book. Writing to his father, he suggested, without much enthusiasm, "Democracy in Crisis: The Jacksonian Tradition"; "Democracy: The Jacksonian Years"; and "Democracy in Action: The Jacksonian Revolution." Finally came "The Age of Jackson and the Democratic Tradition," which his publisher leapt upon. "The Age of Jackson seems OK by me," Schlesinger admitted half-heartedly. "It is not quite accurate, and it sounds a bit too much like an attempt to cash in on Van Wyck Brooks [1937 Pulitzer Prize winner for *The Flowering of New England*]; but on the whole it seems to me the most elevated of the various suggestions." In fact it would turn out to be one of the most famous titles in the writing of American history.[13]

Reading over the proofs, Schlesinger found himself "in the stage of complete non-confidence about it," but whether this had more to do with his general frame of mind than the book is unclear. Life that autumn seemed on a downhill slide for him. He began to drink heavily. Expressions of profound loneliness and absence continued to fill his letters home, and Christmas "undid me." And his deep foreboding about the army continued to intensify.[14]

What made the situation worse for Schlesinger was the dawning realization that William Langer, the head of R&A in Washington, had a personal grudge against him. Schlesinger's boss, Philip Horton, had written to OSS in DC asking them to seek a deferment. On February 21, 1945, Arthur returned to his office to find a crestfallen Horton with a letter from Langer on his desk "expressing total indifference to the problems of trying for a deferment." Unwilling to give up on his young Harvard colleague, Horton went to William Casey, who agreed to go over Langer's head to get the deferment from Charles S. Cheston, acting director of OSS. Cheston cabled back immediately saying OSS did not wish to have Schlesinger deferred. "Dr. Langer in concurrence," Cheston added acidly, the rebuke for trying to subvert the lines of command, which were clear enough. Schlesinger had only worked with Langer for a few months in Washington, including the rambunctious Halperin affair, but clearly it had been enough time for the Washington man to develop a deep antipathy towards his London junior. "If Langer had offered any support, there would have been no question concerning deferment," Schlesinger wrote unhappily, but clearly, "Langer and Washington do not wish to salvage me." No one in Paris tried to disabuse him of that view.[15]

On March 7, 1945, Schlesinger reported to the adjutant of 203rd General Hospital unit. Finding him at lunch, Schlesinger for the last time availed himself of the opportunity to dine in the Officers' Mess. "Then" he told his parents, "I returned, was sworn in, changed my uniform from officer to GI, and dined at the Enlisted Men's Mess." When he got back to OSS by 7 p.m., he removed his uniform and was instructed that from now on he would eat with the cooks above the kitchen. Evicted from his officer's accommodation, he slept in his office or "eight franc a night flop houses." "The queer sensation, at times a bit discouraging," he told Marian, "is that of being excluded all of a sudden from places and prerogatives which one has enjoyed up to now." To console himself, "in my spare time, I devise post-war situations in which I can satisfactorily pull the rug out from under W. L. Langer." Perhaps the only chastening thought was that Arthur's brother, Tom, was in a far worse position. He was now a forward observer for the field artillery on the front line—"a hell of a dangerous job, and his predecessor was killed at it." Despite being a victim of Washington politics, he remained "basically glad as hell that I came over [and] not tormented by the awful feeling that all the important things are being done somewhere else."[16]

There were times, though, when that sense of mission bumped up against his sense of entitlement. He moved to a flat in Montmartre in a room divided by a partition and a long way from the office, but these were circumstances Schlesinger could abide, not least because the house had hot running water. What did plague him was the sense of being crushed beneath the weight of army bureaucracy—and the realization that all these woes were being inflicted upon him rather than happening arbitrarily. Now formally inducted into the army, Schlesinger was informed that he would need to go away for seventeen weeks of basic training ("to provide fodder for the Far Eastern war"). Under normal circumstances, the OSS would have expected to get Schlesinger out of this training. But having not applied for an exemption to stop his joining the army, the agency had by itself implied that he was inessential, and, as only those who were essential could be excused basic training, the army now dug in its heels. "I am probably becoming adolescent on the point," Schlesinger railed to Marian, "but the kicking in the teeth of that little bastard Langer is rapidly becoming an almost obsessive emotion. When I think of the absolutely gratuitous array of complications he has imposed on my life in the past few months (and probably for the next few years), all because of his unwillingness out of some private smugness or aggression to make one small move, and all wasting the time of a lot of people beside myself who might be better engaged in fighting the war, I really get fed to the teeth." In the end, only a personal visit by the OSS/Paris commanding officer to the Army HQ got Schlesinger off the hook.[17]

Escaping basic training coincided with the end of the war in Europe on May 8, 1945, affording Schlesinger a brief uptick in spirits. He was sitting in a cafe again on the Champs-Élysées on VE Day as planes above began dropping colored flares and people everywhere celebrated. That night Schlesinger got to bed at four o'clock in the morning, sleeping on the top floor of the Élysées Park Hotel. "I shall never forget the magnificent panorama of Paris with the great buildings lit up," he wrote to his parents of the view that night, "from Sacre-Coeur past the Opera, the Madeleine, Notre Dame, the Place de la Concorde, the Chamber of Deputies, the Invalides, around to the Arc de Triomphe, with the fountains playing in the Rond Point below and little groups of people singing La Marseillaise faintly in the distance."[18]

The moment for Schlesinger could not have been better. "The peace came along just in time to distract me from myself," he wrote to Marian in a long wail of dejection. "I have been in a state of unprecedentedly low morale, chiefly because of the way this goddam Enlisted Man status mucks up everything":

> I have been told often enough what a devastating effect being in the army machine has on one's self confidence, and in a curious way my strange situation rather intensifies it—since I live in certain

respects pretty much the same life I used to live, except that most of the conveniences and privileges are now closed to me. It is not so much disintegration of confidence as a kind of fatalistic conviction that nothing you yourself can do matters very much to your fate. I feel basically that if my work before could not stave off this business that nothing I do now is going to affect my getting out. In addition to which, I really haven't a hell of a lot to do.[19]

It was not difficult to understand why Arthur was "in a bad frame of mind." Since childhood he had lived within the privileged embrace of Harvard University, always encouraged to think that he was special, and producing results that made such an opinion seem justified. Summa cum laude highest honors, publication of his undergraduate thesis by a renowned press, a prestigious Henry Fellowship to the University of Cambridge, election to Harvard's elite Society of Fellows: these achievements represented the glittering prizes of academic life for one already identified as among the brightest of his generation. Now suddenly in 1945, Private Schlesinger was no longer part of the elite. The loss of status meant more than the absence of comfortable digs and decent food, although the downgrade did help demoralize him. More important was the sense of powerlessness that went with being excluded from the officer class to which he had belonged all his life.

To make matters worse, he felt betrayed (despite earlier disdain for the work) by the bureaucratic Establishment, personified by Langer, that had expelled him from the scholarly environs of the R&A Branch. It is no coincidence that along with his official separation, Schlesinger began voluntarily to remove himself from the company of those who had always been his peers. "The basic trouble, of course," he wrote, "is that I don't want to see most people; for one reason or another they depress me or (I am ashamed to say) make me envious." For the first time in his life, Schlesinger was on the outside. And it was a painful, unwelcome experience.[20]

As always, though, Harvard establishment connections were never far away. Chadbourne Gilpatric, class of '37, had been a year ahead of Schlesinger and was a Rhodes Scholar at Oxford in 1938–1939 when the younger man was at Cambridge. Now as a captain in the US Army seconded to OSS, Gilpatric was in a position to help relieve some of Schlesinger's misery. Gilpatric asked Schlesinger to go to Germany with him as SI chief political reports officer. When it was pointed out that a private (albeit now private first-class) did not have the rank to attend meetings with senior officers and, in an occupied country, would have to live in barracks with the other enlisted men, Gilpatric devised and pushed through a scheme that would allow an elite group of enlisted grade OSS members to mess and billet with officers, and wear paramilitary uniform. "It would mean immunity from reveille, curfew, bed-check, drill and other joys of GI existence," a relieved Schlesinger wrote, although the fear remained that "an arrangement so profoundly contrary to military faith is likely to meet trouble somewhere."[21]

He left on June 20, enduring "a somewhat rough flight," before transferring to Biebrich, a suburb of Wiesbaden in Hessen. His new office was located in the Henkell Trocken factory, which, despite its associations with the Nazi foreign minister Joachim von Ribbentrop, was still producing bottles of sparkling wine on a daily basis. Schlesinger and his OSS colleagues were billeted in a house with views of the Rhine that had "very much the atmosphere of a college fraternity." At last, Schlesinger was back in his Ivy League comfort zone. Even Charles Wintour was nearby at the SHAEF HQ in Frankfurt, where the two friends soon met for "drinks, dinner and an evening of imbibing some excellent Moselle."[22]

Frankfurt brought Schlesinger face to face with the destruction that Allied bombing wrought. His Harvard tutor, Perry Miller, who was also in Germany, had shown "positive delight" in seeing German cities in ruins. Schlesinger did not share that sense of jubilation, but surveying the coverage and magnitude of the aerial bombardment, he did "still tend to feel a certain satisfaction in seeing how low the sons of bitches who talked so big a few years back have been laid." Even ordinary Germans still evoked intense feelings of suspicion and mistrust. "How does one feel about the Germans?" he asked. "My general reaction thus far is that I continue to hate their guts." Most he found "sullen, smug and stubborn," an assessment reinforced by his job, in which he "assisted in interrogation of enemy prisoners."[23]

In July, Allan Evans, a medievalist from Yale, invited Schlesinger to return to London to coordinate R&A reporting on politics in Britain, where a general election had just taken place. The position in many ways ideally suited Schlesinger. Not only did he have a strong interest in the British political world, where he could use a new expense account to consolidate his "business political contacts with probable post-war value," but a condition of the move was that he would serve for only three months before returning to the United States.[24]

To some it might have appeared unseemly to use the war effort to promote his own postwar interests. Certainly that was how it looked to his colleagues in Wiesbaden. On July 21, Schlesinger faced his branch chief, Harry Rositzke, "a very intelligent and hard hitting guy" who would later become the first chief of the CIA's Soviet division. Rositzke lost no time in letting Schlesinger know what he thought about a potential return to London, accusing him of prioritizing "personal preferences to the detriment of the national interest." Schlesinger protested that his job in Germany really didn't amount to much. "Well there would be a job if you wanted one and were not satisfied with simply discharging the day's work," Rositzke fired back. Afterwards, Schlesinger admitted, "There is some truth in this. I have never been fully committed to any job I have had in OSS."[25]

"I am not really an organization man," he explained to Marian. "I have a certain unhappy knack at administration, particularly at handling paper . . . but I probably will never be able to put my full energy into anything unless (a) it is a writing job, and (b) it is altogether my own." It was an important moment of self-awareness. "This is a conclusion which I must remember," he reflected. "Otherwise I can see the postwar world as a succession of well-paying, high-pressure jobs . . . in which I would draw a good salary, expend a lot of physical and nervous energy and be basically frustrated and unhappy, as basically I am now."[26]

On August 12, with his tail between his legs, Schlesinger left for

London, which he found "foggy and drab as ever." Three days later, Japan announced its surrender ("I rushed back to bed and slept"). The end of the war was good news for Schlesinger in that it was likely to hasten his return to the United States, but it also meant that his promising London job dwindled to nothing. "It is very annoying to have to have an artificial job now that the war is well over," he groused. To while away the time, he began using the OWI Library, which in his current mood did little to raise his spirits. Reading American political commentary was "nauseating," particularly the pro-Soviet views of the liberal magazines. His developing anti-Communist fervor would preoccupy him in the postwar world. Reading the scholarly magazines was even worse, albeit for more personal reasons. "I find myself overflowing with that strong resentment possessed by people who have been overseas for a considerable period," he railed, "toward those lucky bastards who remained, made a lot of money and captured secure places in their various professions." It was, he complained, "extremely annoying."[27]

Arthur's petulance continued throughout that summer of 1945 and into the fall, as he focused his energy on getting home. With his lowly army rank compromising his status within OSS, he lived in constant fear that "most of these sons of bitches will be so concerned with saving their own futures that they may very well overlook such minor details as me." Familiar doubts lurked about the OSS hierarchy in Washington, not least that "Langer's sympathetic approach to my problem will certainly result in my staying over the maximum." Any vague concerns turned to real ones on September 20, 1945, when President Truman dissolved OSS. Even though the R&A Branch was transferred to the State Department, it looked for a brief moment as if Schlesinger might be released back to the army, with the unhappy possibility of serving as a noncommissioned officer in an army of occupation. When the news was announced, in utter despair, he telephoned Marian, and "doubtless I sounded somewhat distraught." In the end, he managed to "beat a freeze order by a nose [and] I am slated to leave 7 October on a Liberty ship." It was welcome news for Marian that her husband would be home; Arthur could not have known when he wrote that her father, Walter Cannon, had died that day in Franklin, New Hampshire.[28]

Writing to Marian before he knew about her loss, Arthur had cautioned her in somewhat callow fashion about what to expect on his return. "I am profoundly tired, very antisocial, somewhat irritable; and all I really want to do is to go off with you and the babies," he wrote. "If there are pressing decisions to be made, they will have to be delayed until I am rested up. I do not want to accept any responsibility or whip up any initiative until I am feeling very much better than I am now."[29]

The journey across the Atlantic to Baltimore took almost three weeks. Schlesinger passed the time sleeping, playing bridge with other GIs ("those who had been to college gravitated to one another"), and eating steak twice a day. The wartime experience had not been a happy one for him. It exposed many of his contradictions that goaded those with whom he crossed political and academic swords in the postwar world. He was both a small "d" democrat and a snob; his clever, ironic personality could also be waspish and peevish. Physically and mentally exhausted, demoralized and unsure of his future, Arthur passed a disheartening twenty-eighth birthday. "I am beginning to lose that feeling of being a bright young man on which I have coasted for so long," he had written to Marian before his departure. "I am getting toward thirty without much accomplished, apart from my distinguished achievements in the fields of matrimony and paternity, and I would like to stop marking time."[30]

CHAPTER SIX

THE AGE OF SCHLESINGER

Waiting in London two weeks before his return to the United States in October 1945, Arthur Schlesinger had written to his wife in a "somewhat distraught" condition. He regularly shared with her complaints about his "miserable" wartime experience in which he had been ground down by the bureaucratic infighting of OSS and the drudgery of life in the United States Army. Aside from the thought of his young family at home in Washington, DC, only one thing seems to have kept him going: Little, Brown was about to publish his new book. "I am looking forward to all the reviews," he told Marian in a rare burst of optimism, before adding, "I hope the god damn book sells." In fact, *The Age of Jackson* would exceed all of Schlesinger's most hopeful expectations.[1]

The most important reviews that came in even before he left England set the tone for what followed. Orville Prescott for the *New York Times* praised *The Age of Jackson* as "an original, brilliant and monumentally massive historical work" and drew a moral from it: "that Jacksonian democracy was not only democratic but the lineal and spiritual ancestor of the Rooseveltian New Deal." Two days later, on September 16, the book was the cover review in the *New York Times Sunday Book Review*. The choice of Columbia historian Allan Nevins as reviewer was in many ways a lucky one for Schlesinger. In the years after the publication of *The Age of Jackson*, Columbia University would emerge as the center of a counter-narrative, explicitly anti-Schlesingerian, on the Jacksonian period. But in 1945, Columbia historian Allan Nevins was in London as chief public affairs officer at the American embassy. His office at No. 1 Grosvenor Square was precisely 0.1 mile, or a two-minute walk, from Schlesinger's OSS office at 36 Brook Street. To say that a bad review in the *New York Times* would have been socially awkward for both men, working virtually next door to each other and running into one another at the popular Causerie buffet inside Claridge's Hotel, is an understatement. Luckily or otherwise, Nevins judged *The Age of Jackson* to be "a remarkable piece of analytical history, full of vitality, rich in insights and new facts, and casting a broad shaft of illumination over one of the most interesting periods of our national life," even if it "sometimes rides its thesis a bit too hard."[2]

Glowing notices in the commercial press and academic journals followed these two reviews in the *New York Times*. The praise flowed from those who had taken an interest in Schlesinger since his youth, including Bernard DeVoto and Charles Beard, and from contemporaries, including Richard Hofstadter. A year older than Schlesinger, Hofstadter was exhilarated by *The Age of Jackson*, a work that would act as an important spur to his own historical thinking and eventually produce a counterblast in 1948 when he published *The American Political Tradition and the Men Who Made It*. His review for *New Republic* was glowing. "At a time when such a heavy proportion of second-rate or downright shoddy historical writing is being widely praised and widely read, it is a pleasure to report on a book like this and find oneself part of a general chorus of approval," he purred. "Mr. Schlesinger's book is a major contribution to American historiography." The one dissenting voice amid that chorus of approval, tucked away in the *Journal of Economic History*, was from the financial historian Bray Hamilton, who in 1945 was an assistant secretary to the Federal Reserve Board of Governors in Washington, DC. He conceded that the book was "important and abounds in excellences" but was highly critical of Schlesinger's "manichean naivete with respect to the nobility of all things Jacksonian and sordidness of all things opposed." Hamilton disparaged the "fumbling treatment of economic matters and particularly of the Bank of the United States." That was a theme to which Hamilton would return in his influential book *Banks and Politics in America from the Revolution to the Civil War*.[3]

Sales of *The Age of Jackson* were spectacular for an academic study. The book was serialized in the *New Republic* and was a top pick for the Book Find Club. It quickly entered the *New York Times* bestseller list, where it stayed for twenty-five weeks, selling 90,000 copies in the first year of publication. The following spring put the cap on Schlesinger's achievement when *The Age of Jackson* won the 1946 Pulitzer Prize for History. At only twenty-eight years old, he was thought to be the youngest historian ever to win the prize. Given the critical and popular success of the book, few caviled that he deserved the honor, although as always in his career there had been a few familiar, or more accurately familial, nudges behind the scenes on his behalf. Arthur Schlesinger Sr. had been a member of the history advisory committee for the Pulitzer Prize since 1937. In 1946, he officially withdrew once it became clear that "my son's *Age of Jackson* was in the running," but it is impossible to believe that his fellow committee members were immune to his influence even in his physical absence. It was another example of Bernard DeVoto's maxim that his "meek and mild" friend dominated "every committee he gets on." In 1938, the senior Schlesinger had secured the prize for his PhD student, Paul Buck. In the two years after Arthur won in 1946, James Phinney Baxter III, who had been master of Schlesinger's house at Harvard, and then DeVoto himself both won the Pulitzer. Doubtless Schlesinger's lobbying for his son and *The Age of Jackson* was subtle, not least because the book spoke for itself. But winning the prize was another instance of Arthur Jr. living on the inside track, a placement that had served him well throughout his rise to national prominence, so often giving him a head start in an always competitive race.[4]

The scope and style of the book was audacious. Neither a biography of Andrew Jackson nor a history of his administration (in fact President Martin Van Buren features more strongly than "Old Hickory"), *The Age of Jackson* is, as Donald B. Cole points out, six closely woven essays on the intellectual history of the period. These move from the background of Jacksonian democracy to the president's campaign to destroy the Second Bank of the United States, before examining Jacksonian democracy at the local level and in the context of civil society, culture, industry, and the law, and concluding with a look forward to the Jacksonians in the American Civil War.[5]

Underpinned by vast research and written with great panache, *The Age of Jackson* was generational history at its most powerful and persuasive. Each essay supports and reinforces Schlesinger's argument that the East was a major force in Jacksonian democracy. Stylistically, the book is populated by colorful, often witty, sometimes moving, sketches not just of the main political players, but other familiar faces—Bancroft and Brownson, of course, but also leading artists and writers of the day such as James Fenimore Cooper, Nathaniel Hawthorne, William Cullen Bryant, Washington Irving, Walt Whitman, James Kirke Paulding, the actor Edwin Forrest, the sculptors Horatio Greenough and Hiram Powers, as well as hundreds of lesser known figures who were brought back to life and shown, when taken together, to form an identifiably Jacksonian worldview.[6]

Franklin D. Roosevelt, the president who had died a few months before the book was published, loomed in the shadows throughout the entire text of *The Age of Jackson*. Schlesinger, still in Paris at the time, had been stunned by the "inherently incredible" news of FDR's demise. "With all his faults," he wrote to his parents, "he was an extraordinary man, and this was no time for him to go. Stalin or Churchill might have been much more easily spared." Schlesinger's admiration for Roosevelt went back to his school days at Exeter, when he had been one of the few Democratic supporters during the 1932 presidential election. When Roosevelt came through the town, Schlesinger excitedly lined up to see him, amid other boys shouting out support for Herbert Hoover. In school debates, he spoke for Roosevelt and "made a lot of sarcastic statements about Herb." When one Republican supporter suggested that Washington freed the country, Lincoln the slaves, and Hoover the working man, Schlesinger retorted, "Yeah. Hoover freed the working man from his home and his possessions."

Now in *The Age of Jackson* Schlesinger presented the New Deal as the culmination of the liberal tradition in which "the Jeffersonian case for weak government" was rejected in favor of "executive vigor and government action" on behalf of all the people and against vested interest. To ram home the point, Schlesinger quoted on the last page of his book Roosevelt himself, that "this heritage . . . we owe to Jacksonian democracy—the American doctrine that entrusts the general welfare to no one group or class, but dedicates itself to the end that American people shall not be thwarted in their high purpose to remain the custodians of their own destiny."[7]

Here is not the place to engage with the historiographical debates that would surround *The Age of Jackson* throughout the rest of the twentieth century and beyond. To demonstrate its professional impact, it is enough to point out that by the 1970s historians polled about the most influential book of the postwar era chose *The Age of Jackson*. Furthermore, two of the next three books on the list were revisionist works that *The Age of Jackson* inspired. Although the book, along with political and intellectual history more generally, would fall out of fashion shortly thereafter, it remained a touchstone for the study of nineteenth-century America, even if sometimes a negative one. In 2009, more than sixty years after its publication, a review by Daniel Howe in the *New York Review of Books* was still asking whether new titles under review meant "Goodbye to the 'Age of Jackson'?" A new generation of academic historians such as Jonathan H. Earle in *Jacksonian Antislavery and the Politics of Free Soil* began to rehabilitate some of the ideas set out in *The Age of Jackson*. And the victory of a new kind of popular politics in the 2016 election drew commentators back to both the age of Jackson and to *The Age of Jackson*. "Andrew Jackson represented a farmer-frontier-worker rebellion against the eastern establishment who had maintained control for over a generation," former House Speaker and Donald Trump surrogate Newt Gingrich told the *Washington Post* during the campaign, comparing the Republican nominee to Andrew Jackson. "The elites disliked him so much he got bad press for a century until Schlesinger's 'The Age of Jackson' rehabilitated him."[8]

If a case for the book's importance is needed, it is put well by Sean Wilentz in his own take on the Jacksonian revolution, *The Rise of American Democracy*. "Since *The Age of Jackson* appeared, a revolution in historical studies has focused scholars' attentions on groups of Americans and aspects of American history that held minor interest at best in the historical profession in 1945," he writes, pointing in particular to issues of Indian removal, race, and gender, all of which Schlesinger for the most part had ignored. "Yet if the social history revolution has profoundly changed how historians look at the United States, it has not diminished the importance of the questions *The Age of Jackson* asked about early American democracy," Wilentz continued. "On the contrary, it has made those questions— especially about democratic politics, social class, and slavery—all the more pertinent to our understanding of the dramatic events that led from the American Revolution to the American Civil War."[9]

Schlesinger himself over the years remained proud of the book, although he would later concede that it was a product of its time. "I well know the infirmities of the work," he wrote in 1989. "History reflects the age." In his 1938 Harvard undergraduate thesis, "Young Arthur" had praised Orestes Brownson for having the "courage" of "inveighing against the capitalist" when "most reformers of the day busied themselves with evils that were remote, like slavery, or largely speculative, like intemperance and sex inequality." Half a century later, his regret, painful for a self-confessed liberal, was that "when I wrote *The Age of Jackson*, the predicament of women, of blacks, of Indians was shamefully out of mind." But he stood over the basic argument of the book, despite the fact that "among historians *The Age of Jackson* has had its ups and downs." Its principal value, he believed, "was that it helped awaken professional interest in a complex and abundant period of American history. It stirred controversy, and controversy is always fruitful for historians."[10]

If "history reflects the age," in the case of *The Age of Jackson*, it also reflects the man. In such a vast book, chock full of so many incidents, ideas, and characters, it is easy (perhaps too much so) to pull out examples and present them as autobiography. That said, *The Age of Jackson* does show the continuation of two very strong influences on Arthur— intellectual father figures, if you like, as well as a clear sense of his own developing historical philosophy.

The first of these father figures was a literal one: Schlesinger Sr., to whom Arthur acknowledged he remained "profoundly indebted . . . for his wise counsel and keen criticism." On one level this debt had to do with the literary style passed from father to son: lapidary, companionable, and with a cheerfulness of tone that often hides the unconventional nature of the ideas; both Schlesingers shared an elegance of prose, even if the younger man's was more forceful than his unostentatious father's.

But beyond the command in writing, there was also an important continuity of ideas. Underpinning *The Age of Jackson* was a view about the cycles of history that Arthur Sr. had been writing about since 1924, and which he had set out most recently in 1939 in an essay, "Tides of American History," in the *Yale Review*. Essentially, he identified alternating periods of roughly sixteen and one-half years in American history, as power cycled between liberalism and conservatism. The former, suggested the progressive Arthur Sr., increased democracy through concern for the wrongs against the many while the latter, he said, contained democracy by concern for the rights of the few. The return of conservatism at any given point usually meant acceptance of the changes made during the preceding liberal period.

Arthur would later write his own book on the subject, *The Cycles of American History*, but in 1945 his father's view was used to help locate Jacksonian democracy in the broader sweep of the national story. "American history has been marked by recurrent swings of conservatism and liberalism," Arthur wrote in a clear echo of his father. "During the periods of inaction, unsolved social problems pile up till the demand for reform becomes overwhelming. Then a progressive government comes to power, the dam breaks and a flood of change sweeps away a great deal in a short time. After fifteen or twenty years the liberal impulse is exhausted, the day of "consolidation" and inaction arrives, and conservatism, once again expresses the mood of the country, but generally on the terms of the liberalism it displaces. So with Jacksonian democracy."[11]

Even more significant to the book was Arthur Sr.'s shifting of the focus in the rise of Jacksonianism away from the frontier. For the central thesis of *The Age of Jackson* was one that had been laid out two decades earlier by Arthur Sr. in his quietly seminal book, *New Viewpoints in American History*. Published in 1922, this book had put forward the thesis that Jacksonian democracy was as much a product of northeastern urban labor as the western frontier. "The aims of the organized labor elements harmonized with the new democratic aspirations of the age and did much towards vitalizing those aspirations," Arthur Sr. wrote, continuing with the same flood image that Arthur would later use: "The labor movement reached its floodtide while Andrew Jackson was in office. Indeed, he could not have been elected president if the votes of the laboring men of the Northeast had not been added to those of his followers in the Southeast and the West. Jackson capitalized this support when he waged battle against the great financial monopoly, the United States Bank." It would be both the starting point for *The Age of Jackson* and its conclusion. "We have seen," Schlesinger Sr. wrote in the final chapter, "how the pat contrasts between country and city, honest farmer and demoralized laborer, were tripped up by the realities of Jacksonian politics."[12]

If *The Age of Jackson* identified with the elder Arthur Meier Schlesinger—the name that young Arthur had adopted in his teens to honor his father—the book also showed the equal and opposite influence of the name that Arthur Jr. had abandoned, Bancroft. The historian and politician George Bancroft had fascinated Arthur since childhood. The presumed familial tie piqued his interest, but as Arthur began to take history seriously, he came to realize that Bancroft's work offered a counterweight to that of his father and the limitations of Harvard. He had already shown his Bancroft colors in his 1940 essay "The Problem of Richard Hildreth," where Bancroft was contrasted with the "pedestrian and annalistic" Hildreth. He returned to the theme in *The Age of Jackson*, which had originally started as a projected biography of his former namesake.[13]

It is not difficult to hear a resonance in the description of Bancroft. He was "too clever and too skeptical to accept the values of Boston . . . or to tailor his talents according to specifications laid down by Harvard or State Street [Boston's "Wall Street"]." Like Arthur, "he went to Europe after finishing college" and, like him, "when he returned the Athens of America seemed flat and disappointing." He taught, dabbled in politics, and remained "still the supercilious Harvardian." What changed his life was the decision to write a sweeping history of the United States. "This determination to devote his life to such a history, which he conceived as the story of the invincible progress of human liberty, undoubtedly released his democratic prepossessions in full flood." In 1834, the year he published the first volume of his *History*, Bancroft announced his conversion to the Democrats. Thought became father to the action. Although Bancroft's "ambition led him to insincere flattery and insincere condemnation, to betraying his friends and aiding his enemies" (an accusation soon thrown at Schlesinger too), Bancroft's authentic legacy was created by "the patient and conscientious devotion with which [he], laboring through the years, wrote his *History*." The lesson of this devotion was clear, even if it came with risks: writing the history of the United States was not removing yourself from national politics; it could mean inserting yourself into them as an active player.[14]

Schlesinger's actions over the next few months would give the clearest indication of how he would try to play this difficult game. On the one hand, reinforced by the success of *The Age of Jackson*, he was able to cement his place in the world of the academy, which offered not just prestige but financial security—an important consideration when the Schlesingers had another child, Christina, on the way. Job offers now flooded in from schools across the country, including Yale, Chicago, Minnesota, and Johns Hopkins. But Arthur Schlesinger Jr. was always a Harvard man, and when that university came calling in April 1946 with the offer of an associate professorship (at that time the highest level of junior appointment), there was little doubt which institution he would pick.

As in the 1930s, when Arthur had chosen Harvard both as his undergraduate college and the place to carry out his (in effect) postgraduate research, the question remains why he did not look to cut the apron strings to his alma mater. It was not as if other elite offers were not on the table. To reinforce the point that he was still "Little Arthur" at the university, the *Harvard Gazette* in announcing his appointment printed his father's vita rather than his. "Academic life will probably be confusing enough for both of you in the future without having Cambridge home talent, like the *Gazette*, complicate matters further," the secretary to the Harvard Corporation, David Bailey, apologized afterwards to Junior. Bailey noted that Arthur Sr. had been "most good natured" about the slip.

Harvard postwar was on the verge of asserting its supremacy as the greatest, or certainly the most famous, American university. But in 1947, when Arthur actually took up his position, that outcome was not clear-cut. As Niall Ferguson points out in his biography of Henry Kissinger, who arrived as a freshman that same year, "Harvard in the fall of 1947 was an unwelcoming shambles." Certainly that was the view of a visiting British don, Hugh Trevor Roper, who told the Harvard alumnus and art historian Bernard Berenson that "their standard of education is really very saddening. Harvard depressed me a great deal." In the end, though, for Arthur, coming after a deeply unsettling wartime experience when his Harvard connections and friendships had consistently saved him from disaster, it was not surprising that he looked forward to the reassuring embrace of home. Marian, on the other hand, as another "Harvard child," was less enthusiastic. "He is going to return to the academic trap, i.e. Harvard, where they have offered him an associate professorship," she complained to her sister Wilma. "So I guess we end up in the same rat hole after all."[15]

Before going down that hole, however, the Schlesingers deferred the financial security of Harvard for a year in Washington, which in the postwar environment now seemed—indeed was—the center of the world. The huge sales and media attention for *The Age of Jackson* had made Schlesinger a saleable asset. Grants came in from the Guggenheim Foundation and the American Academy of Arts and Letters. Numerous magazines and newspapers asked for columns and features. "Our plans seem to be these," Marian finally summed up. "A. has been asked by [Eugene] Meyer of the *Washington Post* to write the history of the paper from 1932 and since A. wants to ultimately write a book about the Age of Roosevelt and much of the material will play right into it, he is in the process of accepting it (if Meyer will give him an unrestricted hand). He will also do some pieces for *Fortune* for which they will be paying him whopping prices."[16]

In the end, Schlesinger decided to pass on the *Washington Post* project, telling Meyer that "I would best serve your own purposes as well as my own if I turned down the *Post* offer." He said that the decision had come "after some soul searching." In truth, his experience at OWI and OSS had taught him about the challenges of being a creative figure dancing to the bigger organizational tune. "He just decided he didn't want to be subject to somebody," Marian recalled. "I think that was it: he wanted to be his own master."[17]

Not that writing for *Fortune* didn't come with its challenges. The owner, Henry Luce of *Time* magazine fame, was known to take a high-handed approach with writers, and his editors followed suit. Schlesinger's Harvard friend and classmate, Theodore White, had just resigned from *Time* because of just such interference by foreign editor Whittaker Chambers (soon to achieve notoriety as a Soviet spy and witness in the trial of Alger Hiss). Meeting Luce, Schlesinger was struck by "his combination of genuine intellectual curiosity about everything with stubborn resistance to changing his mind about anything." Concerned, he sought out White, who reassured him that the level of interference at *Fortune* was less pronounced. In the first edition of *Fortune*, Luce had proclaimed that it would be "the Ideal Super-Class Magazine," and a "distinguished and de luxe" publication. Such excellence demanded high-quality writing and with it an acceptance that writers there must be given more leeway. At $10,000 a year, Schlesinger was still a Luce employee, but one with considerable license to follow his own thoughts and instincts in order to capture the interest of the magazine's target audience of high rollers and persons of influence.[18]

Arthur didn't take long to deliver. He wrote several solid pieces on worthy topics such as the "Good Neighbor" policy in Latin America, but his first cause célèbre came with an article in January 1947 about the US Supreme Court. In many ways this seminal piece, which announced him as a genuine public intellectual, represents Schlesinger at his best. In the tradition of the kind of thought-provoking and deeply researched mid-century American journalism that demanded both style and seriousness of its writers, the article literally redefined the way to understand the Supreme Court.

Schlesinger set about interviewing all nine justices, including Felix Frankfurter, who, as a friend of Arthur Sr., had known Arthur Jr. since his childhood. "He duly showed up," Frankfurter recorded in his diary of his meeting with Arthur for the magazine interview. "I asked him what he had done by way of reading and seeing people to equip himself for the job. He then told me what he had read, and he had read all the things that are worth reading. As to people—he had already seen every other member of the Court except the Chief Justice whom he is to see shortly." It was another A+ for "Little Arthur" from Professor Frankfurter.[19]

Entitled "The Supreme Court: 1947," the article profiled the nine justices (Vinson, Black, Frankfurter, Rutledge, Douglas, Murphy, Reed, Burton, and Jackson) and outlined the divisions among them on the "proper function of the judiciary in a democracy."[20] The pen portraits (Justice Reed: "nice, dull, friendly"; Justice Murphy: "his egotism is vast and somewhat messianic") stripped the "supremes" of a little of their dignity and revealed them as men not without their vanities and petty jealousies. Even more significant, Schlesinger outlined the philosophical differences in how each of the nine approached the law and the alliances that had emerged within the Court. Although this was a "Roosevelt" Court, and as such the justices' politics (with only one Republican) were not dissimilar, the legal differences were profound and important. "The conflict may be described in several ways," Schlesinger explained:

> The Black-Douglas group believes that the Supreme Court can play an affirmative role in promoting the social welfare; the Frankfurter-Jackson group advocates a policy of judicial self-restraint. One group is more concerned with the employment of the judicial power for their own conception of the social good; the other with expanding the range of allowable judgment for legislatures, even if it means upholding conclusions they privately condemn. One group regards the Court as an instrument to achieve desired social results; the second as an instrument to permit the other branches of government to achieve the results the people want for better or worse. In brief, the Black-Douglas wing appears to be more concerned with settling particular cases in accordance with their own social preconceptions; the Frankfurter-Jackson wing with preserving the judiciary in its established but limited place in the American system.

To the Black-Douglas school Schlesinger gave a name that would echo down the years: "judicial activist." This camp, wrote the newly appointed Harvard professor, had its roots in the Yale Law School and believed that "the Court cannot escape politics: therefore, let it use its political power for wholesome social purposes." In contrast, the champions of "Self-Denial" believed that "judicial despotism [threatened] the democratic process." Schlesinger then set up a dialogue between the two:

Self-denial has thus said: the legislature gave the law; let the legislature take it away. The answer of judicial activism is: in actual practice the legislature will not take it away—at least until harm, possibly irreparable, is done to a defenseless person; therefore the Court itself must act. Self-denial replies: you are doing what we all used to condemn the old Court [which opposed the New Deal] of doing; you are practicing judicial usurpation. Activism responds: we cannot rely on an increasingly conservative electorate to protect the underdog or to safeguard basic human rights; we betray the very spirit and purpose of the Constitution if we ourselves do not intervene.

This exchange, wrote Keenan D. Kmiec in the *California Law Review* during the period when he clerked for three justices on the Roberts Court, including the chief justice, "is remarkable for its prescience and timelessness. It has been replayed in slightly different words for decades in legal classrooms, public forums, and scholarly journals. Concerns about failures of the political process, basic human rights, and the ghost of *Lochner* [when the Court ruled in 1905 that a New York law setting maximum working hours for bakers was unconstitutional] are just as central and urgent [today] as they were in 1947."[21]

Schlesinger's coining of the term judicial activism made an important and lasting contribution both to legal scholarship and public debate. Kmiec judged almost sixty years later that Schlesinger had written "a thought-provoking, constructive, and balanced article on a topic of great public importance," adding that "though current discussions of judicial activism often fail to live up to this high standard, Schlesinger gave the concept a promising start."[22]

Contemporary figures in and around the Supreme Court may consider Schlesinger's efforts thought-provoking, constructive, and balanced; the members of the Court in 1947 were less sanguine. Justice Reed was hurt to be described as dull. Justice Murphy protested to *Fortune* about a "highly distorted and inaccurate article," and was widely rumored to be considering suing Schlesinger for libel. Even Felix Frankfurter was grumpy at "the many inaccuracies" and the difficult spot that guilt by association put him in with his fellow justices. "Young Arthur Schlesinger's article in *Fortune* has apparently greatly disturbed Brother Murphy," he wrote in a note to other members of the Nine, explaining that while "Young Arthur's father is one of my close friends at Harvard," he had neither seen the draft article nor gossiped about fellow members of the Court. At an initially difficult lunch a few weeks afterwards, Arthur reported home to Arthur Sr., Frankfurter "got the bile out of his system and became very genial." As well he should, having been essentially the hero of the piece. It was another example of Arthur following the "home" line of Harvard and the world as seen through the eyes of those who were friends at 19 Gray Gardens East.

The article in *Fortune* may have given Schlesinger a few uncomfortable moments with some of Washington, DC's most powerful establishment figures. But it also added to his name among the District's cognoscenti, not least the increasingly influential set who dined and schemed together in Georgetown.

The immediate postwar period was an intoxicating time in Washington. Almost without anyone quite noticing until it had happened, the nation's capital became suddenly and indisputably the world's capital. America was the richest country in the world, with gold reserves of $20 billion (almost two-thirds of the global total). It supplied one-third of the world's exports. Militarily, it had the greatest navy, an even more commanding lead in air power, and a monopoly on the atomic bomb—the most destructive weapon in history (with the H-bomb soon on the way). And with these resources of money and might, the United States was operating in a global vacuum, with the other great powers exhausted or in ruins. Even the military might of the Soviet Union was balanced out by its huge population losses and weak economic base. As Paul Kennedy points out, by 1945 few doubted that "the Pax Americana had come of age."[23]

But was Washington, DC, up to the job of serving as capital of the world? Many, not least those who lived in New York, doubted it. *Vanity Fair* had described DC as "a political village which has become a world capital, without becoming a metropolis . . . conspicuously lacking in what might be described as intelligentsia." Although there was "a small group composed chiefly of newspaper correspondents, who live in Georgetown and aspire to create a sort of Greenwich Village or synthetic *rive gauche* on the right bank of Rock Creek," the magazine continued snootily, "hitherto they have failed to produce anything but malicious gossip and political muckraking." Washington may have been the seat of government, but New York was the seat of financial, cultural, and intellectual power. A legal, economic, and political umbilical cord would continue to tie New York to DC. But within the space of just a few years, that same George-town enclave began to rival Manhattan as the center of political influence and fashionable glamour in the newly minted superpower.[24]

Maîtres d'hôtel of this "Georgetown set" were the Alsop brothers, Joseph and Stewart, Roosevelt relatives, who wrote a thrice-weekly syndi-cated *Matter of Fact* column for the *New York Herald Tribune*. With their houses on Dumbarton Street (sometimes called Dumbarton Avenue), the Alsops each hosted bibulous dinners for their friends and acquaintances who became willing (usually) sources for the brothers' columns. At least in the early days, all the friends shared a fixed determination not to let political differences get in the way of social relationships. Most infamous of all were Joe's Sunday night suppers—soon christened the Sunday Night Drunk—where he would serve vast amounts of alcohol to accompany his pungent terrapin soup and then cajole his guests loudly from his place at the head of the table to spill what gossip they knew.[25]

Schlesinger had run across Stewart Alsop, three years his elder, in Paris at the end of the war. He fluffed the connection by asking, to Stewart's apparent irritation, if he was related to the columnist Joseph

Alsop. ("Plainly, he was tired of the question.") He had better luck with another member of the group. Philip Graham was two years older than Schlesinger, but although the two men had overlapped at Harvard, where Graham was at the Law School, they were not friends. Graham clerked for Felix Frankfurter, but when the United States entered the war, he signed up to join the army, rising from private to major (trumping Schlesinger's modest rise from private to corporal). With his quick mind and charismatic personality, Graham seemed destined for politics. When he married Katharine Meyer, her father, Eugene Meyer, harnessed Graham's energy for the *Washington Post* instead. After Meyer (a former chairman of the Federal Reserve) was appointed first president of the World Bank for six months in 1946, he made Graham publisher of the newspaper, subsequently returning as chairman and leaving Graham in place.[26]

Phil Graham gave Schlesinger a path into the Georgetown set. Marooned out in unfashionable Chevy Chase and unable to afford even a modest property on the likes of Dumbarton Street, Schlesinger was outside the Georgetown loop. But Marian did have a useful connection through Wilma Fairbank, her sister. "John Fairbank's mother had this house in Georgetown that backed up on the house that Kay and Phil Graham had when they came back from the war," Marian recalls. "And it was through her that we met the Grahams. They were very nice people." It was the Grahams who suggested Schlesinger for the job of writing the history of the *Post*. "It was a very expanding period of our connections and everything else," Marian remembers. "It was really fun."[27]

It was also somewhat overwhelming. In his letters home to his parents, Schlesinger could barely hide his star-struck feelings, listing the names of the great, the good, and the rising generation with whom he had dined. As a boy at Phillips Exeter Academy he had been emasculated by their kind; now their provenance and power intoxicated him. On one occasion in 1946, he found himself at dinner with Stewart Alsop (great-nephew of President Theodore Roosevelt), Franklin Roosevelt Jr. (fifth child of President Franklin Roosevelt), two members of the Truman administration (Averell Harriman and Clark Clifford), and the speechwriter (Herbert

Bayard Swope of the New York *World*) usually credited with coining the term "Cold War." Schlesinger was "quite favorably impressed" with Secretary of Commerce Averell Harriman, with whom he would go on to develop something of a protégé relationship. It was at these dinners that Schlesinger also had his first proper sight of a direct contemporary, born in 1917, but two years behind him at Harvard in the class of 1940. "Jack Kennedy [was] there," Schlesinger wrote home. "Kennedy seemed very sincere and not unintelligent," he continued, adding presciently, "but kind of on the conservative side." It surely did not occur to either man that Schlesinger would be the chronicler of the thirty-fifth president.[28]

All sorts gathered at the "Sunday Night Drunk" and other Georgetown dinner parties in those early postwar years. If one philosophical point of view broadly held Schlesinger and many of his friends together, it was their growing sense of belonging to the non-Communist Left. Liberals passionately debated how the United States should handle the Soviet Union, with many important and influential figures sharply disagreeing. When Harriman, for example, as ambassador to Moscow at the end of World War II, had said in front of Walter Lippmann, America's most famous columnist, that "our objectives and the Kremlin's objectives are irreconcilable," the latter, who desired wartime cooperation to continue, had ostentatiously risen from his seat and walked out.[29]

Schlesinger admired Lippmann, but for the historian the important element of that debate was the battle going on in Western Europe between democratic socialism and Stalinism and the extent to which American policy might tilt the outcome of that battle. During the 1930s, many young idealists, including Schlesinger, were attracted by elements of Marxism and Communism. As a Harvard undergraduate, he became a member of the American Student Union, which was Popular Front/Communist–controlled, and was influenced somewhat by his junior-year tutor, the Communist fellow traveler F. O. Matthiessen. During his Henry Fellowship at Peterhouse, he became close friends with Eric Hobsbawm, later among the most prominent Marxist historians. And while there, he had run his undergraduate thesis through a Marxist prism, writing an academic article, "Orestes Brownson: An American Marxist before Marx."

Brownson, he explained, "had the set of doctrines—class conflict, the overthrow of the bourgeoisie, and the historic function of capitalism—which form so necessary an apparatus for enlightenment today." But Schlesinger's experience during the Second World War had brought him to the new enlightenment that American patriotism and Communism were incompatible. His battles in OSS with Maurice Halperin had left a deep imprint. Schlesinger had seen at first hand how the system would tolerate and protect an out-and-out Communist (and Soviet spy) working against his own government; Schlesinger's attempt to push back had led to physical intimidation and a lasting suspicion towards him within OSS, with almost disastrous consequences for him during the rest of the war. There was no question that Schlesinger's smarty-pants demeanor could often irritate colleagues, but on this occasion he had been proven right, as would have been known high up in the OSS in 1945 after the Soviet spy Elizabeth Bentley turned informer and named Halperin to them as a Soviet agent.[30]

The lesson that Schlesinger took from this experience was that his own political class could not be trusted to hold the line against Communist sympathizers. William Langer, after all, who had protected Halperin and made Schlesinger's life so wretched in OSS, was a Harvard history professor and friend of Arthur Sr. It was this instinct that drew Arthur into a major preoccupation, both intellectual and political, that would dominate this controversial phase of his life. It began with an investigation into the US Communist Party for *Life*, part of the same Luce empire as *Fortune* and the country's most widely read weekly magazine. This devastating critique combined alarmist language with Schlesinger's trademark trenchant analysis. "Communists are working overtime to expand party influence, open and covert, in the labor movement, among Negroes, among veterans, among unorganized liberals," he wrote, comparing them to proselytizing "Jesuits, the Mormons or Jehovah's Witnesses." He then examined organizations such as the Independent Citizens Committee of the Arts, Sciences and Professions (ICCASP) to illustrate how "groups of liberals . . . organized for some benevolent purpose, and because of the innocence, laziness and stupidity of most of the membership, [were] perfectly designed for control by an alert minority." Then came the thrust to the heart. "The communist party is no menace to the right in the U.S.," Schlesinger wrote. "It is a great help to the right because of its success in dividing and neutralizing the left. It is to the American left that Communism presents the most serious danger. On the record, Communists have fought other leftists as viciously as they have fought fascists. Their methods are irreconcilable with honest cooperation, as anyone who has tried to work with them has found out the hard way." It is not difficult to imagine Schlesinger thinking of Halperin as he wrote those last words.[31]

The *Life* article provoked immediate and strong reaction, with an onslaught against Schlesinger, predictably, as a "Luce Liberal" in the *Daily Worker.* Less predicted was the reaction of some friends and mentors, including F. O. Matthiessen, who cut him off completely. Other individual responses were more sympathetic, including one that would have implications for subsequent American history: Ronald Reagan, then a New Deal Democrat, would later say that the article was a moment of epiphany, showing him for the first time what was going on within organizations such as the Hollywood Independent Citizens Committee of the Arts, Sciences and Professions (HICCASP), which Schlesinger had named in the piece. Critics would later say it was evidence of Schlesinger's culpability in the creation of the blacklist.[32]

The *Life* article plunged Schlesinger into the middle of a sharp national debate that was existential as much as it was strategic: what to do about Communism and the Soviet Union. On one side were figures like Lippmann, who argued there were "no direct conflicts of vital interest as between the Soviet Union and the United States," adding that America's role in the world should be as "mediator, that is, intercessor, reconciler, within the circle of the big powers." Popular Front liberals, including writers Norman Mailer and I. F. Stone, reinforced that view by promoting cooperation with Communists at home and, in 1948, by supporting former vice president Henry Wallace's run for president. "Communists also supported Wallace," Leo P. Ribuffo notes, "too openly for his own comfort" (he won 2.4 percent of the vote). Ranged against them were centrist liberals like Reinhold Niebuhr and Schlesinger plus the "wise men" who coalesced around the new president Harry Truman. Harriman and friends such as Dean Acheson and George Kennan began to put in place new military, economic, and political institutions to contain and, some hoped, even roll back Soviet expansion. On the right, figures such as Robert Taft, the senator from Ohio, feared there was "no limit to the burden" of such commitments, but Arthur Vandenberg, the influential Republican chairman of the Senate Committee on Foreign Relations from 1947 to 1949, helped drive the measures through. Waiting in the wings were the Cold War hawks such as rising Republican congressman Richard Nixon and government official Paul Nitze, who believed the fight against global Communism had not gone far enough and sought to extend it. "The result," worried George Kennan, architect of containment, "is that there is no place in public life for an honest and moderate man."[33]

That was the febrile environment in which those making and writing about policy in the late 1940s found themselves. With the world having been divided into rival camps, the question naturally arose in the United States, was there an "enemy within," and if so, what should be done about them.[34]

Philip Rahv, a former Communist and cofounder of the *Partisan Review*, argued in 1952 that Communism was a threat *to* the United States, it was not a threat *in* the United States. By the late 1940s membership of the Communist Party (CPUSA) hovered around the forty-three thousand mark, a number similar, Stephen Whitfield points out in *The Culture of the Cold War*, to American membership of the Finnish Evangelical Lutheran church. Most CPUSA members, two thousand of whom were sent underground on subversion schemes, were the worst kind of Stalinist fellow travelers; some were in positions of influence at leading universities, on newspapers, and in Hollywood; others could damage the interests of the United States at the Department of State or the new Department of Defense. The number of Communist Party members, however, was more red herring than red threat: important agents throughout the West were usually not indigenous party members or else had their membership expunged. In Britain, for example, MI5 thoroughly penetrated the CPGB but missed the Cambridge Five spy ring that included Philby, Burgess, and Maclean. Soviet spies had already stolen the A-bomb secret from the United States. As pertinently, Communist penetration by the likes of Alger Hiss and Halperin destroyed the bonds of trust among the elite— exactly as the Soviets had intended to do from the moment in 1944 when Stalin recognized that the United States would replace Britain as the leading capitalist power.[35]

Bentley's defection revealed a vast infiltration of US government life by Soviet operatives. "Today nearly every department or agency of this government is infiltrated with them in varying degree," chief special agent Guy Hottel wrote to FBI director Hoover in March 1946 after reviewing the Bentley file. "To aggravate the situation they appear to have concentrated most heavily in those departments which make policy, particularly in the international field, or carry it into effect." State Department security official Samuel Klaus summarized the figures in his department in early 1946 as being twenty Soviet agents including Hiss (director of the Office of Special Political Affairs), with a further twenty-seven Communists or sympathizers, and seventy-seven more suspects. The Venona counterintelligence project would lead to the unmasking of a long-standing network of "atomic spies," including Klaus Fuchs, Julius and Ethel Rosenberg, Harry Gold, and David Greengrass. As agents and cyphers were blown, writes Jonathan Haslam in his history of Soviet intelligence, "the sequence of events had a chilling effect on Kremlin hopes." By June 1952 Stalin would order all operatives to go dark as the means to "function without interruption under any conditions."[36]

Schlesinger's *Life* piece in 1947 was his first step toward developing a sustained analysis on issues surrounding the Communist threat at home and abroad. The eventual result would be an antidogmatic pluralism that became the general liberal consensus and that Schlesinger, George Marsden points out, was "one of the first to define." Temporarily putting aside plans for research on FDR, Arthur now turned to making the case on behalf of the non-Communist Left with a series of articles on the topic: "The future of socialism" for Rahv's *Partisan Review*, "Political Culture in the United States" for *The Nation*, and two articles, "What is loyalty" and "Not left, not right" for the *New York Times Sunday Magazine*. He made a plea for level-headedness and perspective. "The situation cries out for a little less hysteria and a little more calm sense," he wrote in "What is loyalty" in November 1947. After all, he summed up, "A calm survey surely reveals two propositions on which we can all agree: (1) that Americanism is not a totalitarian faith, which can impose a single economic or political dogma or require a uniformity in observance from all its devotees; but (2) that a serious problem for national security has been created by that fanatical group which rejects all American interests in favor of those of the Soviet Union."[37]

In the context of 1947, his two propositions did not evince calm. After FBI investigations and the Venona project revealed the extent of Soviet penetration in the US government, Truman that year had introduced a "Loyalty Order" for federal employees that included FBI background checks on potential Communist links. Congress also joined the fray, reconvening the House Un-American Activities Committee (HUAC), which soon began turning up the heat on suspected Communists, particularly in the film industry. Critics cried foul, pointing to an unpleasant strain of anti-Semitism, anti-intellectualism, and nativism in a process that traded in gossip and innuendo. Even Truman feared what he had unleashed. "We want no Gestapo or Secret Police," the president implored, telling advisors, "this must stop."[38]

Schlesinger plunged headfirst into the bitter disputes that would divide the Left. There was a world of difference between his brand of antidogmatic liberalism and what turned into McCarthyism; the question became whether it fed the same appetites. Opponents argued that Schlesinger's critique was too strident and ignored the rapid decline in size and influence of the Communist movement, particularly in the wake of growing disaffection with rigid Stalinist practices within the Communist Party of the United States of America. He stood accused of being a quisling, a charge made in the most vitriolic terms by Dalton Trumbo, a member of the Communist Party and one of the infamous "Hollywood Ten" brought before HUAC.

"He takes his stand squarely in the tradition of chronic confessors who have plagued the earth since the first establishment of orthodoxy,"

Trumbo wrote. "Whatever inquisitorial courts have been set up, Mr. Schlesinger and his breed have appeared in eager herds to proclaim: 'I do not wish to imply approval of your questions, but I am not now nor have I ever been a dissenter. I am not now nor have I ever been a Communist. I am not now nor have I ever been a trade unionist. I am not now nor have I ever been a Jew. Prosecute those answers differently, O masters, send them to jail, make soap of them if you wish. But not of me, for I have answered every question you chose to ask, full, frankly, freely—and on my belly."

Schlesinger fired back that Trumbo had been the one grubbing around on the floor. While he, Schlesinger, had always affirmed "the basic constitutional principles that men may be questioned and prosecuted for their acts, never their thoughts," Trumbo he found cowardly in his failure to take the stand at HUAC to defiantly proclaim his First Amendment rights to private opinions. "This accusation is a fair one," notes Christopher Trumbo in a biography of his father. "They [the Ten] clearly harmed their case with the general public by evading questions."[39]

Schlesinger was one of the 130 liberals who founded Americans for Democratic Action (ADA) at its inception on January 4, 1947. Others included the theologian Reinhold Niebuhr and the economist John Kenneth Galbraith, both of whom would become friends and powerful influences on Schlesinger's thinking. The organization itself called for an expansion of the New Deal and was given the blessing of FDR's widow, Eleanor Roosevelt, and their son, Franklin Jr. But the central objective of the new group was to become a powerful vehicle for the non-Communist Left in its vehement opposition to Stalinism.

The presence of the Roosevelts was important for Schlesinger. The 1917 generation had not grown up with the utopian notions about Marxism of earlier generations, but in a time of depression when Communism offered the Scylla of Stalinism to the Charybdis of Nazism. That was why progressives like Schlesinger continued to revere the New Deal. "The whole point of the New Deal," he rejoiced, "lay in its belief in activism, its faith in gradualness, its rejection of catastrophism, its indifference to ideology, its conviction that a managed and modified capitalist order achieved by piecemeal experiment could combine personal freedom and economic growth."[40]

The idea of democracy under threat had seared itself into Schlesinger's mind, but others drew a different lesson from the experience of the '30s and '40s. A week before the formation of the ADA, another new organization, the Progressive Citizens of America (PCA), was formed in New York with the support of former FDR-era vice president Henry Wallace. PCA sought a continuation of the wartime alliance through a more cooperative attitude with Stalin, the Soviet Union, and Communists generally. In contrast, the ADA in its first principles declared, "in the great democratic tradition of Jefferson, Jackson, Lincoln, Wilson, and Franklin D. Roosevelt [we] reject any association with Communists or sympathizers with communism in the United States as completely as we reject any association with Fascists or their sympathizers." The consequences would be dramatic. "The historic significance," reported the *New York Times*, not often given to such sweeping statements, "was the cleavage which it creates in the American liberal movement."[41]

But many were baffled, like Lippmann, at why friendly cooperation with the USSR should be such an untenable position, or why, for that matter, Dalton Trumbo shouldn't be allowed to write his screenplays. Others worried that a split on the left might open up an opportunity for extremism, even Fascism, on the right. Those questions would percolate with Schlesinger, who, before doubts set in amid McCarthyism, sallied forth with his first political book—a vehement defense of the "vital center." But first the practicalities of life and profession intervened. For in 1947 Schlesinger and his family packed their belongings together to move from Washington back to Cambridge. After a gap of five years, Arthur was going home to Harvard.

CHAPTER SEVEN

THE VITAL CENTER

"I met [the attorneys] Mr. Boland and Mr. Winslow this morning," the letter to Arthur Schlesinger Jr. announced in the spring of 1947, "and we completed the transfer of 109 Irving Street, Cambridge. I hope you will have as much pleasure in the house as I have had directly and indirectly during the past fifty years." The correspondent's father, Edward Mark, a Harvard zoology professor, who built the house in 1893, lived there for more than half a century until his death at age ninety-nine. The Schlesingers own it to this day, so it has been in the hands of just two families for more than 120 years.

But in 1947, Marian Schlesinger was not enthusiastic about the purchase. Everything about the move seemed dreary. She had grown up just two minutes away on Divinity Avenue. The new house on Irving Street was dark and run-down. Even though the street had been home to the likes of William James and E. E. Cummings, "our neighborhood seemed rather a gray one, occupied by virtuous minded academics and the like," Marian recalled. "We were so much more sophisticated now," she says. "Arthur had been in the war. We had made all sorts of friends in Washington. But Cambridge had changed in the war too. So this rather small society turned out to be a much bigger scene." She painted the inside of the house white and set up her own art studio on the third floor, while Arthur had his own spacious study on the floor below. Each of the three children had their own room, and there was a generous yard in which they could all play. For the first time, the Schlesingers had a family home.[1]

Most mornings Arthur would set out from Irving Street on the fifteen-minute walk to the university, usually taking the more scenic route past the elegant Harvard Divinity School, down Oxford Street, across Harvard Yard, and up the steps of the Widener Library. For him the library served as a home away from home. As a young child, his father had often left him in the basement, where he would happily wade through piles of discarded envelopes looking for foreign stamps to add to his collection. The world-class holdings in this library informed his undergraduate thesis and the research for his Pulitzer Prize–winning *The Age of Jackson*. Now as he stepped between the neoclassical columns to enter the building, he could wander along to greet his father or the mentor-turned-friend Perry Miller, taking care to avoid F. O. Matthiessen, with whom he had fallen out over the non-Communist Left. Often there were visiting colleagues too, including, in 1949, the historian of ideas Isaiah Berlin, who became a lifelong friend (even if one often left bemused by the "slight tiffs" that Arthur had with Marian in his presence).[2]

Harvard in the late 1940s and early 1950s was a family in another way too. Around half of the 448 members of the Faculty of Arts and Sciences had Harvard PhDs, with a long tradition—of which Schlesinger was a prime example—of promoting from within the équipe. This helped to create what Bernard Bailyn, later chair of History and in 1947 Schlesinger's first teaching assistant, called the "Harvard problem": a "ridiculously inflated reputation and self-esteem." In the 1940s this manifested itself in a preference for appointing its own; later it would show itself as a paralyzing inability to appoint almost anyone.[3]

In such an overbearing environment, armed with a Pulitzer Prize and his sense of entitlement, Schlesinger not surprisingly began behaving in a way that many colleagues found arrogant and peremptory. His wartime experience in OWI and OSS had apparently taught him little about office politics and diplomacy. Certainly Samuel Eliot Morison, who had been the only professor to give young Arthur a B grade for a history class, seems not to have revised his opinion upwards after working alongside him as a colleague. "[He] is rather smart-alecky and disagreeable in personality," Morison reported to Winthrop Aldrich, the US ambassador in London in

1954. "He is just the kind of person who would rub the English the wrong way." Years later, when someone unkindly showed Schlesinger that letter, he would say, "Actually I admired him [Morison] greatly, and in later years we became good friends [but] I can well see how as a brash young man (which I fear I was) I could have got on Sam's nerves." Marian did her best to encourage Schlesinger to moderate his outbursts. "I remember trying to calm him down," Marian recalls, "saying for God's sake, don't treat people like that just because they disagree with you. And then of course [colleagues] said, Arthur, don't fight with people; maybe you'll get along much better with them if you just stop this old routine." At the Faculty Club he often spent lunch with colleagues from outside History, including from 1948 onwards the economist John Kenneth Galbraith, who bought the house over the fence from the Schlesingers. "We became the closest of neighbors and, notwithstanding, the most devoted of friends," Galbraith wrote to Schlesinger almost forty years later.[4]

If Schlesinger struggled with his History colleagues, he got on much better with students taking his classes. With veterans arriving on the GI Bill, the incoming class in 1947 was both older and, at more than 1,500 students, bigger than any previous class in the history of the university. That increase in size brought new demands. Many (including Henry Kissinger) could not even be accommodated and ended up sleeping on camp beds in the Indoor Athletic Building. And those who had fought in the war were inevitably different from previous generations of students. "Students who had seen combat in Europe or the Pacific were mature, determined to learn and unimpressed by authority," Schlesinger recalled. "It was an exciting time to teach."[5]

As always, Arthur Sr. helped prepare the way for his son. His popular American social and intellectual history was reconstituted as social and cultural history, leaving Arthur Jr. to teach History 169: American Intellectual History. It soon became the most oversubscribed course in the history curriculum. One important feature of Schlesinger's teaching was the iron rule that politics did not enter the classroom. As a later student, Arthur Aptowitz, recalled, "The outside world was not allowed to enter. Nearly every other undergraduate and graduate instructor in my history and political science classes devoted at least some time to discussing the dramatic events of the day." Schlesinger made it clear to students that the classroom was "only for research and criticism." It was one of the reasons why he was a popular teacher but rarely a controversial one, even at times such as during the early Cold War and later during the Vietnam War, when, contrastingly, he was a divisive public figure.

However, Harold Burstyn, who came up to Harvard in 1947, recalls one rare instance when politics did intervene at a lecture given by "the teacher we called Young Arthur." In the fall of 1948, the day after President Truman was unexpectedly elected, "Professor Schlesinger came in to thunderous applause. He gave a brief analysis of the unexpected result and dismissed the class, suggesting that many of us, like him, may have been up quite late. As he spoke, I looked along the row I was sitting in to see George Cabot Lodge, the [Republican, Massachusetts] senator's son, looking quite glum. It's one of the strongest memories from my college years."[6]

In the lead-up to the 1948 election, Schlesinger had vigorously promoted the Democratic candidacy not of Truman, but of General Dwight D. Eisenhower, when the future 34th president's party allegiance was unknown. ("Never back a presidential candidate whose views are top secret," Schlesinger reflected ruefully afterwards.) When Eisenhower made clear that he was not seeking the nomination of either party, Schlesinger "gloomily" backed Truman, expecting him to lose. The actual result, he told his parents, who were abroad, left him "stunned, overwhelmed and delighted," even if it meant that the ADA was "at sea for the moment."[7]

During the campaign, the White House invited Schlesinger to write a speech for Truman, but it was never used ("no use for a staccato president," Schlesinger said, then "still a novice ghostwriter"). He had better luck with another prominent character, Averell Harriman. "The Crocodile" could not have been a much grander figure. The heir to a vast railroad fortune, he had served as FDR's "special envoy" to Churchill and Stalin during the Second World War, and later in Truman's cabinet as commerce secretary. In 1948, the president sent him to Paris to run the European recovery effort known as the Marshall Plan. With patrician airiness, Harriman thought a Pulitzer Prize–winning Harvard professor had exactly the kind of gifted writing skills to pep up his speeches. So Harriman invited Schlesinger to come to Paris as his special assistant for the entire Harvard 1948 summer vacation. Even though Marian was pregnant with the couple's fourth child, Schlesinger "said yes at once." Arthur was already wearing every academic laurel. Harriman opened a door into a different kind of world. The opportunity to work at close quarters with such an influential political figure, Schlesinger calculated, was simply too good to pass up.[8]

When Harriman left for Paris in April, Schlesinger quickly filled out his own paperwork for the Economic Cooperation Administration (ECA) and waited for confirmation of his position. And he waited. Harriman's office began calling Schlesinger to ask why he had failed to arrive. Schlesinger's own phone calls to the ECA met only with vague responses about things in the pipeline. Slowly it began to dawn on him that his unhappy vetting experience with the US Navy during the war was repeating itself. What made the logjam more perplexing, however, was that Schlesinger was still on the books of the CIA as a consultant after his wartime service in OSS. Turning to his Georgetown friend, Philip Graham, Schlesinger asked him to use his influence to find out what was going on. Graham called FBI chief J. Edgar Hoover directly. He quickly discovered, as the government file would later make clear, that Schlesinger was viewed as "most outspoken and demonstrative with reference to his contempt for the Bureau." Hoover later described the Harvard man as "another jackass which enjoys the braying of his own voice." That spring, word had reached him that Schlesinger had denounced him at a dinner in Boston, saying that the director "represents a more destructive force in public life today than any Fascist who might be named." After Graham's intervention, Hoover grudgingly had his assistant Louis B. Nichols investigate the claim. Nichols personally interviewed Schlesinger, who, the file notes, "denied making such a statement and added that he had confidence in the FBI." Having extracted that applause line, Hoover gave the go-ahead for Schlesinger to be cleared. Finally approved, he left for Paris in mid-July.[9]

Harriman had taken up residence in the city center in the elegant surroundings of the Hôtel de Talleyrand near the Place de la Concorde. It had been a personally provocative choice. At the Potsdam Conference in 1945, Harriman had heard Stalin say he would like to own the building, no doubt, Harriman conjectured, because the headquarters of Napoleon's foreign minister seemed a reminder that he, Stalin, had emulated the victory of Tsar Alexander in the Battle of Paris in 1814. "For no purpose but one-upmanship against Stalin," Harriman's official biographer Rudy Abramson notes, "Averell had taken the initiative for the United States to acquire the use of the building." Once ensconced there, however, Harriman began to wonder if perhaps the building, and particularly his own lavish apartments, were somewhat too grand, so he made sure to leak information that the building, as a national monument, was owned and appointed by the French government. When he bought a Matisse painting, *Lady with a Hat*, that had taken his fancy, Harriman tried to avoid bad optics by instructing an aide, Major Vernon Walters (later US ambassador to the United Nations under President Reagan), to do the bidding for him—much to the astonishment of Walters's visiting mother.[10]

Schlesinger arrived at the Talleyrand Building feeling a mixture of excitement and trepidation. It was well known that Harriman was tough on his staff, even while often inspiring fierce loyalty from them. Chip Bohlen, another of Schlesinger's new Georgetown acquaintances, worked closely with Harriman during the war and later described his mode of operation as a boss. "One thing he does not like is too much contradiction," Bohlen judged, "although he enjoys a good discussion. Above all don't make any smart cracks or anything that smacks of freshness in regard to anything he says or does." The best word to sum up the relationship, Bohlen judged, was "feudal."[11]

One man who had done similar work with Harriman was the diplomat George Kennan, by now famous as the author of the "X" article on the "sources of Soviet conduct" in the July 1947 issue of *Foreign Affairs*. Kennan, who served as counselor of the Moscow embassy when Harriman was ambassador, later described the atmosphere that often existed in a Harriman office. "The place was full of papers, the air vibrating with tense, relentless interrogations about every detail of everything that was going on," Kennan recorded in his diary of a visit to Harriman in the

1950s. "In another room, a harried stenographer, bland, tight-lipped, and philosophic, with an 'I just work here; I ain't saying nothing; you don't know the half of it' air about her. It was all just like Moscow again." Yet like Bohlen, Kennan's admiration for and loyalty to Harriman was vast. "Imperious only when things or people impeded the performance of his duties," summed up Kennan, "the United States has never had a more faithful public servant."[12]

Schlesinger's new job as ghostwriter was a particularly delicate one. The New York Times thought Harriman "a dreadful public speaker, talking in a slow monotone and sounding unsure of himself." After a particularly enervating performance before the House Foreign Affairs Committee by the man known as "Honest Ave the Hairsplitter," a sympathetic House staffer had thrown aside the transcription of Harriman's rambling testimony and replaced it with something altogether crisper.[13]

Soon after Schlesinger arrived in Paris, he encountered the problem at first hand. At a luncheon for the American Chamber of Commerce, Harriman mumbled his way through his speech, casting a soporific pall over his visibly bored audience. Immediately afterwards, Schlesinger and his colleague Al Friendly, later managing editor of the Washington Post and another friend of Philip Graham, could not bring themselves to face their boss. "[We] sought fortification at a convenient café and did not reappear in the office till late in the afternoon," Schlesinger explained. "Averell glared at us and said, 'All right, what did I do wrong?' We told him. He grunted, dismissed us brusquely and returned to work." But later that same day, Harriman reappeared to ask them both to dinner at Maxim's, all without a word about the earlier speech. It was an example that what Kennan called "the anxious needlings" did get through to Harriman, even if they "sometimes upset him." When Harriman returned to the United States in the summer of 1950 as special assistant to the president, he would, Schlesinger recorded, "summon me to Washington to help draft speeches and messages." Harriman thus became Schlesinger's first genuinely top-level political client; a decade later, he would be dealing with Harriman while holding the same White House title himself.[14]

Another important relationship Schlesinger developed in Paris, with the socialite Marietta Tree, was more personal. She was born into a wealthy New England Episcopalian family, and "her ambition," Arthur would later say, "was to be a combination of Mrs. Roosevelt and Carole Lombard." When she walked into a dinner party given by the American diplomat David Bruce that summer, Arthur said, "I fell in love with her the first second I saw her." Whether they actually became lovers is unclear. Certainly Marietta was unhappy in her (second) marriage to her bisexual husband, the British former conservative MP, Ronald Tree. And with Arthur away from home, bowled over by her beauty, intelligence, and charm, there was both opportunity and attraction on his part. "We can only begin to imagine," Holly Brubach, the style editor of the *New York Times Magazine*, recalled, "the desire [she] must have inspired." The unkind truth, however, is that Marietta was probably out of Arthur's league. Like a society version of Marilyn Monroe, she collected intellectuals in and around power. But her lovers were the likes of Hollywood director John Huston and soon-to-be presidential candidate Adlai Stevenson. Certainly Arthur's sons, Stephen and Andrew, believed "they were never lovers, despite the words of endearment in their correspondence." ("Marietta darling," Arthur wrote around this time, "I can only reiterate well beyond the point of boredom what fun it has been seeing you these last weeks, how much I count on it, and how much I love and miss you.") Whether or not the two were lovers, their long friendship was enough to cause serious difficulties in the Schlesingers' marriage. Marietta always represented a fashionable ideal for Arthur that the bluestocking Marian could never live up to. "She was a real thorn in the flesh," Marian says.[15]

Schlesinger returned home in September, ready for a new term at Harvard and the birth of his fourth child. The lessons of his experience in France, however, where one in four voters supported the Stalinist French Communist Party, also remained very much on his mind. Writing to the journalist Max Lerner, editor of the *New York Star* (previously *PM*), which was hostile to the non-Communist Left position, Schlesinger explained why he believed wartime cooperation with the Soviet Union could not be resumed. Certainly it was true that if the Marshall Plan brought about the hoped-for "strengthening of Europe politically, economically and militarily to the point where it becomes relatively immune to Communist activity, then we can perhaps hope for a stable agreement with the USSR." But to appease the Soviets at this point, he continued, to believe that "somehow an international miracle can be achieved . . . is to play into the hands of both the isolationists and the Communists." In short, "we are in this for the long haul; there is no one-shot solution." It was a nuanced position that showed the influence of Harriman and echoed the "long and wearisome process" foreseen by Kennan, with whom Schlesinger was in regular correspondence.[16]

Arthur had been reflecting on the need to move beyond mundane political shibboleths since his undergraduate days working on Brownson. His 1939 article in *The Sewanee Review* outlined how throughout American history conservatives and radicals alike had engaged in "denunciation by formula." Brownson was unusual because when confronted by the Panic of 1837 he came up with a "searching" analysis that was "sharp and fresh." Inevitably he found few takers to "admire the brilliance of [his] analysis or to examine judicially his proposals for the future." Instead, "Little Arthur" concluded, in 1837 and in most crises from "Neandertal days" to FDR, "conservatives and radicals battled" with "the same beautiful predictability," falling back on "old arguments with the same unoriginality."[17]

These considerations had been on Schlesinger's mind throughout 1948 as he began to wrestle with the idea that a changed international landscape required a new kind of politics. He first tested the concept that spring in an essay for the *New York Times*. Eighteenth-century notions of left and right, he ventured, were no longer sufficient as a way to organize politics in a totalitarian age. The revolutionary authoritarianism and totalitarianism of Fascism and Communism both seemed to draw from the traditions and language of right and left. Between these extremes, an idea had emerged in postwar Europe of a so-called Third Force in politics. Led by the veteran socialist leader Léon Blum, it reinforced the notion that the non-Communist Left shared much common ground with the moderate non-Fascist Right—not least a faith in democratic methods against any form of dictatorship. The American Left, Schlesinger said, being opposed to both Fascism and Stalinism, should want to "rush up and shake hands" with those occupying the middle ground of European politics. "Yet the performance of American liberals and labor [has been] generally shocking," he raged, "[as] altogether too many liberals followed Communist cues at every Soviet triumph."[18]

Schlesinger's analysis up to this point in the *Times* essay was forceful without necessarily being penetrating. At the end of the article, however, he took his first step into new territory. "Such developments make it urgent that, in the interests of clear thinking, we abandon the word Left," he wrote, continuing that "the non-Communist Left and the non-Fascist Right share a common faith in free political society." All hope for the future "surely lies in the revival of the Center." The destruction of that middle way, "which unites hopes of freedom and economic abundance," would be the "first priority" of both Fascism and Communism. Quoting the Irish poet W. B. Yeats that "Things fall apart; the centre cannot hold," Schlesinger identified the crucial task ahead as "to make sure that the Center does hold" as "the pattern of conspiracy against the Center is repeated throughout the world." The subeditor at the *New York Times*, perhaps also thinking of *Moby-Dick*, gave Schlesinger's concept a new name: "Not Left, Not Right, But a Vital Center." The historian pilfered it for the title of his 1949 book, *The Vital Center*.[19]

In the Manichean world of the 1930s and 1940s, intellectuals grappled to make sense of the recent horrific experiences of Nazism and Stalinism. Numerous books on freedom appeared in the immediate postwar period, including seminal works such as Hayek's *The Road to Serfdom* (1945), George Orwell's *Nineteen Eighty-Four* (1949), and Hannah Arendt's *The Origins of Totalitarianism* (1951). As Schlesinger would write in 1949, "Tormented by war and by tyrannies worse than war, out of the Soviet offensive against democratic socialism came a renewed sense of the meaning of freedom." The writers who served as his model in this endeavor were those "who refused to swallow the fantastic hypocrisies involved in the defense of totalitarianism." These included the likes of "[Arthur] Koestler, with his probing, insatiable intellectual curiosity; [Ernest] Hemingway, who disliked people who pushed other people around [and] ... George Orwell, with his vigorous good sense, his hatred of cant."[20]

Schlesinger had been in London in 1945 when Orwell's *Animal Farm* was published. He was stunned by this "wonderful anti-Stalinist allegory" and "bought several copies to take back to the United States." The book then became part of his battle with Communist sympathizers. Passing along his British copy to his US publisher, Little, Brown, he was shocked not so much when they turned down American rights—that's business— but by the vehement pro-Communist views he perceived in the company's chief editor, Angus Cameron, and the corresponding hostility to himself. "It is my serious belief," he told Bernard DeVoto, "that my well known views on the Communist party have put me on some ... blacklist."[21]

In 1947, Schlesinger wrote to Alfred McIntyre, company president, to withdraw his publishing contract. When McIntyre did not even bother to reply, Schlesinger followed up with a coruscating attack that gives an indication of the febrile atmosphere of the times. "Each day increases my sense of shame at ever having been associated with your house," he hollered. "I would never have signed up in 1939 if one of your leading members had been an active pro-German and pro-Nazi; and I have no more intention of being published by Little, Brown today when one of your leading members is taking an active part in opposing the democratic effort to check the spread of Soviet totalitarianism."[22]

Decades later, Schlesinger would concede that Cameron, a well-regarded and even beloved editor, had probably not let political views cloud his editorial judgment. But in 1951, when Cameron was named before Senator William E. Jenner's internal security subcommittee, Schlesinger shamefully released his letter of 1947 to the press, telling *Time* magazine that the rejection of an anti-Communist novel as brilliant as *Animal Farm* had set alarm bells ringing.[23]

Orwell's work had a profound influence on Schlesinger, but even its impact paled in comparison to "the tragic sense of the predicament of man" evinced by the theologian Reinhold Niebuhr. Schlesinger had first heard Niebuhr preach in the winter of 1940–1941 when debates raged about whether the United States should join the war against Hitler. Dragged along unwillingly by Marian to Memorial Church in Harvard Yard, he had been transfixed by the homily's "jagged eloquence . . . the dramatics, the argument, . . . cool, rigorous and powerful." Man was sinful, Niebuhr said, but even the sinful man had a duty to act against evil. Our own sins, for example, were no justification for standing apart from the struggle taking place in Europe. "The emphasis on sin startled my generation, brought up on optimistic convictions of human innocence and perfectibility," Schlesinger recalled of the "hushed" congregation. It was an unlikely moment of epiphany for a man who since childhood had shown little interest in religion or signs of faith. But Schlesinger overnight joined the ranks of what Felix Frankfurter described as Niebuhr's believing unbelievers. ("May a believing unbeliever thank you for your sermon?" Frankfurter once inquired. "May an unbelieving believer thank you for appreciating it?" Niebuhr smoothly replied.)[24]

Throughout his life, Schlesinger had benefited from a series of strong advisors and mentors: his father, obviously, but also characters such as his Harvard tutor, Perry Miller, and Bernard DeVoto, who arranged his first book contract. Even Charles Wintour, as a worldly-wise contemporary, was a mentor of sorts during the year at Peterhouse. And it is striking that the one unhappy period in Schlesinger's life, at OSS during the war, even before his loss of officer-equivalent status, came when he was without a strong influence to guide him. In the immediate postwar period, Reinhold Niebuhr became a new mentor and inspiration for Schlesinger. The two men engaged in a regular correspondence throughout the late forties and the fifties, and when Schlesinger visited New York, he would often stay with Niebuhr and his wife, Ursula (herself a theologian), in their apartment in Morningside Heights. Each man read the other's work, and Niebuhr sent Schlesinger the draft of *The Irony of American History* (1952), which "I was most anxious to have you [look at]." Niebuhr also provided a model for the kind of public intellectual that Schlesinger hoped to become, not just for the quality of his ideas, but for thrilling the younger man with reports on being summoned by Secretary of State Dean Acheson "to consider 'various plans of the department for strengthening the non-communist world.'"[25]

Schlesinger now "immersed myself in Niebuhr," particularly the two volumes of the *Nature and Destiny of Man* (1941–1942) and *The Children of Light and The Children of Darkness* (1944). Here he found arguments about the mixed nature of man and what Niebuhr called the "humble recognition of the limits of our knowledge and our power," including how man's wickedness made government both essential and dangerous. The aim of government, therefore, was not "the creation of an ideal society in which there will be uncoerced and perfect peace and justice, but a society in which there will be enough justice, and in which coercion will be sufficiently non-violent to prevent [our] common enterprise from issuing into complete disaster." Niebuhr's approach, often called "Christian realism," provided a key for Schlesinger in its warnings against utopianism, messianism, and perfectionism. "He persuaded me," Schlesinger wrote later, "that original sin provides a far stronger foundation for freedom and self-government than illusions about human perfectibility."[26]

Niebuhr's ideas quickly found their way into Schlesinger's historical and political analysis. In 1945 in *The Age of Jackson*, he had concluded with a favorite Niebuhrian quotation from Pascal's *Pensées*—"Man is neither angel nor brute, and the unfortunate thing is that he who would act the angel acts the brute,"—and added his own line that "The great tradition of American liberalism regards man as neither brute nor angel." By 1949, his tone about the imperfectibility of man had become more acerbic. In a survey essay on the historiography of the causes of the American Civil War, he excoriated the revisionists, notably James G. Randall, for their perceived naïveté about war and the nature of man. "We have here a touching afterglow of the admirable 19th-century faith in the full rationality and perfectibility of man; the faith that the errors of the world would all in time be 'outmoded' (Professor Randall's use of this word is suggestive) by progress," Schlesinger wrote in characteristically Niebuhrian terms. "Yet the experience of the 20th century has made it clear that we gravely overrated man's capacity to solve the problems of existence within the terms of history. That conclusion about man may disturb our complacencies about human nature. Yet it is certainly more in accord with history than Professor Randall's 'enlightened' assumption that man can solve peaceably all the problems which overwhelm him."[27]

Niebuhr also gave Schlesinger both the confidence and the intellectual underpinning for his first overtly political book, *The Vital Center: The Politics of Freedom*, which in turn would do more than perhaps any other book to popularize the theologian's ideas. It was through the experience of Fascism and Communism that his generation had "discovered a new dimension of experience—the dimension of anxiety, guilt and corruption," Schlesinger wrote in the foreword. "Or," he added, paying his philosophical debts, "as Reinhold Niebuhr has brilliantly suggested, that we were simply rediscovering ancient truths which we should never have forgotten."[28]

But if mankind was not perfectible, what was the postwar liberal to do in the face of totalitarianism? If Schlesinger accepted Niebuhr's essentially conservative notion that consistent pessimism about humankind inoculated democracy against authoritarianism and totalitarianism, then, in Schlesinger's own words, "Wherein lies the hope?" Departing from Niebuhr, the answer certainly did not come through traditional religion, which Schlesinger saw as passé in a new scientific age. But equally, the notion "that doubt and anxiety" would be banished by science and a rising standard of living he saw as another false dawn. And although society needed "a revival of the elan of democracy, and a resurgence of the democratic faith," the evolution of democracy into a "political religion," like totalitarianism, was not the answer either. The only way forward was to "recharge the deepest sources of moral energy" to create a society in tune with "the emotional energies and needs of man."[29]

For that notion, Schlesinger found an echo in the American poet Walt Whitman, who wrote that "to work for Democracy is good, the exercise is good—strength it makes and lessons it teaches." So in the end, for Schlesinger in *The Vital Center*, it is the very process of democracy itself, not perfect ends, which forms the bulwark against totalitarianism. "Problems will always torment us, because all important problems are insoluble: that is why they are important," he wrote in the conclusion. "The good comes from the continuing struggle to try to solve them, not from the vain hope of their solution. . . . The totalitarians regard the toleration of conflict as our central weakness. So it may appear to be in an age of anxiety. But we know it to be basically our central strength." Thus it was through a renewed commitment to the very exercise of democracy itself that "the centre" might indeed hold.[30]

What is striking about *The Vital Center* is the gap between gloomy, fatalistic diagnosis and hopeful, confident prescription; "the movement," James Nuechterlein notes, "from conservative assumptions to liberal conclusions." Schlesinger himself was not unaware of this sometimes uncomfortable shift, writing in *Encounter* two decades afterwards that the background of being "much influenced by Reinhold Niebuhr . . . accounts for the combination in the book of a certain operational optimism with a certain historical and philosophical pessimism." That conflict was something in itself that he had inherited from Niebuhr, who, while often an appealing writer for conservatives, considered himself a liberal. But as Schlesinger pointed out in the introduction to a 1998 reissue of the book, these internal traditions within the democratic tradition were not the point. "The vital center was in a global context," he wrote, "liberal democracy as against its mortal enemies, fascism to the right, communism to the left," which made *The Vital Center* "an attempt to strengthen the liberal case against the renewed totalitarian impulse" of the postwar era. Within that framework, different impulses could coexist, because the vital center referred "to the contest between democracy and totalitarianism, not to contests within democracy between liberalism and conservatism." The balancing trick, as Niebuhr later helpfully summed up, was that "Democracy is on the whole the vital center, but it must be worked so that it doesn't go to dead center." It was an analogy that Schlesinger himself would co-opt and reuse. The "vital" center, he would write, was not "the so-called 'middle of the road' preferred by cautious politicians of our own time." That position, after all, is only somewhere to stand if you want to be flattened.[31]

Thus far, Schlesinger, the Pulitzer Prize–winning author of *The Age of Jackson*, had received laudatory reviews throughout his short career. Now matters became more uneven, as the two contrasting reviews in the *New York Times* demonstrate. Certainly Schlesinger continued to have his fans, including Charles Poore in the weekday *Times*, who wrote that *The Vital Center* was "the best guide to our prospects for civilized survival we have seen in a long time." In particular, Poore admired the "wonderful battery of ubiquitous artillery" that Schlesinger deployed as he "blows the Communists and their diminishing flotillas of fellow-travelers out of the water with deadly aim" and "blasts the medieval-minded Colonel Blimps of reaction." On the other hand, Gerald W. Johnson, whose 1927 book on President Jackson had been effectively trashed by Schlesinger in his own more successful book, was withering in the *New York Times Sunday Book Review*. Johnson made little attempt to hide his view that Schlesinger was jejune and an intellectual snob. "One suspects that he has associated too exclusively with the intellectuals," Johnson chided, adding that he should have spent more time observing real politics. "The politician knows the common herd," Johnson concluded damningly, "and the election of 1948 raised at least a suspicion that the common herd is miles ahead of the intellectuals in its grasp of the realities of the situation." What both men agreed on, however, was Schlesinger's ability as a stylist. For Poore, *The Vital Center* was "exuberant, witty and remorselessly penetrating." And even Johnson admitted that the book had an "energy, boldness and certainly . . . a good deal more wit than is to be found in most of its tribe."

Most reviewers concurred on the stylistic verve of the book and took a middle course on the content. "He offers few novel thoughts," summed up the writer Irwin Ross for *Commentary*. "His success, rather, lies in the precision, vitality, and emotional power of his restatement of commonly accepted views. He has seldom written better prose—a lean and pliant style, edged with wit and paradox, equally capable of flashing satire and fine sonorities of exhortation."[32]

Reasonably well reviewed and a modest bestseller in 1949, *The Vital Center* would turn out to be among Schlesinger's most enduring works, with new editions published in 1962, when he was a member of the Kennedy administration, and in 1998, after the original had been extolled by both President Clinton and Republican Speaker of the House, Newt Gingrich. (The Speaker in 1996 had quoted the line that "The conservative must not identify a particular *status quo* with the survival of civilization, and the radical equally must recognize that his protests are likely to be as much the expressions of his own self-interest as they are of some infallible dogma"—a plea for humility, Schlesinger drily noted, "that neither Gingrich nor I have always observed.") Looking back, the *New York Times* would conclude that it was with *The Vital Center* that Schlesinger "solidified his position as the spokesman for postwar liberalism."[33]

CHAPTER EIGHT

EGGHEAD

In June 1950, Arthur Schlesinger Jr. traveled from Cambridge, Massachusetts, to West Berlin to take up his place among the world's leading anti-Communist thinkers. Around two hundred delegates, including illustrious names such as novelist Arthur Koestler, philosopher A. J. Ayer, and playwright Tennessee Williams, landed in West Germany for a gathering of the Congress for Cultural Freedom—an event supported by the US Military Government in Berlin and, covertly, the CIA. Gathered here, Schlesinger wrote to his former boss Averell Harriman, now special assistant to the president, were "potentially the richest intellectual resources" in the West.[1]

Schlesinger made the trip with Sidney Hook, the violently anti-Communist convert from Marxism. He later recalled how excited Hook was by the danger and drama of the situation. The divided former German capital had only recently come through the first major crisis of the Cold War, the Berlin airlift, so the sense of journeying to the front seemed very real. "He had this fantasy about Communist attacks from all sides," Schlesinger recalled. "He was quite excited about it all. I think many of the [delegates] were. They thought they were going to be where the action was—especially those who hadn't been in the war."[2]

No sooner had Schlesinger and his fellow delegates arrived than a new Cold War crisis reinforced their belief in the urgency of their task. As everyone gathered at the Titania Palace on June 26, 1950, news spread that Communist forces in Korea had crossed the 38th parallel into the

US-controlled South of the country—beginning what would become the Korean War. With the Berlin Philharmonic Orchestra present in the hall to provide the suitably tragic-heroic soundtrack of Beethoven's *Egmont* overture, delegates marched in together before standing for a moment of profound silence to remember those who had died fighting for freedom.[3]

Over the next four days, debates raged about a strategy for the non-Communist Left in democratic politics. The hardliner James Burnham, author of *The Managerial Revolution* and, like Hook, another Marxist turned vehement anti-Communist, led the way with his theory of "good" atomic bombs that could destroy all major Soviet cities in a day. Along with Hook, Burnham condemned any descent into moral equivalence, attacking Jean-Paul Sartre and his followers, who "were quite aware of French and American injustices to Negroes when they supported the Resistance to Hitler, but they can see no justice in the western defense against Communist aggression because the Negroes have not yet won equality of treatment." Hook would remember the event as "the most exciting conference I have ever attended, before or since." Others were more skeptical. They found the tone of the language, exemplified by Arthur Koestler's evocation of scripture to "Let your yea be yea, and your nay, nay," too simplistic and Manichean. "I felt, well, what sort of people are we identifying ourselves with?" the British historian Hugh Trevor Roper recalled after hearing Koestler speak. "That was the greatest shock to me. There was a moment during the Congress when I felt that we were being invited to summon up Beelzebub in order to defeat Satan."

Within this combustible atmosphere, Schlesinger underperformed. In fact, Koestler's call to intellectual arms had to some degree been a reaction to Schlesinger's own poor speech. "Schlesinger was there, and he made a dry-as-dust, unemotional statement," the CIA's representative, Lawrence de Neufville, reported. "After that we had Koestler who spoke from the heart, and he moved many people. It was a crusade—Koestler had changed the tone."[4]

Schlesinger's subdued performance reflected his failings as public speaker. He rarely extemporized, almost always reading from a prepared text. A forceful and colorful writer, in person his lack of both physical presence and a larger-than-life stage personality meant he was rarely a charismatic force other than in the university lecture hall. "I found his lectures anything but dull," Harvard undergraduate at the time Harold Burstyn recalls, "but there's a substantial difference between public speeches and classroom lectures. I suspect that his ironic tone and lack of fireworks would have affected the response to his public presentations." Superb if deploying the critic's scorn, Schlesinger struggled to convey the sincerity required of a politician. More often than not he stuck to writing speeches while leaving others to deliver them.[5]

On the substance of the conference, however, Schlesinger returned to America convinced that the meeting had been the beginning of something important. "The Berlin Conference was very useful, I think," he told Harriman, "and, properly developed could become [invaluable] in combating the Communist 'peace' drive in Europe and in fighting neutralism in general."[6]

Schlesinger had spent much of the conference in the company of his friend Nicolas Nabokov, the minor composer and cousin of the more famous Vladimir. The two had met in Washington in 1946 at Joseph Alsop's stag dinner and immediately hit it off. "He overflowed with vitality," Schlesinger remembered, "was a notable raconteur in half a dozen languages, also a notable mimic, and had, what was rare in an artist, a penetrating and ironical political intelligence." In Berlin, the two men went exploring together and sought out those who, like Nabokov after the revolution, had managed to flee the Soviet Union. "According to these Russian escapees, Schlesinger recorded, "Soviet indoctrination has been sufficiently successful to give the Russian people as a whole a profound conviction that any American initiative is ultimately a mask for American expansion." Schlesinger dismissed this notion as nonsense. Nabokov in contrast recognized that the very exercise they themselves were engaged in was something of an exercise in American cultural expansion, commenting to A. J. Ayer that they were being gently "manipulated" by the "occult forces" of the Americans paying for the conference. As it turned out, this fact was one that Nabokov was happy to exploit. In Berlin that summer, the Soviet exile delivered one of the most aggressive speeches of the conference. "Out of this Congress we should build our first fighting organization," he declared. "If we do not, we will sooner or later be hanged. The hour has long struck Twelve." It was a pitch to lead the movement.[7]

A series of exposé articles in the *New York Times* in the late 1960s revealed that the CIA funded the Congress for Cultural Freedom (CCF). Subsequent release of documents and research by historians, notably Frances Stonor Saunders, demonstrated not only that the intelligence service funded CCF, but that it was in fact a CIA front organization, led by a CIA agent, Michael Josselson. "At its peak," Saunders writes, "the Congress for Cultural Freedom had offices in thirty-five countries, employed dozens of personnel, published over twenty prestige magazines, held art exhibitions, owned a news and features service, organized high-profile international conferences, and rewarded musicians and artists with prizes and public performances. Its mission was to nudge the intelligentsia of western Europe away from its lingering fascination with Marxism and Communism towards a view more accommodating of 'the American way.'" The way in which the CIA achieved this end was by recruiting a "consortium" of American artists and public intellectuals who would, knowingly or not, work alongside the CIA "to promote an idea: that the world needed a pax Americana, a new age of enlightenment, and it would be called The American Century." Appropriately enough, Henry Luce, the originator of the phrase "American Century," helped establish the most famous beneficiary of the CIA's cultural largesse. In March 1949, Alfred Barr, founding director of MoMa, which had strong links to the CIA, wrote to Luce encouraging him to promote Abstract Expressionism as representative of American "artistic free enterprise." The August edition of *Life* then featured an extravagant article on Jackson Pollock, with photographs of him at work by Arnold Newman. "It made Pollock famous," Louis Menand says, "the 'action painter,' the very type of the modern American culture hero."[8]

The CIA revelations embarrassed Schlesinger and other prominent CCF members. For many observers, the question became a simple, perhaps simplistic, binary: were you a CIA dupe or a CIA stooge? "It [is] very difficult now to deny that some of these things happened," gloated

Norman Birnbaum, a Georgetown lawyer and founding editorial board member of *New Left Review,* pointing out that the revelations "placed a lot of people living and dead in embarrassing situations."[9]

Some reacted by blaming the system. Nabokov (who died in 1978 before Saunders's revelations), complained after the original *New York Times* exposé, "Had the American government *then* [1950] had the courage and foresight to establish a worldwide fund . . . to subsidize legally and overtly—as did the Marshall Plan in the domain of economic reconstruction—the indispensable anti-Stalinist, anti-Communist, and, in general, anti-totalitarian cultural activities of the Cold War, the whole ugly mess of 1966 or 1967 would not have taken place. Many reputations would have been spared [and the Cold War] fought out, at least in the world of the intellect and culture, openly and frankly."[10]

That seems like cant on the part of Nabokov, who knowingly was on the CIA payroll as CCF general secretary. Others, such as the Oxford philosopher Isaiah Berlin, had greater justification in making a similar argument. Berlin had known vaguely that CCF was getting some kind of US government money. "He knew about our involvement," the CIA's Lawrence de Neufville later said, "I don't know who told him, but I imagine it was one of his friends in Washington." Berlin, as a Russian emigre, had no embarrassment about being called a Cold War intellectual or even taking American money. "I did not in the slightest object to American sources supplying money—I was (and am) pro-American and anti-Soviet, and if the source had been declared I would not have minded in the least," he explained. What bothered Berlin, however, was that publications such as *Encounter* that claimed to be independent, "over and over again, turned out to be in the pay of American secret intelligence."[11]

Schlesinger was less agitated than his friend Berlin. As a former OSS officer, he well understood the nature of cultural propaganda, had routinely been kept on the CIA's books as a consultant after the war, and would have been naïve given his wartime service not to have seen a connection between the agency and CCF. Certainly when he had concerns about the political direction of the CCF branch in the United States, the American Committee for Cultural Freedom, he turned immediately to his CIA contacts, presumably on the grounds that they were in a position to act. In 1952, for example, he wrote a long memo with enclosures to his wartime OSS friend Frank Wisner, appointed that year as head of the CIA Directorate of Plans. The memo presented "a rather alarming picture," wrote Wisner, who immediately ordered an investigation. Schlesinger still claimed later that while he had been aware of the CIA's initial investment in the Congress for Cultural Freedom, the full extent of its involvement surprised him. "[I] assumed the foundations were paying," he maintained. "Like everyone else, I thought they were *bona fide* . . . I didn't know it was the CIA paying for it all."

The extent to which Schlesinger did or did not know about CIA involvement, however, had no impact on his essential view about the episode. When cooperating with Saunders on her book, he made a forceful defense that agency involvement could only have led to corruption "if people were persuaded to do things they wouldn't otherwise have done. And that simply wasn't the case." He himself had quickly become disillusioned with the organization for political reasons, but not because he was concerned about CIA activity. "I still do not see how people who used the Congress to press views they honestly held could be corrupted by the fact, unknown to them, that the Congress was financed by the CIA," he wrote in 1997. "The Congress was not involved in covert action in that sense [regime change]. It was doing no more than providing means of expression to people who felt that Stalinism was a bad thing. Was that so terrible? Suppose it had been Nazism?"[12]

The reason for Schlesinger's memo to Wisner, and for his broader unease with the CCF project, was a growing alarm about the political witch hunt popularly known as McCarthyism. The House Un-American Activities Committee (HUAC) was established in 1938 to look out for Fascist sympathizers, but once committee hearings got going, its focus quickly moved to left-wing radicals, which, it charged, had penetrated the US government. Schlesinger sympathized with that view. His tough experience inside OSS during the war, not least the confrontation with a named Soviet spy, Maurice Halperin, left him with a profound belief that the security of the state had been compromised.

When HUAC investigated Hollywood after the war, Schlesinger was quick to condemn the "imbecility" of the hearings, writing loftily in the *New York Times Magazine* that "the private political views of a Hollywood writer . . . hardly seem to be the proper consideration of the United States Government or a committee of Congress." But when it came to HUAC's most famous case of Soviet penetration, Schlesinger showed his true colors, and they weren't red.

In 1946, when he was living in Washington, DC, and researching a *Life* article about the American Communist Party, Schlesinger had interviewed the brilliant, brooding *Time* editor and writer, Whittaker Chambers. During that interview, Chambers confirmed Schlesinger's belief that Soviet penetration of the US government was extensive, and he named the State Department official Alger Hiss as an example. Unable to use the libelous information in the article, Schlesinger told Philip Graham, publisher of the *Washington Post*, and asked him to pass it along to his contacts in the State Department. Graham told Undersecretary of State Dean Acheson, who in turn told Secretary of State James F. Byrnes. Hiss, when confronted, denied everything, but was not given his accuser's name.[13]

How Hiss found out that Chambers was that accuser also came about inadvertently through Schlesinger and his researcher, Barbara Kerr, a colleague from his Office of War Information days. At a drunken New Year's Day celebration in 1948, Kerr got into a fierce row with Dean Acheson's former assistant, Edward Miller, about Truman's "Loyalty Order" introduced the previous year. Kerr said these tests were a waste of time, because Communists such as Alger Hiss continued working for the government. Miller angrily accused her of lies and malicious slander. Nonsense, she replied, telling him that she had heard Whittaker Chambers name Hiss. Miller stormed out, telling Kerr that he would be informing Hiss and advising him to sue. Afterwards, another Acheson assistant who had been present at the dinner, John Ferguson, asked Kerr why she had been so certain. She showed him the transcript of Schlesinger's 1946 interview. In August that year, Chambers would name Hiss in an executive session of the House Un-American Activities Committee. When Dean Acheson was asked by Hiss's lawyer, William L. Marbury, how his client's name had come into the public domain, he replied, "Everyone knew the name of Chambers. Arthur Schlesinger was mentioning it at every cocktail party in Washington."[14]

What made the situation doubly difficult for Schlesinger was that Marbury was a member of the Harvard Corporation. To Schlesinger's astonishment, Marbury arrived in his office in Widner unannounced, demanding to know on what basis he was spreading rumors about Hiss. "He then went into a long song-and-dance about his own absolute conviction of Hiss's innocence," Schlesinger reported to Joseph Alsop. "I need not state my astonishment and dismay over the action of a member of the Harvard Corporation seeking, in the interests of one of his clients in private law practice, to bring pressure on a member of the Harvard faculty. In any case, he did not get very far."[15]

Whatever Schlesinger's reputation as a gossip, he had felt no compunction about passing along Chambers's allegation about Hiss to the State Department in 1946. By the 1950s, however, he was increasingly alarmed about the witch-hunt atmosphere in Washington for which critics such as Dalton Trumbo said he bore some responsibility. Disgust at the inquisitorial tactics of Senator Joseph McCarthy, who would appear before television cameras brandishing lists of what he claimed were Communist sympathizers (including in 1952 Schlesinger himself), soon edged out older concerns about the penetration of the US government by Soviet agents. "Obviously the central and overriding enemy of cultural freedom in the world is Communism," he wrote anxiously to the novelist James Farrell, "but I doubt very much whether Communism can be plausibly considered the central and overriding enemy of cultural freedom *within the United States* today." The battles of the '30s and '40s did not need to be refought. "As you know, I fought some of those battles too," he reminded Farrell, "but I believe now that we have better things to do than to pay off old scores."[16]

As American politics in the early 1950s turned ever more paranoid and intolerant, divisions within the Left about how to deal with McCarthyism became increasingly rancorous. The debates played out in a series of American Committee for Cultural Freedom meetings in March 1952.

Farrell took the lead, arguing that if "our object in the United States was to deal with conditions of cultural freedom . . . we ought to go after McCarthyism." The majority, however, led by the likes of Sidney Hook and Daniel Bell, resisted a blanket condemnation of McCarthy or his -ism. Writing to the political thinker Hannah Arendt on March 14, the novelist Mary McCarthy despaired, "I can't believe that these people seriously think that Stalinism on a large scale is latent here, ready to revive at the slightest summons. But if they don't think this, what *do* they really think?" To Schlesinger, she complained of "the miserable sophistry," adding, "I wish the Committee would go on record as condemning McCarthy by name."[17]

It was these divisive meetings that provoked Schlesinger to give the CIA's Frank Wisner an account of events and to express his fears about the direction in which the ACCF was heading. Later he also wrote to Cord Meyer, Wisner's deputy, to reinforce the point. "My concern about the ACCF was the role of ex-Communists so obsessed with Communism that they defended Joe McCarthy and argued that critics of McCarthy were 'objectively' (an old Communist Party formulation) pro-Communist," he reported, adding that he thought "the ACCF an increasingly useless body."[18]

In the spring of 1952, just as Schlesinger was losing interest in the ACCF, other political opportunities unexpectedly opened for him. On March 29, Schlesinger's ADA friend, Joseph Rauh, offered him a last-minute spare ticket to hear President Truman address the Jefferson-Jackson Day dinner (an annual Democratic Party fundraiser) in Washington, DC. Borrowing a black tie from Philip Graham and hoping no one would notice that he was wearing a dark blue suit rather than a tuxedo, he soon found himself gossiping with his old boss Averell Harriman, Governor Adlai Stevenson of Illinois, and ADA chairman Wilson Wyatt—"the three nicest men in public life." After the dinner, Truman, apparently preparing to run for a full second term, gave a "lively" speech "delivered with humor and composure"; it was, Schlesinger said afterwards, "a good, fighting campaign speech." Which is a reason why most in the room were astounded when at the end Truman announced that he would not be running in November. "He hurriedly finished the speech, leaving the audience still stunned,"

Schlesinger wrote in his diary. "Half the people did not seem to know what had happened."[19]

Harriman had already asked Schlesinger to join him for a drink at the Metropolitan Club after the dinner. Now Stevenson joined them, for the first of a series of awkward "After you," "No, after you" conversations between two contenders for the nomination, both of whom, it seemed, thought it too vulgar to say they wanted the job. Harriman pressed Stevenson to run "for the sake of the party and of the nation." Stevenson buried his head in his hands and "looked as if he were going to cry," telling Harriman, "at the moment I don't give a goddamn what happens to the party or the country." Either way, Schlesinger now found himself one step closer to the inside track.[20]

His view of Truman had risen since the 1948 election, when he had hoped the thirty-third president would decline to run again. By 1952, he had even written, with the *New Yorker*'s Richard Rovere, a best-selling polemic that praised Truman for firing General Douglas MacArthur, the media-hungry commander of US forces in Korea, on April 11, 1951, for insubordination. Schlesinger had written to Harriman, the president's special assistant, a few days before MacArthur was fired, pointing out that "no general has so systematically lobbied and intrigued against his commander-in-chief since McClellan [sacked by Lincoln]." MacArthur should be recalled, he urged, a decision that might "be greeted favorably" and "break through the present miasmic atmosphere and reestablish the sense of presidential leadership and initiative." Certainly Schlesinger did his best to shape that positive opinion. His three-hundred-page book with Rovere, turned around in just ninety days, added fuel to the flames of an already intense national debate. On one side stood the China Lobby and the Asia First faction; on the other, internationalists and the "Wise Men" of the East Coast foreign policy establishment, notably Harriman. How extraordinary it was, Schlesinger and Rovere told readers, that MacArthur, a general who "had been forced, through apparent bungling on his part, to order one of the most tragic retreats in the history of American arms [from the 38th parallel]," and who had attempted to "usurp the diplomatic function" of the president, then "returned and rode the streets, not in a cart, but in a conqueror's Cadillac." With such rhetoric, *The General and the President* was read and discussed, said the *New York Times*, "as passionately almost as the subject which gave it rise," enthralling anti-MacArthurites but outraging his supporters. "The young man wanting to know how to write so that he can whittle a great man down to any desired dimension," judged S. L. A. Marshall, a chief US Army combat historian, "could use this [book] as a model."[21]

One person who did appreciate the book, however, was Harry Truman, who wrote to "Doctor Schlesinger" on November 5 to say "you analyzed the situation just as it is." As to MacArthur, the president remarked, "like all other egotists do, he wanted to place the blame as far from himself as possible." Schlesinger was delighted, replying that "We felt that the facts ought to be placed squarely on the record; and we are gratified indeed to know that you did not find our analysis too far off the beam." In what might have been a sycophantic flourish had he not already said much the same in print, Schlesinger reassured Truman, correctly, that "the relief of MacArthur will go down, I am confident, as one of the wisest and most courageous of the many wise and courageous decisions of your administration."[22]

But would Truman run again? As the election year came around, Schlesinger prepared a note for Adlai Stevenson urging him to be ready to run. "I do not think President Truman knows yet (any more than FDR at this point in 1940) whether or not he will run again," he said, and "even if he had made his decision, moreover, there would be no point in communicating it." But Stevenson had to prepare in the event that Truman did not run, he urged. "Your name is constantly being mentioned in this connection," he told Stevenson, so "it seems to me that more ought to be done in the next months to acquaint [the] country with you and your record." Keep your name "before the public eye," he advised, pointing out that "after all, a deadlocked convention might lead to anything." To Joseph Rauh, a Stevenson confidant and ADA friend, he added the practical suggestion "that we should get out rather quickly a biography of Adlai—and not a hack job either."[23]

By January 1952, not only had Truman decided against running, he had even quietly informed Stevenson of this fact. "Early in January 1952, I asked Adlai Stevenson, governor of Illinois to come to the Blair House for a talk," Truman recalled that July. "I told him that I would not run for President again and that it was my opinion he was best fitted for the place." Stevenson told him that he would be standing again as governor and would not run for two offices at the same time. Truman tried again on March 4, telling him, "I felt that in Stevenson I had found the man to whom I could safely turn over the responsibility of party leadership."[24]

After this second meeting Stevenson paid a call on Schlesinger in Cambridge to survey the ground, while again taking care to restate his reluctance about entering any race (a familiar posture). Schlesinger advised that, in the event, if Stevenson did not run, the next months "will really tear apart the Democratic Party." "You are the only solution," Schlesinger told him. Afterwards, he wrote to Stevenson "to say that, while I appreciate better the complexity of your position, I still hope like hell that you can see your way clear to becoming a candidate." Four days later, Truman brought the issue to its pressing point by announcing his withdrawal.[25]

On April 16, Stevenson at last appeared to make a decision, announcing that he would not be seeking the nomination, on the previously stated grounds that he was already a gubernatorial candidate in Illinois. His close confidant and protege, George Ball, believed the reluctance was more political, "largely, I think, because he thought he could not beat Eisenhower [the emerging Republican candidate]." Stevenson's sage withdrawal, however, opened up a pathway for Averell Harriman. Except that Stevenson could never quite manage to tear himself away. Only a day after his statement on the presidency, Stevenson turned up for a vast New York fundraising dinner at which Harriman was the guest of honor, and inevitably stole his thunder. Harriman, despite Schlesinger's best efforts, was not a good public speaker, and, unnerved by Stevenson's presence, he blew his chance with a dull, faltering performance. "Probably the trouble was that he tried too hard," the Alsop brothers wrote in their syndicated column, "for he is conscious of his peculiar problem, and he works over his major speeches so endlessly and painstakingly that he tends to go stale before delivering them." Afterward, Stevenson slipped the knife in, noting that while Harriman "would make a very good president," his performance "had not pleased the politicians" and demonstrated that he probably could not beat Eisenhower.[26]

By the time the delegates arrived at the Chicago Democratic convention in late July, matters remained unresolved, with none of the leading candidates, including Harriman, Senator Estes Kefauver of Tennessee, and Senator Richard Russell Jr. of Georgia having anything close to enough votes to secure the nomination. "We are still living in the age of miracles if we believe in them enough," Harriman urged his young speechwriter. Schlesinger had worked hard for Harriman, but by that July he believed the only chance for victory was an endorsement from Truman. "It is my guess that the President will support you and that you will have enough votes to keep Adlai from entering seriously," he advised. "I do not think Adlai wants the nomination if he has to make a real fight for it; I think he means it rather literally when he talks about a draft. So I am tempted to think he may not yet become a really serious candidate." But Harriman had been unable to reach the president, who, for reasons genuine or political, had checked himself into Walter Reed Hospital with a viral infection. Truman thereby avoided delivering the news to his old friend, an unusually rich one, that he had given up on his chances of winning the nomination. Instead, as a courtesy, Truman intended to back the vice president, Alben W. Barkley, who stood little chance of winning. Sensing the shifting tides, Schlesinger warned Harriman that he needed to be nimble at the convention. Go for the win if he could, Schlesinger advised, but be ready to take the kudos as kingmaker too. "If the moment should come when it seems certain [Stevenson] will be nominated," he wrote, "perhaps you ought to consider coming out for him." Schlesinger advised this course "reluctantly" but pointed out the prize it might bring: "If you do it early enough to bring a large number of delegates over, you will be the logical candidate for Secretary of State."[27]

At the convention, Schlesinger became the obvious go-between for Harriman and Stevenson. "You're the only contact I have," Harriman told him. As the convention began, Schlesinger found Harriman "calm, resolute, hopeful, not too bitter about Adlai." Early on the morning of July 22, Harriman phoned to ask Schlesinger to visit Stevenson and extract a promise of public support. Schlesinger finally saw the governor that afternoon. In a "long, meandering conversation," Stevenson eventually revealed his hopes. "I've done everything I could for Averell," he said, adding without apparent irony, "short of coming out for him." But Harriman's political strength was "very discouraging." If he were nominated, Averell would be a "disunity candidate" and "the party would take a terrible beating." Finally, Schlesinger was able to bring Stevenson around to revealing his plan, even if a level of rhetorical hypocrisy remained. "He sketched very clearly his own design as to how he hoped things would work out," Schlesinger recorded in his journal. "He did not want the nomination, he said, and if he had to take it, he hoped it would come only because the available candidates all recognized that none of them could win. Having mutually exhausted each other he hoped they would all come to him and ask him to run."

"My overall impression was that Adlai would reluctantly run," Schlesinger concluded, keeping a straight face. He promised to do his best to prevent the relationship with Harriman hardening into "a permanent grudge," urging Stevenson to phone Averell in person.[28]

Over a "tête-à-tête dinner" with Harriman, Schlesinger delivered the bad news. "Win or lose," he consoled him, "you have done a fine job and it was all worth the effort." The stoic Harriman refrained from shooting the messenger. "He seemed, on the whole, to be in excellent condition, if weary," Schlesinger recorded, "though his prospects . . . seem fairly hopeless." The following day, after taking various soundings, Harriman asked Schlesinger to set up a meeting with Stevenson as quickly as possible.[29]

Harriman took Schlesinger along for the meeting, so he saw close-up the painful traversal of hurt feelings and bruised egos. Stevenson began with the disingenuous claim that "he definitely did not countenance any of the pressure moves on his behalf." He had "little use" for those who had done so. Harriman had to understand that "he had not sought the nomination; he did not want it; if he had to take it, he wanted a genuine draft." Harriman in turn made it clear that he was not withdrawing, that if he could find a way to make a deal with any of the other candidates he would, but that "he preferred Adlai to any other candidate next to himself and would, if necessary, use his strength to support Adlai against Barkley or Kefauver."[30]

When Harriman was comprehensively beaten in the second round, with Stevenson placed second behind Kefauver, Schlesinger's advice about becoming the kingmaker came into operation. "I withdraw as a candidate and urge my supporters to cast their votes for my old friend, Governor Adlai E. Stevenson of Illinois," Harriman declared, although with bad timing, because the press got hold of the statement shortly after President Truman's arrival at the convention, making it look as if he had ordered Harriman to withdraw. Either way, Harriman's endorsement, now coupled with that of the president, was enough to push Stevenson across the line.[31]

Watching Stevenson's acceptance speech in the hall, and having seen him close-up during the convention, Schlesinger anticipated the upcoming campaign with foreboding. Yes, Stevenson was a "complicated, sensitive and distinguished personality." Certainly the speech had "great polish and dignity," with "wonderful passages of political polemic [and it] was suffused throughout with a sense of the immensity and impenetrability of the crisis of our time." And yet, Schlesinger noted, it was like watching an acrobat and waiting for the fall. Stevenson hesitated too much to command confidence, with "too much business . . . about how he had not wanted the job and was not up to it." Ominously, Schlesinger recalled a comment made to him during the convention that a Stevenson presidency would be like having "Hamlet in the White House." The contrast with Ike, the man who defeated Hitler, could hardly have been more pronounced.[32]

Harriman had emerged from the wreckage of a failed presidential campaign with the grudging respect of many observers. "Of all men, the good Lord gave Averell Harriman nearly the least of the natural equipment of a campaigner," New York Post columnist Murray Kempton pointed out, and yet the candidate had persevered with the "rising at six; the press of strangers; the business of learning every step of the way." Certainly Schlesinger's regard for Harriman had grown steadily throughout the process.

"He played a gallant and selfless role," he wrote to Ursula and Reinhold Niebuhr, "made a clearcut stand on the issues; and gave the liberal position a dignity and a strength it might otherwise have lacked. I saw a good deal of him in his most intimate and troubled moments; and he behaved with a dignity, a decency and a clear-sightedness which were most impressive." The respect was mutual. There was little denying that the campaign had been poorly run: in the words of Harriman's official biographer, Rudy Abramson, "He had been a late starter; he had begun without an organization; he had been poorly advised." Still, no blame attached to Schlesinger, whose delicate liaison with Stevenson, in particular, had been well disguised. A few days after the convention, Harriman phoned Schlesinger to say that he had recommended him to Stevenson for the campaign.[33]

At the beginning of August, Schlesinger traveled to Springfield, Illinois, to spend a few days with Stevenson and his campaign manager, Wilson Wyatt. Although Wyatt was the founding chairman of Americans for Democratic Action, Schlesinger was startled to discover how conservative his candidate's positions were. "Adlai was probably even more conservative than I had thought," Arthur complained, "perhaps, indeed, at this stage, the most conservative Democratic candidate since John W. Davis [in 1924]." Issues that would appeal to labor unions, liberals and minorities were all played with a "soft pedal"; instead the target audience was "high-minded' Republicans and voters in the South. Schlesinger left Springfield wondering whether he would even be able to get Stevenson to mention the New Deal at all. But Schlesinger by this time was enough of an operative to understand that in politics you had to fully commit when switching from one team to another. "Eisenhower utters the cliches of the right, Harriman the cliches of the left (with which I agree)," he noted. Only "Stevenson promises the possibility of adjourning the tired old debates, moving beyond them and ushering us into the post-Rooseveltian era, toward which we are groping." It was an important shift: if Schlesinger was going to write for the candidate, he may as well believe in him.[34]

When the speechwriting team convened on August 12 in Springfield, however, "my heart sank as the discussion proceeded." Stevenson's beliefs "were so remote from my beliefs," he decided, "that I had better confine myself to a technical role in the campaign and stay out of policy discussions." That might have been a soulless experience had it not been for the excitement of being at the center of a national campaign and the quality of the speechwriting team. As well as Schlesinger, the writers in the core team included his Harvard friend and neighbor, the economist John Kenneth Galbraith; the *Saturday Evening Post* reporter and Stevenson biographer, John Bartlow Martin; Northwestern law professor (and future Kennedy labor secretary) Willard Wirtz; *Harper's* editor John Fischer; and Truman aide (and later JFK budget director) David Bell. "We almost never had fewer than four Pulitzer Prize winners in residence," Wyatt recalled. "It was probably as accomplished a group of writers as has ever participated in a presidential campaign."[35]

The quality of that team did not come without its complications. As Richard Hofstadter points out in his 1964 Pulitzer Prize–winning book *Anti-Intellectualism in American Life*, "Stevenson became the victim of the accumulated grievances against intellectuals and brain-trusters which had festered in the American right wing since 1933." It was Stewart Alsop during the campaign who gave Schlesinger and his group the name that would forever stick to public intellectuals by describing them in his *Matter of Fact* column as "eggheads." To compound the image, he would soon devise his "cookout" test (the forerunner to the "who would you have a beer with?" test) about Stevenson—"Eisenhower's the kind of guy I'd like to invite over for a cookout," Alsop remarked, despite the fact that he voted for the Democrat. "Can you imagine inviting that Adlai for a cookout?"[36]

From the outset, the campaign was extremely sensitive about jibes that northeastern liberal intellectuals had assumed control. Occasionally events turned to farce. No sooner had John Kenneth Galbraith arrived in Springfield to join the team than he was greeted by a frantic call from Schlesinger ordering him to stay in his hotel room until further notice. "The reason," Galbraith recalled, "was that at a press conference a day before, Stevenson had been asked if his campaign wasn't being taken over by radicals, specifically by dangerous figures from the Americans for Democratic Action."[37]

Stevenson had been a character witness for Alger Hiss, which meant he was, as Hofstadter points out, "especially vulnerable to the common tandem association between intellect and radicalism, radicalism and disloyalty." Schlesinger and his Harvard friends were vulnerable to similar charges. During the campaign the *Chicago Tribune* ran an editorial under the headline, "Harvard Tells Indiana How to Vote," citing Schlesingers Senior and Junior as exhibit one. Added to radicalism and disloyalty was the associated charge of effeminacy. "Adelaide" Stevenson's speeches, said the *New York Daily News*, were filled with "fruity . . . teacup words" more suggestive of "a genteel spinster who can never forget that she got an A in elocution at Miss Smith's Finishing School" than a president of the United States. And it was no wonder when the candidate was surrounded by "typical Harvard lace-cuff liberals," who were no more than "pompadoured lap dogs." In September, Eleanor Roosevelt stepped into the debate with a withering defense of Schlesinger and the writers around Stevenson. The *Chicago Tribune*, she wrote, "is frightened about Governor Stevenson's advisors and says they are a Socialist brain trust. Somehow, I never thought of Arthur Schlesinger Jr. as Socialist. Did you?" Arthur was delighted with the intervention, writing to thank her for "your generous defense." But he was in no doubt that it was "obviously going to be a very dirty campaign." Attacks on Schlesinger would culminate a week before the election when Senator Joseph McCarthy accused him of being pro-Communist because the Harvard professor "thought Communists should be allowed to teach your children."[38]

It was into this kind of fevered atmosphere that Schlesinger released Galbraith from hotel captivity, going on to explain another difficulty to his friend: the candidate liked to maintain the illusion that he wrote his own speeches. Wilson Wyatt later claimed that for all their talent, the writers were like "reporters covering a police beat," providing the governor with information "because of their conviction that Adlai Stevenson was a master of prose himself and that they were not writing his speeches but simply enabling him to extend himself in the preliminary drafting." A *New York Times* story about the campaign bought into the myth, reporting that the writers were in reality "research staff to dig out facts and figures and ideas for speeches." When Stevenson himself was asked whether he wrote his own speeches, he replied, "I am blushing—appropriately I hope." It was a misleading answer that reflected the dying embers of a certain approach to political speechmaking. High-minded observers agreed with Associate Justice of the Supreme Court Robert H. Jackson that "ghost-writing has debased the intellectual currency in circulation here and is a type of counterfeiting which invites no defense." At heart, Stevenson believed that too. "He really feels very sensitive to any suggestion that he does not write his own speeches," Schlesinger groaned during a September campaign trip to Colorado, irritated by the candidate's constant fiddling with texts. "He [Stevenson] spent most of the trip reworking the main Denver draft . . . protest[ing] plaintively about how his own best phrases were always cut out."[39]

The speechwriters, who met on the third floor of the Elks Club building on South Sixth Street in Springfield, soon became known, inevitably enough, as the Elks Club Group. They worked in a 650-square-foot, sparsely furnished main room—the bullpen—dominated by a long central table that ran most of the length of the room. Off this room were four bedrooms, where writers could crash when pulling an all-nighter. Long hours and no exercise were the norm in a punishing regime. It quickly took its toll. David Bell and Bill Tufts both collapsed from exhaustion; Schlesinger had to be hospitalized briefly after his knee swelled up like a balloon. Their day would usually start at 10 a.m. with a group meeting. They would then work until 3 or 4 a.m., with breaks only to drink at Sazerac's dive bar or eat at the local diner, where Schlesinger's principal complaint was the absence of chocolate sauce for his ice cream (a lifelong obsession). All the while, they worked amid the cacophony of clattering typewriters, ringing telephones, and visiting staffers. Schlesinger's sangfroid impressed John Bartlow Martin. "He could, seemingly, simultaneously hold a telephone conversation, write a speech, read source material, and talk to somebody across the desk. He wrote rapidly and well. He wrote basic drafts on major speeches, did heavy rewrite on other people's drafts, and, from his friends around the country, obtained dozens of drafts."[40]

These qualities soon meant that Schlesinger, along with David Bell, was given responsibility for running the Elks Club Group. That put Schlesinger in a bind with Harvard. Most of the academics such as Galbraith returned to their universities once the academic year began, but Stevenson asked Schlesinger to stay on in Springfield. Paul H. Buck, provost of Harvard, was approached about a leave of absence and, as a close friend of Arthur Sr. going back to Ohio in the 1920s, he readily assented, albeit with the vaguely patronizing air of one who could hardly believe that Young Arthur, whom he had known as a small child, was now advising the Democratic candidate for president of the United States. It was a real "opportunity both to serve and to learn," Buck wrote. "I do not know what other participants may get out of this campaign," replied Stevenson laconically, "but I can assure you that my own education is proceeding apace." Either way, "I cannot tell you how much I value" the "willingness to grant a leave of absence to Mr. Arthur Schlesinger Jr."[41]

What made Arthur stand out from most of the other writers in the room, his brilliant prose style, matched his ability to think about the political effect of a speech. Martin remembers learning that latter skill from him. "I began by worrying about the prose and soon learned to worry more about the politics," he said. Initially shocked to hear Schlesinger talking about sections of speeches being aimed at particular voting blocs such as African Americans or Catholics, he quickly "came to see that in a diverse pluralistic democracy like ours, a politician can approach the electorate in no other way."[42]

The writers took turns in accompanying the candidate around the country, when they were often called upon to turn out an instant speech. On the final train trip of the campaign, someone remembered that the next day, October 24, was United Nations Day. That left Schlesinger writing "desperately from midnight to 2:30 the night before" in order to turn out "a sharp speech on the UN and Korea" for delivery in Rochester at 9:30 the next morning. "It proved a great success," he recorded proudly, "so much so that the newspapermen immediately demanded texts and made it their lead for the next day."[43]

Stevenson kept a distance from his writers, usually referring to Arthur as "Mr. Schlesinger" and barely concealing his irritation with him. "A little more sobriety about the difficulties" of peace and prosperity, Stevenson tersely demanded of him that October, "a little more 'sense'—than the continued flat assertion that we Dems can & will continue prosperity and win the peace—a little more challenge to the people to understand the difficulties and help us solve them for their benefit etc."[44]

Moments of success, however, became fewer and fewer as the campaign went on and Stevenson failed to rise to the challenge. Occasionally persuasive, he was rarely compelling and, unlike Eisenhower, he lacked any kind of rapport or common touch with large crowds. He also failed to respond quickly enough to Eisenhower's pioneering use of TV. Both candidates resisted the new medium at first, but Ike relented sooner. He used "Mad Men" advertising executive Rosser Reeves of the Ted Bates agency to create brilliant thirty-second TV spots. Ironically, Stevenson came across well on TV, but his highfalutin nature caused him to minimize it in the campaign. "This is the worst thing I've ever heard of," he scoffed, "selling the presidency like cereal!" That attitude left him behind the curve.[45]

Ignoring his speechwriters compounded the failure. For a major address in St. Louis in October, the team had worked up a powerful speech, with overtones of *The Age of Jackson*, outlining Stevenson's "New Frontier" for America. (Eight years later Schlesinger would be on the team of speechwriters that recycled the idea more successfully for Kennedy.) But when the speech was timed, Schlesinger, on the road with the candidate, realized it was too long for the TV coverage. He produced a shorter text, but Stevenson refused to use it, on the grounds that he liked the original better. Inevitably, the networks cut him off halfway through, amid scenes of the large crowd looking bored and passive. Similarly at one of the final large-scale rallies of the campaign in Madison Square Garden, Stevenson performed woefully. The arena was packed with a large crowd and a smattering of famous faces from stage and screen. "At 10:30 p.m. the Governor came on," Schlesinger wrote. "The excitement was by now overwhelming, and the ovation tremendous." Once again, though, the performance was underwhelming and "the speech itself was unfortunately something of a flop." Only in his home state of Illinois did Stevenson manage to pull off a great performance, leading Schlesinger to comment drily, "The Governor even finished on time."[46]

Flush with the success of the last speech, and from sharing a car ride into town with Humphrey Bogart and Lauren Bacall ("What a beautiful—and delightful—girl Lauren Bacall is!—even more attractive in the flesh than on the screen"), Schlesinger returned to Cambridge "still completely certain that we would win." Within hours of the polls closing on November 4, it quickly became apparent that all his efforts had been for nought. "Tuesday night was sad," he wrote. "I knew as soon as I heard the results from Connecticut (about 8 p.m.) that we had lost. . . . Melancholy settled more heavily on all of us as the evening moved on." Schlesinger had already helped Stevenson with a concession speech, using an anecdote about Lincoln, despite having "assured him he would not have to tell the story." In the end, the result was a landslide, Eisenhower winning 442 electoral votes to Stevenson's 89.

"One consolation about being beaten 56 to 0," Schlesinger wrote stoically, "is that there is no point wondering whether you would have done better if you had had a different left tackle—or a different quarterback."[47]

CHAPTER NINE

POLITICS IS AN
EDUCATIONAL PROCESS

After the presidential election campaign, an exhausted Schlesinger and his family immediately took off for a vacation in a wealthy enclave north of Palm Beach, Florida, courtesy of Averell Harriman. "I cannot say how grateful the Schlesingers are to you for the Hobe Sound interlude," he wrote Harriman afterwards. "I feel a new man as a result of the sun and the surf and the rest. In fact I feel almost capable of coping with the New Era."[1]

Most Americans found they really did "Like Ike." Eisenhower's cheerful reassuring manner, pledge to balance the budget, and decisive Cold War rhetoric played out well on TV sets, which by 1955 would be installed in three-quarters of all American homes. For Schlesinger, however, back in "gray New England" and pointlessly resistant to owning a television set, the period after the election would be an emotional struggle. Like many veterans of an intense campaign, he missed the action. "My new year's toast: *To hell with 1953*," he wrote to Joseph Rauh, adding "glasses to be thrown in the fireplace." And to Marietta Tree (his Paris crush, by this time Adlai Stevenson's lover), he wrote on Inauguration Day, "I feel so depressed today." Yet his reaction to the disappointment of the election was less extreme than others'. Schlesinger only had to look across the garden fence to see the impact that defeat was having on some. John Kenneth Galbraith, already struggling with the grief of losing a son to childhood leukemia, fell that winter into a dangerous cycle of drink and prescription drug addiction. Soon he would be treated for latent manic depression, something, he noted, that was kept "a beautifully guarded secret," even from neighborhood friends.[2]

Yet with both men in various degrees of distress, each helped the other by focusing not on a past defeat, but on the practical application of ideas going forward—in effect, thinking themselves away from the trauma of a losing campaign. In November 1952, Schlesinger wrote to Stevenson urging him to remain engaged. "Roosevelt, as a private citizen and an invalid, managed to make himself a powerful national figure within the Democratic Party by the simple process of correspondence," Schlesinger reminded him. "I know you will do this anyway," he said, "and I think it could be a valuable technique." Now in the spring of 1953, Schlesinger and Galbraith began to develop something altogether more ambitious. "As the party of the well-to-do, the Republicans do not hesitate to make use of their dough," Galbraith explained. "As the party of the egg-heads we should similarly and proudly make use of our brains and experience."[3]

Their idea was to create an elite venue for policymakers and intellectuals to formulate fresh ideas for Stevenson; "to help him," as Schlesinger put it, "to overcome his [patrician] upbringing." A subtext of the move was an attempt to orientate Stevenson and the party towards the more progressive Northeast, particularly New York, where Averell Harriman was considering a run for governor. The hope, Schlesinger explained to journalist James Wechsler, was to establish "New York as a powerful liberal voice in the national Democratic Party." To move the project forward, Schlesinger and Galbraith now approached Thomas Finletter, a close Stevenson friend and former secretary of the Air Force under Truman, who was considering his own run in New York for a US Senate seat. "He was older than [we]," Schlesinger recalled, and "he was identified with air power and hard nosed things like that. This gave weight to his views that Ken Galbraith and I did not have with Stevenson."[4]

Finletter agreed to the idea—something between a brain trust and a think tank—and approached Stevenson, who replied positively. "I shall be coming East, probably around the end of the month," Stevenson told him. "I will be in New York then and could we have an evening perhaps with some others, for skull practice?" In advance of that meeting, Schlesinger sent Stevenson a bundle of study papers, which produced a grateful if somewhat amused, perhaps even bemused, response. "So many thanks for your letter . . . and the fat enclosures," he wrote. "Lord knows when I will have time to read them, but read them I will. . . . I find concentration terribly difficult, what with distractions, weariness and chronic intellectual confusion."[5]

Stevenson's reluctance—his perennial difficulty in committing firmly to anything—would become a consistent feature of what became known as the Finletter Group. "The Gov. did not attend," Finletter recalled wearily. "We couldn't get him to the meetings. . . . I only remember he attended two meetings—one at Galbraith's and one in Chicago." The diplomat George Ball complained, "We could never get Adlai to do his homework." Yet the study group would, in the words of the Stevenson speechwriter turned biographer, John Bartlow Martin, become "one of the most important, influential, and notable movements of modern American politics . . . [and] the basis of the New Frontier and the Great Society" under Presidents Kennedy and Johnson.[6]

Stevenson provided a symbolic focal point for the Finletter Group, but the quality of the ideas stemmed from the distinction of its people. As well as Schlesinger, Ball, and Galbraith, regular participants included the CIA's Richard Bissell, Truman's Director of Policy Planning for the State Department Paul Nitze, Henry Wallace aide Paul Appleby, and diplomat Chester Bowles. Averell Harriman also attended the first meeting and was a frequent visitor thereafter. They met regularly in New York and Cambridge to discuss and revise papers. "I never worked with more intelligent and devoted people in all my born days," Finletter recalled admiringly. "We just made ourselves a place where the best views of the Democratic Party were assembled. The quality of the discussion was the important thing. We spent *hours* together. These were men with first-class brains." If there had been a deficit of ideas and new thinking during the 1952 Stevenson campaign, Schlesinger and Galbraith were doing their best to give the Democrats a fighting chance in 1956 by laying the groundwork for a new vision of modern liberalism.

Eisenhower committed his administration to what he called "the middle way"—the basis both of his political program and his leadership style. The new president believed that increased prosperity and the effects of industrialization, mass production and distribution, and urban growth contained within them the dangers of extreme class conflict (something Schlesinger had described in *The Crisis of the Old Order*). Eisenhower wanted to arrest the momentum of New Deal liberalism or, as Herbert Hoover—antihero of *The Crisis of the Old Order*—advised him, to achieve a "flattening of the curve of this particular trend." But the president also wanted to find a way to ease the tensions arising from the modern state and to steer a reasonable course between capital and labor, the hard Right and the hard Left. The answer, he declared in the 1953 State of the Union Address, "[is] a middle way between untrammeled freedom of the individual and the demands for the welfare of the whole nation."[7]

Schlesinger's response to the challenge of the "middle way" would be an idea summed up in his phrase "the quality of American life." It was a notion that would be used by Stevenson in 1956, and subsequently by Democrats John F. Kennedy and Lyndon Johnson. Even a Republican president, Richard Nixon, would borrow the concept. Liberals, Schlesinger argued, needed to move not away from but beyond the basic goals of the New Deal. In an age of affluence, he argued, the state had to ensure that all Americans enjoyed at least a minimum quality of material comfort. "Instead of the quantitative liberalism of the 1930s rightly dedicated to the struggle to secure the economic basis of life," he wrote, "we need now a 'qualitative liberalism' dedicated to bettering the quality of people's lives and opportunities." America was richer than it had ever been in its history, yet so many citizens remained excluded. "Our gross national product rises; our shops overflow with gadgets and gimmicks; consumer goods of ever-increasing ingenuity and luxuriance pour out of our ears," he would explain in a 1956 essay on the future of liberalism. "But our schools become more crowded and dilapidated, our teachers more weary and underpaid, our playgrounds more crowded, our cities dirtier, our roads more teeming and filthy, our national parks more unkempt, our law enforcement more overworked and inadequate." It was a theme that John Kenneth Galbraith would take up in his best-selling 1958 book, *The*

Affluent Society, which pointed to the uneven experience of the American Dream. "Is this, indeed, the American genius?" he mordantly asked. Galbraith's putting the question was a tribute to the power and importance of friendship in the development of ideas—one of the most important statements in American thinking, honed over the garden fence in Cambridge.[8]

After the 1952 election, in the privacy of his diary, Schlesinger had admitted to a "jaundiced picture of Stevenson." Part of the problem, he had reflected, was that "one tends to overestimate Stevenson's articulateness." Yet in the immediate aftermath of defeat, he had already begun to think that "on a number of things he was right and I was wrong," not least that "Adlai was right" in saying that they should not run as if it were still the Great Depression. Eisenhower had imbued a sense of what unprecedented postwar prosperity might offer for the middle class. The hard-won achievements of the New Deal, it seemed, meant "very little to younger people, for whom Social Security and collective bargaining and economic opportunity were as secure and unalterable parts of the landscape as the trees and bushes." The Finletter Group was a response to that analysis, pushing Schlesinger to come up with new ideas such as "the quality of American life" that would push the party beyond the 1930s New Deal and the governor in a more liberal direction.[9]

But Schlesinger's response to defeat was not only political; it was also historical. Going in to see Harry Truman a few weeks before the thirty-third president left the White House, Schlesinger had found him chipper and confident that "history would vindicate him and his administration." Yet something else also struck Schlesinger. "I noticed," he recorded thoughtfully, "that he still speaks of FDR as 'the President.'"[10]

Truman understood who "the President" was, but young people, it seemed, did not. Reminding them became Arthur's next major intellectual project.

Schlesinger's *Age of Jackson* had been a bold and ambitious project, one that he had delivered with a combination of stylistic panache, depth of research, and a fresh interpretation. The idea for *The Age of Roosevelt* was on an even more grandiose, almost foolhardy, scale. Schlesinger toyed with the format at various stages, but by the time he started in the summer of 1953, the project had turned into a gargantuan five-volume history of the Roosevelt era. As with *The Age of Jackson*, the key theme running throughout would be the war between liberalism and business-dominated conservatism. Volume one, *The Reign of Business, 1920–1933*, would tell the story of the "stupidity and wickedness of business" and "the triumph of business values" in the 1920s, soon followed by a "collapse of faith in business" during the Wall Street Crash, which led to the election of FDR. Running alongside that story was one about the failure of liberals and intellectuals in the 1920s, including "indifference to democracy verging on anti-democracy: Babbitt [from the 1922 novel by Sinclair Lewis], H. L. Mencken," as well as the "impotence of protest before prosperity" and the "essential conservatism" of the Democratic Party under Al Smith. Only with the emergence of "the happy warrior" FDR, supported by a new wave of intellectuals—the "brain trust (Raymond Moley, Rexford Tugwell, Adolf Berle, Samuel Rosenman, Felix Frankfurter)"—did the necessary "radicalization" of ideas take place that allowed the Democrats to win "the campaign for America" in 1932.[11]

The second volume, *The First New Deal, 1933–1935*, was set to show the power of Roosevelt's bold thinking and action in the face of a national emergency. Here was a story of "American revival," an audacious "experiment in national planning," and the "creation of the labor movement." Volume III, *The House Divides, 1935–1937*, would show business interests, led by the Liberty League, fighting back, "mounting Roosevelt hatred" and "proto-fascism," coupled with a new threat, "communist penetration: influence among intellectuals." Throughout all this tumult "FDR as administrator and leader, holding all together" and winning reelection in 1936. The fourth volume would examine *The Crisis of the New Deal, 1937–1940*, before the series ended with *The New Deal Abroad* looking at FDR's wartime administration. Given that these last two volumes would never be written, the detail and argument in the outline for both was already more flat and less detailed than in the previous volumes, suggesting either that Schlesinger had run out of ideas even before he'd started or that he was uncomfortable with these more contested areas of FDR's legacy from the outset. He would collapse those two volumes into a single volume (albeit one that he never completed). Of the overall purpose of the series, however, Schlesinger was confident: "Relation of New Deal to American liberal traditions—how New Deal changed conceptions of democracy (the 'mixed economy' and the recoil from totalitarianism)—how New Deal changed conceptions of foreign policy (relationship between force and freedom)."[12]

The epigraph to open *The Crisis of the Old Order, 1919–1931,* the first of three volumes in *The Age of Roosevelt,* would come from Emerson: "Every revolution was first a thought in one man's mind." Reviewing the book in the *New York Times,* when it was eventually published, Henry Steele Commager would get the political point immediately. "In the bright sunshine of prosperity we have tended to forget, many of us, how black the [Depression] was," he wrote. "It is one of the merits of Mr. Schlesinger's book that it re-creates for us so vividly this tragic chapter of our history."[13]

Schlesinger was well aware of the stakes involved in such an ambitious project, and, uncharacteristically, was nervous about his ability to deliver. "This is the first piece of serious writing that I have done for a long time, and I had forgotten what it was like," he wrote to Marietta. "For years I simply sat down and dashed things off in the expectation that they would meet the day's need and afterward could be forgotten. But this is different; and I had forgotten the *tension* of this kind of writing. It is terribly exciting, when things click, and dismal when they don't, . . . and exhausting all the time." His aim was to attack the first volume during the academic year 1953–1954 in order to have a draft ready well in advance of his publication date of spring 1956—an election year. "I fear that I will not make the deadline," he wrote with a kind of cheerful pessimism, "but it is a tremendous relief to be at last under way." *The Crisis of the Old Order, 1919–1933: The Age of Roosevelt,* vol. I, would, in fact, be published late, in March 1957—too late to help Adlai Stevenson.[14]

Schlesinger had understood the dangers of political distractions, but the temptations had been too great. When Joseph Rauh and James Loeb approached him in the summer of 1953 about the possibility of taking a leadership role in Americans for Democratic Action (ADA), he turned them down flat, saying that he had to work on *The Age of Roosevelt* with "as little distraction as possible." Yes, there were good financial reasons for needing to get the book written—"Years of living beyond our income have put the Schlesinger family in a tough condition, which can be remedied only by a bestselling book (and soon)." Nevertheless, Schlesinger also believed that "the book, if it is any good, will serve the liberal cause far better" than any hands-on political job. By 1955 he had changed his mind. The FDR book, Arthur reassured Stevenson's wealthy friend and personal assistant William M. Blair Jr. when he came calling, "does not mean that I am proposing to retire from political life."[15]

Stevenson, in truth, had been running for president again almost as soon as he lost the 1952 election, most notably making a world tour in 1953 to establish himself as an international statesman. Yet Adlai being Adlai, there was inevitably a great deal of disingenuous vacillation about whether he *really* wanted to run. When Schlesinger traveled to Springfield in the fall of 1954 to discuss the next election cycle, he was not surprised to hear the (non)candidate say, "He definitely will not enter primaries. If he is drafted, he will accept; but realistically he concedes that he will not be drafted twice." The governor, Schlesinger thought, was "as warm and easy as ever," but his prevarication was baffling. Even Stevenson himself conceded, "My present position is morally repugnant, emotionally unbearable and intellectually inconsistent."[16]

Schlesinger returned to his theme over the coming months, putting Stevenson on the spot about whether he had the ambition to run for president. "I am really convinced that the one important doubt the American people have about you is whether you want to be President," he admonished. "(Don't say, 'They are right!') The people regard this as the highest honor they have in their power to bestow; and they do not want to have to force it on people, or to coax them to accept it, or to see them indecisive and Hamletish in the face of it." The dangers of that latter approach were all too apparent. "I think that if the image you present to the electorate in the spring and summer of 1956 is one of reluctance and hesitation, you may win the nomination by default but will lose the election," he went on. "But I think that, if the image you present is one of clarity, vigor and decision, you will have an excellent chance of beating Eisenhower."[17]

Stevenson's indecision was something that vexed his friends as much as it helped his opponents. "An enormously insecure man," his son, Borden, said of his father. Agnes Meyer, wife of *Washington Post* owner Eugene Meyer and a personal friend of Stevenson, judged that he had "a deep psychopathic fear of [his] own greatness and destiny." But events now began to help those who wanted Stevenson to commit to the idea of running properly for the nomination rather than hoping it would fall into his lap. First, in the fall of 1954, the Democrats had put in an unexpectedly strong performance in the midterm elections, with the party regaining control of the House and the Senate, and overturning a 30–18 Republican advantage in state governorships to hold a 27–21 Democratic edge. During the campaign, Stevenson had worked hard in close races around the country, making eighty-eight speeches in thirty-three states. "Toward the end," said Elks Club Group alum John Bartlow Martin, "he was covering thousands of miles by air, touring the countryside in an open car, speaking several times a day, sidestepping local factional feuds, receiving delegations in hotel rooms till late at night, then working on a speech, then arising early to begin the next day's labors." These were not the actions of a man who had given up on politics—or ambition. The midterm results, and Stevenson's role in the campaign, changed political calculations and, as Schlesinger told Stevenson, meant that the Democrats had at least "a reasonable chance of winning" in 1956.[18]

The real problem, however, was that Stevenson would be running against Dwight Eisenhower, one of the most popular presidents—and Americans—of the modern era. During 1955, Eisenhower's approval rating in the Gallup poll ranged between 68 and 79 percent. For his opponents, it made no difference if that popularity was "rooted in the fact that he is the agent of the acceptance by Republicanism of the major policies of the Rooseveltian Revolution of the past two decades," as Schlesinger's friend, Reinhold Niebuhr, wrote in a 1955 essay, "Why Ike is Popular." For Schlesinger, that popularity could not be ignored. "The following assumptions must be made with regard to 1956," Schlesinger wrote to Joseph Rauh in September 1955. "That Eisenhower will run . . . [and] given the continuation of peace and prosperity, nothing will have happened to shatter Eisenhower's popularity and the national mood of complacency and apathy on which his popularity rests and which his personality so well satisfies." A long memo followed, with a comprehensive political analysis and suggestions for a campaign playbook, ending with the upbeat point that the "one great advantage we enjoy over 1952 is that we can begin preparations fourteen months ahead of the election instead of 3 months," a benefit that it was "essential not to squander." Nevertheless, the fundamental assumption remained that they would be running against a formidable and popular candidate in an era of peace and prosperity. Anything that changed that calculation, Schlesinger wrote on September 6, "must be regarded as a windfall."[19]

What fell into their lap came via personal calamity when two weeks later, on September 24, President Eisenhower suffered a heart attack after playing twenty-seven holes of golf in Denver, Colorado. Even when out of immediate danger, writes Nicholas Fortuin in the *New England Journal of Medicine*, Eisenhower's prospect of "recovery was made more difficult, because the prevailing attitudes about patients with coronary artery disease among doctors and the public in the 1950s were uniformly pessimistic; at that time there were no effective palliative treatments, such as surgery or angioplasty, or drugs to improve survival, and ideas about preventive measures were in their infancy. Many patients were consigned to invalidism, and the prognosis for long life was thought to be bleak."[20]

Financial markets went into free fall following Eisenhower's heart attack, and so did the Republican Party. Vice President Richard Nixon recalled that Eisenhower himself went through a long period of deep depression. "He talked like a man who felt his public career was finished," Nixon said. "He did not even want to discuss the possibility of running the following year." When reporters asked Republican national chairman Len Hall about the election, his stock reply was that the ticket would be Ike and Dick. "Finally," Nixon wrote, "one reporter asked the dreaded question: 'What happens if Eisenhower decides not to run?' Hall blurted out, 'We will jump off that bridge when we come to it.' "[21]

Eisenhower's health scare presented Schlesinger with an awkward personal dilemma. By the fall of 1955 he had "written some 350,000 words" of *The Age of Roosevelt*, but still had "a considerable distance to go." If the first volume was to be completed on time, he understood only too well that he must "subordinate everything else to bringing this to completion." And yet the political calculus had changed, and Schlesinger did not want to miss the Stevenson boat. With Eisenhower still bed-ridden, Schlesinger wrote to Bill Blair to pitch his own case. "Now that 1956 begins to look serious," he explained, "I thought I had better write and set forth my situation." He had a sabbatical coming up in 1957–1958, so he would be "free for full time labors from the convention (and before) to the election." In the meantime, he offered to write for Stevenson ("speechwriting is a congenial diversion for me") and to help Finletter "in every way I can on the research side of things." There was, of course, he protested (too much), no sense in which "this letter of mine [should] be construed as an attempt to impose myself on the campaign!" Instead, it was just the thought that "it might help if I could let you know exactly what my availability is." For all that he wanted to "get the manuscript out of the way," this was Schlesinger putting politics first. The result, inevitably, was that *The Age of Roosevelt* was delivered late.[22]

Schlesinger need not have worried about whether Stevenson wanted him. When the core team met in early November to formulate a campaign strategy for 1956, Schlesinger joined the inner circle. Stevenson accepted the need for a fresh approach this time around. "My speeches must be more simple, vivid, concrete," he told Schlesinger, quietly conceding the problems of 1952. "In the past they have been too abstract and philosophical. I've always tried to cover too much. Now I must work hard to get specific instances and examples which will carry over to people and mean something to them."[23]

Before Schlesinger began the process of honing Stevenson's message, starting with his presidential announcement that November, there was one difficult conversation to be had. Averell Harriman, now governor of New York, had been Schlesinger's first entrée into Washington's elite circles. When it became clear that Harriman intended to run in 1956, it soon became equally clear that he expected Schlesinger to help him. It was a sign of Schlesinger's growing confidence that he felt able to resist Harriman's overtures, and of his ruthlessness that he did not hesitate to use his inside knowledge about Harriman to help Stevenson knock him out of the race. What made Harriman an unexpected threat was his support from former president Harry Truman. "As HST begins to get the word around, there is likely to be a definite check to the Stevenson surge," Schlesinger warned, "especially among the pros, unless counteractive measures are undertaken." Schlesinger had worked for Harriman long enough to know that he was often wooden and ineffective on the stump, could appear detached from the concerns of ordinary people, and was perceived as a northeastern liberal too narrowly focused to win a national campaign. "The private Stevenson line on Harriman," Schlesinger advised, "should be that he is just too weak a candidate."[24]

Once the primary season got underway, however, it was not Harriman, but Senator Estes Kefauver of Tennessee who raced ahead of the pack, defeating Stevenson in New Hampshire, Minnesota, and Wisconsin. By April, Kefauver looked unstoppable. Schlesinger, summoned to Illinois for an emergency summit after Stevenson's loss in Wisconsin, found the candidate "exceptionally tired; sad, gentle and charming in manner; and the total impression was rather heartbreaking."[25]

In 1952, Schlesinger had been in awe of Stevenson; now in 1956, older and more experienced, he did not hesitate to hand out forthright advice to save the campaign. In a private note to Stevenson, he gave no quarter, instructing him on how to be a better candidate. First, Schlesinger wrote, "*Don't* say that problems are intricate and complicated. Everyone knows that they are." Second, "*Don't* profess ignorance on questions, or say that you don't know enough to give a definite answer. If you are running for the Presidency, people expect, not necessarily a detailed technical answer, but a clear and definite expression of the way you would propose to tackle the problem." Third, "*Don't* hesitate to give a short answer. . . . Having taken a stand, you then seem to introduce a number of other factors which have the effect of diluting your own position and baffling your audience." And last, "*Do not* think that all this is in any sense a counsel of dishonesty. Politics, at its best, is an educational process. . . . The great educators (and statesmen) are the men whose oversimplifications correspond to correct principles." Summing up, Schlesinger demanded that "You, like Lincoln, Wilson and the Roosevelts, should forget the refinements and concentrate on plain statements of what you think essentially is right."[26]

Stevenson accepted the need for recalibration. "I think it is time to change my methods," he admitted to Schlesinger. The question was how to achieve that objective. In the end it was John Bartlow Martin who made the breakthrough, coming up with a new system that put Schlesinger's four points into action. For each whistle stop, a page or two of "editorial advice" was prepared for Stevenson that outlined the setting, a few historical facts, the expected composition of the crowd, which points to hit and which to avoid, and a few zingers appropriate for the occasion. These notes struck just the right balance between giving Stevenson enough freedom to feel in control while keeping him on message. Before each stop, Martin noted, Stevenson "read them, then turned them over and scribbled notes in longhand, making the pages his own, and he used them, speaking, in effect, extemporaneously from notes, and the crowd liked it." The press began to write about a "new" Stevenson. "He learned to talk with rough-hewn notes," *Time* reported, "and in so doing, he freshened his delivery." The effect was immediate. Crowds grew bigger and more enthusiastic. And primary voters followed suit. On June 5 Stevenson wrested back momentum in the race with a huge win in California, and other victories in Washington, DC, New Jersey, Illinois, Oregon, and Florida. By the time he arrived at the Democratic convention in Chicago that August, Stevenson was the clear front-runner and won easily on the first ballot.[27]

The 1956 convention was another dramatic one for the Democrats, mainly because Stevenson turned the selection of a vice presidential running mate over to the delegates. "This was the most exciting thing I have ever seen at a convention," Schlesinger recorded afterwards. Estes Kefauver and Senator John F. Kennedy of Massachusetts duked it out, with Kennedy at one stage coming within eighteen and a half votes of securing the nomination, before eventually Kefauver won. "I was strongly for Kennedy until the moment of climax in the second ballot," Schlesinger wrote. "Then I was suddenly seized by an unexpected onrush of emotion and found myself shouting wildly for Kefauver. On reflection, this seemed to me right. Jack, who made himself a national political figure in this convention, will have more chances. Estes has earned this chance, if anyone has." Schlesinger, too, would have more chances with Kennedy. Writing to the senator afterwards, he reassured him, "You are bound to be in everyone's mind from now on in any future consideration of national candidates," and urged him to use the forthcoming campaign as the best way "for you to get to know political leaders in all sections—and for them to get to know you."[28]

The vice presidential vote, fully covered on prime-time national television, generated great excitement at the convention. Democrats began to think they really could win back the White House from a popular but sickly president, whose own running mate and potential midterm successor, Richard Nixon, was not widely liked. Everything was set for Stevenson. Former president Harry Truman gave a brilliant, terse speech that fired up the hall. Kefauver's address was, Schlesinger said, "third rate," but as he had seen at Madison Square Garden with Harriman in 1952, a brilliant warm-up act often threatened to steal the thunder of the main event. When the presidential nominee emerged, it was to a fervent ovation. "Stevenson never looked more forceful, and his voice, when he began to speak, was sure and confident," Schlesinger wrote hopefully. "Here seemed the moment to cap the convention by giving the emotional surge of the last 24 hours a fitting expression. Instead there came a diffuse mass of words. After a few moments, the sense of excitement was trickling away."[29]

Schlesinger could hardly contain his fury. The speech "had not benefitted at all from the work done on it or the criticism levelled against it." Revisions had been "nearly all ignored." The lessons learned in the primaries had disappeared into the ether. "One felt that the image of the new Stevenson, this grim, masterful figure, had suddenly disappeared," Schlesinger moaned, "and in its place appeared the old Stevenson, the literary critic, the man obsessed with words and portentous generalization." Running into Phil Graham afterwards, the publisher of the *Washington Post* confirmed the worst. "You know, I thought that the Democrats really had a chance to win," he told Arthur, "until Adlai began to speak."[30]

The 1956 campaign never achieved the optimism of 1952. With the

"Elks Club" writing team now relocated to the Stevenson headquarters in Washington, DC, Schlesinger and John Bartlow Martin reprised their roles as full-time speechwriters and were joined by the lawyer W. Willard Wirtz, who later became labor secretary under Kennedy and Johnson. They worked well together as a team, writing speeches that hit Eisenhower hard, but found themselves in constant opposition to Stevenson's political advisors. "The conflict was never really resolved," Martin recalled, surprised that he and Schlesinger were pushing "hard-nosed political views," while the professional politicians like campaign manager James A. Finnegan and his assistants Hyman Raskin and James Rowe were pushing the "lofty idealistic position." The result was a series of speeches that unhappily straddled both approaches, with the candidate constantly "stepping on applause lines, uttering strong lines without conviction, diluting them in delivery." Schlesinger could barely conceal his frustration. "One trouble is the Governor's own split between his desire to win and his desire to live up to the noble image of himself which exists in the minds of such people as Barbara Ward [who campaigned on third world issues] and Eugenie Anderson [the first woman US ambassador]," he complained at the midway point of the campaign. "When they tell him he should take the high road and educate people about the issues of destruction and survival, he then begins to feel ashamed of his attacks on the Republicans as the party of big business interests"—the very theme that Schlesinger had been developing in his delayed *Age of Roosevelt.*

With just over two weeks left before election day, Schlesinger reluctantly agreed that Stevenson "had to get foreign policy out of his system." No sooner had the switch been made than the Hungarian Uprising started, which triggered a Soviet invasion; and then Israel, soon joined by Britain and France, invaded Egypt, unleashing the Suez Crisis. For a brief moment, Stevenson hoped that world events might tilt the election his way; instead most wavering voters seemed to conclude that the experienced soldier, General Eisenhower, was best placed to keep the United States safe in a world in crisis. On the eve of the election, a desperate Stevenson resorted to a nasty personal attack on Eisenhower's health. "Distasteful as this matter is," he declared at a final rally in Boston, "I must say bluntly that every piece of scientific evidence we have, every lesson of history and experience, indicates that a Republican victory tomorrow would mean Richard M. Nixon would probably be president within the next four years. I say frankly, as a citizen more than a candidate, that I recoil at the prospect."[31]

Many staff and friends watching the speech back at Stevenson's hotel gasped at the personal nature of the attack. Schlesinger was not one of them. As part of the senior speechwriting team, he would certainly have contributed to such a major address. Twenty years later he would go so far—but only that far—as to admit that Bill Wirtz had shown him the passage and asked his opinion. "I'm afraid I said, 'It's true, and the people should know it,' or something like that." He then quickly added, "I wish I had said that it was wrong—because I thought it was. But I gave some terrible answer like that." The fact that Schlesinger was talking at this later point to the third member of the speechwriting team, John Bart-low Martin, who was by then Stevenson's official biographer, only compounds the sense of general buck-passing. "Where the passage originated is not clear," Martin concludes, honoring some kind of speechwriters' code. And no wonder, for the remarks, he concludes, "alienated some of Stevenson's . . . friends and tarnished his reputation." If the matter was a question of judgment, then it is worth adding that when Schlesinger and Martin had attempted to persuade another speaker that night, John F. Kennedy, to launch a personal attack on the Republicans, including Nixon's role in McCarthyism, the senator had refused point blank.[32]

The election resulted in a landslide for Eisenhower. Stevenson won only seven states, with just one (Missouri) from outside the old Confederate States. He carried not a single northern state, putting all Schlesinger's work in the Finletter Group to the sword. Even Louisiana turned Republican for the first time since 1876. Eisenhower gained the highest popular vote in history and a plurality only outstripped by FDR in 1936. "It hurts so badly," Stevenson told Marietta Tree, "even worse than 1952."[33]

The results hardly surprised Schlesinger. He had gone into the campaign fearing that the "old" Stevenson had replaced the newer model, and then been disappointed by the candidate's belated willingness to go for the

POLITICS IS AN EDUCATIONAL PROCESS   179

jugular in addressing Eisenhower's health issues. But defeat also left him in a difficult personal position. He had now been involved in two losing presidential campaigns, in charge of the very part of those campaigns, no less, that observers cited as the reason for successive landslides. If Stevenson was a poor speechmaker, then the speechwriters, it surely followed, were as much to blame as the speaker. To redeem themselves, Schlesinger and Martin, along with the Harvard economist Seymour Harris, began to put together an edited collection of Stevenson's 1956 campaign speeches for publication as *The New America*. Stevenson promised to write a foreword "expressing some views about primaries, the campaign, the successes and failures, etc.," but in this endeavor, as so often, he disappointed. "I suppose it is actually more inertia than pressure, but the period is totally sterile!" Stevenson wrote in response to a letter from the editors in April 1957. "Moreover, I think the material that Arthur and Seymour [Harris] have prepared covers most of what I could have said anyway, and doubtless better." His speechwriters would have been justified in reflecting that their lives would have been much simpler if Stevenson had been so accepting of what they had written on the campaign trail itself.[34]

If *The New America* was about restoring Stevenson's reputation as a thoughtful public speaker, the defeated candidate's "inertia" also pointed toward another difficulty. Stevenson once again said he did not want to run, and this time he even freed those who had worked with him previously to find other contenders. "I have told all my friends who have asked, to go work for 'the candidate of their choice,'" he wrote to Schlesinger. "I think I told *you* that sometime ago. If I didn't, I do herewith!" That release would, once 1960 came around, turn out to be disingenuous; in the aftermath of the 1956 defeat, however, Stevenson's declaration that his race was run freed Schlesinger to look for a new horse in the political stakes.[35]

Past failure did not create a shortage of takers for Schlesinger's political advice. The most important of these new potential clients was Lyndon B. Johnson, the Senate majority leader. On February 1, 1957, clearly irritated by the historian's critique that congressional Democrats were too conservative given that they held a majority in both houses, Johnson wrote a "put up or shut up" style letter to Schlesinger. "From what I have heard, I am inclined to think that you are not convinced that I am going about it in the right way," he wrote. "As Majority Leader of the Senate, I have some problems which I do not think you are too aware of. I hear that you come to Washington quite often. I would appreciate it if you would . . . talk over some of these problems. I suspect that you will find I will go a long way toward convincing you that it is not as easy as you think."

Schlesinger took a full two weeks before replying to this vaguely threatening note, telling Johnson that he would "welcome indeed a chance for a discussion," but adding that while "grateful for your interest in my views," they were "of no importance, however, except as they reflect misgivings prevalent among northern Democrats." The two men met in March 1957, when they talked alone in Johnson's Senate office for an hour and a half. "I found him both more attractive, more subtle and more formidable than I expected," Schlesinger wrote of the man with whom his fortunes would later become entwined. The senator's blunt language was "vivid and picturesque but unforced." Clearly he was a "virtuoso in senatorial operation," existing "almost completely in the realm of tactics," and yet "with a nostalgic identification of himself as a liberal and a desire, other things being equal, to be on the liberal side."[36]

Johnson, employing a tactic that Schlesinger had become accustomed to working for Stevenson, assured the younger man that he was "a sick man," had "no interest at all" in the presidential nomination, and did not even mean to run again for the Senate. Thus being "entirely disinterested," the leader only wanted to do what he could for the party and the nation. "One almost heard violins in the background," Arthur smirked, before adding, "yet he may well have been perfectly sincere."[37]

Either way, Johnson now asked Schlesinger to send a memo setting out a future agenda for the party. A week later, Schlesinger wrote, saying he had "greatly enjoyed our conversation the other day, and I much appreciate your suggestion that I send along any thoughts I might have." His principal focus was the budget, taking aim at those who believed that the Democratic Party should follow the Republican lead by promising retrenchment and economy. "For Democrats to take this position is really madness," he explained. "It will persuade nobody. It is contrary to the

historic position of the modern Democratic Party and to the public welfare: it makes neither political, moral nor economic sense." Obviously the
Democratic Party should "stand strong against waste and extravagance
in government." But the party should not fall into the trap of promising to
cut "vital public services in the name of 'economy.' " The nation was richer
than at any point in its history, yet spending in the public sector had not
kept pace. "Our great historic position as the party which believes in the
use of government to promote the general welfare will," Schlesinger told
Johnson loftily, "continue for a long time, I believe, to be the main source
of our political strength."[38]

As in 1952, Schlesinger's reaction to defeat was a belief that the Democratic Party had lost touch with its roots, betraying the progressive ideals
and values of the liberal tradition—a neat example of what social psychol-
ogist Jonathan Haidt calls "*confirmation bias*, the tendency to seek out and
interpret new evidence in ways that confirm what you already think." Two
months later, now writing to "Lyndon" as "Arthur," Schlesinger returned
to his theme. "If we try to identify ourselves with government retrenchment, who will ever take us seriously as a party again," he asked. "The
great tradition of the Democratic Party," he urged, "is the tradition of
affirmative government—the tradition of Jackson, [William Jennings]
Bryan, Wilson and FDR."[39]

And it was to the task of restoring that tradition that Schlesinger now
finally turned, not this time as a political operative, but as the author of a
transformational new narrative of America's recent history.

CHAPTER TEN

A Saint's Life

"**N**othing is worse than the pre-publication limbo," Schlesinger wrote in February 1957 to his friend James Wechsler at the *New York Post*. The nervousness was understandable. His previous scholarly book, *The Age of Jackson*, had won him a Pulitzer Prize at the precociously tender age of twenty-eight years. As the *New York Times* helpfully reminded readers when *The Age of Roosevelt: The Crisis of the Old Order, 1919–1933* was finally published on March 4, "At the age of 39 Arthur M. Schlesinger Jr. is firmly established as one of our leading younger historians and as one of the shining lights of the Harvard faculty." Even a man of Schlesinger's intellectual assurance would have been foolhardy not to recognize the risk involved in such a "grandiose" new project. He had risen high and fast, and now had a long way to fall.[1]

The first volume was a year late, but two more volumes—*The Coming of the New Deal* and *The Politics of Upheaval*—would be published in quick succession in 1959 and 1960. Thus by the time of the next presidential election in 1960, Schlesinger had established his narrative on Franklin Roosevelt and the New Deal as the major statement on progressive liberalism in US history.

Franklin Roosevelt had hovered as a spectral presence throughout Schlesinger's 1945 book, *The Age of Jackson*, finally being summoned to the forefront of the narrative in the last pages. Now Schlesinger offered a thesis that presented Roosevelt as the ultimate expression of three major traditions in the Republic. FDR had decisively committed the country to Hamiltonian progressivism, building on the work of Theodore Roosevelt and Woodrow Wilson, and acting upon the need for "executive vigor and government action." Alongside this activism, FDR had also displayed a Jeffersonian respect for the dangers inherent in the new instruments of public power created by this executive vigor. "In the hands of a people's Government this power is wholesome and proper," Roosevelt had cautioned, "but in the hands of political puppets of an economic autocracy such power would provide shackles for the liberties of the people." As the measure for what was "wholesome and proper," Schlesinger pointed to the third tradition, the Jacksonian heritage, which FDR summed up as "the American doctrine that entrusts the general welfare to no one group or class, but dedicates itself to the end that the American people shall not be thwarted in their high purpose to remain the custodians of their own destiny." For Schlesinger, it was this last tradition that assumed a special significance, because its spirit provided the key for Roosevelt to make an "earnest, tough-minded, pragmatic attempt to wrestle with problems as they come, without being enslaved by a theory of the past, or by a theory of the future." Through these values, Schlesinger concluded, Roosevelt had been able to steer the United States away from "social catastrophe" during the Great Depression and to the brink of victory in a global war. These were themes that Schlesinger then addressed at length.[2]

In the prologue to *The Crisis of the Old Order*, Schlesinger brings us to the White House on the eve of Roosevelt's inauguration, conjuring a scene in which America stood teetering at the edge of an abyss:

The White House, midnight, Friday, March 3, 1933. Across the country the banks of the nation had gradually shuttered their windows and locked their doors. The very machinery of the American economy seemed to be coming to a stop. The rich and fertile nation, overflowing with natural wealth in its fields and forests and mines, equipped with unsurpassed technology, endowed with boundless resources in its men and women, lay stricken. "We are at the end of our rope," the weary President [Herbert Hoover] at last said, as the striking clock announced the day of his retirement. "There is nothing more we can do."[3]

It was in many ways a typical Schlesinger paragraph: the style vivid, appealing, and dramatic; the narrative clear, with the politics subtle yet unmistakable. The midnight hour, the sense of uncertainty as the banking system shut down; how unnecessary the crisis was in a country of such abundance in people and resources; and at the heart of it all, a leader who had run out of ideas and hope: here was the America that the old order had laid to waste and for which it offered no remedies.

Uncertainty was everywhere. As dawn broke "gray and bleak" in the streets around the Capitol Building, "the colorless light of the cast-iron skies, the numb faces of the crowd, created almost an air of fantasy." The Washington and New York Establishment, "the well groomed men, baffled and impotent in their double breasted suits," began to gather. And yet here riding into the middle of the crisis, not quite to the strains of Handel's *Judas Maccabaeus*, came Franklin Roosevelt. On the journey to the inauguration ceremony, the outgoing president sat glum and monosyllabic. Expectant crowds pressed in for some sign of hope. Suddenly Roosevelt understood that "the two men could not ride on forever like graven images." While Hoover's face remained "heavy and expressionless," the president-elect "began to smile to the men and women along the street and to wave his top hat." Optimism and good cheer in the face of adversity began to take effect. "Men and women now curiously awakened from apathy and daze," Schlesinger writes. In Washington the weather remained cold and gray, but "across the land the fog began to lift."[4]

The Crisis of the Old Order sets out to explain how the United States in 1933 had arrived at such a perilous state of affairs and why Franklin D. Roosevelt, a patrician from the Gilded Age estates of the Hudson Valley, embodied the best hopes of the American people. At the heart of Schlesinger's story was the corruption of the Age of Business in the 1920s. "If the business of America was business," he writes, "then business meant more to Americans than the making of money." Capitalism seemed to have "transcended its individualism and materialism, becoming social and spiritual." Business became a "new faith [that] permeated the churches, the courts, the colleges, the press. It created a literature of complacency. . . . It developed an economics of success and a metaphysics of optimism." For some, like Calvin Coolidge, "the process went even farther: the factory was the temple, work was worship, and business verged on a new religion." With scorn seeping through the page, Schlesinger cites the example of Bruce Barton, best-selling author of *The Man Nobody Knows* (1925). "Barton assimilated Jesus Christ into the new cult," Schlesinger records, "observing admiringly of the Son of God that He had 'picked up twelve men from the bottom ranks of business and forged them into an organization that conquered the world.'" Salvation, then, was to be "measured by success; and success thus became the visible evidence of spiritual merit."[5]

The problem with the new faith, however, was that it "knew no skepticism." The nation seemed to have reached "a permanent plateau of prosperity." Business was expanding and foreign trade growing; the stock market was going up and up; national leadership "could not now be in more expert or safer hands." Speaking in his inaugural address in March 1929, the new president, Herbert Hoover, confidently announced, "I have no fears for the future of our country. It is bright with hope."[6]

The 1929 Wall Street Crash and the Depression that followed may not have been Hoover's fault, but it was his job to sort them out. "The American system remained essentially a presidential system," Schlesinger writes, and "in the end, all things come down to the man in the White House." For Hoover (as it would be for Roosevelt, although Schlesinger does not say so), the "battle in [his] mind" was between a scheme of public works and his mounting concern about balancing the budget. In the end, "the infatuation with the balanced budget thus destroyed a major plank of Hoover's first anti-depression plan—the expansion of public works." Schlesinger's judgment on Hoover was a harsh one, but not entirely out of keeping with the president's subsequent historical reputation. Revisionists Patrick D. O'Brien and Philip Rosen point out that the traditional image of Hoover (which they blame on Schlesinger) "as an irresponsible reactionary who lacked a sense of humanity ... has gradually and largely been supplanted in historical writing as historians now often describe a humane reformer with an idealistic vision of America." Yet as Robert Merry sums up in his book on presidential historical standings, it may well be that "Hoover attacked the problem with vigor [and] was a far more activist president than history has acknowledged. But his efforts didn't work, and he was tossed aside."[7]

For Schlesinger, it was not just the Republican Party that posed a threat to Roosevelt's plans. Skeptics lurked everywhere among Democrats too, with key figures working to "commit the party to conservatism." During the 1932 presidential campaign, FDR's own vice presidential running mate, the famously scatological John Nance "Cactus Jack" Garner IV, warned Roosevelt that if he went "too far with some of these wild-eye ideas, we are going to have the shit kicked out of us." Garner at least told FDR "he is the boss and we will all follow him to hell if we have to."

Other defeated rivals and party figures proved more troublesome. Al Smith, the party's nominee in 1928 and by now deeply embittered that FDR had usurped him, warned that we should "stop talking about the Forgotten Man and about class distinctions." Smith wanted government retrenchment, not investment, as did other influential figures such as Governor Albert Ritchie of Maryland and former US Treasury Secretary Carter Glass. The 1924 (losing) Democratic nominee, John W. Davis, summed it up by accusing Hoover of traveling "the road to socialism" and warning Roosevelt not to follow suit.[8]

But Schlesinger's Roosevelt was not to be persuaded by conservatives inside or outside the party. "Washington observers began to note that liberals making the pilgrimage to Warm Springs [FDR's retreat in Georgia] returned more cheerful than conservatives," he writes. In January 1933, the president-elect outlined to reporters a broad vision of multipurpose development, linking waterpower, forestry, flood control, conservation, reclamation, agriculture, and industry in a vast experiment, beginning in Tennessee and spreading throughout the country.[9]

Here at last was a leader who had the moral and intellectual leadership to meet the challenge of the times, Schlesinger concludes in the first volume of *The Age of Roosevelt*. And what times they were, he writes, when "the American experiment in self-government was now facing what was, excepting the Civil War, its greatest test . . . even more perhaps hung on the capacity to surmount crisis than in 1861, [for] in 1933 the fate of the United States was involved with the fate of free men everywhere."

"Many had deserted freedom, many more had lost their nerve," Schlesinger writes exultantly on the last page. "But Roosevelt, armored in some inner faith, remained calm and inscrutable, confident that American improvisation could meet the future on its own terms." That was the character on display as FDR traveled with President Hoover to the inauguration ceremony:

> Deep within, he seemed to know that the nation had resources beyond its banks and exchanges; that the collapse of the older order meant catharsis rather than catastrophe; that the common disaster could make the people see themselves for a season as a community; as a family; that catastrophe could provide the indispensable setting for democratic experiment and for presidential leadership. If this were so, then crisis could change from calamity to challenge. The only thing Americans had to fear was fear itself. And so he serenely awaited the morrow. The event was in the hand of God.[10]

Schlesinger's prose seems cloyingly purple by contemporary standards, but reviewers in 1957 had few complaints about his bravura and elan. Orville Prescott in the daily *New York Times* noted that "Mr. Schlesinger is as industrious in research as a history professor ought to be [but] he writes much more skillfully than all but a very few professors of history." Despite some "massively detailed . . . heavy going" passages, here was "an account of the intellectual and political climate of the first third of this century [that] is sometimes brilliant, often entertaining and always informative and educational." Academic reviewers similarly enjoyed Schlesinger's style. Columbia's William E. Leuchtenburg admired the "verve" and "slashing vigor" of the book. G. M. Craig at Toronto recognized an "exciting and absorbing read." Frank Thistlethwaite, the founding chairman of the British Association for American Studies, enjoyed a "sustained, fluent and often brilliant narrative." John D. Hicks at Berkeley acknowledged Schlesinger's "gifts of a high order" in the ability to "write with verve and vigor, know how to make the most of every dramatic possibility, and be able to exploit the reader's appetite for suspense."

Some reviewers did object, however, to the overtly political nature of the book. "*The Crisis of the Old Order* is a frankly Democratic interpretation of recent history," Prescott wrote in the *Times*, "and it will certainly antagonize many Republicans." But fellow historians, too, worried about the partisan nature of the book. Craig thought, "the informed reader will often cringe at the author's almost diabolical pursuit of his villains, and at his easy tolerance of the occasional failings of his hero." Oberlin's Thomas LeDuc huffed that "the book is so passionate in tone and so meager in new research that it need not be dignified by an extensive review." Even the sympathetic Thistlethwaite worried that the book was an example of "partisan history, written, one suspects, in Mr. Adlai Stevenson's words on the jacket, to demonstrate 'how the democratic process can shake off despair and produce vigorous leadership,'" and that it did not adequately complete its advertised task of addressing "all the important questions raised by America's 'struggle to come of age in the modern world.'"[11]

Yet the most penetrating review of all came from Leuchtenburg, who was at work on his own outstanding history of the New Deal that would win both the Bancroft Prize and (like *The Crisis of the Old Order*) the Parkman Prize. "One marvels at the apparent effortlessness with which Schlesinger writes, his mastery of the material, and the great scope of this ambitious project," he wrote. "Yet, for all of this, one puts down the book with a sense of disappointment." Leuchtenburg's complaint was that Schlesinger had put contemporary politics above historical objectivity. Because the book presented the period as "a conflict between good (liberal, Democratic) men against bad (conservative, Republican) men," it had left the reader with "little sense of the men of the times as prisoners of historical forces or a particular historical situation." Moreover, this Manichean struggle left no room for nonpolitical figures such as T. S. Eliot or William Faulkner, who themselves spoke to the broader crisis of the old order.[12]

Although the Columbia school had set its stall out in opposition to Schlesinger's *Age of Jackson*, Leuchtenburg himself was not personally or professionally hostile to Schlesinger and later he would express admiration for his work.[13] Even this unfavorable review was essentially constructive in nature (which, of course, made it all the more damning), concluding, "It is precisely because he [Schlesinger] is such a gifted historian that it is important to explore the shortcoming of this first volume in some detail." Moreover, Leuchtenburg added, "If in his forthcoming volumes, Schlesinger will permit himself to be disciplined by his material, instead of committing to an inhibiting thesis, *The Age of Roosevelt* will be one of the benchmarks of historical writing this century."

Debates about objectivity in history had been raging within the profession since at least the first decades of the century when New Historians such as Charles Beard and Carl Becker repeatedly argued that the usual professional standard of icy impartiality was intellectually dishonest. Arthur Schlesinger Sr. had been one of those who stood out against the trend, arguing, for example, when it was put to him by Perry Miller that the first world war had prompted the "rewriting of American history," that "I am not aware that it had any such effect." For Arthur Jr. the lens was subtly different. For him it was not so much the impact of the immediate past on the writing of history that mattered, as the reverberations of history with the present, particularly the political present. "I have long been fascinated and perplexed," he would write in 1966, "by the interaction between history and public decision: fascinated because, by this process, past history becomes an active partner in the making of new history; perplexed because the role of history in this partnership remains both elusive and tricky."[14] To enemies on the other side of the political divide, such as neoconservative Norman Podhoretz, Schlesinger's view made him "an exceptionally bad historian: incapable of doing justice to any idea with which he disagreed, and so tendentious that he invariably denigrated and/or vilified anyone who had ever espoused any such idea"—a judgment not far removed from the view, albeit expressed with more academic *politesse*, by Leuchtenburg that Schlesinger's was "a tortured reading" of the 1920s.[15]

Twice in his review, Leuchtenburg reached casually for religious language to rebuke Schlesinger, suggesting that he had become "the captive of a theological interpretation of history which views America as swaying between two traditions—one liberal, one conservative," and that in *The Crisis of the Old Order* "he has presented a morality play." Other critics of the book, such as Arthur Page, who famously drafted President Truman's statement on the dropping of the first atomic bomb at Hiroshima in August 1945, used similarly religious language, believing it to be a New Deal "hagiography."[16]

The term *hagiographer* and its like were ones that would be thrown around a great deal later in Schlesinger's career, particularly in relation to his books on President John F. Kennedy and the president's brother Robert Kennedy. By the time, for example, Schlesinger was awarded the National Humanities Medal in 1999, the *Financial Times* ran a profile under the headline "Loyal Keeper of the Kennedy Flame," which described how "Arthur Schlesinger has defended Kennedy's reputation at no little cost of his own. . . . He has been denounced as a 'servant,' a 'poodle' and one of the US's 'more purchasable intellectuals.'" Similarly when Schlesinger signed a letter against the impeachment of President Clinton as part of a grouping called Historians in Defense of the Constitution, the contrarian critic Christopher Hitchens (himself no stranger to accusations of being a sellout) noted scathingly in *The Nation* that Schlesinger "was not known to me before as a historian of any kind, but [he] presumably squeezed in as a composer of profiles in Democratic opportunism." Schlesinger liked to treat such attacks as a humorous part of the game. "I have not enjoyed such a fusillade for a third of a century," he quipped nonchalantly in 1999, "it makes me feel young again." But when friends like Princeton professor Sean Wilentz balanced the unflattering remarks of others with their own judgments that "He is the great liberal Democratic intellectual of our time," Schlesinger took the time to note down such a "nice quote" in his journal, implying that he was less immune to the barrage of criticism than he liked to pretend.[17]

Contemporary writers were using "hagiography" and "Manichean-ism" in a general vernacular sense rather than in any specific scholarly way. Although "hagiography" in particular has become a term of abuse today, Schlesinger's work does have indirect parallels with older notions of the idea. Saints' lives (vitae) of the fourth or fifth century such as Athanasius's *Life of Antony* or Sulpicius Severus's *Life of Martin* demonstrated how a holy existence could be transformed into a powerful literary form and widely disseminated, spreading a saint's reputation and influence. What gave a life coherence was not so much its details or structure but its *purpose*. "Every hagiographic work is 'an exercise in persuasion,'" writes historian Robert Bartlett, "and its purpose was to persuade the reader that its subject was a saint."[18]

On one level, *The Age of Roosevelt*, like *The Age of Jackson*, had a fairly straightforward ideological agenda coming out of Progressive history. Both projects were in some senses intellectual and political tributes to Arthur Sr. But unlike his father, Arthur Jr. was a public intellectual. He believed in the uses of history and in useful history. That instinct, which was present right from the outset in *Orestes Brownson*, had been accentuated by the wartime experience and writing *The Vital Center*. Schlesinger did use pseudo-religious language, but the spiritual enterprise for this atheistic historian was to influence the battle he saw going on between the forces of light and darkness in postwar America and in the Cold War. That was his purpose. "The book, if it is any good," Arthur told his friend Joseph Rauh, "will serve the liberal cause."[19]

For Schlesinger the character of the president was instrumental. "A cheerful strength radiated from him," Schlesinger writes of FDR, which roused in others "exhilaration and a sense of their own possibilities." He could "communicate confidence by the intonation of his voice, the tilt of his head, the flourish of a cigarette holder." His depths were such that "beyond the screen, the real Roosevelt existed in mystery, even to himself." His eyes were "friendly but impenetrable, the smile genial but non-committal, the manner open but inscrutable—all signified the inaccessibility within." The inner man was "tougher than the public man, more ambitious, more calculating, more petty, more puckish, more selfish, more profound, more complex, more interesting." Roosevelt had been through his own time of trial with poliomyelitis in 1921, a "brush with death [that] increased his joy in living" and "developed in him latencies and potentialities that gave him a new power, a new sympathy, a new self-control, a new specific gravity." Taken all together, "Franklin Roosevelt was a man without illusions, clearheaded and compassionate, who had been close enough to death to understand the frailty of human striving, but who remained loyal enough to life to do his best in the sight of God."[20]

In volume II of *The Age of Roosevelt*, Schlesinger set about showing the works that the new president had wrought. The stakes in 1933 were high, "a matter of seeing whether a representative democracy could conquer economic collapse . . . even (at least some so thought) revolution." Again religious imagery came to the forefront. "Faith in a free system was plainly waning." Roosevelt's first hundred days provided "resurgent hope." The new president sent fifteen messages to Congress, pushed through fifteen major laws, delivered ten speeches, gave press conferences and held cabinet meetings, undertook talks with foreign leaders and sponsored an international conference, "made all the major decisions in domestic and foreign policy, and never displayed fright or panic and rarely even bad temper."

"His mastery astonished many who thought they had long since taken his measure," Schlesinger writes of the president at the end of those first hundred days. "Norman Davis, encountering Raymond Fosdick outside the presidential office, expressed the incredulity of those who had worked with him during the Wilson administration. 'Ray, that fellow in there is not the fellow we used to know. There's been a miracle here.' "[21]

The "miracle" of the hundred days began the process of healing "a people who had lost faith." A raft of legislation and reforms followed in the next two years, including a new farm policy, experiments in industrial policy such as the National Recovery Administration, the rise of federal relief, public works and social security, the development of a national labor policy, and attempts at controlling the stock exchanges. By the time of the midterm election in 1934, the New Deal achieved what Arthur Krock in the *New York Times* described as "the most overwhelming victory in the history of American politics"—and certainly the best result for a sitting president since the Civil War. "It shows how faithful the American people are to the true spirit of democracy," William Randolph Hearst, owner of the nation's largest newspaper chain, wrote afterwards to Roosevelt.[22]

"Make no mistake," Schlesinger quotes Carl Jung saying after seeing FDR in 1936, "He is a force." Those who despised the president did so not "from honest opposition" but from "an emotion of irrational violence, directed against Roosevelt's personality rather than his program." This hostility shared "not just a common psychopathological impulse but a common social source," namely, "the American upper class." It was, Schlesinger said, "a disease of the rentier class" made worse for them in constituting "apostasy" by "one of their own." Ordinary people, however, admired Roosevelt. Portraits "now stood on the mantle" as icons, because "FDR cared for people, battled for them, and exulted in the battle." His was the image of "human warmth in a setting of dramatic national action which made people love him."[23]

Behind Roosevelt's force, Schlesinger concludes in the final pages of *The Coming of the New Deal*, lay a sense of providence. "I doubt if there is in the world a single problem, whether social, political, or economic," FDR himself wrote, "which would not find ready solution if men and nations would rule their lives according to the plain teaching of the Sermon on the Mount." To which Schlesinger adds, "If nothing ever upset him, if his confidence seemed illimitable, it was because he deeply believed, with full reverence and humility, that he was doing his best in the eyes of God, that God was blessing his purpose, that he was at one with the benign forces of the universe."[24]

When the book came out in January 1959, reviewers followed its author's lead in maintaining this religious language about Roosevelt. "What *anni mirabiles* they were!" Henry Steele Commager exclaimed in the *New York Times Sunday Book Review*. Furthermore, he pointed out, "In the last analysis—so Schlesinger concludes—the energies that fed him

[FDR] were moral," adding his own judgment that "however clever, however elusive and indirect he was in tactics, his grand strategy was always simple and clear: it involved faith in the triumph of the right, faith in the ability of men to overcome evil and achieve peace and dignity."[25]

Reviews of *The Coming of the New Deal* were more consistently positive than for the previous volume, *The Crisis of the Old Order*. Two clear themes emerge from these notices. First, the new book was elegantly and persuasively written. Reviewers marveled that he had produced another volume so quickly without apparently having compromised on quality. "It is possible that other energetic scholars could accomplish as much work in the same interval," Orville Prescott observed in the *Times* review. "It is unlikely that many could have done it so well, for Mr. Schlesinger is a writer as well as a historian." Therefore the "brightly entertaining" book was written with "skill and dash." Academic reviewers, who might have sniffed out more weaknesses, instead concurred. "There is no evidence of shoddy writing," George C. Osborn glowed in the *Annals of the American Academy of Political and Social Science*, "of any lack of acquaintance with the materials, of any conclusions hastily drawn." Other reviewers praised the "sparkling" way in which characters were brought to life, "the literary talents and orderly intelligence" that could pull off "history with appropriate ingredients of narrative, drama, biography, analysis and interpretation," and the "first-rate piece of historical writing" that made *The Coming of the New Deal* such a "highly readable narrative." Few, if any, would have doubted by 1959 that Schlesinger was established as a leading, perhaps the preeminent, contemporary stylist writing American history.

The second theme to emerge was that whereas many reviewers of the first volume of *The Age of Roosevelt* felt that Schlesinger had crossed a line into political partisanship, most saw him stopping just short of that line in this new volume. "Although essentially favourable to the New Deal," G. M. Craig wrote in the *International Journal*, "this second volume is less of an anti-Republican tract than was the first." It was a view echoed in the *American Historical Review*, where Robert E. Burke noted, "If Schlesinger's sympathies are clearly with his hero throughout, in this volume he seems less partisan than in the introductory one. He affords little aid and comfort to the anti-New Dealers, but he does permit them to state their cases." Other reviewers pointed out that there was "never any doubt" about Schlesinger's feelings about the New Deal, and even complained he was "too ready" to explain the New Deal through "the Roosevelt personality." But the broad tone of the reviews matched that of Commager in the *Times*, who proclaimed of *The Age of Roosevelt*, "spacious and monumental in form, scholarly and authoritative in character, spirited and affluent in style, it promises to be one of the major works in American historical literature."[26]

The week after that rhapsodic review appeared, Schlesinger's publisher Houghton Mifflin threw a book party for him in Manhattan. Schlesinger was already on a high by the time he arrived to celebrate, having just met one of his childhood idols, Greta Garbo, at the home of a mutual friend, the journalist John Gunther. ("She is the greatest actress ever to play in the movies," Arthur gushed to his children. "I had somehow expected her to be older, but . . . her face is as young and lovely as a girl in her twenties.") After the Houghton Mifflin party, attended by friends ranging from Averell Harriman to Teddy White, the Schlesingers headed out to Idlewild (now JFK) Airport to catch a flight to England; Arthur was taking Roosevelt on tour.[27]

The occasion was the 1959 Commonwealth Fund Lectures at University College London, for which Schlesinger would deliver a series of eight talks on "Franklin D. Roosevelt and the Coming of the War"—essentially the first reading of ideas for the proposed fourth volume of *The Age of Roosevelt*. It was in many ways an evocative invitation, as Arthur Sr. had delivered lectures in the same series in 1934, taking Arthur Jr. with him as part of a round-the-world tour that made such a dramatic impact on the boy. It was just before that trip that Arthur Bancroft Schlesinger had legally changed his name to Arthur Meier Schlesinger Jr. in honor of his father; now two decades later, he was following in his father's footsteps, not just as the Commonwealth Fund Lecturer, but doing so, like his father, as a professor of history at Harvard. Arthur had dedicated *The Coming of the New Deal* to his parents. It was left to his more demonstrative mother to express what that dedication meant to the couple. "I just wanted to tell you again how supremely happy we are over your great success," she wrote to him that month. "Your tribute to us, so unexpected and cherished, gave us a joy which I hope you will experience in your turn and when it comes you will really understand what great happiness it has brought us." The more taciturn Arthur Sr. demonstrated his appreciation by agreeing to come out of retirement to cover his son's classes at Harvard while Arthur was in London. "It was like an old horse returning to pasture!" he quipped.[28]

The relationship between father and son—the "bloodstock stable"— was one that caught the attention of the London press in their coverage of the lectures. "Dr. Arthur Meier Schlesinger, second of his name and line to be professor of history at Harvard, had shouldered his way to the front rank of his profession before he was 30," gushed a profile in the *Times*, "and now at 41 he has a row of brilliant yet solid books behind him." For the *Observer*, he was an "important American prophet in London now, Professor Arthur M. Schlesinger Junior, professor of history at Harvard, not to be confused with Professor Arthur M. Schlesinger Senior, former professor of history at Harvard." The slightly irreverent *Observer* profile, which appeared under the headline "Charm and Bourbons," went on to describe Schlesinger as "a smallish, birdlike man with the quicksilver quality . . . of great charm, no chips on shoulder, and a capacity for warm friendships and very large Bourbons on the rocks."[29]

This last phrase drew a quick apology from the columnist "Pendennis"—in reality the bohemian socialite Philip Toynbee, himself a famous alcoholic and the son of an eminent historian (Arnold Toynbee). "I wrote that 'Pendennis was surprised and delighted by the size of the whiskies which were offered,'" he explained. "This was transformed, but by a piece of irritating editorial shorthand, into a tiresome implication that you yourself are a gargantuan drinker. I hope you'll forgive this!" Schlesinger lightly brushed it off, but writing home to his family, he did express puzzlement at "increasingly grim and fatuous" publicity. "Do I strike any of you as smallish? birdlike?" he asked his children, but did not neglect to tell them to pass along the clippings to Grandpa and Grandma Schlesinger.[30]

Aside from the lectures, "London University leaves me alone," Schlesinger cheerily reported home, but "no one else does, and we are now at a point where we have no lunch or dinner free for the rest of our time here." Poor Marian "goes to so many luncheons, cocktail parties and dinners that she says she is tired all the time." Arthur on the other hand thrived on the attention and the company, which blended academia, politics, and the arts. ("Lunched with Lady Pamela Berry," notes a typical daily report. "Present were Hugh Gaitskell, Isaiah Berlin, and Mr. and Mrs. Graham Sutherland. . . . Later in the afternoon we went to a party given by *Encounter* for the Stephen Spenders, who were leaving for the US. Graham Greene was there.")[31]

As well as time in the capital, Schlesinger made trips to both Oxford and Cambridge, where he continued the pattern of lecturing a little and socializing a lot. For all the agreeable company in both universities, including dinner with the likes of good friend Isaiah Berlin, Maurice Bowra, and A. J. P. Taylor at Oxford, and a happy return to Peterhouse, Cambridge, Arthur nevertheless felt a certain ennui about these academic towns in comparison to London. "Each visit," he told his father, "confirms me in my belief that it would drive me mad to spend an entire year at either of these institutions."[32]

This apparently off-hand comment marks the beginning of a shift in Schlesinger's attitude toward academic life, one in which his professorship gradually became little more than a useful title, a salary, and a means to store his books. The Commonwealth Lectures, strikingly in his letters, are the element of his stay in England that seemed to interest Schlesinger the least. In part this was because the broad topic was foreign policy, with lectures on isolationism, relations with Britain and Russia, and policy in the Far East. Schlesinger's lack of enthusiasm flags a longer-term difficulty in engaging with FDR's foreign policy that later would make completing *The Age of Roosevelt* such a troubling, almost existential, experience for him over several decades. Arriving now at University College London on the day of the first lecture, "I realized with all these dignitaries, the lecture would have to be rewritten and rushed back and added a few new bits." In the end, Schlesinger had "no idea how it went." Not all the lectures had even been written, and having been "busy for luncheon, dinner and usually cocktails every day" he "only got round" to working on each one at the last minute. In the end the most memorable aspect of visiting UCL was not giving the lectures, but viewing the preserved body of Jeremy Bentham, utilitarian founder of the college, whose unusual predicament—his corpse on display, fully dressed, and sitting in his favorite chair—Arthur took delight in describing in grisly detail to his children, not least the philosopher's head, "which is kept in a mummified state in a box nearby."[33]

Schlesinger arrived back in Massachusetts at the end of February 1959 apparently energized by his visit to London, for he immediately got to work on the massive third volume of *The Age of Roosevelt*, which was published the following year. Any ideas about FDR's foreign policy were themselves "mummified," as he focused a further 750 pages on the domestic history of the Roosevelt administration, now taking the story through the presidential election of 1936.[34]

The second volume had left off with Roosevelt's triumph when the Democrats swept all before them in the midterm elections of 1934. Yet volume III opens in more uncertain times, as "thoughtful New Dealers knew that all was not so well as it looked." Certainly there had been "no doubt impressive" accomplishments. The "downward grind" of 1933 had been stopped. But in the Manichean world of Schlesinger's *Age of Roosevelt*, "by transforming the national mood from apathy to action, the New Deal was invigorating its enemies as well as its friends." And for once the president seemed unsure of himself and how to act. "People tire of seeing the same name day after day in the important headlines of the papers, and the same voice night after night over the radio," FDR wearily told a friend. To fill the vacuum, Schlesinger wrote, "clamorous new voices, like those of Huey Long and Father Coughlin, were seizing the headlines . . . [in the absence] of a lead of any sort from the White House."[35]

In part, Schlesinger put this sudden collapse of the national sense of well-being down to the effects of trauma. "In the half dozen years before 1935, the American people had been through two profound shocks," he writes. "The first was the shock of the depression, bringing the sudden fear that the national economy could no longer assure its citizens jobs or perhaps even food and shelter." The second was the shock of the New Deal itself. That second shock "terminated the national descent into listlessness" and initiated a new period of aspirational energy. "But soon," Schlesinger added darkly, "it began to spread through the country and shoot off in several different directions." In short, "the people . . . regained the energy to fight among themselves."[36]

To explain the effects of this phenomenon and how Roosevelt overcame its consequences, Schlesinger continued the religious theme he had developed so strongly in the first and second volumes. The entire first section of the book expounded on "The Theology of Ferment" and featured "crusades" and "The Messiah of the Rednecks," namely Huey Long Jr., the populist senator from Louisiana. Long he viewed as a man "who gave off a sense of destiny," but "as a technique of political self-aggrandizement, not as a gospel of social reconstruction." This alternative to Roosevelt was "part traveling salesman, part confidence man, part gang leader, [with] at most a crude will toward personal power. He may not have been a Hitler or a Mussolini, Schlesinger ventured, but was more like "a Latin American dictator, a Vargas or a Perón . . . like them, he was most threatened by his own arrogance and cupidity, his weakness for soft living and his rage for personal power." Taken together with the anti-Semitic, pro-Hitler "radio priest" Father Coughlin, whose weekly broadcasts attracted tens of millions, these demagogues, though "preaching competing gospels . . . seemed to represent a common group and to express a common impulse," namely "Old America in resentful revolt."[37]

This popular swell, supplemented by an unholy alliance of the business community, the "underground creature, pallid but vicious" of the "communist conspiracy," and attacks on the legality of the New Deal from the judiciary, provoked in Roosevelt an "ordeal by indecision" and momentarily put him "in retreat." Only when he recognized the "posture of indiscriminate, stupid, and vindictive opposition" did he summon "a group of progressives to the White House" for "candid and unrestrained talks" that signaled he "meant to take a progressive stand and force the fighting on that line." The result was the second New Deal, a program, says Schlesinger, that deployed, often nervously, the concepts embraced by the likes of Supreme Court justice Louis Brandeis and economist John Maynard Keynes, moving the emphasis of the New Deal from a managed to a mixed economy.[38]

Looking toward the 1936 presidential election, Herbert Hoover, FDR's predecessor as president, announced that the campaign would be another "holy crusade for liberty." But it was the apparent economic miracle of 1936 that would give Roosevelt "a propitious climate for a presidential election," Schlesinger writes, listing the spectacular data that showed how national income had risen by 50 percent and unemployment fallen by nearly half since 1933, with gross earnings in the second quarter of the year 70 percent higher than in the first. On the back of such gains, Roosevelt won by a landslide in November, carrying forty-six of the forty-eight states against Alf Landon, an amiable but lightweight Republican candidate who lacked Long's extremism (The Kingfish was assassinated in 1935) but also his fire. Roosevelt succeeded by blending ideas with pragmatism. "This fluidity was Roosevelt's delight," Schlesinger wrote, using a familiar naval analogy, "and he floated upon it with the confidence of an expert sailor, who could detect currents and breezes invisible to others, hear the slap of the waves on distant rocks, smell squalls beyond the horizon and make infallible landfalls in the blackest of fogs." With this critical vision blended with the reality of politics, Roosevelt had recovered from the torpor of 1935 and restored his command in time to win a second term and see off the demagogues, Fascists, Communists, and their like who had threatened the Republic. "The whole point of the New Deal," Schlesinger summed up, "lay in its faith in 'the exercise of Democracy.'"[39]

Schlesinger's notion of the two New Deals became one of the defining metaphors by which people came to understand a shift in priorities in 1935 as the planners gave way to the decentralizers. Like many successful interpretations, this one opened a rich vein of scholarship that eventually dismissed it as overly simplistic because it blurred the ways in which planning and regulation occurred throughout the entire period. In the 1960s, New Left historians such as Barton Bernstein and Paul Conkin attacked FDR as a capitalist lackey and the New Deal itself as a continuous attempt to prop up a failing system. More persuasively, subsequent New Deal historians such as Jordan A. Swartz, Theda Skocpol and Kenneth Finegold, and Alan Brinkley presented the period as an exercise in state capitalism and state-building. Schlesinger's individual ideas, particularly the links back to Andrew Jackson, may have been "consigned to the historiographical dustbin," Morton Keller points out, but even by the beginning of the twenty-first century, "the major conceptual framework of the literature is the distinction between a recovery-minded First New Deal rooted in the past, and a reform-minded Second New Deal that under the political, intellectual, and demographic pressures of change unfolded into something broader and more original." It was Schlesinger, along with the likes of Richard Hofstadter and William Leuchtenburg, who created that enduring and influential framework.[40]

Reviewers at the time lauded *The Politics of Upheaval*. Orville Prescott, who apparently had a monopoly on the series in the daily *New York Times*, continued to praise Schlesinger as "one of the ablest contemporary American historians" and for "his mastery of a lively and readable style"; as importantly, he judged that long after the author's writings as a "busy participant in partisan politics" were forgotten, "Mr. Schlesinger's monumental history, *The Age of Roosevelt*, seems destined to survive." For the *New York Times Sunday Book Review*, Schlesinger was lucky enough to get a notice from his friend, the British historian Denis Brogan ("Lunched with Denis Brogan," Schlesinger had reported from London the previous year).[41] Brogan praised Schlesinger's "masterly achievement" and echoed the religious language and purpose of the series. The current volume made evident that "the serpent was loose in Eden," while "the New Dealers were not at all a band of brothers, unless we take Cain and Abel as a representative sample of fraternal relations." His reservation, one echoed in other reviews, was that the "outer world is remote." In the *American Historical Review*, Robert E. Burke pointed out that "we must continue to withhold judgment on whether the exclusion of foreign policy for systematic handling in later volumes is worth the cost of a loss in the sense of sequence."[42]

Toward the end of *The Politics of Upheaval*, Schlesinger, in a paean to liberal pragmatism, praised Roosevelt and the New Deal for their "denial of either-or" and "indifference to ideology," which allowed the president "to steer between the extreme of chaos and tyranny." It was in many ways a devious piece of counter-intuition, because "either-or" was precisely what Schlesinger had offered readers of *The Age of Roosevelt*. If his subject in all three volumes had been what he called the "battlefield of ideas," then he knew that his books were an exercise in intellectual warfare in his own times.

That warfare would form the basis of much of the historiographical debate about the books and the New Deal more generally in the years to come, as revisionists rehabilitating the presidencies of Calvin Coolidge and Herbert Hoover took aim at Schlesinger's overtly political worldview. "Schlesinger's selectivity," noted one, T. B. Silvers in *Coolidge and the Historians*, "puts him in the role of a prosecutor who wrenches one damaging remark out of a witness' mouth and then shuts him up before he can say anything else." Yet even among those who disagreed with Schlesinger, or had even been his victim, many recognized that he played an enterprising role within a profession that could often be timid and narrow. "As a historian, Schlesinger is bold, opinionated, somewhat arrogant, and occasionally wrong," ventured Gerald W. Johnson, author of *Andrew Jackson: An Epic in Homespun*. "But at least Schlesinger has the enormous merit of saying something; he is committed to the old-fashioned and perhaps illiberal theory that there is not only a difference, but a perceptible difference between a scoundrel and an honest man, and he never ends a study with the arid recommendation that the subject deserves further study."[43]

Schlesinger knew what he wanted to say, but so too, it appears, did he know when to keep his mouth shut. At the end of volume III, he left Roosevelt enjoying the spoils of victory, looking forward to a second term. Ahead for the historian lay the choppy waters of the "court packing plan" and stunted economic growth along with the foreign policy that had failed to capture Schlesinger's imagination during the Commonwealth Lectures in London.

In the final lines of *The Politics of Upheaval*, Schlesinger quotes the reelected president declaring, "I accept the commission you have tendered me." The same could not be said of Schlesinger himself: he would leave FDR in 1936 and never publish another line in *The Age of Roosevelt* series. The continuation of Schlesinger's grand liberal narrative of American history would require another heroic figure to propel the story into a new age.[44]

CHAPTER ELEVEN

ARE YOU READY TO WORK AT THE WHITE HOUSE?

D *emocratic convention, Los Angeles, July 15, 1960.* "My own pleasure in national politics is coming to an end," Arthur Schlesinger wrote gloomily in his journal that summer. An era was drawing to a close. Inside Adlai Stevenson's suite at the Sheraton-West Hotel, veterans of the '52 and '56 presidential campaigns milled around, making low-key small talk and trying to affect nonchalance in the face of disappointment. "As I saw them there together, I suddenly saw one great reason for Stevenson's failure," Schlesinger wrote. "The Stevenson crowd consisted almost entirely of such nice people." Four days earlier John F. Kennedy had outmaneuvered Stevenson to be the Democratic nominee and then chosen Lyndon B. Johnson as his running mate. These events confirmed the arrival of a new order, signifying the triumph of "the professional" candidate over "the amateur." It was, Schlesinger recognized, "inevitable" that Kennedy should have beaten the two-time presidential loser, but he could not shake the sense that a certain civilized quality "has gone out of national politics."

As for the Kennedy campaign to come, "I don't really much care whether I get into it or not." Certainly he admired JFK's "strength and ability." But the candidate himself, Schlesinger found cold, and the ruthlessness he displayed during the convention ensured that "my affection for him and personal confidence in him have declined." Indeed he dreaded having done too good a job on the senator from Massachusetts. Kennedy, a keen historian, had read the first two volumes of *The Age of Roosevelt* carefully. "I fear he may have learned too well the lesson of the last part of *The Coming of the New Deal*," its author worried. "He has commented to me several times in the past how illuminating he found my discussion of FDR's executive methods. I am quite sure now that Kennedy has most of FDR's lesser qualities. Whether he has FDR's greater qualities is the problem for the future."[1]

Like Schlesinger, "Jack" Kennedy had been born in 1917 and attended Harvard, where the two men should have been classmates. But Arthur had been fast tracked, so rather than join the class of 1940, he found himself the "runt of the litter" in the class of 1938 with Jack's older brother Joe Jr., with whom he had no contact. It is impossible to know whether Schlesinger and the younger Kennedy might have become Harvard friends, although given that Arthur was a brainiac and Jack roomed with college athletes and, said his contemporary, Lem Billings, was "more fun than anyone I've ever known," it seems unlikely. Nevertheless, Arthur's accelerated career meant that in the relationship he always played catch-up socially. Kennedy's Harvard roommate, Jimmy Rousmaniere, believed that loyalty meant everything to Jack, pointing out how he kept close to school friends such as Congressman Torby Macdonald and Billings throughout his life even as he rose to power. Later he would develop another similar circle comprising Kenny O'Donnell, Dave Powers, and Larry O'Brien ("the Irish Brotherhood') in which loyalty was paramount. The relationship, when it did come for Schlesinger, would be of another less visceral, more intellectual kind, and was one that Kennedy himself would acknowledge as important. Reading the book by Theodore White (also Harvard '38), *The Making of the President: 1960* the following year, JFK pointed out the parallel with Schlesinger's "men around the president" in *The Age of Roosevelt*. "When I read your Roosevelt books, I thought what towering figures those men around Roosevelt were," Schlesinger records him saying. "Then I read Teddy's book and realized that they were just [Theodore] Sorensen and [Richard] Goodwin and you." Interestingly, White actually cites Sorensen, Goodwin, and JFK's chief of legislative research, Mike Feldman, as Kennedy's "personal" brain trust, putting Arthur instead in the "academic" brain trust that also included the likes of future national security advisor, Harvard's McGeorge Bundy. Either way, Schlesinger would finally bond with Kennedy, but theirs was essentially a meeting of minds rather than personalities.[2]

Kennedy's enthusiasm for history and historical biography was certainly genuine. Like Schlesinger, it took family connections to publish his Harvard senior thesis, *Why England Slept*, a study of British appeasement in the 1930s. All the same he maintained a keen interest in history throughout his life. "He would read walking, he'd read at the table, at meals, he read after dinner, he'd read in the bathtub," Jacqueline, his wife, would say, recalling how Kennedy each Sunday would circle the new books in the *New York Times Sunday Book Review* that he wanted to read. Schlesinger said of Kennedy, "History was full of heroes for him and he reveled in stately cadences of historical prose. Situations, scenes and quotations stuck in his mind for the rest of his life." Even in the middle of the Democratic race in the summer of 1960, Kennedy would suddenly, but to no one's surprise, compare Lyndon Johnson to the nineteenth-century British prime minister, Sir Robert Peel, both of whom he thought "were omnipotent in Parliament but had no popularity in the country." Kennedy had a particular taste for political biography, with favorites including David Cecil's *The Young Melbourne*, a tale of sexual scandal and high politics, and *John Quincy Adams and the Union* by Samuel Flagg Bemis, the story of a son trying to shake off the legacy of a famous but unpopular father. When asked by a reporter in 1957 what he was reading, he cited *Wilson: The Road to the White House* by Arthur S. Link, and *The Crisis of the Old Order* by Arthur M. Schlesinger Jr.[3]

Kennedy and Schlesinger ran across each other in Washington immediately after the war, usually as part of Joe Alsop's Georgetown dining circle, but it was not until the 1950s that the beginnings of a working relationship emerged. In June 1955, Kennedy, now a senator, told Schlesinger that during recuperation from serious back surgery he had written a book on the political courage of US senators and asked him to read it. "I would certainly be appreciative for whatever you could do to improve its historical accuracy, style and interest, and general contribution," Kennedy wrote, "and if you feel that any or all of these chapters are inadequate, I would be most grateful if you would frankly tell me so."[4]

Schlesinger read what would become *Profiles in Courage* while on vacation that summer. Years afterwards he would write that his "only assistance ... was to suggest some books that he might look at." His actual contribution was more forthright: a 2,000-word manuscript review as if this were a draft by an academic colleague. "I have read your book with great interest and admiration," Schlesinger wrote in early July. "It seems to me, in the main, historically sound, skillfully written and a genuine contribution to political courage." So far, as expected. But among Schlesinger's greatest assets was his ability to speak truth unsparingly to power and influence. He followed with an interrogation of the text that ranged from the correction of factual inaccuracies to criticism of flaws in structure and analysis. He noted, for example, that the chapter on Daniel Webster, one of the eight senators profiled, was "not particularly persuasive to me" for reasons that were outlined, not least that Schlesinger believed in fact that President Zachary Taylor, not Webster, "was right" on the famous Compromise of 1850. Even more problematic was the chapter on Senator Robert A. Taft, who had taken a stand against the Nuremberg Trials for trying Nazi war criminals under ex post facto laws. "I am not persuaded by this chapter at all," Schlesinger wrote. "The Taft incident took place elsewhere [outside the Senate]. For another, I find it hard to recollect Taft's doing anything else which required political courage. . . . He showed no courage at all in the face of McCarthy." This last comment, perhaps innocently delivered, must have stung, as it was a criticism often thrown at the Kennedys about McCarthyism. (Patriarch Joe Sr. was friends with McCarthy; JFK's brother Bobby briefly worked for him; their sisters Eunice, Pat, and Jean went on dates with him; and Jack would be the only Democratic senator not to call for McCarthy's censure in 1954, a fact he explained away by citing convalescence from back surgery.) Concluding, Schlesinger noted that he had "put my doubts about the Webster and Taft chapters in strong language to save time, and because I know you would like these doubts to be expressed vigorously while there is still time." But, he added, "it is your book and you cannot expect to please every reader!"[5]

Kennedy replied effusively, thanking Schlesinger for "your very helpful comments and corrections," and saying that "I have, to the extent possible, followed every one of your suggestions, and they were of considerable help in sharpening the manuscript." Specific changes included making it clear in chapters where "there is disagreement as to whether their position was necessarily the right one" and an effort "to eliminate some of the overstatement." Kennedy concluded warmly with "sincere thanks for your very real help." The tone of the letter and the detailed response and changes Kennedy made suggest genuine gratitude. However, Schlesinger's "strong language to save time" may have annoyed Ted Sorensen, the coauthor. Even though only Kennedy's name appeared on the title page of *Profiles in Courage*, the book was a collaborative work with Sorensen, who was JFK's assistant and speechwriter. "JFK worked particularly hard and long on the first and last chapters, setting the tone and philosophy of the book," Sorensen would recall, "I did a first draft of most chapters, which he revised with a pen and through dictation." When Kennedy sent Schlesinger the manuscript, the senator noted, "unfortunately, I have not yet completed the introductory and concluding chapter." The first draft that Schlesinger was reading was likely as much Sorensen's as Kennedy's. Thus when Arthur replied, thinking that he was speaking truth to power, he was in fact speaking truth to a staffer, and one, moreover, with a reputation for intellectual arrogance and a thin skin.

Schlesinger's tone, pitch perfect for a senator, had taken apart a staffer's work in front of his boss. Sorensen and Schlesinger would go on to have a prickly relationship, as each strove to be Kennedy's premier intellectual influence (Sorensen was closer to JFK; Schlesinger, as a Harvard professor and Pulitzer Prize–winning author, more distinguished). That rivalry would continue even after the president's assassination in 1963 as each competed to write the first and definitive insider's account of Kennedy's life and work. It is no stretch to see the roots of this long-standing rivalry in the letter that Schlesinger sent Kennedy after reading Sorensen's first draft of *Profiles in Courage*.[6]

Kennedy continually turned to Schlesinger for historical advice during the 1950s, including working closely with him as chair of a special committee to choose five senators whose portraits would be placed in the Senate Reception Room. Politically, however, the relationship took longer to gel. Freed by Stevenson after the 1956 defeat, Schlesinger gently played the field among Democrats who were considering a run in 1960. There were the early meetings with Lyndon Johnson, who wanted Schlesinger to help him be "sensitive to liberal criticism." As late as February 1960, Johnson was still writing, "I hope you will continue to let me have the splendid products of your wonderful mind and deft hand." Schlesinger also enjoyed friendly relations with Hubert Humphrey, the liberal senator from Minnesota, for whom he occasionally wrote speeches, including a highly successful one delivered at the 1960 Jefferson-Jackson Day Dinner. And all the time, there remained the seemingly perennial question of Adlai.[7]

Over Christmas 1959, on the eve of the primary season, the "Hamlet" of the Democratic Party was still worrying away about whether he needed to issue a statement saying that "if the convention wants me, I could not, of course, decline the nomination." Patiently Schlesinger warned against such a statement, explaining that it "would only magnify the impression of coyness."[8]

Dealing with the Stevenson problem is how Schlesinger became useful to Kennedy. In the lead-up to the campaign, Kennedy had certainly made an effort to court Schlesinger, inviting him and his family to Hyannis Port ("less grand than I had imagined") for sailing and political gossip. Schlesinger found him "exceedingly open," enjoying what, he recorded in the summer of 1959, "was, indeed, the freest, as well as the longest talk I have ever had with him." Once the primary season got underway, however, the two men were only occasionally in touch, so it was not until May, with Kennedy ahead but not by enough, that Schlesinger came into play. On May 14 the candidate phoned Schlesinger to ask him to intercede with Stevenson. "He does not see why Stevenson won't help him," Schlesinger recorded. Clearly neither did Arthur, because the following day he went to Libertyville, Illinois, to see Stevenson. Would the governor support Kennedy? he asked. Stevenson tried to wriggle off the hook. "It would look as if I were jumping on the bandwagon," he protested. "It would look as if I were angling for a job." But would you at least let Kennedy come see you?" Arthur pressed. Stevenson reluctantly agreed. The meeting a week later was a disaster. "AES did not intend to do anything for the moment,"

Schlesinger noted. "Jack said that he was not much impressed by AES's account of why he did not wish to act; but supposed this to be because he did not wish to disclose his real reason—that, if he said nothing, there might still be a possibility that he would emerge out of the scramble as the candidate."[9]

Kennedy may not have convinced Stevenson, but he had converted Schlesinger. "I have come, I think, to the private conclusion that I would rather have Kennedy as President," Arthur confided to his journal at the beginning of June. "Stevenson is a much richer, more thoughtful, more creative person; but he has been away from power too long; he gives me an odd sense of unreality." Kennedy, in contrast, "gives a sense of cool, measured, intelligent concern with action and power." But, Schlesinger added, "I cannot mention this feeling to anyone."[10]

In the end, Schlesinger agreed that he would come out for Kennedy in a public letter that would include his friends John Kenneth Galbraith, Joseph Rauh, and Henry Steele Commager. But the announcement was woefully bungled, leading to extreme distress and embarrassment for Schlesinger. On June 5, Adlai Stevenson stayed overnight with the Schlesingers in Cambridge, during which visit the governor expressed his feeling that "talk from the Kennedy camp" about him was "quite aggravating." Schlesinger by and large was not politically deceitful, his views often expressed unsparingly in the face of personal relationships. That summer, for example, he would infuriate Felix Frankfurter, whom he had known since childhood, for the way in which he characterized the associate justice's behavior on the Supreme Court in *The Politics of Upheaval*. But on this occasion, for whatever reasons of embarrassment or last-minute indecision, he declined to inform Stevenson of his thinking. Only forty-eight hours later, the *Chicago Sun-Times* in Stevenson's home state broke the story that Schlesinger and other "eggheads" were jumping ship. "I felt sick about it," Arthur wrote, "and still feel guilty and sad." He issued a public statement saying that Stevenson was best qualified to be candidate, but as the governor was not a candidate, he was supporting Kennedy. He also wrote to Stevenson, who replied "rather casually, I thought; a little cool and hurt?" (Stevenson would write graciously on June 13 to Marian, however, who had stayed loyal to him, that "I am distressed by all that has happened, and that I should be the cause of any embarrassment to Arthur whom I love as dearly as ever.") Schlesinger would continue to think that "Kennedy, with his cool, sharp mind and his Rooseveltian political genius, would be the better president," but he admitted to feeling "guilty and unhappy over appearing to abandon AES," not least when Stevenson's candidacy briefly sparked as some Democrats got cold feet about Kennedy's youth and Catholicism. All told, Arthur reflected wearily, "Politics requires a toughness in human relations which in this case I find hard to achieve." No wonder he left for the Democratic convention in Los Angeles that July "with considerable trepidation and in considerable bafflement," not least with a harangue from Marian, still a Stevenson loyalist, ringing in his ears. "Can't you control your own wife," Bobby Kennedy teased, "or are you like me?"[11]

It was the second time that Schlesinger had felt buyer's remorse with Jack Kennedy. In 1956, Kennedy reported to his father about the vice presidential nomination, "Arthur Schlesinger wrote to me yesterday and stated that he thought it should be done and that he was going to do everything that possible he could." Yet at the convention that summer Arthur had found himself "shouting wildly for Kefauver." Now in 1960, he harbored similar doubts, even wondering whether Kennedy had duped him both politically and personally. "I believe him to be a liberal, but committed by a sense of history rather than consecrated by inner conviction," he wrote grandly, returning to the pseudo-religious language of *The Age of Roosevelt*. "I also believe him to be a devious and, if necessary ruthless man. I rather think, for example, that Ken [Galbraith] and I were in a sense had by him; that he sought our support when he considered it useful before the convention to have liberal Democratic names behind him, but that, if he thinks our names would cause the slightest trouble when he starts appealing to Republicans, he will drop us without a second thought."[12]

Certainly that was the tenor of a piece run in the August 29 edition of *Newsweek*, which reported that Schlesinger was "hurt" by Kennedy's failure to use his speeches and that relations between the two men were "strained." Schlesinger immediately wrote a letter for publication refuting the story as "not true" and deprecating the impression that the rumors had come from him. "To invent statements of a defamatory sort and then to attribute them to the person defamed is enterprising but hardly responsible journalism," he fumed. Yet while the story may have overstated the case, the essential point that Schlesinger, and the liberals more broadly, felt excluded was on the mark. Writing to Kennedy after an ADA national board meeting to pick a presidential endorsement, Schlesinger reported, "I was prepared for apathy on the part of grassroots liberals. I was not prepared for the depth of hostility which evidently exists." He then went on unsparingly to catalogue that hostility in great detail, freely admitting to JFK that "It may be that after this you won't want to hear anything from me for the rest of the campaign, which I would wholly understand."[13]

In fact, Kennedy did the opposite and sought Schlesinger out, inviting him to the Cape and generally treating him "with his usual affability" and "utmost cordiality." Others within the campaign, however, took great care to keep Schlesinger at arm's length that fall. Ted Sorensen, Schlesinger would later write, "had come to feel that no one knew the candidate's mind so well or reproduced his idiom so accurately [and], justifiably proud of his special relationship, he tended to resent interlopers." Schlesinger was not the only unwelcome gatecrasher, as Archibald Cox, the Harvard law professor whom Kennedy had asked to head up his Brain Trust, discovered. Cox complained bitterly about Sorensen's unwillingness to use any of the material his thirty or so academic writers generated for the campaign trail. "It was one of the few elements of discord within the campaign," Sorensen would later admit. To get around the Sorensen problem, Schlesinger at the beginning of October sought out John Bartlow Martin, his old Elks Club compatriot from the '52 and '56 campaigns, to ask for advice about his position. Martin, a less prickly character than Schlesinger, had reached an accommodation with Sorensen, providing JFK's principal speechwriter with the kind of "editorial advance" for speeches that he had pioneered for Stevenson in 1956. Now he urged Schlesinger to find a similar compromise. Sorensen had asked Arthur to submit drafts for major speeches, such as the Al Smith Memorial Dinner at the Waldorf-Astoria Hotel, New York, on October 19, but "it was evident," Schlesinger complained, "he wanted them done at a distance." Such speeches could not be "written in a vacuum," Schlesinger told Martin, so he was going to say no and "apply myself to other things." Martin urged him to hold fire and comply with Sorensen's request on the grounds that eventually as "fatigue caught up with them, they would need more outside help, and I would be the logical person to join them."[14]

Schlesinger took Martin's advice and wrote the Al Smith speech, but eventually he felt compelled to raise the matter directly with Kennedy at a meeting in the candidate's duplex apartment in The Carlyle in mid-October. "We talked a bit about my situation," Schlesinger recorded afterward. "Jack said that this had to be looked at coolly. He would like me along—might need me, since his own people were getting tired and running out of ideas—but there would be certain publicity reactions which had to be taken into account. He feared that my joining the group would be played up as 'Kennedy's team is collapsing and Stevenson's ace speech writer is coming to take over.'" His suggestion in the end was purely pragmatic. "Ted is indispensable to me," he told Arthur, but if you want to get material to me directly, "communicate through Jacqueline." It was, Arthur wrote later, a channel designed "to simplify his relations with immediate staff." That October he would soon be taking regular calls "from Jackie Kennedy (who seems to have become my channel of communication with the candidate) . . . [saying] Jack had asked her to call me." It was the beginning of a relationship that would be accepted by all parties as another direct means of access not just to the candidate but shortly thereafter to the president.[15]

In the end, perhaps Schlesinger's most important contribution to the campaign was not any speech, but rather the production of a short book, *Kennedy or Nixon: Does It Make Any Difference?*, which became an immediate bestseller. The aim of the book was simple: to dispel "the favorite cliché of 1960" that the two candidates "are essentially the same sort of men, stamped from the same mold, committed to the same values, dedicated to the same objectives—that they are, so to speak, the Gold Dust Twins of American politics."[16]

Kennedy or Nixon touched on differences of party and policy, but around two-thirds of the book focused on the central issue of comparing the two candidates as men. The likes of Eric Sevareid, one of Ed Murrow's "boys" at CBS, had complained that "The managerial revolution has come to politics and Nixon and Kennedy are its first completely packaged products. The Processed Politician has finally arrived." It may have been true, Schlesinger conceded, that both men "take a cool, professional pleasure in politics for its own sake," but "beyond this, Kennedy and Nixon seem to me vastly different in their interests, their skills, and their motivations."[17]

The portrait he drew of Nixon showed Schlesinger writing at his most brilliant and polemical best. The Republican was "unique among major American politicians of this century" because his "name invokes no substantive position at all." He was "in his way, a serious political personality; yet he stands for almost nothing." His qualities were those of "an almost disembodied alertness and intelligence." And, Schlesinger went on, "Because [Nixon] has no political philosophy, he has no sense of history . . . he is disembodied, not only in relation to any inward substance of conviction, but also in relation to the past experience of his own country." He was "a lonely man" who lacked "an instinct for dignity—for one's own dignity, and for the dignity of others." The key to Nixon was "provided by the word to which he has been long devoted—the word 'image.' " Nixon was "not a bad man." He would "make a better president than men like [Barry] Goldwater," but, echoing T. S. Eliot, "he remains a strangely hollow man." And what happens, Schlesinger asks, "to such a man in the moment of stark crisis when public issues become irreducible and nothing can meet them except a rock-bottom philosophy of politics and life?"[18]

Kennedy on the other hand "could hardly be more different" from Nixon. "If both men appear at times cool in their attitude toward issues," Schlesinger suggests, "this is, I would say, because Kennedy reasons about them and Nixon doesn't much care." Kennedy possessed "a genuine, rather than a manipulative, interest in issues and ideas." While not "precisely an intellectual himself, [like] Franklin D. Roosevelt, he can enjoy the company of intellectuals with perfect confidence in his capacity to hold his own." His habits of thought were "unusually detached, consecutive, and explicit." His mind was "a first class instrument, strong, supple

ARTHUR MEIER SCHLESINGER, JR.

CAMBRIDGE, MASS.

"Art."

Entered Upper Middle Year; Winter Track Squad (2); *The Exonian* (2), Associate Editor, Alumni Editor; Golden Branch Literary Society (2); Herodotan Society; Honor Man, First Group (2); Honor Man, Second Group; Bandler Latin Prize (Honorable Mention); Pennell Prize; Bandler Latin Prize; College Preference, Harvard.

"Think of school as an opportunity for future advancement": At Phillips Exeter Academy (class of 1933). *(Phillips Exeter Academy Archives, Class of 1945 Library)*

The Schlesinger clan, 1950s. Back row (left to right): Arthur Jr., Ban and Tom (AMS Jr.'s brother and sister-in-law), Marian (AMS Jr.'s wife), Stephen (AMS Jr.'s son). Sitting (left to right): Susan (Tom's daughter), Elizabeth (AMS Jr.'s mother), Christina (AMS Jr.'s daughter), Katharine (AMS Jr.'s daughter), Arthur Sr., and Andrew (AMS Jr.'s son). *(Steve Schlesinger)*

"I am betting on you!": With Arthur Sr., Harvard, 1958.
(*Burt Glinn / Magnum Photos*)

"History depends on who writes it":
With John F. Kennedy in the Oval Office, July 1962.
(*Cecil Stoughton / JFK Library*)

The darker side of Camelot? With Bobby Kennedy, Marilyn Monroe, and JFK at a birthday party for the president in New York, May 1962. (*Cecil Stoughton / JFK Library*)

"As I was standing on the side of the crowd, a man brushed by. It was
Lyndon Johnson." The new president addresses the nation at Andrews Field,
November 22, 1963, with Schlesinger, far left of picture.
(*Cecil Stoughton / JFK Library*)

"By far the hardest thing I have ever tried": in his D.C. office making final changes to the manuscript of *A Thousand Days*, July 1965.
(*Arnold Newman / Getty Images*)

With Jackie Kennedy, January 1967. "It takes wings,"
she wrote of *A Thousand Days*, "and when you read it—Jack is alive again."
(*Bettmann / Getty Images*)

Alexandra and Arthur Schlesinger at the second annual Robert F. Kennedy
Pro-Celebrity Tennis Tournament, 1973. (*Ron Galella / Getty Images*)

Pundit: Schlesinger making his point
during the taping of *The David Susskind Show*, 1979.
(*Bettmann / Getty Images*)

and disciplined." He was not faultless: "Kennedy's record on McCarthy, as I told him at the time, seemed to me discreditable." But the experience had provoked in him a process of clarification about "his conception of the place of individual freedom and due process in a democracy." So while Kennedy may not have been with them by instinct, Schlesinger reassured his liberal readers, "Today he seems to me a committed liberal." This allegiance had come through "intellectual analysis" rather than "spontaneous visceral reactions in the usual pattern of American liberals. . . . But his conclusions are no less solidly grounded or less firmly held."

In terms of style, too, the candidates could hardly have been more different. While Nixon "imports histrionics into politics" with "vulgar rhetoric" and he "even weeps," Kennedy's manner was by contrast "studiously unemotional, impersonal, antihistrionic." Taken together, it meant that Kennedy and Nixon stood "in sharp contrast" to each other, leaving voters with a decision about whether the country should "muddle along" or "recover control over our national destiny." For Nixon "the Presidency seems essentially a source of private gratification." For Kennedy it was "a means of public achievement." That was the real choice of character facing the people in the election of 1960.[19]

The success of Schlesinger's pamphlet threw the Nixon campaign into a panic. Wealthy Republican donors immediately banded together to set up Free World Press just to publish a hastily written rejoinder, *John F. Kennedy: What's Behind the Image?* by Victor Lasky, a former journalist at the *New York World-Telegram and Sun* who had previously written a book about the Alger Hiss case. "The Nixon camp had all this material," Lasky told the *New York Times*, going off message. "They could have done this months ago." The impetus, Lasky said, "came last month" after publication of Schlesinger's "pro-Kennedy analysis, *Kennedy or Nixon: Does it make any difference?*" The *Times* called Lasky's book a "literary attack on Senator Kennedy and his family," quoting him as saying that the Democrat was "everything that the liberals say Nixon is," and adding intemperately that the candidate's brother and campaign manager, Robert F. Kennedy, was "a fascist." Schlesinger himself came under attack in the book as "Kennedy's leading apologist among intellectuals" and the "liberal demonologist" author of "an agit-prop-like contribution to the Kennedy cause." The Nixon campaign immediately handed out copies at events and press conferences. But published on November 1, the book was too late to counter Schlesinger's narrative. Between *John F. Kennedy: What's Behind the Image?* and *Nixon or Kennedy,* clearly it was Arthur Schlesinger who made the biggest difference.[20]

"No political leader can guarantee anything, and no one can guarantee any political leader," Schlesinger had concluded at the end of *Nixon or Kennedy,* "but the election of Kennedy, like that of Wilson in 1912 and Franklin Roosevelt in 1932, would plainly keep open vital options in our life." The question for Schlesinger himself was whether he had done enough in the campaign to keep open vital options in his own life. Looked at in the fall of 1960, a best-selling book and regular phone calls with the candidate's wife seemed to add up to a most vexatious and disappointing campaign. The only light relief came when William Buckley, iconoclastic founder of *National Review,* had a "Democratic" real donkey sent to Schlesinger at 109 Irving Street accompanied by a caustic note about *Kennedy or Nixon.* Marian Schlesinger, thinking on her feet, had it sent back on the grounds that their underage son had signed for delivery; Buckley thereafter kept the animal and named it "Arthur." Practical jokes aside, having been a central figure in 1952 and 1956, Schlesinger was only too aware that he had been marginal this time around. "I was sorry, of course, not to have taken a greater part in the campaign," he recorded despondently in his journal at the election's conclusion. "I love the drama of campaigning—the airplanes and motorcades, the hotel rooms and telephone calls and speeches crises, the policy conferences and the tense decisions and the constant air of excitement and anxiety and passion and fatigue. I missed it all terribly." Only now did Schlesinger the academic understand the extent to which he had developed a near addiction to the narcotic of political battle.[21]

An anxious period followed as he waited to see if a job was in the offing. Always somewhat highly strung, he was plagued by his shredded nerves, particularly when it looked as if Kennedy was shunning liberals and appointing a predominantly conservative administration. Dining with his friend Philip Graham in Washington, DC, on November 16, he completely lost his temper when Graham was "euphorically insistent" on Douglas Dillon as secretary of the treasury. "Phil and I had our first serious wrangle in years," Schlesinger wrote, "and I left for the airport in a state of extreme irritation." Graham "charmingly" phoned the next day to make up, but it was Dillon, a Republican who had served in the Eisenhower administration, who got the Treasury job.[22]

Schlesinger was no more reassured about the prospects of liberals in the Kennedy administration when he finally saw the president-elect again in December. There were a few minutes of awkwardness as the unathletic professor attempted to throw a football with three-year-old Caroline ("The Kennedys apparently believe in breaking them in early") before matters turned to senior political appointments. One by one, JFK batted away Schlesinger's suggestions, including Averell Harriman, who had been on the phone to Arthur a great deal in the previous weeks. ("Too old hat," Kennedy said dismissively.) JFK did try to reassure him that liberals "shouldn't worry" as "we are going down the line on the program." But then came the killer punch. "How about you?" Kennedy asked. "Wouldn't you like to be an ambassador?" When Schlesinger quickly responded that he didn't think so, Kennedy joked that he would like to be one himself, but then put the question again: "Are you sure you wouldn't want one?" Schlesinger held his ground, repeating that he "didn't think so" (carefully constructed so as not to absolutely refuse an incoming president), but it was a deeply dispiriting and disquieting experience. Afterwards, he reflected that Kennedy had torpedoed the liberals. "My broad impression is that he is much more on the defensive," Schlesinger recorded, and "much more impressed, for example, by the need to appoint people who will get along with a conservative Congress." He listed all the names of liberals who had been overlooked for cabinet positions, and added sadly, "Hence (perhaps) the desire to export Galbraith [who had been offered the ambassadorship to India] and Schlesinger."[23]

After two weeks of anxious thumb-twiddling and marking Harvard term papers, Schlesinger finally got a hint that a place might still be found for him in the White House. On December 15, the day before the new president announced his brother as attorney general, Bobby Kennedy took Schlesinger to lunch. "As we were chatting," Arthur recalled, "he abruptly asked me what I intended to do for my country." Flustered, Schlesinger mentioned that there had been mention of an ambassadorship, which prospect had not "attracted me much." RFK then asked whether it would be okay "if he suggested to his brother that I come down as a Special Assistant to the President and serve as a sort of roving reporter and trouble shooter." Schlesinger could not hide his relief and excitement. "I would of course be delighted to come," he enthused, saying that the "assignment could not have appealed to me more." Kennedy promised to bring it up with his brother, telling Schlesinger that he would "probably" hear from JFK in the new year.[24]

Bobby's idea thrilled Schlesinger. For one brief moment it looked as if the job might even be better. Just after Christmas, Galbraith went down to see JFK at Kennedy's winter house in Palm Beach, Florida, and came back reporting that Schlesinger was being considered for national security advisor. A few days later, the job went to their Harvard colleague, McGeorge Bundy. "This is all right," Arthur told Marietta Tree, clearly disingenuously, despite his having had no previous interest or expertise in national security issues. Earlier in the letter, he had complained about those who were "Democrats and actively worked for the Kennedy-Johnson ticket" being overlooked, and thought any young person "might well conclude that they will have a better chance for preferment under a Democratic administration if they remain Republicans or neutralists." Bundy was precisely such a person: a Republican until 1960, he had voted twice against Stevenson and played no role in Kennedy's campaign in 1960 other than endorsing him. But as dean of arts at Harvard and part of a family that had a long tradition in foreign affairs, his was the kind of appointment Schlesinger identified as "designed to win applause in the respectable press." Kennedy had discussed several assistant secretary positions at the State Department with him before finally offering administrative affairs. Bundy turned the post down, partly on the advice of his Harvard colleague, Henry Kissinger, who warned him, "You don't want that." Kennedy then offered Bundy the position as national security advisor, thereby trumping his other Harvard colleague, Arthur Schlesinger. "He was so good that when he left I grieved for Harvard and I grieved for the nation," commented one colleague, the Harvard sociologist David Riesman, "for Harvard because he was the perfect dean, for the nation because I thought that very same arrogance and hubris might be very dangerous."[25]

At least Bundy's elevation gave Schlesinger a lesson in how to play his own cards. Once Bundy was appointed, word now came through that Kennedy wanted to offer Schlesinger an assistant secretaryship at the State Department, putting him in charge of cultural affairs. Schlesinger promptly turned it down, which brought another message from Kennedy saying that "he didn't mean the State Dept idea too seriously, that he is still thinking of me in terms of the White House." More concretely, Kennedy told him that "he wants to talk about it" during a planned visit to Cambridge on January 9, 1961.[26]

That meeting would turn out to be one of the political high points of Schlesinger's life. Kennedy was coming to Cambridge to address the Massachusetts Legislature and to attend a meeting of the Harvard Board of Overseers. He didn't want to hold political meetings inside the university, so Fred Holborn, Kennedy's legislative assistant and soon to be special assistant to the White House, asked Schlesinger if they could use his house.

"This was an exciting day for the Schlesingers," Arthur recorded in his journal. "Secret service men vetted the house; Harvard and Cambridge police surrounded it; and around 2 p.m. a small crowd of curiosity seekers and fans began to collect." Kennedy arrived at 2:20 p.m. "Inside," Marian Schlesinger recalled, "he shook hands with members of the household shyly lined up in awe to greet him, various children and their lucky best pals, and two sweet Irish cleaning women." Then he went into the living room, "sat on the couch" and began interviewing people. At one stage during the afternoon, Kennedy needed to use the telephone privately, so Arthur sent him upstairs to the room into which, it turned out, Marian had "thrown all the general refuse of the family," thinking no one, "much less a future president of the United States," would venture. "He was so charming," Marian recalls, "so outgoing and friendly." He could "not have cared less" that she had been "found out."[27]

During the course of the afternoon, various Harvard people arrived to see the new president. Mac Bundy rode his bike, which he nonchalantly left propped against the gate. Others, including Schlesinger, were less cocksure. But during a brief lull in the proceedings, Kennedy turned to his host and finally asked the question Arthur had been waiting to hear: "Are you ready to work at the White House?" Schlesinger was suitably modest, telling Kennedy, "I am not sure what I would be doing as Special Assistant, but if you think I can help, I would like very much to come." Kennedy, with that charming lightness of touch that was already a trademark of his political style, replied, "Well, I am not sure what I will be doing as President either, but I am sure there will be enough at the White House to keep us both busy." Schlesinger asked if he should now formally apply for leave at Harvard; Kennedy told him to wait until after Chester Bowles was confirmed as assistant secretary of state for political affairs, as "I don't want the Senate to think that I am bringing down the whole ADA." That meant Schlesinger being kept at arm's length until after the inauguration; most tellingly, Kennedy did not ask Schlesinger to work on the inaugural address, which he planned to finalize in the coming week. That left Arthur in Cambridge quite literally in the cold.[28]

Another anxious period of waiting followed. Arthur and Marian went to Washington to watch the inauguration. At a party given by Kennedy's sister, Jean Smith, the new president asked them cheerfully whether they had found a house in Washington yet, a remark, Arthur wrote, that "gave me some relief, because I had heard nothing about my supposed White House appointment since the talk in my house in Cambridge three weeks earlier." He returned disconsolately to Harvard, now thinking about the semester ahead, as "silence resumed" from the White House. Only at the end of January did the call finally come through. The Senate had confirmed Bowles's appointment, so now the president wanted to announce Schlesinger's own appointment. He should call Ralph Dungan, the special assistant in charge of personnel.

"Your appointment as what?" Dungan asked him when he called.

"As I understand it, Special Assistant to the President," Schlesinger replied, exasperated.

"That's the first I've heard of it," Dungan retorted unhelpfully, but told him to report the next Monday anyway.[29]

By the time Schlesinger arrived at the White House on Monday, January 30, 1961, Dungan had recovered himself sufficiently to apologize. "Things are happening so fast around here," he said, "that no one knows what is going on."

Dungan then called in Richard Neustadt, the author of *Presidential Power*, who had held the same position under Harry Truman and was now advising Kennedy, and together the two men stood with Schlesinger as he swore his oath of office as special assistant to the president. It was a remarkable point not just in the arc of Schlesinger's ambition but in that of the 1917 generation. Here was one of its brightest intellectual stars, Harvard luminary, Pulitzer Prize winner, and best-selling writer Arthur Schlesinger, joining forces as a Camelot insider with his generation's leading political light. A Thousand Days had begun.

CHAPTER TWELVE

THE GADFLY

"I settled down in an office in the East Wing of the White House and tried to find out what I was supposed to do," wrote newly minted Special Assistant to the President Arthur Schlesinger Jr. at the end of his first week. "I had the impression that JFK was equally baffled, and he had somewhat more weighty matters on his mind." It was, Schlesinger would later recall, an "uncertain and confusing" beginning.[1]

Schlesinger's own confusion about his role in the White House reflected a debate that would rumble on for several decades among Kennedy staffers and loyalists: What exactly had been the professor's influence within the White House, at least compared to their own? Certainly some staffers were irritated from the outset when Richard Rovere, Schlesinger's coauthor of *The General and the President*, wrote a profile in the *New Yorker* that installed his friend as "court philosopher" at the White House. "It is an extraordinary assignment, and one that has no precedent in American history," Rovere enthused, "or, probably," he went on, overstretching the image, "in the history of any modern democracy."

Others later would offer a more sour assessment. Press secretary Pierre Salinger dismissed Schlesinger as "not a policy maker" and suggested his "official role was that of White House liaison with United Nations Ambassador Adlai Stevenson." The location of Schlesinger's office in the East Wing of the White House offered evidence that Schlesinger was a peripheral figure (even though McGeorge Bundy was installed even further away in the Executive Office Building). After all, as a popular TV series later dramatized, the action was in the West Wing. Salinger sneered that the "calmer atmosphere he must have found more congenial to his cerebrations." Another staffer contemptuously recalled, "You have to understand that *Arthur* was over in the *East Wing*, drinking tea with *Jackie*," not realizing, presumably, that Kennedy had instructed Schlesinger to use the First Lady as a way to circumvent the kind of toxic jealousies so perfectly illustrated by that petty remark. Even so, the room allocation stung. "He complained a little bit," Christina Schlesinger, his daughter, recalls. "His office was in the East Wing and, as you know, the West Wing is where everything was happening."[2]

Still, Schlesinger was habitually in conversation with the president, usually at the end of each day, when part of his job was to round up issues from across the board to make sure that Kennedy knew what he needed to know. A memo written a month after Schlesinger moved into the White House, unimportant for its details, gives a vivid insight into how this function worked.

"These are the points left over from last night," Schlesinger wrote on March 6, 1961:

1. You wanted to tell Adlai Stevenson to talk to Dr. Nkrumah [president of Ghana] and get some idea what Nkrumah means to say in the UN tomorrow.
2. Bolivia: check Stepansky—what is holding his [ambassadorial] appointment up? If there is a problem, consider the possibility of shifting Loeb from Peru to Bolivia.
3. Israel: what has happened to inspection of atomic installation?
4. Egypt: what about the plan to save the ruins at Assuan.
5. Iran: letter to the Shah.
6. You wanted to talk to Rostow [deputy national security advisor] about organizing a citizens committee on the foreign aid program.
7. Eisenhower-Khrushchev minutes: you wanted to circulate?

Two other points:

1. George McGovern is holding a Food for Peace press conference
   this afternoon to discuss our Latin American trip. He wants
   me to appear with him . . .
2. Is there anything you want me to do about the electoral commission? I have been in touch with Dick Neustadt . . .[3]

Speechwriting was among Schlesinger's other duties. Not the least of
the sensitivities to navigate here concerned Ted Sorensen, the president's
principal speechwriter. If a draft speech was unsatisfactory, Kennedy
might give it to Schlesinger, but, recalls Richard Goodwin (Sorensen's
embattled deputy), he would say, "Rework this a little, but don't tell Ted
I asked you." Sorensen always fought hard to keep his rival away from
speech drafts. He later claimed Schlesinger's most important role, as well
as being "a source of innovation, ideas and occasional speeches" (note the
subtle dig of the qualifying adjective), was to act as a "constant contact
with liberals and intellectuals both in this country and abroad."

Kennedy's own attitude toward Schlesinger was often more difficult
to gauge. Evelyn Lincoln, who as the president's personal assistant saw life
in the Oval Office close up, judged that Kennedy "admired Schlesinger's
brilliant mind, his enormous store of information, and his ability to turn
a phrase," but felt that "Schlesinger was never more than an ally and assistant." Robert Kennedy said, "He didn't do a helluva lot, but he was good
to have around."

David Halberstam in *The Best and the Brightest* also says Kennedy
appointed Schlesinger to assuage the disappointed Stevenson Democrats,
and to gain credibility with the liberals whom he disdained as elitist and
ineffectual. Schlesinger often worried that Kennedy was no liberal; certainly the president was easily irritated by those such as Chester Bowles
and Adlai Stevenson within his own administration, who were liberals.
"Boy, when those liberals start mixing into policy," Ben Bradlee recalled
the president complaining, "it's murder." Schlesinger became an important *via media* for the White House with "those liberals" because, unlike
most of them, Schlesinger believed Kennedy's tactic was to use conserva-

tive figures "to execute a liberal policy." Moreover, if he was an ambassador to the liberals outside the administration, inside it his roving role was to be the in-house liberal who acted, in the words of Patrick Anderson, a press secretary to Robert Kennedy, as "an intellectual gadfly, skitting here and there to seek out new ideas and sting the slothful bureaucratic beast into action."[4]

Yet while Kennedy sometimes ignored Schlesinger's policy advice, as will become clear, the president, far from being "baffled," actually seemed to have a very clear idea about why he wanted Schlesinger around. "He wanted to be remembered as a great President," Anderson again points out, "and he therefore thought it was wise to have in attendance a great historian." Kennedy often commented to Sorensen, "history depends on who writes it." As a Harvard professor and Pulitzer Prize–winning author of two vast histories of Democratic presidents, and moreover, a contemporary who had abandoned Stevenson to come out for Kennedy at a crucial moment, Arthur had credentials for the job that were second to none.[5]

Schlesinger, predictably, took the historian's role seriously. Writing to Carl Bridenbaugh, a distinguished colonial historian, Schlesinger explained, "My primary commitment is to writing and scholarship and I hate the thought of suspending work on the Roosevelt series," he disclosed. "On the other hand, no American historian has had the good luck to be able to watch an unfolding of public policy from this particular vantage point, and I did not feel I could decline such an opportunity." In *The Age of Roosevelt*, he had recounted how Robert F. Sherwood, FDR's speechwriter and later author of the Pulitzer Prize–winning *Roosevelt and Hopkins: An Intimate History*, had struggled to fathom FDR, commenting, "I could never really understand what was going on in there." Now Schlesinger, believing that he could succeed where Sherwood failed, wanted the new president to give future historians the strongest possible lead.[6]

When, within days of Schlesinger's arrival, Kennedy raised with him the question of which papers a president might properly take away at the end of his presidency, the new special assistant used the opportunity to write him a three-page memo on the importance of maintaining the historical record—in effect a mission statement. "The answer is that you are expected to take away *all* your papers," Schlesinger began, pointing out that while cabinet members could establish a distinction between personal and public papers, "it is not feasible to establish such a distinction in the case of the President [because] the various aspects of Presidential personality are not easily separable, and even his most official acts are sufficiently tinged with his private personality to rate as personal papers." President Eisenhower, for example, had "removed everything except a few routine files." Writing the history of the Kennedy administration, Schlesinger went on, would depend on two fundamental points.[7]

First, "It is obviously essential that the Presidential files contain as near as possible to a full record." Schlesinger had been involved in helping draw up a new White House Filing Manual. Critical to its success, however, was the question of Kennedy's handwritten notes and instructions. "Mrs. Lincoln should be asked never to mail a handwritten letter without making a xerox copy for the files," he urged, "and she should always copy handwritten postscripts on the carbons of typed letters." A similar procedure was needed for times when "someone brings you a paper, you write 'OK, JFK,' and he takes it away." "All this," Schlesinger urged the president, "is for your own protection as well as for the historical record." (In July 1962, Kennedy would take that advice one step further by installing a tape system in the Oval Office, but not to Arthur's knowledge.)

Second, the question arose over "kiss and tell" accounts of the administration. "I think you should make it clear to anyone who seems to have a literary glint in his eye that you expect nothing will be written about the Kennedy administration without prior discussion with you," Schlesinger urged. This latter point also gave him the opportunity to clarify his own position. "As for myself, I might add that I do not regard myself as being here on an historical mission," he told Kennedy, somewhat ingenuously. "I have no work of contemporary history under contemplation, except to finish *The Age of Roosevelt*; and that, unless you wish me to do so, I plan nothing personally in the way of collecting materials on the Age of Kennedy."

On this second point, Kennedy soon put Schlesinger right during an exchange the two men had after the Bay of Pigs invasion a few weeks later. Kennedy agreed that he did not want aides recording White House conversations and keeping diaries, but in Schlesinger's case, that was to be his most important job. "We'd better make sure we have a record over here," Kennedy instructed, "so you go ahead." From then on, Schlesinger would keep 8x4–inch cards in his pocket wherever he went, transferring his notes to foolscap on the weekends, ready to put them at Kennedy's disposal when the time came. Eventually they would become the basis for his own book, *A Thousand Days*. He regularly sat in on meetings in the Oval Office and meetings of committees (although not Ex-Comm). His frequent presence contributed to the "gadfly" reputation, but he was history-making as much as policymaking. "Schlesinger scooped up information like a vacuum cleaner," *Time* magazine would later say.[8]

As part of this process, Schlesinger looked for ways to enhance the historical record in further innovative ways, as Ted Sorensen recalled. "At the urging of the eminent historian on his staff, Arthur Schlesinger, Jr., he [JFK] agreed that procedures should be established to record the first-hand recollections of participants in crucial events while our memories were still fresh," Sorensen wrote. Kennedy "never found time to do it," because he was, Sorensen judged, "in some ways deliberately elusive in his approach." But Schlesinger continued to prod and nag Kennedy throughout his presidency. In March 1963, in a memo entitled "Your Obligation to Future Historians," Schlesinger, as the "representative of the historical interests of the Administrations," wrote to "beg" him "to dictate the circumstances" of major decisions "while they are still fresh in your mind," and to adopt the habit "to set aside five or ten minutes every afternoon to note the major events of the day." At the same time, and aside from any account he might write himself, Schlesinger also wrote to the president about an official history of the administration, which, he advised, could either be produced by a single "house historian," or else by a series of specialists who would write about specific topics as case studies in presidential decision-making (an idea Schlesinger had developed with Richard

Neustadt). "You decided," Schlesinger wrote in exasperation, "that you did not want either a continuing White House historian or ad hoc specialists brought in from the outside to write up specific episodes."

The most obvious explanation for Kennedy's casual attitude is that he believed Schlesinger had the matter under control. In 1963 Schlesinger, as probably America's most famous historian, had seen the administration from the inside. Kennedy's reputation, the president himself seems to have decided, was safe in Arthur's hands. That conclusion had not been a given. "Those bastards, they are always there with their pencils," Ben Bradlee recalled Kennedy saying after reading *The Ordeal of Power*, speechwriter Emmet Hughes's insider account of the Eisenhower administration. This epithet, uniquely for Kennedy, did not apply to Schlesinger, "whom," Bradlee concluded, "he admired as a historian, [and] liked enormously as a person."

Schlesinger would have multiple goes at writing and shaping that history, including his White House journal, oral history interviews with Jacqueline Kennedy, his 1965 book, *A Thousand Days: John F. Kennedy in the White House*, a biography of the president's brother Robert Kennedy, and a stream of reviews and articles about Kennedy, particularly after revelations were made about the president's health and private life. In all of these works, it seems fair to say that he would honor the implicit understanding made between the two men in 1961 that his role would be to protect the president's legacy and establish the Age of Kennedy as a worthy successor to the Age of Roosevelt. Schlesinger was not so much court philosopher, as Richard Rovere had suggested, but Kennedy's court historian.[9]

In February Schlesinger wrote to his friend, the Oxford don Isaiah Berlin, "I wish you would come over this spring, before the bloom goes off the rose." Sure enough, Schlesinger quickly found himself thrust into the middle of the first major crisis of the Kennedy administration, and on the wrong side of the president. It had all started well, with Schlesinger making his first trip abroad as a member of the administration. George McGovern, newly appointed as head of the understaffed Food for Peace program, was leaving for talks in South America. Kennedy offered to lend him a special assistant and, wrote Schlesinger, "knowing my interest in

Latin America, he wondered whether I was the person to go." Schlesinger's interest in the region went back to his wartime days in OSS, when he had tussled over Latin American issues and Roosevelt's Good Neighbor policy with the Communist Maurice Halperin. He had written frequently on the area ever since, so was an obvious choice to accompany McGovern. But the invitation was also an introduction to the way things worked for those who served at the pleasure of the president and a reminder that no one still quite knew what to do with Schlesinger. "I had no real choice but to go," the troubled special assistant grumbled, "though JFK put it up to me in a manner which would have permitted me to decline."[10]

Schlesinger did not know McGovern well, but as fellow historians they quickly found common ground that would prove the basis of a long friendship. He was unnerved to discover that "like everyone else" in the Kennedy administration, McGovern was five years younger than himself, "a fact," he recalled later, "which continued to disconcert one who had been accustomed to regarding himself as the youngest man in the room." As well as this personal connection, the trip did provide some political and social insights for Schlesinger. He was, for example, deeply shocked by the poverty on display in the favela slums of Rio de Janeiro. "Once one becomes sensitized to the existence of favelas, one begins to see them everywhere," he wrote. "The result is to give a sinister undertone to the quality of life in this lively and lovely city. . . . No doubt all this has value as reminder of morality; the *favela* in Rio is certainly a constant symbol of the skull beneath the skin." Even more telling was the political reality of the intensity of hostility among hemispheric elites toward the Castro regime in Cuba. In a meeting with the Bolivian president, Victor Paz, Schlesinger (having left McGovern in Brazil) carefully outlined the administration's line that while the Cuban revolution had begun as a national revolution, it had now been seized by forces from outside the hemisphere that wanted to establish a Communist state. "What could the hemisphere do with this focus of infection?" Schlesinger inquired of the president. "Castro must be eliminated," the president answered, "without hesitation."[11]

The notion of eliminating Fidel Castro was one already transfixing the Kennedy administration by February 1961. The previous year, President

Eisenhower had approved a plan to establish training camps in Guatemala, where CIA operatives would prepare Cuban exiles to overthrow
the regime. Kennedy, having inherited the operation, came under great
pressure from the CIA to push the plan to its logical conclusion. That
meant US assistance, including air strikes, for an invasion. When Kennedy asked Schlesinger to look into the Cuban situation, Schlesinger was
aghast at how thin plans for the operation were. As early as February 11,
1961, two months before the operation actually took place, he was writing
to the president in a top secret memorandum that while a "plausible argument" existed for action if only focusing on Cuba, "as soon as one begins
to broaden the focus beyond Cuba to include the hemisphere and rest of
the world, the arguments against this decision begin to gain force." However well disguised the action might be, it would be ascribed to the United
States. There would be "a wave of massive protest" and "at one stroke,
it would dissipate all the extraordinary good will which has been rising
toward the new Administration through the world [and] fix a malevolent
image of the new Administration in the minds of millions." Such drastic
action should only be taken, he concluded, "after we had exhausted every
conceivable alternative."[12]

Schlesinger now embarked on a two-pronged strategy that would, first,
make clear his opposition to the operation and, second, should the operation go ahead, make sure that the political implications of such an action
were fully considered and the president protected. After returning from
his Latin America trip, he immediately asked Kennedy if he could "look
into" the question of "launching a comprehensive campaign" to learn the
facts about the Castro regime. "Such a campaign," he advised, "would
seem an indispensable preliminary to any hard decisions on Cuba." Kennedy gave him the go-ahead to prepare a white paper on Cuba. Writing it
gave Schlesinger even more concerns about any planned invasion.[13]

With his customary ability to write both effectively and quickly, Schlesinger turned around the white paper in a week. "The function of this
document," he explained when circulating the first draft, was "to win over
those who had some initial sympathy for the Cuban Revolution, to give
them reasons for a change of mind and thus to provide them a bridge

by which they can return to the hemisphere." The issue was not one of "criticizing [Castro's] right to have his own internal social and economic policy." Obviously Castro's "internal regimentation, etc., is bad, but by itself it would not serve as an occasion for intervention." Instead the launch of such drastic action would turn on the question of "Castro's subservience to the Communists and his intervention in the affairs of other Latin nations."[14]

The white paper itself was a blend of social science analysis, journalism, and purple prose. "The people of Cuba remain our brothers," it concluded. "We acknowledge our own past omissions and errors in our relationship with them. In future we pledge them our active support in their brave efforts to achieve freedom, democracy and social justice for their nation." It was "not too late" for the Castro regime to "sever its links with the international movement, to return to the original purposes . . . and integrity of the Cuba Revolution." But if Castro did not turn away from Communism, "we are confident that Cuban patriots will arise against this new tyranny."[15]

While working on the draft, he continued writing to Kennedy to urge caution and restraint. "The military aspects of the problem," he warned, "had received more thoughtful attention than the political aspects." Indeed, "it did not seem to me that the political risks had been adequately assessed or that convincing plans had been laid to minimize them." What, for example, would the president himself say in any press conference following an operation? "It would seem to me absolutely essential to work out in advance a consistent line which can hold for every conceivable contingency," he advised. "Otherwise we will find ourselves in a new U-2 [spy plane] imbroglio, with the government either changing its story midstream or else clinging to a position which the rest of the world will regard as a lie." Moreover, Schlesinger confided to the president, he had an overwhelming sense of "danger of our being rushed into something because the CIA has on its hands a band of people it doesn't quite know what to do with." He reported back a comment by Allen Dulles, director of the CIA: "We have a disposal problem. If we take these men [Cuban exiles] out of Guatemala, we will have to transfer them to the US, and we can't have them wandering around the country telling everyone what they have been doing." "Obviously this is a genuine problem," Schlesinger judged, "but it can't be permitted to govern US policy."[16]

Kennedy took the paper away to Palm Beach on the weekend of March 25 and met Schlesinger in the Oval Office the following Tuesday. "He was surprisingly generous in his comment," Schlesinger recorded. "He made a few specific criticisms . . . wondered whether [one] phrase was snide and suggested its omission. As usual, he was temperate, quick and effective." As Schlesinger was leaving, he finally steeled himself and asked the president the most important question:

"What do you think of this damned invasion?"

"I think about it as little as possible."

Schlesinger left somewhat cheered after the two men "agreed that the critical point—and the weak part of the case for action—lay in the theory of an immediate local response to a landing."[17]

The State Department published the pamphlet at the beginning of April. The *New York Times* devoted an editorial to it, describing the pamphlet as "a document of high quality" and pointing out that "it is noteworthy that the document makes no threats." According to "informed sources" (which surely referred to Schlesinger himself), the paper reported, "the pamphlet was written largely by Mr. Schlesinger," although the same source emphasized, "President Kennedy devoted many hours to the pamphlet personally, going over it with Mr. Schlesinger."[18]

Arthur had provided the rationale he thought Kennedy needed for a Cuba policy that stopped short of invasion. Perhaps it was the excitement of his first public display of policy influence that caused Schlesinger to flunk his moment with the president about Cuba. When Kennedy asked him on April 4 after a meeting with staff whether the invasion should go ahead, in his own words of apology to the president, "I'm afraid that I did not give a properly ordered answer." But returning to his desk, Schlesinger had written a five-page memorandum to the president that set out in a clearer fashion his views on the issue. To give the memo even greater clarity, he included an executive summary at the beginning that was free of the usual nuances of analysis. The latest plan for Cuba, he wrote, would represent "a change of phase in our Cuban policy." If it worked, it would have "the highly beneficial result of getting rid of the Castro regime." If that could be done "by a swift, surgical stroke, I would be for it." "But in present circumstances," Schlesinger went on, nailing his colors to the peace party mast, "I am against it."[19]

He then laid out a more detailed case against the operation. Hazards included that any protracted struggle would inevitably involve "the commitment of American prestige . . . [and] increasing pressure on us to guarantee the success of the operation." It would give the Soviet Union the opportunity "to wage political warfare," as Cuba "will become our Hungary [1956]." To allies, the operation will seem "gross, unprovoked and bullying imperialism." There would be the embarrassment of evasions and even lies to the press. "Whatever we do," Schlesinger continued, "the effect will be to spoil the new US image—the image of intelligence, reasonableness and honest firmness which has already had such an extraordinary effect in changing world opinion about the US and increasing world confidence in US methods and purposes."[20]

By the staff meeting of April 7, Schlesinger knew he had lost the debate. "We seem destined to go ahead," he recorded. He met privately afterwards with Dick Goodwin, who also had reservations, about "making one more try" to reverse the decision; when they approached McGeorge Bundy, he shot down the notion. Still, Schlesinger persisted. Seeing Kennedy that afternoon, he raised the issue again, pointing out that political and diplomatic contingency planning remained woeful, a point the president accepted "with vigor." Yet still, Schlesinger recorded, "It is apparent that he has made his decision and is not likely now to reverse it."[21]

Even now Schlesinger did not give up. Both he and Goodwin decided to see Dean Rusk, secretary of state, who was known to harbor some reservations about the operation. Rusk, clearly punting, said that he had "for some time" wanted to "write up a balance sheet on the project" and would now do so over the weekend in order to discuss it with the president the following week. Goodwin described how Rusk in his meeting "listened patiently to my monologue, then—I'll never forget it—leaned back in his chair, pressed his fingertips together, hovered for a moment in this pose of thoughtful concentration, and then, slowly, pausing between each phrase: 'You know, Dick, maybe we've been oversold on the fact that we can't say no to this thing.'" It was, Goodwin noted, the moment he understood "the secret of Rusk's extraordinary staying power—say little, and above all, go with the flow."[22]

Finally in desperation, Schlesinger sought out Bobby Kennedy, the president's brother and closest advisor. It was a brutal experience. "So Arthur Schlesinger came to my house sometime that week," Bobby recalled afterward to John Bartlow Martin. "I can remember having a conversation with him in which he said that he was opposed to it. I said that I thought everybody had made up their minds and that he was performing a disservice to bring it back to the President. I remember telling him that once the President had made up his mind—once it seemed to have gone so far—we should all make efforts to support him. And he [Schlesinger] should remain quiet."[23]

For Schlesinger that process of "remaining quiet" actually meant completing a number of disagreeable tasks. An immediate test involved Gilbert Harrison, the owner and editor of the influential *New Republic* magazine. Harrison sent him a draft copy of a piece to run in the next edition. It was, in Schlesinger's words, "a careful and substantially accurate account of CIA activities in Miami." Schlesinger felt overwhelmed by "a predictable moral struggle." On the one hand, clearly the article represented "trouble" for the White House. Equally, there were questions of whether or not "one should intervene in such matters of editorial judgment." In the end, Schlesinger resolved the dilemma, not altogether to his own satisfaction, by passing the article to Kennedy, who quickly told him to do everything possible to stop the story. "So I called Gil, who accepted the suggestion promptly and without questions," Schlesinger noted, "a gentlemanly and patriotic act, which made me feel rather unhappy."[24]

Another matter that made Schlesinger unhappy was having to be less than completely frank with Adlai Stevenson, now the US ambassador to the United Nations. Schlesinger traveled to New York along with Tracey Barnes of the CIA to brief the ambassador on Saturday, April 8. In *A Thousand Days*, Schlesinger said that Kennedy had instructed him, "the integrity and credibility of Adlai Stevenson constitute one of our great national assets, [so] I don't want anything to be done which might jeopardize that." In fact, the next week would see Stevenson compromised in a way that exactly damaged his reputation—something for which Schlesinger was in large part responsible. "We told him about the exile group. We told him we were training them, supplying them weapons, I'm not sure we told him that there would be U.S. planes, but we told him there would be no U.S. combat troops," Schlesinger recalled of the meeting with Stevenson. "But there was a failure of communication" about the full extent to which the planned invasion was a CIA operation.

The ambassador's reaction, as Schlesinger's own had been, was immediately to oppose the attack. "Look I don't like this," he said. "If I were calling the shots, I wouldn't do it. But this is Kennedy's show." The unpleasantries over, they all retired to the Century Club for lunch. "He is substantially a good soldier about it," Schlesinger recorded in his journal afterwards, "and is prepared to try and make the best possible U.S. case." A week later Stevenson would find not Schlesinger but McGeorge Bundy on his doorstep on behalf of the president. "I told him all about it," Bundy later recalled. "We should have done that a week earlier." As Francis Plimpton, Stevenson's second in command at the UN, bitterly reflected of Schlesinger's briefing, "Certainly there was great lack of candour in that interview."[25]

The invasion, launched on April 17, quickly developed into precisely the calamity that Schlesinger had feared. A combination of bad weather and poor planning meant that the Cuban émigrés struggled to get ashore, and when they finally did, Castro's forces were waiting for them. The CIA asked Kennedy for permission to send in further American planes or even ground troops, but the president, still thinking he could hide US involvement, turned them down flat. Effectively the operation was over. "How could I have been so stupid as to let them go ahead?" Kennedy asked Ted Sorensen. Historians have asked the same question. Castro, capitalizing on nationalist sentiment, used the opportunity to announce his intention to make Cuba a Communist state. Privately he agreed to let the Soviets take a leading role in the Cuban security service and in external defense. "The Bay of Pigs had brought John Kennedy the worst possible outcome," write Aleksandr Fursenko and Timothy Naftali. "A coup-proof Cuba in a Caribbean even more unwilling to approve the use of outside force. He now faced a Communist state, a short flight away from Miami. The question that the world asked in the aftermath of this personal debacle was whether the United States could come to terms with a Soviet beachhead in its backyard. . . . The very nature of the rivalry between the superpowers rested on the answer to that question."[26]

If Schlesinger felt "unhappy" about misleading the "gentlemanly" Harrison and the "good soldier" Stevenson, his determination throughout to protect the president overrode all other concerns. In a nine-page memo for Kennedy a week before the invasion, copied to Rusk and to Bundy, Schlesinger had laid out his suggestions to overcome problems identified in his often repeated overall objection that "the operational planning for the Cuban project seems much farther advanced than the political, diplomatic and economic planning which properly should accompany it." Central to Schlesinger's argument was the good name both of the United States and the president himself. The United States "is emerging again as a great, mature and liberal nation, coolly and intelligently dedicated to the job of stopping Communism, strengthening free and neutral nations and working for peace, " he wrote, echoing an earlier memo. "It is this reawakening world faith in America which is at stake in the Cuban operation." Therefore a key element of the coming days was to guard that, including "protection of the President."

Curiously using the words that in *A Thousand Days* he would put in Kennedy's mouth about Stevenson, he explained, "The character and repute of President Kennedy constitute one of our greatest national resources. Nothing should be done to jeopardise this invaluable asset." Then Schlesinger went on to spell out how this protection might be accomplished in practical terms. "When lies must be told, they should be told by subordinate officials," he urged. "At no point should the President be asked to lend himself to the covert operation. For this reason, there seems to me merit in Secretary Rusk's suggestion that someone other than the President make the final decision and do so in his absence—someone whose head can later be placed on the block if things go terribly wrong."[27]

Those looking for a scapegoat have used these final words to bring down opprobrium and condemnation on Schlesinger. For example, historian and Kennedy biographer Robert Dallek writes that the phrase "someone whose head can later be placed on the block" was one that "may have ingratiated him with the president but does no credit to his historical reputation." Moreover, Dallek judges more generally about Schlesinger and the invasion, "On balance, he favored continued quiet anti-Castro actions but opposed an invasion. Against his better judgment, however, he fell into line with Kennedy's command. It is an example of a brilliant critic who sacrificed his independent judgment to the attractions of continuing access to power."[28]

But is it? Dallek is a reputable historian, but in this instance he seems naïve about how governmental decision-making actually takes place and strangely affronted both personally and on behalf of his profession. Surely it is an obvious point that Schlesinger was no longer a critic: as a special assistant to the president, he was a government official. An argument might be made that he never should have joined the administration in the first place, but it is absurd to say that once there he should, or even could, have held out on Cuba once the president had made up his mind. Resignation was always a final recourse. Otherwise, he served at the pleasure of the president. More broadly, as a member of an administration, he was bound by the usual conventions of collective responsibility. He came out hard against the operation, repeatedly making clear his opposition both to the president and to senior cabinet ministers such as Dean Rusk, to such an extent that Robert Kennedy, presumably on the instructions of his brother, had told him to desist. Thereafter, Schlesinger got on with his job of helping the president execute his policy, converting Schlesinger not into a supporter of the operation, but into someone trying to plug the holes that had led him to oppose it in the first place. That governments mislead the press, the public, allies, and even members of their own administration—disagreeable as it may often be—is hardly news, as Eisenhower's U-2 escapade the previous year had demonstrated and countless operations thereafter would demonstrate, including the Grenada invasion, with President Reagan's barefaced lie to his closest ally, the British prime minister Margaret Thatcher. Schlesinger as a younger man, such as during his wartime experience at the Office of War Information, might have reacted petulantly and resigned in a huff. Instead he acted with a certain maturity in the middle of a crisis not of his own making, showing a willingness not to quit the arena to return to a spectator's seat at the first sign of trouble. He lost the argument, so moved on. The pragmatic Schlesinger had trumped the principled one, calculating that he would live to fight another day for something else important.

As a historian, later, Schlesinger reflected on some of the practical and ethical difficulties of this position. Certainly he laid out in successive memoranda to the president his opposition to the plan, and followed them up by "speaking truth to power" inside the Oval Office. However, he worried that while such actions "look nice on the record," they actually represented "of course, the easy way out." Schlesinger would reproach himself for not speaking out more vigorously in a series of meetings of principals and staff held in the Cabinet Room during which he contributed little, "although my feelings of guilt were tempered by the knowledge that a course of objection would have accomplished little save to gain me a name as nuisance."

Then in one of his most reflective passages in *A Thousand Days*, he made a forthright appraisal while staring into the looking glass at the historian in government standing before him. "It is one thing for a Special Assistant to talk frankly in private to a President at his request," he writes, "and another for a college professor, fresh to government, to interpose his unassisted judgment in open meeting against that of such august figures as the Secretaries of State and Defense and the Joint Chiefs of Staff, each speaking with the full weight of his institution behind him." In part, the problem was rhetorical. Soldiers and spooks were always able to "strike virile poses and talk of tangible things—fire power, air strikes, landing craft and so on." Diplomats and special advisors had only intangibles to invoke: "the moral position of the United States, the reputation of the

President, the response of the United Nations, 'world public opinion,' and other such odious concepts." The tendency for advisors and State Department officials to back the former over the latter was often overwhelming, driven by a desire to demonstrate "they were not soft-headed idealists but were really tough guys, too."

A few voices, such as that of William Fulbright, chairman of the Senate Foreign Relations Committee, stood against the prevailing wind when they were brought into the discussion. Fulbright provided an instructive contrast for Schlesinger's own behavior during the crisis. Hitching a ride to Palm Beach on March 30, Fulbright had presented Kennedy with a memorandum opposing any military action. Kennedy then brought him in a few days later for the final review of the Cuban operation, during which Fulbright faced down the CIA and military top brass, saying the planned invasion was a constitutional and operational disaster. "Fulbright speaking in an emphatic and incredulous way denounced the whole idea," Schlesinger recalled, judging his remarks "a brave, old-fashioned American speech, honorable, sensible and strong." It was a lesson for him in how an advisor to the president might communicate opposition with clarity and force.[29]

Fulbright aside, Schlesinger left most meetings "fearful that only two of the regulars present were against the operation: but since I thought the President was the other, I kept hoping that he would avail himself of his own escape clause and cancel the plan." Once it became clear that the president had signed off, it was game over for Schlesinger's objections. "We all succumbed," wrote Dick Goodwin afterwards. "Even those who opposed the plan (except for Arthur Schlesinger) failed to challenge the imperative of a swift decision."[30]

Lying in bed in the early hours of April 19, turning events of recent days over in his mind, Schlesinger was shaken from his thoughts when the telephone rang. He had only just returned home to Georgetown, but now here was McGeorge Bundy on the line saying the president wanted to see him right away. Dressing quickly and driving to the White House, Schlesinger entered the Oval Office to find the president gathered with his senior team, including Vice President Johnson, secretaries Rusk and

McNamara, and the army chief of staff, General Lyman Lemnitzer—all dressed incongruously in white tie and tails for a congressional reception that had been going on inside the building. Adolf Berle, Kennedy's advisor on Latin American affairs, was going to Florida to placate the Cuban Revolutionary Council, the émigré group formed by the CIA nominally to coordinate and direct the invasion. ("I can think of happier missions," Berle sardonically noted.) The president asked Schlesinger to go with him. Arthur dashed home to Georgetown to pack a bag before heading out to the airport. On board the Military Air Transport Service plane, he and Berle apprehensively discussed tactics over a "dreary" Service meal. In Miami they found the waiting Cuban Revolutionary Council despondent and angry. Calling Washington, the two men were told that matters had further deteriorated; even evacuation was now impossible. "How to break the news that the CIA had shattered their hopes and sent their sons to death or captivity?" Schlesinger pondered. "How to do so, and at the same time dissuade them from calling a press conference, telling all they knew and issuing public denunciations of the CIA and the Kennedy administration." Turning to Berle, Schlesinger said, "Can't we do something to bring the President into it?" Berle suggested taking the Council to Washington, DC, to meet the president. They phoned the White House, but Dean Rusk stalled. They waited a few minutes and then tried to get hold of the president personally. Kennedy told them to bring the Council to the White House, where a few hours later he "expressed his regret over the events of the last 48 hours."[31]

Schlesinger was struck by how "quiet but plain impressive" the president seemed. Others were less convinced. Jacqueline Kennedy later recalled how, after the congressional reception, her husband had "just put his head in his hands and sort of wept." Sorensen around the same time found his boss "depressed and lonely." Senator Albert Gore of Tennessee, visiting the Oval Office after the congressional reception, was shocked to find an "extremely bitter" Kennedy "dishevelled" and talking "too fast."

"All you bright fellows have gotten the President into this," Bobby Kennedy, a vocal advocate of the operation, raged during a meeting in the

Cabinet Room, "and if you don't do something now, my brother will be regarded as a paper tiger by the Russians."[32]

Certainly Jack Kennedy himself had a strong sense his clever advisors had let him down. "There is only one person in the clear," he fumed in a breakfast meeting with staff on April 21, "that's Bill Fulbright." Mac-George Bundy piped up that, in fairness, Schlesinger had opposed the operation too. Only a week before, Kennedy had been laughing at a remark made by Bundy in a meeting that the president was "surrounded by five ex-professors." Now Kennedy rounded on them. "Oh sure," he jabbed, "Arthur wrote me a memorandum that will look pretty good when he gets around to writing his book on my administration. Only he better not publish that memorandum while I'm still alive." The president even had a title for Schlesinger's book: *Kennedy: The Only Year.*

The meeting was a dispiriting end to the first hundred days of the new administration. Schlesinger's only hope was that they had all learned a lesson. The president should have overruled his senior advisors and called the operation off. "Next time," he wrote hopefully, "I am sure he will." By sticking around, Schlesinger gave himself the chance to find out.[33]

CHAPTER THIRTEEN

PLAYING CASSANDRA

*F*riday, April 21, 1961. Settling into his seat on the Rome-bound flight from New York, Arthur Schlesinger Jr. had every reason to be nervous. Not only was he flying into a storm of opprobrium in Europe, but there was the worry of leaving the White House as everyone cast about for a Bay of Pigs scapegoat. Schlesinger had been one of the few who had opposed the operation, yet, as any student of politics knows, no prince wants to be reminded of his own failure. It is easier to banish the offending courtier and start again with someone new. Kennedy would sideline Chester Bowles, the assistant secretary of state who was telling anyone who would listen that he had opposed the operation in Cuba, within the year. This trip to a conference in Bologna had been long planned. Before leaving, a nervous Schlesinger had suggested postponing, but with Kennedy himself due to leave for Europe in a month, the president had been keen to have someone to conduct reconnaissance and effect damage control. "Maybe you can explain to them over there what we have been doing," Kennedy told him. "Do your best."[1]

In the last few weeks, Schlesinger had been constantly on the move and almost always awake, working late into the night as the crisis escalated. Now in the radio silence of the flight, he was able to consider what really had gone wrong. "How does one add all this up?" he asked plaintively in his journal. Over the next few months, he would draw some broader conclusions about the machinery of foreign policymaking and how it could better serve the president.[2]

His more immediate task, however, was to weather the storm of European reaction to recent events in Cuba. Arriving in Bologna to address an international conference on American foreign policy, he found a baffled audience given to embarrassment. European participants talked of "everything but" Cuba. "One felt as if there had been a frightful scandal in one's family," Schlesinger wrote, "which friends refrained from mentioning for reasons of delicacy." The press were less tactful. "In one day," blared the *Corriere della Sera*, "American prestige collapses lower than in eight years of Eisenhower timidity and lack of determination." Then too he had to face Dean Acheson at the conference. The doyen of American diplomacy had been "present at the creation" of the postwar world under Roosevelt and Truman. Acheson listened to Schlesinger's account with amused disdain, before quoting an aphorism of Konrad Adenauer, the chancellor of Germany: "In view of the fact that God limited the intelligence of man it seems unfair that he did not also limit his stupidity."[3]

Schlesinger left Bologna concluding that the Bay of Pigs had done "immense damage" to the Kennedy administration's reputation. "We not only look like imperialists," he wrote, "we look like ineffectual imperialists, which is worse; and we look like stupid, ineffectual imperialists, which is worst of all." Traveling on to London and Paris, Schlesinger found more bemusement and dismay. "I've staked my whole political career on the ability of Americans to act sensibly," Denis Healey, the Labour foreign affairs spokesman, complained, recalling Britain's own imperial bungling five years earlier at Suez. Healey's colleague Richard Crossman warned, "Faith still remains in Kennedy . . . but one more mistake like this, and you really will be through."[4]

Schlesinger returned to Washington humiliated. On the plane home, he began drafting a memo for Kennedy outlining his experience and its implications for American policy. It was a document that spared no one's feelings, including those of the commander in chief. "The new American President in three months had reestablished confidence in the maturity of American judgment and the clarity of American purposes," Schlesinger wrote to Kennedy. "Now, in a single stroke, all this seemed wiped away. After Cuba, the American Government seemed as self-righteous, trigger-happy and incompetent as it had ever been. . . . 'Kennedy has lost his magic,' one person said to me."[5]

As "baffled and incredulous" as European opinion was about how "incompetent, irresponsible and stupid" the administration had been, the "unfortunate and unnecessary" fact that embassy staff had not been briefed about the operation exacerbated matters. "The State Department appears to have sent out no instructions to American Embassies how to explain what happened in Cuba," Schlesinger wrote. "As a consequence, our Ambassadors remain in the dark, . . . forced to mouth official generalities or to confess ignorance or to rely on [columnist James "Scotty"] Reston or *Time*."[6]

Having prepared his memorandum, Schlesinger went to see Kennedy in the Oval Office. The recently agitated figure of the Cuban crisis had reverted to a leader who "seemed, as usual, cool and composed." The two men talked about Cuba, with Kennedy again incredulous about the quality of the advice he was still getting from the CIA and the military, saying they wanted him to "intervene in Laos now." Schlesinger's downbeat report from Europe he brushed off with a joke. Showing his special assistant new Gallup polling that put him at an unprecedented 82 percent approval rating with US voters, he laughed, "It's just like Eisenhower. The worse I do, the more popular I get."[7]

Schlesinger had always admired Kennedy's coolness and composure, believing, as in the summer of 1960, that it was the quality that better equipped him to be president than, for example, Adlai Stevenson. Yet for all the bonhomie and self-deprecating wit, Schlesinger over the next weeks noticed a palpable dent in the president's self-assurance. "I surmise a rather profound shock to the President's own self-confidence," he recorded in his diary at the beginning of June. "Beneath his total self-control, he saw from the moment things began to go wrong the whole proportions of the catastrophe. . . . He has not spared himself when it comes to postmortems." Certainly the Soviet leader, Nikita Khrushchev, recognized that potential insecurity and tried to pulverize the president when the two leaders met in Vienna for their first summit on June 4. Khrushchev threatened to take West Berlin and talked airily of nuclear war. "Pretty rough?" the journalist Reston asked afterwards. "The roughest thing in my life," Kennedy replied, "he just beat the hell out of me." The face-to-face meeting combined with the incompetence of the Bay of Pigs convinced Khrushchev he could take advantage of a young and inexperienced leader by ratcheting up tensions in the Cold War. Washington and the allied community lost a measure of confidence in the president. "Khrushchev scared the poor little fellow dead," spat Vice President Johnson with his Texan's contempt for any sign of weakness. British prime minister Harold Macmillan saw Kennedy as "completely overwhelmed by the ruthlessness and barbarity" of the Soviet leader. "It reminded me in a way," he wrote ominously, "of Lord Halifax or Neville Chamberlain trying to hold a conversation with Herr Hitler."[8]

Schlesinger did not travel to Europe with Kennedy. Thus he had an opportunity to think more about the broader issues of governance that had bothered him since the Cuban failure. Incompetence and poor advice defined the operation; its aftermath generated a blend of torpor and risk aversion. "Because this bold initiative flopped," he complained, "there is now a general predisposition against boldness in all fields." Reinvigoration required not simply the president getting his "magic" back, but also a systemic overhaul.[9]

Schlesinger the historian was deeply interested in the ways in which a president imposed his will on his own administration; now as a political operative he wanted to apply some of those lessons. In *The Coming of the New Deal*, he had dedicated the last part of the book to the evolution of the presidency, with an entire chapter on the "dynamics of decision." In particular, Schlesinger had emphasized Roosevelt's habit of breaking down formal lines of demarcation, often to the irritation of advisors and cabinet officials. Harold Ickes complained in his diary about "what he [FDR] does frequently, namely, calling in members of my staff for consultation on [Interior] Department matters, without consulting me or advising with me." Sometimes those visitors would find themselves asked for advice completely outside their area of expertise. "He had a great habit," Schlesinger quotes FDR's commerce secretary, Jesse H. Jones, saying, "of talking to one caller about the subject matter of his immediately preceding interview." So officials brought in to discuss economic policy might suddenly find themselves talking about foreign policy. "All this," Schlesinger concluded of Roosevelt's leadership philosophy, "irritating as it was to tidy minds, enlarged the variety of reactions available to [FDR] in areas where no one was infallible and any intelligent person might make a contribution."[10]

After the Bay of Pigs, Schlesinger made it one of his principal activities to try to break down fences within the federal government, open the Oval Office to a wider range of advice, and thereby find ways to push presidential ideas more firmly through the system. He captured the frustrations of that challenge in the chapter in *A Thousand Days* entitled "In The White House," which mirrors the chapter on decision-making in *The Coming of the New Deal*. On taking office "aglow with ideas," the Kennedy administration, Schlesinger writes angrily, "promptly collided with the feudal barons of the permanent government, entrenched in their domains and fortified by their sense of proprietorship; in turn, the permanent government, confronting this invasion, began almost to function . . . as a resistance movement." He then stressed, "This was especially true in foreign affairs."[11]

In the summer of 1961, Schlesinger's specific fear was that nothing had been learned from the experience of Cuba. He was appalled to learn that the CIA had drawn up another Cuban covert plan. "Stop this paper in its present form and demand that it be recast to make political sense," Schlesinger wrote urgently to Dick Goodwin. "It is a fallacy to suppose that clandestine activity can be carried out in a political vacuum," Schlesinger despaired.[12]

These individual cases were dangerous examples of what Schlesinger believed was a systemic problem, so he sought constantly to act as a disruptive force within that system. It began with the CIA. Writing to Kennedy days after the Bay of Pigs, he urged "reconsideration and reorganization" of the agency, reminding the president that "I served in OSS during the war, and I have been a CIA consultant for a good deal of the period since; so that, while I am far from a professional in this field, I am a relatively experienced amateur."[13] Kennedy told him to think further on the issue. The result was a fifteen-page report at the end of June. It contained some philosophical reflections on the nature of an intelligence agency, with "the conclusion that secret activities are permissible so long as they do not corrupt the principles and practices of our society, and that they cease to be permissible when their effect is to corrupt those principles and practices." But its most radical contribution was the recommendation for a major overhaul of intelligence gathering and analysis, with the CIA stripped of its independence. The Agency's failure at the Bay of Pigs operation, at root, had come about because the intelligence branch (DDI) of the agency had been subservient to the operations branch. Even low-level agents hanging around the Cuban bars of Miami had known more about the Bay of Pigs operation than top officials of the intelligence branch.

Schlesinger's plan for reorganization required creating greater separation of activities. The State Department would be granted general clearance over all "clandestine activity," and a new assistant secretary of state for intelligence would take responsibility for convening a Joint Intelligence Board to coordinate "all elements in the intelligence community." The CIA itself would be split into an operating agency and a separate research agency (the latter charged with collation and interpretation). It was, Schlesinger admitted, "a fairly drastic rearrangement of our present intelligence set-up." But as he warned the president, "The important thing to recognize today, in my judgment, is that the CIA, as at present named and constituted, has about used up its quota [of visible errors]. Its margin for future errors is practically non-existent."[14]

In some ways Schlesinger was pushing at an open door. Kennedy privately cursed the "CIA bastards" who had led him into trouble, and expressed a wish to "splinter the CIA into a thousand pieces and scatter it to the winds." That summer, after affording Allen Dulles a period of grace, Kennedy summoned the CIA director and fired him, along with his deputy Richard Bissell. "Under a parliamentary system of government, it is I who would be leaving office," Kennedy consoled Dulles, "but under our system it is you who must go." For one tantalizing moment Kennedy, perhaps thinking out loud, seemed to consider bringing in Schlesinger as a new reforming director of the CIA, even though, as Schlesinger recognized, "it would cause consternation on the Hill." In the end, however, Kennedy followed the model of his earlier appointments by putting a well-regarded Republican into a controversial appointment as a way of blunting criticism of his policies from the right. In this case he preferred Truman veteran Clark Clifford but instead chose businessman John McCone, chair of the Atomic Energy Agency under President Eisenhower. Schlesinger took the news of his own non-appointment phlegmatically. "I imagine that the President was joking," he said of the idea that he might have gone to the CIA.[15]

That summer Schlesinger also found his name under consideration for the position of assistant secretary of state for Latin American affairs. Schlesinger fought a rearguard action against having to move from the White House, telling his parents of "my effort to disengage" from matters Latin. Dick Goodwin, who later in 1961 would get the State Department job himself, brilliantly captures how such a departure felt to an insider. Kennedy told him, "You know, Dick, maybe we'd be better off if you were in the State Department, closer to the action." Politics, Goodwin realized, was not love, even though he felt jilted. "I was not in the White House because John Kennedy liked me (although he may have) but for my contribution to his ambitions and objectives," he wrote afterwards. "In return I received a title, a significant office, and the opportunity to help shape the course of public power. If my presence caused difficulties, if my value declined, then I must go. It was a simple matter of transaction; not ruthless at all, but rational, the inevitable deduction from the syllogism of power."[16]

Schlesinger was aware that he himself had been an irritant in the lead-up to Cuba without being effective. He "saw little" of Kennedy in the early summer, and when he did, Schlesinger found him colder than before, as "the customary wit and relaxation were missing." In part, Kennedy's "back was causing him definite trouble," but there was also a marked sense of despondency in the West Wing after the twin setbacks of Cuba and the Vienna summit, with another crisis brewing in Berlin.[17]

Looking elsewhere to focus his attention, Schlesinger settled on Italy, whose prime minister, Amintore Fanfani, was due to visit the White House that summer. Just as Schlesinger had been drawn to thinking about decision-making and the bureaucracy in a Rooseveltian context, so too did his policy interest in Italy stem from earlier writings. Throughout the late 1940s and early 1950s, Schlesinger had written often and controversially about the importance of the non-Communist Left, most famously in his best-selling book, *The Vital Center* (1949). Arguably the most powerful postwar Communist force in the West was the Italian Communist Party. But in the late 1950s, the Socialists led by Pietro Nenni moved away from the Communists, eventually breaking with them by 1960. This split provided an *apertura a sinistra* (opening to the left) for a government that excluded Communists. In *The Vital Center*, Schlesinger had written that "the health of the democratic left requires the unconditional rejection of totalitarianism," and that in this and most other regards, the Italian socialist party was "broken and helpless." Now in 1961 he believed that Nenni's move presented a real opportunity for the non-Communist Left in Italy and for the United States to nudge things along.

Briefing Kennedy the weekend before Fanfani arrived, he laid out the context for the president. "The issue here is whether the Christian Democrats [Fanfani's party] should be encouraged to undercut the Italian Communist Party, which is the largest and most formidable Communist party in the free world . . . by adopting the policy of the so-called 'opening to the left.'" Answering the question, Schlesinger advised Kennedy that "what you might wish to do is . . . solicit Fanfani's views on the opening to the left [and] make it clear that, if there is a real prospect through closer relations with the Nenni Socialists of rescuing a large segment of the Italian working class without corrupting the Italian position in NATO, the U.S. would welcome such a development."[18]

Schlesinger found the president's meeting with the Italian prime minister "less interesting than it sounded," as he wrote home, "because Fanfani had very little on his mind and is not a deeply interesting man." Schlesinger and Robert Komer, a national security assistant, however, had sufficiently convinced Kennedy to communicate to Fanfani American encouragement of the "opening to the left." The key to this maneuver, Schlesinger advised, was to do it quickly. "Obviously the Communists are as well aware as we are that the final defection of the Nenni Socialists would be a terrific blow to their prestige and to their hope of getting anywhere in Italy," he told Kennedy. "Accordingly they are doing everything they can to stop it; hence time is important."[19]

To Schlesinger's frustration, the State Department took a different view. Writing to Walt Rostow, soon to become director of policy planning at the State Department, Schlesinger complained that the department's policy on Italy was just "a shopping list of desirable objectives . . . rather than a coherent statement of strategy." The idea that "it is OK for us to stand by until the situation has evolved" was "too complacent" and "a misreading of the situation."[20]

Dean Rusk, secretary of state, had another perspective on that same situation. "There were times when I had trouble with Arthur Schlesinger," he recalled witheringly. "Not content with life in the East Room with the social secretaries, Schlesinger liked to play a role in policy matters." Schlesinger's letter on Cuba had been "strong and sensible." On other matters, however, "he was less helpful," including on Italy. "A question arose over whether the Italian government should shift toward the left and build a broader coalition of political parties," Rusk wrote. "Schlesinger wanted the United States to use some pressure and nudge the Italians in that direction. However, our ambassador in Rome, Frederick Reinhardt, and I felt that this was not our job. I stonewalled Arthur, believing 'an opening to the left,' as Schlesinger called it, was a matter for the Italians to decide. They later made their move and indeed shifted to the left, but not because of American pressure." It was, Rusk spat contemptuously, just one example of how "Schlesinger was a fifth wheel in decision making."[21]

That contempt was mutual. When Schlesinger traveled to Bologna in the immediate aftermath of the Bay of Pigs, searching around for someone to blame, his eye had fallen on the inscrutable secretary of state. Certainly the CIA's and the military's "calculations were mistaken." But Rusk more than anyone else had failed to recognize the flaws in the planned operation. "The person who should have raised these points with vigor and who should have told the President to cancel the whole thing was the secretary of state," Schlesinger fumed. "I would regard his failure as almost the most reprehensible of all." That calculation would prove consequential for Rusk's historical reputation: *A Thousand Days* would portray the secretary of state throughout as a hapless mediocrity, well out of his depth and lacking in courage. The effect would be summed up in a *Washington Star* cartoon illustrating a Buddha-like figure skewered on a fountain pen under the title, "Secretary of State Dean Rusk stabbed in the back by Arthur Schlesinger."[22]

Rusk's own passivity and caution was, in Schlesinger's view, only the tip of an institutional iceberg for a department lacking in fearlessness and imagination. Subsequent historians would point to the impact of the McCarthyite attacks of the 1940s and 1950s, when many had been driven from the service and accused of being traitors, to explain the lack of independent voices. Averell Harriman, on being appointed assistant secretary of state for Far Eastern Affairs in December 1961, described the department as "a disaster area filled with human wreckage."[23]

"The basic problem springs, I believe, from the nature of the Foreign Service itself," Schlesinger told Kennedy. While most officials were "well above the average in decency, intelligence and devotion," they were also "emasculated so far as policy decision is concerned." The reason for this unsatisfactory situation was that "the whole Foreign Service training has the effect of discouraging the Foreign Service officer from strong views on substantive policy." The broader culture was one in which "officers are taught that their job is to carry out [policy], however idiotic they may personally consider the policy to be." Obviously the State Department could not be "a collection of freewheelers pursuing their independent foreign policies." But the "inherent indifference to substance and tendency toward caution," Schlesinger advised, "have increased the importance of strong [political] leadership." David Halberstam would later point out that the fault lay with Kennedy. "Those who had applauded the idea of the weak Secretary of State," he writes, "had gotten what they wanted and deserved."[24]

Schlesinger's overwhelming sense of déjà vu as the administration lurched from one international crisis to another compounded his sense of urgency. Throughout the summer of 1961, the Soviet Union had been making ominous threats about the status of Berlin, with heavy hints that

East Germany might seal the East Berlin border, through which two and a half million East Germans had moved permanently to the West since 1949. In the starkest terms, Soviet leader Nikita Khrushchev warned Kennedy that if the Americans decided to go to war over the issue, it would be nuclear from the outset.[25]

As Schlesinger came to be involved in planning for any Soviet incursion in Berlin, he quickly concluded that his fears that Cuba had taught the administration nothing were sadly real. He also recognized that having made the right call about Cuba but not voicing it forcefully enough, he had failed to be proactive. "I do not wish to play the role of Cassandra, and this, strictly speaking, is absolutely none of my business," he wrote in a memo to Kennedy on July 7, "but I cannot resist the feeling that the present stages of planning for Berlin are ominously reminiscent of comparable stages in the planning for Cuba." In particular, he was concerned that the basic US plan "comes, as the Cuban plan did, as if with the full endorsement of the various departments involved" and that "there has been no adequate presentation of alternatives."[26]

Schlesinger had wanted more independent voices, unafraid to speak the truth to the president, and what he had acquired was Dean Acheson—an example of "be careful what you wish for." Truman's secretary of state thought Kennedy—whose father the Waspy diplomat abhorred as an upstart bootlegger and an appeaser—was emotionally and intellectually unimpressive. After the disaster at the Bay of Pigs, Acheson made a speech to an audience of Foreign Service officials in which he described the widely held view that they were "watching a gifted young amateur practice with a boomerang when they saw, to their horror, that he had knocked himself out." Soon afterward, Acheson smirked that Kennedy had heard about the speech and "didn't like it at all." Nevertheless, as Berlin sent temperatures rising, Kennedy asked Acheson what he would do as the crisis unfolded. Acheson was blunt in his advice. The Eisenhower administration had drawn up three red lines on Berlin: access to the city by air and ground; a continued military presence in West Berlin; and the freedom and survival of the western sector. Khrushchev, Acheson advised, must be told that the

United States was "irretrievably committed" to these three "essentials" even if that meant nuclear war.[27]

Schlesinger was horrified. "Are the Acheson premises adequate?" his July 7 memo asked the president. "What other premises ought to be brought into the Berlin discussion?" As always for Schlesinger, the problem was that everyone had rallied too quickly behind a plan. "We would have been better off in the Cuba discussions if someone had been appointed as a devil's advocate and charged with the exercise of picking holes in the plan," he suggested. But today, he admitted, "This is harder to do here, when the proponent is someone so brilliant, charming and formidable as Dean Acheson." He told the president to bring in other big guns to challenge Acheson from among such contemporaries as David Bruce, the ambassador in London, Averell Harriman, or Adlai Stevenson, "before all thinking is frozen in the present mold."[28]

Schlesinger's own analysis was that Acheson's plan ignored political realities. "It appears to contain no long-run political strategy, except the view that, if we can win the 'clash of political wills,' then we can impose our own terms (unspecified) on the enemy," he wrote, adding the warning that "we may well be left exposed and even immobile before Soviet political warfare" unless "a more systematic effort" was made "to prepare for the political as well as the military issues implicit in the Berlin situation."[29]

In a note to McGeorge Bundy taking up a view remarkably like the actual strategy followed during the Cuban missile crisis, Schlesinger urged thinking about "providing an escape hatch" for the Soviet leader. "We must not shove him against a closed door," Schlesinger warned, "we must figure a way by which he can back down from the more extreme implications of his present course without inviting an unacceptably large political humiliation." Plans needed to include "a sketch as to how we think Khrushchev is going to get out of the hole he has dug for himself."[30]

When Schlesinger finally saw the president alone just after lunch on July 7, he expressed these "misgivings about the course of the Berlin planning." Kennedy read Schlesinger's memo there and then. The president had always admitted that Schlesinger was right about the Bay of Pigs. Now here he was telling him that the same mistakes were being repeated. After reading the paper, Kennedy conceded that Acheson's paper was too narrowly focused and that "Berlin planning had to be brought back into balance." So expand on this memo, Kennedy told Schlesinger, and give me an alternative. And do it by the time I leave for Hyannis Port at 5 p.m.

Schlesinger rushed back to his office and his typewriter. He feared that "the issue is being gradually defined, to put it crudely, as—are you chicken?" This approach was another "Cuban resemblance. . . . People who had doubts about Cuba suppressed those doubts lest they seem 'soft.'" Schlesinger now called in reinforcements to bolster the case: two sympathetic Harvard colleagues working within the administration: the international lawyer Abram Chayes, who was legal advisor to the State Department, and the political scientist and future secretary of state Henry Kissinger, then a consultant at the White House. Over the next few hours, with Schlesinger at the keyboard, the three men hammered out a four-page memo for the president, which Schlesinger ripped from the typewriter a few minutes before five o'clock and just got into Kennedy's bag before Marine One took off from the White House lawn.[31]

The memo was divided into two parts. The first attempted to undercut the premise of Acheson's paper, which it said had characterized Khrushchev as using the Berlin question as a pretext for a test of will with the United States. The United States could win that test only by showing that it was prepared for nuclear war over the issue. Thus, the memo argued, "the test of will becomes an end in itself rather than a means to a political end." According to Schlesinger, Acheson's premise avoided a number of major issues. At worst it "casts the U.S. as rigid and unreasonable and puts us on the political defensive." Moreover, Acheson's paper "hinges on our willingness to face nuclear war, but this option is undefined." And Acheson made no effort to address the question of "what happens if our allies decline to go along."

Part two of the memo offered thoughts about "unexplored alternatives." These alternatives covered predictions, premises, policies, conceptions, and assumptions, with suggestions about "what procedure can be devised to make sure that alternatives are systematically brought to the surface and canvassed." Among the most important of these was the alternative premise as to Soviet behavior, notably that "Khrushchev may be seeking to stabilize his own situation and relations in Germany and Eastern Europe." The paper urged a wider discussion of opinions, with as many different voices brought in as possible, including "non-Achesonians" such as Bruce, Harriman, and Stevenson. Equally important, "The White House staff should be directed to question all existing proposals, especially from the viewpoint of the effect the pressure of events will have on decisions; and it should be directed to take an active role in stimulating exploration of the various alternatives listed above (and others which reflection and analysis will bring to mind)."[32]

The two July 7 memos were among the most influential that Schlesinger wrote during his time in the White House. His memo before the Bay of Pigs had been essentially right, but it failed to impinge. The lesson he learned from that experience—to be bolder—informed his actions in the summer of 1961. The impact on the president this time was direct and immediate. The next morning in Hyannis Port, Kennedy hauled Dean Rusk and his deputy, Chip Bohlen, over the coals for their department's pacificity on Berlin. Holding Schlesinger's second memo, as the secretary of state perched uncomfortably in his dark business suit on the fantail of JFK's docked speedboat, Kennedy barked, "What's wrong with the goddamned department of yours? I can never get a quick answer, no matter what the question." The attack was so ferocious that Secretary of Defense Robert McNamara and General Maxwell Taylor, who were also on the boat, quietly slipped away to grab hot dogs on shore. Once everyone came together again, Kennedy demanded a plan for dealing with Berlin that did not involve nuclear weapons. He wanted alternatives, Kennedy told them, beyond the current choice between "holocaust or humiliation." The Schlesinger view had taken hold.[33]

Buoyed by his success, Schlesinger now overreached. Not content with influencing the internal debate, he tried to apply pressure on the White House from the outside. He briefed Scotty Reston at the New York Times that not enough was being done for political planning on Berlin. Reston's Times article pointed the finger of blame at Schlesinger's antagonist in the State Department. When the secretary called Reston to ask about his source and was told the briefing came from the White House, Rusk called Kennedy to complain. Summoning Schlesinger to his stateroom on Air Force One, "JFK looked at me shrewdly and asked whether I had recently talked with Reston." When Schlesinger confirmed that he had, "JFK said mildly that he wished hereafter I would make my complaints directly to the State Department rather than through the *New York Times*." The mildness of tone did not hide the force of the rebuke. "What the hell Scotty was doing telling Rusk that he got the story from the White House I shall never know," Schlesinger grouched, irritated at being sold down the river by one of his most useful journalistic contacts. It was naïve to have expected otherwise: Reston was unlikely to have sacrificed lines to Rusk to protect those with Schlesinger.[34]

The embarrassment over Reston was not the only difficulty Schlesinger had in trying to shift policy during the Berlin political discussions. Another had its roots in Harvard Yard, as Professor Schlesinger drew on Professor Kissinger for advice. Despite being a White House consultant on national security problems, Kissinger was well known to be playing on both sides of the political aisle. Here the difficulty was not so much Rusk, but the former dean of arts, now national security advisor, McGeorge Bundy, who (to say the least) disliked Kissinger personally and mistrusted his scheming. "Mac had never once asked his advice on anything," Schlesinger recorded after a conversation with Kissinger that summer, "and had not even responded in any way to the very intelligent series of memoranda Henry had been writing about Berlin."[35]

The second memorandum that Schlesinger had handed the president on July 7 had—not surprisingly, given that Kissinger had coauthored it—advised unambiguously that "Henry Kissinger should be brought into the center of Berlin planning." Presumably Kissinger had been pleased to include that line, but Schlesinger, who believed it himself, had already included Kissinger's ideas in his own memoranda to the president, even though they sometimes contradicted Schlesinger's own more dovish views.

Kissinger was less accommodationist than Schlesinger. "The West," he wrote that summer, "must stand for the unity of Germany despite the experiences of two world wars" and should continue to argue for issues such as freedom of movement and free elections in East Berlin not because they would be accepted by the Soviets, but precisely because they would not." But Schlesinger persisted in inserting Kissinger's voice, emphasizing forcefulness and intimidation, into the debate because he believed his Harvard friend was one of those disruptive voices essential to strong policymaking, someone who was unafraid to speak out against the conventional wisdom or the bureaucratic "line to take."

Sustaining that diversity became harder after the Berlin crisis reached its climax. On August 13, East German security forces sealed off the border with West Berlin by erecting barbed wire fences that soon evolved into the Berlin Wall. Kissinger's view, expressed to General Maxwell Taylor, former army chief of staff, was that "the Soviets have made us look like monkeys, weak monkeys, and we can't wait to demonstrate our masochism by crawling back and begging them please to negotiate, so that we can give up something else to them." Instead, Kissinger urged, the United States should "inform them that we will go to war before we forgo our rights in and access to Berlin, calmly carry on with our military buildup, and let them sweat for a change." This sabre-rattling, which his biographer Niall Ferguson contentiously presents as an example of Kissinger's "idealism," stood in contrast to the "realism" adopted by the White House and summed up by the president's phrase that "a wall is a helluva lot better than a war," not least a nuclear war.[36]

Kissinger believed that once the wall went up the president needed to "stand before the ruddy bar of history and choose from among carefully and sharply presented alternatives." Instead he was being "confronted with faits accomplis by the bureaucracy which he can ratify or modify but which preclude a real consideration of alternatives." That was precisely the argument Schlesinger had been pushing from within the White House in memo after memo to the president. So even as Kissinger excoriated the administration, Schlesinger continued urging that his voice be included.

When Kissinger wrote an eleven-page letter railing against his exclusion from policymaking, describing himself as "a kibitzer shouting random comments from the sidelines," Schlesinger took the letter to Kennedy and urged him to intervene. There followed an awkward meeting between Kissinger and Bundy. "MB made a great attempt to grovel," Kissinger wrote afterwards, "and since he covered almost every point in the letter to AS, it seems obvious that he was schooled to make these points." It was all to no avail. Kissinger's role in the Kennedy administration, such as it had been, was essentially over. As he exited in November, he expressed his disdain to Schlesinger about "the lack of an overall strategy which makes us prisoners of events."

Forwarding the resignation letter, Schlesinger told the president that Kissinger remained "devoted to you and to the Administration and would like to help wherever he can." Moreover, Kissinger would not be consulting for Republicans, because "he feels that foreign policy will be in much safer hands under a Democrat than a Republican Administration." That turned out to be wishful thinking on Schlesinger's part. As Kissinger later told Arthur's son, Stephen, it was the unwillingness of the Kennedy administration to give him a proper job that "put me on the path to a post with Nixon."[37]

Yet Schlesinger in the summer of 1961 had been key to the Berlin decision-making process. His memos to the president on July 7 had promoted JFK's demand to hear more voices and explore a wider range of alternatives. That approach, successfully applied during the Berlin crisis, would become the hallmark of the administration's decision-making process, especially during the missile crisis the following year. Running concurrently with Berlin that summer was another Cold War crisis about nuclear testing that again saw Schlesinger centrally involved, although this time he found himself on the wrong side of the debate.

During the 1950s, as both superpowers had built up frightening destructive capabilities through their thermonuclear weapons programs, each had come to recognize that mutual self-interest demanded some kind of self-restraint. On the American side, President Eisenhower, increasingly anxious about the buildup of nuclear weapons, committed himself to working out an agreement to ban nuclear testing as the capstone on his presidency. In April 1958, Hans Bethe, who had been head of the Theoretical Division at Los Alamos, told the president that technology now existed to detect even the smallest atmospheric and underground nuclear tests. In other words, verification of any agreement was now possible. Eisenhower wrote to Khrushchev calling for "technical talks" and offering to observe an informal moratorium on testing in the meantime. Khrushchev readily agreed. By 1960, however, with agreement on a treaty at hand, the U-2 incident crashed those hopes.[38]

The collapse of the test ban talks was a bitter moment for Eisenhower, who failed to strike (as Ronald Reagan would in 1987–89) a defining peacemaker's note on which to leave office. But his disappointment was about more than vanity and an appeal to legacy. "What worried Eisenhower most wasn't what happened on his watch," White House Staff Secretary and future NATO Supreme Allied Commander Andrew Goodpaster recalled. "He knew he could handle the military people. It was what would happen to another president—one who hadn't had his preparation or experience."[39]

A few weeks into office, Kennedy got to see some of those problems for himself. During a White House luncheon with his top foreign policy, defense, and arms control officials, an intense row broke out. Were continuing test ban talks simply a tactic by the Soviets that would allow them to further increase their nuclear capability? Kennedy defused tension in the room through humor, wrapping up the meeting, Glenn Seaborg of the Atomic Energy Commission recalled, "with a smile in his voice," thanking everyone for speaking openly, and saying, to great laughter, that he was "glad to see that there was agreement on the U.S. side." Then he added that it only remained "to get the Russians to agree also."[40]

But for all the humor, Kennedy understood that nuclear matters were the most onerous and deadly aspect of his job. That same spring, in a meeting with General Curtis LeMay, chief of the air force, and Harold Brown, director of defense research, he was informed that 60 million Americans would die if the Soviet Union launched a first-strike nuclear attack, with the number being "probably 20–30 million" Americans if the United States struck first. "I don't see there is very much difference," Kennedy said, shaken. "The answer is the same: there must never be a nuclear war."

Even a return to testing he found dangerous. "We test and then they test and we have to test," he complained, "and you build up until somebody uses them." But as he also explained in a press conference in June, following difficult discussions with Khrushchev at Vienna weeks earlier and with the Soviet leader now dropping heavy hints that the USSR would soon return to testing, it was "a serious question about how long we can safely continue on a voluntary basis a refusal to undertake tests in this country without any assurance that the Russians are not testing."[41]

In this context Kennedy asked Schlesinger to prepare a white paper on nuclear testing that would look at the political context of any decision to resume. Working with Edward R. Murrow, the legendary reporter who now headed the United States Information Agency, he also drew up a paper setting out a strategy for how the United States might present a decision to resume testing. "Unless we persuade our allies and the uncommitted nations of the rightness of our course on the nuclear test ban issue," it read, "we stand in grave danger of losing their support on other issues, notably general disarmament and Berlin." Therefore it was essential to begin a "political warfare effort" immediately to convince world opinion that the United States had done "everything in its power" to get agreement, and that the Soviet Union had "not negotiated in good faith."[42]

Meeting with Kennedy a few days later, Schlesinger was struck by "his lack of enthusiasm over the resumption of tests" despite the "rising pressure at home for immediate resumption." As Schlesinger and Murrow had written in their note on political strategy, much of this pressure came from the Atomic Energy Commission. "Those fellows," Kennedy complained in agreement, "think that they invented the bomb themselves and look on everyone else as Johnny-come-latelies and amateurs." Matters weren't helped, Schlesinger slyly pointed out, because the long-awaited State Department brief was still outstanding.[43]

Meeting to renew discussions at the beginning of August, the president "expressed general approval" for the papers Schlesinger had written. "The

President's immense reluctance to resume testing became increasingly apparent in the course of the talk," Schlesinger wrote, "He also said ... that the risk of being caught was so great that ... even the Soviet Union would be extremely stupid to try and get away with anything." A technical report by the president's Science Advisory Committee reinforced that judgment. The panel concluded that there was no evidence to suggest the Soviet Union had begun testing again and that, as a consequence, the United States could compensate for a lack of testing opportunities through other means. If, however, the Soviets did renew testing, then the United States could not maintain the test ban without harming its military position.

The joint chiefs of staff filed an opposition paper—"semi-literate and generally unimpressive," Schlesinger judged—that sought to undermine the premise and findings of the Advisory Panel report. But after a tense conference in the middle of August, over which Kennedy presided, Schlesinger remained convinced that "JFK has no wild passion to resume testing" and that "pressure for resumption seems to have subsided." In the meantime, talks between the powers continued in Geneva, where a joint US-UK proposal for a test ban treaty was under review.[44]

Before long the issue reignited. Khrushchev's modus operandi throughout much of Kennedy's brief tenure was to place the president under maximum stress in multiple arenas. Many, including Dean Acheson, believed that the Soviet leader's actions in Berlin had been more about pretext than context; that Berlin was just a convenient issue over which to bully Kennedy on the world stage. Schlesinger profoundly disagreed, but events that took place at the end of August gave it greater force, when the Soviet leader initiated another provocative move in the confrontation between East and West.

On August 30 at a routine press conference, Kennedy expressed cautious optimism about the Geneva test ban talks. No sooner was the conference over than Ted Sorensen told him that the Soviets had announced a planned resumption of nuclear tests. "Fucked again," Kennedy roared, losing his customary cool. "The bastards. That fucking liar." Bundy would later claim that "of all the Soviet provocations of these two years, it was the resumption of testing that disappointed Kennedy most." At a top-level meeting the next day, Dean Rusk presented a draft statement saying that the United States would soon begin testing.

Kennedy went along with the thrust of the message, diluting it slightly to say that he was ordering preparations that would make testing possible. Schlesinger saw even this watered-down version as a disaster. "This lets the Russians off the hook," he hissed to Ted Sorensen, who nodded agreement. "Tell Murrow," Sorensen whispered back. Schlesinger edged over to the USIA director, who reassured him that he was about to say something similar. "If we issue that statement," he said, "we destroy the advantages of the greatest propaganda gift we have had for a long time." Murrow's intervention sufficed to stall the announcement. "It is all too typical of Rusk," Schlesinger spat afterwards, "that, instead of speaking for the interests of U.S. foreign policy, he capitulated and put forward a statement which might have been drafted in the Defense Department or the Joint Committee."[45]

Schlesinger was tasked to draft a statement if and when it became clear that a first test had taken place. They didn't have to wait long. Mid-afternoon on September 1, Schlesinger was working in his office when McGeorge Bundy called to say that there now was evidence that the Soviets had resumed testing. "We are trying to figure out what to say," he said. "You had better come over." Schlesinger pressed for the statement he had drafted only that morning. John McCloy, director of the US Disarmament Commission, and Arthur Dean, the lead negotiator at the talks in Geneva, argued for announcing a decision to resume testing immediately. Reaching no conclusion, they decided to take two statements to the president. Standing in his bathrobe, Kennedy listened "a little impatiently" to both sides of the argument, "completed our sentences, slashed each statement to bits . . . and briskly ushered us out." Although "not inclined" to announce a resumption of tests immediately, the president really "did not know how much longer he could refrain from doing so." The whole discussion, Schlesinger felt, "was all over a little too quickly."[46]

Schlesinger's instinct that the president had almost made up his mind proved correct. Over the next two days, British prime minister Harold Macmillan called for a summit meeting with Khrushchev and a joint

US-UK proposal to ban atmospheric tests (a forerunner of the limited test ban treaty that would be negotiated two years later). That briefly encouraged Schlesinger's hope that the United States would not resume testing. But when Kennedy called him forward to the state rooms on Air Force One on September 5, and there joshed him good-naturedly about a film review Schlesinger had just written for *Show* magazine, the special advisor knew the game was up. "One thing we did not discuss was the question of our resuming nuclear tests," Schlesinger wrote afterwards. At five o'clock that same afternoon, the statement appeared, "without much consultation among his advisers," that the United States would resume nuclear testing.[47]

"I assume that he did not raise this question with me," Schlesinger concluded miserably, "because he had heard my view and was not interested in listening to more liberal guff on this matter." As in divorce, the president didn't want expert mediation once he'd decided to bail out.[48]

CHAPTER FOURTEEN

LOOKING SO ARTHURISH

O n the evening of Monday, September 11, 1961, Arthur Schlesinger
Jr. set out to walk from his office in the East Wing of the White
House to Georgetown. His doctor had constantly urged him to exercise
more and lose weight ("You certainly have a problem with your weight,
and I hope that you are successful in reducing it somewhat"), so Arthur
tried to walk home as often as possible, particularly in the more temperate
fall weather. On this occasion he was not heading for the crumbling old
Federal Period house that the Schlesingers had rented on O Street ("People
came to see us not for our interior decor, I can promise you," Marian tartly
observed). Instead he kept going past O Street to 29th and Q Streets to
the home of former New Dealer Chester Bowles, now no. 2 at the State
Department. There waiting for him was his old friend and Harvard colleague John Kenneth Galbraith, now US ambassador to India, and Adlai
Stevenson, the man both had supported in 1952 and 1956 and current UN
ambassador.[1]

These four downcast liberals, Galbraith recorded afterwards, "all
talked mournfully about our foreign policy." A few days earlier, Stevenson
had endured a testy meeting with the president. After hearing Stevenson's
critique of his decision to resume nuclear testing and his argument that
it gave away an advantage in the propaganda war, Kennedy dismissed the
ambassador out of hand. "What does that mean?" Kennedy had asked
about the propaganda war. "Anyway," he added dismissively, "the decision has been made." Later that evening Stevenson would be further out-

264

raged when Schlesinger began "toying provisionally" with an idea of John McCloy's. "World opinion?" the president's principal disarmament advisor had scoffed, "I don't believe in world opinion. The only thing that matters is power." For Stevenson, it was a phrase that would stick and to which he would return a year later in the most famous speech of his life. Chester Bowles shared Stevenson's dismay. The last months, he had written in his diary, demonstrated "how far astray a man as brilliant and well-intentioned as Kennedy can go who lacks a basic moral reference point." The disillusionment was mutual; Kennedy would sack him two months later in the so-called Thanksgiving Day Massacre.

"The President snuck up on him one day," Robert Kennedy recalled, "and got him fired." In fact the attorney general was no fan of Bowles either, both for his disloyalty in the aftermath of the Bay of Pigs and for his opposition to RFK's plan for intervention in the Dominican Republic after the assassination of President Rafael Trujillo Molina earlier in 1961. The problem, Schlesinger would write later, was that the Kennedys "put a premium on quick, tough, laconic, dedicated people and [were] easily exasperated by more speculative types" like Bowles. It was a judgment Schlesinger feared might apply to the four who gathered around the dinner table that night.[2]

A month earlier, knowing his relationship to Stevenson was close, Kennedy had charged Schlesinger in advance of the upcoming UN General Assembly with managing the ambassador. Stevenson's high moral tone increasingly irritated Kennedy. "He didn't want to be lectured," Bobby Kennedy judged—so he handed off the problem to another liberal. Schlesinger was stuck with the task for the remainder of his time at the White House. That left his ill-wishers like press secretary Pierre Salinger free to make contemptuous remarks that his only "official role was that of White House liaison with United Nations Ambassador Adlai Stevenson." Schlesinger himself had immediately recognized the internal political dangers of the assignment. "I imagine that this will put me unhappily in the middle between JFK and AES," he complained in his diary, "but I have been through this before and I guess I can survive."

In fact it took just days before the awkwardness arose. When the Soviets announced a resumption of nuclear testing, Stevenson suggested introducing a resolution at a meeting of the UN Security Council calling on the Soviet Union to rescind the decision and on all other powers to refrain from testing. When Schlesinger took the idea to Kennedy, the president "thought aloud for a minute, then sat silent in his chair, obviously going through a process of visible concentration on the problem." He eventually decided that it would "look hypocritical" to appeal to the UN when he had already decided to resume US testing. Then with a wave, "he left cheerily for Hyannis Port," abandoning Schlesinger to the unhappy task of telling the ambassador.[3]

Throughout that fall, Schlesinger increasingly came to feel that he was an embattled liberal minority in the White House, constantly forced to fight his corner as the administration settled into an essentially conservative character. Later in September, he was appalled to read in the *New York Times* that the president was considering appointing the chair of the US Atomic Energy Commission, John McCone, as the next head of the CIA. Schlesinger was not galled simply because he had offered to be Kennedy's point man in recruiting a new director, and had even been spoken of by the president as a potential candidate. What really bothered Schlesinger was that the appointment of the Republican McCone confirmed what he saw as Kennedy's political caution. Firing off a memo to the president, Schlesinger complained that "Mr. McCone, for all his able administrative qualities, is a man of crude and undiscriminating political views (or, to put it more precisely, political emotions)."

Once again, Schlesinger tried to play his Cuban trump card. "My guess," Schlesinger judged, "is that if McCone had been head of CIA in March, we would have got, not a discriminating and careful advocacy of the Cuban operation, but an emotional and moralistic presentation." In fact, Schlesinger concluded witheringly, "I would consider him far less inclined than [outgoing head] Mr. Dulles to weigh the political significance of proposed clandestine operations." Schlesinger's intervention made no difference, since McCone was announced that same day. "I am sure JFK knows what he's doing and possibly my concern here will turn

out to be as unwarranted as my concern last December over the appointment of Doug Dillon," Schlesinger noted uncertainly in his diary, "but I
doubt it."[4]

Perhaps to soften the blow of McCone's appointment, the following
week Kennedy invited Schlesinger and his wife, Marian, to dine together
with himself and the First Lady in the Residence. "JFK was, as usual,
exceedingly relaxed, pungent and charming," Arthur wrote afterwards.
"The talk, as usual, encompassed a tremendous range of subjects, with
swift transitions from one to another." The two experiences—McCone
and dinner with the Kennedys—in many ways summed up Schlesinger's
experience of life as a special assistant in the White House. There was no
question that he had regular and privileged access to the president, which
he greatly enjoyed. Most days, when he called by the Oval Office, Kennedy usually beckoned him to join whatever conversation was already
ongoing. ("The Vice President was sitting by his desk, but he invited me
in. We talked about the CIA.") Save for his brother Bobby, JFK always
maintained a certain aloofness in personal relations. "He and I," remarked
even Ted Sorensen, "continued to be close in a peculiarly impersonal way."
As Robert Dallek shrewdly observes, "There was no one who could readily
describe himself as a close Kennedy friend—not any of the White House
insiders, not Sorensen or Schlesinger, nor any of the three members of the
Irish mafia, O'Brien, O'Donnell, and Powers." But within these param-
eters, Schlesinger had his own easy relationship with Kennedy. He was
not instrumental in Sorensen's technical way, nor a "jock" in the social
bantering way of the Irish boys. (Sometimes he was able to make a joke
out of the latter: "As the prime example of physical unfitness in the White
House, I have given the draft everything I could," said the note from
"Arthur 'Butch' Schlesinger Jr.," which accompanied a draft speech for
the Football Hall of Fame.) Yet the president was also a keen historian, so
he enjoyed having Schlesinger around to discuss books and ideas. Kennedy relished Schlesinger's effortless ability to draw some interesting parallel between events of the day and, say, those of the Founders or Chester
Arthur and Grover Cleveland. Kennedy would often invite Schlesinger in

at the end of the day, when the two men would enjoy a drink, often a dai-
quiri, and chat about whatever was on the president's mind, particularly
what he was reading at the time.[5]

Schlesinger himself understood that the easy and informal relationship was part of the problem too. Having arrived at the White House in
January with little or no idea "what I was supposed to do" and with JFK
"equally baffled," Schlesinger never quite found a place in the formalized
structure of governance, because, in fact, his position was essentially ad
hoc. Galbraith had perceptively diagnosed this problem from the outset.
"I had a long talk with Arthur Schlesinger who is unhappy and uncertain concerning his White House assignment," Galbraith had noted in his
diary in February 1961, with Arthur only days in the door. "He has a good
address, but no clear function. It will soon straighten out, but it confirms
my view that no sane man should ever take a staff position as distinct from
some line responsibility in Washington. One should get his power, not
from the man above but from the job below. One should be not one of the
people the President wants to see but one that he must see."[6]

Clearly Schlesinger was one of the people the president wanted to see.
That ensured that Arthur always got a hearing and entered into policy
debates. And when he caught the president's ear, his influence could
be great, as with the two July 7 memoranda that helped shift decision-
making during the Berlin crisis, or when, as for the 1962 state of the
union address, he was able "to give a philosophical coherence" to the
speech and added his own paragraph "to tie the program together and
relate it to the New Frontier." Moreover, as perhaps the most liberal voice
among Kennedy's advisors, he was the embodiment of his own philosophy of government, vigorously promoted after the Bay of Pigs, that a
president needed to hear as wide a variety of voices as possible in the
decision-making process.[7]

Yet the limitations and frustrations of his role were obvious too. When
Schlesinger's ideas captured the president's attention, his influence could
be marked. But when those ideas fell flat, Schlesinger was often stuck.
On some issues, it was simply a question of the president telling him to
keep his nose out. ("Ted Sorensen called me urgently that morning to say

that the president . . . did not wish me to touch on government-business relations," Schlesinger wrote, for example, in June 1962. "I explained that I was sticking to foreign policy.") But neither was there any institutional weight to fall back on. When an assistant secretary of state felt that he was not getting a fair hearing on an issue, he had the collective brain and muscle of the State Department to draw on in order to reframe the argument and push it through other venues. Moreover, echoing Galbraith, if the issue was within that person's administrative bailiwick, they could be marginalized, but still stood more chance of avoiding being entirely cut out of the decision-making process.

Schlesinger, on the other hand, was a one-man band. Not only was he ultimately dependent on the patronage of the president, he was constantly having to build alliances, as he did with Henry Kissinger and Abram Chayes over Berlin, on an issue-by-issue basis. That was harder for him than for other key figures in the White House such as McGeorge Bundy or Theodore Sorensen, not least because each of these had their own staff to provide back-up and advice. As a consequence, Schlesinger might often find himself out of the loop at any given moment, as for example he often was when debate arose over one of the most consequential foreign policy issues of the decade.[8]

Vietnam had been an international problem since at least the Paris Peace conference of 1919, when a young Ho Chi Minh had tried to petition President Woodrow Wilson about Vietnamese independence from France. After his Communist Viet Minh forces occupied Hanoi in 1954 and proclaimed a provisional government, the Eisenhower administration had gambled on supporting a newly formed South Vietnam and its unproven leader, Ngo Dinh Diem, as a bulwark against the spread of Communism in the region. Diem quickly proved arbitrary, incompetent, and out of touch with most of his people, including the Buddhist majority. In 1959, Eisenhower had authorized US military advisors to accompany South Vietnamese Army battalions on operational missions. Thus began active American military engagement that would last until 1973. When Kennedy assumed office, in the words of one White House aide at the time, US interest in Vietnam "was simply a given, assumed and unquestioned."

The one person for whom that statement was not entirely true was the new president himself, who could claim to know as much about the situation as any Democratic politician in Washington. He had first visited Vietnam as a young congressman in 1951 and maintained a close interest thereafter. He had been scathing about French attempts to crush Ho Chi Minh, recognizing, moreover, that any free and fair vote would likely sweep the Communists to power. To act "apart from and in defiance of innately nationalistic aims spells foredoomed failure," he remarked presciently after that early visit to the country.[9]

"Kennedy," writes Fredrik Logevall in his Pulitzer Prize–winning book *The Embers of War*, "more than most national political figures of the time might have gone against the grain and ordered a full-scale review of Vietnam policy." Yet the closest the new president came to that reevaluation came in 1961 when he sent his most trusted military figure, General Maxwell Taylor, and White House aide Walt Rostow to report on South Vietnam. With the regime teetering on the brink of collapse, Kennedy gave them clear instructions. He wanted to know now whether the United States was any better off than the French had been ten years earlier. The implication in the question could hardly have been clearer: was he heading toward "foredoomed failure"?[10]

Later on, Schlesinger would identify the Taylor-Rostow mission as a crucial turning point in Vietnam, and he attached blame for its failure to Dean Rusk and State. "The very composition of the mission," he would write, "headed by a general, with a White House aide as deputy and no figure of comparable rank from the State Department, was significant. It expressed a conscious decision by the Secretary of State to turn the Vietnam problem over to the Secretary of Defense." Kennedy acquiesced to the shift in responsibility, Schlesinger suggested, "because he had more confidence in McNamara and Taylor than in State." The effect, however, was to "color future thinking about Vietnam in both Saigon and Washington with the unavowed assumption that Vietnam was primarily a military rather than a political decision."

At the time, however, Schlesinger seems to have taken little interest in Vietnam. He had a conversation with Kennedy after Taylor and Rostow submitted their report, during which he listened to the president's concerns about committing troops. "They want a force of American troops," Kennedy said, "but it will be just like Berlin. The troops will march in; the bands will play; the crowds will cheer: and in four days everyone will have forgotten. Then we will be told we have to send in more troops. It's like taking a drink. The effect wears off, and you have to take another." But Schlesinger's own views remained opaque. Unlike with Cuba, Berlin, and nuclear testing, he had limited interest in southeast Asia. There seem to have been no urgent memos to the president, no briefings to favorite journalists, or prodding of various department officials. Was this because he already had his influence through other means, particularly after his old friend and mentor Averell Harriman became assistant secretary of state for Far Eastern affairs that November? As likely, it was his Eurocentric worldview coupled with the fact that even Laos was more important than Vietnam at the time and neither loomed that large. There was also an element of pique. When Kennedy wanted another perspective on Vietnam and the Taylor-Rostow report, it was not to Arthur Schlesinger that he turned, but his other Harvard professor, John Kenneth Galbraith, US ambassador to India, whom he also sent to Saigon to take a look.

These missions offer an insight into one way in which Kennedy used the academics in his administration. When he wanted to know what was going on in Vietnam, he sent Walt Rostow, a professor at MIT and an anti-Communist hawk. When he needed a counterbalancing view, he asked Galbraith of Harvard to visit. What all of these professors, including Schlesinger, offered the president was an ability to analyze and write at the highest levels of expression. Not only were they rigorous thinkers and good stylists, but each was unafraid to reject the pieties and conventional wisdom of the day, giving the president access to the thoughts of clever men who were prepared to say what they thought even if each saw only part of the problem. Kennedy thought they gave him a vital edge. As Jackie recalled, when Schlesinger returned from Europe after the Bay of Pigs disaster, JFK had been so anxious to read his report that he left in the middle of a reception for a visiting head of state to read it.[11]

Galbraith, like Harriman, now warned Kennedy that the Vietnamese regime was a disaster. "The only solution must be to drop Diem," he urged in his cable. Given the friendship and political alignment among the three men, it is not unreasonable to imagine that Schlesinger concurred, but he remained curiously indifferent on the issue. Yes, when Galbraith was in Washington shortly before heading off to Saigon the three had discussed the matter. Again, Schlesinger recorded their views—Harriman on how the State Department always underestimated the dynamics of revolution, and Galbraith's opinion that "our trouble is that we make revolutions so badly"—but Schlesinger did not bother to express his own opinion. Certainly there seems to have been no ill will toward Galbraith personally; the two men met for breakfast, lunch, and dinner regularly during those few weeks that Galbraith was in Washington, coinciding with the visit by Indian prime minister Jawaharlal Nehru. On one occasion he even managed to hook Galbraith up with the Hollywood actress Angie Dickinson (who quickly made herself scarce after he attempted to kiss her; she was rumored to have a bigger presidential fish on the hook). Schlesinger's uncharacteristic reticence may have reflected a genuine lack of interest in the subject, or he might have simply deferred as he usually did to a person he liked and respected on an issue where he believed that he himself had little expertise. Whatever the answer, it is an odd lacuna in Schlesinger's political career that he opted out at one of the crucial turning points in American foreign policy, but also it is an indication of the limitations of his role as special advisor without any particular portfolio.[12]

The anxieties Schlesinger had about his first year as a special assistant in the White House came to a head as 1961 turned to 1962. That January, the president of Harvard, Nathan Pusey, inquired whether Schlesinger would be returning from leave in the fall. If he did not, he would be expected to resign his professorship. His departmental chair, Robert Wolff, who had been a couple years ahead of Schlesinger as a student and served with him in OSS, brought the additional unwelcome news that he had lost his intellectual history courses (among the most popular in the school).[13]

Schlesinger felt the dilemma keenly. On the one hand, he was only just finding his feet at the White House, which, for all its occasional frustrations, had its exhilarating moments. He was playing a role in major international crises and (as he did that January) sitting next to greats like composer Igor Stravinsky, who at dinner whispered conspiratorially to him, "I am drunk." A year earlier, Schlesinger explained to Pusey why he wanted to extend the six-month leave of absence he had taken for the 1960 election to the maximum allowable two years. "I felt that I could not in all conscience reject a job at the White House," he reported. "No professional historian in all our history has ever been privileged to see events from this vantage point, and I know I would always regret it if I declined the opportunity." But he would be back in 1962, he assured Pusey, because his "basic commitment is to writing and scholarship, and I would hate to suspend 'The Age of Roosevelt' for a longer period than eighteen months."[14]

Schlesinger now asked Mac Bundy for advice. Only a year and a half earlier, Bundy as dean of arts had been writing to Schlesinger to inform him that his Harvard salary was going up to $18,000 per annum. Now the two men were working together at the center of government in the White House. But did the president really need him? Bundy told him that Jerome Wiesner, an MIT professor and the president's science advisor, had come to him immediately beforehand with a similar question, so he would ask Kennedy about both of them. After an anxious wait, Bundy gave Schlesinger an answer. "According to Mac," Schlesinger recorded, glowing, "JFK said that he would be sorry to see Wiesner go but he imagined that he could find another scientist to take his place, but I was irreplaceable." Then he caught himself and added, "I expect that the presidential reaction has been improved by Mac's generosity" (not a quality for which Bundy was renowned). Nevertheless, fortified by the endorsement, Schlesinger concluded, "It is probable that he [JFK] would like me to stay; and since I do not feel that I have come close to exhausting the value of the experience for myself, or the fun, I feel that I should do it a little longer." He now raised the issue with Kennedy himself, who told him, "I think you would be more useful down here than teaching those sons of privilege up there." Schlesinger set out for Cambridge on January 16 to tell Pusey in person, from whom he received a cold welcome. "At one point he burst forth against scholars and government, suggesting that he regarded it as a corrupting relationship." Many others echoed that view with Schlesinger much in mind, not the least of whom was Arthur Schlesinger Sr. He was deeply upset at his son resigning his Harvard professorship. To him it was the essential condition of whatever else Arthur did. To cut that tie was to risk the danger of being nothing more than a political hack. Arthur resigned anyhow, quickly receiving a letter to confirm that at a meeting of the president and fellows on February 5, 1962, "the resignation of Arthur Meier Schlesinger, Jr. as Professor of History and Associate of Adams House was received and accepted to take effect June 30, 1962." The decision, breaking Arthur Sr.'s heart, would be a source of tension between the two for the rest of the father's life. "It was sorrow," recalls his grandson Stephen Schlesinger, a student at Harvard, "sorrow for my father not following the strict routine of a scholar. That's what he thought life was about."[15]

If Schlesinger needed reassurance from other quarters that he had done the right thing, it came courtesy of Bobby Kennedy. Waiting at Andrews Field to board a flight to Montevideo for an Organization of American States conference, he was summoned to the phone. "The president is mad at you," RFK told him. "I have just been talking to him, and he said, 'Let's check that with Arthur.' I said that you had gone off to South America. He blew up at that and said he knew nothing about it, and that everyone was leaving him." Schlesinger was nonplussed and offered to return immediately to the White House. "No, you go ahead," Bobby told him. Afterwards, Schlesinger reflected that he "could not make out how seriously to take Bobby's rendition of this." But he also admitted to himself that "in a way [I] was a little relieved, since I had somewhat the impression . . . that the President might be getting impatient about his liberal advisers." Better a cross JFK missing him, after all, than a president who couldn't care less whether he was there or not. Confident in that knowledge, Schlesinger boarded the plane for Uruguay.[16]

For Schlesinger it was the start of a marathon tour involving three continents. He traveled first to South America for the conference in Punta del Este, before flying to Asia for a meeting of the US-Japan Committee on Educational and Cultural Cooperation in Tokyo, followed by a tour of India with George McGovern of Food for Peace. Then he moved to Europe, where he went to Rome and Berlin with Bobby and Ethel Kennedy, before rounding off his trip with talks in Paris and London. In total, he was out of the United States for forty-two days. During that same period, JFK would fight hard with the State Department to reduce the length of a tour the First Lady had planned for India (Schlesinger's visit was part of the "advance"), complaining that they were "trying to make this jaunt to India last forever, and I don't want Mrs. Kennedy overscheduled." In the end, that visit was settled at nine days. But it is an indication of the demands put on White House staff that Schlesinger was expected to be away from home for well over a month. To help alleviate the burden, his wife Marian was at least allowed to join him for the second half of the tour.[17]

The conference in Punta del Este found Schlesinger, as usual, despairing about Dean Rusk's performance and, again as usual, he seized the occasion to undermine him with the president. The gathering of foreign ministers of the Organization of American States took place amid growing division and acrimony over what to do about Cuba. The Americans had proposed a hard line, effectively expelling Cuba from the club and imposing punitive sanctions. "The present Government of Cuba, which has officially identified itself as a Marxist–Leninist government," declared the draft resolution, "is incompatible with the principles and objectives of the inter-American system." In order to pass that resolution, a two-thirds majority (fourteen states) was required. After some last-minute negotiations, including, in a nod to future policy in the region, a deal with the authoritarian regime of François Duvalier in Haiti, the United States got its fourteen votes. But for Schlesinger it was an opportunity missed. Argentina had proposed a compromise motion (expulsion but more moderate sanctions) that all twenty states might easily have supported. "In these terms, the decision taken at Punta del Este to prefer a hard resolution and a divided hemisphere to milder resolution and a united hemisphere may have been an error," Schlesinger wrote to the president. He praised Rusk for his "great patience and tact in dealing with the Latinos," but twisted the knife by suggesting that "at the end he may have been overborne by the pressure of the North American legislators and the Central American diplomats." The importance of achieving unanimity among the

OAS nations would come to the fore later in 1962 during the missile crisis when the question was whether to impose a quarantine on Cuba. Now it was just one more misstep in American diplomacy on Cuba that overall, Schlesinger complained, was causing "general bafflement" among allies.[18]

From the drama of Punta del Este, Schlesinger traveled on to the educational and cultural meeting in Japan. "I guess this conference was a good idea," he complained, "[but] the meetings were about the most tedious I have ever attended anywhere." Things looked up once George McGovern arrived in Japan to travel on to India—the Food for Peace program's number one client state. Schlesinger liked McGovern, found him "intelligent, persuasive, tactful, and a splendid embodiment of American liberalism and of tough-minded humanitarianism." His program was committed to sending India $1.4 billion worth of wheat and other agricultural produce—the equivalent of a shipment of wheat every day for the next four years. As they toured India together, McGovern and Schlesinger witnessed the effect of this aid at first hand, not least in the popular school lunch program that reached one in every five Indian children and would help double school attendance by 1964. Schlesinger would later describe the Food for Peace program as "the greatest unseen weapon of Kennedy's third world policy." Its broader political impact in 1962, he reported back to the president, was such that he "could find little evidence of a serious Communist threat in the country"—an important development in a nonaligned nation during the Cold War.[19]

Schlesinger's tour across India with McGovern was thrilling but exhausting. "I evidently overscheduled Arthur a bit," ambassador J. K. Galbraith noted laconically. The two men nevertheless enjoyed the time they spent together in New Delhi, not least the opportunity to bitch about Rusk. "Arthur agrees that Rusk is a dull foundation type," Galbraith recorded, "necessarily dependent on the military and a passionate and indiscriminate exponent of all the Establishment clichés." All that seemed to matter to Rusk, they concluded, was that "he is in, which is the basic position of all Establishmentarians."[20]

Such lofty professorial disdain came easily around the dinner table at the ambassador's residence, but these Harvard men were Establishmentarians of their own kind too, having to endure a drubbing that in all other circumstances they would have disdained. Flying from New Delhi, still gossiping, this time about Kenneth O'Donnell and the "Irish mafia" in the White House, the two arrived at Dum Dum Airport in time to greet Bobby Kennedy, with whom Schlesinger would be traveling on to Rome and Berlin. "Bobby looked very tired," Galbraith noted, and when Schlesinger showed him the keynote address he was due to give in Berlin, Kennedy, in front of Galbraith, ripped it to shreds for its "conventional praise of the bravery of Berliners, [and] strictly conventional damnation of Communists." Galbraith had actually looked it over and "thought it all right." Now, however, "On second thoughts, I was forced to conclude, as did Arthur, that the criticism was sound." Rusk, it turned out, was not the only one who was beholden. As Thomas Parrot, a White House note-taker, would later say of the dynamic between Bobby and any official, "[He'd] sit there, chewing gum, his tie loose, feet up on his desk, daring anyone to contradict him. He was a little bastard, but he was the president's brother, the anointed guy, and you had to listen to him. Everybody felt that he would tell Big Brother if you didn't go along with what he was proposing."[21]

Loyalty to the Kennedys, a prerequisite of service, was particularly difficult to sustain during these next weeks, as their behavior on tour became more and more difficult to explain away. Ethel Kennedy, Bobby's wife, and Teddy Kennedy, Jack and Bobby's younger brother, had always been exuberant up to, and often beyond, the point of embarrassment. The previous summer, Schlesinger had recorded in his journal a party for Bobby and Ethel's wedding anniversary that had seen "wild dancing," Ethel and Teddy singing, and the latter "plunging fully dressed into the swimming pool." Schlesinger liked to explain this as "great fun—a perfect expression of the rowdier aspects of the New Frontier." To Ben Bradlee, editor of the Washington Post and no shrinking violet himself, the scene was "just like a horror movie." At the following year's party, Arthur found himself dumped fully clothed into the swimming pool with Ethel, causing him to offer his resignation to the president. "Don't worry about it," an amused JFK told him. Interior secretary Stewart Udall's wife, Lee, later confessed, saying "he was standing there holding forth and looking so Arthurish, and something came over me."[22]

Excessiveness at private parties might be considered one thing, but when the younger Kennedys were abroad representing their country, their public antics were more difficult to dismiss. In Rome, at the famous Alfredo's restaurant, a champagne-fueled lunch that went on for five hours reportedly ended with Ethel riding a Vespa between the tables, causing chaos and embarrassment. An appalled Marian Schlesinger said the "mayhem" represented "the Kennedy party at its adolescent worst."[23]

Even worse was to come in Berlin when Teddy Kennedy joined the party. At a dinner given by Willy Brandt, the mayor of Berlin and future chancellor, before Bobby's lecture at the Free University, events once again got out of hand. During the toasts, Brandt drank to "the President, government and people of the United States." The attorney general, responding lamely, said, "That's the three of us—the President, that's my brother [Jack]; the government, that's me; and [pointing at Teddy] you're the people." This remark, Brandt wrote afterwards, made him view the whole Kennedy project with "disquiet." Leaden humor then gave way to farce. Bobby rose again at the end of the dinner and made the unwelcome announcement that Teddy, who turned thirty that day, was "going to sing some songs from South Boston." To the astonishment of the West German worthies gathered at the banquet, the birthday boy now proceeded to give excruciating renditions of "When Irish Eyes Are Smiling" and "Danny Boy." "Teddy was obviously high and the tension was almost unbearable," Marian wrote. "The Kennedys often did this sort of thing, turning so many occasions into little private parties of their own, full of private jokes and silly by-play," she continued witheringly. "They were so self-centered that if something happened to them, then it had to be of overwhelming importance to everyone concerned whether it be the burghers of Berlin or the shopkeepers of Rome." Arthur, writing to the president afterwards, reported, "Bobby handled himself with immense poise and skill and did not make a false step." For Marian, on the other hand, the trip to Berlin was "one of the most embarrassing occasions I ever witnessed."[24]

The darker side of Camelot was in marked contrast to the sobering experience of the Berlin Wall. "It was more barbaric and sinister than one could have imagined," Arthur remembered, "the crude, gray concrete blocks, the bricked-in windows of the apartment houses along the sector line, the vicious tank traps, the tall picket fences erected to prevent East Berliners from even waving to relatives or friends in West Berlin, the plain white crosses marking places where people had jumped to their death." Surveying the depressing sight before him gave Schlesinger pause. Should the allies, he wondered, "have done something to halt the wall or to tear it down?" As his thoughts now turned homeward, it was a grim reminder, if he needed it, that policymaking in Washington affected real lives on the front line of the Cold War. He could hardly have known that within months, Washington, DC, itself would stand on that same front line.[25]

CHAPTER FIFTEEN

WE'RE COUNTING ON YOU

*W*hite *House cinema, Saturday, March 7, 1962.* Since childhood, Arthur Schlesinger had always been a film buff. At school he had kept a notebook in which he recorded his thoughts on every movie he saw. Always the academic, he even graded them. As special assistant to the president, he continued to write movie reviews for *Show: The Magazine of the Performing Arts* ("Do they pay you well?" Kennedy wanted to know). So now, having returned a few days earlier from a forty-two-day trip encompassing three continents and thousands of miles of travel, Schlesinger found himself in the screening room in the White House. The selection that night, the dreamlike *Last Year in Marienbad* directed by Alain Resnais, was unusual in an era dominated by Westerns. Schlesinger thought it "one of the most enthralling" films he had ever seen. But when the president left the White House screening room halfway through the movie, Schlesinger was caught in a diplomatic movie conundrum. Should he leave Marian Schlesinger and the First Lady to watch the movie alone? Take advantage of his boss leaving to grab him for a private word? What was a special advisor to do? In the end, discretion was the better part of valor, and he stayed behind, transfixed not just by the film but also by how Jackie watched "with fascination."[1]

Afterwards, when Kennedy returned to the room and the two couples chatted over late night drinks, the subject of families and how to raise children came up. How was it, Schlesinger sycophantically asked JFK, that the Kennedys had turned out so well when the Churchills and the Roosevelts

280

had done so badly? Kennedy's reply was remarkable for the consummate skill of his acting:

> Well no one can say that it was due to my mother. It was due to my father. He wasn't around as much as some fathers; but, when he was around, he made his children feel that they were the most important things in the world to him. He seemed terribly interested in everything we were doing. He held up standards for us, and he was very tough when we failed to meet his standards. This toughness was important. If it hadn't been for that, Teddy might be just a playboy today. But my father cracked down on him at a crucial time in his life, and this brought out in Teddy the discipline and seriousness which have made him a possible political figure.

Marian in particular must have found it hard not to choke on her drink, but the question makes Arthur look like a fool or a stooge. The fact that he asked it and Kennedy replied in that fashion tells us something about the relationship between the two men. Given what we now know about the "dark side of Camelot," it is impossible really to understand the extent to which Schlesinger was naïve about or complicit in the vagaries of the president's personal life. Certainly the way in which Arthur, in comparison to Marian, later glossed over the events in Rome and Berlin in his biography of Robert Kennedy, suggests that he was capable of turning a blind eye to the excesses of this family. He dismissed those who did otherwise as members of "the *National Enquirer* school of biographers." On the other hand, the question also displays a guileless quality. Certainly it was not a question that Kennedy would have had been asked by the likes of Dave Powers, for whom close friendship often entailed pimping for the president. Kennedy's answer shows how adept he was at maintaining the public facade. But it also illustrates the limits of the relationship man-to-man with Schlesinger, who surely otherwise would have steered well clear of the subject in front of Jackie.[2]

Whatever the nature of their personal friendship, Schlesinger's presence that weekend in the White House, where he dined two out of three consecutive nights, exemplifies the easy access that he enjoyed with Kennedy. A few weeks afterwards, John Kenneth Galbraith, following dinner with Schlesinger and the president, wondered whether he himself was "far less effective as an adviser than a year ago," because Kennedy now "knows so much more, has much greater confidence" than when he came into office. But Galbraith and Schlesinger were also learning to play the game a little better themselves, as events would soon demonstrate.[3]

In those weeks liberals in the administration—Schlesinger, Galbraith, and Chester Bowles (now special representative and advisor on African, Asian, and Latin American Affairs)—began a concerted push back on increasing American involvement in Vietnam. Both Schlesinger and Bowles visited India in consecutive weeks in February. On March 2, in a letter purportedly about the First Lady's visit to India, Galbraith told Kennedy that the United States looked doomed to repeat the mistakes of the French in Vietnam. Further US involvement was "political poison" and "could kill us." It was vital that the president keep the door open to a political settlement involving "even the Russians," Galbraith urged, reminding him shortly afterwards "that the Soviets are not particularly desirous of trouble in this part of the world."[4]

Three days later, Schlesinger opened his report on his global travels with a long disquisition on the state of Communism, reporting how "the Russo-Chinese tension has become a dominating issue throughout the world." There was, he wrote, "no question that this tension has already had a serious effect on Communist operations outside the bloc," adding that "the Russo-Chinese divergence has seriously impaired the broad appeal of Communism." The key for the United States was to encourage pluralism, but not do anything that might "stimulate Russia and China to try to get together again." Schlesinger did not mention Vietnam by name, but his strategic meaning could not have been clearer.[5]

Kennedy got the message and invited Schlesinger and Galbraith down to Glen Ora, his Virginia family retreat. (In a further indication of how dependent advisors were on the patronage of the president, Kennedy never bothered to see Chester Bowles, who also wrote him a fifty-four-page memorandum on Vietnam; the man who had backstabbed JFK after the

Bay of Pigs fiasco was "out.") Schlesinger and Galbraith arrived in Virginia in the late afternoon on April 1, with both surprised at the lack of security ("a gate with a single guard") and the "relatively modest" surroundings. Before dinner, everyone sat down to watch an NBC documentary about Jackie's visit to India. "Well, while you and Ken watch yourselves on television," Kennedy quipped, "Arthur can read his books and I will listen to some of my old speeches." After dinner, the talk turned to more serious matters—"South Vietnam as usual," said Galbraith.[6]

At the end of the evening, Kennedy asked for a formal memo on the subject. It arrived three days later on April 4, under Galbraith's signature, although the repeated use of "we" suggests that Schlesinger had a hand in its composition. The memo warned in stark terms that a "growing military commitment" in Vietnam "could expand step by step into a major, long-drawn-out, indecisive military involvement." The United States was "backing a weak and, on the record, ineffectual government." There was a "consequent danger we shall replace the French as the colonial force in the area and bleed as the French did." But what to do? "In the light of the foregoing we urge the following," the memo continued, recommending "that it be our policy to keep open the door for political solutions . . . seize any good opportunity to involve other countries and world opinion in settlement and its guarantee . . . [and] measurably reduce our commitment to the particular leadership of the government of South Vietnam." The United States should "approach the Russians to express our concern about the increasingly dangerous situation that the Vietcong is forcing in Southeast Asia." In the meantime, Kennedy should "resist all steps which commit American troops to combat action and impress upon all concerned the importance of keeping American forces out of actual combat zones." A personal note from Galbraith that accompanied the memo thanked JFK for "the other evening at Glen Ora, our survey of the problems of the nation and the world, and the chance to reflect on the unique capacity of your advisers to solve them."[7]

When the secretary of defense, Robert McNamara, and the chiefs of staff got hold of the Vietnam memo, they pressured the president to reject both its premise and recommendations. "The Department of Defense cannot concur in the policy advanced by Ambassador Galbraith," the joint chiefs told Kennedy, "but believe strongly that present policy toward South Vietnam should be pursued vigorously to a successful conclusion." In truth, Kennedy himself was skeptical about negotiating with Hanoi, but he also remained fearful that the United States was being dragged into a colonial war that could only end badly, so he sent word to Galbraith that he wanted him to explore the option of using India as a go-between with the North Vietnamese to find a way out. Galbraith's official biographer, Richard Parker, claims that Averell Harriman, now assistant secretary of state, disobeyed a direct instruction from the president and did not pass along that message to Galbraith. Yet Galbraith made the approach to the Indians anyway and sent a blistering telegram condemning Harriman.

Schlesinger may well have been the one to pass along the president's message, although George Ball, another assistant secretary at the State Department who opposed escalation in Vietnam, would also have been a candidate. Either way, it showed that the liberals were learning to work together effectively as political players. They had by no means won the argument on Vietnam, but they had at least successfully provided the president with an alternative strategy and point of view—a vital lesson learned from the Bay of Pigs disaster.[8]

The spring of 1962 also saw Schlesinger playing more of a role in crafting Kennedy's speeches, which in turn meant a subtly more liberal tone for the president. After all, Kennedy gave more progressive speeches once Schlesinger was brought in to help the more conservative Ted Sorensen. This arrangement also brought management challenges. Everyone, including the president, knew that working with the brilliant but possessive Sorensen was often a nightmare. Take, for example, the experience of Richard Goodwin, who had been in the speechwriting office with Sorensen from the beginning despite having told Kennedy after the 1960 campaign that "I don't think I can work with Ted." Kennedy persuaded him otherwise but was forced to move him on after less than a year when the relationship with Sorensen proved too fraught. Goodwin, born in 1931, was only three years younger than Sorensen, but the (slightly) older man treated him like some kind of ungrateful apprentice.

Schlesinger, on the other hand, as an older Pulitzer Prize–winning historian and Harvard professor who had been the chief speechwriter to Adlai Stevenson, was harder to ignore or dismiss. In January 1962, Kennedy asked Schlesinger to pep up Sorensen's draft of the state of the union address. Sorensen then stayed up the night before the speech, writing another competing version. Kennedy passed them both to Bundy and said, "Weave them together." According to Schlesinger's son Robert, even moments before the speech, Sorensen was trying to have Schlesinger's sections removed. "Ted certainly doesn't go for additions to his speeches!" Kennedy joked. But he kept the insertions, one of which—"To make society the servant of the individual and the individual the source of progress, and thus to realize for all the full promise of American life"—was highlighted as the "Quotation of the Day" in the next morning's *New York Times.* "Ted will die when he sees that," JFK told Schlesinger.[9]

In March, Kennedy asked Schlesinger to write a speech for Charter Day at the University of California, Berkeley. Kennedy was tired of headlines that talked only of a world in crisis; he wanted something that spoke of a democratic vision. He had read the long memorandum "Around the world in 42 days," in which Schlesinger had argued that the most basic difference between Communism and the democratic world was pluralism (an idea that he had picked up from his Oxford friend Isaiah Berlin). "Pluralism is incompatible with the Communist system," the memo stated, "but it is wholly compatible with—indeed, should be the basis of—our system. What we must do is both to emphasize that our objective is a pluralist world and to rethink our international relationships in these terms." Now in a further memo, Schlesinger urged that the Berkeley speech might show how "we have already made great progress in putting flesh and bones on the concept of the pluralistic world."[10]

Kennedy told Schlesinger to go ahead, but again Sorensen wrote a competing draft, this time on the "age of hate or the age of knowledge." On March 22, the day before the speech, Kennedy called both men up to his private office in the Family Quarters, passing a scowling FBI director, Edgar Hoover, on the threshold. ("I didn't introduce you," Kennedy explained, "because I did not want to upset Mr. Hoover.") Looking over the two drafts, Kennedy explained that he liked the "age of knowledge" but not the "age of hate" from Sorensen and "pluralism" from Schlesinger. "Weave them together," Kennedy again instructed, this time passing both drafts to Schlesinger. Each man "protested" that they were two different speeches, with Sorensen no doubt further irritated that Schlesinger got the assignment. Kennedy waved these concerns aside, telling them to have it done by 5 p.m.

"This reminds me of my father," Kennedy told them. "When someone gave him an idea or a memorandum, he would say, " 'This is lousy. It's no good.' Then they would ask what he wanted, and he would say, 'That's up to you,' and walk out of the room. That's what I am doing now." And he did precisely that, leaving for his swim and a nap. "By five," Arthur recorded, "I dutifully returned with a new draft." Just as the president had wanted, it combined both themes.

"The pursuit of knowledge itself implies a world where men are free to follow out the logic of their own ideas," Kennedy would say at Berkeley the next day. "It implies a world where nations are free to solve their own problems and to realize their own ideals. . . . We must reject oversimplified theories of international life—the theory that American power is unlimited, or that the American mission is to remake the world in the American image. We must seize the vision of a free and diverse world—and shape our policies to speed progress toward a more flexible world order." Afterwards, Schlesinger proudly recorded that Walter Lippmann described the speech as Kennedy's best since the inaugural address.[11]

The Berkeley speech established a pattern for Schlesinger and Sorensen. "My first draft seemed to him [JFK] too mild," Schlesinger wrote of the commencement address for Yale in 1962, "and he asked me to 'sharpen' it up, which with Galbraith's help I did. The result was too sharp." So of course "Sorensen now produced a new draft," Schlesinger explained, but "this was not right either." Eventually, to Sorensen's evident irritation, Schlesinger and Bundy (Yale '40) knocked out the final copy.

The theme, government-business relations, came at a time of economic sluggishness and industrial disputes. Interestingly, given the strident tone that Schlesinger had adopted toward business interests in his books, notably *The Crisis of the Old Order*, the main point of the speech was a call for common sense and pragmatism, not renewed ideological warfare.

"What is at stake in our economic decisions today is not some grand warfare of rival ideologies which will sweep the country with passion but the practical management of a modern economy," Kennedy said at Yale on June 11. "What we need is not labels and cliches but more basic discussion of the sophisticated and technical questions involved in keeping a great economic machinery moving ahead."

It was, Schlesinger wrote afterwards, an expression of Kennedy's "economic thought, with its pragmatic and managerial instincts." Years afterward, to Harvard's Daniel Bell, he noted, "the general problem of 'myth' and reality' was much on Kennedy's mind in that period," so that while he had written "the basic draft . . . the theme was Kennedy's own, expounded to me at some length when he asked me to prepare a draft." It was an example of how as a speechwriter Schlesinger had the capacity to be the servant not the master of the message. He did, however, follow it up with a long memorandum on "Business and Government: An Historian's View," which forcefully asserted that "an American president, to win world confidence, *must* convince the world that he is independent of the American business community."[12]

As a side note, it is worth pointing out that the Yale speech also demonstrated Schlesinger's natural ear for humor, on this occasion making good use of JFK's (as well as his own) background as a Harvard man. "It might be said now," Kennedy began, having received his honorary doctorate, "that I have the best of both worlds, a Harvard education and Yale degree." To great laughter he continued, "I am particularly glad to become a Yale man, because as I think about my troubles, I find that a lot of them have come from other Yale men."[13]

Important speeches such as those at Berkeley and Yale were part of Schlesinger's role as Kennedy's liaison with intellectuals and the universities. As he had written to Kennedy in 1961, "It might also be of use to have someone in the White House in whom labor and liberals would find what you once called 'visual reassurance' and whom they could trust as a channel of communication." Since the summer of 1961, that had involved being

Kennedy's point of contact for UN ambassador Adlai Stevenson. And it was in that role that Schlesinger would write perhaps the most important speech of his political career.[14]

––––––

THROUGHOUT THE SUMMER OF 1962, memos from the CIA began reporting that the Soviets were supplying Cuba with "large quantities of transportation, electronic and construction equipment" that included "possible limited quantity weapons." Several prominent Republicans, including Senator Kenneth Keating of New York, accused the administration of ignoring the buildup, including the prospect of missiles in Cuba. Schlesinger wrote to McGeorge Bundy on August 22, "The evidence suggests a striking change in Soviet policy toward Cuba." He explained how Raul Castro, brother of Fidel, had visited Moscow a few weeks earlier and that "it now appears that Raul succeeded and that the USSR may have decided to make a major investment in Cuba." But as to what that investment might be, Schlesinger urged caution. "Any military construction will probably be defensive in function," he wrote, because "a launching pad directed against the U.S. would be too blatant a provocation. Probably they want to listen in on Canaveral [space center]—or to shoot down a U-2." Then he added, "Mr. McCone is going to take this up with the President this afternoon."[15]

That apparently innocuous last line to Bundy was in fact a warning that CIA director John McCone took a much less benign view of Soviet activity. The Soviets were creating a major air defense system as part of what the CIA believed was "the most extensive campaign to bolster a nonbloc country ever undertaken by the U.S.S.R." Surely, McCone advised the president, the Soviets were not putting such an elaborate system in place unless there was something in Cuba they did not want the Americans to see. He believed that the something had to be preparations for nuclear weapons. Kennedy was skeptical about the claim, looking at it in the context of McCone's rabid anti-Communism. "The major danger is the Soviet Union with missiles and warheads," the president cautioned, "not Cuba."[16]

Schlesinger was relieved at Kennedy's circumspection, but two weeks later he returned to the subject of Cuba in a memo to the president. "I know very little about the present state of our Cuban policy," he began. "However, as an old Cuba hand, it seems to me that there are increasingly dangerous potentialities in the existing situation." Schlesinger then went on to say that he had heard about "a planned uprising in Cuba in the next few weeks," which he feared would be a disastrous repeat of the Bay of Pigs. "Our world prestige would suffer a terrific blow," he warned. "I would therefore hope that CIA *be given the clear cut and definite responsibility to make sure that no such premature insurrection takes place.*"

Kennedy's reply was guarded. "I read your memorandum of September 5th on Cuba," it said. "I know of no planned 'uprisings inside Cuba within the next few weeks.' Would you send me the intelligence reports to which you refer. In any case, I will discuss the matter with the CIA." In fact, as Schlesinger had seemingly picked up around the White House, the president at the end of August had already approved a top-secret directive to begin phase B of Operation Mongoose—the plan, coordinated by Bobby Kennedy, to murder Castro and overthrow his Marxist regime. Schlesinger later claimed circumstantial evidence pointed neither to Bobby nor to the president knowing about the specific plans to assassinate Castro. But either way, he would write, Operation Mongoose remained "Robert Kennedy's most conspicuous folly."[17]

Schlesinger's forceful posture on Cuba helps explain why JFK kept him out of the loop in the coming weeks as the Missile Crisis unfolded. Unlike Sorensen and Bundy, Schlesinger would not sit in on EXCOMM meetings from October 16 onwards. Thus he had no voice in shaping America's response to the discovery of Soviet nuclear-tipped missiles in Cuba. In fact, not only was Schlesinger absent from the meetings, such was their secrecy that he did not even know they were taking place. Given the need for absolute discretion, Schlesinger's loose lips may also have been part of the reason for his exclusion. ("I am filled with contrition over my loose talking yesterday," he had recently apologized in familiar fashion to the president. "I will stay away from the press for a while.") Either way, it meant that he was out of the room when decisions were made during one of the most important moments of the Cold War.[18]

That exclusion, however, did not mean he had no significant role to play as the events unfolded. In many ways, the crisis was the high point of his political career. On the afternoon of Friday, October 19, Adlai Stevenson phoned Schlesinger to say that he was in Washington and could they meet up early the next day. Stevenson was staying across the street from Schlesinger in Georgetown, and when the younger man walked the few short steps for the meeting, he found the ambassador's official car already waiting with the engine running. But Stevenson beckoned Schlesinger inside the house, telling him that he didn't want to risk being overheard by the driver.

"Do you know what the secret discussions this week have been about?" Stevenson asked him. Schlesinger had not even heard of any secret discussions. "Berlin?" he replied weakly. "No, Cuba," Stevenson said, and then went on to reveal what was going on. "The secret was superbly kept," Schlesinger wrote somewhat ruefully in his diary afterwards. Stevenson now came quickly to the point. He had to make a speech to the UN Security Council justifying any American action: would Schlesinger write it for him?[19]

That same Saturday, Stevenson was involved in the most intense EXCOMM meeting of the entire crisis, as the president's advisors debated whether to bomb or blockade Cuba. Stevenson supported the latter course, but also proposed a series of other measures, including a guarantee of the territorial integrity of Cuba, UN inspection teams, and a summit meeting with Khrushchev. He also suggested handing back Naval Station Guantanamo Bay and withdrawing US missiles in Turkey in exchange for withdrawal of missile capacity in Cuba. At one stage, an incandescent Bobby Kennedy called a halt and pulled Stevenson aside into a separate room to continue the discussion in private, making clear, he later wrote, that he "disagreed strongly with his recommendations." Many of Stevenson's suggestions, including the offer to withdraw missiles from Turkey, would in fact become a decisive and highly secret part of the resolution of the crisis, but at the time they were sharply rejected.[20]

Stevenson's performance that Saturday afternoon led to accusations not only that he was a Cold War dove, but also that he was too soft or even a 1930s style appeaser.[21] John F. Kennedy, however, was at least impressed by Stevenson's fortitude in defending his line in the face of direct attacks. "You have to admire him for sticking to it," the president told Sorensen, later adding to deputy national security advisor Carl Kaysen that Stevenson had shown "a lot of guts to come in here and say what he thought was right." Kennedy might have admired Stevenson's mettle, but it also left him with a problem. Robert Lovett, Truman's secretary of defense, warned about the ambassador's state of mind and advised Kennedy to send someone up to New York to look after him when he presented America's case at the UN. Adopting a strategy of "good cop/bad cop," for the latter Kennedy summoned John McCloy back from Europe to sit next to Stevenson during the UN debate. The pretext was bipartisan support; the subtext was that as a Cold War hardliner McCloy would stiffen the ambassador's sinews. "I am confident," Schlesinger would write in a note drafted for the president to send Stevenson, "that no one can interpret this in any way as a departure from your continuing authority and leadership in New York." Understandably Stevenson did not agree, protesting to Kennedy that the Republican's presence was an outrage. Schlesinger knew it too, which may be why he deleted the phrase in the final draft.[22]

If McCloy was the bad cop, then Kennedy's pick as good cop was an obvious choice. "On Monday the President told me to go to New York and work with Stevenson on the UN side of things," Schlesinger wrote. He already had a completed draft of Stevenson's speech, which he now discussed with JFK, Dean Rusk, and Robert Kennedy. "It was generally applauded," he reported. But Bobby pulled him aside afterwards to make clear that his role was about more than writing the speech. "We're counting on you to watch things in New York," he warned him. "That fellow [Stevenson] is ready to give everything away."[23]

"The next three days," Schlesinger recalled, "were a kind of continued pandemonium." He arrived in New York just in time to watch with Stevenson as the president outlined to the nation in a TV address the quarantine of offensive military equipment and his warning that any missile launched from Cuba would be regarded as an attack on the United States by the Soviet Union. As they discussed the president's speech, Schlesinger thought Stevenson seemed in "good shape" and reconciled to the strategy. Even McCloy's arrival did not seem to rattle the ambassador.

Some familiar frustrations remained, however, as Schlesinger found the experience of working with Stevenson as maddening as ever. "The actual speech process was dismally reminiscent of the 1952 and 1956 campaigns," he complained. "Adlai Stevenson worked hard on the draft, but at the last moment, so that both the main speech, delivered on Tuesday, and the rebuttal, delivered on Thursday, were still in the works when he had to go over to the Security Council to begin speaking."[24]

Nevertheless, amid the "sense of continuous and unrelenting crisis" at the UN that week, Schlesinger thought Stevenson proved "unperturbed and effective." On Tuesday, October 23, the ambassador, using the speech and notes Schlesinger drafted, outlined the "grave threat to the Western Hemisphere and to the peace of the world." In a bone-chilling conclusion, he declared, "We hope that Chairman Khrushchev has not made a miscalculation, that he has not mistaken forbearance for weakness. We cannot believe that he has deluded himself into supposing that, though we have power, we lack nerve; that, though we have weapons, we are without the will to use them." Immediately afterwards, a delighted Kennedy cabled him a message. "I watched your speech this afternoon with great satisfaction," it read. "It has given our cause a great start. . . . The United States is fortunate to have your advocacy. You have my warm and personal thanks."[25]

Stevenson's finest hour, however, was yet to come. On Thursday, October 25, armed again with a Schlesinger speech, the ambassador returned to the chamber of the Security Council for his famous confrontation with his Soviet counterpart, Valerian Zorin (who was also in the chair). "All right, sir," he demanded at the height of their exchange, "let me ask you one simple question: Do you, Ambassador Zorin, deny that the USSR has placed and is placing medium and intermediate range missiles and sites in Cuba. Yes or No? Do not wait for the translation. Yes or no?" When Zorin told Stevenson he was not in a courtroom, Stevenson fired back, using a phrase that he had discussed with Schlesinger and Galbraith a year earlier, "You are in the courtroom of world opinion right now, and can answer yes or no." Zorin hedged again, saying Stevenson would get an answer in due course. To which Stevenson replied, somewhat illogically but brilliantly, "I am prepared to wait for my answer until Hell freezes over, if that is your decision. I am also prepared to present evidence in this room," which he promptly did—displaying huge presentation boards of the U-2 reconnaissance photographs showing the presence of nuclear sites in Cuba.

"Stevenson had his confrontation with Zorin in the Security Council," Schlesinger wrote afterwards in his diary. "Zorin, who seemed to be laboring without instructions, was not effective, and Stevenson even won a favorable notice from the *Daily News.*" Perhaps more pertinently, Stevenson got another favorable notice from the president. "Terrific," he announced, watching the speech on TV in the Oval Office, before adding more waspishly, "I never knew Adlai had it in him. Too bad he didn't show some of this steam in the 1956 campaign."[26]

Stevenson was not the only one of his old clients that Schlesinger helped rehabilitate that week in New York. In between Stevenson's two speeches, Averell Harriman contacted Schlesinger to express his concern about how the crisis was developing. Although Harriman was an assistant secretary at the State Department, he was conspicuously outside the policymaking loop. But Harriman was not going to let that stop him from involving himself in the current crisis, when, he believed rightly, he had as much experience in reading Soviet intentions as anyone in Washington. Khrushchev was desperate to find a way off the hook, he now told Schlesinger. "We must give him an out," Harriman urged. "If we do this shrewdly, we can downgrade the tough group in the Soviet Union which persuaded him to do this. But if we deny him an out, then we will escalate this business into a nuclear war." Have you told anyone this? Schlesinger asked him. "I haven't talked to Rusk," Harriman admitted. So Schlesinger promised to pass along his view directly to Kennedy.

"Accordingly I reported his view in a memorandum which I sent that night to the President," he recalled, "who apparently read it because he called Harriman the next day and asked him questions about it." In that conversation, Harriman, as Stevenson had, would raise the prospect of withdrawing US missiles from Turkey—a crucial part of the deal between

Kennedy and Khrushchev that would emerge over the coming weekend. Bobby Kennedy, who noticed how useful Harriman's Soviet credentials had been during the crisis, recommended that Harriman soon afterwards become assistant secretary of state for political affairs, putting him once again back on the inside track.[27]

Going in to see the president on Monday, October 29, once the crisis had passed, Schlesinger found JFK "relaxed and chipper but far from complacent." The problem, Kennedy told him, was that "too many people will think now that all we have to do in dealing with the Russians is to kick them in the balls." Kennedy asked him to put some thoughts on paper about how they might present the lessons from these traumatic thirteen days. That paper, written the same afternoon, would point to the crisis as marking "an end and a beginning—an end to violent adventures designed to overturn the equilibrium of world power; and a beginning of fresh initiatives for peace," particularly on nuclear testing. "[We] should interpret the nature of the victory in such a way as to accustom the nation to the future use of limited force for limited purposes," he told Kennedy, "while at the same time pointing out that our success in Cuba does not prove that force can solve everything." After all, a relieved Schlesinger reflected in the privacy of his own diary, it had all been "a near thing."[28]

At the end of the meeting, the two men conversed about the judgments of history. A survey of seventy-five historians, published that year by Arthur's father in the New York Times Magazine, fascinated Kennedy. The poll had appeared under a photograph not of a past president but of the current one, with the question underneath, "How will he be rated by historians?" Kennedy had expressed astonishment at the high rankings for Woodrow Wilson and Theodore Roosevelt in the survey over, say, Polk or Truman. "What is interesting," Schlesinger reported to his father, "is that his criterion is obviously that of concrete achievement rather than political education." Talking later to Walter Reuther of the United Automobile Workers, Schlesinger put it another way: the shift from the New Deal to the New Frontier was one from "evangelists who want to do something because it is just and right, to technocrats who want to do something because it is rational and necessary."

Writing to his mother to thank her for the gift of cigars for his birthday ("I have been smoking them regularly throughout the crisis and could hardly have survived without them"), Schlesinger now offered his own first draft of the judgment of history on the president. "Everyone here says that the President was superb," he told her, "cool, judicious, clear, and wholly impervious to the pressures, at times quite extreme, to get him to commit himself to one or another rash policy." Life in Washington, DC, had returned to normal, Arthur reassured her. "Last night among the trick or treaters, there appeared a little girl dressed in a mask with a collection of friends," he reported. "Behind them a masked mother directed their activities. It turned out to be Jackie and Caroline."[29]

CHAPTER SIXTEEN

THE WATCHMAN WAKETH BUT IN VAIN

The missile crisis boosted the president's national approval ratings, with one Gallup poll saying he was the most admired man in the world. That in turn bolstered Kennedy's confidence about reelection in 1964. The midterm elections had delivered the second-best result for a party in a century. The favorite to win the Republican nomination, Barry Goldwater, the senator from Arizona, was someone Kennedy believed would frighten moderate conservatives into his camp. All told, his political prospects looked better than at any time since before the Bay of Pigs disaster shortly after he took office in 1961.[1]

Schlesinger had clear ideas about how the president should spend that political capital in 1963. The missile crisis, we saw him tell Kennedy days after the crisis passed, represented "an end and a beginning." For Schlesinger that meant both a reengaging on the whole question of nuclear testing that had complicated superpower relations since the summer of 1961, and the minting of a new evangelizing language addressing the broader question of peace. Yet Arthur himself remained frustratingly at arm's length in this process.

Over the course of the next year, with the memory still fresh of how close the two sides had come to a nuclear exchange, the United States and the Soviet Union worked steadily toward a nuclear test agreement. In July 1963 Averell Harriman went to Moscow, where an agreement was reached on the terms of a limited test ban treaty. The US Senate ratified the treaty on September 24 by a majority of 80–19.[2]

Kennedy described the test ban treaty as "a shaft of light cut into the darkness." That language reflected for Kennedy in 1963 a rhetorical shift in the way he discussed the Cold War. On June 10, wanting to give the test ban talks a boost, Kennedy gave the commencement address at American University in Washington, DC. There he broke with the Wilsonian tradition of making "the world safe for democracy" by declaring that he wanted peace for all mankind, "not a Pax Americana enforced on the world by American weapons of war." It was time to reexamine relations with the Soviet Union, he said. The huge losses that the Soviets had endured in defeating Hitler must be acknowledged and honored. Pluralism of political systems need not be a barrier to good relations. And the two countries had to work together to ensure that the world avoided another war—this one nuclear. "For in the final analysis," Kennedy declared in one of his most eloquent pieces of rhetoric, "our most basic common link is that we all inhabit this small planet; we all breathe the same air; we all cherish our children's future; and we are all mortal." Twelve days later, Kennedy embarked on a ten-day European tour, where he was greeted, the presidential historian Herbert Parmet would later write, "as though he was a new prince of peace and freedom."[3]

In all these developments, Schlesinger remained at best distant, at worst completely out of the loop. The American University speech showed how successful Sorensen had been in repelling Schlesinger's advances in the battle of the speechwriters. During the previous year, Kennedy had often set the two men up against each other, telling them to sort out their differences for important speeches such as the Yale commencement address. Or, as in the 1962 State of the Union address, he told Sorensen to include specific paragraphs from Schlesinger's drafts. By 1963 Sorensen was clearly in command and Schlesinger on the bench. "Feel free to recommend deletions and improvements in grammar and style as well as substance," Sorensen had written offhandedly to him about the 1963 State of the Union message, adding the curt instruction, "It is imperative, however, that specific changes in wording are suggested, not general comments." Provocatively, Schlesinger rewrote the entire speech, telling Sorensen, "It seemed to me simplest to run it through the typewriter." For the American University speech, Sorensen sent copies to Schlesinger, Mac Bundy, and Walt Rostow, who then met to discuss it. "We all thought the speech was fine and suggested only minor changes," Schlesinger noted in his diary. Then Sorensen joined Kennedy on a trip to Hawaii, where the two men worked alone on the speech aboard the new "Air Force One" presidential plane. When they returned to Washington, DC, on the morning of June 10, an unkempt Sorensen, text in hand, went straight to American University rather than accompanying the president back to the White House. It was yet another example of the lengths to which he would go to keep others away from his handiwork.

For all the personal irritation in his relationship with Sorensen, Schlesinger could not help but admire the results and the way in which the American University speech circumvented the bureaucratic constraints that so often blunted the key messages. "I suppose from that, from the viewpoint of orderly administration, this was a bad way to prepare a major statement on foreign policy," he mused, "but the State Department could never in a thousand years have produced this speech. The President is fortunately ready to assert control over the policy of his administration, however deeply it may offend the bureaucracy." Or his other speechwriters, he might have added.[4]

Sorensen's highly defensive attitude about being the sole voice for the president could explain Schlesinger's minimal involvement with the American University address. Other areas of exclusion were more puzzling. Two years earlier, when the test ban issue once again became a point of conflict between the United States and the Soviet Union, Kennedy had asked Schlesinger to draft a white paper. Schlesinger had then been closely involved in advising the president throughout the summer, even if he eventually ended up on the losing side about whether or not the United States should resume atmospheric testing. By 1963, however, even though the debate had moved in his direction, Schlesinger played almost no role in the White House discussion of the issue. What makes this exclusion even more surprising is that Averell Harriman, the politician to whom, along with Adlai Stevenson, Schlesinger was closest, became deputy undersecretary of state in April and then led the discussions in Moscow that brought agreement.[5]

Schlesinger's exile was similarly evident in European affairs. Again in 1961, pushing a theme he had developed in *The Vital Center* about the importance of the non-Communist Left, Schlesinger had argued hard that the United States should take advantage of an "opening to the left" in Italy. That intervention loosed an avalanche of opprobrium on Schlesinger's head. State Department officials dismissed him as an amateur and Secretary of State Dean Rusk could scarcely hide his contempt. But by 1963, just as Kennedy prepared to leave for Europe, the "opening to the left" had come off, with the Socialists about to join a government for the first time since 1947. It was a moment of great personal and political satisfaction for Schlesinger, and an area, moreover, in which he could justifiably claim to have greater expertise than others in the president's team. Not only that, but Kennedy was also visiting Berlin and London, both places where Schlesinger had connections and expertise. Hence he might reasonably have expected a seat on the presidential plane. Yet while the likes of Sorensen, Bundy, Dave Powers, and Kenny O'Donnell all accompanied the president to Europe, Schlesinger remained behind. He could not quite bring himself to beg for a seat, but he did quietly try to maneuver himself onto the plane. When the draft speeches from the State Department came in for use in Europe, Schlesinger told the president they were pretty much rubbish. "My general impression is of their predominant banality and vapidity," he wrote. "These speeches could have been given just as easily by President Eisenhower—or by President Nixon. They fail to convey any sense of a fresh American voice or distinctive Kennedy approach." Perhaps, Schlesinger suggested, picking up on a casual remark the president made in the Oval Office, it might be worth "sending Ted Sorensen and myself over a few days in advance to get the feel of things," before adding hastily, "I am not bucking for a trip for myself." In the end it did not happen. "Ted does not consider this necessary," Schlesinger wrote forlornly.[6]

Sorensen had cut Schlesinger out of the loop; other personality clashes also took a toll. On European affairs, Schlesinger found himself blocked off by Rusk. The secretary believed "Schlesinger was a fifth wheel in decision making." He purposely "stonewalled" to keep him away from policymaking and foreign trips. How keenly Schlesinger felt that personal animosity is evident in *A Thousand Days*, where he delivered the only real insider hatchet job in the book. In six pages on "The Enigma of Rusk," he headed and gutted the man who was still secretary of state as a character of "imperturbable blandness" who constantly "perplexed and disappointed" Kennedy. "Inscrutability was splendid as a negotiating stance," Schlesinger hissed, "but inadequate as a principle of life."[7]

Schlesinger recognized as well that the Kennedy team ultimately viewed him as a Stevenson man. Some of that distrust went back at least to the 1960 Democratic convention, when Schlesinger, uneasy at the ruthlessness of the Kennedy campaign, appeared to flirt with the idea that Stevenson should get a third tilt at the presidency. He served the White House in part as a liaison with the liberal faction faithful to Stevenson. That function had paid great dividends for the administration during the missile crisis, when Kennedy sent Schlesinger to work with Stevenson on his UN speeches, but in its aftermath, the special assistant again seemed to show where his loyalties lay. A few weeks after the crisis, the *Saturday Evening Post* proclaimed, "Adlai Wants a Munich. He Wanted to Trade U.S. Bases for Cuban Bases." The authors, Stewart Alsop and Charles Bartlett, were both friends of the president, who had seen the article in draft and who was the "non-admiring official" referred to in the story. Kennedy, whose undergraduate thesis and a subsequent book condemned appeasement, even seems himself to have penciled in "Munich." Schlesinger urged the president to refute the story. Afterwards, he sent a memo in which he took the story apart line by line. "The Alsop-Bartlett story on Stevenson seems to be wrong in almost every particular" he charged. At the time, Schlesinger was not among the handful who knew that Kennedy had done a deal to remove US missiles in Turkey in exchange for Soviet withdrawal of those in Cuba. Kennedy had fed the Stevenson story to Alsop and Bartlett, partly because it enabled him to look strong in comparison to the ambassador. Schlesinger, outraged by the attack on his old boss, called on his new one to come to the ambassador's aid. "The suggestion in the Alsop-Bartlett story that Stevenson favored a Caribbean Munich is grossly unfair," he told Kennedy, "and shows the number of people who still have their knives out for him." Clearly he did not realize that Kennedy was one of them. Reluctantly, Kennedy agreed to write to Stevenson emphasizing the importance of the ambassador's role at the UN during the crisis and that the letter could be leaked to journalists.[8]

In defending Stevenson, Schlesinger embarrassed the president by calling him out in front of his own Georgetown set. That contributed to his drift to the margins. But so too did the sense, often self-inflicted, that Schlesinger was not *un homme sérieux*. The president "liked Arthur Schlesinger," his brother, Robert Kennedy, would say, "but he thought he was a little bit of a nut sometimes."

By 1963, that nuttiness was beginning to irk. Schlesinger embroiled himself in embarrassing public spats with the likes of William F. Buckley Jr., the founder and editor of the conservative magazine *National Review*. Buckley liked nothing better than tweaking Schlesinger as a high priest of the liberal establishment. Recall that during the 1960 election he had sent a donkey to Schlesinger's house in Cambridge. In a similar vein of devilment, in February 1963, Buckley advertised his new book with a quotation from Schlesinger: "He has a facility for rhetoric which I envy, as well as wit which I seek clumsily and vainly to emulate." Rather than playing along with the joke, or at least rising above it, Schlesinger wrote immediately to demand that the publisher furnish him with "the source of this statement or else discontinue its use." On and on the correspondence went, with a delighted Buckley never failing to up the stakes. "Would you be so kind as to ask Mr. Schlesinger to okay the translation of his quotation into French," Buckley asked in April, including the text. Then he put out a press release saying Schlesinger was suing him and trying to censor the book. Furious, Schlesinger wrote a public letter to *Publishers Weekly* protesting that "both claims are false." Inevitably Buckley responded, happy to keep the row going. He would stop using the quotation, he wrote, if Schlesinger sent him a letter "requesting me to do him the personal favor of removing it." Otherwise, "so long as he tries to get me to drop it under the pressures of Messrs. Greenbaum, Wolff and Ernst [attorneys], I'll go to the electric chair first, and instruct my heirs to put on my tombstone, Wm. F. 'Envy His Rhetoric' Buckley Jr."

Such a row between two literary figures might have been entertaining; Buckley, after all, regularly sparred with liberal writers such as Norman Mailer and Gore Vidal. But Schlesinger was no longer simply a literary figure; he was a political one, and such exchanges often seemed beneath the dignity of a special assistant at the White House. When added to embarrassing headlines that he had fallen into the swimming pool with Ethel Kennedy at Hickory Hill, called a journalist an "idiot," or accepted payment for articles in contravention of the government code of conduct, the impression emerged of a man who was more a liability than an asset. Schlesinger himself conceded the point after the swimming pool incident in 1962, writing to the president with "a heartfelt apology for the trouble I was causing him and a statement that I would resign at any time." Yet his behavior over the next year did not noticeably change.[9]

Irritation with Schlesinger's working methods inside the White House compounded concern over his outside nuttiness. Kennedy often seemed to tire of Schlesinger's barrage of ideas and proposals. "His suggestions would reach the President's desk in a constant stream of memoranda," Pierre Salinger recalled. "Although many of Schlesinger's recommendations were put to use, JFK occasionally was impatient with their length and frequency, and felt that many of the memos should have gone to staff specialists."[10]

At times Schlesinger's demands on the president's time went beyond frivolous. In the spring of 1963, as Kennedy grappled with the implications of the Birmingham civil rights campaign, one of the most influential struggles of the civil rights movement, Schlesinger chose to ask him about the state of the White House tennis court. "The President listened skeptically," Schlesinger recorded, but told him he saw "no particular need to resurface the court." Yet Schlesinger persisted until Kennedy said somewhat testily that he would "take a look himself." The next day he ended the debate. "I went down to take a look at the court," he told his special assistant, "and it looks fine to me." Schlesinger admitted defeat ("at least until the fall" he added in his diary). He seems not to have recognized that he might have irritated the president or wasted both men's time in the face of what Schlesinger called "a Negro revolution." "It has been a long time since I felt things to be so vividly in motion in our country," he added with no reference to tennis.[11]

These flaps in and out of the White House came together during the Birmingham campaign. Kennedy had been cautious on introducing civil rights legislation, but the aftermath of police attacks on black demonstrators in Birmingham, Alabama, finally convinced him to ask Congress for a civil rights law. On June 11, 1963, George Wallace, the controversial governor of Alabama, in the face of the federalized Alabama National Guard, allowed two black students to register at the University of Alabama, thereby ending segregation of admissions in the school. Robert Kennedy, as attorney general, bore the brunt of this confrontation. He urged his brother to use the occasion to inform the nation on television that he was calling on Congress to act on civil rights. Given that Wallace left the campus at 5:40 p.m. Washington time, the White House had just over two hours to meet the 8 p.m. TV deadline for the address. Both Kennedys handed their notes to Sorensen. There was also a draft speech on civil rights from Richard Yates, Bobby's new speechwriter and the acclaimed author of *Revolutionary Road* (although characteristically Sorensen later claimed never to have read the Yates draft). Within the hour, Sorensen had his own first draft, which he took to the waiting president and his brother. RFK, thinking of 1964, was appalled by its confrontational tone, which included phrases like "the cesspool of discrimination" and "a social revolution is at hand," and he pronounced it "unsatisfactory." The president agreed the draft was inadequate. Waving away Sorensen's protests, he told Evelyn Lincoln to get hold of Arthur Schlesinger right away.[12]

Four hundred miles away in Boston, Arthur was drinking whisky with his Harvard contemporaries, war correspondent Richard Tregaskis and journalist Teddy White. The three members of the class of '38 were marking their twenty-fifth reunion. But Arthur and his friends were doing so privately, taking a rain check as the rest of the class gathered at Symphony Hall to hear Arthur Fiedler and the Boston Pops Orchestra. The three men had agreed to enjoy some gossip and a few drinks before watching the president speak on TV at eight o'clock.

As they drank, back in Symphony Hall an announcement came over the public address system paging Schlesinger. After a few minutes, the message came again, this time more urgent. "Attention Mr. Schlesinger! Attention Mr. Schlesinger! Urgent message from the White House. Call the President!" No doubt eyes rolled among those gathered in the hall. As one of the youngest members of the class, there had always been something immature about Little Arthur. Had he paid someone on the hall staff to make such a self-aggrandizing announcement? Over at Winthrop House, the undergraduate hall where Schlesinger was staying for the reunion, other urgent messages from Mrs. Lincoln also piled up, but Arthur could not be found.

Back at the White House, with the minutes ticking down before JFK spoke to the nation, the atmosphere was becoming increasingly agitated. "It was," Sorensen recalled, "the only time in my three years at the White House that JFK came to my office to ask about a speech." Sorensen's deputy, Lee White, remembers, "The President was extremely nervous. Normally he's not nervous, but he was awfully damn nervous about this one. . . . He wasn't sure exactly what was going to come out of the typewriter . . . he was scrounging around for more information and he remembered he'd read something in the New York Times two days before, could we find that? People were flying around trying to get it." When National Security Advisor McGeorge Bundy arrived at Joe Alsop's house for dinner shortly before 8 o'clock, he told the assembled group, "There isn't going to be a speech. I just left the White House 30 minutes ago and Sorensen didn't have a draft yet." ("That was true," Sorensen admits.) And still Arthur Schlesinger was M.I.A. Finally, at 7:55 p.m., Schlesinger got a message and immediately called the White House. It was too late: Kennedy was on air in five minutes.[13]

In the end Sorensen admitted defeat and simply gave the president what he had. "When the text did arrive, Kennedy had no more than two minutes to look it over," writes Andrew Cohen in Two Days in June. "It was a jumble of fragments and different pieces of paper; he made changes in pen, striking words, adding others. . . . In some accounts of this *opéra bouffe* pages continued to arrive even after he began speaking." Certainly Kennedy extemporized the last eight paragraphs. This last section, "to give a chance for every child," Lee White later judged, "was probably the most moving part of the whole thing."[14]

Kennedy's call for social justice was controversial, but everyone seemed to recognize the address itself as a tour de force. "It was one of the most eloquent, profound and unequiv[ocal] pleas for justice and freedom of all men ever made by any President," Martin Luther King Jr. wrote to Kennedy immediately afterwards. Sorensen, judging his own efforts, was more modest. "It turned out fine," he recalled. In some ways Sorensen had been hoisted by his own petard. He never lost an opportunity to make clear that others had made little or no contribution to important speeches. Even Kennedy's extemporized conclusion to the civil rights speech was parsed ("there is a discernable point where the rhythm and style change slightly," Sorensen wrote). Had he developed a team around him, perhaps he would not, in his own words, have left JFK with four minutes to go before 8 p.m. "scribbling while waiting for me, fearing I might produce nothing and he would have no text at all."[15]

Schlesinger regarded Kennedy's TV address as "the best speech in his administration on civil rights." But he felt intensely the personal embarrassment at not having been available to help amid the chaos. Not only had he missed an opportunity to upstage Sorensen, he was perhaps the only person in the White House who would have had both the skill set and the personal authority to bang out sections of the speech and then put them directly into the hands of the president. He was a faster, more fluent and prolix writer than Sorensen, and his first drafts were usually better.

As the night of June 11 went on, the full extent of White House efforts to contact him became apparent. "At first, I thought it was a joke," he said on hearing about Symphony Hall, "but it became evident that something had happened." When he returned to Winthrop House, he received Mrs. Lincoln's messages urging him to call the president. "I suppose that, at the peak of uncertainty, he was collecting opinions as to what he should do," he wrote, adding a somewhat forlorn, "Anyway, it came out right."

In his more private moments, however, Schlesinger understood that the events confirmed the unfavorable impression developing about him. Of course, he had informed the president in a note that he was "scheduled to be in Cambridge until Thursday night [June 13] at my 25th reunion [but] I can break away at a moment's notice, however, if I can be helpful here." Yet when the moment came, he had neither broken away nor been helpful. That made him look both hapless and lightweight. It was something about which he had been anxious throughout his time at the White House. "I feel that I lack some sort of specific gravity of the kind that is required for effectiveness in government," he confessed. "I guess I convey an ineradicable impression of dilettantism—partly because I am spread so thin and partly because at bottom I must prefer it that way." The events of June 11 did nothing to dispel that impression.[16]

Throughout that summer, Schlesinger remained on the fringes. Kennedy was in Europe throughout much of June and July, leaving Arthur in Washington, DC, while Sorensen supplied another hit with the famous "Ich bin ein Berliner" speech (even if the German phrase implied that the president was a doughnut). Soon afterwards, Averell Harriman made the surprisingly fast breakthrough in Moscow that led to a limited test ban treaty with the Soviets.

While others bestrode the world stage, Schlesinger was left in the White House managing a project for the First Lady, who wanted to provide the building with a proper library. "As you know, Mrs. Kennedy is deeply interested in realizing the full potentialities of the White House as an expression of American culture and the American experience," he had explained to Fred Adams, the director of the Pierpont Morgan Library in New York. "Her redecoration program has included the Library on the ground floor, and it is her hope that this Library may contain the books which will best represent the history and culture of the United States." Now having begun the process of housing the books, Schlesinger was trying to maneuver Jackie into putting the library to use. "I had supposed that members of the White House staff, who need to consult a book in a hurry, might feel free to go to the shelves of the White House Library," he gently pleaded with her. "It is true that the Library of Congress is available; but it takes half a day to get books from the other side of town; and, as you know, there are occasions when something has to be written in half an hour." The library matter was a far cry from what Schlesinger anticipated when he left his tenured professorship at Harvard to join the president's staff.[17]

This last thought seemed to nag at Schlesinger. The previous year he had cheerfully given up tenure at Harvard to remain as special assistant to the president. Now when the early modern historian W. K. Jordan wrote somewhat bashfully saying that the Widener Library had offered him Schlesinger's old room, Arthur reacted with barely concealed alarm. "Have you any suggestions as to how I should answer this question," he asked his father plaintively. Clearly there was "no substantial ground for continuing to reserve Widener." And yet "on the other hand, it is an agreeable office, and I should be sorry to relinquish it." Glumly he concluded, "I imagine that there is no alternative." But more than at any point during his time in Washington, DC, the letter seemed to show not just that Schlesinger had doubts about his role in the White House, but that also, really for the first time, he was thinking about an eventual return to his old life in Cambridge.[18]

If Schlesinger felt dejected that summer, Phil Graham's suicide compounded his dismay. The publisher of the *Washington Post* was "in some ways the most brilliant member of my generation" (which, it should be remembered, included the president). Graham had been ill for some time, spending most of that year in Chestnut Lodge, a private sanatorium in Rockville, Maryland. A conversation he had with the president during a late-night call illustrated a deteriorating state of mind that bewildered his friends. "Do you have any idea who you're talking to," Graham asked angrily at one point. "I know," Kennedy replied gently, "I'm not talking to the Phil Graham I have so much admiration for." For all the warning signs, his death was a profound shock. "Suicide always remained a possibility," Arthur wrote disbelievingly, "but I had subconsciously supposed that his innate vitality would win out over the demons within." Graham was "my closest friend in Washington."[19]

Adding to the air of melancholy around the White House was the sad death of the president's infant son, Patrick, a few days later. Arthur expressed his condolences to the Kennedys and received a handwritten reply from Jackie saying, "some letters really do help." But Patrick's death also led to an excruciating conversation in the Oval Office with JFK, who, "almost shyly," told him that Adlai Stevenson had not bothered to write to Jackie. "Everyone else who ought to write has written—she got a very nice letter from you—except Adlai," he said. "I can't believe that he didn't write; but, if he hasn't, I wish you would tell him to send her a letter." It was just one more way in which Schlesinger's association with Stevenson tarred in the Kennedys' eyes.[20]

Sometimes Arthur's position as "White House liaison with United Nations Ambassador Adlai Stevenson" seemed to be all that was left for him. At least that summer he managed to make the most of it by shooting for the moon. The rest of August and September he acted as the go-between with Stevenson as the president prepared to address the United Nations General Assembly. That did free him to make one eye-catching policy contribution. "The moon proposal is a vagrant thought of my own," Schlesinger told Stevenson on September 16, "which has been discussed with no one." When Kennedy gave his speech four days later, it included the proposal that the United States and the Soviet Union should cooperate on a joint expedition to the Moon—an idea that the president had gratefully seized upon as helping him to find a way out of—or at least share— the expensive pledge he had made in 1961 to land a man there by the end of the decade. The idea had occurred to Schlesinger more as a response to a dull speech draft from the State Department about the "Alliance of Man" than from any particular interest in space exploration. The space race, like the arms race, had been a point of conflict between the two superpowers; the suggestion of cooperation there provided a neat symbol for the better relationship that was emerging after the dangers of the missile crisis.

Schlesinger tested the idea on Bundy and Sorensen, who both told him to show the president. "The bracketed proposal on the moon project has been cleared with no one," he told the president, "I put it in to see how it sounded." Once Kennedy said he liked it, Schlesinger then made a few hasty phone calls to the head of the space agency, and to State, Defense, and the Arms Control agency. "Established procedures nearly always prevent anything new from happening," John Bartlow Martin, his old colleague and fellow Stevenson speechwriter, noted. "In the main only by such end-runs as Schlesinger's can new things be accomplished." It was Arthur at his best in his other role as the White House "gadfly."[21]

Throughout the rest of that fall important discussions continued inside the White House about the future of American involvement in Vietnam. The question arose of what the United States should do in the aftermath of the military coup against President Diem in November. Gadflies had no say in such weighty matters. Instead Schlesinger was left to drift back "against my inclination" to "doing more and more in the way of speechwriting." He did at least do his best to make the most of the situation. He drafted a fine address for the president to mark the hundredth anniversary of the National Academy of Sciences, setting out the challenge of how, "as we begin to master the destructive potentialities of modern science, we move toward a new era in which science can fulfill its creative promise." And a few days later Kennedy handed him Sorensen's draft for a speech at the groundbreaking for the Robert Frost Library at Amherst College on October 27. Since the president dismissed it as "thin and stale," Schlesinger completely rewrote it to reflect Frost's legacy, which included his reading at Kennedy's inauguration and his ideas about power and the arts.

The night before the Amherst speech, Kennedy called Schlesinger to ask him to come along on the trip. "The President's mood was gay," Schlesinger recalled. On Air Force One the two men worked on the draft toning down the "fancier passages," with Kennedy adding his own personal reflections on the responsibilities of those born into wealth. "The result, I think," Schlesinger reflected proudly, "was most successful. Certainly no previous President has ever talked this way about the arts."

"At bottom," Kennedy/Schlesinger had said in a beautiful passage, "he [Frost] held a deep faith in the spirit of man, and it's hardly an accident that Robert Frost coupled poetry and power, for he saw poetry as the means of saving power from itself. When power leads man towards arrogance, poetry reminds him of his limitations. When power narrows the areas of man's concern, poetry reminds him of the richness and diversity of his existence. When power corrupts, poetry cleanses. For art establishes the basic human truths which must serve as the touchstone of our judgment."[22]

It was a rare moment for Schlesinger. As October turned to November and he remained out of the policy loop, other worlds seemed to beckon him. On November 21, with the president already in Texas, Schlesinger took a last look over the final copy for a routine speech to be delivered the following day to the Citizens Council at 1:00 EST/12:00 CST in the Trade Mart in Dallas. Then he grabbed his coat and left the office. With the president away, he would be flying to New York City the next day with Katharine Graham to discuss ideas for the "back of the book" at *Newsweek* magazine, as he drifted back toward a world of letters. His old friend Ken Galbraith would be there too. All told, it was going to be a fun day.

Behind him in his East Wing office sat the copy of the speech that would never be delivered. "For as was written long ago," read the final sentence, " 'except the Lord keep the city, the watchman waketh but in vain.' "[23]

CHAPTER SEVENTEEN

A THOUSAND PAGES

*S*aturday, November 23, 1963. In the early hours of the morning, when Richard Goodwin discovered Schlesinger at his typewriter, the eminent author and presidential advisor already had history on his mind. In his diary, Schlesinger reflected on how the Kennedy court quickly divided after the events in Dallas. Realists such as Mac Bundy and J. K. Galbraith who were "ready to face facts and make the best of them" joined one camp; the "sentimentalist[s]" like himself and Kenny O'Donnell whose hearts were "not in it" joined the other. Galbraith thought, "Like most people interested in politics, [Arthur] was reacting too much to the chemistry of the moment." Yet Schlesinger was a realist in his own way: his job was to forge Kennedy's historical reputation.[1]

The day after the assassination, having already sent a letter of condolence, Schlesinger wrote to Jacqueline Kennedy to ask about her husband's archive. "When you have a moment," he wrote, "I hope we may perhaps have a talk about the President's papers and about your own." He had, he told her, already had a similar conversation with the dead president's brother, Bobby, and brothers-in-law Sargent Shriver and Steve Smith. The National Archives had set in motion the process to segregate Kennedy administration papers throughout the government. Schlesinger explained that he would be seeing "the Archives people" on Monday to work out the next steps. He would also meet Bobby "later in the week" to discuss the "general problems" in the "preparation" of the presidential library. "I don't know whether you will wish to join this meeting or not," he asked Jackie. "In any case, I will keep you fully up to date on progress."[2]

Schlesinger intimately involved himself with the development of the Kennedy Library; at the same time he moved to extricate himself quickly from the White House. Both actions laid the groundwork for the task that would obsess him for the next two years: writing the book that implicitly or otherwise John F. Kennedy had always expected of him.

Extricating himself from the White House was harder than Schlesinger anticipated. He wrote immediately to the new president to resign his post. A message came back from Johnson within hours asking him to withdraw his resignation. "You have a knowledge of the program, the measures, the purposes, of the history of the country and of progressive policies, you know writers and all sorts of people," Johnson told him. "I need all that, and you must stay." Reluctantly, Schlesinger agreed to remain on in the national interest. "I am a little perplexed as to what to do," he brooded. "I am sure that I must leave, but I can see that the problem of disengagement is going to be considerable."[3]

In fact, Johnson effectively took the problem out of his hands. When it came to his first address to Congress as president, it was not Schlesinger, but the historian's friend Galbraith and rival Sorensen to whom LBJ turned to write the draft. When the press picked up on that fact, Johnson invited Schlesinger to sit in the First Lady's box during the address. "Reason?" Arthur pondered. "Personal kindness? Liberal reassurance? A quick way to knock down stories which spread around town yesterday . . . that I had had a disagreement with Johnson about the speech and resigned or been fired?" Over the course of the next month, Johnson hardly consulted Schlesinger at all. Rumors circulated that Eric Goldman, the Princeton historian ("not much of an historian," Arthur Jr. sniffed to Arthur Sr.) was set to become LBJ's new Schlesinger. "My own position remains baffling—or perhaps not," Arthur wrote at the year's conclusion, noting that he had not received a single communication from the president or his staff for the last month. "It seems clear that they are prepared to have me fade away, which is OK by me." (Within the year, Johnson would regret that decision. "We've lost Schlesinger and Sorensen and Salinger," he complained to George Reedy, his press secretary. "They [the secretaries of state and defense] say the White House staff is in shambles.")[4]

Schlesinger was happy to fade away as his other enterprise came into sharper focus. Writing to his parents in the new year, he reported on his "tentative" book plans. "I have discussed it in a preliminary way with Bobby and have sent a note to Jackie about it (I am going to Jackie's for dinner tonight and will perhaps get her provisional reaction)," he told them, adding that he intended "to set out my thoughts in an ordered way" in a few days' time.

His plans remained tentative in large part because Jacqueline Kennedy held strong views about the historical profession. "What bothered her was history," Schlesinger's friend Theodore White recalled of a conversation with the grieving First Lady a week after the assassination (following which he would write his famous "Camelot" article for *Life* magazine). She wanted JFK rescued from "all these 'bitter people' who were going to write about him. She did not want Jack left to the historians." But in December 1963, in response to an address that Schlesinger had given on JFK to the Massachusetts Historical Society that month, Jacqueline now urged the historian on, telling him to write a book "while all is fresh— while you remember his exact words." Schlesinger's letter to her at the beginning of January, therefore, artfully set out to reinforce that point by saying that his book would be written as a Kennedy insider not a historian. "The book I have in mind would not be a systematic or comprehensive history of the administration," he reassured. "That will have to be done later and by someone who was not personally involved. It would rather be an account of the way John F. Kennedy ran the presidency, an attempt to define the achievement and impact of these years, and also an attempt to set forth the legacy of the President for those who come after." Nevertheless, he promised, "I would not of course wish to undertake such a work unless you and Bobby thought it a good idea."[5]

What gave the matter more urgency than Schlesinger would have liked was the unwelcome news that Ted Sorensen was telling everyone with typical bluntness that he intended to write a book of his own. "He [JFK] had planned to write such a book with me after the presidency," Sorensen claimed. "Now that he was gone, I felt some obligation to write it." Where Schlesinger had walked softly, Sorensen had a heavy foot. In fact, not only had he announced his intention to write the book, he had already secured a contract ("generous," he boasted) from Harper & Row, who earlier had published *Profiles in Courage*. Walking into the Oval Office on January 14, 1964, Sorensen handed the president a letter of resignation that repeated the "obligation to devote the next several months to writing a book about the late President and my eleven years of service with him." Johnson protested, but eventually agreed, later writing to him, "as the Nation has been made stronger by your service, so will the memory of John F. Kennedy be made richer by your book."[6]

News that Sorensen intended to write a book caused Schlesinger at least a momentary pause. "I plan to leave [the White House] at times and places of my own choosing," he had told his parents on January 8. "I am inclining more and more to the idea of writing a book about the Kennedy Administration, though I understand that Ted Sorensen has this in mind too. He was more deeply involved in a wider range of public policy than I; but I still think I might have something to contribute." Sorensen's resignation a few days later, with its specific line about the book, changed Schlesinger's calculation and fortified his resolve.[7]

Thirteen days after Sorensen, Schlesinger submitted his own resignation to the president. "As I told you when you so generously urged me to stay on after President Kennedy's death," he advised Johnson, "I had long since resolved that in any case the time had come for me to return to scholarly work." The resignation, Schlesinger noted in his journal, "was accepted with alacrity. LBJ received it at 8 p.m. Monday evening, and his letter of acceptance was in my hands by noon the next day." Johnson's letter, however, was a model of graciousness. "I know the academic world will be richer for your return," he wrote. "But the White House will not be quite the same without you. We shall miss the fresh insights of your scholarship and the liberality of your spirit."[8]

Perhaps not wanting to set off a "book race" with Sorensen, Schlesinger had implied that his reason for leaving was a desire to return to academic life. In fact, he had no such thought. "Galbraith and [Seymour] Harris are waging a campaign in the *Crimson* to make it possible for me to return to Harvard!" he told his parents. "My view on that is that I do not want to exclude this as an eventual possibility, but that I want to spend at least a couple of years, and perhaps more, on my own work."[9]

Once his letter was submitted, Schlesinger began preparing for his new life. In part, that involved trying to recover from the sheer exhaustion of life in the White House since 1961 and the trauma of the assassination. At the end of February, while still officially working at the White House, Schlesinger headed down to Florida to be "swathed in sunshine and luxury" courtesy of treasury secretary Douglas Dillon, who had a house at Hobe Sound. "In the main I have been trying to catch up on my sleep," he wrote, "and store up energy for the next few weeks." That energy was required not just for the move out of the White House; it was in preparation for what lay ahead. "Before leaving Washington [for Hobe Sound], I finally found what appears to be a quite promising office," Schlesinger wrote his mother. "I can get the entire top floor of a 3-story building on 18th St., just off Conn Ave, a few blocks above the Mayflower. It is light and has plenty of space. Gretchen Stewart [his secretary] has got leave of absence from the White House and," he added significantly, "will stay with me until I finish the JFK book."[10]

The decision to write the book having been made, and Ted Sorensen having left the White House on February 29, 1964, Schlesinger departed the following day. "The Former Friends of Arthur Schlesinger, Jr. invite you to a Gala! Joyous! Exultant! Celebration of his departure from the Government of the United States," said the invitation to his leaving-do, "and the opening of his new offices CASH (Center for the Advanced Study of History)." It promised "Many door prizes—a favorable mention in his History of the Kennedy Administration." The cake decorations that night featured two cowboys, identified by their initials AMS and TCS, fighting each other to get to a pot of gold, which bore the legend "May the Better Man Win."

The battle to be the official chronicler of the Kennedy years fascinated the media and obsessed the rival protagonists for the next eighteen months. "Our friendship," Sorensen wrote understatedly, "was temporarily strained."[11]

Sorensen had held the whip hand over Schlesinger in the White House. Not only did he have greater access to Kennedy, but he was acknowledged even at the time as one of the greatest presidential speechwriters. Now, though, he was moving back onto Schlesinger's territory. "I was still unfamiliar with the challenges of writing a book," Sorensen later admitted, adding that "I started writing in June, optimistically hoping to have a completed draft by Labor Day 1964. . . . I was lucky to finish it by Labor Day 1965."[12]

Schlesinger had another advantage over Sorensen: the Kennedys. Sorensen would later write that it was incorrect that the family "pressured me with demands" about the book. Nevertheless, he did admit that his book "was written in solitude" with just his own "files, piles [of notes and cuttings] and memories" to assist him. Given Sorenson's brittle temperament and his closeness to the president, the other Kennedys had become suspicious of him. That was a situation Schlesinger milked for his own benefit and that of his book. "She does not like Ted Sorensen," he recorded gleefully after visiting Jackie in March, "and the reason is that in 1956 he gave people around Washington the impression that he, not JFK, had written *Profiles in Courage.*" When Schlesinger discovered that Sorensen, who had constantly moaned about being unrecognized for his role in writing the book, had all along been getting the royalties for *Profiles*, he squealed in delight at the gossip, "That's fantastic!"

Jackie was not the only Kennedy who suspected Sorensen. "Bobby was also exceedingly cool about Ted," Schlesinger wrote that month. Schlesinger had pointed out that Sorensen "served the President well in the White House." Bobby's reply was acid. "Yes, Ted loved only two people in his life. In the White House he decided that he loved one more than the other." "Who was the other?" Schlesinger "stupidly" asked. "Himself," Bobby said.[13]

Arthur on the other hand was now drawn into the Kennedy circle perhaps more fully than he had ever been during the White House years.

He was a regular at dinners and receptions to raise funds for the Kennedy Library. He was a frequent weekend guest of Bobby and Ethel, as well as of Jackie and the Smiths. Those visits often included lines in his journal such as "I had a long talk with JBK. She started to tell me about the trip back from Dallas . . ." That process was formalized the day after his resignation from the White House took effect, when Schlesinger began a series of interviews with Jacqueline Kennedy about her life with JFK as part of the "crash" oral history project he had urged on the Kennedys "as a matter of urgency."[14]

Before November 1963, Schlesinger had been on the periphery of the circle. There were times like the Berlin Crisis when he wrote policy papers that hit home. Sometimes, as with the speech on Robert Frost, he managed to outmaneuver Sorensen to get eloquent words into the president's mouth. But the White House experience had been an ambiguous one for him. After Kennedy's assassination, Schlesinger moved to the center, because the legacy project mattered for everyone: for Jackie in reinforcing the Camelot myth; and for Bobby, who had to position himself in relation to the dead president, not just the living one. At stake was the political agenda for the '60s.

For Schlesinger this project was not the one he had imagined writing. When he formally resigned from Harvard in 1962, he might reasonably have expected to complete a full two terms—eight years in the White House. Afterwards surely would come *The Age of Kennedy*, the multivolume considered history written in his fifties, if not exactly as a retirement project, then rounding off his trilogy of progressive "Ages"—Jackson, Roosevelt, and JFK. Dallas overturned all the assumptions in American politics, including Arthur's. The book could no longer be a reflective work of history. Instead it would be run off his diary, his Kennedy contacts, and his index cards, and be written in white heat.

The Kennedys were also the main distraction that kept Schlesinger from his new book. He was marginal to Johnson's 1964 presidential election campaign, but when Bobby Kennedy decided to throw his hat into the ring for the US Senate election in New York, Schlesinger continued to play his traditional role as ambassador to the liberal wing of the Democratic

Party and to the *New York Times*. "His record of accomplishment is formidable," Schlesinger wrote in late August, after the *Times* had denounced
RFK's candidacy. "He has shown himself in the most difficult situations a
man of strong and consistent character, liberalism, imagination and idealism." When the newspaper failed to print the letter, Schlesinger went
to see Arthur Sulzberger, the publisher. "Sulzberger is amiable and fairly
open-minded," Schlesinger reported back to Bobby, but the *Times* was
going to need "strong reassurance" about his liberal reform credentials
"before there is any possibility of their endorsing you."[15]

The *New York Times* attack on Kennedy as a "ruthless" machine politician who "never manifested much passion for reform" while in office was
the public expression of what most liberals said in private. When Schlesinger went to see Adlai Stevenson, he was astonished at his former boss's
vehemence. "The avarice of the K's really makes me sick. I'd almost like to
do it [run in New York] to challenge him," Stevenson railed, citing the
"rising protest against the Kennedy invasion from the liberal party."[16]

Stevenson's attitude was based in part on personal animus towards the
Kennedys. Despite having lost two presidential campaigns in disastrous
fashion, he somehow imagined with his patrician sense of entitlement
that the Boston upstarts had stolen the White House from him. Schlesinger had been disgusted in the days after JFK's assassination to find
Stevenson "smiling and chipper, as if nothing at all had happened." It was,
Schlesinger recorded bitterly, "a most disappointing reaction, and one that
it will take me long to forgive."[17]

It was Stevenson's personal callousness, not his political analysis, that
Schlesinger rejected. For Arthur himself had his own reservations about
Kennedy's commitment to progressive ideas. "I believe him to be a liberal, but committed by a sense of history rather than consecrated by inner
conviction," he had written after Kennedy's victory in November 1960.
Even in the White House, Sorensen later recalled, Schlesinger and Ken
Galbraith would be heard complaining about the president's "Republican
dogma and [William] McKinley-like phrases." As *Newsweek* had pointed
out in 1962 in an article entitled "Why are some 'liberals' cool to the Ken-

nedy Administration?" JFK "never was really one of the visceral liberals [and] many liberal thinkers never felt close to him."

Schlesinger would later write that one night Kennedy observed to him, "Liberalism and conservatism are categories of the thirties, and they don't apply any more." Since Schlesinger believed they did apply, he had a problem, for as Ira Stoll points out, "Kennedy's tax cuts, his domestic spending restraint, his military buildup, his pro-growth economic policy, his emphasis on free trade and a strong dollar, and his foreign policy driven by the idea that America had a God-given mission to defend freedom all make [Kennedy], by the standards of both his time and our own, a conservative." By 1964 these questions of character and the liberal tradition had become the central conundrum for Schlesinger in writing his age of Kennedy.[18]

A Thousand Days mixed personal recollection, a broad chronology of the Kennedy years, and a number of thematic chapters reflecting on life in Washington and inside the White House. In 1985, Schlesinger would tell his friend, the Yale historian John Morton Blum, that he "never did a JFK oral history, regarding *A Thousand Days* as the moral equivalent thereof." At the beginning of the book, Schlesinger offered a professional disclaimer. "This work is not a comprehensive history of the Kennedy Presidency," he wrote in the first line of the foreword. "It is a personal memoir by one who served in the White House during the Kennedy years." It was therefore by definition "only a partial view" and one that "inevitably tends to overrate the significance of the things" he knew about. The perspective from the Oval Office was "tragically and irretrievably lost." But in the future some historian would "immerse himself in the flood of papers in the Kennedy Library and attempt by the imaginative thrust of his craft to recover that perspective. He will not attain it," Schlesinger continued. But "I hope that this and similar books published in the time between may advance his task."

Later, revisionist historians and critics would take him to task for how he addressed that problem. Christopher Hitchens, for example, reviewing a collection of books on Kennedy in 1998, began his review with a reference to "Arthur Schlesinger's court history, *A Thousand Days: John F. Kennedy in the White House*, which might without unfairness be called the founding breviary of the cult of JFK." And in some ways, Hitchens was right (or perhaps more accurately, he was not wrong). For in writing about Kennedy, Schlesinger would turn to his own model in *The Age of Roosevelt*: what gave a life coherence was not so much its details or structure but its *purpose*.[19]

For Schlesinger in *A Thousand Days*, the purpose of the life of the martyred president was national renewal: the historian claiming him as part of the long arc of the broad progressive tradition that he had already chronicled in the ages of Jackson and Roosevelt, and which went back to the Founding Fathers themselves. "Lifting us beyond our capacities, he [JFK] gave his country back to its best self, wiping away the world's impression of an old nation of old men, weary, played out, fearful of ideas, change and the future," Schlesinger would write of this Founding Father for the contemporary age. "He reestablished the republic as the first generation of our leaders saw it—young, brave, civilized, rational, gay, tough, questing, exultant in the excitement and potentiality of history. He transformed the American spirit." To emphasize the point, Schlesinger on page one of *A Thousand Days* describes Kennedy, on his way to deliver his own inaugural, reading Thomas Jefferson's first inaugural address.[20]

Historian Garry Wills would later write that Schlesinger "was the craftsman of the framework within which Kennedys have been most often studied—the claim that Kennedys mature late; but that the maturity, when it comes, is spectacular." That trajectory is established in *A Thousand Days* right from the outset, when Schlesinger artfully acknowledges that huge doubts surrounded Kennedy in 1961, and that he himself shared many of them. Some of these concerns were political, notably that "many liberal Democrats regarded him with suspicion." There had been Kennedy's "silence" in the 1950s, when he had not taken Senator Joseph McCarthy "very seriously." Schlesinger does not try to absolve him, but he does point out that "Kennedy's actual position was not better and no worse than that of most Democrats, including those more clearly in the liberal stream of things." But in fact, Schlesinger argued, it was precisely the experience of the 1950s that enabled Kennedy to find his liberal instincts. "Some people have their liberalism 'made' by the time they reach their late twenties," he quotes Kennedy telling the historian James MacGregor Burns. "I didn't. I was caught in cross currents and eddies. It was only later that I got into the stream of things."

Helping Kennedy to find the way to his liberalism, says *A Thousand Days*, was none other than his contemporary Arthur M. Schlesinger Jr., and Schlesinger's Harvard friend and colleague John Kenneth Galbraith. They found liberal distrust of their senator from Massachusetts "unfair and unwarranted." Indeed, "we found ourselves, as we saw more of him, bound to him by increasingly strong ties of affection and respect." As such they set out both to "combat the continuing mistrust . . . declared our confidence in Kennedy's basic liberalism . . . [and] tried to help recruit people for his growing brain trust." In this way, Schlesinger implied, he and Galbraith played their part in the liberal education of a president. When in July 1959 Kennedy read an earlier memorandum that Schlesinger had written called "The Shape of National Politics to Come," which proposed that a new liberal era would resemble the Progressive Era, Schlesinger judged that "this argument—the belief that we stood on the threshold of a new political era, and that vigorous public leadership would be the essence of the next phase—evidently corresponded to things which Kennedy had for some time felt himself." Thus, like the ancient philosopher Seneca and the emperor Nero, so the pupil became the political master.[21]

Schlesinger also dealt immediately with other doubts about Kennedy, notably that his health and character disqualified him from being president. Questions about Kennedy's physical fitness circulated even before he ran for president; certainly by 1960 Lyndon Johnson backers would publicly call for Kennedy to release his medical records in the Democratic primaries, and the question would come up again during the November general election. In July 1959, Kennedy had invited Schlesinger to the family compound at Hyannis Port, Massachusetts, for the first time. "I asked him about the rumors that he had Addison's disease and was taking regular doses of cortisone for adrenal deficiency," Schlesinger wrote (and his journal confirms). Kennedy said that war fevers had caused his adrenal glands to malfunction, but that this had been brought under control. "He pointed out that he had none of the symptoms of Addison's disease—yellowed skin, black spots in the mouth, unusual vulnerability to infection," Schlesinger wrote, adding Kennedy's own words to him: "No one who has the real Addison's disease should run for the Presidency, but I do not have it."

Two years after *A Thousand Days* was published, a report in the *Journal of the American Medical Association* entitled "President Kennedy's Adrenals," by Dr. John Nichols of the University of Kansas Medical Center, Kansas City, began the process that demonstrated this last statement was likely to be false. When Robert Dallek examined some of Kennedy's medical files in 2002, the 85-year-old Schlesinger reflected that Kennedy "did draw a distinction between true Addison's and broadly construed Addison's," but added that he did not know why. He also said that he had never been aware of the president's discomfort, other than back pain. "I mean, he never uttered a word of self-pity or complaint," Schlesinger said. But by having put the question in 1959, he claimed to have done due diligence on the matter by asking the candidate outright.[22]

On other matters, Schlesinger turned a more oblivious eye both at the time and in *A Thousand Days*. The 1965 book presented the Kennedys as the ideal couple, happy and in love. "Her husband's delight in her was visible," he recalled. "His eyes brightened when he talked of her or when she unexpectedly dropped by the office. . . . Life for herself and her husband and children was never more intense and more complete. It turned out to be the time of greatest happiness." After revelations about the Kennedys' marriage came out later in books such as *The Dark Side of Camelot* or *A Question of Character*, Schlesinger, in a new introduction to *A Thousand Days* in 2002, would say that nothing he had seen in the White House suggested that Kennedy's womanizing interfered with the dispatch of business. Quoting Ben Bradlee, editor of the *Washington Post* and friend of Kennedy, he also pointed out, "It is now accepted history that Kennedy jumped casually from bed to bed with a wide variety of women. It was not accepted history then" (although Bradlee's own sister-in-law, Mary Pinchot Meyer, was in fact one of Kennedy's many lovers). Schlesinger's own attitude at the time had been one of skepticism blended with "don't ask, don't tell." When Adlai Stevenson put the rumors to him in 1960, Schlesinger told his old boss, "though I have no knowledge at all of the facts, my impression is that the stories in circulation are greatly exaggerated. . . . The stories about his private life seem to date from 1955 and before. I have heard no reliable account of any such incident in recent years."[23]

Later, as revelations about Kennedy's private life put Schlesinger on the defensive, and accusations flew that he was, at best, credulous or, worse, a Kennedy stooge, Schlesinger's response was to hit back hard. "We live in an age obsessed with sex," he fumed in his 1986 book, *The Cycles of American History.* "It titillates us to know that Jefferson, FDR, Eisenhower, Johnson, and Martin Luther King, Jr., had (or may have had) mistresses. This obsession has bred the *National Enquirer* school of biographers . . . [who] collect unsubstantiated and unattributed rumors, treat them as if they were undisputed facts, and use them as the basis for a highly speculative character analysis." The result was to tear down "anyone who attains a high place" in national life.

By 1995, he could joke of JFK that "I guess he played around a bit, but this was not evident to the staff at the time and did not interfere with his conduct of public affairs. There was no parade of bimbos through the oval office!" Yet the more revealing assessment came in a passage in *The Cycles of American History,* written two decades after *A Thousand Days,* when Schlesinger conceded that "Kennedy revisionism has kindled in some people a growing resentment bordering on rage." He added, "Remembering their days of naive faith and ingenuous hope, they feel that they were manipulated, seduced, betrayed and abandoned. Did he fool us? Did we fool ourselves?"

Schlesinger left the question hanging, not answering an inquiry that seems as much directed at himself as the reader. It was a powerful, painful moment.[24]

Jacqueline Kennedy even reprimanded Schlesinger in 1965 for using information that was "too personal" in the draft of his book and extracts in *Life* magazine. "The world has no right to his private life with me," she complained, "I shared all those rooms with him—not with the Book of the

Month Club readers." It is beyond imagination what her reaction would
have been if Schlesinger had hinted at JFK's marital infidelity. That might
seem the compromise of one who was bound too inextricably to the Kennedys; certainly the elision is questionable by the standards of modern
biography, let alone the "*National Enquirer* school" that Schlesinger so
despised. But it does fit the older model of one whose aim was the presentation of the exemplary life in order to serve a broader purpose—in Schlesinger's case, liberal progressive politics. That was only possible in the era
before Watergate, Chappaquiddick, and Fannie Fox, when a politician's
foibles were largely off limits to the press.[25]

Drawing points of comparison with FDR was the most obvious way
in which Schlesinger built the case for the liberal Kennedy. Readers of
Schlesinger's first volume of *The Age of Roosevelt* would immediately
have recognized in Schlesinger's description in *A Thousand Days* a pre-
Kennedy "old nation of old men, weary, played out, fearful of ideas, change
and the future," a direct allusion to "the image [in 1933] of a nation as it
approached zero hour: the well-groomed men, baffled and impotent in
their double-breasted suits . . . the confusion and dismay . . . the fear . . ."
as America faced the "crisis of the old order" before Franklin Roosevelt
"awakened [the country] from apathy and daze."

Both books open with a similar use of metaphor that shows a country
struggling to emerge from deep winter into the light. Friday, March 3,
1933, had dawned "gray and bleak . . . heavy winter clouds hung over the
city . . . the darkness of the day intensif[ying] the mood of helplessness."
Friday, January 20, 1961, similarly, had been a day when "the winds blew in
icy, stinging gusts and whipped the snow down the frigid streets." Just as
outgoing president Herbert Hoover, symbol of a barren old order, had "sat
motionless and unheeding" next to Roosevelt on their way to the inauguration, so too the unresponsive outgoing president Eisenhower talked
to his successor only "formally and inconsequentially." When Roosevelt
spoke the words of the oath of office, "a few rays of sunshine broke for a
moment through the slate clouds upon the inaugural stand." As Kennedy
waited to take the same oath, the sunshine was so bedazzling that his

favorite poet, Robert Frost, had to stop reading a new poem and instead recited "The Gift Outright" from memory.[26]

So too Kennedy and Roosevelt were alike in sharing the right temperament and ease of manner for the presidency. "Our last natural President [before JFK] had been Franklin Roosevelt," Schlesinger writes:

> Roosevelt and Kennedy had so much in common: both were patrician, urbane, playful, cultivated, inquisitive, gallant; both were detached from the business ethos, both skeptical of the received wisdom, both devoted to politics but never enslaved by it, both serene in the exercise of power, both committed to the use of power for the ends of human welfare and freedom: both too had more than their share of physical suffering.

Each man, in short, was committed to the exercise of power not for personal gain, but to extend freedom at home and abroad, for the benefit of the many, not the moneyed elite.

Yet the younger man was no imitation of the four-time president. "Kennedy, the child of a darker age, was more disciplined, more precise, more candid, more cautious, more sardonic, more pessimistic," Schlesinger writes of this president for the Atomic Era. "His purpose was hardened and qualified by the world of ambiguities and perils. Underneath the casualness, wit and idealism, he was taut, concentrating, vibrating with inner tension under iron control, possessed by a fatalism which drove him on against the odds to meet his destiny."

When Kennedy was alive, some said that "he concentrated on 'selling himself' and his family rather than his ideas; that he was excessively preoccupied with his 'image'; and that he was unwilling to convert personal popularity into political pressure for his program." In this way he was compared "invidiously with the Roosevelts, Wilson and other Presidents celebrated for their skill in rallying the electorate behind controversial policies." Yet, Schlesinger goes on, "in later years the age of Kennedy was seen as a time of quite extraordinary transformation of national values and purposes—a transformation so far-reaching as to make the America of the sixties a considerably different society from the America of the fifties." Indeed, those same critics now sometimes said "he tried to do too much too quickly."

For Schlesinger, Kennedy embodied what it meant to be Modern. "The Kennedy message—self-criticism, wit, idea, the vision of a civilized society," he wrote, opened up a new era in the American political consciousness. "The President stood, in [political scientist and early JFK adviser] John P. Roche's valuable phrase, for the politics of modernity. . . . His hope was to lead the nation beyond the obsessive issues of the past and to call for the new perceptions required for the contemporary world." "He had accomplished so much," Schlesinger writes at the end of *A Thousand Days*, highlighting various achievements including the nuclear test ban, the "emancipation of the American negro," the "concern for poverty," the "new hope for peace," a reordering of defense and economic policies, the spur to the arts, and "the fight for reason against extremism and mythology."

"Above all," Schlesinger finishes, "he gave the world for an imperishable moment the vision of a leader who greatly understood the terror and the hope, the diversity and the possibility, of life on this planet and who made people look beyond nation and race to the future of humanity." In this way, he established Kennedy, like Roosevelt before him, as the kind of "tough-minded" and "pragmatic" liberal that Schlesinger had first identified (with an intellectual debt to the philosopher William James) in *The Age of Jackson*, one who could "wrestle with new problems as they come, without being enslaved by a theory of the past, or a theory of the future."

That argument also reasserts another central element of *The Age of Jackson*, namely that "American history has been marked by recurrent swings of conservatism and of liberalism." Periods of "inaction, unsolved social problems pile up till the demand for reform becomes overwhelming," he had written. "Then a liberal government comes to power, the dam breaks and a flood of change sweeps away a great deal in a short time." The ages of Jackson and Roosevelt had seen this process fulfilled. The tragedy of the age of Kennedy was that an unnatural event had stopped him from completing his task. As Schlesinger writes in the last line of *A Thousand Days*, linking a poignant day in Washington on December 22, 1963 to the inaugural blizzard with which he began the book, the age of Kennedy "all ended, as it began, in the cold."

Thus *A Thousand Days*, while establishing Kennedy as part of the progressive cycle of American history, had one crucial difference to his portraits of *The Age of Jackson* and *The Age of Roosevelt*. For while *The Age of Jackson* was in many ways a defense of Roosevelt (written while FDR was still alive), and *The Age of Roosevelt* was a defense of Adlai Stevenson and then John F. Kennedy—the error of "presentism," Schlesinger's historical critics called it—the cold ending of *A Thousand Days* was a vote for no one other than the dead president. The election of Martin Van Buren in 1836 had given "the Jacksonian revolution . . . its third term," but the election of Lyndon Johnson in 1964 elicited no such accolade. Instead, standing outside the White House on that freezing December 1963 day, Schlesinger found the presidential mansion "ghostly and strange." Inspiration would come from elsewhere. "The energies [Kennedy] released, the standards he set, the purposes he inspired, the goals he established," Schlesinger wrote, "would guide the land he loved for years to come."[27]

A Thousand Days had been a bravura performance in terms of both presentation and sheer effort—more than a thousand pages of memoir and history written in not much more than a year. "I compose on the typewriter, aim at 3000 words a day, rewrite as I go along and smoke cigars," Schlesinger told *Life* magazine. That regimen had clearly worried his parents. "Under cross examination I will say that I am fine in spite of writing 12 hours a day," he had reassured them during the process. "I have brought my weight down to 165 [pounds] and would feel perfect if I only could get more sleep!" To his children, he described the same ordeal of "getting up at 7:30 every morning and working fifteen hours a day." His friend John Blum told his graduate students at Yale that Churchill and Schlesinger were the two authors he knew of who could "virtually write for galleys."[28]

Schlesinger was not the only one who suffered during the arduous process of writing such a high-profile book. "The pressure—for which I am paying in health, happiness and probably quality," Ted Sorensen wrote to Schlesinger at the end of March 1965, "is to have [my book] come out in early fall." But could they "conclude a pact on the timing of our books," he asked Schlesinger, suggesting that the latter delay, "thereby relieving some pressure from us both and better serving JFK's memory with better books."[29]

It was an astonishingly brazen request, not least in enlisting the memory of the dead president to his cause. Schlesinger lost no time in rejecting the idea. "My problem," he told Sorensen, "is that, like you I am under an obligation to my publishers, to the magazine [Life], etc., to finish the book as soon as I decently can . . . in time for publication before the end of 1965." Naturally, he was "not going to rush the book or lower its quality to win a non-existent race." But having "accepted a substantial advance on the expectation that I would finish this summer, [I] feel I must do my best to do so." It was the first skirmish in a race (for certainly it was that) that soon would turn nasty.[30]

When *Life* magazine published extracts from *A Thousand Days* that summer—"Start of a series: A famous historian's intimate recollections"— Schlesinger immediately found himself in the middle of a political and social storm. Much of the tut-tutting was about whether it was vulgar to write about private conversations between JFK and Jacqueline Kennedy, but most of the serious press coverage focused on Dean Rusk, the current secretary of state, whom Schlesinger alleged Kennedy was going to sack in 1964.[31]

"At times one wondered whether the harshness of life—the seething planet of revolutionary violence, ferocity and hate, shadowed by nuclear holocaust—ever penetrated the screen of clichés, ever shook that imperturbable blandness," Schlesinger wrote in *Life* of the "Buddha-like" secretary. He was "the perfect No. 2, but his "inscrutability" made him "a baffling leader" who had "no command." Kennedy was quoted as saying that Rusk's State Department was "a bowl of jelly."

Schlesinger, with his unerring ability to generate attention for his books, had whipped up a storm around *A Thousand Days*. "For the better part of a month," William V. Shannon, Washington correspondent for the *New York Post* (and later US ambassador to Ireland), observed, "the name of Schlesinger was front-page news and a prime topic of conversation at Washington and New York cocktail parties." Newspapers around the country, yet to receive the book, now weighed in on the issue of whether he had broken faith with the late president. "When it takes advantage of a dead man who can neither confirm nor deny published statements, it becomes extraordinarily dirty," fumed the *Philadelphia Inquirer*, "especially when it is done for personal profit and political revenge." The *Salt Lake Tribune* chided Schlesinger for committing "a grave breach of historical propriety." The *Richmond Times-Dispatch* in Virginia noted that "if Arthur Schlesinger, Jr., is an admirer of John F. Kennedy, he has a strange way of demonstrating the fact in his highly questionable memoirs." The *Christian Science Monitor* thought Rusk as "an appointed official still in office should not be subjected to such private voices from the grave."

The extracts also drew a rebuke from Lyndon Johnson, who told a press conference that such gossip did "a great disservice to one of the most able and most competent and most dedicated men that I've ever known." Hubert Humphrey, the vice president, followed up on CBS TV Morning News: "I think it has been harmful," he said, "I think it has been mischievous. I don't think it has helped the country." A former colleague at Harvard briefed journalists off-the-record that such "keyhole history" was unworthy of Schlesinger. A New Jersey Republican, William Widnall, even denounced Schlesinger on the floor of the House of Representatives. As for Rusk himself, dignified under fire, he simply told reporters that his colleagues at least "can rest on the assurance that when they deal with me on the basis of confidence that confidence will be respected." Rusk, said the *New York Times*, "gave the back of his hand—diplomatically but with a noticeable chop—to Arthur M. Schlesinger, Jr."[32]

Schlesinger would address the question of "keyhole history" in a more considered fashion five years later in an academic article on the historian as participant. ("This revival [in eyewitness history] has met with a certain skepticism and resistance from professional historians . . . ," he wrote waspishly, "[but] there is nothing new, of course, in the idea that historians should write from their own direct experience. 'Of the events of the [Peloponnesian] war,' observed Thucydides, 'I have described nothing but what I either saw myself, or learned from others of whom I made the most careful and particular enquiry.'") In 1965, however, he was somewhat less academic, brushing off press queries with a dismissive observation that "he didn't care less" about the criticism he was attracting.[33]

That sentiment was almost true. Friends reported Schlesinger "upset" and "so surprised" at Humphrey's comments. He regarded the vice president as a friend for whom he had often written speeches. In public, however, Schlesinger accused the vice president of making those comments to suck up to his boss. It would take until December for the two friends finally to make up, after Humphrey wrote generously to Schlesinger saying, "I know that I may have offended you, and for this I am sincerely regretful."[34]

Only one other comment seemed genuinely to have riled Schlesinger: Theodore Sorensen, at a press conference on August 14, said he "did not wish to be drawn" on Schlesinger's comments about Rusk, but then briefed some of the same journalists off-the-record that he wished to dissociate himself both from Schlesinger and *A Thousand Days*. When Ben Bradlee of the *Washington Post* phoned to tell him, Schlesinger issued his own withering statement to the press and then fired off a note to Sorensen. "I really do not see that you are in a position to claim great moral superiority," he fumed. "It really is most unseemly that you and I should end up this way in the newspapers. It does not serve the memory of the man we love most, not does it serve ourselves, or our books, or anything else. I have been shoved around a good deal recently and, in the interests of my self-respect, could not let your animadversions go without challenge."

To Paul Brooks, his publisher at Houghton Mifflin, Schlesinger wrote, "Obviously Harper's put Sorensen up to this. Can't you explain to them how this kind of nonsense is hurting both our books." Others thought the opposite. "The clamor over Arthur M. Schlesinger Jr.'s forthright narrative . . . and Theodore Sorensen [weighing] in with his own inside account," predicted *New York Times Book Review* veteran Charles Poore, was "a flood" that had not "come anywhere near cresting yet."[35]

Sorensen at the beginning of October beat Schlesinger out of the gate with publication of *Kennedy*. "I refused all suggestions," Sorensen wrote later, "that the publication be delayed until the November 22 anniversary." Schlesinger had no such misgivings, bringing out A *Thousand Days: John F. Kennedy in the White House* in the week of the anniversary. Sorensen's letter of March that year had expressed his concerns, perhaps fears, about the two books being reviewed alongside each other. Even with the gap in publication dates, comparison was inevitable. Certainly the *New York Times Book Review* invited that comparison when they sent both books to the political scientist and presidential biographer James MacGregor Burns. Burns had full access to Kennedy in 1958–1960 to write a biography of the presidential candidate.

"Sorensen writes from so central a vantage point in Kennedy's inner circle," Burns judged, "that he knows a great deal—but his perspective is stunted." The book lacked "the authenticity and perhaps the generosity" of its subject. Of course the book was "indispensable for its facts about the Kennedy Administration" but, he concluded witheringly, it was "disappointing in its examination of Kennedy the man."[36]

A month later, when Burns weighed in with his view on A *Thousand Days*, the contrast was pronounced. Unlike Sorensen, "Schlesinger the historian is not dependent on Schlesinger the White House aide." Indeed, it was "exciting in this book to see the historian take over." Closeness to the scene had "not dulled the author's ability or willingness to portray [contemporaries] in diamond-bright vignettes." Moreover, Schlesinger had caught the "sweep and the ferment of the thousand days" in the "widest historical and intellectual frame" of what was "virtually a history of the Age of Kennedy." It was an "astounding" achievement.

"History will reassess both the Thousand Days and [A] *Thousand Days*," Burns concluded, "but I will offer one man's verdict now. This is Arthur Schlesinger's best book. A great president has found—perhaps he deliberately chose—a great historian."[37]

Ted Sorensen's book had gone straight to No. 1 in the bestseller lists. A *Thousand Days* now quickly replaced it. "Welcome to the No. 1 spot," Sorensen wrote to his rival. "As No. 2, we try harder," he remarked, adding somewhat sourly, "and Truman Capote [with *In Cold Blood*] will soon displace us both." Jacqueline Kennedy was more generous. Writing to Schlesinger from Rome, she sent her congratulations and told him that she was "so proud" he had written the book. "I think you will be a Plutarch or Thucydides when as many years separate us from now as they are behind us," she told him, adding that already people "fall back on your book to understand what now seems the mystery of those days."[38]

Those thousand days for John F. Kennedy had in reality been exactly 1,037. The main text of *A Thousand Days* totaled 1,031 pages, plus one for the title page that came immediately before them. There were 1,032 pages for the 1,032 days from January 25, 1961, the announcement of Schlesinger's appointment as special assistant, to Kennedy's assassination on November 22, 1963: Schlesinger's own thousand days with JFK in the White House. They had, he told Jacqueline Kennedy soon afterwards, "been the most exciting and fulfilling of my life." Certainly they had become so in the retelling.[39]

THE SWINGING SOOTHSAYER

D ays before Christmas 1965, Arthur Schlesinger received a cheerful telegram from one of his oldest friends, the British journalist Charles Wintour, congratulating him on making the cover of *Time* magazine. "Far more glamorous" than *Newsweek*, Wintour teased, alluding to the rival magazine's cover that featured the "new darling of the movies" in a black evening gown with plunging neckline. Schlesinger was not so sure. "I must say the description of the author fully lived up to the sulky and petulant figure on the cover," Schlesinger complained of the snarky *Time* profile. "Personally I prefer Julie Christie."[1]

Achieving the front cover of *Time* signified Schlesinger's arrival as a national figure. Hero or villain, making the front cover meant you were somebody. And by the end of 1965, Schlesinger was certainly that. The "Combative Chronicler," as *Time* called him, had already sold 175,000 copies of *A Thousand Days*, with a fifth printing under way and No. 1 spot on the bestseller list beckoning. The book itself, said *Time*, had been "a virtuoso demonstration of the skills that helped make Schlesinger a Pulitzer prizewinner at 28" and showed off his "unique combination of encyclopedic knowledge, sharp reporter's eye, extraordinary facility and a literary style any novelist would be proud of."

More glittering prizes would soon follow. In March, Schlesinger won the National Book Award. Two months later, he took his second Pulitzer. ("Sincerest congratulations on the Pulitzer Prize!" his rival Ted Sorenson wrote wearily: "Had I been on the panel I can certainly say that your book would have been one of my top two choices.") That same year City University of New York (CUNY) appointed Schlesinger to the Albert Schweitzer chair in the humanities; the Graduate Center post required him only to contribute a Monday afternoon seminar each week for an overall remuneration and support package, staggering for the time, of $100,000 (around $750,000 in today's money). Gretchen Stewart, the loyal administrator with a knack for straightening up people that Arthur bent out of shape, came with him as part of the deal. "My colleagues on the selection committee and I are confident that, if we can persuade you to accept this chair," the university's chancellor wrote to Schlesinger on making the offer, "we shall have found the international leadership we need."[2]

Schlesinger had elite and popular society at his feet; so why, in his own estimation, did he seem both "sulky and petulant"? Part of the answer was sheer fatigue. *A Thousand Days* had been written at full tilt in half that time. Prepublication, including the *Life* extracts, had drained him. There were the constant on- and off-the-record barbs from envious former colleagues to be endured. Some White House staffers griped that Schlesinger's inside account was written by someone who was "more part of the atmosphere than the substance of the New Frontier." Academic colleagues, too, happily lobbed grenades. "Arthur liked everything about Harvard except the students," one professorial colleague remarked. "And most of the faculty," chimed in another. Even self-proclaimed friends did not help much. "He always leaves me exhausted," said one, "because I find myself slightly on edge all the time trying to hold his interest."

"I am getting old," Schlesinger complained to his children of the attention. "I have given 14 speeches in the last 14 days and feel that way," he told them: "A different audience every evening, a different sponsor, a different bed every night, except they are all the same and merge indistinguishably in retrospect as well as prospect. I can hardly remember where I was yesterday and where I am supposed to be tomorrow." No wonder that *Time* saw not just the "man with the professorial air," but also one fighting a losing battle against "retreating hairline and advancing waistline." Schlesinger, it unkindly judged, "hardly looked the part of the New Frontiersman."[3]

Lethargy and disillusion increasingly enveloped Schlesinger in this period. Beyond professional exhaustion he also had other, deeper troubles. The year 1965, as well as the triumph of his book, had brought with it a number of personal and highly emotional setbacks.

In July, Adlai Stevenson had died suddenly while in London. Schlesinger had been upset and offended by Stevenson's lack of empathy in the aftermath of Kennedy's assassination. And yet for all Stevenson's personal failings, he "had somehow the quality of inciting and fortifying one's better self." Schlesinger the historian was attracted to John Kennedy, ultimately, because the relationship entailed the study of power. But his political heart always remained with the more liberal Stevenson. While on his book tour in February 1966, Schlesinger made a pilgrimage to Stevenson's old house in Libertyville, Illinois. There he found John Bartlow Martin, who had worked alongside Schlesinger on the governor's 1952 and 1956 presidential campaigns, researching away on Stevenson's official biography. "It was sad," Schlesinger wrote afterward, "to be in that nice house so filled with pleasant memories."[4]

That sadness was nothing compared to the loss of his father, aged 77, just weeks before the publication of *A Thousand Days*. Arthur Sr. had spent October 29 at his desk revising an article on the state of the American people at the time of independence. The next morning, preparing to work in the garden he loved so much, Arthur Sr. suffered a massive heart attack and died that same day. His death, Arthur Jr. wrote in an obituary for *Saturday Review*, was "the conclusion of a life of exceptional serenity, happiness, and fulfillment, out of which he distilled absolute integrity and rare wisdom."[5]

Arthur's exceptionally close relationship with his father had been somewhat strained in the years leading up to the latter's death. Arthur Sr. had just about understood why his son took a leave of absence from Harvard to experience life in the White House. "I cannot help hoping, although I know I should not say so," he later wrote to him, "that your [years] in government will gain for you all the benefits that I think you rightly ascribe to such an experience for historians." But when Arthur resigned his professorship in 1962, Arthur Sr. was heartbroken. "I did things which I am sure disappointed him," the son admitted, pointing specifically to "not returning to Harvard after the White House."[6]

Sometimes the tension between the two had broken to the surface. "Forgive my asperity on the telephone," Arthur had written to his father a year before his death; the row had been about Bobby Kennedy (a candidate in the US Senate election in New York), whom Arthur Sr. had publicly declined to support. "You are absolutely right to declare for [Republican incumbent Kenneth] Keating if that is the way you feel," Arthur said. "My only regret is that I did not have an opportunity to submit what seems to me some relevant considerations before you reached your decision." The father's rejection of a Kennedy seemed almost calculated to hurt and embarrass his son, who had to ask RFK to excuse him.[7]

At this dark point in their relationship, historical scholarship inevitably pulled them back together. Arthur Sr. read and commented closely on the draft text of *A Thousand Days*. He was genuinely excited at the prospect of his son returning to academic life at City University, whose commitment to civic education he greatly admired. And he was quietly delighted when Arthur helped him publish an updated and expanded edition of his 1949 book, *Path to the Present*, with Houghton Mifflin, to which Arthur added an introduction. "The opportunity for one historian to express admiration for the work of another who happens to be his father is probably rare," he wrote. "I make no apologies for seizing this chance," which he then did in fulsome style. "Your foreword to Dad's book touched us both very deeply, in fact it brought tears," his mother wrote afterwards to him. "What a privilege for us all that you should write as you did and that your father could see it and that I could share the happiness of it all with both of you."[8]

Schlesinger in that introduction wrote about his father's "profound effect on his associates and students"; nowhere had that effect been more intense than with Arthur Jr. To begin with, there was the adoption, aged 15, of his father's name, replacing Arthur Bancroft Schlesinger with Arthur Meier Schlesinger Jr. Then came the adoption of his father's profession, which included training at the university where his father was a professor and taking the classes that he taught. His rise as a historian came in the field of intellectual and social history—his father's field—and his first two books—on Orestes Brownson and the age of Jackson—drew heavily on his father's ideas. Had war not intervened, he would have written the Jackson book as a doctoral dissertation under his father's supervision. When he returned to Harvard after the war, now a professor himself, he took over his father's intellectual history courses. Subsequently, he would use another of his father's concepts, about the cyclical nature of political power, for his book *Cycles of American History* (1986).

In all these scholarly endeavors, Arthur freely acknowledged his filial debt. "I remember reading it some years later," he said in 1968 of his father's book, *New Viewpoints in American History* (1922), and being surprised at the extent to which I was developing insights he had already set forth. I have no doubt that he had communicated to me the substance of these insights in the incessant (and fascinating) conversations we held through the years on all manner of historical topics." Sometimes the "incessant" quality of that dialogue had become too intense, even suffocating. "His father directed him," Marian Cannon Schlesinger recalls. "He saw to it that everything that could be done was done. [Arthur] can't help having been irritated by it." Yet few, least of all Arthur himself, doubted the intellectual and emotional debt that he owed, not to mention the professional one. "Your counsel and support throughout my life," Arthur wrote to his father on his 77th and last birthday, "have meant more to me than I could ever possibly express." Both men, said Arthur Jr.'s friend, the British historian Marcus Cunliffe, seemed to understand Arthur Senior "as the first stage of the rocket; Arthur Junior's success was a second-stage development."[9]

His father's passing devastated Arthur. "It was a hard blow, but he went at the height of his powers and this was as he would have wished it," he told former Truman aide George Elsey. "However, it caught the rest of us psychologically unprepared." What intensified the experience was that it came at the exact moment that his marriage to Marian was disintegrating. The Schlesingers had always endured a stormy relationship, beginning when Arthur was still an undergraduate at Harvard. Each had entertained doubts before their marriage about whether they were right for each other, and their relationship had enjoyed more downs than ups. "My parents didn't have a great relationship when we were young," Christina Schlesinger, born in 1946, remembers. "There was a lot of arguing. When we were in Cambridge, my parents fought in so many ways. My friends describe coming over to visit me and there was always so much yelling in the house. So the marriage was very frayed before we went to Washington. They were not in a good place."[10]

Life in Washington, DC, during the Kennedy years had given the family a reprieve. "I loved it!" Marian recalls. "My relationship with Arthur was still not very good, but I made a lot of friends, I played tennis and went to parties. I had a wonderful time!" She set up an artist's studio in a room above the kitchen where she could paint and illustrate. With Arthur so busy, and both so energized, they seemed to find some kind of equilibrium. That stability did not survive Kennedy's death. "I think he was actually heartbroken over it," Marian says. "But not only was he heartbroken over the president's horrible death, but also in a way he was heartbroken over his own career. His life had fallen apart in that sense. What was he going to do next?"[11]

Arthur's son Robert remembers his father telling him years afterwards that he realized his first marriage was over when riding back from Kennedy's funeral. "The trauma of JFK's death," Robert says, "had given him a certain clarity about what was important in his life." Christina experienced the emotional consequences of her father's insight. "My parents were both enjoying themselves so much in Washington, but soon after Kennedy's assassination the marriage fell apart," she says. "So in some weird way, the Kennedy assassination really impacted the nation and it also impacted my family in a very personal way."[12]

Writing of "the frustration and agony of your rejection and coldness and the growing isolation between us," Marian unleashed her rage on her husband. "I have felt for years like a caged animal not knowing where to turn," she told him, "proud and hurt and tense—trying not to show how much pain I felt at every rebuff—hopelessly withdrawing. And now I am free . . ." Arthur seemed at least to empathize with her pain. "She is sometimes careless and self-centered," he told his mother (who was worried about Marian's imminent return to Cambridge), "but she is not mean, and this has been a terribly upsetting and difficult time for her."[13]

Basic incompatibility had not helped their relationship, but neither too had Arthur's infidelity. "He might have been kind of nerdy when he was at Harvard," says Christina, "but then he becomes, you know, a kind of sexy intellectual and young women were attracted to him. And he was a flirt and he wanted to have some fun. That drove my mother crazy." Even worse for Marian was the ambiguous relationship he enjoyed with Marietta Tree, the socialite lover of, among others, Adlai Stevenson. "Mother lived under the implicit and sometimes explicit model and shadow of Marietta Tree," remembers Andrew Schlesinger, their youngest son. "The beloved Marietta," Marian concurs. "She was sort of a thorn in the flesh." Whatever the physical relationship between Arthur and Marietta, there was no doubt that Schlesinger adored her. "He went gaga over her," says Christina. Andrew agrees, pointing out that each had something to offer the other. "She terribly wanted to be an intellectual," he says, "and my father said she was educable. But he also said that she had a New England mind and a New York style and that was for my father the perfect combination."[14]

While Marian vented "all the things that have been buried in frustration for so many years," neither was Arthur immune to the pain of the separation. Schlesinger, although a prolific correspondent and diarist, was not a man often given to personal reflection. His letters and even his journals are usually a formal commentary on public events, not those of the heart. There is a pattern, however, to the few instances of emotional turmoil that found their way onto the written page. These occasions coincided with periods when he was away from home in an institutional environment. At Harvard as an undergraduate in the 1930s he poured his troubles and ambitions into his personal diary; during the unhappy period overseas when he was conscripted into the army, he wrote a series of heartrending letters to Marian; and now in 1966, having left Marian and while in residence for a semester at the Institute for Advanced Study in Princeton, he wrote to his mother to express his sense of anguish and shame. "Life is difficult all round," he told her frankly, continuing:

But the one thing one can do, I think, is accept the frustrations and forget them and dwell on the affections which bind people together. I do know that it is a good deal easier to say this than to do it; but I have been unable to come up with any other formula for making life tolerable. I have just finished an excellent new biography of Mark Twain by Justin Kaplan—*Mr. Clemens and Mark Twain*—and it reminded me of the agony and chaos with which he struggled through so much of his life. Disappointment and wretchedness would seem to make up a very large part of the human condition. Anyway I love you and am sorry when I disappoint you but hope that this matters much less than the steadiness of love.[15]

Just as with the relationship with his father, Schlesinger hoped that historical scholarship would help him put his life back together. "Only one more week," he wrote to his children in February while on the road promoting *A Thousand Days*, "and I can return to Princeton and my own work. I can hardly wait." Others nudged him in that direction too. "Not surprisingly you got the Pulitzer prize again and I am very glad," wrote Adolf A. Berle, a member of FDR's original "brain trust" who had briefly served with Schlesinger in the Kennedy administration. "What I do hope is that you now get a chance to finish the Roosevelt book. The record ought to be straight on that also." Yet even this fallback failed Schlesinger now. Princeton would mark the beginning of a struggle that would last the rest of his life: to complete his multi-volume *The Age of Roosevelt*. "I am glad to say that I will be starting writing the fourth volume of THE AGE OF ROOSEVELT this autumn," he wrote twenty years later in correspondence that was characteristic of almost any point in the next forty years. "When I finished the third volume a quarter of a century ago, my scheme required that the next volume deal with foreign policy in the 1930s. At that time many crucial documents were still classified. In the next years I got involved in other matters. In recent times nearly everything of consequence has been opened in the United States and Britain. I have substantially completed the research, and the next volume will be about FDR and the coming of the Second World War." That serious archival work had been done with enthusiasm. "After spending a couple of days at the Public Record Office, I have found quite a lot of interesting material," he wrote cheerfully to Gretchen Stewart during one trip to London. "Accordingly I am postponing my return by a week." But the book would never be written.[16]

Over the summer of 1966 Schlesinger moved into an apartment at 166 East 61st Street in Lenox Hill on New York's Upper East Side. Marian kept the house in Cambridge, which, with children Stephen, Christina, and Andrew all at various stages in their Harvard careers, remained the focus for the family (Kathy married that same year and moved to West Virginia). Teaching for Arthur began in September at the Graduate Center, where he found himself nervously out of practice. "I guess we survived," he wrote of his first seminar, "but I also have to spend a lot of time getting caught up on the Jackson period, so that I will not be exposed. I feel such a fake; this, it is now evident, is the real reason for my disquietude as a teacher." In fact, as he told his friend, the Yale historian John Blum, the time commitment was slight. "It will provide a base," he told him, "and at the same time I will have plenty of time for my own work."

He had completed some serious work, including an article for *Foreign Affairs* on the origins of the Cold War, which, he told former secretary of state Dean Acheson, was a first draft on the topic for the last volume of *The Age of Roosevelt*, "when I will be able to repair deficiencies and errors in the present account." Schlesinger even threw himself into the academic lion's den by agreeing to attend a seminar on the article organized by George Kennan in Princeton with many of the leading revisionist historians present. "Surprisingly mild," a relieved Schlesinger reported of the revisionists. "congenial and not confrontational at all." One of their number, Walter LaFeber, recalls of him: "There were other historians of his stature that marked us out as the enemy, but Arthur wasn't one of them." In fact, both sides agreed that the perpetually contrary Kennan was the trickiest character present.[17]

Yet the Princeton seminar, important though it was, was only Schlesinger dipping his toe back into the academic waters. His publisher Houghton Mifflin, rather than urging him on with Roosevelt, now asked him to set that book aside in order to turn an article he had written for the *New York Times Magazine* about the heavy bombing in Vietnam into a book. That counterblast, published as *The Bitter Heritage*, was an undisguised attack on the Johnson administration. "Alas, Kennedy's profound insight was forgotten," Schlesinger concluded, "when his successor plunged ahead with the foreign policy of overkill."

That observation reveals that the distance Schlesinger had traveled in the space of a few short years was pronounced. In 1963 he had pulled together a series of essays for a book called *The Politics of Hope* that exuded the gusto of the New Frontier. Four years later, with Kennedy dead, Schlesinger back in academe, and the United States mired in the Vietnam War, the new book, points out Sean Wilentz, Schlesinger's friend and editor of a later edition, showed that "he knew that by 1967 Lyndon B. Johnson's heedless military escalation had dashed many liberal dreams, including Johnson's own"—and, we might add, Schlesinger's. "*The Bitter Heritage* is not exactly a cry of defeat," says Wilentz, "but its prevailing tone is tragic, and it says precious little about hope." The analysis prompted a public spat between Schlesinger and his friend Joseph Alsop, who accused him of defeatism and going soft on Communism, a view Schlesinger told him was "grotesque." Writing to another friend, George Kennan, Schlesinger suggested that the administration and the war lobby had simply "swallowed its own propaganda." The essential problem was the "general error" of "supposing that a political problem will yield to military and technological solutions." The United States had "plunged into this terrible war without a persuasive explanation of what our interests in Vietnam are and what our peace aims will be." The whole "ghastly situation" was a tactical and strategic calamity.[18]

The Bitter Heritage and his private correspondence were the intellectual manifestations of the personal and professional gloom that had enveloped Schlesinger in this next phase of his life. Perhaps in reaction against it, and without the baleful gaze of his father, he threw himself into the glamour of life as a famous intellectual in New York. *Time* magazine, which had put him on the cover in 1965, concluding that *A Thousand Days* ensured that "few of the men who served Kennedy will leave a mark so durable or so valuable," now profiled him and his Manhattan lifestyle in rather more sardonic fashion in 1967 as "the Swinging Soothsayer":

> Since he joined the faculty of the City University of New York last year, Schlesinger, 49, has led the hectic life of a much-sought-after bachelor—he is separated, at least geographically, from his wife Marian. . . . His jaunty bow tie has been seen at Arthur—a discothèque that might well have been named for him—and his every date and dictum seem to end up in the gossip columns. . . . "Any party with Arthur Schlesinger and me in it," proclaims perpetual starlet Monique Van Vooren, "can't be a failure." Not that his life is all fox trot and froth (he has yet to learn to frug). Magazines besiege him for articles, TV producers beg him to open his mind before the big eye, colleges beseech him to lecture. Reporters solicit his opinions on all manner of subjects, making him sometimes sound like Instant Delphi.

Attendance at louche nightclubs and at society events such as Truman Capote's infamous Black and White Ball may have seemed unlikely for a man with features "expressing, all in one, the horn-rimmed wisdom of the scholar [and] the sophistication of balding middle age." But whatever midlife crisis Arthur was going through, his new existence as a carefree (soon-to-be) divorcé did him less damage than the other growing perception: that his intimacy with the Kennedys had cost him "his historian's objectivity." "Few can doubt that, at the very least, he would be the chronicler of a new Kennedy Administration," *Time* said, adding snidely, "even if that entailed forsaking Manhattan's fleshpots and his life as a swinging soothsayer."[19]

When Bobby Kennedy ran for the US Senate in 1964, Schlesinger took a month off from writing *A Thousand Days* to help him win a faltering campaign. "The New York senatorial contest is the only thing I really care about in this whole damned election," he told RFK as the candidate struggled to fend off accusations (including from Arthur Sr.) that he was a carpetbagger. Kennedy, lacking his brother's gracefulness and still weighed down by grief, had turned out to be a poor campaigner. In particular, he was a weak public speaker, often tripping over his words and misjudging pauses, leading to embarrassing silences. Schlesinger warned Kennedy frankly that he was "concerned" about his prospects and urged him to put more of himself into the campaign. "Personally, I think you would be best advised to throw all the drafts away," he suggested, adding that "You have to get more of yourself into your speeches." Why not, he asked, first "dictate a rough draft and then let . . . me polish it up? I am sure you would find the exercise beneficial, and the end result would be much more satisfactory." Kennedy won in the end, but he did so with two million fewer votes than Johnson received in the presidential poll in New York. In his victory speech, he spoke about how he had won "an overwhelming mandate to continue the policies" of his brother. Almost immediately the question then became whether the next step in continuing those policies would be a tilt at the presidency in 1968.[20]

Schlesinger all along had thought he should run. In the immediate hours after the assassination of John F. Kennedy, he had made the instinctive judgment that his political and personal loyalty now lay not with Lyndon Johnson, the new president, but with Robert Kennedy. "Bobby obviously has no confidence in and no taste for Johnson and wants to be President himself," he wrote two weeks after the assassination in Dallas, "(an ambition I thoroughly applaud and will support)."

In those first days, unwisely, he had even believed RFK should run for president in 1964. Now Schlesinger's thoughts increasingly turned to how to convince him to go for it in '68. He found an ally in his friend Dick Goodwin, and together the two men took Bobby to dinner in the summer of 1966 to urge him to rally resistance to Johnson and the war. "Bobby suffers from a sense of bafflement," Schlesinger judged afterwards, but the two aides came away believing "for the first time [in] the possibility of RFK's going for the nomination in 1968." Johnson's decision to widen the bombing campaign in Vietnam was the most visible wedge issue between the president and Kennedy. At another lunch in New York with Goodwin and their friend Ken Galbraith, all three men "decided to do what little we could to stir public opinion." The result was a book from each of them, including Schlesinger's *The Bitter Heritage*, that made the case against Johnson's war policy.[21]

As the war went from bad to worse and Johnson's poll ratings slumped throughout 1967, the stage seemed set for Bobby. Except that he continued to procrastinate. "The situation is perplexing and time is passing awfully fast," Schlesinger wrote to him in November 1967, as Eugene McCarthy, senator from Minnesota, signaled that he intended to challenge the president but, crucially, would likely step aside for RFK. "Johnson is not going to come up with anything new or different and we must therefore have a new President," Schlesinger told Kennedy. "Take a fresh look at the situation," he pleaded, "I think you could beat LBJ."

On December 10, RFK "finally summoned a council of war" to discuss the issue. Schlesinger led off by "putting the case for his running." Almost inevitably, he found himself on the opposite side of the argument from his familiar rival Ted Sorensen, as well as Edward Kennedy, who both "put the case for waiting." Each argued, "LBJ is sure of reelection in 1968 and . . . Bobby is sure of nomination in 1972." Schlesinger and Dick Goodwin countered that, if reelected, Johnson would do everything possible to block Kennedy's nomination in 1972. ("He would die and make [Vice President] Hubert [Humphrey] president," RFK quipped, "rather than let me get it.") The meeting broke up inconclusively, with Kennedy telling everyone to "keep brooding" on the problem. Consultations continued over the holiday. "The ordeal continues," complained Schlesinger as the year ticked over from 1967 to 1968. Finally at the end of January the decision came down. "He is not going to do it," Schlesinger recorded gloomily.[22]

Everything changed on March 12, though, when Eugene McCarthy enjoyed an unexpected moral victory in the New Hampshire primary, winning 42 percent of the vote and showing Johnson's deep vulnerability among Democrats who opposed the war. The result threw Kennedy back into a paroxysm of indecision. Another "council of war" gathered at Hickory Hill, RFK's house in McLean, Virginia. But having previously urged him to jump in, Schlesinger now joined Sorensen in urging Kennedy to stay out, particularly when word filtered back that McCarthy had rebuffed an overture from Edward Kennedy suggesting that the Minnesotan with-draw in favor of his brother. Asleep in one of the guest rooms, Schlesinger was soon awakened by Bobby padding in "rather gloomily" in his pajamas. "What should I do?" he asked Schlesinger. "Why not come out for McCarthy?" Arthur told him bravely, calling his bluff. "He looked at me stonily," the historian wrote afterwards, "and said, 'I can't do that. It would be too humiliating. Kennedys don't act that way.'" The next day RFK announced that he was running for president.[23]

"Are you glad I'm doing this?" Kennedy asked him immediately after the announcement was made. Schlesinger told him he was and now felt he had been wrong in telling him not to run in the early hours of Sunday morning. "Well, you were right earlier," RFK said, "and I was wrong then."[24]

By the time Arthur Schlesinger had this conversation he was fifty years old and adorned with every intellectual laurel. Yet for all that success, and a certain arrogance that accompanied it, Schlesinger still had a perspective on himself and his work that allowed him to remain an accomplished advisor. Not only did he have the courage to speak truth to those with power and influence, he understood the essential nature of the relationship. Writing in his diary on the day that Robert Kennedy declared, he cut to the heart of the matter. "So this has been his own decision," Schlesinger wrote, ". . . which confirms my general theory that the principal knows better than his advisers, which is why they are only advisers and he is the principal." This moment of remarkable insight helps explain why he still remained in the middle of the political huddle after more than three decades in the game.[25]

That same perspective also alerted Schlesinger to the dangers of staleness in politics, as the same old advisors, himself included, refought the battles of an earlier era using tactics that were no longer relevant. He put these thoughts down on paper for Kennedy in a long memorandum written in April called "The Old Politics and the New." This note included an analysis of the impact of mass media, especially television. ("Underneath his nonsense," Arthur pointed out, "[Marshall] McLuhan has a fundamental point.") And the changed media environment, he went on, had practical implications for Kennedy.

First, the candidate himself had to change. McCarthy "lets down" audiences who hear him in the hall, but "he comes over well on television" and "sounds reasonable, thoughtful, reassuring to the great audience." RFK, on the other hand, already getting mixed reviews for speeches, on television can "seem emotional, pressing too hard, even demagogic in a two minute excerpt before the great audience." This was a matter that "depends less on content than on style," Schlesinger explained. RFK needed to be more "low-key . . . not retreating at all on issues but stating his views with sobriety and precision."

Just as important, however, was the question of how to deal with the Kennedy old guard. "JFK won in 1960 in part because he brought in a group of young men unknown to national politics," Schlesinger explained (in itself a self-deprecating point, because he had been one of the old Stevenson hands the new men had pushed out). But McCarthy was "threatening to win today for the same reason." That represented a major challenge for RFK. "Obviously putting a campaign together from scratch in a short time requires people with previous experience," he recognized. "But all of us—Schlesinger, Sorensen, O'Brien, O'Donnell—should stay in the background and work behind the scenes. . . . RFK must run on his own record and character. He must run as a contemporary figure. He must not appear to be surrounded by figures from the past."[26]

That analysis was reinforced when Lyndon Johnson electrified the race by withdrawing at the end of March. ("He [LBJ] is a bully who likes to flex his muscles and beat up his inferiors," Schlesinger spat contemptuously, "but avoids trouble with his peers.") Yet even in this changed dynamic, Schlesinger continued to worry about the campaign misfiring. He just couldn't put his "finger on what's wrong." In part, it was because McCarthy was running a high-energy campaign that emphasized his daring in having shaken up the race. Yet there were some deeper problems at work. "I am baffled by the intensity of feeling some people have against RFK," he wrote on May 5, 1968. The problem, he concluded, was the way that Kennedy had entered the contest, which had "revived the earlier image of [RFK] which his senatorial performance had so successfully obscured, as an unprincipled and ruthless opportunist." In retrospect, progressives would see this 1968 campaign as a moment of hope, admiring Bobby's stance on the war, poverty, civil rights, and race relations (his famous speech after the death of Martin Luther King Jr. being a much-heralded case in point). Schlesinger later would help create that narrative about RFK. But seen from inside the campaign at the time, his overwhelming emotion was one of deep alarm at the "bitterness" he witnessed everywhere, perhaps even "greater than the bitterness against JFK." "Hysteria," Schlesinger wrote at the end of May, "has turned this into real hatred."[27]

That bitterness seems to have had little to do with the reasons why, a few days later, a twenty-four-year-old Palestinian, Sirhan Sirhan, shot and killed Robert Kennedy in the kitchens of the Embassy Hotel in Los Angeles. The febrile atmosphere of the election, however, might help explain why RFK—"unsettled and frightened even" by the "frenzied crowd," suggests Thurston Clarke in *The Last Campaign*—surprised his security detail by exiting through the kitchen in the first place.[28]

Schlesinger was in Chicago (Kennedy's next campaign stop) when he received the news. "It is beyond belief, but it has happened—it has happened again," he wrote forlornly in his diary. While RFK lay in the hospital dying, Arthur mournfully returned home to New York, where he was due to give his inaugural lecture at City University. "I could hardly eat," he wrote. "Bourbon was again the great means of getting through the day, as on November 23." He gave the address, making some reference to events of the previous night. The next morning, June 6, he received the news that RFK was dead. In two days he would stand as an honorary pallbearer at Kennedy's funeral. "As I rode up the Central Valley [California] with him on May 30," Schlesinger reflected, "who could have known that nine days later I would be riding with him on another train, from St. Patrick's Cathedral [New York] to Arlington Cemetery?"[29]

Robert Kennedy's death stunned Schlesinger, perhaps even more so than the president's assassination five years earlier. "JFK was urbane, imperturbable, always in control, invulnerable, it seemed, to everything, except the murderer's bullet," he reflected. "RFK was far more vulnerable. One wanted to protect him." What kind of a president would he have made? "I think very likely a greater one than JFK," was Schlesinger's instant judgment. RFK was "more radical" and would have "restored the idealism of America." The "poignancy" of him being killed, "before he had a chance to place his great gifts at the service of the nation in the presidency," was almost too much to bear. "My personal feeling is one of such outrage and despair that I do not want to get involved in politics again," Arthur lamented. "Every political leader I have cared about is dead."

His feeling of grief and despondency was natural enough after the assassination of two Kennedys whom he loved and admired so much. Yet there was also a sense that their deaths represented the destruction of a broader idea. As he brooded in his journal, those deaths, and that of the civil rights leader Martin Luther King Jr. just a few weeks before RFK's, brought to an ugly, violent end the optimism that framed much of Schlesinger's life—the New Deal, the "greatest generation," and the confidence of the postwar era. "We have now murdered the three men who more than any other incarnated the idealism of America in our time," he despaired. "Something about our social ethos has conferred a kind of legitimacy on hate and violence." These events represented nothing less than "the decomposition of the system," he concluded. "One shudders at future possibilities."[30]

Schlesinger experienced much of that hate personally. He now increasingly found himself a target of the New Left, whose supporters often howled him down at events. He had always enjoyed courting controversy, and willingly entered the rough and tumble of debate. But this was something more disturbing. "At the end of the evening," he wrote after an event with Herbert Marcuse, the New Left's foremost theorist (and someone Arthur liked personally), "a bearded little man, stoned on something . . . came out of the audience and sat down beside me in an ominous way."

"You know what you are? You're a murderer, a murderer, and a traitor, and a mother fucker. It's against the wall for you. Do you know what is going to happen? You are going to be executed."[31]

For Schlesinger, this upsetting encounter, with a leader of Students for a Democratic Society (SDS), was not untypical of his daily life. "Now I am hissed at practically every public appearance in this city [NYC]," he lamented in 1968. Walking to the newsstand on Third Avenue each morning to get his *New York Times* became a routine in which "inevitably someone harangued and denounced me." Even cinema visits, a constant source of escape and sanctuary for Schlesinger throughout his life, led to confrontations. On one night at the movies, a man in the row behind, provoked simply by Schlesinger's presence, began a tirade about Kennedy, the war, and Arthur being "one of the biggest fascists in America." Schlesinger should not even be allowed to walk the streets. "We're going to fix that, and very soon," the man menaced him. "We're going to rub you out."[32]

"I think these people are crazy," Schlesinger sighed, "but I do feel curiously isolated here." Ironically, such confrontations had the effect of making him nostalgic for the ideological battles of his youth. "The Stalinists of the thirties were equally rigid, dishonest and fanatical," he wrote, "but they did not have the cult of violence, nor the associated contempt for the mind." It seemed no coincidence to him that it was a 1930s veteran of the Abe Lincoln Brigade and the Spanish Civil War who came to his aid during the altercation in the cinema. "I know what revolution is like," the man told Schlesinger's tormenter. "This man [pointing at AMS] is OK." It was the saving grace of a highly disagreeable situation that the "shrill, incoherent anger" of such an encounter "occasionally brings together members of the old left who previously might have been deeply divided over the merits of things like communism." (Not all his old opponents, however, felt the same: in 1969 the screenwriter and member of the Hollywood Ten, Dalton Trumbo, was still raging that a recent letter from the "intellectually disgraceful" Schlesinger was "sheer mindless gabble; garbage, as some call it; dreck, pure *merde*.")[33]

For those like Trumbo, the excoriation was rooted in their belief that Schlesinger and the non-Communist Left had betrayed essential First Amendment rights during the McCarthy era. Schlesinger's participation in the Kennedy administration compounded their sense of him as a mealy-mouthed Establishment stooge, too tepid on central issues surrounding Vietnam and civil rights. Schlesinger responded in turn that the "noxious rubbish" of the likes of Marcuse, who elevated violence and espoused "repressive tolerance," was a direct "assault on rationality in politics." The New Left's belief in its own doctrinal purity, he warned, was promoting "an atmosphere which destroys the process of democracy itself" and which in due course would only benefit "those who use violence best"—the far Right. The challenges ahead for America were not easy, Schlesinger argued, but the answer to them could not be found in violence, cynicism, and intolerance. "Let us not yield to that awful despair which dissolves all distinctions in thought and reason and hurtles us on to the politics of apocalypse," he pleaded. "In the long run, any sane society must rest on freedom and reason. If we abandon this, we abandon everything."[34]

This 1968 cri de coeur was written in the immediate aftermath of the assassination of Bobby Kennedy. Schlesinger, now in his early fifties, would never again return to the political role he had played as advisor since at least 1952, first for Adlai Stevenson, and then for Jack and Bobby Kennedy. In July 1969 Ted Kennedy drove his car into a tidal channel at Chappaquiddick on Martha's Vineyard, saving himself but leaving his companion, Mary Jo Kopechne, to die. The resulting national scandal blunted, at least until 1980, the Massachusetts senator's presidential aspirations, and with them any possibility that Schlesinger might become the éminence grise in a Kennedy Restoration. "With some reluctance" he was dragooned into drafting the acceptance speech for his friend George McGovern at the 1972 Democratic Convention, but Schlesinger was never to be in the thick of the action again. Instead, his reaction to the events of the sixties—"the worst and saddest decade of one's life," he called it on New Year's Eve, 1969, "the decade of the murder of hope"—was primarily intellectual. The result would be the last two major books of his career as a historian, which together would capture both his grief for a passed age and his fury at the world that had replaced it.[35]

CHAPTER NINETEEN

A LONG TIME AGO

A month after Bobby Kennedy's murder, his widow, Ethel, asked Schlesinger to write her husband's biography. It was a request that Arthur had anticipated, although not relished, telling a friend in the days after Kennedy's death that "I do not think that I would have the heart" to undertake such a book. But other factors weighed too, not least that he had already been through the mill with *A Thousand Days*. He had faced the sensitivity of dealing with Jacqueline and the family, and then the political storm when *Life* magazine published controversial extracts. Did he really have the stomach to go through all that again? "You know how much I loved and admired your husband," Schlesinger told Ethel, whom he regarded as more volatile and emotional than Jackie. Could she tolerate "things in the book . . . [the family] might think unnecessary or inappropriate"? Playing for time, he warned that it might be better to forestall "complaints about 'instant history,'" pointing out that in any case, "I would not be able to work on it until I complete the fourth volume of *The Age of Roosevelt*," which would "probably" take another two years. "Remember [William] Manchester," he advised, recalling the controversy surrounding *The Death of a President*, "and do nothing rashly."[1]

He soon changed his mind. It is tempting to say that an old rivalry kicked in. "Have you heard that Ted Sorensen is planning a book about JFK and RFK," he told Jackie later that July, aghast. It was true, as with *A Thousand Days*, that he thought no one could do the job better. But he also sought and got reassurances about greater authorial control. Burke Marshall, who had been an assistant attorney general under RFK, handled the delicate negotiation on this point. "I took the liberty of telling her [Ethel] that you would not write the book on the basis that the manuscript had to be acceptable to the Kennedy family," he told Schlesinger, "and that I thought you were right about that." It was, he said, a situation that "will be most difficult to her," but eventually she agreed to the principle of authorial independence.

That was the green light that Schlesinger needed. Writing to Ethel in February 1969, he confirmed that "If you [are] definite in your own mind about it, I [am] quite clear in mine that I would like to go ahead with the biography of Bobby." The final Roosevelt volume, "so long delayed," would again be deferred "until I finished the book on Bobby." Work would start that year, he told her—"*if* you are still sure you want me to do it." [2]

Schlesinger's original projection for publication was "early fall of 1971, or otherwise in 1973" (thereby avoiding the 1972 presidential election). In fact, he struggled with the project, which would take nine years to complete. In between times, however, he would make one of his most enduring contributions to the language of American politics with a new book, *The Imperial Presidency*.

Written in the style of his 1949 polemic, *The Vital Center*, the new book addressed Richard Nixon and the unfolding Watergate crisis. It also afforded him the opportunity to finally grasp the foreign policy nettle that he had been avoiding with the last volume of *The Age of Roosevelt*. In doing so, the book would show what Schlesinger called the "absolutely persuasive" influence of the realist George F. Kennan, a regular, detailed correspondent and reader of his work since the late sixties, who, like Reinhold Niebuhr for *The Vital Center*, added a conservative underpinning to Arthur's essentially liberal worldview.[3]

Schlesinger's first thought in the spring of 1973 had been to write a quick pamphlet. "I began it in March, expecting that it could be done in a few weeks," he wrote after producing a quick-fire 200,000 words in five months, "but the book grew as I got further into it and as I thought harder about the inner pattern of the Nixon presidency. Then Watergate came along to provide the climax and, I trust, denouement."[4]

In *The Imperial Presidency*, Schlesinger wrote in the foreword, he faced a conundrum. "The first concern is that the pivotal institution of the American government, the Presidency, has got out of control and badly needs new definition and restraint," he asserts. "The second concern is that revulsion against inordinate theories of presidential power may produce an inordinate swing against the Presidency and thereby do essential damage to our national capacity to handle the problems of the future." How then to strike a balance between restraint and flexibility?

Schlesinger freely admitted his own culpability over many years, in both word and action, in perpetuating "an exalted conception of presidential power." American historians and political scientists, "this writer among them," labored to give the "expansive theory" of the presidency historical sanction, he conceded. "Overgeneralizing from the [pre-1941] contrast between a President who was right and a Congress which was wrong," scholars had developed "an uncritical cult of the activist Presidency." In thus presenting the presidency as "the great engine of democracy" and the American people's "one authentic trumpet," Schlesinger writes, the dominant narrative treated the presidency as the answer to almost everything. "By the early 1970s," he continued, "the American President had become on issues of war and peace the most absolute monarch (with the possible exception of Mao Tse Tung of China) among the great powers of the world." This decisive executive power as commander in chief had a knock-on effect, as "the claims of unilateral authority in foreign policy soon began to pervade and embolden the domestic presidency." Thus "The Imperial Presidency, created by war abroad has made a bold bid for power at home."

Beginning with the Founding Fathers and their struggles with the separation of powers, Schlesinger sketches how presidents throughout the history of the Republic, "usually under the demand or pretext of an emergency," all engaged in acts of "presidential usurpation." Whether it was Lincoln's imposition of martial law and suspension of habeas corpus, McKinley's decision to send troops to China, Teddy Roosevelt's sending the Great White Fleet around the world without congressional approval, or any number of other examples, Schlesinger argued there had been a gradual shift of power away from Congress to the White House.

A crucial turning point came with World War II and the beginning of the Cold War, as Roosevelt and Truman each saw both reason and opportunity to expand executive authority. After Pearl Harbor, when Congress declared war, "Roosevelt seized on the role of Commander in Chief with relish." Increasingly he came to rely on the various emergency powers that he asserted as "Commander in Chief in wartime." Roosevelt was careful to consult Congress, especially Republican senator Arthur Vandenberg, but he kept "the military and diplomatic reins of war . . . very much in his own hands." In this way war "nourished" the presidency. "The towering figure of Franklin Roosevelt," Schlesinger writes in a hint of what volume four of *The Age of Roosevelt* might have been, "his undisputed authority as Commander in Chief after Pearl Harbor, the thundering international pronouncements from wartime summits of the Big Two or the Big Three—all these gave Americans in the postwar years an exalted conception of presidential power."[5]

Americans turned to this reassuring model in the alarming new environment of the Cold War and the arms race. Many feared that democracy lacked the mettle to withstand the totalitarian Soviet threat. "The menace of unexpected crisis hung over the world, demanding, it was supposed, the concentration within government of the means of instant decision and response," Schlesinger writes. "All this, reinforcing the intellectual doubt about democratic control of foreign relations, appeared to argue more strongly than ever for the centralization of foreign policy in the Presidency." Congress would soon "thresh around" without success to recover its lost authority. During this period of "The Presidency Ascendant," broad consultation relied on the good judgment of the commander in chief. Although John F. Kennedy only informed rather than consulted congressional leaders during the missile crisis—"the most authentic national emergency since the Second World War"—he used the storied EXCOMM meetings to encourage "vigorous and intensive debate," so that "major alternatives received strong, even vehement, expression." In this way, while he took decision-making into his own hands, "it is to be noted that he did not make it in imperial solitude."[6]

For Schlesinger it was Johnson who crossed the line the Founders had established. He "overrode the written checks of the Constitution" and "began to liquidate unwritten checks." His belief that warfare anywhere in the world might constitute an attack on the United States meant that "it was hard to see why" any future president would go to Congress before leading the nation into war. "There is only one that has been chosen by the American people to decide," Schlesinger quotes LBJ saying, adding his own acid judgment: "American history had traveled a long distance from Lincoln's proposition that 'no one man should hold the power' of bringing the nation into war."[7]

"So the imperial presidency grew at the expense of the constitutional order," Schlesinger concludes his foreign policy review. "Like the cowbird, it hatched its own eggs and pushed the others out of the nest." The process reached its apotheosis in the presidency of Richard Nixon, who "for all his conventionality of utterance and mind was a genuine revolutionary" whose "inner mix of vulnerability and ambition impelled him to push the historical logic to its extremity." Unprecedented attacks on the Constitution followed, including, as Sidney Warren, author of *The President as World Leader*, neatly summed up in his review of the book, Nixon's "usurpation of war-making power, his interpretation of the appointing power, his unilateral termination of statutory programs, his enlargement of executive privilege, his theory of impoundment, his deliberate disparagement of his cabinet, his discrediting of the press."[8]

Ultimately, "the recalcitrance of institutions—the independent judiciary, the free press, the investigative power of Congress" held Nixon in check. However, Schlesinger warned, "it was a very near thing." The fact that now "Americans tended to preen themselves on the virtues of the American form of government: *the system worked*" failed to take into account how "it came terribly close to not working." In the end, the political order rallied itself to "stop the revolutionary Presidency," Schlesinger reports, adding a call for Congress to go all in by impeaching Nixon.

But recent events would only provide a temporary halt on the Imperial

Presidency unless people recognized Nixon as its symptom, not a cause. Other elements of the system could draw "new confidence as institutions from the exercise of power they had forgotten they possessed." Watergate, he concluded optimistically, by provoking the reassertion of congressional authority, "was potentially the best thing to have happened to the Presidency in a long time," because "many, many years would pass before another White House staff would dare take the liberties with the Constitution and the laws the Nixon White House had taken." (When the Iran-Contra scandal broke thirteen years later, Schlesinger sighed, "If a presidency is inclined to do dumb things, it is far better that it be weak rather than strong."[9])

Reviewers by and large embraced the central idea of the book, not least because, as Garry Wills pointed out in the *New York Times*, Schlesinger "puts his own name in the list of 'uncritical' men . . . [and] since he here means to write like a scholar, he is not afraid to apologize forthrightly." Such "generous confessions . . . [earn] him the hearing he deserves." The New York intellectual Alfred Kazin paid a similar, albeit more backhanded, compliment in the *New York Review of Books*. "His attack on Nixon comes wrapped in a more theoretical and seemingly even-handed consideration of presidential authority," he rasped, "than I would have expected from that politically scrappy, but as a historian, old-fashioned hagiographer." Academic reviewers also welcomed the book, and Schlesinger even picked up some unexpected friends among those historians of the New Left who had in part forged their name as revisionists of his earlier work. "I was very interested in what he had to say in *The Imperial Presidency*," says Cornell professor Walter LaFeber, who had recently published *Origins of the Cold War: 1941-47.* "I used *The Imperial Presidency* in my lecture course, my senior seminar and my graduate seminars. It was a very important book, not only because it was easy to read and made his points very clearly, but also because it had a particular point of view which could be discussed in general terms, not just as historical evidence."[10]

Having completed *The Imperial Presidency*, a revivified Schlesinger returned "with a certain feeling of confidence" to the life of Robert Kennedy. By 1976, he was telling the historian James MacGregor Burns that "the book is turning out to be far longer than expected—500 pages, and I'm only up to 1960!" He completed a massive draft three times that size by the middle of 1977, when he moved "from creation to destruction" in a desperate effort to prune the text. "The RFK book is finished," he told a friend, "but is overlong and I am now struggling to cut." Even after this process, the book came in around the thousand-page mark when it was published the following fall.[11]

Unlike *The Age of Roosevelt* and *A Thousand Days*, which both began with the optimism of Inauguration Day, Schlesinger opens Robert Kennedy's story at the end, as the author travels aboard RFK's funeral train from New York to Washington, DC, on a "sweltering June afternoon" in 1968. Thousands crowded along the railroad tracks, some joining hands and singing "The Battle Hymn of the Republic." The train's whistle "blew in long, piercing, melancholy blasts." Most touching of all to Schlesinger were those moments as the train moved south through the Pennsylvania countryside when "one occasionally saw a man or woman, far from any visible town, standing gravely and alone, enveloped in private grief."[12]

Schlesinger's beginning with the train ride embeds in the reader's mind the idea of a long if unfulfilled journey. In the foreword, he describes Kennedy's life as "a labor of education." These are notes that he will sound time and again throughout the book, summed up by Bobby quoting a well-known saying often attributed to Mark Twain that "Good judgment is usually the result of experience and experience is frequently the result of bad judgment."

This mechanism of education through experience becomes the way in which Schlesinger deals with two problematic ideas that had already taken hold in the public mind about Robert Kennedy by 1978. First, that he was a nasty piece of work, a man with a sharp tongue and even sharper elbows, whose ruthless political and personal ambition knew no bounds; that he was, in the words of his father Joe Kennedy, "as hard as nails" and someone who "hates like me." Second, that RFK's appetite for advancement and power was not matched by any great ability or quality of mind and temperament; that in the words of one who might know, former president Dwight D. Eisenhower, "It is difficult for me to see a single qualification that the man has for the presidency. I think he is shallow, vain and untrustworthy—on top of which he is indecisive."[13]

Describing a journey of self-education gave Schlesinger room to acknowledge these criticisms. At Harvard, Bobby was a D student put on academic probation, although he did stand out in sports by playing on the football team (alongside his roommate Ken O'Donnell). Harvard revealed the start of a pattern. Those like O'Donnell who got inside the Kennedy circle developed a fierce and protective loyalty toward him. Those outside saw only arrogance and entitlement. John Knowles, later head of the Rockefeller Foundation, regularly sat next to Bobby in lectures (with students arranged alphabetically) and found him "kind of a nasty, brutal, humorless little fellow when he got going." Ted Sorensen, whose relationship was with JFK alone, took a similar view once Bobby was working in Congress for Joe McCarthy, finding him to be "militant, aggressive, intolerant, opinionated, somewhat shallow . . . more like his father than his brother."

That view, Schlesinger writes, teeing up his own first proper encounter, "was widely shared." In 1956 Bobby helped on the Stevenson campaign. Initially Schlesinger found Bobby cold, "making notes, always making notes," speaking only "occasionally . . . but in a rather solitary way." But there were also glimpses of hidden emotion. Visiting the Lincoln house in Springfield, Illinois, Bobby "grew even more silent than usual," so that older hands "understood there were depths of feeling in him I had never suspected."[14]

By the time JFK ran for the presidency in 1960, Bobby was his brother's most trusted consigliere. But as *Robert Kennedy and His Times* moves onto this territory and the subsequent Kennedy administration, Schlesinger hits a problem quite literally of his own making: he has already told the guts of the story before in *A Thousand Days*. This presents him with a number of challenges, which he surmounts with only limited success. At the outset, Arthur explains that he will "avoid retelling familiar stories," but the reader is often left with the uncomfortable sense of him falling between stools. Have we been here before, or not? Jack inevitably pushes Bobby out of the limelight. The younger brother is often relegated to "Robert Kennedy" in the text, while Jack gets the stand-alone "Kennedy," with the result that Bobby can seem a bit player in his own biography. Schlesinger attempts to sidestep this problem through a series of thematic chapters, including on J. Edgar Hoover, the Mob, civil rights, poverty, and Martin Luther King Jr. These overlong chapters create problems of their own by slowing the pace to a crawl and losing the narrative thrust of Bobby's life.

For all the problems of the middle four hundred pages of an eleven-hundred-page book, there were still moments when Schlesinger could hit the high notes. The chapter on the relationship between Bobby and Jack is brilliantly done. We see the impact that office had on the younger brother as "unrelenting pressure was etching lines in his face." We find him "still diffident and often uneasy" among strangers, a man "at once magical and desperate." Yet between Jack and Bobby there seemed an absolute trust. For Schlesinger, drawing on his favorite historical parallel, "Jack Kennedy used Robert in part as Franklin Roosevelt used Eleanor—as a lightning rod, as a scout on far frontiers, as a more militant and somewhat discountable alter ego, expressing the President's own idealistic side while leaving the President room to maneuver and to mediate." At the same time, Schlesinger continues, "the Attorney General was John Kennedy's Harry Hopkins, Lord Root of the Matter, the man on whom the President relied for penetrating questions, for follow-up, for the protection of the presidential interest and objectives." The brothers were two perfectly balanced personalities. "John Kennedy was a realist brilliantly disguised as a romantic," the man who had worked for both concluded. "Robert Kennedy was a romantic stubbornly disguised as a realist."[15]

The chapter on the two brothers is an immediate prelude to the tragedy of JFK's assassination and the final third of *Robert Kennedy and His Times*. As Bobby becomes the central character in his own story again, the pace and quality of the book pick up, with Schlesinger recapturing the tone of *A Thousand Days*, not least in seamlessly inserting his own experiences into the narrative. The tempestuous relationship with LBJ is parsed ("Robert Kennedy baffled Johnson. Johnson repelled Robert Kennedy"), as are his opposition to the administration's policy on the war, and a growing commitment to social justice, civil rights, and overcoming poverty. Schlesinger does his best to explain why Bobby aroused such hostility when he ran in 1968. "Kennedy's greatest disappointment," he writes, "was the young," who gravitated to his opponent Eugene McCarthy. For them, as with Clinton versus Sanders in 2016, Kennedy represented the Establishment machine, while McCarthy was the populist outsider. Schlesinger in 1968 had shared qualms about Kennedy declaring when McCarthy had been the one brave enough to face down LBJ. Now he let the poet Robert Lowell do his talking for him. "I personally like and admire Senator Kennedy," Schlesinger quotes Lowell saying. "Still, it's hard to forgive Kennedy his shy, calculating delay in declaring himself, or forgive the shaggy rudeness of his final entrance."

While Schlesinger could never completely hide Bobby's sharp elbows, the recurring theme of growth is never far away. "The most striking thing about Bob," he quotes Ramsey Clark, assistant attorney general under RFK, "was his desire and capacity for growth." Peter Maas, a writer on the Mob, elaborated the point. "He continually embraced new things and he didn't reject something just because it didn't fit in with an earlier period," not least his own brother's presidency. "Most people," Anthony Lewis, a pioneer in legal journalism, observed, "acquire certainties as they grow older; he lost his. He changed—he grew—more than anyone I have known."[16]

Writing in his diary on the day that Robert Kennedy died, Schlesinger had recorded that Bobby was "more vulnerable" than his brother. "One wanted to protect him; one never felt that Jack needed protection." That instinct comes out in the two books that in other circumstances might have been Schlesinger's "Age of Kennedy." The life of Robert Kennedy is more emotional and defensive than his book on John F. Kennedy. Although he says at one point that RFK's story "was a damned long time ago," its telling feels rawer and more overblown. A Thousand Days, in contrast, is cooler in tone and more consistently assured despite being written in the immediate emotive aftermath of the events it portrays. In short, the two books reflect their subjects: le style, c'est l'homme.

Robert Kennedy and His Times would go on to win a National Book

Award and become a TV miniseries, but most critics thought it a disappointment after the vitality of *A Thousand Days*. Some reviewers were sympathetic. Garry Wills in the *Times* thought it a "balanced yet affectionate book." Others were less kind. Stephen B. Oates, under way with a biography of Martin Luther King Jr., found "such muddled organization" that it "is astonishing for a writer of Schlesinger's artistic and dramatic talents." Marshall Frady, the controversial biographer of another 1968 figure, George Wallace, was even more biting in the *New York Review of Books*. Schlesinger, to be sure, had been "one of the most generous spirits among that curia of intellectual ministers to the Republic over the years. But," he went on, "his chronicle of memorial to Robert Kennedy induces a question about the degree one is compromised after having engaged in an exercise something like a [1,000]-page promotional pamphlet of exculpation and eulogy." The book was an "unremitting serial of absolutions" in which Schlesinger "systematically takes up each complaint" and answers "in a vast rehabilitationist effort." Frady's conclusion was harsh to the point of rudeness: "It is an indiscriminate defensiveness," he judges, "the strenuous deferentiality of an infatuation which, given the harsher aspects of Robert Kennedy's nature, is somehow oddly unbecoming and embarrassing in so distinguished and magisterially endowed a historian."[17]

Frady's review was the worst among those generally panning *Robert Kennedy and His Times*. The critics agreed that the excessively long biography lacked the narrative drive of earlier works, with transitions that felt forced or even jejune. Schlesinger's judgment was off-kilter, they argued—too personal, too defensive about the Kennedys. It seemed, in short, more apologia than historical biography.

On most issues, when weighing probabilities, Schlesinger chose for RFK. On the plan to kill Castro, for example, he concludes that "Plainly [RFK] had known nothing about assassination plots" and more generally that "several circumstantial points strengthen the conclusion that the Kennedys knew nothing about the continuing assassination policy." Even if that was a legitimate judgment, more recent historians such as Michael Dobbs have used similar evidence to come to an alternate assumption:

"While there is no smoking gun tying the Kennedy brothers to the Castro assassination plot, there is some circumstantial evidence."

On other questions, Schlesinger had found it harder to square the various circles. John F. Kennedy's deal with Khrushchev over Turkish missiles, negotiated by Bobby with Soviet ambassador Anatoly Dobrynin, not only contradicts Schlesinger's own account in *A Thousand Days*, it provides a textbook example of a commander in chief subverting due process with a unilateral foreign policy initiative; in other words, the act of an imperial president. "Was this secret diplomacy justified?" Schlesinger asks readers, "a testing question for those who think that no President should ever make a secret commitment." His lame conclusion is that "Perhaps there may be a place for secret diplomacy, at least when nuclear war is involved." It is difficult for the reader not to wince as Schlesinger pulls the punch.[18]

He might easily have argued that Kennedy was acting responsibly in using outmoded missiles essentially as a bargaining chip. Part of the problem was that the argument of his own *Imperial Presidency* bedeviled Schlesinger. As new information emerged in the 1970s about controversies such as the covert diplomacy of the missile crisis, RFK's bugging of Martin Luther King Jr., the decision to suppress the Sherman Adams case (a scandal involving Eisenhower's chief of staff), and the plan to assassinate Castro, it became harder not to see Robert Kennedy, as Stewart Alsop had pointed out to Arthur in 1969, as the natural and inevitable harbinger of Nixon. At the time, Schlesinger was outraged, telling Alsop that there was "a radical and fundamental difference between the Nixon policy and the RFK policy." By 1978, that was becoming more difficult to argue, and the crisis of analysis showed in the baggy, uncharacteristically flat writing in the middle section of an otherwise engaging book.[19]

The fact that Schlesinger himself had been immersed in the revelations only exacerbated the problem. Recently declassified documents had included Schlesinger's April 10 memorandum to the president on how to mislead the press during the Bay of Pigs operation in 1961. ("It really should be read in association with a memorandum I sent JFK on April 5," Schlesinger wailed to John Kenneth Galbraith. "Unfortunately the earlier

memorandum has not been declassified and I cannot get hold of a copy.")
Old adversaries were quick to call him on his apparent hypocrisy. "Could
Nixon have improved on that one?" William F. Buckley Jr. inquired in
the *New York Post*. "No sir, this is Grade A, Harvard BA, Harvard PhD
Quality Lying."[20]

Stewart was not the only Alsop who had tried to counsel Schlesinger
about the pitfalls of writing about Bobby Kennedy and the fate that
might await him if he did. "I point this out to you as an old friend," Stew's
brother, Joe, had written frankly to Arthur in 1975. "If I sense the way the
wind is blowing correctly, the time is overripe for a really nasty reaction
to a hagiographical book about Bobby. I can positively see the enormous
piece in the *New York Review*," he warned prophetically, "making all the
points above listed and a lot more, too; and calling you every name in the
historical lexicon."[21]

Part of Schlesinger's problem was changing fashions as the boundaries
of discourse shifted away from him. As the English historian J. H. Plumb
noted, his friend Arthur's style and subjects now had "an old-fashioned
air" about them. Loyal readers still bought *Robert Kennedy and His Times*
in sufficiently large quantities to send it into the bestseller charts, but,
unlike *A Thousand Days*, the number-one spot by the '70s was the preserve of the Nixon/Ford-era Woodward and Bernstein, not the Kennedy-
era Schlesinger. Conservatives and neoconservative intellectuals that
soon would help bring Ronald Reagan to power did so while rejecting
the liberal progressive narrative Schlesinger laid down in his books on
Jackson, Roosevelt, and the Kennedys. Within the academy, questions
about gender, race, and class had superseded his more traditional frame
of reference. "The terms that had dominated post-World War II intellectual life began to fracture," Daniel T. Rodgers sums up. "One heard less
about society, history, and power and more about individuals, contingency, and choice."[22]

For the first time in forty years of publishing, Schlesinger now found
the balance of reviews and opinion weighted against him. "All this gives
me moments of depression," he wrote in his journal, perplexed because
the "same criticism—excessive partiality" had not cooled the reception

for his other books. But what was there to do, he reflected, other than to take recourse in the words of a famous wartime leader. "I recall Churchill explaining how it was possible for him to go to sleep every night when he was being so vehemently criticized," Schlesinger wrote defiantly, " 'I simply say *God damn them all*, and then I sleep like a baby.' "[23]

CHAPTER TWENTY

BEING ARTHUR SCHLESINGER

"I return to face the ordeal of my 60th birthday," Schlesinger wrote to his Oxford friend Isaiah Berlin in October 1977. "I don't feel 60—sometimes 90 and more often about 35, but never 60." Certainly this contradiction, encapsulating both renewed vigor and at the same time a sense of utter weariness, was true in his personal life. The beginning of the decade had seen him divorce Marian in a bitter and expensive settlement. "I cannot believe you really need nearly $1000 a week," he complained in a note to her in September 1970, "nor can I possibly afford anything like that." He had been tempted to abandon the whole process. "One would prefer to observe the niceties," Arthur told his lawyers, "but, if the terms proposed are impossible, then to hell with it. I can live my own life without the benefit of legalities." Marian and her lawyers were "living in a dream world" if they thought "they have me over a barrel." After all, "society no longer demands divorces as it once did."

In the end, he relented. On November 23, 1970, the *Boston Evening Globe* ran a story under the headline, "Mrs. Schlesinger gets divorce, $4700 a month." The grounds were "cruel and abusive treatment." In fact, as his new set of lawyers at Hill & Barlow pointed out to him in 1971, the figures were actually worse than reported when taking into account cost-of-living increases. "This is obviously a lot of money," he wrote to his children. "The reason I agreed to a settlement like this, apart from the fact that it was the only way to get out of a dismal situation, was that presumably most of the money (plus the Cambridge and Wellfleet houses [which he had relinquished]) would eventually go to all of you."[1]

That letter written in 1972 to his four grown-up children, Stephen, Katharine, Christina, and Andrew, told them that their trust fund "will be exhausted in another couple of years" and that "I don't quite know where to go from here." Typed and xeroxed as usual, it was characteristic of the formal and often complicated relationship he had with them. Kathy, his eldest daughter, later poured out her sense of disappointment in the life he had provided. "Too many times I have been depressed, angry, pissed off when I see . . . people who are not as bright or intelligent as myself living a secure existence [on inherited wealth], who have gained their successes because they have never had to support themselves," she wrote to him. "I am jealous of that—because we were led to believe that our world would be like that—and it turned out not to be."[2]

Another difficult transition for Arthur's children came when he remarried just a few weeks after the divorce from Marian was made final. "This new life you are entering into," Kathy pleaded with him, "don't let it overshadow your children." In fact, eventually it seemed to help their relationships, because for the first time in many years, Arthur found contentment in his personal life and the agitation that had characterized his domestic circumstances began to abate for everyone. "They weren't screaming and yelling at each other the way my parents were," says Christina, who "adored" her father's new wife. "You're never sure what's going to happen, but she kept everybody intact as a family," Christina says. "It was just wonderful."[3]

Arthur had first met Alexandra Emmet in Cambridge in 1955 when she, as a student at Radcliffe, had attended his lectures and cocktail parties for students. After he moved to New York in 1966, when she was working at the *New York Review of Books*, the two had begun an affair (she was also married), and by 1969 they were openly a couple. They married in July 1971 at the apartment they already shared at 118 East 82nd Street. His children and his mother were among the handful of guests. Marian would later say, "Arthur, when he went to New York, he had to have a

New York wife" (who, she added, "turned out to be a very nice person"). When Arthur married the bluestocking Marian, with her famous academic father, she had represented the Harvard world that he hoped to conquer. By the mid-1960s, the "Swinging Soothsayer" of *Time* magazine seemed to want something altogether more glamorous. And Alexandra, twenty years younger and daughter of the artist Lily Emmet Cushing, was certainly that.

Everyone who encountered the couple recognized how happy they made each other. Friends and colleagues who had always known Arthur as a more combative figure were often astonished at his conspicuous displays of affection and how completely besotted he was with her. "I was talking with Arthur in his office just before we went in to meet his graduate seminar," remembers Walter LaFeber. "Alexandra came in and was very friendly, very nice and very tall. He introduced her to me as his wife and then reached up and kissed her flush on the lips as he stood on his tiptoes to do it. That was not the image I had of Arthur Schlesinger, kissing his wife that way!"[4]

Arthur's second marriage also gave him a stepson, six-year-old Peter Allen. He remembers Arthur making that transition easy for him, not least in always welcoming the boy's father to stay during visits to the city. "My mother and father divorced when I was very little and I don't even remember living with them when they were married, so I really grew up in the house with Arthur," Peter says of life at 171 E. 64th Street (purchased in 1973 for $200,000). "We had a great relationship and I really liked spending time with him. He had his study on the third floor and usually he was in there, but you could always go in even if he was writing—it wasn't 'the maestro is working, be quiet' sort of thing. And then later he would come down and have his Jack Daniels and play backgammon." Whereas Schlesinger's older children, like Arthur before them with Arthur Sr., had often felt the oppressive weight of parental expectation, Peter experienced a more relaxed figure. "He wasn't there standing over you watching you do your homework every night," Peter says, "but if you asked him to take a look at a paper he would help and make suggestions."[5]

On June 27, 1972, Peter was joined by a baby brother, Robert Emmet

Kennedy Schlesinger (named for Robert Kennedy and for the eighteenth-century Irish nationalist Robert Emmet, to whom the newborn was directly related on his mother's side). Like Peter, Robert remembers a contented childhood. "A very happy household is how I would describe it," he says. "It was a happy time growing up." Arthur did more of the fatherly duties with Robert than he had with his older children. Once Robert started kindergarten, his father most mornings would walk him to school on 62nd Street accompanied by their Cavalier King Charles Spaniels. When Robert got home, Arthur would usually be in his office, where the two would work alongside each other when the boy was older. "His study was on the third floor and overflowing with books," Robert recalls. "There were two desks in it—one was his and then another second desk was where Peter or I could do schoolwork. Afterwards, I would sit in JFK's rocking chair that he had in there, reading or watching the TV, and Dad would be smoking his cigar, working on whatever he was writing." All told, Robert says, "It was a very nice relationship."[6]

Alexandra believes that Arthur's bond with Robert and Peter left him with feelings of "guilt about his older children" because "he had just never been interested." His younger daughter Christina holds that her father learned from his earlier mistakes and the frequent disagreements with the children from his first marriage. "He was more absent than present and when he was present he was preoccupied," she says of her own childhood. "He expected us to do well but we were on our own. He was more relaxed the second time round both because he was more experienced and because he was happier in a less contentious marriage. I think he was a more present parent."[7]

Christina felt that greater sense of engagement when she came out to him in 1977. "I don't want to make a big deal of it, but that's the colored in version of my life" she wrote, explaining that she was "afraid of disappointing and hurting" him. ("I don't have the courage yet to tell Mother," she added.) Alexandra says Arthur was "appalled" by the news, but he quickly came around, saying, "She's my daughter, I will support her no matter what." He wrote to Chrissie to affirm his commitment, prompting another letter from her admitting, "I feel greatly relieved by your love and your understanding—and that I do not have to hide a part of my life." One or two awkward moments followed, but Christina felt that her father was genuinely doing his best. "I remember a rather uncomfortable lunch at the Century Association on this topic and an equally uncomfortable visit when he came to [her partner] Cheryl's and my apartment in West LA," she recalls. "He was definitely trying, but I think he found accepting my sexuality a bit awkward. In this way I think he was very much a product of his times."[8]

Christina's letter formed part of an emotional few months for Schlesinger leading up to his sixtieth birthday that October. His mother, Elizabeth Bancroft Schlesinger, died that summer, aged 90. Her death prompted an uncharacteristically personal reflection in his journals, where he usually held emotion at bay. "She was a quite marvelous woman in her spirit, her range of interest, her high standards, her absence of righteousness and rigidity and her passion," he wrote. Marian Schlesinger, who had observed the relationship close at hand, always thought, "he was not close to his mother at all." Schlesinger himself seemed to acknowledge that fact. "Her acuteness of concern used to get on my nerves," he admitted ("You are doing too much," she had written recently, "please slow down!")—"a fact I naturally regret bitterly now, but I think she knew how much I loved her." But although he was closer to his father, whose influence on his life and career was more obvious, Schlesinger understood that he combined characteristics of both parents. "I know I owe a lot of my better qualities to her," he reflected warmly, "my strength of feeling, my readiness to trust intuition, my capacity for affection; not to mention," ever the pragmatist, "my reading speed."[9]

One of the delights for Arthur had been that his mother's last years were "infinitely brightened for her" by his new family. "I don't suppose any grandmother ever loved any little boy as Mother loved Robert," Arthur wrote after her death, recalling how he would "burst into the room" shouting, "I want to speak to Grandma! I want to speak to Grandma!" That same vitality now lifted Arthur as the "ordeal" of 60 arrived. Above all, he wrote on October 15, 1977, this was a time to celebrate "the miracle that incorporated Alexandra and Robert and Peter into my life."[10]

A profile in *People* magazine provides a vivid picture of his working day while finishing his vast biography of Robert Kennedy that year. "Up at 7 every morning, Arthur goes immediately to his study, a comfortable room filled with books on the [second] floor of his townhouse, and he writes," the profile noted. "After finishing 10 pages without fail, Schlesinger breaks for lunch. . . . Afternoons he works in a big white garret office at the City University of New York on 42nd Street. There, as Albert Schweitzer Professor of the Humanities (a chair set up to bring prominent intellectuals to the university), Schlesinger does research for [his] two-hour seminar on American cultural history. . . . In the evenings the Schlesingers often go out, and their pictures and names regularly appear in New York society pages. It is an unusual life for an academic, but no matter how late he stays out, Schlesinger, a light drinker in the evening, is always at work early next day."[11]

The *People* profile appeared under the headline, "Arthur Schlesinger Is Halfway Through His Book on Bobby and Enjoying His Life to the Hilt." And indeed he was. But there was also a sense of an ending contained in the subtext of the article. Noticeably missing in this 1976 account of his day was any sense of contemporary political engagement, not least during what was a presidential year. As a younger man, Schlesinger had combined both writing and politics with equal gusto, producing, for example, *The Age of Roosevelt* while working for Stevenson and then JFK, and *A Thousand Days* while helping RFK run for the US Senate. Those days had now passed. James Fallows, chief speechwriter for Democratic candidate Jimmy Carter, remembers that Schlesinger "gave useful advice about the nuts and bolts of speechwriting . . . when I saw him briefly at a campaign stop in 1976." Otherwise, Schlesinger was mostly detached from the process. He seemed sanguine about that transition. "[Carter] doesn't know anybody," he wrote to his old friend J. K. Galbraith. "I regard it as an advantage. . . . There is a better chance that something creative might emerge from a new man than from an old political hack surrounded by old intellectual hacks."[12]

For Schlesinger, it was all part of the code of the guild of speechwriters. Later, he would describe this evolutionary process when Al Gore asked him to write a draft for the 1992 Democratic convention. "Of course, like an old firehorse responding to the bell, I was delighted by the invitation," he wrote. "I also had foreboding. Speechwriting is a young man's game, and you have to be in the thick of things to do it right." Back in 1952, the young Schlesinger had been thrilled to meet Robert Sherwood and Sam Rosenman, FDR's speechwriters, who had agreed to do something for Stevenson. An "uproarious" lunch followed, but when Schlesinger read their speech drafts his heart sunk. "Sherwood and Rosenman had been out of things too long," he remembered forty years later, "So have I." Fallows makes the same point with similar affection and respect. "[Schlesinger] barely knew me, and our few dealings were across a huge eminence gap more or less like that of the first freshman-dorm encounter," he recalls, adding warmly that "nothing in his bearing indicated his awareness of that fact. Many big shots carry themselves like big shots; he did not."[13]

In 1980, a possible Kennedy restoration briefly flared and then fizzled when Teddy ran unsuccessfully against Carter, the sitting president. But even here Schlesinger was peripheral as new boys Carey Parker and Robert Shrum had taken the lead in crafting the senator's message. "Contrary to my expectations, the speech was an enormous triumph," Schlesinger wrote of Kennedy's address to the 1980 Democratic National Convention in New York. "My representations may have somewhat moderated the capitulationist aspects, but it remains essentially the Parker-Shrum version, and they deserve the credit." As happened to Sherwood and Rosenman before him, the times were moving on and, as he had noted after attending the opening of the JFK Library in November 1979, he must "accept the fact that a whole new generation was coming of age for whom John Kennedy was as remote and historical a figure as, say, Theodore Roosevelt and Woodrow Wilson had been for us."

The sense of Arthur Schlesinger being a "big shot" always guaranteed him a courteous hearing in the years that followed, so there was some 1950s-style false modesty to his "old firehorse" diary entries. Presidents of all stripes and Democratic Party nominees would reply to his letters and sometimes ask for his advice. He remained unafraid to speak truth to power. ("Dear Mr. President," he wrote in 1994, "a prime purpose of this year's State of the Union, I would think, would be to restore Bill Clinton's credibility as a President and as a man.") Such sentiments, while always "candid," were usually offered, as he did to the Democratic nominee in 1988, Michael Dukakis, as "from an aging veteran" away from the current scene. But even as he worried about being too old for speechwriting, he could still hit the occasional home run. "Al Gore's big line from that 1992 convention speech, 'It's time for them to go,' came from Dad's draft," Robert Schlesinger recalls, "so he hadn't lost his touch entirely."[14]

At other moments, Arthur seemed to be going back to the future. Out promoting the paperback of *Robert Kennedy and His Times* in Chicago in the fall of 1979, Schlesinger was astonished when Alexandra phoned him to say they had a new neighbor over their garden wall. "It's not someone you like very much," she told him, asking him to guess who it was moving into 142 East 65th Street. When he drew a blank, she gave him a clue: "Someone you think ought to be in prison." The penny dropped. "I can't believe it," he told her in astonishment. "Richard M. Nixon!" Two days later, after the story was picked up in the *New York Times*, news crews turned up at Schlesinger's doorstep to ask him what he thought. "There goes the neighborhood," he joked. Robert, aged 7, piped up, "I think it is just fine." Why, a reporter asked. "So I can trick or treat him" came the reply that would make the news that night.[15]

Nixon was hardly much happier to discover the identity of his new neighbor. "He certainly believes that *The Imperial Presidency* was a catalyst in his downfall!" the British MP, Jonathan Aitken, had told Schlesinger after visiting the disgraced former president. Occasionally Arthur would see "the unmistakable figure" himself gathering logs in the winter or in a deckchair, fully suited, in the summer. When Nixon's secret service agent told Schlesinger's stepson, Peter, to stop climbing his wall, a row ensued. "Arthur was so furious that he climbed up and said 'How dare you kick my son off this wall,'" Peter remembers. "'Your man should be in prison, not here, telling people what to do.'" Peter was impressed—"he didn't take any bunk at all, even though it was an ex-president"—and the message seemed to get through. "The next time I was up on the wall, Nixon waved," says Peter. "And my mother said, 'Oh, you see, he's not so bad.' And Arthur said 'No, he didn't, he was saying get off the wall.' I think, in his awkward Nixonian way, he *was* trying to wave, but Arthur wouldn't budge on that!" In the end, Nixon threw in the towel first, moving in 1981 to New Jersey. "I felt a little badly for him," Peter says.[16]

While Schlesinger was refighting past battles across his garden fence, so too did his more elevated thoughts turn to his own past. Although he never gave up talking about a return to *The Age of Roosevelt*, his remaining major book projects would focus on his own life and the influence of his father, Arthur Schlesinger Sr., whose concern with the fate of progressive reform he shared. In 1986, having made little headway on FDR, Arthur Jr. gathered together a quarter of a century of essays in a new volume, *The Cycles of American History*. As one reviewer noted, "the marvelous boy of 1945 (when he published *The Age of Jackson*) is now in his seventieth year," with the consequence that *Cycles* "strongly resembles a testament." The title of the book and the subject of its best-known essay was an act of intellectual homage to his father. It drew on Arthur Sr.'s 1924 lecture (and subsequent 1949 essay) on the cyclical nature of American history, which Arthur Jr. had himself used so decisively in *The Age of Jackson*. "I inherit [an] interpretation of this cyclical phenomenon from my father," Arthur said, "who defined the swing as between conservatism and liberalism, between periods of concern for the rights of the few and periods of concern for the wrongs of the many." Arthur Sr. had identified eleven periods of around sixteen and a half years, when "in six of the periods the object was to increase democracy; in five to contain it." Each reform and retrenchment pairing formed a roughly thirty-year cycle. Of course, Arthur being (Little) Arthur, there was a political point to his reiteration of the cycle in 1986: "if the rhythm holds," he wrote, "then the 1980s will witness the burnout of the most recent conservative ascendancy, and the age of Reagan, like its earlier versions in the 1950s, 1920s and 1890s, will fade into historical memory." Or as the *New York Times* book reviewer, Benjamin Barber, put it, *The Cycles of American History* "might better be understood as an extended elaboration on the theme 'long live liberalism.'"[17]

To this essentially domestic cycle Arthur added his own foreign policy dimension—a product of his preparatory work on his fourth Roosevelt volume. Here Schlesinger saw competing visions of America abroad in which John Winthrop's puritan ideal of "a city upon a hill" that was tempered by "the corruptibility of men and the vulnerability of states" gave way to "the delusion of a sacred mission and a sanctified destiny." The answer for Schlesinger was that the original conviction stood "rooted in realistic conceptions of history and of human nature—conceptions that waned as the republic prospered." Moral values, he concluded, "do have a fundamental role" in the conduct of moral affairs, but that role was not to provide universal principles for decision-making. "It is rather to illuminate and control conceptions of national interest." In that way, the national interest provided "an indispensable magnetic compass for policy" without which "there would be no order or predictability in international affairs." It was, said George Kennan (architect of containment and doyen of conservative realism) in the *New York Review of Books*, "a conclusion, firmly rooted in Federalist thinking, which could scarcely have been better expressed."[18]

The Cycles of American History was Schlesinger's last major book in the field as a historian. As he turned seventy, he settled into the routine of enjoying his renown as one of America's most famous and distinguished public intellectuals of a bygone era—of being, in fact, Arthur Schlesinger.

That venerable status did not mean retirement. Schlesinger maintained his ability to provoke controversy and continued to produce a steady stream of polemics in the form of reviews, op-eds, and short books that often caused outrage. In 1991 he published his controversial take on the culture wars, *The Disuniting of America: Reflections on a Multicultural Society*. Setting out with the question, "What is it that holds a nation together?" he answered with two elements, referencing John Stuart Mill, that it was "the desire on the part of the inhabitants to be governed together and the 'common sympathy' instilled by shared history, values and language." The "melting pot," he argued, had achieved that in practice over the course of two centuries: identity politics was now in danger of destroying it. America's record on racism was shameful, but the "use of history as therapy . . . means the corruption of history as history." Every civilization had "skeletons in its closet . . . but what kind of history do you have if you take out the bad things?" Taking full aim at what he described as "self-ghettoizing" black history, he declared, "the best way to keep a people down is to deny them the means of improvement and achievement and cut them off from the opportunities of the national life. If some Kleagle of the Ku Klux Klan wanted to devise an educational curriculum for the specific purpose of handicapping and disabling black Americans, he would not be likely to come up with anything more diabolically effective than Afrocentrism." Attacking a common American identity, and indeed the broader Western "canon," was "the culmination of the cult of ethnicity." This dagger to the heart of the Republic was a potentially mortal blow to the Founding Fathers' notion of *E Pluribus Unum* (out of many, one). "What then is the American, this new man?" a French immigrant to New York had asked in the 1760s, providing the answer that "Here individuals of all nations are melted into a new race." It was, Schlesinger concluded his book, "Still a good answer—still the best hope."[19]

With Americans entering the "Big Sort" rather than the Melting Pot, Schlesinger's *The Disuniting of America* anticipated many of the debates and controversies about diversity today. At the time, reaction to the book was ferocious. Even supporters such as the literary Frank Kermode, who thought it a "sane and a temperate" defense of the canon, recognized that "in the present climate he will make few converts, and his rare bursts of indignation may prove inflammatory." Kermode wasn't wrong. Henry Louis Gates Jr., newly appointed at Harvard that year, characterized Schlesinger's arguments as a demand for "cultural white-face." The novelist and Berkeley professor Ishmael Reed denounced Schlesinger as a "follower of David Duke," the former Ku Klux Klan leader. It was left to conservatives such as Heather MacDonald to defend the book. "While predictable, the hostile response to *The Disuniting of America* is nevertheless particularly discouraging," she wrote in *Commentary* magazine, "for it is difficult to imagine a book expressing greater compassion for . . . racial frustrations." Whether Schlesinger found himself more discomforted by this conservative defense than the original attacks is not clear. He expressed himself nonplussed about the controversy when questioned by the *Washington Post*, saying "What the hell! You have to call them as you see them. This too shall pass." In the privacy of his journal he wrote more tentatively, "I suppose outrage over the way the cult of ethnicity leads to flagrant abuse of history is why I am involved. Or it may be simply the folly of old age."[20]

Folly or not, controversy around the book only confirmed that Schlesinger, now approaching his seventy-fifth birthday, still had it in him to shape and enflame national debate as a public intellectual. The milestone saw him celebrated in grand fashion for that lifetime contribution. The day before his birthday, Daniel Patrick Moynihan, senator from New York, arranged for the Stars and Stripes to fly over the US Capitol for the day to honor a man "who had rendered his country and his flag uncommon service, on the occasion of his 75th birthday." The following night at the Century Association, friends threw a celebratory dinner in Schlesinger's honor. It was a lavish occasion, with organizers including Katharine Graham and Pamela Harriman, with a Schlesinger fund set up, chaired by Jacqueline Kennedy, to finance young historians researching in the JFK and FDR libraries. Ted Sorensen, J. K. Galbraith, and Graham all made speeches. Betty Comden (born the same year) and Adolph Green, along with Phyllis Newman, provided music for the occasion. Caroline Kennedy, JFK's daughter, and Linda Stevenson Weicker, wife of the late FDR Jr., presented mementos on behalf of each family. "I can only think how lucky I have been," Schlesinger responded gratefully in his speech, but he revealed one perpetual worry: "I may yet finish *The Age of Roosevelt*. That still remains my goal."[21]

Schlesinger would never finish *The Age of Roosevelt*, but he would in his own way write a personal age of Roosevelt. He had been thinking about a memoir since the early 1980s, though he worried that he was not a "natural memoirist." He began in earnest in 1994, in part to cover the loss of salary caused by his retirement from City University that same year (the advance from Houghton Mifflin was $350,000). The process suffered a major setback when his house on 64th Street was gutted in a fire. "We have been driven out of our house by a disastrous fire—hence the new address [4 East 62nd Street]," he told his friend John Blum. "The fire could have been worse (no one hurt; no vital papers lost), but the house is a wreck and will require months of restoration, and my library is in storage." Henry

Kissinger called "anxiously" to ask about the fate of Schlesinger's papers, and to say that he himself had immediately ordered fireproofing for his basement. The "damned fire" plunged Schlesinger into a "depression" not experienced "since the murders of JFK and RFK." Aside from anything else, he wrote, "this disruption of life is the last thing I need in my 78th year with a book to write." The memoir would take another six years to complete and was published in 2000 as *A Life in the Twentieth Century: Innocent Beginnings, 1917–1950*. Schlesinger had warned himself and readers against the dangers of what Charles Bohlen had called "hindmyopia," namely the "refusal to see the specific circumstances, the particular pressures, the full context that shaped decisions." He therefore took the greatest pleasure when, among a plethora of "semi-raves" in the reviews, the *Economist* magazine concluded its notice by comparing the book to *The Education of Henry Adams*. That, "of course," he purred happily, "is the comparison I have always secretly had in mind."[22]

Even now, well into his ninth decade, Schlesinger was not done. After the critical and popular success of *Innocent Beginnings*, he began work on a second volume of memoirs. And when George W. Bush led the United States into wars in Afghanistan and Iraq, Schlesinger pulled together a series of op-ed and review articles to publish an attack on the forty-third president in book form, *War and the American Presidency*, in the hope it would influence the election that fall. The 2004 book, in truth, was far from his best work. It drew poor reviews from across the political spectrum that ranged from the withering—"reads like a magazine article rather than a serious investigation by a major scholar" (Kevin Drum, *New York Times*), to the outright brutal—"Pure baloney" (Angelo Codevilla, *Claremont Review of Books*). Worse for Schlesinger, George W. Bush, destined to be the last president of the historian's lifetime, was reelected, beating John Kerry, who, although a Yale man, was the senator from Schlesinger's adoptive state of Massachusetts.[23]

Now aged eighty-seven and already suffering from the symptoms of Parkinson's disease, Schlesinger seemed finally to be on a downward trajectory. The death from cancer of his daughter, Kathy, in 2004 was another crushing reversal. "My father was really stricken," says Kathy's sister,

Christina. "After she died I looked at my father and I thought he doesn't look like he's going to be around long either."

There was, however, still one last intellectual gem to come. Three decades earlier, Schlesinger had written in his journal, "It is odd to me how little read [Reinhold] Niebuhr seems these days." Certainly, Schlesinger told his son Robert in 1991, the theologian's "interpretation of history and of human nature had a great impact on me." By 2005 interest in Niebuhr was sparking again in specialist circles in the context of the War on Terror. Schlesinger now tried to bring the theologian's ideas to a broader public, writing a widely noticed essay for the *New York Times Sunday Book Review*, "Forgetting Reinhold Niebuhr," that made a far more persuasive case about US foreign policy than the shrill efforts of *War and the American Presidency*.[24]

"Why, in an age of religiosity," Schlesinger began, "has Niebuhr, the supreme American theologian of the 20th century, dropped out of 21st-century religious discourse?" In part the answer lay with the experience of 9/11, which "revived the myth of our national innocence." Niebuhr had regarded national innocence as a delusion. He emphasized the mixed nature of humankind, which was both creative and destructive. "The notion of sinful man," Schlesinger explained, "was uncomfortable for my generation . . . brought up to believe in human innocence and even in human perfectibility." But Niebuhr's concept of original sin also "solved certain problems for my generation." His argument both accounted for Hitler and Stalin, and for the necessity of standing up to them. But it also cautioned against national self-righteousness. "From the earliest days," Schlesinger quoted Niebuhr writing in 1952, "there is a deep layer of messianic consciousness in the mind of America. We never dreamed that we would have as much political power as we possess today; nor for that matter did we anticipate that the most powerful nation on earth would suffer such an ironic refutation of its dreams of mastering history." Without pumping the pedal too hard, Schlesinger brought readers to his conclusion about why Niebuhr was as relevant in the post-9/11 world as he had been during earlier periods of global crisis. "To be effective in the world," he wrote, "we need 'a sense of modesty about the virtue, wisdom and power available to us' and 'a sense of contrition about the common human frailties and foibles which lie at the foundation of both the enemy's demonry and our vanities.'" If America should perish, Schlesinger said, quoting the last lines of *The Irony of American History* (1952), "the ruthlessness of the foe would be only the secondary cause of the disaster. The primary cause would be that the strength of a giant nation was directed by eyes too blind to see all the hazards of the struggle; and the blindness would be induced not by some accident of nature or history but by hatred and vainglory.'"[25]

The essay was a perfectly formed miniature of Schlesinger the public intellectual, popularizing a scholarly idea with an elegance of style and clarity of argument that seemed effortless. Certainly the piece had its effect, helping advance the revival of interest in Niebuhr's work that was already percolating in think tanks, political magazines, and universities. Niebuhr would become, *Slate* later reported, "The Philosopher of the Post 9/11 Era"—a celebrated status for which his old friend Arthur Schlesinger could take a lion's share of the credit.[26]

Schlesinger's powers now began to fail as his health gave way. It was a gradual decline, and one that he continued to fight with tenacity, his enthusiasm for ideas undimmed. Robert Caro, celebrated biographer of Lyndon Johnson and a friend since the early 1980s, recalls meeting Schlesinger in these last years for lunch periodically at Jubilee, near Sutton Place on the East Side. Schlesinger would arrive cane in hand, waving away any offers of help. "How did you get here?" Caro once made the mistake of asking. "I walked," Schlesinger replied, scowling. Towards the end, Parkinson's had made it difficult for him to speak clearly. "His voice began to fail, but his mind never did," Caro says. "I remember once he asked me, 'How long do you sleep?' I said only five to six hours. And he said that was the same for him. 'Do you realize if you sleep eight hours a night, you're wasting one-third of the only life you've been given?'" It was that work ethic that had maximized his talent.[27]

It was at another restaurant, Bobby Van's Steakhouse on Park Avenue, that the end finally came. On February 28, 2007, now in his ninetieth year, Schlesinger was out for a family dinner to celebrate his stepson Peter's engagement when he was stricken with sudden chest pains. Life left him quickly. He was rushed to New York Downtown Hospital, where he was declared dead that same evening. As to what might come next, Arthur liked to quote Luis Buñuel, the Spanish film director, who when asked about his faith replied, "I'm an atheist. Thank God." But for Schlesinger his credo was found elsewhere. "The future outwits all our certitudes," he had said just a few weeks earlier at an event organized in his honor in New York. "History is the best antidote to delusions of omnipotence and omniscience."[28]

REWRITING HISTORY

"The measure of what is historically important," the 20-year-old Schlesinger wrote in 1938, "is set by the generation that writes the history, not by the one that makes it." The next phase in the battle over his own reputation began a few months after his death when his journals were posthumously published. On one side were critics like Christopher Hitchens, who concluded that Schlesinger would have written "not just more books but better ones" if he had not "squandered so much time and energy being a compulsive socialite and an insecure *valet du pouvoir*." Ernest May, an academic observer of the Kennedy administration from the outside, formed a similar conclusion about his one-time Harvard colleague. Schlesinger's skills, he said, were "put to little use" after his great works on Jackson and Roosevelt. Instead, he had allowed "political and social pursuits to consume his time and talent." May pointed specifically to the failure to complete *The Age of Roosevelt* as Exhibit A in the case against Schlesinger. Others were less censorious. Sure, *The Age of Roosevelt* had not been finished, said the Pulitzer Prize–winning journalist Joseph Lelyveld after reading the *Journals*. "But honestly, wouldn't you rather have this book than volume four?"[1]

Some of the disdain displayed toward Schlesinger could be attributed, the Rutgers historian David Greenberg points out, "to the snarls of professional jealousy that greet any colleague who writes best sellers, let alone consorts with the Kennedys." But Schlesinger's friends too had worried at the time. A letter on March 1, 1961, from C. Vann Woodward, a generation older than Schlesinger, captures the ambiguity that many historians felt. With Schlesinger now in the White House, Woodward admitted, "I go daily to my appointed task the more serene in the knowledge that you are where you are." But in the same letter, having just read Schlesinger's draft chapters for *The National Experience*, the influential college text for which both were authors, he worried about the direction in which his friend was heading. "I only hope, Arthur, that you are not really as confirmed a partisan" as it appears, Woodward wrote. "But I confess there are times when I wonder."[2]

Schlesinger sometimes wondered too. Was he simply "the power-loving stablemate of statesmen" rather than a serious historian? In 2000 he confessed his doubts in a *New York Times* interview. Of course he had enjoyed politics, but he was "essentially" a historian. For that reason, he said, "I feel that I should have spent much more time writing history and less time writing op-ed pieces or speeches for candidates." Even in 1968, when still at the height of his powers and fame, he had his doubts. "What have I been doing?" he wrote to his daughter Christina. "As usual, writing too many transitory pieces and not doing enough serious work."[3]

The Age of Jackson, The Crisis of the Old Order, The Vital Center, A Thousand Days, and *The Imperial Presidency*: these books alone comprise enough "serious work" in their very different ways to establish Schlesinger as one of the foremost historians of the postwar era. Just as significant, his life and work lived up to the vision he set out for himself as a young man at Harvard. History, the undergraduate Arthur had decided in 1937, was "the only possible career" for him, but he was desperate to avoid the ivory tower if that meant "cutting myself off" from "the currents that electrify vital life." For the undergraduate Schlesinger the answer to that conundrum was that "knowledge and experience should be intimately related."[4]

Over the next seventy years Schlesinger turned that principle into action, experiencing life on the frontline of war and politics, and fashioning that experience into history and polemic. He identified as part of an older tradition of historian-participants stretching back to Thucydides and including the likes of Guicciardini and Machiavelli, Bacon and Raleigh, Macaulay, Tocqueville and Guizot, Henry Adams and, of course, his own relative George Bancroft. "They were all involved in the public world," Schlesinger wrote. "They were not men just of the study and the lamp." One such writer, Edward Gibbon, another imperial historian, wrote that his time as "the captain of the Hampshire grenadiers (the reader may smile) has not been useless to the historian of the Roman Empire." Some of Schlesinger's readers too may have smiled, and his critics smirked, about this "gadfly" in the White House. But like Gibbon, Schlesinger believed that his experience as special assistant to the president had not been useless to the historian of the American Empire.[5]

The question was whether it had in any serious way skewed his vision as well as expanded it. For some historians, all political engagement was an anathema. When Woodward, who worried about Schlesinger, had written *The Strange Career of Jim Crow* in the wake of the *Brown v. Board of Education* Supreme Court decision, he found himself upbraided by the historian of the South David M. Potter for engaging in activism, not history. Woodward believed the compromise was worth it, because the book suggested that segregation was not a facet of human nature, but a historical construct. Humans, having created it, were free to undo it. In 1965 Martin Luther King Jr. quoted Woodward in Montgomery, Alabama. Yet when Woodward's friend Richard Hofstadter published his Pulitzer Prize–winning and most popular work, *Anti-Intellectualism in American Life*, it was Woodward who had done the upbraiding. "Dick, you just can't do this," he exclaimed, accusing his friend of selling out history when he "let go with both barrels" to make a political point about the supposed superiority of liberal cosmopolitanism.[6]

Still others argued that Schlesinger was the inevitable and extreme consequence of the Progressive school of history that included not only Arthur, but also his father Arthur Sr., Charles A. Beard, and Frederick Jackson Turner. When in 1967 the New Left produced their seminal essay collection *Towards A New Past: Dissenting Essays in American History*, the editor Barton J. Bernstein took full aim at the Schlesingers and their Progressive notion that historical inquiry might promote liberal reform. "Logically, there was no conflict between their aims of writing objective history and of influencing change," he wrote. "But in practice a tension developed, and their history was sometimes distorted by their commitments, provoking hostile criticism from a later generation."[7]

Even for historical practitioners inside the White House, Arthur Jr. remained a dubious role model. When Bill Clinton told Taylor Branch in 1993 that he wanted him to be "an Arthur Schlesinger," Branch recoiled from the idea, telling the president, "no 'court history' by me could earn much credit for either of us." (Branch's own eventual attempt, *The Clinton Tapes*, presented as many problems as it solved.)[8]

Somewhere, possibly sometime in the twelfth century, there was a historian-monk who passed these various purity tests, but he was surely the last to do so. As Schlesinger foresaw in 1937, really none of his books was closeted in the environs of the abbey or the ivory tower. Beginning with *Orestes Brownson* and *The Age of Jackson*, each of his works engaged in one way or another with public debates, even if some were more in the crucible of events than others. His most famous scholarly book, *The Age of Jackson*, has a political point of view, but it came essentially from the archives; a more ideological book like *The Vital Center* reversed the process, using history as a backstop for a political idea. In books like *A Thousand Days*, and *Robert Kennedy and His Times*, the historian emerged as both participant and chronicler.

Unlike his contemporaries, the colonial historian Edmund S. Morgan (born in 1916) or the historian of slavery John Hope Franklin (1915), Schlesinger did not write books that redefined an entire subfield. Neither did he, like Frederick Jackson Turner, the midwestern historian whom Arthur Sr. replaced at Harvard, introduce a seminal theory of history (although the "cycles of history" had its followers). But Schlesinger can claim to have made two essential contributions to historical scholarship—one summative, the other formative. The summative contribution came through *The Age of Jackson*, which represents the apotheosis of the Progressive commitment to the pragmatic function of historical inquiry. Here Schlesinger showed how Jackson wrenched control of the Republic back from a wealthy oligarchy to return it to its egalitarian roots. Although he recalibrated that process, moving the beating heart away from Turner's frontier in the West to the urban East, the book remains a lesson about how reform was forged on the anvil of popular democracy—a thesis that Schlesinger would reinforce with *The Age of Roosevelt*. As David S. Brown, biographer of Richard Hofstadter, wryly points out, in universities throughout America Schlesinger's famous dictum that "more can be understood about Jacksonian democracy if it is regarded as a problem not of sections but of classes" was "a line memorized by a generation."[9]

Schlesinger's formative books on Kennedy matched his work on Jackson. *A Thousand Days* (and to a lesser extent *Robert Kennedy and His Times*) is a foundational text on the Kennedy administration. Not only did Schlesinger establish the "first draft" of history on the Kennedy years, but he offered an invaluable personal account of life on the inside. Few doubt that the book represented a case for the defense. But even Schlesinger's critics at the time, among whom Christopher Lasch was the most vehement (calling him a "kept intellectual"), did not accuse Schlesinger of bad history. Later revisionist accounts of the administration overturned much of Schlesinger's analysis, yet the book remains a must for any historian working on Kennedy. Richard Reeves in his biography of the president judges that *A Thousand Days* is one of "the two essential Kennedy books" (the other being Sorensen's). President Clinton made this point to Branch after he read Reeves, saying that "after all these years" Schlesinger's book still worked; more than ever, the president said, he wanted his own Schlesinger "to take care of the history."[10]

Schlesinger understood the tensions in his own position as historian-participant. From inside the Kennedy White House he set down his notion that "to smell the dust and sweat of battle, is surely to stimulate and amplify the historical imagination." Experience gave the historian an insight into the emotions and pressures of real power. "The observer who once witnesses the making of decisions under pressure," he wrote, "is unlikely ever to write in the same disdainful way about the agonizing of Madison in 1812 or Lincoln in 1861 or Roosevelt in 1941." Once outside the White House, he continued the theme. Most historians, Schlesinger later explained, like "to tidy things up," imposing order on events and giving them meaning. The eyewitness historian on the other hand was able "to preserve the felt texture of events and to recognize the role of such elements as confusion, ignorance, chance, and sheer stupidity." "Obviously we need both and the dialectic between them is a major part of the historical exercise," he concluded. His singular contribution was to represent that dialectic in one person.[11]

Schlesinger carried off the role of participant with some aplomb. In office he learned that it was not enough to be right if ignored, as during the Bay of Pigs. An advisor must pick up how to make himself heard, as he did during the Berlin Wall crisis. Kennedy enjoyed Schlesinger's company and sometimes took his advice, but both men knew that Arthur's real job was yet to come. That task became something different from what either man had imagined after the president was assassinated. The need for instant history denied the opportunity for leisurely post-presidency reflection, yet Schlesinger managed its demands with both style and substance. Those who tried to repeat the trick as White House participant-historian found out how difficult it was. Eric Goldman (LBJ), Edmund Morris (Reagan), and Branch—prize-winning historians all, and in the latter two cases, outstanding experienced biographers—struggled in various ways to do what Schlesinger had made look easy.[12]

Schlesinger at different times was a professor, an "action-intellectual," and a court historian. Winning the Pulitzer Prize at 28 was a precocious first act; what followed—more prize-winning books, a role as a major public figure, and his own thousand days in the White House—proved that there were second acts in some American lives. Schlesinger was a multifaceted historian, writing in different styles and formats, whose crossover often defied categorization. While he took the academic world by storm as a young man, he worried about his "serious work" later in life. But he also wanted to get to the inside of the political world, which he was intent on bringing to life for a popular audience. Sometimes he paid a reputational price. His choice demeaned him in the eyes of many peers who believed that he had sold out. Yet he did become an instrumental eyewitness to history. And he did bring the past very much to life as one of the finest narrative historians America has ever produced. But whether as a man of thought or as a man of action, he retained the same idée fixe: to put himself and his ideas at "the vital center."

Schlesinger was aware of the contested nature of this vital life, the more so as the older figure bearing the scars of battles in the public arena replaced the brash young "daddy's boy" of the 1930s and 1940s. "We are prisoners of our own times and own experiences," he acknowledged at his eightieth birthday dinner at the Century Association in 1997. "New times bring new contexts and new perspectives—and new histories." But Schlesinger's life had fulfilled the words of Oscar Wilde that he quoted that night. "The one duty we owe to history," he said, "is to rewrite it."[13]

ACKNOWLEDGMENTS

For help in a variety of ways, I wish to thank the following: Daniel Akst, Maurice Bric, Ian Buruma, Sir David Cannadine, Eliot Cohen, Deirdre d'Albertis, Mark Danner, Omar Encarnación, Lucy Flamm, Rory Kennedy, Cynthia Koch, Walter LaFeber, Michael Mandelbaum, Sean McMeekin, Brian Murphy, Mike Riley, Declan Ryan, Michael Staunton, Karen Sullivan, David Swanson, Rachel Thompson, Noel Whelan, Harry White, and David Woolner; the president, faculty, staff, and students of Bard College, particularly the members of my first-year seminar classes; Walter Russell Mead, Damir Marusic, Jamie Horgan, and everyone at *The American Interest*; the archivists of the JFK Library and the New York Public Library, with particular thanks to Tal Nadan and Brandon Westerheim; Peter Nelson, head of archives at Phillips Exeter Academy; David Reynolds, Fredrik Logevall, Mark Lytle, and Simon Ball for their immense generosity in taking time away from their own research to read all or part of my first draft; my superb editor Tom Mayer, his assistant Sarah Bolling, and the entire team at W. W. Norton; the indefatigable Georgina Capel of Georgina Capel Associates; Stephen Graham and Andrew Wylie for facilitating the connection with the Schlesinger family, and the Schlesingers themselves for their kindness in welcoming this project, with special thanks to Alexandra Schlesinger, Robert Schlesinger, and Peter Allan, Marian Cannon Schlesinger, Stephen Schlesinger, Christina Schlesinger, and Andrew Schlesinger; my wife, Kathryn Aldous, for once again reading an entire manuscript; my mother, Patricia Aldous, and my late father,

John Aldous, who first introduced me to *A Thousand Days*. Finally this book is dedicated to my daughter Elizabeth. She's nobody's "Junior," but I am every bit as proud of her as Arthur Sr. was of Young Arthur.

Richard Aldous
Annandale-on-Hudson, New York
March 2017

NOTES

Prologue: Where He Was

1 Accounts of Schlesinger on Nov. 22/23, 1963: Richard N. Goodwin, *Remembering America: A Voice from the Sixties* (Boston: Little, Brown, 1988), 226–231; diary entry, Nov. 23, 1963, Arthur Schlesinger, *Journals: 1952–2000,* ed. Andrew Schlesinger and Stephen Schlesinger (New York: Penguin Press, 2008), 203–206; William Manchester, *The Death of a President: November 1963* (New York: Harper & Row, 1967), 420, 437, 442–443; Katharine Graham, *Personal History* (New York: Alfred A. Knopf, 1997), 353; "The Combative Chronicler," *Time,* Dec. 17, 1965; AMS, "The Historian and History," *Foreign Affairs* (April 1963), https://www.foreignaffairs.com/articles/1963-04-01/historian-and-history.

Chapter One: Becoming Arthur Schlesinger Jr.

1 **Key: NYPL**—Arthur M. Schlesinger Jr. Papers. Manuscripts and Archives Division. The New York Public Library. Astor, Lenox, and Tilden Foundations. **AMS Memoirs**—Arthur M. Schlesinger Jr., *A Life in the 20th Century: Innocent Beginnings, 1917–1950* (Boston: Houghton Mifflin, 2000). **AMS Letters**—Arthur M. Schlesinger Jr., *The Letters of Arthur Schlesinger, Jr.,* ed. Andrew Schlesinger and Stephen Schlesinger (New York: Random House, 2013). **JFKL**—Arthur M. Schlesinger Jr. Personal Papers. John F. Kennedy Presidential Library and Museum.

Three generations of Schlesingers have told the story of Arthur's early life, and I draw on each of them in this chapter. There are Arthur's own memoirs, his father's memoirs, and an account by his sons, Andrew and Stephen, in the prologue to the published letters. Andrew has also written a study of Arthur's alma mater, Harvard University. Arthur's first wife, Marian Cannon, who, like him, grew up in Cambridge, Massachusetts, wrote her own memoir of a Harvard childhood. Arthur M. Schlesinger Jr., *A Life in the 20th Century: Innocent Begin-*

nings, 1917–1950 (Boston: Houghton Mifflin, 2000), 59; Arthur M. Schlesinger Sr., *In Retrospect: The History of a Historian* (New York: Harcourt, Brace and World, 1963); Arthur M. Schlesinger Jr., *The Letters of Arthur Schlesinger, Jr.*, ed. Andrew Schlesinger and Stephen Schlesinger (New York: Random House, 2013); Andrew Schlesinger, *Veritas: Harvard College and the American Experience* (Chicago: Ivan R. Dee, 2005); Marian Cannon Schlesinger, *Snatched From Oblivion: A Cambridge Memoir* (Boston: Little, Brown, 1979); Niall Ferguson, *Kissinger, 1923–1968: The Idealist* (New York: Penguin Press, 2015), 447; Walter LaFeber, interview by author, June 4, 2014.

2 Marian Cannon Schlesinger, interview by author, Mar. 9, 2014.

3 AMS Memoirs, 13.

4 "Ohio, Marriages, 1800–1958: Bernhard Schlesinger and Katie Feurle, 20 Feb 1873," *FamilySearch*, citing Greene, Ohio, reference, FHL microfilm 0535126 V. 5–7, https://familysearch.org/ark:/61903/1:1:XDNW-JYD; Helen Hooven Santmyer, *Ohio Town: A Portrait of Xenia* (New York: Harper, 1961).

5 Schlesinger, *In Retrospect*, 195.

6 Ibid., 51.

7 "Ohio, Deaths, 1908–1953," Arthur Schlesinger in entry for Katherine Bancroft Schlesinger, 18 July 1916, *FamilySearch*, citing Columbus, Franklin Co., Ohio, reference fn 42891; FHL microfilm 1,983,750, https://familysearch.org/ark:/61903/1:1:X8N2-DBN; Schlesinger, *In Retrospect*, 52; Note by AMS on his sister's death, Feb. 23, 1994, NYPL 506/1.

8 "United States World War I Draft Registration Cards, 1917–1918," Arthur Meier Schlesinger, 1917–1918, *FamilySearch*, citing Columbus City no 4, Ohio, United States, NARA microfilm publication M1509 (Washington, DC: National Archives and Records Administration, n.d.); FHL microfilm 1,832,032, https://familysearch.org/ark:/61903/1:1:K6FN-D4N.

9 "The Great Pandemic: The United States in 1918–19," *Center for Disease Control*, http://www.flu.gov/pandemic/history/1918/your_state/midwest/ohio/index.html.

10 Children's Bureau reports, 1918 and 1921; State University of Iowa Welfare Research Station reports, Dec. 18, 1923 and May 24, 1924, NYPL 506/1.

11 Schlesinger, *In Retrospect*, 6; Gerald Mansheim, *Iowa City: An Illustrated History* (Norfolk, VA: Donning, 1989), 72–73.

12 AMS Memoirs, 23.

13 Reviews of *Before Head Start: The Iowa Station and America's Children*, by Hamilton Cravens; Joseph M. Hawes, *History of Education Quarterly* 34, no. 4 (Winter 1994): 507–508, http://www.jstor.org/stable/369294, DOI: 10.2307/369294;

Peter C. Holloran, *The American Historical Review* 99, no. 5 (1994): 1763-1764, http://www.jstor.org/stable/2168549; Roberta Wollons, *Isis* 85, no. 4 (1994): 729-730, http://www.jstor.org/stable/235351; AMS Memoirs, 24; Bird Baldwin, ed., *University of Iowa Studies In Child Welfare* (Iowa City: University of Iowa, 1921), https://babel.hathitrust.org/cgi/pt?id=mdp.39015039710721;view=1up;seq=9; "Iowa Child Welfare Research Station, 1917-1974," *University of Iowa,* http://digital.lib.uiowa.edu/ictcs/icwrs.html.

14 On the work of Arthur Schlesinger (Sr.): Arthur M. Schlesinger Jr., "Arthur M. Schlesinger, Sr.: New Viewpoints in American History Revisited," in *The New England Quarterly* 61, no. 4 (Dec. 1988): 483-501; review by R. W. Kelsey, "New Viewpoints in American History by Arthur Meier Schlesinger," *The American Historical Review* 28, no. 1 (Oct. 1922): 131-132; review by Clement Eaton, "In Retrospect: The History of a Historian, by Arthur M. Schlesinger Sr.," *The Journal of Negro History* 49, no. 3 (July 1964): 210-211; James Chace, "The Age of Schlesinger," *New York Review of Books,* December 21, 2000, http://www.nybooks.com/articles/archives/2000/dec/21/the-age-of-schlesinger; David Milne, *Worldmaking: The Art and Science of American Diplomacy* (New York: Farrar, Straus and Giroux, 2015), 126-131.

15 Wilcomb E. Washburn, "Samuel Eliot Morison, Historian," *The William and Mary Quarterly* 36, no. 3 (July 1979): 325-352; P. A. M. Taylor, "Samuel Eliot Morison: Historian," *Journal of American Studies* 11, no. 1 (Apr. 1977): 13-26; William Bentinck-Smith, "Samuel Eliot Morison," *Proceedings of the Massachusetts Historical Society* 88 (1976): 121-131; review by R. W. Kelsey, "New Viewpoints in American History by Arthur Meier Schlesinger," *The American Historical Review* 28, no. 1 (Oct. 1922): 131-132; Jill Lepore, "Plymouth Rocked: Of Pilgrims, Puritans, and Professors," *The New Yorker,* Apr. 24, 2006, http://www.newyorker.com/magazine/2006/04/24/plymouth-rocked.

16 Arthur M. Schlesinger, Jr., "Arthur M. Schlesinger, Sr.: New Viewpoints in American History Revisited," 483-501.

17 Schlesinger, *In Retrospect,* 55-56; Frederick Jackson Turner, "The Significance of the Frontier in American History" (1893), republished in *Rereading Frederick Jackson Turner: 'The Significance of the Frontier in American History' and Other Essays* (New Haven, CT: Yale University Press, 1994), 31-60, http://www.jstor.org/stable/j.ctt32bv5g.5.

18 AMS Memoirs, 24.

19 "Thomas Bancroft Schlesinger, 1922-1983," Sept. 14, 1983, NYPL 515/3.

20 Schlesinger, *In Retrospect,* 79.

21 Andrew Schlesinger, *Veritas*, 163–165; Ferguson, *Kissinger: The Idealist, 1923–1968*, 211–214.

22 Morton Keller and Phyllis Keller, *Making Harvard Modern: The Rise of America's Universities* (New York: Oxford University Press, 2001), 81.

23 Schlesinger, *In Retrospect*, 131.

24 AMS to S. Regensberg, undated, NYPL 532/5; Schlesinger, *In Retrospect*, 7; Arthur M. Schlesinger Jr., *The Disuniting of America: Reflections on a Multicultural Society* (New York: W. W. Norton, 1998, revised and enlarged edition), 60–63; Antonio Monda, *Do You Believe? Conversations on God and Religion* (New York: Vintage, 2007), 146.

25 *Wonderful Town* (1953) with lyrics by Betty Comden and Adolph Green and music by Leonard Bernstein; Schlesinger, *In Retrospect*, 80–82; Joseph P. Lash, ed., *From the Diaries of Felix Frankfurter* (New York: Norton, 1975), 4–5.

26 Edward C. Kirkland, review of *In Retrospect: The History of a Historian*, by Arthur M. Schlesinger Sr., *The New England Quarterly* 37, no. 2 (June 1964): 263–265.

27 Keller and Keller, *Making Harvard Modern*, 85; Jacques Barzun, "Reminiscences of the Columbia History Department 1923–1975," *Living Legacies*, Winter 2000, http://www.columbia.edu/cu/alumni/Magazine/Winter2000/Barzun.html.

28 Milne, *Worldmaking*, 127; Schlesinger (Sr.), *In Retrospect*, 77–79; Edward C. Kirkland, review of *In Retrospect*, by Arthur M. Schlesinger Sr., 263–265.

29 Schlesinger, *In Retrospect*, 79.

30 Christina Schlesinger, interview by author, Apr. 16, 2014; AMS Memoirs, 36.

31 Undated "when I am a man" note [c. 1925], NYPL 508/1.

32 AMS letters to his mother and grandmother, May 7, June 4, June 5, 1926, Arthur Schlesinger (Sr.) to Elizabeth Schlesinger, June 9, 1926, NYPL 506/1–2.

33 Camp Wonalancet, NH, director to Elizabeth Schlesinger, July 7, 1927, AMS to Elizabeth Schlesinger, with postscript by Arthur Schlesinger (Sr.), June 4, 1926, NYPL 296.1–5, 506/1–2.

34 Schlesinger, *In Retrospect*, 80–81.

35 AMS diary, April 24, 25, 30, May 7, 1929; Elizabeth Schlesinger to Arthur Schlesinger, May 2, 1929, NYPL 296/1–2; "Woolworth Building," *Cass Gilbert Society*, http://www.cassgilbertsociety.org/works/nyc-woolworth-bldg.

36 Schlesinger, *Snatched from Oblivion*, 208–209.

37 Cleveland to Arthur Schlesinger (Sr.), May 6, 1929, Dec. 17, 1929, NYPL 506/1–2.

39 AMS Memoirs, 41, 60; Camp report, 1930; Arthur Schlesinger (Sr.) to AMS, July 2, 1930, NYPL 296/1–2.

39 Schlesinger, *Snatched from Oblivion*, 208–209; Schlesinger (Sr.), *In Retrospect*, 81.

40 AMS Memoirs, 81; AMS to Arthur and Elizabeth Schlesinger, undated letters from Exeter, NYPL 508/4.

41 AMS to Arthur and Elizabeth Schlesinger, undated letters from Exeter, NYPL 508/4.

42 AMS to Elizabeth Schlesinger, undated letter from Exeter, NYPL 508/4.

43 "How to be a student," undated, NYPL 506/2; John Brewer, "Educational Guidance," as reprinted in Los Angeles Educational Research Bulletin: Los Angeles City Schools, January 7, 1924.

44 AMS to Elizabeth Schlesinger, undated letter from Exeter [1933], NYPL 508/4.

45 Lewis Perry, Exeter reference for Harvard, June 8, 1933; Harvard Entrance Board to Arthur Schlesinger (Sr.), July 17, 1933, NYPL 508/4-5.

46 Harvard Application Form, date stamped, Apr. 21, 1933; College entrance exam scores, June 24, 1933, NYPL 508/4-5.

47 Marian Cannon Schlesinger, interview by author, Mar. 9, 2014; Schlesinger, In Retrospect, 157.

48 AMS Memoirs, 93.

49 Around the World Trip, diary entries, Sept. 5, Oct. 15, Dec. 31, 1933, July 31, 1934, NYPL 309.

50 Around the World Trip, diary entries, Jan. 1-5, June 25-30, 1934, NYPL 309.

51 Around the World Trip, diary entry, Oct. 14, 1933, NYPL 309.

52 Around the World Trip, diary entry, Dec. 8, 1933, NYPL 309.

53 Around the World Trip, diary entries, Sept. 25-30, Oct. 19, 1933, July 15, July 21, 1934, NYPL 309.

54 Around the World Trip, diary entries, Jan. 31, April 19, 1934, NYPL 309; AMS Memoirs, 102.

55 Around the World Trip, diary entries, Dec. 20, 1933, June 16, 1934, NYPL 309.

56 Around the World Trip, diary entries, Dec. 31, 1933, Jan. 31, 1934, NYPL 309; Douglas Martin, "Arthur Schlesinger, Historian of Power, Dies at 89," New York Times, Feb. 28, 2007, http://www.nytimes.com/2007/02/28/washington/28cnd-schlesinger.html?pagewanted=1&_r=0.

57 Around the World Trip, diary entry, Aug. 29, 1934; Itinerary of trip, 1933-34, NYPL 309.

Chapter Two: A Pilgrim's Progress

1 Ian Hamilton, Robert Lowell (New York: Vintage, 1983), 45-47; Ian S. MacNiven, "Literchoor Is My Beat": A Life of James Laughlin, Publisher of New Directions (New York: Farrar, Straus and Giroux, 2014), 36-37; Isaiah Berlin, Letters, 1928-1946, ed. Henry Hardy (New York: Cambridge University Press, 2004),

367–368; Niall Ferguson, *Kissinger: The Idealist, 1923–1968* (New York: Penguin, 2015), 206–207.

2 Nicholas Lemann, *The Big Test: The Secret History of the American Meritocracy* (New York: Farrar, Straus and Giroux, 2000 paperback edition), 21; AMS Memoirs, 114; Theodore H. White, *In Search of History* (New York: Harper and Row, 1978), 41–43.

3 James P. Baxter to Harvard Admissions, May 4, 1933, NYPL 508/5.

4 AMS to Clara Bancroft, Sept. 23, 1934, NYPL 299/9; White, *In Search of History*, 40.

5 AMS Memoirs, 115.

6 Timothy Jack Ward, "Changes to Union Divide Harvard," *New York Times,* Feb. 15, 1996, http://www.nytimes.com/1996/02/15/garden/changes-to-union-divide -harvard.html; AMS to Clara Bancroft, Oct. 9, 1934, NYPL 299/9.

7 Samuel Eliot Morison, *Three Centuries of Harvard* (Cambridge, MA: Belknap Press, 1986), 476–478; AMS Memoirs, 112–113.

8 AMS to Clara Bancroft, March 16, 1935, NYPL 299/9; Movie viewing log, NYPL 508/6; AMS Memoirs, 126–127; Leo P. Ribuffo, *Right Center Left: Essays in American History* (New Brunswick, NJ: Rutgers University Press, 1992), 134–135.

9 J. Michael Lennon, *Norman Mailer: A Double Life* (New York: Simon and Schuster, 2013), 37; MacNiven, *Literchoor Is My Beat*, 91–92; AMS Memoirs, 119; Madeline Schwartz, "Sesquicentennial Soirée: Harvard Advocate alumni take stock," *The Harvard Magazine*, Sept./Oct., 2016, http://harvardmagazine.com/2016/09/ sesquicentennial-soiree.

10 AMS Memoirs, 121; AMS to Clara Bancroft, Nov. 21, 1934, NYPL 299/9.

11 AMS to Clara Bancroft, Oct. 9, Dec. 28, 1934, NYPL 299/9; Harvard transcript, NYPL 506/5.

12 White, *In Search of History,* 44–45; "Schlesinger Given Briggs Prize for History 1 Essay," *Harvard Crimson*, Mar. 7, 1935, http://www.thecrimson.com/article/1935/ 3/7/schlesinger-given-briggs-prize-for-history.

13 Harvard Freshman Adviser's Report, Mar. 4, 1935, NYPL 506/5; AMS Memoirs, 172.

14 AMS to Clara Bancroft, Mar. 11, 1935, NYPL 299/9; Morison to Winthrop Aldrich, April 20, 1954; AMS to Ray Helsel, May 24, 1993, *Argosy,* http://www.argosybooks .com/shop/argosy/218104.html; Harvard transcript, NYPL 506/5.

15 Marcus Cunliffe and Robin Winks, eds., "Arthur M. Schlesinger, Jr.," in *Pastmasters: Some Essays on American Historians* (New York, Harper and Row, 1969), 183; AMS Memoirs, 162; Schlesinger and Morgan later worked together on John M. Blum, William S. McFeely, Edmund S. Morgan, Arthur M. Schlesinger Jr., and

Kenneth M. Stampp, *The National Experience: A History of the United States* (New York: Harcourt, Brace and World, 1963).

16 Cunliffe and Winks, eds., *Pastmasters*, 183; Bernard DeVoto, *The Hour: A Cocktail Manifesto* (New York and Portland: Tin House Books, 2010); Wallace Stegner, *The Uneasy Chair: A Biography of Bernard DeVoto* (New York: Doubleday, 1974), 105.

17 Stegner, *The Uneasy Chair*, 170–171; AMS Memoirs, 168–169.

18 AMS Memoirs, 176.

19 Marian Cannon Schlesinger, *Snatched from Oblivion: A Cambridge Memoir* (Boston: Little, Brown, 1979), 237; Marian Cannon Schlesinger, *I Remember: A Life of Politics, Painting and People* (Cambridge, MA: TidePool Press, 2012), 79.

20 AMS diaries, May 25, 1937, NYPL 309 (volume 5).

21 "Riverside Statue Stumps Historians," *New York Times*, July 1, 1937, http://query .nytimes.com/mem/archive/pdf?res=9807E0DA1F3AE23ABC4953DFB166838C6 29EDE; Handwritten diaries, May 25, 1937, NYPL 309 (volume 5); AMS Memoirs, 176.

22 Handwritten diaries, Oct. 16, 1937, NYPL 309 (volume 5); AMS Memoirs, 163, 178.

23 AMS, "Orestes Brownson: A Pilgrim's Progress" (undergraduate thesis, Harvard University, 1938), Harvard University Archives, 1, 53–54; Thomas T. McAvoy, review of *Orestes Brownson: A Pilgrim's Progress*, by AMS, *The Review of Politics* 1, no. 3 (1939): 364–365, http://www.jstor.org/stable/1403964; Granville Hicks, review of *Orestes Brownson: A Pilgrim's Progress*, by AMS, *The New England Quarterly* 12, no. 3 (1939): 582–588, DOI:10.2307/360849.

24 Handwritten diaries, Oct. 16, 1937, NYPL 309 (volume 5); AMS Memoirs, 176.

25 White, *In Search of History*, 53; Arthur Schlesinger (Sr.) to AMS, Oct. 27, 1938, NYPL 293/4.

26 Arthur Schlesinger (Sr.) to AMS, Oct. 27, 1938, NYPL 293/4.

27 "Appeasement at Munich," *HOLLIS Catalog*, http://id.lib.harvard.edu/aleph/ 003744011/catalog; Nigel Hamilton, *JFK: Reckless Youth* (London: Arrow, 1992), 380.

28 Arthur Schlesinger (Sr.) to AMS, Oct. 27, 1938, NYPL 293/4.

29 "Four Harvard Men Are Recipients of the Henry Awards," *Harvard Crimson*, February 14, 1938, http://www.thecrimson.com/article/1938/2/14/four-harvard -men-are-recipients-of; Marian Cannon Schlesinger, interview by author, March 9, 2014.

30 AMS diaries, Aug. 2, Sept. 6, 1938, NYPL 309; Marian Cannon to AMS, Aug. 4, Aug. 25, 1938, NYPL 299/1–3.

31 Telegram to AMS, Sept. 5, 1938; AMS diaries, Sept. 19, 1938, NYPL 506/5 and 309.

Chapter Three: Another Cambridge

1 AMS diaries, Sept. 29 and 30, 1938, NYPL 309.

2 "Four Harvard Men Are Recipients of the Henry Awards," *Harvard Crimson*, Feb. 14, 1938, http://www.thecrimson.com/article/1938/2/14/four-harvard-men -are-recipients-of; Eric Hobsbawm, *Interesting Times: A Twentieth Century Life* (London: Pantheon, 2007), 1871 (Kindle).

3 Charles Wintour to AMS, Apr. 15, 1939, NYPL 148/4; Michael Leapman, "Obituary: Charles Wintour," *The Independent,* Nov. 4, 1999, http://www.independent .co.uk/arts-entertainment/obituary-charles-wintour-1123476.html.

4 AMS diaries, Oct. 27, 1938, NYPL 309; Hobsbawm, *Interesting Times*, 2044 (Kindle).

5 AMS diaries, Oct. 27, Dec. 13, 1938, April 14, June 4, 1939, NYPL 309; AMS Memoirs, 195.

6 John Fairbank to AMS, Nov. 26, 1938, NYPL 166/1; Charles Wintour to AMS, June [30], 1939, NYPL 148/4.

7 AMS diaries, Nov. 11, 1938, NYPL 309; Arthur Schlesinger (Sr.) to AMS, Feb. 2, 1939, NYPL 506/3-5; Perry Miller to AMS, April 22, 1939, NYPL 95/3; Record of Union Society vote, NYPL 506/3-5. The no teller was John Donaldson, future master of the rolls, who also presided over the infamous Guildford Four trial.

8 Samuel Eliot Morison, *Three Centuries of Harvard* (Cambridge, MA: Belknap Press, 1986), 380; Arthur Schlesinger (Sr.) to AMS, Feb. 2, 1939, NYPL 506/5.

9 Arthur Schlesinger (Sr.) to AMS, Feb. 2, 1939, NYPL 506/3-5.

10 Office of the President and Fellows of Harvard College to AMS, April 24, 1939, NYPL 506/5; Henry Steele Commager, "That Sturdy but Erratic Reformer, Orestes Brownson," *New York Times*, April 23, 1939, https://www.nytimes.com/ books/00/11/26/specials/schlesinger-brownson.html.

11 Perry Miller to AMS, Apr. 22, 1939, NYPL 95/3.

12 A. C. Hanford to AMS, July 24, 1939, NYPL 166/1; AMS to Jacob Neusner, July 9, 1992; AMS toast at Harvard Club of Cambridge, c. May 15, 1939, NYPL 506/3-5.

13 AMS to Arthur and Elizabeth Schlesinger, Mar. 16, 1939, AMS Letters, xxiv.

14 AMS diaries, May 23, 1940, NYPL 309; AMS Memoirs, 217.

15 His student days over, "Arthur" henceforth becomes "Schlesinger." For clarity his father is referred to as "Arthur Sr." or "Schlesinger Sr."

16 Charles Wintour to AMS, Sept. 12, 1939, NYPL 148/4; AMS toast at Harvard Club of Cambridge, c. May 15, 1939, NYPL 506/3-5.

17 Wintour to AMS, June 8, July 11, 1940, NYPL 506/3–5; AMS journal, May 23, 1940, NYPL 309.

18 Unidentified press clipping announcing junior fellows at Society of Fellows, NYPL 506/5; George C. Homans and Orville T. Bailey, "The Society of Fellows, Harvard University, 1933–1947," in *The Society of Fellows*, ed. Crane Brinton (Cambridge, MA: The Society of Fellows of Harvard University, 1959), 32.

19 AMS journal, May 25, 1937, NYPL 309 (volume 5).

20 Arthur M. Schlesinger Jr., "The Problem of Richard Hildreth," *New England Quarterly* 13, no. 2 (June 1940): 223–245.

21 AMS to Marcus Cunliffe, July 9, 1968, AMS Letters, 361.

22 Lilian Handlin, "George Bancroft," *American National Biography Online*, February 2000, http://www.anb.org/articles/14/14-00034.html; AMS Memoirs, 225.

23 AMS Memoirs, 227; Stuart Bruchey, *Roots of American Economic Growth 1607–1861: An Essay on Social Causation* (London: Routledge, 2013), 2000; AMS, *The Age of Jackson* (Boston: Little, Brown, 1945), 263; Alan Brinkley, "Where Historians Disagree: The Age of Jackson," in *American History: A Survey* (New York: McGraw-Hill, 1995), http://glencoe.mheducation.com/sites/0012122005/student_view0/chapter9/where_historians_disagree.html.

24 Charles Wintour to AMS, June 8, 1940, NYPL 148/4.

25 AMS diaries, May 23, 1940, NYPL 309; Charles Wintour to AMS, Mar. 17, June 8, 1940, NYPL 148/4.

26 AMS to "Dear Family," Aug. 19, Aug. 24, 1940, NYPL 506/5.

27 Marian Cannon Schlesinger, *I Remember: A Life of Politics, Painting and People* (Cambridge, MA: TidePool Press, 2012), 80–81.

28 Perry Miller to AMS, Apr. 22, 1939, NYPL 95/3; AMS Memoirs, 251; AMS to his parents, May 10, May 27, 1941, NYPL 506/3.

29 Proposal quoted in AMS Memoirs, 255; NYPL 365/5.

30 Harvard University Appointment Office registration, May 11, 1942, NYPL 506/4; note by Bernard DeVoto, May 16, 1941, NYPL 506/5.

31 Marian Cannon Schlesinger, interview with author, Mar. 9, 2014; note by Bernard DeVoto, May 16, 1941, NYPL 506/5.

32 AMS Memoirs, 265–266.

Chapter Four: A Knee-Pants Genius

1 John King Fairbank, *Chinabound: A Fifty Year Memoir* (New York: Harper and Row, 1982), 155–156, 339; Stephen Schlesinger, email to author, Jan. 5, 2017.

2 AMS Memoirs, 268.

3 Allan M. Winkler, *The Politics of Propaganda: The Office of War Information, 1942–1945* (New Haven, CT: Yale University Press, 1978), 24; AMS Memoirs, 267.

4 Ibid., 55–56, 67; William Strand, "Senate Kills Dry Rider to 18 Year Draft," *Chicago Tribune*, Oct. 23, 1942, http://archives.chicagotribune.com/1942/10/23/page/1/article/senate-kills-dry-rider-to-18-year-draft.

5 Notes on Biloxi, undated [November 1942], NYPL 522/1-5; AMS Memoirs, 269; Marian Schlesinger to AMS, undated [Nov. 1942], NYPL 299/1-3.

6 AMS to Pringle, memorandum on drinking, undated [Nov. 1942], NYPL 522/3; Office of War Information, "Coast to Coast Survey of Drinking Conditions in and Around Army Camps" (Washington, DC: US Government Printing Office, 1942).

7 AMS to Henry Pringle, annotated memorandum on race relations, undated [Nov. 1942], NYPL 522/3; Marian Schlesinger to AMS, undated [Nov. 1942], NYPL 299/1-3.

8 AMS to Henry Pringle, annotated memorandum on race relations, undated [Nov. 1942], NYPL 522/3.

9 AMS Memoirs, 272–273; AMS to Henry Pringle, annotated memorandum on race relations, undated [Nov. 1942], NYPL 522/3.

10 AMS Memoirs, 272–274; AMS to Henry Pringle, annotated memorandum on race relations, undated [Nov. 1942], NYPL 522/3.

11 Jean Edward Smith, *FDR* (New York: Random House, 2008 edition), 400–402.

12 On the context of OWI and the walkout of the writers, I follow Winkler, *The Politics of Propaganda*, 63–68.

13 AMS to Bernard DeVoto, Mar. 9, 1943, NYPL 522/4; ibid., 64–65.

14 AMS to Bernard DeVoto, Mar. 9, 1943; AMS to Bernard DeVoto, undated [Apr. 1943]; AMS to Elmer Davis, Apr. 14, 1943, NYPL 522/4; Winkler, *Politics of Propaganda*, 23.

15 *Washington Post*, April 18, 1943; *Washington Daily News*, Apr. 14, 1943.

16 AMS to Bernard DeVoto, undated [Apr. 1943], 1943, NYPL 522/4.

17 Ibid.

18 AMS to "Dear Family," June 20, 1943, NYPL 521/1; Arthur M. Schlesinger, *In Retrospect: The History of a Historian* (New York: Harcourt, Brace and World, 1963); Robert Schlesinger, "Arthur Schlesinger Jr.'s Not-So-Secret Career as a Spy," *US News & World Report*, Aug. 20, 2008, http://www.usnews.com/opinion/articles/2008/08/20/arthur-schlesinger-jrs-not-so-secret-career-as-a-spy.

19 AMS to "Dear Family," June 20, 1943, NYPL 521/1.

20 Ibid.

21 Rhodri Jeffreys-Jones, *In Spies We Trust: The Story of Western Intelligence* (Oxford: Oxford University Press, 2013), 73–75; Louis Menand, "Wild Thing," *The New Yorker*, Mar. 14, 2011; AMS to "Dear Family," undated [May 1943], NYPL 521/6.

22 AMS to "Dear Family," undated [May 1943], NYPL 521/6; Robin Winks, *Cloak and Gown: Scholars in the Secret War, 1939–1961* (New Haven, CT: Yale University Press, 1987), 61.

23 Winks, *Cloak and Gown*, 62–63; AMS to "Dear Family," undated [May 1943], NYPL 521/6; AMS diaries, May 25, 1937, NYPL 309 (volume 5); Nelson MacPherson, *American Intelligence in Wartime London: The Story of OSS* (London: Routledge, 2014), 101.

24 Winks, *Cloak and Gown*, 90–91; AMS Memoirs, 297–300.

25 Interview with Arthur Schlesinger Jr., OSS Oral History Project, NYPL 521/1; Petra Marquardt-Bigman to AMS, Aug. 27, 1997, NYPL 521/1; Barry M. Katz, *Foreign Intelligence: Research and Analysis in the OSS, 1942–1945* (Cambridge, MA: Harvard University Press, 1989), 65–67.

26 AMS to "Dear Family," undated [May 1943], NYPL 521/6.

27 Winks, *Cloak and Gown*, 90–91.

28 J. L. Granatstein, review of *Cold War Exile: The Unclosed Case of Maurice Halperin*, by Don S. Kirschner, *Political Psychology* 18, no. 2 (1997): 511–514, http://www.jstor.org/stable/3791780. The description of "Venona" is from Calder Walton, *Empire of Secrets: British Intelligence, the Cold War, and the Twilight of Empire* (New York: Overlook Press, 2013), 117.

29 Interview with Arthur Schlesinger Jr., OSS Oral History Project, NYPL 521/1.

30 "Revolution in La Paz," *New York Times*, December 21, 1943, http://timesmachine.nytimes.com/timesmachine/1943/12/21/88587915.html?pageNumber=26; Arnaldo Cortesi, "La Paz Regime Out," *New York Times*, Dec. 21, 1943, http://timesmachine.nytimes.com/timesmachine/1943/12/21/88587204.html?pageNumber=1; "Hull is Hesitant on Bolivia Regime," *New York Times*, December 23, 1943, http://timesmachine.nytimes.com/timesmachine/1943/12/23/88588213.html?pageNumber=5.

31 Don S. Kirschner, *Cold War Exile: The Unclosed Case of Maurice Halperin* (Columbia: University of Missouri Press, 1995), 97.

32 Kirschner, *Cold War Exile*, 88; AMS Memoirs, 302.

33 Leo P. Ribuffo, *Right Center Left: Essays in American History* (New Brunswick, NJ: Rutgers University Press, 1992), 141–142; Cold War International History Project, "Was Robert Oppenheimer a Soviet Spy? A Round Table Discussion," *Woodrow*

Wilson Center for International Scholars, July 7, 2011, https://www.wilsoncenter .org/publication/was-oppenheimer-soviet-spy-roundtable-discussion.

34 Katz, *Foreign Intelligence,* 14–15.

35 Kirschner, *Cold War Exile,* 88–89.

36 Kirschner, *Cold War Exile,* 89–90; AMS memoirs, 302–303.

37 "AS Jr. war chronology," July 11, 1991, NYPL 521/4.

38 AMS to Marian Cannon Schlesinger, July 8, 1991; FBI Report, July 12, 1948, NYPL 517/2.

39 Crane Brinton and Harold Deutsch to William L. Langer, Feb. 22, 1944, NYPL 521/2.

40 FBI Report, July 12, 1948, NYPL 517/2; AMS memoirs, 316–317.

41 AMS, "The London Operation," July 11, 1991, NYPL 521/4.

42 AMS to Marian Cannon Schlesinger [June 27, 1944].

Chapter Five: The Real Education of Arthur Schlesinger Jr.

1 AMS to Marian Cannon Schlesinger, July 9, 1944, NYPL 299/3.

2 AMS to Marian Cannon Schlesinger, July 9, 16, 30, Aug. 31, Sept. 10, 20, 1944, NYPL 299/3; AMS to Bernard DeVoto, Aug. 8, 1943, NYPL 35/4; Charles Wintour to AMS, June 8, July 11, 1940, NYPL 506/3–5; AMS journal, May 23, 1940, NYPL 309.

3 AMS to Arthur and Elizabeth Schlesinger, July 7, Aug. 28, Nov. 20, 1944, NYPL 298/3; AMS to Marian Cannon Schlesinger, July 24, Aug. 17, Sept. 10, 18, 1944, NYPL 299/3; AMS Memoirs, 320; AMS, "The London Operation," July 11, 1991, NYPL 521/4; Charles Wintour to AMS, June 8, July 11, 1940, NYPL 506/3–5.

4 AMS to Marian Cannon Schlesinger, Aug. 17, 1944, NYPL 299/3.

5 Richard Brown Baker, *The Year of the Buzz Bomb: A Journal of London, 1944* (Pickle Partners Publishing: Kindle Formatted edition, 2015); AMS, "The London Operation," July 11, 1991, NYPL 521/4; Nelson MacPherson, *American Intelligence in Wartime London: The Story of OSS* (London: Routledge, 2014), 100.

6 AMS to Marian Cannon Schlesinger, Aug. 10, 1944, NYPL 299/3; AMS to Arthur and Elizabeth Schlesinger, Oct. 23, 1944, NYPL 298/3.

7 AMS to Bernard DeVoto, Aug. 8, 1943, NYPL 35/4; Marian Cannon Schlesinger to AMS, Oct. 9, 1944, NYPL 299/3; AMS to Marian Cannon Schlesinger, Sept. 10, 1944, NYPL 299/3.

8 AMS to Arthur and Elizabeth Schlesinger, Oct. 23, 1944, NYPL 298/3.

9 AMS to Marian Cannon Schlesinger, Oct. 22, 1944, NYPL 299/3; MacPherson, *American Intelligence in Wartime London,* 147–149; AMS to Arthur and Elizabeth Schlesinger, Oct. 23, Nov. 20, 1944, NYPL 298/3; AMS Memoirs, 330.

10 Gertrude G. Johnson, "Manpower Selection and the Preventative Medicine Pro-

gram," Office of Medical History, US Army Medical Department, http://history
.amedd.army.mil/booksdocs/wwii/PrsnlHlthMsrs/chapter1.htm; AMS Memoirs,
342.

11 AMS to Marian Cannon Schlesinger, Nov. 4, 17, 1944, NYPL 299/3.

12 AMS Memoirs, 337–338.

13 AMS to Marian Cannon Schlesinger, Nov. 17, 1944, Jan. 28, 1945, NYPL 299/3;
AMS to Arthur and Elizabeth Schlesinger, Nov. 10, 1944, NYPL 298/3.

14 AMS to Arthur and Elizabeth Schlesinger, Nov. 10, Dec. 25, 1944, NYPL 298/3.

15 AMS to Marian Cannon Schlesinger, Feb. 22, 25, 1945, NYPL 299/3.

16 AMS to Marian Cannon Schlesinger, Jan. 14, Feb. 6, Mar. 3, 11, 29, 1945, NYPL
299/3; AMS to Arthur and Elizabeth Schlesinger, Mar. 12, 1945, NYPL 298/3.

17 AMS to Marian Cannon Schlesinger, Apr. 5, May 3, 1945, NYPL 299/3.

18 AMS to Arthur and Elizabeth Schlesinger, May 9, 1945, NYPL 298/3.

19 AMS to Marian Cannon Schlesinger, May 8, 1945, NYPL 299/3.

20 AMS to Marian Cannon Schlesinger, May 25, June 13, 1945, NYPL 299/3.

21 AMS to Marian Cannon Schlesinger, May 25, 28, 1945, NYPL 299/3.

22 AMS to Marian Cannon Schlesinger, June 10, 19, 24, 1945, NYPL 299/3.

23 AMS to Marian Cannon Schlesinger, June 24, July 8, 1945, NYPL 299/3; Army of
the United States, Separation Qualification Record, Dec. 6, 1945, NYPL 532/5.

24 AMS to Marian Cannon Schlesinger, July 15, 1945, NYPL 299/3.

25 Paul Lewis, "Harry Rositzke, 91, Linguist and American Spymaster," New York
Times, Nov. 8, 2002, http://www.nytimes.com/2002/11/08/us/harry-rositzke-91
-linguist-and-american-spymaster.html; AMS to Marian Cannon Schlesinger,
July 21, 1945, NYPL 299/3.

26 AMS to Marian Cannon Schlesinger, July 21, 1945, NYPL 299/3.

27 AMS to Marian Cannon Schlesinger, Aug. 16, 17, 1945, NYPL 299/3.

28 AMS to Marian Cannon Schlesinger, July 28, Aug. 8, 22, Sept. 3, 20, Oct. 1, 1945,
NYPL 299/3.

29 AMS to Marian Cannon Schlesinger, Oct. 1, 1945, NYPL 299/3.

30 AMS to Marian Cannon Schlesinger, Aug. 3, Oct. 1, 1945, NYPL 299/3. AMS
Memoirs, 357.

Chapter Six: The Age of Schlesinger

1 AMS to Marian Cannon Schlesinger, Sept. 22, 1945, NYPL 299/3.

2 Orville Prescott, "Books of the Times," New York Times, Sept. 14, 1945; Allan
Nevins, "At the Roots of Democracy," review of The Age of Jackson, by AMS Jr., New
York Times, Sept. 16, 1945, http://www.nytimes.com/books/00/11/26/specials/
schlesinger-jackson.html.

3 Richard Hofstadter, "Democracy in the Making," review of *The Age of Jackson*, by AMS, *New Republic*, October 22, 1945, https://newrepublic.com/article/74429/democracy-the-making; Bray Hammond, review of *The Age of Jackson*, *The Journal of Economic History* 6, no. 1 (1946): 79–84, http://www.jstor.org/stable/2112998. For academic reviews of *The Age of Jackson*, see, for example: Russel B. Nye, review of *The Age of Jackson*, *The American Historical Review* 51, no. 3 (1946): 510–513, http://www.jstor.org/stable/1840130, DOI:10.2307/1840130; "What Are the Outstanding Books of 1945?" *ALA Bulletin* 39, no. 12 (1945): 509–510, http://www.jstor.org/stable/25692238; Culver H. Smith, review of *The Age of Jackson*, *The Journal of Southern History* 12, no. 1 (1946): 123–126, http://www.jstor.org/stable/2197735, DOI: 10.2307/2197735; Thomas T. McAvoy, "Leaders of Democracy," review of *The Age of Jackson*, et al., *The Review of Politics* 8, no. 1 (1946): 135–137, http://www.jstor.org/stable/1403976; Carl Brent Swisher, review of *The Age of Jackson*, *The New England Quarterly* 19, no. 1 (1946): 122–123, http://www.jstor.org/stable/361216, DOI:10.2307/361216.

4 AMS Memoirs, 42; Arthur M. Schlesinger (Sr.), *In Retrospect: The History of a Historian* (New York: Harcourt, Brace and World, 1963); Harry Hansen, "Pulitzer Award to Schlesinger for Jackson Book Commended," *Chicago Sunday Tribune*, May 12, 1946, http://archives.chicagotribune.com/1946/05/12/page/106/article/pulitzer-award-to-schlesinger-for-jackson-book-commended.

5 On the "six essays," I follow Donald B. Cole, "The Age of Jackson: After Forty Years," review of *The Age of Jackson*, by AMS, *Reviews in American History* 14, no. 1 (1986), http://www.jstor.org/stable/2702131, DOI: 10.2307/2702131; Stuart Bruchey, *Roots of American Economic Growth 1607–1861: An Essay on Social Causation* (London: Routledge, 2013), 2000.

6 Arthur M. Schlesinger Jr., "The Ages of Jackson," *New York Review of Books*, Dec. 7, 1989, http://www.nybooks.com/articles/1989/12/07/the-ages-of-jackson/.

7 AMS to Arthur and Elizabeth Schlesinger, Apr. 16, 1945, NYPL 298/3; AMS to Elizabeth Schlesinger, undated [fall 1932], NYPL 296.

8 Cole, "The Age of Jackson: After Forty Years"; Daniel Howe, "Goodbye to the 'Age of Jackson'?" *New York Review of Books*, May 28, 2009, http://www.nybooks.com/articles/2009/05/28/goodbye-to-the-age-of-jackson/; John Sacher, review of *Jacksonian Antislavery and the Politics of Free Soil, 1824–1854*, by Jonathan H. Earle, *Indiana Magazine of History* 101, no. 4 (2005): 383–384, http://www.jstor.org/stable/27792675; Chris Cillizza, "Newt Gingrich Explains How Donald Trump Happened," *Washington Post*, December 17, 2015, https://www.washingtonpost.com/news/the-fix/wp/2015/12/17/newt-gingrich-says-donald-trump-reminds-him-of-andrew-jackson.

9 Sean Wilentz, *The Rise of American Democracy: Jefferson to Lincoln* (New York: W. W. Norton, 2005), xix–xx.

10 AMS, "The Ages of Jackson," *New York Review of Books*, Dec. 7, 1989; AMS, "Orestes Brownson: A Pilgrim's Progress" (undergraduate thesis, Harvard University, 1938), Harvard University Archives, 230.

11 Arthur Schlesinger (Sr.), *Paths to the Present* (New York: Macmillan, 1964); AMS, *The Cycles of American History* (New York: Mariner Books, 1999 edition), 24–25; AMS, *The Age of Jackson* (Boston: Little, Brown, 1945), 391.

12 Arthur M. Schlesinger (Sr.), *New Viewpoints in American History* (New York: Macmillan, 1922), 209, https://archive.org/details/newviewpointsina00sch; Cole, "The Age of Jackson: After Forty Years"; AMS, *The Age of Jackson*, 512.

13 Arthur M. Schlesinger Jr., "The Problem of Richard Hildreth," *New England Quarterly* 13, no. 2 (1940): 223–245.

14 AMS, *Age of Jackson*, 161–162.

15 Secretary to the Harvard Corporation to AMS, Apr. 11 & 25, 1946, NYPL 59/3; Marian Cannon Schlesinger to Wilma Cannon Fairbank, Feb. 25, 1946, NYPL 515/1; "The New Tenure Track," *Harvard Magazine*, Sept.–Oct. 2010, http://harvard magazine.com/2010/09/the-new-tenure-track; Niall Ferguson, *Kissinger: The Idealist* (New York: Penguin Press, 2015), 212, 222.

16 Marian Cannon Schlesinger to Wilma Cannon Fairbank, Feb. 25, 1946, NYPL 515/1.

17 AMS to Eugene Meyer, Apr. 13, 1946, AMS Letters, 15; Marian Cannon Schlesinger, interview by author, Mar. 9, 2014.

18 Theodore H. White, *In Search of History* (New York: Harper and Row, 1978), 209–210; Henry Luce, "Fortune Prospectus," *Fortune*, Sept. 1, 1929, http://fortune.com/1929/09/01/fortune-prospectus-september-1929-volume-one-number-zero/; AMS Memoirs, 375–376, 394.

19 Joseph P. Lash, ed., *From the Diaries of Felix Frankfurter* (New York: Norton, 1975), 275.

20 AMS, "The Supreme Court: 1947," *Fortune*, January 3, 1947. For the legal analysis of AMS's argument, I follow the excellent essay by Keenan D. Kmiec, "The Origin and Current Meanings of Judicial Activism," *California Law Review* 92 (2004), http://scholarship.law.berkeley.edu/californialawreview/vol92/iss5/4, DOI: 10.15779/Z38X71D.

21 Kmiec, "The Origin and Current Meanings of Judicial Activism," 1449.

22 Ibid., 1450.

23 Paul Kennedy, *The Rise and Fall of the Great Powers* (London: Fontana Press, 1989 edition), 463, and more generally 460–467.

24 Quoted in Gregg Herken, *The Georgetown Set: Friends and Rivals in Cold War Washington* (New York: Alfred A. Knopf, 2014), 17.

25 Ibid., 20–21; Robert Merry, *Taking on the World: Joseph and Stewart Alsop— Guardians of the American Century* (New York: Viking, 1996), 154–156.

26 AMS Memoirs, 332; Philip Graham Profile: Herken, *The Georgetown Set*, 15–16.

27 Katharine Graham, *Personal History* (New York: Alfred A. Knopf, 1997), 163; Marian Cannon Schlesinger, interview by author, March 9, 2014.

28 AMS to Arthur and Elizabeth Schlesinger, undated [1946], AMS Letters, 16–17.

29 David Milne, *Worldmaking: The Art and Science of American Diplomacy* (New York: Farrar, Straus and Giroux, 2015), 215.

30 M. Stanton Evans and Herbert Romerstein, *Stalin's Secret Agents: The Subversion of Roosevelt's Government* (New York: Threshold Editions, 2012), 102; Ferguson, *Kissinger: The Idealist*, 221; AMS, "Orestes Brownson: An American Marxist before Marx," *The Sewanee Review* 47, no. 3 (1939): 317–323, http://www.jstor.org/stable/27535562.

31 AMS, "The U.S. Communist Party," *Life*, July 29, 1946; see Bob Colacello, *Ronnie and Nancy: Their Path to the White House, 1911 to 1980* (New York: Warner Books, 2004), 97; Andrew Hemingway, *Artists on the Left: American Artists and the Communist Movement, 1926–1956* (New Haven, CT: Yale University Press, 2002), 195–197.

32 Stephen Vaughn, *Reagan in Hollywood: Movies and Politics* (Cambridge: Cambridge University Press, 1994), 124; Bob Colacello, *Ronnie and Nancy*, 97.

33 David Milne, *Worldmaking*, 214–215, 287; H. W. Brands, *The Devil We Knew: Americans and the Cold War* (Oxford: Oxford University Press, 1993), 23–26; Lawrence J. Haas, *Harry & Arthur: Truman, Vandenberg and the Partnership that Created the Free World* (Lincoln, NE: Potomac Books, 2016), 253; Ribuffo, *Right Center Left*, 143.

34 Stephen J. Whitfield, *The Culture of the Cold War* (Baltimore: Johns Hopkins University Press, 1996, 2nd edition), 4.

35 Ibid., 3-4; Ribuffo, *Right Center Left*, 142–143; Jonathan Haslam, *Near and Distant Neighbors: A New History of Soviet Intelligence* (New York: Farrar, Straus and Giroux, 2015), 143.

36 Haslam, *Near and Distant Neighbors*, 171–173; M. Stanton Evans, *Blacklisted by History: The Untold Story of Senator Joe McCarthy and His Fight Against America's Enemies* (New York: Three Rivers Press, 2007), 126, 153, 170.

37 George M. Marsden, *The Twilight of the American Enlightenment: The 1950s and the Crisis of Liberal Belief* (New York: Basic Books, 2014), 57; AMS, "What is Loy-

alty? A Difficult Question," *New York Times*, Nov. 2, 1947, https://www.nytimes
.com/books/00/11/26/specials/schlesinger-difficult.html.

38 David Reynolds, *Empire of Liberty: A New History* (London: Allen Lane, 2009),
396; Whitfield, *The Culture of the Cold War*; Marsden, *The Twilight of the American Enlightenment*, 57–59; Brands, *The Devil We Knew*, 34.

39 Larry Ceplair and Christopher Trumbo, *Dalton Trumbo: Blacklisted Hollywood Radical* (Lexington: University Press of Kentucky, 2015), 203–206.

40 Alonzo L. Hamby, *Beyond the New Deal: Harry S. Truman and American Liberalism* (New York: Scribner's, 1971), 279–280; Daniel F. Rice, *Reinhold Niebuhr and his Circle of Influence* (Cambridge: Cambridge University Press, 2013), 116–121; Marsden, *The Twilight of the American Enlightenment*, 57–59.

41 *New York Times*, Jan. 5, 1947.

Chapter Seven: The Vital Center

1 Marian Cannon Schlesinger, interview by author, March 9, 2014; Marian Cannon Schlesinger to AMS, June 30, 2006, NYPL 299/3; Marian Cannon Schlesinger, *I Remember: A Life of Painting, Politics and People* (Cambridge, MA: TidePool Press, 2012), 95–97; Corydon Ireland, "Storied Irving Street Paves Way to History," *Harvard Gazette*, May 19, 2016, http://news.harvard.edu/gazette/story/2016/05/storied-irving-street-paves-way-to-history.

2 AMS Memoirs, 57; Isaiah Berlin to Corinne Alsop, July 5, 1949, Isaiah Berlin, *Enlightening: Letters, 1946–1960*, ed. Henry Hardy and Jennifer Holmes (London: Chatto & Windus, 2009), 101.

3 Morton Keller and Phyllis Keller, *Making Harvard Modern* (Oxford: Oxford University Press, 2007 updated edition), 211, 223.

4 Samuel Eliot Morison to Winthrop Aldrich, Apr. 20, 1954; AMS to Ray Helsel, May 24, 1993, *Argosy*, http://www.argosybooks.com/shop/argosy/218104.html; Marian Cannon Schlesinger, interview by author, Mar. 9, 2014; J. K. Galbraith to AMS, Oct. 15, 1987, NYPL 523/1.

5 Andrew Schlesinger, *Veritas: Harvard College and the American Experience* (Chicago: Ivan R. Dee, 2005), 196; AMS Memoirs, 441.

6 Arthur D. Aptowitz, "Letter," *New York Times Sunday Book Review*, Jan. 22, 2014; Harold L. Burstyn, email to author, Jan. 24, 2015.

7 AMS to Elizabeth and Arthur Schlesinger, Nov. 4, 1948, AMS Letters, 22; AMS Memoirs, 458.

8 AMS Memoirs, 465, 480–481.

9 Application for Federal Employment, Consultant for ECA (Paris-OSR), 1948,

NYPL 532/5; U.S. Government Memorandum, "Arthur Meier Schlesinger Jr.," Nov. 14, 1960, NYPL 517/2; AMS Memoirs, 467–469.

10 Rudy Abramson, *Spanning the Century: The Life of Averell Harriman, 1891–1986* (New York: William Morrow, 1992), 428.

11 Walter Isaacson and Evan Thomas, *The Wise Men: Six Friends and the World They Made* (New York: Simon and Schuster, 2013), 228.

12 George F. Kennan, *The Kennan Diaries*, ed. Frank Costigliola (New York: W. W. Norton, 2013), 393–394; John Lewis Gaddis, *George F. Kennan: An American Life* (New York: Penguin Press, 2011), 174.

13 AMS Memoirs, 480–481; Alan S. Oser, "Ex-Gov. Averell Harriman, Adviser to 4 Presidents, Dies," *New York Times*, July 27, 1986, http://www.nytimes.com/1986/07/27/obituaries/ex-gov-averell-harriman-adviser-to-4-presidents-dies.html?pagewanted=all.

14 Isaacson and Thomas, *Wise Men*, 425; AMS Memoirs, 471; Gaddis, *George F. Kennan*, 173.

15 Richard Severo, "Marieta Tree, Former U.N. Delegate, Dies at 74," *New York Times*, Aug. 16, 1991, http://www.nytimes.com/1991/08/16/nyregion/marietta-tree-former-un-delegate-dies-at-74.html; AMS Memoirs, 473; AMS to Marietta Tree, Jan. 20, 1953, AMS Letters, 57–59 and fn.; Marian Cannon Schlesinger, interview by author, Mar. 9, 2014; Holly Brubach, "Running Around in High Circles," review of *No Regrets,* by Caroline Seebohm, *New York Times,* Nov. 9, 1997, http://www.nytimes.com/books/97/11/09/reviews/971109.09brubact.html.

16 AMS to Max Lerner, Nov. 15, 1948, AMS Letters, 24.

17 AMS, "Orestes Brownson: An American Marxist before Marx," *The Sewanee Review* 47, no. 3 (1939): 317–323, http://www.jstor.org/stable/27535562.

18 AMS, "Not Left, Not Right, But a Vital Center," *New York Times*, Apr. 4, 1948, https://www.nytimes.com/books/00/11/26/specials/schlesinger-centermag.html.

19 Ibid.

20 AMS, *The Vital Center: The Politics of Freedom* (Boston: Houghton Mifflin, 1949), 147.

21 AMS to Bernard DeVoto, Nov. 16, 1946, NYPL 35/4; AMS Memoirs, 432.

22 AMS to Alfred McIntyre, Dec. 21, 1947, AMS Letters, 20.

23 Michael Wreszin, "Arthur Schlesinger, Jr., Scholar-activist in Cold War America: 1946–1956," *Salmagundi* 63/64 (1984): 255–285, http://www.jstor.org/stable/40547663.

24 AMS, "Reinhold Niebuhr's Long Shadow," *New York Times*, June 22, 1992, http://

www.nytimes.com/1992/06/22/opinion/reinhold-niebuhr-s-long-shadow.html. On AMS and Reinhold Niebuhr more generally, Daniel F. Rice, *Reinhold Niebuhr and His Circle of Influence* (Cambridge: Cambridge University Press, 2013), 113–144.

25 Reinhold Niebuhr to AMS, Nov. 14, 1951, AMS, NYPL 100/4.

26 Barton Swaim, "Sifting the Wheat from the Chaff," review of *Major Works on Religion and Politics*, by Reinhold Niebuhr, *Wall Street Journal*, June 26, 2015, http://www.wsj.com/articles/SB11292601245819683363204581056111883885634; AMS Memoirs, 511; AMS, "Reinhold Niebuhr's Long Shadow"; AMS, *Age of Jackson*, 523.

27 AMS, "The Causes of the Civil War," in *The Politics of Hope and The Bitter Heritage*, ed. Sean Wilentz (Princeton, NJ: Princeton University Press, 2008), 64.

28 AMS, *The Vital Center*, ix; Rice, *Reinhold Niebuhr and His Circle of Influence*, 116. On the Vital Center more generally, James A. Nuechterlein, "Arthur M. Schlesinger, Jr., and the Discontents of Postwar American Liberalism," *The Review of Politics* 39, no. 1 (1977): 3–40, http://www.jstor.org/stable/1406576; Christopher P. Loss, "Educating Global Citizens in the Cold War," in *In Between Citizens and the State: The Politics of American Higher Education in the 20th Century* (Princeton, NJ: Princeton University Press, 2012), 121–162, http://www.jstor.org/stable/j.ctt7shbr.9.

29 AMS, *The Vital Center*, 4, 170, 246–248.

30 Ibid., 251.

31 Nuechterlein, "Arthur M. Schlesinger, Jr., and the Discontents of Postwar American Liberalism," 10; AMS, "The Vital Center Reconsidered," *Encounter*, Sept. 1970, 89–93; AMS 1998 introduction to *The Vital Center* quoted in Rice, *Reinhold Niebuhr and His Circle of Influence*, 117.

32 Reviews of *The Vital Center*: Charles Poore, "Books of the Times," *New York Times*, Sept. 8, 1949, http://query.nytimes.com/gst/abstract.html?res=9A0CEED7173BE 23BBC4053DFBF668382659EDE&legacy=true; Gerald Johnson, "In Defense of Liberalism," *New York Times*, Sept. 8, 1949, http://query.nytimes.com/gst/abstract .html?res=9507E3DE113DE03ABC4952DFBF668382659EDE&legacy=true; Irwin Ross, *Commentary*, Oct. 1, 1949, https://www.commentarymagazine.com/articles/the-vital-center-by-arthur-m-schlesinger-jr.; Joseph L. Rauh Jr., *Harvard Law Review* 63, no. 4 (1950): 724–727, http://www.jstor.org/stable/1336015, DOI:10.2307/1336015; George H. Sabine, *The Philosophical Review* 59, no. 2 (1950): 246–249, http://www.jstor.org/stable/2181509, DOI: 10.2307/2181509; Charles O. Lerche Jr., *The Western Political Quarterly* 3, no. 2 (1950): 292–294,

http://www.jstor.org/stable/443514, DOI: 10.2307/443514. David McCord Wright, *The American Economic Review* 41, no. 1 (1951): 217–219, http://www.jstor.org/stable/1815990.

33 Douglas Martin, "Arthur Schlesinger, Historian of Power, Dies at 89," *New York Times*, Mar. 1, 2007, http://www.nytimes.com/2007/03/01/washington/01 schlesinger.html.

Chapter Eight: Egghead

1 AMS to Averell Harriman, July 19, 1950, AMS Letters, 31.

2 On the Congress for Cultural Freedom, I follow Frances Stonor Saunders, *Who Paid the Piper? The CIA and the Cultural Cold War* (London: Granta, 1999), 72–84.

3 Ibid., 76.

4 Ibid., 77–79.

5 Harold L. Burstyn, email to author, Dec. 9, 2016.

6 AMS to Averell Harriman, July 19, 1950, AMS Letters, 31.

7 Vincent Giroud, *Nicolas Nabokov: A Life in Freedom and Music* (Oxford: Oxford University Press, 2015), 229–235; AMS Memoirs, 377; AMS to Averell Harriman, July 19, 1950, AMS Letters, 31; "C.I.A. Tie Confirmed by Cultural Group," *New York Times*, May 10, 1967, http://query.nytimes.com/mem/archive/pdf?res=9804 EEDA1E3CE63ABC4852DFB366838C679EDE.

8 Saunders, *Who Paid the Piper?*, 1–2. Louis Menand, "Unpopular Front: American Art and the Cold War," *New Yorker*, Oct. 17, 2005.

9 Laurence Zuckerman, "How the C.I.A. Played Dirty Tricks with Culture," *New York Times*, Mar. 18, 2000, http://www.nytimes.com/2000/03/18/books/how-the -cia-played-dirty-tricks-with-culture.html?pagewanted=all.

10 Giroud, *Nicolas Nabokov*, 230.

11 Michael Ignatieff, *Isaiah Berlin* (London: Vintage, 2000), 199–200; Saunders, *Who Paid the Piper?*, 1–2.

12 Frances Stonor Saunders to AMS, Oct. 27, 1997; AMS to Saunders, Nov. 25, 1997, NYPL 4/3; Saunders, *Who Paid the Piper?*, 200–201.

13 Walter Goodman, "A Farewell to HUAC," *New York Times*, Jan. 19, 1975, http:// query.nytimes.com/mem/archive/pdf?res=9A03E1D7143AE034BC4152DFB766 838E669EDE; AMS Memoirs, 490.

14 AMS Memoirs, 497; Sam Tanenhaus, *Whittaker Chambers* (New York: Random House, 1997), 212–218; Walter Goodman, *The Committee* (New York: Penguin, 1969), 254–256.

15 AMS to Joseph Alsop, Mar. 17, 1953, NYPL 2/5.

16 AMS to James T. Farrell, Mar. 16, 1955, NYPL 4/3.

17 James T. Farrell to AMS, Mar. 6, 1952, NYPL 4/3; Mary McCarthy to Hannah Arendt, March 14, 1952, in Frances Kiernan, *Seeing Mary Plain: A Life of Mary McCarthy* (New York: W. W. Norton, 2000), 337; Mary McCarthy to AMS, April 3, 1952, NYPL 89/2.

18 AMS to Saunders, Nov. 25, 1997, NYPL 4/3.

19 Diary entry, Mar. 29, 1952, AMS Journals, 3-4.

20 Ibid.

21 AMS to Averell Harriman, Apr. 8, 1951, AMS Letters, 38; Richard Rovere and Arthur Schlesinger, *General MacArthur and President Truman: The Struggle for Control of American Foreign Policy* (New Brunswick, NJ: Transaction, 1992), 10-11; Arthur Herman, *Douglas MacArthur: American Warrior* (Random House, 2016), 844-845; S. L. A. Marshall, "The MacArthur of Fact, Legend and Just Plain Myth," review of *The General and the President: The Future of American Foreign Policy,* by AMS, *New York Times,* Oct. 28, 1951, http://query.nytimes.com/mem/archive/pdf?res=9E05E2DD1F39E23ABC4051DFB667838A649EDE.

22 Harry Truman to AMS, Nov. 5, 1951; AMS to Harry Truman, Nov. 28, 1951, AMS Letters, 43-45.

23 AMS to Joseph Rauh, with "I propose to take this line" enclosure, Jan. 15, 1952; AMS to Joseph Rauh, Jan. 30, 1952, NYPL 112/2.

24 Longhand note of President Harry S. Truman, July 11, 1952, Truman Papers, President's Secretary's Files, Harry S. Truman Library, https://www.trumanlibrary.org/whistlestop/study_collections/trumanpapers/psf/longhand/index.php?documentVersion=both&documentid=hst-psf_naid735322-01&pagenumber=2; Truman on March 4, 1952, quoted in Porter McKeever, *Adlai Stevenson: His Life and Legacy* (New York: William Morrow, 1989), 181.

25 AMS to Adlai Stevenson, March 25, 1952, AMS Letters, 47.

26 Ball quoted in McKeever, *Adlai Stevenson,* 198; Rudy Abramson, *Spanning the Century: The Life of Averell Harriman, 1891-1986* (New York: William Morrow, 1992), 490-491.

27 Harriman to AMS, June 19, 1952; AMS to Harriman, July 9, 1952, JFKL, Series 01, Box P16, Harriman.

28 Diary entry, July 22, 1952, AMS Journals, 5-6.

29 Diary entries, July 23, July 24, 1952, AMS Journals, 5-6.

30 Diary entry, July 25, 1952, AMS Journals, 8-9.

31 Abramson, *Spanning the Century,* 501-502.

32 Diary entry, July 25, 1952, AMS Journals, 8–9.

33 AMS to Ursula and Reinhold Niebuhr, Aug. 6, 1952, AMS Letters, 49–50; Abramson, *Spanning the Century*, 498, 503.

34 Diary entry, Aug. 8, 1952, AMS Journals, 11–12.

35 Diary entry, Aug. 12, 1952, AMS Journals, 12–13; McKeever, *Adlai Stevenson*, 207; Fletcher Farrar, "The Tallest Elk in Springfield," *Illinois Times*, May 4, 2006, http://illinoistimes.com/mobile/articles/articleView/id:2990; Wilson W. Wyatt, *Whistle Stops: Adventures in Public Life* (Lexington: University Press of Kentucky, 1985), 97.

36 Stewart Alsop, *Stay of Execution: A Sort of Memoir* (Philadelphia: J. B. Lippincott, 1973), 106.

37 Richard Parker, *John Kenneth Galbraith* (New York: Farrar, Straus and Giroux, 2005), 254.

38 See, particularly, Richard Hofstadter, *Anti-Intellectualism in American Life* (New York: Vintage Books, 1963 edition), 221, 225–227; Gregg Herken, *The Georgetown Set: Friends and Rivals in Cold War Washington* (New York: Alfred A. Knopf, 2014), 159; AMS to Eleanor Roosevelt, Oct. 2, 1952, AMS Letters, 51; "McCarthy May Attack Schlesinger In Radio and TV Broadcast Tonight," *Harvard Crimson*, Oct. 27, 1952.

39 Wyatt, *Whistle Stops*, 98; Robert Bendiner, "Ghosts behind the Speechmakers," *New York Times*, Aug. 17, 1952, http://query.nytimes.com/mem/archive/pdf?res=9C07E2DC1039E632A25754C1A96E9C946392D6CF; diary entry, Sept. 4, 1952, AMS Journals, 15. Ray E. Boomhower, *John Bartlow Martin: A Voice for the Underdog* (Bloomington: Indiana University Press, 2015), 128.

40 An outstanding account of the Elks Club Group is found in Boomhower, *John Bartlow Martin*, 121–154.

41 *The Papers of Adlai Stevenson, Volume 4*, ed. Walter Johnson et al. (Boston: Little, Brown, 1974), 87–88.

42 Boomhower, *John Bartlow Martin*, 131.

43 Diary entry, Oct. 24, 1952, AMS Journals, 17.

44 *The Papers of Adlai Stevenson, Volume 4*, 150.

45 Jean Edward Smith, *Eisenhower in War and Peace* (New York: Random House, 2012), 544–545.

46 Boomhower, *John Bartlow Martin*, 140–142; diary entries, Oct. 28, Nov. 1, 1952, AMS Journals, 18–19.

47 Diary entry, Nov. 26, 1952, AMS Journals, 21.

Chapter: Nine: Politics Is an Educational Process

1 AMS to Marie and Averell Harriman, Nov. 20, 1952, AMS Letters, 52.

2 AMS to Joseph L. Rauh Jr., undated [December 1952], NYPL 112/2; AMS to Marietta Tree, Jan. 20, 1953, AMS Letters, 57; David Reynolds, *Empire of Liberty: A New History* (London: Allen Lane, 2009), 399-401; Richard Parker, *John Kenneth Galbraith* (New York: Farrar, Straus and Giroux, 2005), 262; AMS, "The Political Galbraith," *Journal of Post-Keynesian Economics* 7, no. 1 (1984): 7-17, http://www.jstor.org/stable/4537860.

3 AMS to Adlai Stevenson, Nov. 21, 1952, AMS Letters, 53; Parker, *John Kenneth Galbraith*, 265.

4 Parker, *John Kenneth Galbraith*, 265; AMS to James Wechsler, Aug. 28, 1953, AMS Letters, 86.

5 Adlai Stevenson to Thomas K. Finletter, Sept. 5, 1953; Stevenson to AMS, Sept. 5, 1953, *The Papers of Adlai Stevenson*, vol. 4, ed. Walter Johnson et al. (Boston: Little, Brown, 1974), 267-268; John Bartlow Martin, *Adlai Stevenson and the World: The Life of Adlai E. Stevenson* (New York: Doubleday, 1977), 82-83.

6 Martin, *Adlai Stevenson and the World*, 82-83; 89.

7 On Eisenhower's "middle way," I follow Robert Griffith, "Dwight D. Eisenhower and the Corporate Commonwealth," *The American Historical Review* 87, no. 1 (1982): 87-122 (especially 89-92), DOI:10.2307/1863309; Stephen Ambrose, *Eisenhower: The President* (New York: Simon and Schuster, 1984), 158-159; *State of the Union: Presidential Rhetoric from Woodrow Wilson to George W. Bush*, ed. Deborah Kalb, Gerhard D. Peters, and John Turner Woolley (Washington, DC: CQ Press, 2006), 465.

8 Martin, *Adlai Stevenson and the World*, 82-83, 88; AMS, "The Future of Liberalism: The Challenge of Abundance," *Reporter*, May 3, 1956; Adam Rome, "'Give Earth a Chance': The Environmental Movement and the Sixties," *The Journal of American History* 90, no. 2 (2003): 525-554, DOI: 10.2307/3659443.

9 Diary entry, Nov. 26, 1952, AMS Journals, 21.

10 Diary entry, Dec. 29, 1952, AMS Journals, 22-23.

11 AMS, *The Age of Roosevelt* working outline, 1952, NYPL 532/5.

12 Ibid.

13 AMS, *The Crisis of the Old Order, 1919-1933: The Age of Roosevelt*, vol. 1 (Boston: Houghton Mifflin, 1957), epigraph; Henry Steele Commager, "After the Decline and Fall, the Promise of a New Day," review of *The Crisis of the Old Order*, by AMS, *New York Times*, March 3, 1957, https://www.nytimes.com/books/00/11/26/specials/schlesinger-crisis1957.html.

14 AMS to Marietta Tree, Aug. 16, 1953, AMS Letters, 83.

15 AMS to Joseph Rauh and James Loeb, May 12, 1953, NYPL 112/2; AMS to William M. Blair Jr., Oct. 4, 1955, AMS Letters, 118.

16 Diary entry, Sept. 10, 1954, AMS Journals, 32.

17 AMS to Adlai Stevenson, Feb. 15, 1955, AMS Letters, 103.

18 Borden Stevenson and Agnes Meyer quoted in Jonathan A. Cowden, "Self-effacing and Self-defeating Leadership: Adlai E. Stevenson," *Political Psychology* 20, no. 4 (1999): 845–874, http://www.jstor.org/stable/3792197; Ray E. Boomhower, "A New America," in *John Bartlow Martin: A Voice for the Underdog* (Bloomington: Indiana University Press, 2015), 156; Reinhold Niebuhr, *Major Works on Religion and Politics*, ed. Elizabeth Sifton (New York: The Library of America, 2015), 671.

19 AMS to Joseph Rauh, Sept. 6, 1955, NYPL 112/2; "Dwight D. Eisenhower: Campaigns and Elections," Miller Center, University of Virginia, http://millercenter.org/president/biography/eisenhower-campaigns-and-elections.

20 Nicholas Fortuin, "Eisenhower's Heart Attack: How Ike beat heart disease and held on to the presidency," *The New England Journal of Medicine* 338 (1998): 1703–1704, DOI: 10.1056/NEJM199806043382321.

21 Richard Nixon, *In the Arena* (New York: Simon and Schuster, 1990), 171–172.

22 AMS to William M. Blair Jr., Oct. 4, 1955, AMS Letters, 118.

23 Diary entry, Nov. 5–6, 1955, AMS Journals, 37.

24 Rudy Abramson, *Spanning the Century: The Life of Averell Harriman, 1891–1986* (New York: William Morrow, 1992), 535; AMS to Adlai Stevenson, Oct. 10, 1955, AMS Letters, 423.

25 Martin, *Adlai Stevenson and the World*, 300.

26 AMS to Adlai Stevenson, May 15, 1956, AMS Letters, 134–135.

27 Diary entry, Nov. 5–6, 1955, AMS Journals, 17. On the speechwriters in 1956, I follow Ray E. Boomhower, *John Bartlow Martin: A Voice for the Underdog* (Bloomington: Indiana University Press, 2015), 166.

28 Diary entry, Aug. 17, 1956, AMS Journals, 43; AMS to John F. Kennedy, Aug. 21, 1956, AMS Letters, 136.

29 Diary entry, Aug. 17, 1956, AMS Journals, 43.

30 Ibid.

31 Boomhower, *John Bartlow Martin*, 167; diary entries, Oct. 9, 16, 1956, AMS Journals, 45; Craig Allen, *Eisenhower and the Mass Media: Peace, Prosperity, and Prime-time TV* (Chapel Hill: University of North Carolina Press, 1993), 127–149; Porter McKeever, *Adlai Stevenson: His Life and Legacy* (New York: William Morrow, 1989), 388.

32 Martin, *Adlai Stevenson and the World*, 389–390.

33 The election results are taken directly from Martin, *Adlai Stevenson and the World*, 391.

34 Stevenson to John Fischer, Apr. 23, 1957, *The Papers of Adlai E. Stevenson*, vol. 6, ed. Walter Johnson (Boston: Little, Brown, 1976), 524; John L. Steele, "Two Books By and About Stevenson," review of *The New America*, by Adlai E. Stevenson, *New Republic*, Sept. 2, 1957, 17.

35 McKeever, *Adlai Stevenson*, 425.

36 LBJ to AMS, Feb. 1, 1957, AMS to LBJ, Feb. 14, 1957, JFKL, Series 1, Box P17, Lyndon Johnson, 1953–1960; diary entry, Mar. 30–31, 1957, AMS Journals, 49–50.

37 Diary entry, March 30–31, 1957, AMS Journals, 49–50.

38 AMS to Lyndon B. Johnson, Apr. 3, 1957, AMS Letters, 141.

39 AMS to LBJ, June 17, 1957, AMS Letters, 143; Jonathan Haidt, *The Righteous Mind: Why Good People Are Divided By Politics and Religion* (New York: Vintage, 2013), 93.

Chapter Ten: A Saint's Life

1 AMS to James Wechsler, Feb. 5, 1957, NYPL 143/1; Orville Prescott, "Books of the Times," *New York Times*, Mar. 4, 1957.

2 AMS, *The Age of Jackson* (Boston: Little, Brown, 1945), 520–523.

3 AMS, *The Crisis of the Old Order, 1919-1933* (Boston: Houghton Mifflin, 1957), 1.

4 Ibid., 1–8.

5 Ibid., 71.

6 Ibid., 155.

7 Robert W. Merry, *Where They Stand: The American Presidents in the Eyes of the Voters and Historians* (New York: Simon and Schuster, 2012), 94; Patrick O'Brien. "Hoover and Historians," *The Annals of Iowa* 49 (1988): 394–402, http://ir.uiowa .edu/annals-of-iowa/vol49/iss5/5; AMS, *The Crisis of the Old Order*, 231–233.

8 AMS, *The Crisis of the Old Order*, 416–417.

9 Ibid., 454.

10 Ibid., 485.

11 Reviews of AMS, *The Crisis of the Old Order, 1919-1933*: Orville Prescott, "Books of the Times," *New York Times*, Mar. 4, 1957; William E. Leuchtenburg, *Political Science Quarterly* 73, no. 3 (1958): 460–463, http://www.jstor.org/stable/2145855, DOI:10.2307/2145855; G. M. Craig, *International Journal* 12, no. 4 (1957): 311–312, http://www.jstor.org/stable/40198360, DOI: 10.2307/40198360; Thomas LeDuc, *Journal of Southern History* 23, no. 3 (1957): 405–406, http://www.jstor

.org/stable/2954908, DOI: 10.2307/2954908; George C. Osborn, *The Annals of the American Academy of Political and Social Science* 313 (1957): 153–154, http://www.jstor.org/stable/1031778; Frank Thistlethwaite, *The English Historical Review* 73 (1958): 329–331, http://www.jstor.org/stable/556989; W. R. Brock, *The Historical Journal* 1 (1958): 89–91, http://www.jstor.org/stable/3020375.

12 William E. Leuchtenburg, review of *The Crisis of the Old Order, 1919–1933*, by AMS, *Political Science Quarterly* 73, no. 3 (1958): 460–463, http://www.jstor.org/stable/2145855, DOI:10.2307/2145855.

13 See for example, William Leuchtenberg, *The Wall Street Journal*, Jan. 8, 2016, http://www.wsj.com/articles/william-leuchtenburg-1452278787.

14 Peter Novick, *That Noble Dream: The Objectivity Questions and the American Historical Profession* (Cambridge: Cambridge University Press, 1988), 270–271; Stephen P. Depoe, *Arthur M. Schlesinger Jr., and the Ideological History of American Liberalism* (Tuscaloosa: University of Alabama Press, 1994), 19.

15 Norman Podhoretz and Ron Radosh, "Arthur Schlesinger, Jr.: Exchange Between Norman Podhoretz & Ron Radosh," *History News Network*, Mar. 1, 2007, http://historynewsnetwork.org/article/36075#sthash.1i8cqQ9E.dpuf.

16 William E. Leuchtenburg, review of *The Crisis of the Old Order, 1919–1933*, by AMS, *Political Science Quarterly* 73, no. 3 (1958): 460–463, http://www.jstor.org/stable/2145855, DOI:10.2307/2145855; James T. Sparrow, William J. Novak, and Stephen W. Sawyer, eds., *Boundaries of the State in U.S. History* (Chicago: University of Chicago Press, 2015), 304.

17 Marc J. Selverstone, *A Companion to John F. Kennedy* (Hoboken, NJ: Wiley, 2014); diary entry, Nov. 23, 1999, AMS Journals, 840; David Woolner and Jack Thompson, *Progressivism in America. Past, Present, and Future* (Corby, UK: Oxford University Press, 2015), 45, 44n.

18 On medieval hagiography, I follow Robert Bartlett, *Why Can the Dead Do Such Great Things: Saints and Worshipers from the Martyrs to the Reformation* (Princeton, NJ: Princeton University Press, 2013), 18, 505, 519.

19 Diary entry, Nov. 26, 1952, AMS Journals, 21; AMS to Joseph Rauh and James Loeb, May 12, 1953, NYPL 112/2; AMS, *A Thousand Days: John F. Kennedy in the White House* (Boston: Houghton Mifflin, 1965), x–xi.

20 AMS, *The Crisis of the Old Order*, 405–410.

21 Cf. Isaiah 26:12 (KJV): "Lord, thou wilt ordain peace for us: for thou also hast wrought all our works in us"; AMS, *The Coming of the New Deal, 1933–1935* (Boston: Houghton Mifflin, 1958), 13, 20–21.

22 AMS, *The Coming of the New Deal*, 508; Leroy D. Brandon under the direction of

South Trimble, Clerk of the House of Representatives, "Statistics of the Congressional Election of November 6, 1934," US House of Representatives: Office of the Clerk, http://clerk.house.gov/member_info/electionInfo/1934election.pdf.

23 AMS, *The Coming of the New Deal*, 533, 567–569, 573, 576.

24 Ibid., 587; Athanasius, *Nicene and Post-Nicene Fathers*, ed. Philip Schaff and Henry Wace (New York: Christian Literature Company, 1892).

25 Henry Steele Commager, "Two Years That Shaped Our Lives," *New York Times*, Jan. 4, 1959, http://www.nytimes.com/books/00/11/26/specials/schlesinger-age2.html.

26 Reviews of AMS, *The Coming of the New Deal, 1933–1935*: Commager, "Two Years That Shaped Our Lives"; Orville Prescott, "Books of the Times," *New York Times*, January 5, 1959; Florence Kiper Frank, *The Yale Law Journal* 68, no. 8 (1959): 1723–1727, DOI:10.2307/794381; George C. Osborn, *The Annals of the American Academy of Political and Social Science* 324 (1959): 149–150, http://www.jstor.org/stable/1034073; Robert E. Burke, *The American Historical Review* 65 (1959): 148–150, http://www.jstor.org/stable/1846650, DOI: 10.2307/1846650; G. M. Craig, *International Journal* (15): 89–90, http://www.jstor.org/stable/23595822; James A. Tinsley, *The Journal of Southern History* 25, no. 3 (1959): 407–409, http://www.jstor.org/stable/2954784, DOI:10.2307/2954784; "Background Books: The New Deal," *The Wilson Quarterly* 6, no. 2 (1982): 94–97, http://www.jstor.org/stable/40256267.

27 AMS to "Dearest Children," Jan. 23, 1959, NYPL 531/7.

28 Elizabeth Bancroft Schlesinger to AMS, undated [Jan. 1959]; *Harvard Crimson*, Feb. 3, 1959, NYPL 531/7.

29 *The Observer*, Jan. 18, 1959; *The Times*, Jan. 20, 1959, NYPL 531/7.

30 Philip Toynbee to AMS, undated [January 1959]; AMS to "Dearest Children," Jan. 21, 1959, NYPL 531/7.

31 AMS to "Dearest Children," Jan. 21, 26, 1959, NYPL 531/7; Lady Pamela Berry, socialite and political hostess; Hugh Gaitskell, leader of the Labour Party; Isaiah Berlin, Oxford philosopher and friend of AMS; Graham Sutherland, artist; Stephen Spender and Graham Greene, writers.

32 AMS to "Dearest Children," Jan. 26, 1959; AMS to Arthur and Elizabeth Schlesinger, Feb. 2, 1959, NYPL 531/7.

33 Ibid.

34 AMS, *The Politics of Upheaval, 1935–1936* (Boston: Houghton Mifflin, 1960).

35 Ibid., 1–10.

36 Ibid., 15.

37 Ibid., 42–44, 68.

38 Ibid., 273–274, 547.

39 Ibid., 273–274, 648, 651–657.

40 Morton Keller, "The New Deal: A New Look," *Polity* 31, no. 4 (1999): 657–663, DOI:10.2307/3235241; Thomas A. Krueger, "New Deal Historiography at Forty," *Reviews in American History* 3, no. 4 (1975): 483–488, DOI:10.2307/2701507.

41 AMS to Arthur and Elizabeth Schlesinger, Feb. 2, 1959, NYPL 531/7.

42 Reviews for AMS, *The Politics of Upheaval, 1935–1936*: Orville Prescott, "Books of the Times," *New York Times,* Sept. 7, 1960; Clarke A. Chambers, *The Mississippi Valley Historical Review* 47, no. 4 (1961): 731–733, DOI:10.2307/1889643; Norman Hunt, *International Affairs* 38 (1962): 132–133, DOI: 10.2307/2611478; Robert E. Burke, *The American Historical Review* 66, no. 3 (1961): 765–766, DOI: 10.2307/1847026.

43 On critical responses to Schlesinger's *The Age of Jackson* and *The Age of Roosevelt*, see Stephen P. Depoe's thoughtful *Arthur M. Schlesinger Jr., and the Ideological History of American Liberalism* (Tuscaloosa: University of Alabama Press, 1994), 27–30 passim; Robert Allen Rutland, ed., *Clio's Favorites: Leading Historians of the United States, 1945–2000* (Columbia: University of Missouri Press, 2000), 161–162.

44 AMS, *Politics of Upheaval*, 657.

Chapter Eleven: Are You Ready to Work at the White House?

1 Diary entry, July 14, 15, 1960, AMS Journals, 73–79.

2 Nigel Hamilton, *JFK: Reckless Youth* (London: Arrow, 1992), 204–205. Helen O'Donnell, *The Irish Brotherhood: John F. Kennedy, His Inner Circle, and the Improbable Rise to the Presidency* (Berkeley, CA: Counterpoint, 2015); Robert Allen Rutland, ed., *Clio's Favorites: Leading Historians of the United States, 1945–2000* (Columbia: University of Missouri Press, 2000), 162; "James Rousmaniere, 86, Skilled Yachtsman, Dies," *New York Times,* Oct. 31, 2004, http://www.nytimes .com/2004/10/31/nyregion/james-rousmaniere-86-skilled-yachtsman-dies .html?_r=0; Theodore H. White, *The Making of the President: 1960* (New York: Harper Perennial, 2009), 284: it is the only reference to AMS in the book.

3 John T. Shaw, *JFK in the Senate: Pathway to the Presidency* (New York: Palgrave Macmillan, 2013), 124–125; diary entry, June 16, 1960, AMS Journals, 70.

4 JFK to AMS, June 11, 1955, AMS Letters, 106–107.

5 AMS to Stephanie Adwar (fourth grade student writing to him about *Profiles in Courage*), March 11, 1975, NYPL 1/4; AMS to JFK, July 4, 1955, AMS Letters, 112–117; Shaw, *JFK in the Senate*, 126–127.

6 Ted Sorensen, *Counselor: A Life at the Edge of History* (New York: Harper, 2008), 146; AMS to JFK, July 4, 1955, AMS Letters, 112–117.

7 LBJ to AMS, Feb. 5, 1960, JFKL, Series 1, Box P17, Lyndon Johnson, 1953–1960.

8 JFK to AMS, May 2, 1957, NYPL 77/1; diary entries, March 30–31, 1957, July 19, Dec. 27, 1959, AMS Journals, 51, 57, 59.

9 Diary entries, May 14, 15, 22, 1960, AMS Journals, 66–68.

10 Diary entries, June 16, 1960, AMS Journals, 66–68.

11 Diary entries, June 16, July 9, 1960, AMS Journals, 70–71; Stevenson to Arthur and Marian Schlesinger, June 7, 1960; Stevenson to Marian Schlesinger, June 13, 1960, Walter Johnson et al., eds., *The Papers of Adlai Stevenson*, vol. 7 (Boston: Little, Brown, 1977), 507–513; AMS to Stevenson, June 8, 1960, AMS Letters, 203; Marian Cannon Schlesinger, *I Remember: A Life of Politics, Paintings and People* (Cambridge, MA: TidePool Press, 2012), 132.

12 JFK to Joseph P. Kennedy, June 29, 1956, in Amanda Smith, ed., *Hostage to Fortune: The Letters of Joseph P. Kennedy* (New York: Viking, 2001), 672; diary entry, July 15, 1960, AMS Journals, 78–79.

13 AMS to the Editors of *Newsweek*, Aug. 26, 1960, AMS Letters, 217; AMS to JFK, Aug. 30, 1960, AMS Letters, 219.

14 Diary entry, Oct. 16, 1960, AMS Journals, 85–89; AMS, *A Thousand Days: John F. Kennedy in the White House* (Boston: Houghton Mifflin, 1965), 70; Ray E. Boomhower, "The New America," in *John Bartlow Martin: A Voice for the Underdog* (Bloomington: Indiana University Press, 2015), 155–192; Sorensen, *Counselor*, 134.

15 Diary entry, Oct. 16, 1960, AMS Journals, 87.

16 AMS, *Kennedy or Nixon: Does It Make Any Difference?* (New York: Macmillan, 1960). The Gold Dust Twins, "Goldie" and "Dusty," advertised washing powder. The phrase was often used to signify two characters working together as a team.

17 Ibid., 1–2.

18 Ibid., 2–18.

19 Ibid.

20 Peter Braestrup, "G.O.P. uses a book scoring Kennedy," *New York Times*, Nov. 2, 1960; Victor Lasky, *John F. Kennedy: What's Behind the Image* (Washington, DC: Free World, 1960), 114–115.

21 AMS, *Kennedy or Nixon*, 18–34; diary entry, Oct. 20–Nov. 8, 1960, AMS Journals, 93.

22 Diary entry, Nov. 21, 1960, AMS Journals, 93.

23 Diary entry, Dec. 1, 1960, AMS Journals, 94–96.

24 AMS, *A Thousand Days*, 143; diary entry, Feb. 2, 1961, AMS Journals, 102.

25 AMS to Marietta Tree, Jan. 1, 1961, AMS Letters, 239–241; Kai Bird, *The Color of Truth: McGeorge Bundy and William Bundy, Brothers in Arms* (New York: Simon and Schuster, 1998), 152.

26 AMS to Marietta Tree, Jan. 1, 1961, AMS Letters, 239–241; diary entry, Feb. 2, 1961, AMS Journals, 102.

27 Marian Cannon Schlesinger, interview by author, March 9, 2014; Marian Cannon Schlesinger, *I Remember*, 128.

28 AMS, *A Thousand Days*, 162.

29 Ibid., 167.

Chapter Twelve: The Gadfly

1 Diary entry, Feb. 6, 1961, AMS Journals, 102.

2 Here I follow Patrick Anderson's superb sketch in *The President's Men: White House Assistants* (New York: Doubleday, 1968), 213–220; Christina Schlesinger, interview with author, April 16, 2014.

3 AMS to JFK, March 6, 1961, JFKL, Schlesinger, Series 6, Memoranda to the President, Box WH 66, 1961.

4 Ira Stoll, *JFK: Conservative* (Boston: Houghton Mifflin Harcourt, 2013), 82–83; Anderson, *The President's Men*, 216; Tevi Troy, *Intellectuals and the American Presidency: Philosophers, Jesters, or Technicians?* (Lanham, MD: Rowman and Littlefield, 2002), 28–29; David Halberstam, *The Best and The Brightest* (New York: Ballantine Books, 1993 edition), 28–29.

5 Anderson, *The President's Men*, 214–215.

6 AMS to Carl Bridenbaugh, Jan. 30, 1960, JFKL, Series 09.1, Box WH 54, Jan. 30, 1961–Feb. 5, 1961; AMS, *The Coming of the New Deal, 1933–1935* (Boston: Houghton Mifflin, 1958), 576.

7 AMS to JFK, memorandum for the president, Disposition of Presidential Papers, Feb. 6, 1961, JFKL, Schlesinger, Series 09.1, WH 54, Feb. 6--9, 1961.

8 AMS to JFK, memorandum for the president: Disposition of Presidential Papers, Feb. 6, 1961, JFKL, Schlesinger, Series 09.1, WH 54, Feb. 6–9, 1961; AMS, *A Thousand Days: John F. Kennedy in the White House* (Boston: Houghton Mifflin, 1965), x–xi; *Time*, Dec. 17, 1965; Ted Wilmer, ed., *Listening In: The Secret White House Recordings of John. F. Kennedy* (New York: Hyperion, 2012), 1.

9 Theodore C. Sorensen, *Kennedy* (New York: Harper and Row, 1965), 5; Benjamin C. Bradlee, *Conversations with Kennedy* (New York: Norton, 1975), 127–128; Troy, *Intellectuals and the American Presidency*, 31.

10 AMS to Isaiah Berlin, Feb. 11, 1961, AMS Letters, 244; AMS, *A Thousand Days*, 168; diary entry, Feb. 6, 1961, AMS Journals, 103.

11 Diary entries, Feb. 20, Feb. 24, 1961, AMS Journals, 103–106; Robert Sam Anson, *McGovern* (New York: Holt, Rinehart and Winston, 1972), 106–109.

12 AMS to JFK, Feb. 11, 1961, JFKL, Schlesinger, Series 09.2, Box WH 69, 3/20/61–7/18/61.

13 AMS to JFK, Mar. 10, 1961, JFKL, Schlesinger, Series 09.2, Box WH 69, 3/20/61–7/18/61.

14 AMS to Adolf Berle, Mar. 20, 1961, JFKL, Schlesinger, Series 09.2, Box WH 69, 3/20/61–7/18/61.

15 AMS, draft white paper on Cuba, undated, JFKL, Schlesinger, Series 09.2, Box WH 69, 3/20/61–7/18/61.

16 AMS to JFK, Mar. 10 & Mar. 15, 1961, JFKL, Schlesinger, Series 09.2, Box WH 69, 3/20/61–7/18/61.

17 Diary entry, Mar. 28, 1961, AMS Journals, 108.

18 E. W. Kenworthy, "Kennedy Helps Draft Appeal on 'Struggle' for Hemisphere," *New York Times*, Apr. 4, 1961; "White Paper on Cuba," *New York Times*, Apr. 5, 1961.

19 AMS to JFK, Apr. 5, 1961, JFKL, Schlesinger, Series 09.2, Box WH 69, 3/20/61–7/18/61.

20 Ibid.

21 Diary entry, Apr. 7, 1961, AMS Journals, 109.

22 Diary entry, Apr. 12, 1961, AMS Journals, 110; Richard N. Goodwin, *Remembering America: A Voice from the Sixties* (Boston: Little, Brown, 1988), 176–177.

23 Edwin O. Guthman and Jeffrey Shulman, eds., *Robert Kennedy: In His Own Words* (New York: Bantam Books, 1988), 242.

24 Patricia Sullivan. "Gilbert Harrison, 92, Longtime Editor of New Republic," *Washington Post,* Jan. 8, 2008, http://www.washingtonpost.com/wp-dyn/content/article/2008/01/07/AR2008010703193.html; diary entry, Apr. 7, 1961, AMS Journals, 109.

25 AMS to JFK, memorandum for the president, Apr. 7, 1961, JFKL, Schlesinger, Series 09.2, Box WH 69, 3/20/61–7/18/61; AMS, *A Thousand Days*, 271; diary entry, Apr. 12, 1961, AMS Journals, 110; Walter Johnson et al., eds., *The Papers of Adlai Stevenson*, vol. 8 (Boston: Little, Brown, 1979), 53; John Bartlow Martin, *Adlai Stevenson and the World: The Life of Adlai E. Stevenson* (New York: Doubleday, 1977), 624, 628.

26 Alan Brinkley, *John F. Kennedy* (New York: Times Books/Henry Holt, 2012), 68–

69; Michael Beschloss, *Kennedy v. Khrushchev: The Crisis Years 1960–63* (London: Faber, 1991), 132; Jim Rasenberger, *The Brilliant Disaster: JFK, Castro and America's Doomed Invasion of Cuba's Bay of Pigs* (New York: Scribner's, 2011), 227ff.; Aleksandr Fursenko and Timothy Naftali, *"One Hell of a Gamble": Khrushchev, Castro, and Kennedy 1958–1964* (New York: W. W. Norton, 1997), 99–100.

27 AMS to JFK, memorandum for the president, Apr. 10, 1961, JFKL, Schlesinger, Series 09.2, Box WH 69, 3/20/61–7/18/61.

28 Robert Dallek, *Camelot's Court: Inside the Kennedy White House* (New York: Harper, 2013), 136–146.

29 William J. Fulbright, *The Arrogance of Power* (New York: Random House, 1966), 47–48; Randall Bennett Woods, *Fulbright* (Cambridge: Cambridge University Press, 1995), 265–268.

30 AMS, *A Thousand Days*, 255–256; Richard N. Goodwin, *Remembering America: A Voice from the Sixties* (Boston: Little, Brown, 1988), 173.

31 Diary entry, Apr. 21, 1961, AMS Journals, 113–116.

32 Brinkley, *John F. Kennedy*, 71–72; Beschloss, *Kennedy v. Khrushchev*, 128.

33 Diary entry, Apr. 21, 1961, AMS Journals, 118.

Chapter Thirteen: Playing Cassandra

1 AMS, *A Thousand Days: John F. Kennedy in the White House* (Boston: Houghton Mifflin, 1965), 290.

2 Diary entry, Apr. 21, 1961, AMS Journals, 119.

3 Ibid., AMS, *A Thousand Days*, 291.

4 AMS to JFK, memorandum for the president, May 3, 1961, JFKL, Schlesinger, Series 09.2, Box WH 69, 3/20/61–7/18/61; diary entry, Apr. 22, 1961, AMS Journals, 120.

5 AMS to JFK, memorandum for the president, May 3, 1961, JFKL, Schlesinger, Series 09.2, Box WH 69, 3/20/61–7/18/61.

6 Ibid.

7 Diary entry, May 7, 1961, AMS Journals, 120; "The Laos Crisis, 1960–1963," United States Department of State: Office of the Historian, https://history.state.gov/milestones/1961-1968/laos-crisis.

8 Diary entry, June 7, 1961, AMS Journals, 121; David Reynolds, *Summits: Six Meetings that Shaped the Twentieth Century* (London: Penguin, 2007), 195; Michael Dobbs, *One Minute to Midnight: Kennedy, Khrushchev, and Castro on the Brink of Nuclear War* (New York: Alfred A. Knopf, 2008), 6–7.

9 Diary entry, June 7, 1961, AMS Journals, 121.

10 AMS, *The Coming of the New Deal, 1933–1935* (Boston: Houghton Mifflin, 1958), 524–525.

11 AMS, *A Thousand Days*, 681.

12 AMS to Richard Goodwin, July 8, 1961, JFKL, Schlesinger, Series 09.2, Box WH 69, 3/20/61–7/18/61.

13 AMS to JFK, memorandum for the president, "CIA," Apr. 21, 1961, JFKL, Schlesinger, Series 09.2, Box WH 69, 3/20/61–7/18/61.

14 AMS to JFK, memorandum for the president, "CIA reorganization," June 30, 1961, JFKL, Schlesinger, Series 09.2, Box WH 69, 3/20/61–7/18/61.

15 Stephen Kinzer, *The Brothers: John Foster Dulles, Allen Dulles, and Their Secret World War* (New York: Times Books/Henry Holt, 2013), 303.

16 AMS to Arthur and Elizabeth Schlesinger, undated [mid-June 1961], AMS Letters, 245; Richard N. Goodwin, *Remembering America: A Voice from the Sixties* (Boston: Little, Brown, 1988), 212.

17 Diary entry, June 18, 1961, AMS Journals, 121.

18 AMS, *The Vital Center* (Boston: Houghton Mifflin, 1949), 149; AMS to JFK, memorandum for the president, Fanfani visit, June 10, 1961, JFKL, Schlesinger, Series 09.2, Box WH 69, 3/20/61–7/18/61.

19 AMS to Arthur and Elizabeth Schlesinger, undated [mid-June 1961], AMS Letters, 245.

20 AMS to Walt Rostow, July 6, 1961, JFKL, Schlesinger, Series 09.2, Box WH 69, 3/20/61–7/18/61.

21 Dean Rusk, *As I Saw It: A Secretary of State's Memoirs* (London: I. B. Tauris, 1991), 454–455.

22 Diary entry, April 21, 1961, AMS Journals, 119; *Washington Star* cartoon: http://www.loc.gov/pictures/item/acd1996003110/PP/.

23 David Halberstam, *The Best and The Brightest* (New York: Ballantine Books, 1993 edition), 189.

24 AMS to JFK, memorandum for the president, "State Department Changes," June 12, 1961, JFKL, Schlesinger, Series 09.2, Box WH 69, 3/20/61–7/18/61; Halberstam, *The Best and The Brightest*, 36.

25 Beschloss, *Kennedy v. Khrushchev*, 268.

26 AMS to JFK, memoranda for the president, "Berlin" and "Berlin Planning," July 7, 1961, JFKL, Schlesinger, Series 09.2, Box WH 69, 3/20/61–7/18/61.

27 Beschloss, *Kennedy v. Khrushchev*, 242–243.

28 AMS to JFK, memoranda for the president, "Berlin" and "Berlin Planning," July 7, 1961, JFKL, Schlesinger, Series 09.2, Box WH 69, 3/20/61–7/18/61.

29 AMS to JFK, memorandum for the president, "Berlin Planning," July 7, 1961, JFKL, Schlesinger, Series 09.2, Box WH 69, 3/20/61–7/18/61.

30 AMS to McGeorge Bundy, July 13 & July 18, 1961, JFKL, Schlesinger, Series 09.2, Box WH 69, 3/20/61–7/18/61.

31 AMS to JFK, memorandum for the president, "Berlin Planning," July 7, 1961, JFKL, Schlesinger, Series 09.2, Box WH 69, 3/20/61–7/18/61; diary entry, July 28, 1961, AMS Journals, 125; Niall Ferguson, *Kissinger, 1923–1968: The Idealist* (New York: Penguin, 2015), 497–498; Frederick Kempe, *Berlin 1961: Kennedy, Khrushchev, and the Most Dangerous Place on Earth* (New York: Putnam's, 2011), 298–299.

32 AMS to JFK, memorandum for the president, "Berlin," July 7, 1961, JFKL, Schlesinger, Series 09.2, Box WH 69, 3/20/61–7/18/61; Kempe, *Berlin 1961*, 298–299.

33 Kennedy in Hyannis Port: Kempe, *Berlin 1961*, 306–307.

34 Diary entry, Aug. 1, 1961, AMS Journals, 125.

35 Ferguson, *Kissinger, 1923–1968*, 495–496, and on the Berlin crisis more generally, 493–503; diary entry, July 28, 1961, AMS Journals, 124.

36 Ferguson, *Kissinger, 1923–1968*, 497–499.

37 AMS to JFK, memorandum for the president, Nov. 10, 1961, JFKL, Schlesinger, Series 09.2, Box WH 69, 3/20/61–7/20/61; Ferguson, *Kissinger, 1923–1968*, 499–501.

38 John Newhouse, *The Nuclear Age: From Hiroshima to Star Wars* (London: Michael Joseph, 1989), 138–143.

39 Ibid., 147.

40 Robert Dallek, *Camelot's Court: Inside the Kennedy White House* (New York: Harper, 2013), 209; Glenn T. Seaborg, *Kennedy, Khrushchev, and the Test Ban* (Berkeley: University of California Press, 1981), 47–48.

41 Gordon S. Barrass, *The Great Cold War: A Journey Through the Hall of Mirrors* (Stanford, CA: Stanford University Press, 2009), 136; AMS, *A Thousand Days*, 455.

42 AMS to JFK, memorandum for the president, "The nuclear test ban issue," July 17, 1961, JFKL, Schlesinger, Series 09.2, Box WH 69, 3/20/61–7/20/61.

43 Diary entry, July 22, 1961, AMS Journals, 122–123.

44 Diary entry, Aug. 1, 1961, AMS Journals, 125. For a summary of Penkofsky report see Seaborg, *Kennedy, Khrushchev, and the Test Ban*, 74–75.

45 Dallek, *Camelot's Court*, 211; Seaborg, *Kennedy, Khrushchev, and the Test Ban*, 84; diary entry, Sept. 4, 1961, AMS Journals, 131–132.

46 Diary entry, Sept. 4, 1961, AMS Journals, 132–133.

47 Christopher Sandford, *Harold and Jack: The Remarkable Friendship of Prime*

Minister Harold Macmillan and President Kennedy (Amherst, NY: Prometheus, 2014), 127.

48 Diary entry, Sept. 5, 1961, AMS Journals, 135.

Chapter Fourteen: Looking So Arthurish

1 Annual physical conducted by Willard Dalrymple, MD, May 14, 1959, NYPL 532/1; Marian Cannon Schlesinger, *I Remember: A Life of Politics, Painting and People* (Cambridge, MA: TidePool Press, 2012), 139.

2 John Kenneth Galbraith, *Ambassador's Journal: A Personal Account of the Kennedy Years* (Boston: Houghton Mifflin, 1969), 205–206; John Bartlow Martin, *Adlai Stevenson and the World: The Life of Adlai E. Stevenson* (New York: Doubleday, 1977), 662; Howard B. Schaffer, *Chester Bowles: New Dealer in the Cold War* (Cambridge, MA: Harvard University Press, 1993), 227; diary entry, Sept. 4, 1961, AMS Journals, 134; Walter Johnson, ed., *The Papers of Adlai E. Stevenson*, vol. 8 (Boston: Little, Brown, 1979), 119; Albin Krebs, "Chester Bowles is Dead at 85; Served in 4 Administrations," *New York Times*, May 26, 1986, http://www .nytimes.com/1986/05/26/obituaries/chester-bowles-is-dead-at-85-served-in-4 -administrations.html?pagewanted=all.

3 Martin, *Adlai Stevenson and the World*, 653–655; Patrick Anderson, *The President's Men: White House Assistants* (New York: Doubleday, 1968), 213–220; diary entry, Sept. 4, 1961, AMS Journals, 133.

4 AMS to JFK, memorandum for the president, "John McCone," Sept. 27, 1961, JFKL, Series 09.2, Box WH 54, 3/20/61–7/20/61; diary entries, Apr. 21, Oct. 8, 1961, AMS Journals, 118, 137.

5 Diary entry, October 17, 1961, AMS Journals, 137; Theodore C. Sorensen, *Kennedy* (New York: Harper and Row, 1965), 263; Robert Dallek, *An Unfinished Life: John F. Kennedy, 1917–1963* (Boston: Little, Brown, 2003), 470–471; AMS to JFK, undated [Dec. 1961], JFKL, AMS, Series 11.2, Box WH 67, Football Hall of Fame, 12/5/61.

6 Diary entry, Feb. 6, 1961, AMS Journals, 102; diary entry, Feb. 4, 1961, Galbraith, *Ambassador's Journal*, 28.

7 Diary entry, Jan. 14, 1962, AMS Journals, 143.

8 Diary entry, June 17, 1962, AMS Journals, 157.

9 On the background of US involvement in Vietnam, I follow Fredrik Logevall, *Embers of War: The Fall of an Empire and the Making of America's Vietnam* (New York: Random House, 2012), 698–699, 702–703 [*sic*] passim.

10 Ibid., 703; AMS, *A Thousand Days: John F. Kennedy in the White House* (Boston: Houghton Mifflin, 1965), 545.

11 Barbara Leaming, *Mrs. Kennedy: The Missing History of the Kennedy Years* (New York: The Free Press, 2001), 100–101.

12 AMS, *A Thousand Days*, 545–547; Rudy Abramson, *Spanning the Century: The Life of Averell Harriman, 1891–1986* (New York: William Morrow, 1992), 607; Richard Parker, *John Kenneth Galbraith* (New York: Farrar, Straus and Giroux, 2005), 372–374.

13 Diary entry, Jan. 14, 1962, AMS Journals, 145.

14 AMS to Nathan Pusey, Jan. 11, 27, 1961, NYPL 59/3.

15 Stephen Schlesinger, interview with author, Jan. 17, 2014; diary entry, Jan. 21, 1961, AMS Journals, 145; Secretary to the Harvard President and Fellows to AMS, Feb 5, 1962, NYPL 532/1.

16 Diary entry, Jan. 21, 1962, AMS Journals, 146.

17 Clint Hill, *Mrs. Kennedy and Me* (New York: Gallery Books, 2012), 127.

18 AMS to JFK, memorandum for the president, "Around the world in 42 days," JFKL, Schlesinger, Series 09.2, Box WH 69, 1962; "Resolutions Adopted at the Eighth Meeting of Consultation of Ministers of Foreign Affairs, Punta del Este, Uruguay, January 22–31, 1962," *The Avalon Project: Documents in Law, History, and Diplomacy,* Lillian Goldman Law Library at Yale Law School, http://avalon .law.yale.edu/20th_century/intam17.asp.

19 AMS to JFK, memorandum for the president, "Around the world in 42 days," JFKL, Schlesinger, Series 09.2, Box WH 69, 1962; Robert Sam Anson, *McGovern* (New York: Holt, Rinehart and Winston, 1972), 111–112.

20 Diary entry, February 19, 1962, Galbraith, *Ambassador's Journal*, 304–305.

21 AMS, *Robert Kennedy and His Times* (New York: Houghton Mifflin, 1978), vol. 2, 599; diary entry, Feb. 21, 1961, Galbraith, *Ambassador's Journal*, 304–305; Michael Dobbs, *One Minute to Midnight: Kennedy, Khrushchev, and Castro on the Brink of Nuclear War* (New York: Alfred A. Knopf, 2008), 10.

22 Diary entries, June 19, 1961, June 25, 1962, AMS Journals, 121, 159; Sandra Hochman, "Arthur Schlesinger Halfway Through His Book on Bobby and Enjoying His Life to the Hilt," *People*, August 16, 1976, http://people.com/archive/arthur -schlesinger-is-halfway-through-his-book-on-bobby-and-enjoying-his-life-to -the-hilt-vol-6-no-7.

23 Marian Cannon Schlesinger, *I Remember*, 166.

24 AMS, *Robert Kennedy*, 600; Marian Cannon Schlesinger, *I Remember*, 166–167; AMS to JFK, memorandum for the president, "Around the world in 42 days," JFKL, Schlesinger, Series 09.2, Box WH 69, 1962.

25 AMS, *A Thousand Days*, 402.

Chapter Fifteen: We're Counting on You

1 *Last Year in Marienbad,* directed by Alain Resnais, Cocinor, 1961, http://www .imdb.com/title/tt0054632; diary entry, Mar. 31, 1962, AMS Journals, 150.

2 Diary entry, March 31, 1962, AMS Journals, 150; Seymour Hersh, *The Dark Side of Camelot* (London: HarperCollins, 1998 paperback edition), 226ff.; Thomas C. Reeves, *A Question of Character: A Life of John F. Kennedy* (New York: Free Press, 1991), 10, and more generally on JFK's personal life, 328-364; AMS, *The Cycles of American History* (New York: Mariner Books, 1999), 407.

3 John Kenneth Galbraith, *Ambassador's Journal: A Personal Account of the Kennedy Years* (Boston: Houghton Mifflin, 1969), 340.

4 Galbraith to JFK, March 2, April 4, 1962, Galbraith, *Ambassador's Journal,* 310, 342.

5 AMS to JFK, memorandum for the president, "Around the world in 42 days," JFKL, Schlesinger, Series 09.2, Box WH 69, 1962.

6 Diary entry, April 5, 1962, AMS Journals, 153-154; diary entry, Mar. 27-Apr. 8, 1962, Galbraith, *Ambassador's Journal,* 340; Bowles to JFK, Apr. 4, 1962, Glenn W. LaFantasie, ed., *Foreign Relations of the United States,* 1961-1963, vol. 2, Vietnam, 1962, United States Department of State: Office of the Historian, https://history .state.gov/historicaldocuments/frus1961-63v02/d142.

7 Galbraith to JFK, April 5, 1962, Galbraith, *Ambassador's Journal,* 342-344.

8 Richard Parker, *John Kenneth Galbraith* (New York: Farrar, Straus and Giroux, 2005), 390-391; Robert Dallek, *An Unfinished Life: John F. Kennedy, 1917-1963* (Boston: Little, Brown, 2003), 272-274.

9 "Quotation of the Day," *New York Times,* Jan. 12, 1962, http://timesmachine .nytimes.com/timesmachine/1962/01/12/87312516.html?pageNumber=36; diary entry, Jan. 14, 1962, AMS Journals, 144. On JFK's speechwriting process, I follow Robert Schlesinger, *White House Ghosts: Presidents and Their Speechwriters* (New York: Simon and Schuster, 2008), 120.

10 AMS to JFK, memorandum for the president, "Around the world in 42 days," JFKL, Schlesinger, Series 09.2, Box WH 69, 1962; AMS to JFK, memorandum for the president, "Berkeley Speech," March 9, 1962, JFKL, AMS, Series 11.2, Box WH 67, Berkeley, 3/23/62.

11 "The age of hate or the age of knowledge," TCS [Sorensen] draft, Mar. 3, 1962, text of an address by the president at Charter Day, University of California, Berkeley, Mar. 23, 1962, JFKL, AMS, Series 11.2, Box WH 67, Berkeley, 3/23/62; AMS, *A Thousand Days: John F. Kennedy in the White House* (Boston: Houghton Mifflin, 1965), 614-616; Robert Schlesinger, *White House Ghosts,* 122.

12 Remarks by President John F. Kennedy at Yale, June 11, 1962; AMS to JFK, memorandum for the president, "New Haven Speech draft 2," June 6, 1962; AMS to Galbraith, June 4, 1962, JFKL, AMS, Series 11.2, Box WH 67, Yale 6/11/62; AMS, *A Thousand Days*, 645–648; AMS to JFK, memorandum for the president, "Business and Government: An Historian's View," July 11, 1962, JFKL, AMS, Series 09.2, Box WH 69, 1962; AMS to Daniel Bell, Sept. 10, 1985, NYPL 11/1.

13 John F. Kennedy, "Commencement Address at Yale University, New Haven, Connecticut," JFKL, June 11, 1962, http://www.jfklibrary.org/Asset-Viewer/Archives/JFKWHA-104.aspx.

14 Tevi Troy, *Intellectuals and the American Presidency: Philosophers, Jesters, or Technicians?* (Lanham, MD: Rowman and Littlefield, 2002), 27; Don Munton and David Welch, *The Cuban Missile Crisis: A Concise History* (Cambridge: Oxford University Press, 2007), 40.

15 AMS to Bundy, Aug. 22, 1962, JFKL, AMS, Series 09.2, Box WH 69, 1962; Alan Brinkley, *John F. Kennedy* (New York: Times Books/Henry Holt, 2012), 113–114.

16 Michael Beschloss, *Kennedy v. Khrushchev: The Crisis Years 1960–63* (London: Faber, 1991), 411–413.

17 AMS to JFK, memorandum for the president, "Cuba," Sept. 5, 1962, JFKL, AMS, Series 09.2, Box WH 69, 1962; Beschloss, *Kennedy v. Khrushchev*, 412; Michael Dobbs, *One Minute to Midnight: Kennedy, Khrushchev, and Castro on the Brink of Nuclear War* (New York: Alfred A. Knopf, 2008), 10; AMS, *Robert Kennedy and His Times* (New York: Houghton Mifflin, 1978), 515, 545–546, 558.

18 AMS to JFK, memorandum for the president, June 6, 1962, JFKL, AMS, Series 11.2, Box WH 67, Yale 6/11/62.

19 Diary entry, Oct. 28, 1962, AMS Journals, 172–173; AMS, *A Thousand Days*, 808–809.

20 John Bartlow Martin, *Adlai Stevenson and the World: The Life of Adlai E. Stevenson* (New York: Doubleday, 1977), 723–724; Ernest May and Philip D. Zelikow, eds., *The Kennedy Tapes: Inside the White House during the Cuban Missile Crisis* (Cambridge, MA: Belknap Press, 1997), 198–199.

21 See Sheldon M. Stern, *The Cuban Missile Crisis in American Memory: Myth versus Reality* (Stanford, CA: Stanford University Press, 2012), 129–133.

22 Martin, *Adlai Stevenson and the World*, 724; AMS to Stevenson (draft), Oct. 29, 1962, JFKL, AMS, Series 09.2, Box WH 69, 1962.

23 Diary entry, Oct. 28, 1962, AMS Journals, 175; Martin, *Adlai Stevenson and the World*, 724. AMS later left out the phrase "that fellow is ready to give everything away," AMS, *A Thousand Days*, 811.

24 Diary entry, Oct. 28, 1962, AMS Journals, 175.

25 Martin, *Adlai Stevenson and the World*, 725–728; text of Stevenson's speech, Oct. 23, 1962: *The Papers of Adlai Stevenson*, 309–325.

26 Ibid., 325–335; Dobbs, *One Minute to Midnight*, 129–132.

27 Diary entry, Oct. 28, 1962, AMS Journals, 176; Rudy Abramson, *Spanning the Century: The Life of Averell Harriman, 1891-1986* (New York: William Morrow, 1992), 593–594.

28 Diary entries, Oct. 28, Oct. 29, 1962, AMS Journals, 177–178.

29 AMS to Elizabeth Schlesinger, Dec. 1, 1964, NYPL 294–295.

Chapter Sixteen: The Watchman Waketh But in Vain

1 Summary of electoral position: Robert Dallek, *Camelot's Court: Inside the Kennedy White House* (New York: Harper, 2013), 335–336.

2 Thomas C. Reeves, *A Question of Character: A Life of John F. Kennedy* (New York: Free Press, 1991), 401.

3 Ted Sorensen, *Counselor: A Life at the Edge of History* (New York: Harper, 2008), 325–327; Parmet quoted in Reeves, *A Question of Character*, 399.

4 AMS to Theodore Sorensen, Jan. 7, 1963, AMS Series 11.2, WH 67, State of the Union, 1/14/63; Andrew Cohen, *Two Days in June: John F. Kennedy and the 48 Hours That Made History* (New York: Signal, 2014), 9–11, 21; diary entry, June 16, 1963, AMS Journals, 194.

5 AMS to JFK, memorandum for the president, "The nuclear test ban issue," July 17, 1961, JFKL, Schlesinger, Series 09.2, Box WH 69, 3/20/61–7/20/61.

6 AMS to JFK, memorandum for the president, "The nuclear test ban issue," July 17, 1961, JFKL, Schlesinger, Series 09.2, Box WH 69, 3/20/61–7/20/61; AMS to JFK, memorandum for the president, "The European Tour," June 8, 1963, JFKL, Schlesinger, Series 09.2, Box WH 69, 3/20/61–7/20/61.

7 AMS, *A Thousand Days*, 432–437.

8 Stewart Alsop and Charles Bartlett, "In Time of Crisis," *Saturday Evening Post*, December 12, 1962, http://www.saturdayeveningpost.com/wp-content/uploads/satevepost/1962-12-08-missile-crisis.pdf. On the Trollope ploy, see Sheldon M. Stern, *The Cuban Missile Crisis in American Memory: Myth versus Reality* (Stanford, CA: Stanford University Press, 2012), 133–137. Gregg Herken, *The Georgetown Set: Friends and Rivals in Cold War Washington* (New York: Alfred A. Knopf, 2014), 278–279; AMS to JFK, memorandum for the president, "Alsop-Bartlett story and Stevenson," Dec. 2, 1962, JFKL, Schlesinger, Series 09.2, Box WH 69, 1962.

9 AMS to G. P. Putnam's Sons, Feb. 5, 1963; AMS to Editor of Publishers Weekly, April 13, 1963; William F. Buckley Jr. to Editor of Publishers Weekly, Apr. 19,

1963: AMS Letters, 257–263. On Buckley and the "liberal establishment," see Kevin M. Schultz, *Buckley and Mailer: The Difficult Friendship That Shaped the Sixties* (New York: W. W. Norton, 2015), 42–43; Marian Cannon Schlesinger, *I Remember: A Life of Painting, Politics and People* (Cambridge, MA: TidePool Press, 2012), 131; diary entry, June 25, 1962, AMS Journals, 159.

10 Pierre Salinger, *With Kennedy* (New York: Doubleday, 1966), 69.

11 Diary entry, May 21, 1963, AMS Journals, 190–191.

12 On the story of Kennedy's civil rights TV address, I follow Cohen, *Two Days in June,* 175ff. and particularly 326–331.

13 Sorensen, *Counselor,* 278–280.

14 Cohen, *Two Days in June,* 330–331, 336.

15 Sorensen, *Counselor,* 282.

16 Diary entry, June 16, 1963, AMS Journals, 195; Cohen, *Two Days in June,* 328–329; AMS to JFK, memorandum for the president, June 8, 1962, JFKL, Schlesinger, Series 09.2, Box WH 69, 1963–1964.

17 AMS to Fred Adams, May 1, 1962, NYPL 293/4; AMS to Jacqueline Kennedy, May 9, 1963, NYPL 102/6.

18 AMS to Arthur Schlesinger (Sr.), Feb. 20, 1963, NYPL 293/4.

19 Diary entry, August 11, 1963, AMS Journals, 199; Herken, *The Georgetown Set,* 288–291.

20 Jacqueline Kennedy to AMS, Aug. 26, 1963, NYPL 102/6; diary entry, August 20, 1963, AMS Journals, 200.

21 AMS to Adlai Stevenson, Sept. 16, 1963, JFKL, Schlesinger, Series 09.2, Box WH 68, Address to the 18th General Assembly of the UN, 9/20/63; Gerard DeGroot, *Dark Side of the Moon: The Magnificent Madness of the American Lunar Quest* (London: Jonathan Cape, 2007), 180–181; John Bartlow Martin, *Adlai Stevenson and the World: The Life of Adlai Stevenson* (New York: Doubleday, 1977), 772; AMS to JFK, "Memorandum for the President," Sept. 16, 1963, JFKL, Schlesinger, Series 09.2, Box WH 68, Address to the 18th General Assembly of the UN, 9/20/63.

22 AMS to JFK, "Memorandum for the President," Oct. 18, 1963, JFKL, Schlesinger, Series 09.2, Box WH 68, National Academy of Sciences; diary entry, Oct. 27, 1963, AMS Journals, 201; AMS, *A Thousand Days,* 1015; John F. Kennedy, "Remarks at Amherst College, October 26, 1963," JFKL, October 26, 1963, https://www.jfklibrary.org/Asset-Viewer/80308LXB5kOPFEJqkw5hlA.aspx. See also "Annotated Draft of Kennedy's Convocation Speech, prepared by Arthur Schlesinger, Jr." Amherst College Archives and Special Collections, October 26, 1963, https://www.amherst.edu/library/archives/exhibitions/kennedy/documents#Draft.

23 Remarks by the president at the Trade Mart, Dallas, Texas: for release 1 PM EST, Nov. 22, 1963, JFKL, Schlesinger, Series 09.2, Box WH 68, "Trade Mart, Dallas, TX."

Chapter Seventeen: A Thousand Pages

1 Diary entry, Nov. 23, 1963, AMS Journals, 206; diary entry, Nov. 23, 1963, John Kenneth Galbraith, *Ambassador's Journal: A Personal Account of the Kennedy Years* (Boston: Houghton Mifflin, 1969), 592.

2 AMS to Jacqueline Kennedy, Saturday [Nov. 23. 1963], NYPL 102/6.

3 Diary entry, Nov. 26, 1963, AMS Journals, 209.

4 Diary entry, Nov. 28, Dec. 30, 1963, AMS Journals, 209, 218–219; Tevi Troy, *Intellectuals and the American Presidency: Philosophers, Jesters, or Technicians?* (Lanham, MD: Rowman and Littlefield, 2002), 48–49; AMS to Arthur and Elizabeth Schlesinger, Jan. 8, 1964, NYPL 294–295; LBJ phone call, Nov. 16, 1964: Michael Beschloss, ed., *Reaching for Glory: Lyndon Johnson's Secret White House Tapes, 1964–1965* (New York: Simon and Schuster, 2001), 143.

5 Theodore H. White, *In Search of History* (New York: Harper & Row, 1978), 520; AMS to Arthur and Elizabeth Schlesinger, Jan. 8, 1964, NYPL 294–295; AMS to Jacqueline Kennedy, Jan. 6, 1964, NYPL 102/6; AMS, *Jacqueline Kennedy: Historic Conversations on Life with John F. Kennedy: Interviews with Arthur M. Schlesinger Jr.,* ed. Michael Beschloss (New York: Hyperion, 2011), xxi.

6 Ted Sorensen, *Counselor: A Life at the Edge of History* (New York: Harper, 2008), 389–390.

7 AMS to Arthur and Elizabeth Schlesinger, Jan. 8, 1964, NYPL 294–295.

8 Diary entry, Jan. 31, 1964, AMS Journals, 224; Troy, *Intellectuals and the American Presidency,* 47.

9 AMS to Arthur and Elizabeth Schlesinger, Jan. 8, 1964, NYPL 294–295.

10 AMS to Elizabeth Schlesinger, Feb. 22, 1964, NYPL 294–295.

11 "The former friends of Arthur Schlesinger Jr. invite you . . ." [1964], NYPL 102/4; Sorensen, *Counselor,* 408–409.

12 Sorensen, *Counselor,* 402, 407.

13 Diary entry, March 27, 1963, AMS Journals, 226–227; *Jacqueline Kennedy: Historic Conversations on Life with John F. Kennedy,* 62.

14 These interviews, including the original recordings, would be published after her death as AMS, *Jacqueline Kennedy: Historic Conversations on Life with John F. Kennedy: Interviews with Arthur M. Schlesinger Jr.,* ed. Michael Beschloss (New York: Hyperion, 2011); "Oral History Program," JFKL, https://www.jfklibrary .org/Research/About-Our-Collections/Oral-history-program.aspx.

15 Diary entry, June 16, 1963, AMS Journals, 227; AMS to Robert Kennedy, Aug. 31, 1964, and AMS to the editor of the *New York Times*, Aug. 29, 1964, AMS Letters, 277–280; "The Kennedy Blitzkrieg," *New York Times*, Aug. 22, 1964, http://www .nytimes.com/1964/08/22/the-kennedy-blitzkrieg.html?_r=0.

16 AMS, *Robert Kennedy and His Times* (Boston: Houghton Mifflin, 1978), 697.

17 Diary entry, Nov. 26, 1963, AMS Journals, 208.

18 Theodore C. Sorensen, interview by Carl Kaysen, "Theodore C. Sorensen Oral History Interview—JFK #6, 5/20/1964," JFKL, https://www.jfklibrary.org/Asset -Viewer/Archives/JFKOH-TCS-06.aspx; diary entry, July 15, 1960, AMS Journals, 78–79; Ira Stoll, *JFK: Conservative* (Boston: Houghton Mifflin Harcourt, 2013), 3–5.

19 Christopher Hitchens, "Brief Shining Moments," *London Review of Books*, February 19, 1998, http://www.lrb.co.uk/v20/n04/christopher-hitchens/brief-shining -moments.

20 Robert Bartlett, *Why Can the Dead Do Such Great Things: Saints and Worshipers from the Martyrs to the Reformation* (Princeton, NJ: Princeton University Press, 2013), especially 18, 505, 519; AMS, *A Thousand Days: John F. Kennedy in the White House* (Boston: Houghton Mifflin, 1965), 1030–1031; AMS to John Blum, Sept. 5, 1985, NYPL 15/4.

21 AMS, *A Thousand Days*, 11–19; Garry Wills, "Fierce in His Loyalties and Enmities," *New York Times*, Nov. 12, 1978.

22 Schlesinger, *A Thousand Days*, 19. For questions on Addison's disease in 1960 and 1967, see W. H. Lawrence, "Johnson Backers Urge Health Test," *New York Times*, July 5, 1960, http://timesmachine.nytimes.com/timesmachine/1960/07/05/ 99503749.html?pageNumber=19; "Candidates Pressed on Data of Any Ills," *New York Times*, November 6, 1960, http://timesmachine.nytimes.com/timesmachine/ 1960/11/06/100888445.html?pageNumber=132; Howard Rusk, "Health of Presidents," *New York Times*, August 6, 1967, http://timesmachine.nytimes.com/ timesmachine/1967/08/06/94109957.html?pageNumber=56; Schlesinger quoted in Lawrence Altman, "In J.F.K. File, Hidden Illness, Pain and Pills," *New York Times*, Nov. 17, 2002, http://www.nytimes.com/2002/11/17/us/in-jfk-file-hidden -illness-pain-and-pills.html?_r=0.

23 AMS, *A Thousand Days*, 671; Seymour Hersh, *The Dark Side of Camelot* (London: HarperCollins, 1998 paperback edition); Thomas C. Reeves, *A Question of Character: A Life of John F. Kennedy* (New York: Free Press, 1991); AMS to Adlai Stevenson, Sept. 4, 1960, AMS Letters, 224–225 and fn.

24 A summary of revisionist books on Kennedy can be found in Hitchens, "Brief Shining Moments."

25 AMS, *The Cycles of American History* (New York: Mariner Books, 1999), 407; AMS, *Jacqueline Kennedy*, xxxi; AMS to Robert J. Alexander (Rutgers), Mar. 27, 1995, NYPL 1/1.

26 AMS, *The Crisis of the Old Order, 1919-1933* (Boston: Houghton Mifflin, 1957), 5-8; AMS, *A Thousand Days*, 1-5.

27 AMS, *A Thousand Days*, 676-678, 714, 739, 1030-1031. On Schlesinger's view of history, see Marcus Cunliffe and Robin Winks, eds., "Arthur M. Schlesinger, Jr.," in *Pastmasters: Some Essays on American Historians* (New York: Harper & Row, 1969), especially 354-358.

28 AMS to Arthur and Elizabeth Schlesinger, undated [1965], NYPL 293/4; AMS to his children, Oct. 26, 1965, NYPL 293/1; AMS, "A Thousand Days: The First Close Portrait of John Kennedy," *Life*, July 16, 1965, 5; Mark Lytle, email to author, November 10, 2016.

29 Theodore Sorensen to AMS, Mar. 31, 1965, NYPL 125/6.

30 AMS to Theodore Sorensen, Apr. 8, 1965, NYPL 125/6.

31 AMS, "A Thousand Days: The First Close Portrait of John Kennedy."

32 *New York Times*, July 25, 29, Aug. 3, 6, 8 (newspaper roundup), Nov. 21, 1965; John Goshko, "Rusk Replies Indirectly to Schlesinger," *Washington Post*, August 3, 1965; AMS, "A Thousand Days: The First Close Portrait of John Kennedy."

33 AMS, "The Historian as Participant," *Daedalus* 100, no. 2 (1971): 339-358, http://www.jstor.org/stable/20024007; "At Home and Abroad," *New York Times*, Aug. 8, 1965.

34 Hubert Humphrey to AMS, Dec. 7, 1965, AMS Letters, 303.

35 AMS to Theodore Sorensen, Aug. 14, 1965; AMS to Paul Brooks (Houghton Mifflin), Aug. 14, 1965, NYPL 125/6; Charles Poore, "The Presidency Makes Its Rules for Succession," *New York Times*, July 29, 1965; M. S. Handler, "Sorensen Tells of Kennedy Fears," *New York Times*, Aug. 14, 1965.

36 James MacGregor Burns, review of *Kennedy*, by Theodore C. Sorensen, *New York Times*, Oct. 31, 1965.

37 James MacGregor Burns, review of *A Thousand Days: John F. Kennedy in the White House*, by AMS, *New York Times*, Oct. 31, 1965.

38 Theodore Sorensen to AMS, Jan. 27, 1966, NYPL 125/6; Jacqueline Kennedy quoted in AMS to "the children," Feb. 21, 1961, AMS Letters, 308.

39 AMS to Jacqueline Kennedy, January 6, 1964, NYPL 102/4.

Chapter Eighteen: The Swinging Soothsayer

1 AMS to Charles Wintour, Dec. 17, 1965, AMS Letters, 305; "A Brief, Not a History," *Newsweek*, Dec. 20, 1965; "The Combative Chronicler," *Time*, Dec. 17, 1965.

Julie Christie was the star of a new film, *Far From the Madding Crowd*, directed by Arthur's British namesake, John Schlesinger.

2 Theodore Sorenson to AMS, May 13, 1965, NYPL 125/6; Peter Kihss, "Pulitzer Drama Prize Omitted; Schlesinger's '1,000 Days' Wins," *New York Times*, May 3, 1966, https://www.nytimes.com/books/00/11/26/specials/schlesinger-pulitzer66 .html; "Schlesinger Captures National Book Award," *Harvard Crimson*, March 17, 1966, http://www.thecrimson.com/article/1966/3/17/schlesinger-captures-national -book-award-parthur/; Albert H. Bowker, CUNY chancellor, to AMS, Feb. 2, 1965, NYPL 299/3; AMS to Jack Blank, CUNY, July 18, 1966, NYPL 128/1.

3 William Shannon, "Controversial Historian of the Age of Kennedy," *New York Times*, Nov. 21, 1965; "The Combative Chronicler," *Time*; AMS to "Dearest Children," Feb. 21, 1966, AMS Letters, 308.

4 Diary entry, July 16, 1965, AMS Journals, 239; AMS to "Dearest Children," Feb. 21, 1966, AMS Letters, 308.

5 "Arthur M. Schlesinger Sr., Historian, Dies at 77," *New York Times*, Oct. 31, 1965, http://www.nytimes.com/books/00/11/26/specials/schlesinger-senior.html; AMS, "A Father Remembered," *Saturday Review*, Nov. 27, 1965.

6 Arthur Schlesinger Sr. to AMS, Jan. 8, 1963, NYPL 293/4; AMS to Marcus Cunliffe, July 9, 1968, AMS Letters, 361.

7 AMS Jr. to Arthur Schlesinger [Sr.], Oct. 25, 1964, NYPL 293/4; AMS to Robert Kennedy, October, 21, 1964, JFKL, Series 3, Box P06, 1964 campaign correspondence 1964, RFK & AMS.

8 Arthur M. Schlesinger [Sr.], *Paths to the Present* (Boston: Houghton Mifflin, 1964), viii; Elizabeth Schlesinger to AMS, undated [c. 1964], NYPL Schlesinger Papers, 294.

9 Marcus Cunliffe and Robin Winks, eds., "Arthur M. Schlesinger, Jr." in *Pastmasters: Some Essays on American Historians* (New York: Harper & Row, 1969), 347–348; Marian Cannon Schlesinger, interview with author, March 9, 2014.

10 AMS to George Elsey, Dec. 21, 1965, NYPL 512/5; Christina Schlesinger, interview with author, April 16, 2014.

11 Marian Cannon Schlesinger, interview with author, March 9, 2014.

12 Christina Schlesinger, interview with author, April 16, 2014; Robert Schlesinger, email to author, Nov. 27, 2016.

13 Marian Cannon Schlesinger to AMS, undated [c. 1965], NYPL 515/2; AMS to Elizabeth Schlesinger, June 13, 1966, NYPL 294.

14 Andrew Schlesinger, interview with author, March 9, 2014; Christina Schlesinger, interview with author, Apr. 16, 2014; Marian Cannon Schlesinger, interview with

author, March 9, 2014; Marie Brenner, "Marietta Tree: Serious Money," *Vanity Fair*, Dec. 1991.

15 AMS to Elizabeth Schlesinger, June 13, 1966, NYPL 294.

16 AMS to Adolf A. Berle, May 2, 1966, NYPL 12/2; AMS to David M. Brown (Dean, University of Minnesota Medical School), Sept. 2, 1986, NYPL 18/5; AMS to "Dearest Children," Feb. 21, 1966, AMS Letters, 308; AMS to "Dearest Children," Oct. 2, 1966, NYPL 299/7; AMS to Gretchen Stewart, July 11, 1970, NYPL 531.

17 AMS to "Dearest Children," Oct. 2, 1966, NYPL 299/7; AMS to John Blum, March 25, 1966, NYPL 15/4; AMS to Dean Acheson, Sept. 21, 1967, NYPL 01/4; AMS, "Origins of the Cold War," *Foreign Affairs* 46 (1967): 22–52; AMS to "Dearest Children," Feb. 19, 1968, NYPL 299/7; Walter LaFeber, interview with author, June 4, 2014.

18 AMS, *The Politics of Hope and The Bitter Heritage: American Liberalism in the 1960s* (Princeton, NJ: Princeton University Press, 2008), ed. Sean Wilentz, vii–viii, 520; Louis B. Zimmer, *The Vietnam War Debate: Hans J. Morgenthau and the Attempt to Halt the Drift Into Disaster* (Lanham, MD: Lexington Books, 2011), 150, 347; AMS to George Kennan, Oct. 23, 1967, NYPL 176/3.

19 "New York: Swinging Soothsayer," *Time*, March 3, 1967.

20 AMS to RFK, June 18, 1964, Sept. 28, 1964, JFKL, AMS Series 3, Box P06, 1964 campaign correspondence, RFK & AMS; Ronnie Eldridge, "The Carpetbagger, 1964," *New York Times*, Feb. 23, 1999, http://www.nytimes.com/1999/02/23/opinion/the-carpetbagger-1964.html.

21 Diary entries, Dec. 5, 1963, July 28, 1967, AMS Journals, 213; Zimmer, *The Vietnam War Debate*, 150. On RFK's decision to run in 1968, see Thurston Clarke, *The Last Campaign: Robert F. Kennedy and 82 Days That Inspired America* (New York: Henry Holt, 2008), 19–38.

22 AMS to Robert Kennedy, Nov. 3, Dec. 13, 1967, NYPL 77/6; diary entries, Dec. 10, 1967, January 25, 30, 1968, AMS Journals, 268–276.

23 Diary entry, March 17, 1968, AMS Journals, 283.

24 Diary entry, March 19, 1968, AMS Journals, 285.

25 Diary entry, March 17, 1968, AMS Journals, 283.

26 AMS to Robert Kennedy, "The Old Politics and the New," Apr. 9, 1968, NYPL 183/4.

27 Diary entries, April 3, 24, May 5, 1968, AMS Journals, 286.

28 Clarke, *The Last Campaign*, 272.

29 Diary entry, June 9, 1968, AMS Journals, 290–295.

30 Ibid.

31 Diary entry, May 5, 1968, AMS Journals, 288.

32 Diary entry, June 9, 1970, AMS Journals, 322–323.

33 Larry Ceplair and Christopher Trumbo, *Dalton Trumbo: Blacklisted Hollywood Radical* (Lexington: University Press of Kentucky, 2015), 478; diary entry, June 9, 1970, AMS Journals, 322–323.

34 Steven V. Roberts, "Schlesinger and Hughes: Observations On Left Politics," *Harvard Crimson*, Feb. 26, 1963, http://www.thecrimson.com/article/1963/2/26/schlesinger-and-hughes-observations-on-left/; AMS, "America 1968: The Politics of Violence," *Harper's Magazine*, August 1968, quoted in Stephen P. Depoe, *Arthur M. Schlesinger Jr., and the Ideological History of American Liberalism* (Tuscaloosa: University of Alabama Press, 1994), 96–97 passim.

35 AMS, *The Imperial Presidency* (Boston: Houghton Mifflin, 1973); AMS, *Robert Kennedy and His Times* (Boston: Houghton Mifflin, 1978); diary entry, December 31, 1969, AMS Journals, 318; diary entry, July 8, 1972, AMS Journals, 354.

Chapter Nineteen: A Long Time Ago

1 AMS to Edward Chase, June 7, 1968; AMS to Ethel Kennedy and Edward Kennedy, June 20, 1968; AMS to Ethel Kennedy, July 16, 1968, NYPL 77/7.

2 AMS to Jacqueline Kennedy, July 24, 1968; AMS to Ethel Kennedy, Feb. 18, 1969; Burke Marshall to AMS, Feb. 18, 1969, NYPL 77/7.

3 For example, the eleven-page exchange on contemporary foreign policy and the origins of the Cold War: George F. Kennan to AMS, Aug. 10, Oct. 17, 1967; AMS to George F. Kennan, Sept. 6, Oct. 23, 1967, NYPL 176/3.

4 Diary entry, Aug. 13, 1973, AMS Journals, 374.

5 AMS, *The Imperial Presidency*, 114–115, 118, 122.

6 Ibid., 126–128, 150, 173.

7 Ibid., 178, 184–185.

8 See Sidney Warren, review of *The Imperial Presidency*, by AMS, *Journal of American History* 61, no. 4 (1975): 1156–1157, http://www.jstor.org/stable/1890722; Donald R. Wolfensberger, "The Return of the Imperial Presidency?" *The Wilson Quarterly* 26, no. 2 (2002): 36–41, http://www.jstor.org/stable/40260602; AMS, *The Imperial Presidency*, 208, 216.

9 AMS, *The Imperial Presidency*, 269, 273, 277, 417; diary entry, Dec. 18, 1986, AMS Journals.

10 Garry Wills, "A Pattern of Rising Power," review of *The Imperial Presidency*, by AMS, *New York Times*, Nov. 18, 1973, http://www.nytimes.com/books/00/11/26/specials/schlesinger-imperial.html; Alfred Kazin, "No, Thank You, Mr. President," *New York Review of Books*, Dec. 13, 1973, http://www.nybooks.com/

articles/1973/12/13/no-thank-you-mr-president/; Jonathan Aitken to AMS, June 29, 1976, NYPL 01/5. Examples of positive academic reviews of *The Imperial Presidency* include: Harold A. Larrabee, *New England Quarterly* 47, no. 1 (1974): 132–135; D. K. Adams, *International Affairs* 50, no. 4 (1974): 682–684, http://www.jstor.org/stable/2615984.

11 AMS to James MacGregor Burns, Jan. 6, 1976, NYPL 20/5; diary entry, Jan. 1, 1975, Jan. 1, 1978, AMS Journals, 392, 443; AMS to Isaiah Berlin, Oct. 17, 1977, NYPL 12/3–5; AMS, *Robert Kennedy and His Times* (Boston: Houghton Mifflin, 1978).

12 AMS, *Robert Kennedy and His Times*, 1–2.

13 Ibid., xiii, 101, 896.

14 Ibid., 68, 110, 139.

15 Ibid., 610–629.

16 Ibid., 619, 651, 936–939; diary entry, June 9, 1968, AMS Journals, 294.

17 Garry Wills, "Fierce in His Loyalties and Enmities," review of *Robert Kennedy and His Times,* by AMS, *New York Times,* Nov. 12, 1978, http://www.nytimes.com/books/00/11/26/specials/schlesinger-robert.html; Marshall Frady, "The Transformation of Bobby Kennedy," review of *Robert Kennedy and His Times,* by AMS, *New York Review of Books,* Oct. 12, 1978, http://www.nybooks.com/articles/1978/10/12/the-transformation-of-bobby-kennedy/; Stephen B. Oates, "Tribune of the Underclass," review of *Robert Kennedy and His Times,* by AMS, *American History* 7, no. 2 (1979): 286–292, http://www.jstor.org/stable/2701107; diary entry, June 9, 1968, AMS Journals, 294; AMS, *Robert Kennedy and His Times,* 610.

18 Michael Dobbs, *One Minute to Midnight: Kennedy, Khrushchev, and Castro on the Brink of Nuclear War* (New York: Alfred A. Knopf, 2008), 154–155; AMS, *Robert Kennedy and His Times,* 515, 545–546.

19 AMS to Stewart Alsop, Oct. 15, 1969, NYPL 02/5.

20 AMS to J. K. Galbraith, May 9, 1977, NYPL 19/5; *New York Post,* May 3, 1977.

21 Joseph Alsop to AMS, April 4, 1975, NYPL 02/5.

22 J. H. Plumb, *The Collected Essays of* J. H. *Plumb,* vol. II, *The American Experience* (Athens: University of Georgia Press, 1989), 131; Daniel T. Rodgers, *Age of Fracture* (Cambridge, MA: Belknap Press of Harvard University Press, 2011), 5–7.

23 Diary entry, Sept. 21, 1978, AMS Journals, 452.

Chapter Twenty: Being Arthur Schlesinger

1 AMS to Isaiah Berlin, Oct. 17, 1977, NYPL 12/3–5; AMS to Ely, Bartlett, Brown & Proctor law firm, April 12, 1970; AMS to Marian Cannon Schlesinger, Sept. 10,

1970 & draft; Hill & Barlow law firm to AMS, Nov. 10, 1971, NYPL 519/2; AMS to "Dearest Children," June 27, 1972, NYPL 516/9.

2 AMS to "Dearest Children," June 27, 1972, NYPL 516/9; Katharine Schlesinger to AMS, July 9, 1969, NYPL 511/1.

3 Katharine Schlesinger to AMS, June 16, 1969, NYPL 510/1; Christina Schlesinger, interview with author, Apr. 16, 2014.

4 Marian Cannon Schlesinger, interview with author, March 9, 2014; Walter LaFeber, interview with author, June 4, 2014; Alexandra Emmet Schlesinger, interview with author, June 17, 2015.

5 Peter Allan, interview with author, Dec. 19, 2014; closing statement on 171 E. 64th Street, NYPL 516/3–8.

6 Robert Schlesinger, interview with author, Nov. 14, 2016.

7 Alexandra Emmet Schlesinger, interview with author, June 17, 2015; Christina Schlesinger, emails to author, Oct. 26–28, 2016.

8 Christina Schlesinger to AMS, Aug. 24, Sept. 10, 1977, NYPL 293/5; Christina Schlesinger, email to author, Oct. 26, 2016; Alexandra Emmet Schlesinger, interview with author, June 17, 2015.

9 Elizabeth Bancroft Schlesinger to AMS, undated [1970s], NYPL 514/3; Marian Cannon Schlesinger, interview with author, Mar. 9, 2014; diary entry, June 1, 1977, AMS Journals, 431.

10 Diary entry, June 1, 1977, AMS Journals, 431–432; diary entry, Oct. 15, 1977, AMS Journals, 435.

11 Sandra Hochman, "Arthur Schlesinger Halfway Through His Book on Bobby and Enjoying His Life to the Hilt," *People*, Aug. 16, 1976, http://people.com/archive/arthur-schlesinger-is-halfway-through-his-book-on-bobby-and-enjoying-his-life-to-the-hilt-vol-6-no-7.

12 James Fallows, "Arthur Schlesinger Jr.," *The Atlantic*, Mar. 2007.

13 AMS to J. K. Galbraith, June 21, 1976, NYPL 49/3; diary entry, July 21, 1992, AMS Journals, 725; Fallows, "Arthur Schlesinger Jr."

14 AMS to Bill Clinton, Feb. 6, 1994, NYPL 8/1; diary entry, Aug. 13, 1980, AMS Journals, 499; AMS to Michael Dukakis, Sept. 1, 1988, NYPL 38/5; "Arthur Schlesinger Tells of J.F.K. Remembered on a Sunny Autumn Saturday in Boston," *People*, Nov. 5, 1979; Robert Schlesinger, interview with author, Nov. 14, 2016.

15 Diary entries, Oct. 3, 5, 1979, AMS Journals, 474–475.

16 Jonathan Aitken to AMS, June 29, 1976, NYPL 01/5; diary entry, March 4, 1980, AMS Journals, 490; Robert Thomas Jr., "Nixons Reported to Have Bought East Side House," *New York Times*, Oct. 5, 1979, http://www.nytimes.com/1979/10/05/archives/nixons-reported-to-have-bought-east-side-house-drop-condominium

.html; Kevin Coyne, "Final Days for a Moldy Nixon Retreat," *New York Times,* May 6, 2007, http://www.nytimes.com/2007/05/06/nyregion/nyregionspecial2/06colnj.html.

17 AMS, *The Cycles of American History* (Boston: Mariner Books, 1986); Hugh Brogan, review of *The Cycles of American History,* by AMS, *Reviews in American History* 15, no. 4 (1987): 521–526, http://www.jstor.org/stable/2701925; Arthur Schlesinger (Sr.), *Paths to the Present* (New York: Macmillan, 1964); AMS, *The Cycles of American History,* 24–25, 45; Benjamin Barber, "America as a Monumental Gamble," review of *The Cycles of American History,* by AMS, *New York Times,* Nov. 16, 1986, http://www.nytimes.com/1986/11/16/books/america-as-a-monumental-gamble.html?pagewanted=all.

18 See Frank Freidel, review of *The Cycles of American History,* by AMS, *The American Historical Review* 93, no. 1 (1988): 213–214, http://www.jstor.org/stable/1865820; AMS, *The Cycles of American History,* 16; George F. Kennan, "In the American Mirror," *New York Review of Books,* Nov. 6, 1986, http://www.nybooks.com/articles/1986/11/06/in-the-american-mirror.

19 AMS, *The Disuniting of America: Reflections on a Multicultural Society* (New York: W. W. Norton, 1998 revised edition), 13, 19, 98–99, 125, 147.

20 Frank Kermode, "Whose History Is Bunk?" *New York Times,* Feb. 23, 1992, http://www.nytimes.com/1992/02/23/books/whose-history-is-bunk.html; Douglas Martin, "Arthur Schlesinger, Historian of Power, Dies at 89," *New York Times,* March 1, 2007; Heather MacDonald, review of *The Disuniting of America,* by AMS, *Commentary,* June 1, 1992, https://www.commentarymagazine.com/articles/the-disuniting-of-america-by-arthur-m-schlesinger-jr; diary entry, Feb. 25, 1991, AMS Journals, 704.

21 "Happy Birthday Arthur"; AMS, "75," Oct. 15, 1992, NYPL 523/3.

22 Publishing Agreement, Dec. 15, 1993, NYPL 172/6; diary entry, Nov. 4, 2000, AMS Journals, 855; "The Education of an American Liberal," *Economist,* Oct. 26, 2000, http://www.economist.com/node/404588; AMS, *A Life in the 20th Century: Innocent Beginnings, 1917–1950* (Boston: Houghton Mifflin, 2000).

23 AMS, *War and the American Presidency* (New York: W. W. Norton, 2005); Angelo Codevilla, "Get Serious," review of *War and the American Presidency,* by AMS, *Claremont Review of Books* 10, no. 2 (2005), http://www.claremont.org/crb/article/get-serious/; Kevin Drum, "'War and the American Presidency': Dire Conclusions," *New York Times,* Sept. 5, 2004, http://www.nytimes.com/2004/09/05/books/review/war-and-the-american-presidency-dire-conclusions.html.

24 Diary entry, June 10, 1971, AMS Journals, 337; AMS to Robert Schlesinger, Nov. 10, 1991, NYPL 299/4.

25 AMS, "Forgetting Reinhold Niebuhr," *New York Times*, Sept. 18, 2005, http://www
.nytimes.com/2005/09/18/books/review/forgetting-reinhold-niebuhr.html?_r=0.

26 Jordan Michael Smith, "The Philosopher of the Post-9/11 Era," *Slate*, Oct. 17, 2011,
http://www.slate.com/articles/arts/books/2011/10/john_diggins_why_niebuhr_
now_reviewed_how_did_he_become_the_phil.html.

27 Caro quoted in Hillel Italie, "Arthur Schlesinger Remembered," *Boston Globe*,
March 1, 2007, http://archive.boston.com/ae/theater_arts/articles/2007/03/01/
arthur_schlesinger_remembered.

28 Robert B. Semple Jr., "A Historian's Valedictory," *New York Times*, March 2, 2007,
http://www.nytimes.com/2007/03/02/opinion/02fri4.html; AMS, "Forgetting
Reinhold Niebuhr"; AMS, "History's Folly," *New York Times*, Jan. 1, 2007, http://
www.nytimes.com/2007/01/01/opinion/01schlesinger.html.

Epilogue: Rewriting History

1 AMS, "Orestes Brownson: A Pilgrim's Progress" (undergraduate thesis, Harvard University, 1938), Harvard University Archives, 1; Christopher Hitchens,
"The Courtier," *The Atlantic* (Dec. 2007), http://www.theatlantic.com/magazine/
archive/2007/12/the-courtier/306429/; May quoted in Vivek Viswanathan, "Arthur
M. Schlesinger, Jr. and the Kennedy Legacy in American Politics, 1964-1980
(M.Phil thesis, University of Cambridge, 2010), 108; Joseph Lelyveld, "The Adventures of Arthur," *New York Review of Books*, Nov. 8, 2007, http://www.nybooks
.com/articles/2007/11/08/the-adventures-of-arthur/.

2 David Greenberg, "Not Just Camelot's Historian," *Slate*, March 1, 2007, http://
www.slate.com/articles/news_and_politics/obit/2007/03/not_just_camelots_
historian.html; C. Vann Woodward to AMS, March 1, 1961, *The Letters of C. Vann
Woodward*, ed. Michael O'Brien (New Haven, CT: Yale University Press, 2013),
216.

3 Alexander Star, "His Liberal Imagination," Q&A with AMS, *New York Times*,
Nov. 26, 2000, http://www.nytimes.com/books/00/11/26/reviews/001126.26int
.html; AMS to Christina Schlesinger, Nov. 24, 1968, NYPL 293/5.

4 AMS diaries, May 25, 1937, NYPL 309 (volume 5).

5 AMS, "The Historian as Participant," *Daedalus* 100, no. 2 (1971): 353-355, http://
www.jstor.org/stable/20024007; *The Works of Edward Gibbon: Autobiography*, ed.
John Murray (New York: DeFau & Company, 1907), 336.

6 Robert H. Ferrell, "C. Vann Woodward," in *Clio's Favorites: Leading Historians of
the United States, 1945-2000*, ed. Robert Allen Rutland (Columbia: University of
Missouri Press, 2000), 175; David S. Brown, *Richard Hofstadter: An Intellectual
Biography* (Chicago: University of Chicago Press, 2006), 138-139.

7 Barton J. Bernstein, *Towards A New Past: Dissenting Essays in American History* (New York: Vintage Books, 1969), v–vi.

8 *The Clinton Tapes: Wrestling History with the President,* ed. Taylor Branch (New York: Simon and Schuster, 2009), 32–33.

9 Brown, *Richard Hofstadter,* 57.

10 Christopher Lasch, "The Cultural Cold War: A Short History of the Congress for Cultural Freedom," in *Towards A New Past,* 354; Marcus Cunliffe, "Arthur M. Schlesinger Jr.," in *Pastmasters: Some Essays on American Historians,* ed. Marcus Cunliffe and Robin Winks (New York: Harper and Row, 1969), 369–371; Richard Reeves, *President Kennedy: Profile of Power* (New York: Simon and Schuster, 1994), 18; Branch, *The Clinton Tapes,* 35.

11 AMS, "The Historian and History," *Foreign Affairs* (Apr. 1963), https://www.foreignaffairs.com/articles/1963-04-01/historian-and-history; AMS, "The Historian as Participant," *Daedalus* 100, no. 2 (1971): 353–355, http://www.jstor.org/stable/20024007.

12 Tevi Troy, *Intellectuals and the American Presidency* (Lanham, MD: Rowman and Littlefield, 2002), 48–74; Edmund Morris, *Dutch: A Memoir of Ronald Reagan* (London: HarperCollins, 2000); Branch, *The Clinton Tapes.*

13 AMS, "On Making Eighty," NYPL 524/3.

WORKS CITED

Primary Sources

Arthur M. Schlesinger Jr. Papers. Manuscripts and Archives Division. The New York Public Library. Astor, Lenox, and Tilden Foundations.

    Series I: Correspondence. 1923–2007.

        I.A: Alphabetical Correspondence, 1934–2006.

        I.B: Subject Correspondence, 1950s–1990s.

        I.F: Family Correspondence, 1923–2006.

    Series II: Journals, circa 1930, 1950–2003.

    Series V: Personal and Family Files. 1922–2007.

Arthur M. Schlesinger Jr. Personal Papers. John F. Kennedy Presidential Library and Museum.

    Series I: Personal Files

        Alphabetical Subject File, 1960–1965.

        Incoming Correspondence, 1945–1960.

    Series II: White House Files

        Chronological File, 1961–1964.

        Remarks for the President, 1961–1963.

        Classified Chronological File, 1961–1964.

Secondary Sources

Abramson, Rudy. *Spanning the Century: The Life of Averell Harriman, 1891–1986*. New York: William Morrow, 1992.

Adams, D. K. Review of *The Imperial Presidency*, by Arthur M. Schlesinger Jr. *International Affairs* 50, no. 4 (1974): 682–684, http://www.jstor.org/stable/2615984.

Allan, Peter. Interview with Richard Aldous. Personal interview. December 19, 2014.

Allen, Craig. *Eisenhower and the Mass Media: Peace, Prosperity, and Prime-time TV.* Chapel Hill: University of North Carolina Press, 1993.

Alsop, Stewart. *Stay of Execution: A Sort of Memoir.* Philadelphia: J. B. Lippincott, 1973.

Alsop, Stewart, and Charles Bartlett. "In Time of Crisis." *Saturday Evening Post,* December 12, 1962, http://www.saturdayeveningpost.com/wp-content/uploads/satevepost/1962-12-08-missile-crisis.pdf.

Altman, Lawrence. "In J.F.K. File, Hidden Illness, Pain and Pills." *New York Times.* November 17, 2002. http://www.nytimes.com/2002/11/17/us/in-jfk-file-hidden-illness-pain-and-pills.html?_r=0.

Ambrose, Stephen. *Eisenhower: The President.* New York: Simon and Schuster, 1984.

Anderson, Patrick. *The President's Men: White House Assistants.* New York: Doubleday, 1968.

"Annotated Draft of Kennedy's Convocation Speech, prepared by Arthur Schlesinger, Jr." Amherst College Archives and Special Collections. October 26, 1963. https://www.amherst.edu/library/archives/exhibitions/kennedy/documents#Draft.

Anson, Robert Sam. *McGovern.* New York: Holt, Rinehart and Winston, 1972.

"Appeasement at Munich." *HOLLIS Catalog.* http://id.lib.harvard.edu/aleph/003744011/catalog.

Aptowitz, Arthur D. "Letter." *New York Times Sunday Book Review.* January 22, 2014.

"Arthur M. Schlesinger Sr., Historian, Dies at 77," *New York Times,* Oct. 31, 1965.

"Arthur Schlesinger Tells of J.F.K. Remembered on a Sunny Autumn Saturday in Boston." *People.* November 5, 1979.

"At Home and Abroad." *New York Times.* August 8, 1965.

"Background Books: The New Deal." *The Wilson Quarterly* 6, no. 2 (1982): 94–97. http://www.jstor.org/stable/40256267.

Baker, Richard Brown. *The Year of the Buzz Bomb: A Journal of London, 1944.* Pickle Partners Publishing, Kindle Formatted edition, 2015.

Baldwin, Bird. *University of Iowa Studies In Child Welfare.* Iowa City: University of Iowa, 1921.

Barber, Benjamin. "America as a Monumental Gamble." Review of *The Cycles of American History,* by Arthur M. Schlesinger Jr. *New York Times.* November 16, 1986. http://www.nytimes.com/1986/11/16/books/america-as-a-monumental-gamble.html?pagewanted=all.

Barrass, Gordon S. *The Great Cold War: A Journey Through the Hall of Mirrors.* Stanford, CA: Stanford University Press, 2009.

Bartlett, Robert. *Why Can the Dead Do Such Great Things: Saints and Worshipers from the Martyrs to the Reformation*. Princeton, NJ: Princeton University Press, 2013.

Barzun, Jacques. "Reminiscences of the Columbia History Department 1923–1975." *Living Legacies*. Winter 2000. Accessed September 29, 2015. http://www.columbia .edu/cu/alumni/Magazine/Winter2000/Barzun.html.

Bendiner, Robert. "Ghosts behind the Speechmakers." *New York Times*. Aug. 17, 1952. http://query.nytimes.com/mem/archive/pdf?res=9C07E2DC1039E632A25754C1 A96E9C946392D6CF.

Bentinck-Smith, William. "Samuel Eliot Morison." *Proceedings of the Massachusetts Historical Society* 88 (1976).

Berlin, Isaiah. *Enlightening: Letters, 1946–1960*. Edited by Henry Hardy and Jennifer Holmes. London: Chatto and Windus, 2009.

Berlin, Isaiah. *Letters, 1928–1946*. Edited by Henry Hardy. New York: Cambridge University Press, 2004.

Bernstein, Barton J. *Towards A New Past: Dissenting Essays in American History*. New York: Vintage Books, 1969.

Beschloss, Michael. *Kennedy v. Khrushchev: The Crisis Years 1960–63*. London: Faber, 1991.

Beschloss, Michael, ed. *Reaching for Glory: Lyndon Johnson's Secret White House Tapes, 1964–1965*. New York: Simon and Schuster, 2001.

Bird, Kai. *The Color of Truth: McGeorge Bundy and William Bundy, Brothers in Arms*. New York: Simon and Schuster, 1998.

Blum, John M., William S. McFeely, Edmund S. Morgan, Arthur M. Schlesinger Jr., and Kenneth M. Stampp. *The National Experience: A History of the United States*. New York: Harcourt, Brace and World, 1963.

Boomhower, Ray E. *John Bartlow Martin: A Voice for the Underdog*. Bloomington: Indiana University Press, 2015.

Bradlee, Benjamin C. *Conversations with Kennedy*. New York: Norton, 1975.

Braestrup, Peter. "G.O.P. uses a book scoring Kennedy." *New York Times*. November 2, 1960.

Branch, Taylor, ed. *The Clinton Tapes: Wrestling History with the President*. New York: Simon and Schuster, 2009.

Brandon, Leroy, under the direction of South Trimble, Clerk of the House of Representatives. "Statistics of the Congressional Election of November 6, 1934." US House of Representatives: Office of the Clerk. http://clerk.house.gov/member_ info/electionInfo/1934election.pdf.

Brands, H. W. *The Devil We Knew: Americans and the Cold War*. Oxford: Oxford University Press, 1993.

Brenner, Marie. "Marietta Tree: Serious Money." *Vanity Fair.* December 1991.

Brewer, John. "Educational Guidance." As reprinted in *Los Angeles Educational Research Bulletin: Los Angeles City Schools.* January 7, 1924.

"A Brief, Not a History." *Newsweek.* December 20, 1965.

Brinkley, Alan. *John F. Kennedy.* New York: Times Books/Henry Holt, 2012.

———. "Where Historians Disagree: The Age of Jackson." In *American History: A Survey.* New York: McGraw-Hill, 1995. http://glencoe.mheducation.com/sites/ 0012122005/student_view0/chapter9/where_historians_disagree.html.

Brock, W. R. Review of *The Crisis of the Old Order, 1919–1933,* by Arthur M. Schlesinger Jr. *The Historical* Journal 1 (1958): 89–91. http://www.jstor.org/stable/ 3020375.

Brogan, Hugh. Review of *The Cycles of American History,* by Arthur M. Schlesinger Jr. *Reviews in American History* 15, no. 4 (1987): 521–526. http://www.jstor.org/ stable/2701925.

Brown, David S. *Richard Hofstadter: An Intellectual Biography.* Chicago: University of Chicago Press, 2006.

Brubach, Holly. "Running Around in High Circles." Review of *No Regrets,* by Caroline Seebohm. *New York Times.* November 9, 1997. http://www.nytimes.com/ books/97/11/09/reviews/971109.09brubact.html.

Bruchey, Stuart. *Roots of American Economic Growth 1607–1861: An Essay on Social Causation.* London: Routledge, 2013.

Burke, Robert E. Review of *The Coming of the New Deal, 1933–1935,* by Arthur M. Schlesinger Jr. *The American Historical Review* 65 (1959): 148–150. http://www .jstor.org/stable/1846650, DOI: 10.2307/1846650.

———. Review of *The Politics of Upheaval, 1935–1936,* by Arthur M. Schlesinger Jr. *The American Historical Review* 66, no. 3 (1961): 765–766, DOI: 10.2307/1847026.

Burns, James MacGregor. Review of *A Thousand Days: John F. Kennedy in the White House,* by Arthur M. Schlesinger Jr. *New York Times.* October 31, 1965.

———. Review of *Kennedy,* by Theodore C. Sorensen. *New York Times.* October 31, 1965.

Burstyn, Harold L. Emails to Richard Aldous. January 24, 2015, December 9, 2016.

"Candidates Pressed on Data of Any Ills." *New York Times.* November 6, 1960. http:// timesmachine.nytimes.com/timesmachine/1960/11/06/100888445.html?page Number=132.

Ceplair, Larry, and Christopher Trumbo. *Dalton Trumbo: Blacklisted Hollywood Radical.* Lexington: University Press of Kentucky, 2015.

Chace, James. "The Age of Schlesinger." Review of *A Life in the Twentieth Century: Innocent Beginnings, 1917–1950,* by Arthur M. Schlesinger Jr. *The New York*

Review of Books. December 21, 2000. Accessed September 24, 2015. http://www
.nybooks.com/articles/archives/2000/dec/21/the-age-of-schlesinger.

Chambers, Clarke A. Review of *The Politics of Upheaval, 1935–1936,* by Arthur M.
Schlesinger Jr. *The Mississippi Valley Historical Review* 47, no. 4 (1961): 731–733.
DOI:10.2307/1889643.

"C.I.A. Tie Confirmed by Cultural Group." *New York Times.* May 10, 1967. http://
query.nytimes.com/mem/archive/pdf?res=9804EEDA1E3CE63ABC4852DFB36
6838C679EDE.

Cillizza, Chris. "Newt Gingrich Explains How Donald Trump Happened." *The Washington Post.* December 17, 2015. https://www.washingtonpost.com/news/the-fix/
wp/2015/12/17/newt-gingrich-says-donald-trump-reminds-him-of-andrew-jackson.

Clarke, Thurston. *The Last Campaign: Robert F. Kennedy and 82 Days That Inspired
America.* New York: Henry Holt, 2008.

Codevilla, Angelo. "Get Serious." Review of *War and the American Presidency,* by
Arthur M. Schlesinger Jr. *Claremont Review of Books* 10, no. 2 (2005). http://www
.claremont.org/crb/article/get-serious/.

Cohen, Andrew. *Two Days in June: John F. Kennedy and the 48 Hours That Made History.* New York: Signal, 2014.

Colacello, Bob. *Ronnie and Nancy: Their Path to the White House, 1911 to 1980.* New
York: Warner Books, 2004.

Cold War International History Project. "Was Robert Oppenheimer a Soviet Spy? A
Round Table Discussion." *Woodrow Wilson Center for International Scholars.* July
7, 2011. https://www.wilsoncenter.org/publication/was-oppenheimer-soviet-spy
-roundtable-discussion.

Cole, Donald B. "The Age of Jackson: After Forty Years." Review of *The Age of Jackson,*
by Arthur M. Schlesinger Jr. *American History* 14, no. 1 (1986). http://www.jstor
.org/stable/2702131. DOI: 10.2307/2702131.

"The Combative Chronicler." *Time.* December 17, 1965.

Commager, Henry Steele. "After the Decline and Fall, the Promise of a New Day."
Review of *The Crisis of the Old Order, 1919–1933,* by Arthur M. Schlesinger Jr.
New York Times. March 3, 1957. https://www.nytimes.com/books/00/11/26/
specials/schlesinger-crisis1957.html.

———. "That Sturdy but Erratic Reformer, Orestes Brownson." *New York Times.*
April 23, 1939. https://www.nytimes.com/books/00/11/26/specials/schlesinger
-brownson.html.

———. "Two Years That Shaped Our Lives." *New York Times.* January 4, 1959. http://
www.nytimes.com/books/00/11/26/specials/schlesinger-age2.html.

Cortesi, Arnaldo. "La Paz Regime Out." *New York Times.* December 21, 1943. http://times machine.nytimes.com/timesmachine/1943/12/21/88587204.html?pageNumber=1.

Cowden, Jonathan A. "Self-effacing and Self-defeating Leadership: Adlai E. Stevenson." *Political Psychology* 20, no. 4 (1999): 845–874. http://www.jstor.org/stable/3792197.

Coyne, Kevin. "Final Days for a Moldy Nixon Retreat." *New York Times.* May 6, 2007. http://www.nytimes.com/2007/05/06/nyregion/nyregionspecial2/06colnj.html.

Craig, G. M. Review of *The Coming of the New Deal, 1933–1935,* by Arthur M. Schlesinger Jr. *International Journal* 15, no. 1 (1959–1960): 89–90. http://www.jstor.org/stable/23595822.

———. Review of *The Crisis of the Old Order, 1919–1933,* by Arthur M. Schlesinger Jr. International *Journal* 12, no. 4 (1957): 311–312; http://www.jstor.org/stable/40198360, DOI: 10.2307/40198360.

Cunliffe, Marcus, and Robin Winks, eds. "Arthur M. Schlesinger, Jr." In *Pastmasters: Some Essays on American Historians.* New York: Harper and Row, 1969.

Dallek, Robert. *Camelot's Court: Inside the Kennedy White House.* New York: Harper, 2013.

———. *An Unfinished Life: John F. Kennedy, 1917–1963.* Boston: Little, Brown, 2003.

DeGroot, Gerard. *Dark Side of the Moon: The Magnificent Madness of the American Lunar Quest.* London: Jonathan Cape, 2007.

Depoe, Stephen P. *Arthur M. Schlesinger Jr., and the Ideological History of American Liberalism.* Tuscaloosa: University of Alabama Press, 1994.

Devoto, Bernard. *The Hour: A Cocktail Manifesto.* New York and Portland: Tin House Books, 2010.

Dobbs, Michael. *One Minute to Midnight: Kennedy, Khrushchev, and Castro on the Brink of Nuclear War.* New York: Alfred A. Knopf, 2008.

Drum, Kevin. "'War and the American Presidency': Dire Conclusions." *New York Times.* September 5, 2004. http://www.nytimes.com/2004/09/05/books/review/war-and-the-american-presidency-dire-conclusions.html.

"Dwight D. Eisenhower: Campaigns and Elections." Miller Center, University of Virginia. http://millercenter.org/president/biography/eisenhower-campaigns-and-elections.

Eaton, Clement. Review of *In Retrospect: The History of a Historian,* by Arthur M. Schlesinger Sr. *The Journal of Negro History* 49, no. 3 (July 1964). DOI: 10.2307/2716660.

"The Education of an American Liberal." *Economist.* October 26, 2000. http://www.economist.com/node/404588.

Eldridge, Ronnie. "The Carpetbagger, 1964." *New York Times*. February 23, 1999. http://www.nytimes.com/1999/02/23/opinion/the-carpetbagger-1964.html.

Evans, M. Stanton. *Blacklisted by History: The Untold Story of Senator Joe McCarthy and His Fight Against America's Enemies*. New York: Three Rivers Press, 2007.

Evans, M. Stanton, and Herbert Romerstein. *Stalin's Secret Agents: The Subversion of Roosevelt's Government*. New York: Threshold Editions, 2012.

Fairbank, John King. *Chinabound: A Fifty Year Memoir*. New York: Harper and Row, 1982.

Fallows, James. "Arthur Schlesinger Jr." *The Atlantic*. March 2007.

Farrar, Fletcher. "The Tallest Elk in Springfield." *Illinois Times*. May 4, 2006. http://illinoistimes.com/mobile/articles/articleView/id:2990.

Ferguson, Niall. *Kissinger, 1923–1968: The Idealist*. New York: Penguin Press, 2015.

Fortuin, Nicholas. "Eisenhower's Heart Attack: How Ike beat heart disease and held on to the presidency." *The New England Journal of Medicine* 338 (1998). DOI: 10.1056/NEJM199806043382321.

"Four Harvard Men Are Recipients of the Henry Awards." *Harvard Crimson*. February 14, 1938. http://www.thecrimson.com/article/1938/2/14/four-harvard-men -are-recipients-of.

Frady, Marshall. "The Transformation of Bobby Kennedy." Review of *Robert Kennedy and His Times*, by Arthur M. Schlesinger Jr. *New York Review of Books*. October 12, 1978. http://www.nybooks.com/articles/1978/10/12/the-transformation-of -bobby-kennedy/.

Frank, Florence Kiper. Review of *The Coming of the New Deal, 1933–1935*, by Arthur M. Schlesinger Jr. *The Yale Law Journal* 68, no. 8 (1959): 1723–1727. DOI:10.2307/794381.

Freidel, Frank. Review of *The Cycles of American History*, by Arthur M. Schlesinger Jr. *The American Historical Review* 93, no. 1 (1988): 213–214. http://www.jstor .org/stable/1865820.

Fulbright, William J. *The Arrogance of Power*. New York: Random House, 1966.

Fursenko, Aleksandr, and Timothy Naftali. *"One Hell of a Gamble": Khrushchev, Castro, and Kennedy 1958–1964*. New York: W. W. Norton, 1997.

Gaddis, John Lewis. *George F. Kennan: An American Life*. New York: Penguin Press, 2011.

Galbraith, John Kenneth. *Ambassador's Journal: A Personal Account of the Kennedy Years*. Boston: Houghton Mifflin, 1969.

Giroud, Francis. *Nicolas Nabokov: A Life in Freedom and Music*. Oxford: Oxford University Press, 2015.

Goodman, Walter. *The Committee.* New York: Penguin, 1969.

——. "A Farewell to HUAC." *New York Times.* January 19, 1975. http://query.nytimes.com/mem/archive/pdf?res=9A03E1D7143AE034BC4152DFB766838E669EDE.

Goodwin, Richard N. *Remembering America: A Voice from the Sixties.* Boston: Little, Brown, 1988.

Goshko, John. "Rusk Replies Indirectly to Schlesinger." *Washington Post.* August 3, 1965.

Graham, Katharine. *Personal History.* New York: Alfred A. Knopf, 1997.

Granatstein, J. L. Review of *Cold War Exile: The Unclosed Case of Maurice Halperin,* by Don S. Kirschner. *Political Psychology* 18, no. 2 (1997): 511–514. http://www.jstor.org/stable/3791780.

"The Great Pandemic: The United States in 1918–19." *Center for Disease Control.* http://www.flu.gov/pandemic/history/1918/your_state/midwest/ohio/index.html.

Greenberg, David. "Not Just Camelot's Historian." *Slate.* March 1, 2007. http://www.slate.com/articles/news_and_politics/obit/2007/03/not_just_camelots_historian.html.

Griffith, Robert. "Dwight D. Eisenhower and the Corporate Commonwealth." *The American Historical Review* 87, no. 1 (1982): 87–122. DOI:10.2307/1863309.

Guthman, Edwin O., and Jeffrey Shulman, eds. *Robert Kennedy: In His Own Words.* New York: Bantam Books, 1988.

Haas, Lawrence J. *Harry & Arthur: Truman, Vandenberg and the Partnership that Created the Free World.* Lincoln, NE: Potomac Books, 2016.

Haidt, Jonathan. *The Righteous Mind: Why Good People Are Divided By Politics and Religion.* New York: Vintage, 2013.

Halberstam, David. *The Best and The Brightest.* New York: Ballantine Books, 1993.

Hamby, Alonzo L. *Beyond the New Deal: Harry S. Truman and American Liberalism.* New York: Scribner's, 1971.

Hamilton, Ian. *Robert Lowell.* New York: Vintage, 1983.

Hamilton, Nigel. *JFK: Reckless Youth.* London: Arrow, 1992.

Hammond, Bray. Review of *The Age of Jackson,* by Arthur M. Schlesinger Jr. *The Journal of Economic History* 6, no. 1 (1946): 79–84. http://www.jstor.org/stable/2112998.

Handler, M. S. "Sorensen Tells of Kennedy Fears." *New York Times.* August 14, 1965.

Handlin, Lilian. "George Bancroft." *American National Biography Online.* February 2000. http://www.anb.org/articles/14/14-00034.html.

Hansen, Harry. "Pulitzer Award to Schlesinger for Jackson Book Commended." *Chicago Sunday Tribune.* May 12, 1946. http://archives.chicagotribune.com/1946/05/12/page/106/article/pulitzer-award-to-schlesinger-for-jackson-book-commended.

Haslam, Jonathan. *Near and Distant Neighbors: A New History of Soviet Intelligence.* New York: Farrar, Straus and Giroux, 2015.

Hawes, Joseph M. Review of *Before Head Start: The Iowa Station and America's Children,* by Hamilton Cravens. *History of Education Quarterly* 34, no. 4 (Winter 1994). DOI: 10.2307/369294.

Hemingway, Andrew. *Artists on the Left: American Artists and the Communist Movement, 1926–1956.* New Haven, CT: Yale University Press, 2002.

Herken, Gregg. *The Georgetown Set: Friends and Rivals in Cold War Washington.* New York: Alfred A. Knopf, 2014.

Herman, Arthur. *Douglas MacArthur: American Warrior.* Random House, 2016.

Hersh, Seymour. *The Dark Side of Camelot.* London: HarperCollins, 1998 paperback edition.

Hicks, Granville. Review of *Orestes Brownson: A Pilgrim's Progress,* by Arthur M. Schlesinger Jr. *The New England Quarterly* 12, no. 3 (1939): 582–588. DOI:10.2307/360849.

Hill, Clint. *Mrs. Kennedy and Me.* New York: Gallery Books, 2012.

Hitchens, Christopher. "Brief Shining Moments." *London Review of Books.* February 19, 1998. http://www.lrb.co.uk/v20/n04/christopher-hitchens/brief-shining-moments.

———. "The Courtier." *The Atlantic.* December 2007. http://www.theatlantic.com/magazine/archive/2007/12/the-courtier/306429/.

Hobsbawm, Eric. *Interesting Times: A Twentieth Century Life.* London: Pantheon, 2007. Kindle edition.

Hochman, Sandra. "Arthur Schlesinger Halfway Through His Book on Bobby and Enjoying His Life to the Hilt." *People.* August 16, 1976. http://people.com/archive/arthur-schlesinger-is-halfway-through-his-book-on-bobby-and-enjoying-his-life-to-the-hilt-vol-6-no-7.

Hofstadter, Richard. *Anti-Intellectualism in American Life.* New York: Vintage Books, 1963 edition.

———. "Democracy in the Making." Review of *The Age of Jackson,* by Arthur M. Schlesinger Jr. *New Republic.* October 22, 1945. https://newrepublic.com/article/74429/democracy-the-making.

Holloran, Peter C. Review of *Before Head Start: The Iowa Station and America's Children,* by Hamilton Cravens. *The American Historical Review* 99, no. 5 (1994). DOI: 10.2307/2168549.

Homans, George C., and Orville T. Bailey. "The Society of Fellows, Harvard University, 1933–1947." In *The Society of Fellows.* Edited by Crane Brinton. Cambridge, MA: The Society of Fellows of Harvard University, 1959.

Howe, Daniel. "Goodbye to the 'Age of Jackson'?" *New York Review of Books.* May 28, 2009. http://www.nybooks.com/articles/2009/05/28/goodbye-to-the-age-of -jackson/.

"Hull is Hesitant on Bolivia Regime." *New York Times.* December 23, 1943. http://times machine.nytimes.com/timesmachine/1943/12/23/88588213.html?pageNumber=5.

Hunt, Norman. Review of *The Politics of Upheaval, 1935–1936,* by Arthur M. Schle-singer Jr. *International Affairs* 38 (1962): 132–133. DOI: 10.2307/2611478.

Ignatieff, Michael. *Isaiah Berlin.* London: Vintage, 2000.

"Iowa Child Welfare Research Station, 1917–1974." Iowa City Town and Campus Scenes Digital Collection, University of Iowa Libraries. http://digital.lib.uiowa .edu/ictcs/icwrs.html.

Ireland, Corydon. "Storied Irving Street Paves Way to History." *Harvard Gazette.* May 19, 2016. http://news.harvard.edu/gazette/story/2016/05/storied-irving-street -paves-way-to-history.

Isaacson, Walter, and Evan Thomas. *The Wise Men: Six Friends and the World They Made.* New York: Simon and Schuster, 2013 edition.

Italie, Hillel. "Arthur Schlesinger Remembered." *Boston Globe.* March 1, 2007. http:// archive.boston.com/ae/theater_arts/articles/2007/03/01/arthur_schlesinger _remembered.

"James Rousmaniere, 86, Skilled Yachtsman, Dies." *New York Times.* October 31, 2004. http://www.nytimes.com/2004/10/31/nyregion/james-rousmaniere-86 -skilled-yachtsman-dies.html?_r=0.

Jeffreys-Jones, Rhodri. *In Spies We Trust: The Story of Western Intelligence.* Oxford: Oxford University Press, 2013.

Johnson, Gerald. "In Defense of Liberalism." *New York Times.* September 1949. http:// query.nytimes.com/gst/abstract.html?res=9507E3DE113DE03ABC4952DFBF668 382659EDE&legacy=true.

Johnson, Gertrude G. "Manpower Selection and the Preventative Medicine Program." Office of Medical History: US Army Medical Department. http://history.amedd .army.mil/booksdocs/wwii/PrsnlHlthMsrs/chapter1.htm.

Johnson, Walter, et al., eds. *The Papers of Adlai Stevenson.* 8 vols. Boston: Little, Brown, 1972–1979.

Kalb, Deborah, Gerard D. Peters, and John Turner Woolley, eds. *State of the Union: Presidential Rhetoric from Woodrow Wilson to George W. Bush.* Washington, DC: CQ Press, 2006.

Katz, Barry M. *Foreign Intelligence: Research and Analysis in the OSS, 1942–1945.* Cambridge, MA: Harvard University Press, 1989.

Kazin, Alfred. "No, Thank You, Mr. President." *New York Review of Books*. Dec. 13, 1973. http://www.nybooks.com/articles/1973/12/13/no-thank-you-mr-president/.

Keller, Morton. "The New Deal: A New Look." *Polity* 31, no. 4 (1999): 657–663. DOI: 10.2307/3235241.

Keller, Morton, and Phyllis Keller. *Making Harvard Modern: The Rise of America's Universities*. New York: Oxford University Press, 2007.

Kelsey, R. W. Review of *New Viewpoints in American History*, by Arthur Meier Schlesinger. *The American Historical Review* 28, no. 1 (1922).

Kempe, Frederick. *Berlin 1961: Kennedy, Khrushchev, and the Most Dangerous Place on Earth*. New York: Putnam's, 2011.

Kennan, George F. "In the American Mirror." *New York Review of Books*. November 6, 1986. http://www.nybooks.com/articles/1986/11/06/in-the-american-mirror/.

———. *The Kennan Diaries*. Edited by *Frank Costigliola*. New York: W. W. Norton, 2013.

Kennedy, John F. "Commencement Address at Yale University, New Haven, Connecticut, 11 June 1962." John F. Kennedy Presidential Library and Museum. June 11, 1962. http://www.jfklibrary.org/Asset-Viewer/Archives/JFKWHA-104.aspx.

———. "Remarks at Amherst College, October 26, 1963." John F. Kennedy Presidential Library and Museum. October 26, 1963. https://www.jfklibrary.org/Asset-Viewer/80308LXB5kOPFEJqkw5hlA.aspx.

Kennedy, Paul. *The Rise and Fall of the Great Powers*. London: Fontana Press, 1989.

"The Kennedy Blitzkrieg." *New York Times*. August 22, 1964. http://www.nytimes.com/1964/08/22/the-kennedy-blitzkrieg.html?_r=0.

Kenworthy, E. W. "Kennedy Helps Draft Appeal on 'Struggle' for Hemisphere." *New York Times*. April 4, 1961.

Kermode, Frank. "Whose History Is Bunk?" *New York Times*. February 23, 1992. http://www.nytimes.com/1992/02/23/books/whose-history-is-bunk.html.

Kiernan, Frances. *Seeing Mary Plain: A Life of Mary McCarthy*. New York: W. W. Norton, 2000.

Kihss, Peter. "Pulitzer Drama Prize Omitted; Schlesinger's '1,000 Days' Wins." *New York Times*. May 3, 1966. https://www.nytimes.com/books/00/11/26/specials/schlesinger-pulitzer66.html.

Kinzer, Stephen. *The Brothers: John Foster Dulles, Allen Dulles, and Their Secret World War*. New York: Times Books/Henry Holt, 2013.

Kirkland, Edward C. Review of *In Retrospect: The History of a Historian*, by Arthur M. Schlesinger. *The New England Quarterly* 37, no. 2 (1964).

Kirschner, Don S. *Cold War Exile: The Unclosed Case of Maurice Halperin*. Columbia: University of Missouri Press, 1995.

Kmiec, Keenan D. "The Origin and Current Meanings of Judicial Activism." *California Law Review* 92 (2004). http://scholarship.law.berkeley.edu/californialawreview/vol92/iss5/4. DOI: 10.15779/Z38X71D.

Krebs, Albin. "Chester Bowles is Dead at 85; Served in 4 Administrations." *New York Times*. May 26, 1986. http://www.nytimes.com/1986/05/26/obituaries/chester -bowles-is-dead-at-85-served-in-4-administrations.html?pagewanted=all.

Krueger, Thomas A. "New Deal Historiography at Forty." *American History* 3, no. 4 (1975): 483–488. DOI:10.2307/2701507.

LaFantasie, Glenn W., ed. "Foreign Relations of the United States, 1961–1963, vol. 2, Vietnam, 1962." United States Department of State: Office of the Historian. https://history.state.gov/historicaldocuments/frus1961-63v02/d142.

LaFeber, Walter. Interview with Richard Aldous. Personal interview. June 4, 2014.

"The Laos Crisis, 1960–1963." United States Department of State: Office of the Historian. https://history.state.gov/milestones/1961-1968/laos-crisis.

Larrabee, Harold A. Review of *The Imperial Presidency*, by Arthur M. Schlesinger. *New England Quarterly* 47, no. 1 (1974): 132–135.

Lash, Joseph, ed. *From the Diaries of Felix Frankfurter*. New York: Norton, 1975.

Lasky, Victor. *John F. Kennedy: What's Behind the Image*. Washington, DC: Free World, 1960.

Last Year in Marienbad. Directed by Alain Resnais. Cocinor. 1961. http://www.imdb .com/title/tt0054632.

Lawrence, W. H. "Johnson Backers Urge Health Test." *New York Times*. July 5, 1960. http://timesmachine.nytimes.com/timesmachine/1960/07/05/99503749.html ?pageNumber=19.

Leaming, Barbara. *Mrs. Kennedy: The Missing History of the Kennedy Years*. New York: The Free Press, 2001.

Leapman, Michael. "Obituary: Charles Wintour." *The Independent*. November 4, 1999. http://www.independent.co.uk/arts-entertainment/obituary-charles-wintour -1123476.html.

LeDuc, Thomas. Review of *The Crisis of the Old Order*, by Arthur M. Schlesinger Jr. *Journal of Southern History* 23, no. 3 (1957): 405–406. http://www.jstor.org/ stable/2954908. DOI: 10.2307/2954908.

Lelyveld, Joseph. "The Adventures of Arthur." *New York Review of Books*. Nov. 8, 2007. http://www.nybooks.com/articles/2007/11/08/the-adventures-of-arthur/.

Lemann, Nicholas. *The Big Test: The Secret History of the American Meritocracy*. New York: Farrar, Straus and Giroux, 2000.

Lennon, J. Michael. *Norman Mailer: A Double Life*. New York: Simon and Schuster, 2013.

Lepore, Jill. "Plymouth Rocked: Of Pilgrims, Puritans, and Professors." *The New Yorker*. April 24, 2006. http://www.newyorker.com/magazine/2006/04/24/plymouth -rocked.

Lerche, Charles O., Jr. Review of *The Vital Center*, by Arthur M. Schlesinger Jr. *The Western Political Quarterly* 3, no. 2 (1950): 292–294. http://www.jstor.org/ stable/443514. DOI: 10.2307/443514.

Leuchtenburg, William E. Review of *The Crisis of the Old Order, 1919–1933*, by Arthur M. Schlesinger Jr. *Political Science Quarterly* 73, no. 3 (1958): 460–463. http://www.jstor.org/stable/2145855. DOI:10.2307/2145855.

———. *The Wall Street Journal*. January 8, 2016. http://www.wsj.com/articles/william -leuchtenburg-1452278787.

Lewis, Paul. "Harry Rositzke, 91, Linguist and American Spymaster." *New York Times*. November 8, 2002. http://www.nytimes.com/2002/11/08/us/harry-rositzke-91 -linguist-and-american-spymaster.html.

Logevall, Fredrik. *Embers of War: The Fall of an Empire and the Making of America's Vietnam*. New York: Random House, 2012.

Loss, Christopher P. "Educating Global Citizens in the Cold War." In *In Between Citizens and the State: The Politics of American Higher Education in the 20th Century*. Princeton, NJ: Princeton University Press, 2012. http://www.jstor.org/ stable/j.ctt7shbr.9.

Luce, Henry. "Fortune Prospectus." *Fortune*. September 1, 1929. http://fortune .com/1929/09/01/fortune-prospectus-september-1929-volume-one-number-zero/.

Lytle, Mark. Email to author. Personal email. November 10, 2016.

MacDonald, Heather. Review of *The Disuniting of America*, by Arthur M. Schlesinger Jr. *Commentary*. June 1, 1992. https://www.commentarymagazine.com/articles/ the-disuniting-of-america-by-arthur-m-schlesinger-jr.

MacNiven, Ian S. *"Literchoor Is My Beat": A Life of James Laughlin, Publisher of New Directions*. New York: Farrar, Strauss and Giroux, 2014.

MacPherson, Nelson. *American Intelligence in Wartime London: The Story of OSS*. London: Routledge, 2014.

Manchester, William. *The Death of a President: November 1963*. New York: Harper and Row, 1967.

Mansheim, Gerald. *Iowa City: An Illustrated History*. Norfolk, VA: Donning, 1989.

Marsden, George M. *The Twilight of the American Enlightenment: The 1950s and the Crisis of Liberal Belief*. New York: Basic Books, 2014.

Marshall, S. L. A. "The MacArthur of Fact, Legend and Just Plain Myth." Review of *The General and the President: The Future of American Foreign Policy,* by Arthur M. Schlesinger Jr. *New York Times.* October 28, 1951. http://query.nytimes .com/mem/archive/pdf?res=9E05E2DD1F39E23ABC4051DFB667838A649EDE.

Martin, Douglas. "Arthur Schlesinger, Historian of Power, Dies at 89." *New York Times.* February 28, 2007. http://www.nytimes.com/2007/02/28/washington/28cnd -schlesinger.html?pagewanted=1&_r=0.

Martin, John Bartlow. *Adlai Stevenson and the World: The Life of Adlai E. Stevenson.* New York: Doubleday, 1977.

May, Ernest, and Philip D. Zelikow, eds. *The Kennedy Tapes: Inside the White House during the Cuban Missile Crisis.* Cambridge, MA: Belknap Press, 1997.

McAvoy, Thomas T. "Leaders of Democracy." Review of *The Age of Jackson,* by Arthur M. Schlesinger Jr. *The Review of Politics* 8, no. 1 (1946): 135–137. http:// www.jstor.org/stable/1403976.

———. Review of *Orestes Brownson: A Pilgrim's Promise,* by Arthur M. Schlesinger Jr. *The Review of Politics* 1, no. 3 (1939): 364–365. http://www.jstor.org/ stable/1403964.

McKeever, Porter. *Adlai Stevenson: His Life and Legacy.* New York: William Morrow, 1989.

Menand, Louis. "Unpopular Front: American Art and the Cold War." *The New Yorker.* October 17, 2005.

Mend, Louis. "Wild Thing." *The New Yorker.* March 14, 2011.

Merry, Robert. *Taking on the World: Joseph and Stewart Alsop—Guardians of the American Century.* New York: Viking, 1996.

———. *Where They Stand: The American Presidents in the Eyes of the Voters and Historians.* New York: Simon and Schuster, 2012.

Milne, David. *Worldmaking: The Art and Science of American Diplomacy.* New York: Farrar, Straus and Giroux, 2015.

Monda, Antonio. *Do You Believe?: Conversations on God and Religion.* New York: Vintage, 2007.

Morison, Samuel Eliot. *Three Centuries of Harvard.* Cambridge, MA: Belknap Press, 1986.

Morris, Edmund. *Dutch: A Memoir of Ronald Reagan.* London: HarperCollins, 2000.

Munton, Don, and David Welch. *The Cuban Missile Crisis: A Concise History.* Cambridge: Oxford University Press, 2007.

Murray, John, ed. *The Works of Edward Gibbon: Autobiography.* New York: DeFau & Co., 1907.

Nevins, Allan. "At the Roots of Democracy." Review of *The Age of Jackson,* by

Arthur M. Schlesinger, Jr. *New York Times*. September 16, 1945. http://www
.nytimes.com/books/00/11/26/specials/schlesinger-jackson.html.

Newhouse, John. *The Nuclear Age: From Hiroshima to Star Wars*. London: Michael
Joseph, 1989.

"The New Tenure Track." *Harvard Magazine*. September–October 2010. http://harvard
magazine.com/2010/09/the-new-tenure-track.

"New York: Swinging Soothsayer." *Time*. March 3, 1967.

Niebuhr, Reinhold. *Major Works on Religion and Politics*. Edited by Elizabeth Sifton.
New York: The Library of America, 2015.

Nixon, Richard. *In the Arena*. New York: Simon and Schuster, 1990.

Novick, Peter. *That Noble Dream: The Objectivity Questions and the American Historical Profession*. Cambridge: Cambridge University Press, 1988.

Nuechterlein, James A. "Arthur M. Schlesinger, Jr., and the Discontents of Postwar
American Liberalism." *The Review of Politics 39*, no. 1 (1977): 3–40. http://www
.jstor.org/stable/1406576.

Nunley, Kathie. "The Caffeine Craze of Youth." Layered Curriculum. Accessed July
28, 2008. http://help4teachers.com/caffeine.htm.

Nye, Russel B. Review of *The Age of Jackson,* by Arthur M. Schlesinger Jr. *The American Historical Review* 51, no. 3 (1946): 510–513. http://www.jstor.org/stable/
1840130. DOI:10.2307/1840130.

Oates, Stephen B. "Tribune of the Underclass." Review of *Robert Kennedy and His
Times,* by Arthur M. Schlesinger Jr. *American History* 7, no. 2 (1979): 286–292.
http://www.jstor.org/stable/2701107.

O'Brien, Michael, ed. *The Letters of C. Vann Woodward*. New Haven, CT: Yale University Press, 2013.

O'Brien, Patrick. "Hoover and Historians." *The Annals of Iowa* 49 (1988): 394–402.
http://ir.uiowa.edu/annals-of-iowa/vol49/iss5/5.

O'Donnell, Helen. *The Irish Brotherhood: John F. Kennedy, His Inner Circle, and the
Improbable Rise to the Presidency*. Berkeley, CA: Counterpoint, 2015.

Office of War Information. "Coast to Coast Survey of Drinking Conditions in and
Around Army Camps." Washington, DC: US Government Printing Office, 1942.

"Ohio, Deaths, 1908–1953." Arthur Schlesinger in entry for Katherine Bancroft Schlesinger. July 18 1916. FamilySearch. Citing Columbus, Franklin Co., Ohio, reference fn 42891; FHL microfilm 1,983,750. Accessed September 16, 2015. https://
familysearch.org/ark:/61903/1:1:X8N2-DBN.

"Ohio, Marriages, 1800–1958: Bernhard Schlesinger and Katie Feurle, 20 Feb.
1873." FamilySearch. Citing Greene, Ohio, reference; FHL microfilm 0535126

V. 5–7. Accessed September 16, 2015. https://familysearch.org/ark:/61903/1:1:
XDNW-JYD.

"Oral History Program." John F. Kennedy Presidential Library and Museum. https://
www.jfklibrary.org/Research/About-Our-Collections/Oral-history-program
.aspx.

Osborn, George C. Review of *The Coming of the New Deal, 1933–1935,* by Arthur M.
Schlesinger Jr. *The Annals of the American Academy of Political and Social Science*
324 (1959): 149–150. http://www.jstor.org/stable/1034073.

———. Review of *The Crisis of the Old Order, 1919–1933,* by Arthur M. Schlesinger Jr.
The Annals of the American Academy of Political and Social Science 313 (1957):
153–154. http://www.jstor.org/stable/1031778.

Oser, Alan S. "Ex-Gov. Averell Harriman, Adviser to 4 Presidents, Dies." *New York
Times.* July 27, 1986. http://www.nytimes.com/1986/07/27/obituaries/ex-gov-averell
-harriman-adviser-to-4-presidents-dies.html?pagewanted=all.

Parker, Richard. *John Kenneth Galbraith.* New York: Farrar, Straus and Giroux, 2005.

Plumb, J. H. *The Collected Essays of J. H. Plumb.* Vol. II. *The American Experience.*
Athens: University of Georgia Press, 1989.

Podhoretz, Norman, and Ron Radosh. "Arthur Schlesinger, Jr.: Exchange Between
Norman Podhoretz & Ron Radosh." *History News Network.* March 1, 2007. http://
historynewsnetwork.org/article/36075#sthash.1i8cqQ9E.dpuf.

Poore, Charles. "Books of the Times." *New York Times.* September 1949. http://query
.nytimes.com/gst/abstract.html?res=9A0CEED7173BE23BBC4053DFBF668382
659EDE&legacy=true.

———. "The Presidency Makes Its Rules for Succession." *New York Times.* July 29,
1965.

Prescott, Orville. "Books of the Times." *New York Times.* March 4, 1957.

———. "Books of the Times." *New York Times.* January 5, 1959.

———. "Books of the Times." *New York Times.* September 7, 1960.

"Quotation of the Day." *New York Times.* January 12, 1962. http://timesmachine
.nytimes.com/timesmachine/1962/01/12/87312516.html?pageNumber=36.

Rasenberger, Jim. *The Brilliant Disaster: JFK, Castro and America's Doomed Invasion
of Cuba's Bay of Pigs.* New York: Charles Scribner's Sons, 2011.

Rauh, Joseph L., Jr. Review of *The Vital Center,* by Arthur M. Schlesinger Jr. *Harvard Law Review* 63, no. 4 (1950): 724–727. http://www.jstor.org/stable/1336015.
DOI:10.2307/1336015.

Reeves, Richard. *President Kennedy: Profile of Power.* New York: Simon and Schuster,
1994.

Reeves, Thomas C. *A Question of Character: A Life of John F. Kennedy.* New York: Free Press, 1991.

"Resolutions Adopted at the Eighth Meeting of Consultation of Ministers of Foreign Affairs, Punta del Este, Uruguay, January 22–31, 1962." *The Avalon Project: Documents in Law, History, and Diplomacy,* Lillian Goldman Law Library at Yale Law School. http://avalon.law.yale.edu/20th_century/intam17.asp.

"Revolution in La Paz." *New York Times.* December 21, 1943. http://timesmachine.nytimes.com/timesmachine/1943/12/21/88587915.html?pageNumber=26.

Reynolds, David. *Empire of Liberty: A New History.* London: Allen Lane, 2009.

———. *Summits: Six Meetings that Shaped the Twentieth Century.* London: Penguin, 2007.

Ribuffo, Leo P. *Right Center Left: Essays in American History.* New Brunswick, NJ: Rutgers University Press, 1992.

Rice, Daniel F. *Reinhold Niebuhr and His Circle of Influence.* Cambridge: Cambridge University Press, 2013.

"Riverside Statue Stumps Historians." *New York Times.* July 1, 1937. http://query.nytimes.com/mem/archive/pdf?res=9807E0DA1F3AE23ABC4953DFB166838C629EDE.

Roberts, Steven V. "Schlesinger and Hughes: Observations On Left Politics." *Harvard Crimson.* February 26, 1963. http://www.thecrimson.com/article/1963/2/26/schlesinger-and-hughes-observations-on-left/.

Rodgers, Daniel T. *Age of Fracture.* Cambridge, MA: Belknap Press of Harvard University Press, 2011.

Rome, Adam. " 'Give Earth a Chance': The Environmental Movement and the Sixties." *The Journal of American History* 90, no. 2 (2003): 525–554. DOI: 10.2307/3659443.

Ross, Irwin. Review of *The Vital Center,* by Arthur M. Schlesinger Jr. *Commentary.* October 1, 1949. https://www.commentarymagazine.com/articles/the-vital-center-by-arthur-m-schlesinger-jr.

Rovere, Richard, and Arthur Schlesinger. *General MacArthur and President Truman: The Struggle for Control of American Foreign Policy.* New Brunswick, NJ: Transaction, 1992.

Rusk, Dean. *As I Saw It: A Secretary of State's Memoirs.* London: I. B. Tauris, 1991.

Rusk, Howard. "Health of Presidents." *New York Times.* August 6, 1967. http://timesmachine.nytimes.com/timesmachine/1967/08/06/94109957.html?pageNumber=56.

Rutland, Robert Allen, ed. *Clio's Favorites: Leading Historians of the United States, 1945–2000.* Columbia: University of Missouri Press, 2000.

Sabine, George H. Review of *The Vital Center,* by Arthur M. Schlesinger Jr. *The Philosophical Review* 59, no. 2 (1950): 246–249. http://www.jstor.org/stable/2181509. DOI: 10.2307/2181509.

Sacher, John. Review of *Jacksonian Antislavery and the Politics of Free Soil, 1824–1854,* by Jonathan H. Earle. *Indiana Magazine of History* 101, no. 4 (2005): 383–384. http://www.jstor.org/stable/27792675.

Salinger, Pierre. *With Kennedy.* New York: Doubleday, 1966.

Sandford, Christopher. *Harold and Jack: The Remarkable Friendship of Prime Minister Harold Macmillan and President Kennedy.* Amherst, NY: Prometheus, 2014.

Santmyer, Helen Hooven. *Ohio Town: A Portrait of Xenia.* New Yorker: Harper, 1961.

Saunders, Frances Stonor. *Who Paid the Piper? The CIA and the Cultural Cold War.* London: Granta, 1999.

Schaffer, Howard B. *Chester Bowles: New Dealer in the Cold War.* Cambridge, MA: Harvard University Press, 1993.

Schlesinger, Alexandra Emmet. Interview with Richard Aldous. Personal interview. June 17, 2015.

Schlesinger, Andrew. Interview with Richard Aldous. Personal interview. March 9, 2014.

———. *Veritas: Harvard College and the American Experience.* Chicago: Ivan R. Dee, 2005.

Schlesinger, Arthur M., Jr. "Orestes Brownson: An American Marxist Before Marx." *The Sewanee Review* 47, no. 3 (1939): 317–323. http://www.jstor.org/stable/27535562.

———. "The Problem of Richard Hildreth." *New England Quarterly* 13, no. 2 (1940): 223–245.

———. *The Age of Jackson.* Boston: Little, Brown, 1945.

———. "The U.S. Communist Party." *Life.* July 29, 1946.

———. "The Supreme Court: 1947." *Fortune.* January 3, 1947.

———. "What is Loyalty? A Difficult Question." *New York Times.* November 2, 1947. https://www.nytimes.com/books/00/11/26/specials/schlesinger-difficult.html.

———. "Not Left, Not Right, But a Vital Center." *New York Times.* April 4, 1948. https://www.nytimes.com/books/00/11/26/specials/schlesinger-centermag.html.

———. *The Vital Center: The Politics of Freedom.* Boston: Houghton Mifflin, 1949.

———. "The Future of Liberalism: The Challenge of Abundance." *Reporter.* May 3, 1956.

———. *The Crisis of the Old Order, 1919–1933: The Age of Roosevelt,* vol. 1 (Boston: Houghton Mifflin, 1957).

———. *The Coming of the New Deal, 1933–1935: The Age of Roosevelt,* vol. 2 (Boston: Houghton Mifflin, 1958).

———. *The Politics of Upheaval, 1935–1936: The Age of Roosevelt*, vol. 3 (Boston: Houghton Mifflin, 1960).

———. *Kennedy or Nixon: Does It Make Any Difference?* (New York: Macmillan, 1960).

———. "The Historian and History." *Foreign Affairs* (April 1963). https://www.foreignaffairs.com/articles/1963-04-01/historian-and-history.

———. *A Thousand Days: John F. Kennedy in the White House.* Boston: Houghton Mifflin, 1965.

———. "A Thousand Days: The First Close Portrait of John Kennedy." *Life.* July 16, 1965.

———. "A Father Remembered." *Saturday Review.* November 27, 1965.

———. "Origins of the Gold War." *Foreign Affairs* 46 (1967): 22–52.

———. "The Vital Center Reconsidered." *Encounter.* September 1970, 89–93.

———. "The Historian as Participant." *Daedalus* 100, no. 2 (1971): 339–358. http://www.jstor.org/stable/20024007.

———. *The Imperial Presidency.* Boston: Houghton Mifflin, 1973.

———. *Robert Kennedy and His Times.* Boston: Houghton Mifflin, 1978.

———. "The Political Galbraith." *Journal of Post-Keynesian Economics* 7, no. 1 (1984): 7–17. http://www.jstor.org/stable/4537860.

———. "Arthur M. Schlesinger, Sr.: New Viewpoints in American History Revisited." *The New England Quarterly* 61, no. 4 (1988).

———. "The Ages of Jackson." *New York Review of Books.* December 7, 1989. http://www.nybooks.com/articles/1989/12/07/the-ages-of-jackson/.

———. "Reinhold Niebuhr's Long Shadow." *New York Times.* June 22, 1992. http://www.nytimes.com/1992/06/22/opinion/reinhold-niebuhr-s-long-shadow.html.

———. *The Disuniting of America: Reflections on a Multicultural Society.* New York: W. W. Norton, 1998.

———. *The Cycles of American History.* Boston: Mariner Books, 1986; New York: Mariner Books, 1999.

———. *A Life in the 20th Century: Innocent Beginnings, 1917–1950.* Boston: Houghton Mifflin, 2000.

———. *War and the American Presidency.* New York: W. W. Norton, 2005.

———. "Forgetting Reinhold Niebuhr." *New York Times.* September 18, 2005. http://www.nytimes.com/2005/09/18/books/review/forgetting-reinhold-niebuhr.html?_r=0.

———. "History's Folly." *New York Times.* January 1, 2007. http://www.nytimes.com/2007/01/01/opinion/01schlesinger.html.

———. *Journals: 1952–2000.* Edited by Andrew Schlesinger and Stephen Schlesinger. New York: Penguin, 2008.

———. "The Causes of the Civil War." In *The Politics of Hope and The Bitter Heritage: American Liberalism in the 1960s.* Edited by Sean Wilentz. Princeton, NJ: Princeton University Press, 2008.

———. *Jacqueline Kennedy: Historic Conversations on Life with John F. Kennedy: Interviews with Arthur M. Schlesinger Jr.* Edited by Michael Beschloss. New York: Hyperion, 2011.

———. *The Letters of Arthur Schlesinger, Jr.* Edited by Andrew Schlesinger and Stephen Schlesinger. New York: Random House, 2013.

Schlesinger, Arthur M., Sr. *In Retrospect: The History of a Historian.* New York: Harcourt, Brace and World, 1963.

———. *New Viewpoints in American History.* New York: Macmillan, 1922. https://archive.org/details/newviewpointsina00sch.

———. *Paths to the Present.* New York: Macmillan, 1964.

Schlesinger, Christina. Interview with Richard Aldous. Personal interview. April 16, 2014.

———. Email to Richard Aldous. Personal email. October 26, 2016.

Schlesinger, Marian Cannon. Interview with Richard Aldous. Personal interview. March 9, 2014.

———. *I Remember: A Life of Politics, Painting and People.* Cambridge, MA: TidePool Press, 2012.

———. *Snatched from Oblivion: A Cambridge Memoir.* Boston: Little, Brown, 1979.

Schlesinger, Robert. "Arthur Schlesinger Jr.'s Not-So-Secret Career as a Spy." *US News & World Report.* August 20, 2008.

———. *White House Ghosts: Presidents and Their Speechwriters.* New York: Simon and Schuster, 2008.

Schlesinger, Stephen. Interview with Richard Aldous. Personal interview. January 17, 2014.

"Schlesinger Captures National Book Award." *Harvard Crimson.* March 17, 1966. http://www.thecrimson.com/article/1966/3/17/schlesinger-captures-national-book-award-parthur/.

"Schlesinger Given Briggs Prize for History 1 Essay." *Harvard Crimson.* March 7, 1935. http://www.thecrimson.com/article/1935/3/7/schlesinger-given-briggs-prize-for-history.

Schneider, Herbert W. Review of *Orestes Brownson: Yankee, Radical, Catholic,* by Theodore Maynard. *Church History* 13, no. 4 (1944): 322–325. http://www.jstor.org/stable/3160246.

Schultz, Kevin. *Buckley and Mailer: The Difficult Friendship That Shaped the Sixties.* New York: W. W. Norton, 2015.

Schwartz, Madeline. "Sesquicentennial Soirée: Harvard Advocate alumni take stock." *The Harvard Magazine.* September/October, 2016. http://harvardmagazine.com/2016/09/sesquicentennial-soiree.

Seaborg, Glenn T. *Kennedy, Khrushchev, and the Test Ban.* Berkeley: University of California Press, 1981.

Selverstone, Marc J. *A Companion to John F. Kennedy.* Hoboken, NJ: Wiley, 2014.

Semple, Robert B., Jr. "A Historian's Valedictory." *New York Times.* March 2, 2007. http://archive.boston.com/ae/theater_arts/articles/2007/03/01/arthur_schlesinger_remembered.

Severo, Richard. "Marieta Tree, Former U.N. Delegate, Dies at 74." *New York Times.* August 16, 1991. http://www.nytimes.com/1991/08/16/nyregion/marietta-tree-former-un-delegate-dies-at-74.html.

Shannon, William. "Controversial Historian of the Age of Kennedy." *New York Times.* November 21, 1965.

Shaw, John T. *JFK in the Senate: Pathway to the Presidency.* New York: Palgrave Macmillan, 2013.

Smith, Amanda, ed. *Hostage to Fortune: The Letters of Joseph P. Kennedy.* New York: Viking, 2001.

Smith, Culver H. Review of *The Age of Jackson,* by Arthur M. Schlesinger Jr. *The Journal of Southern History* 12, no. 1 (1946): 123–126. http://www.jstor.org/stable/2197735. DOI: 10.2307/2197735.

Smith, Jean Edward. *Eisenhower in War and Peace.* New York: Random House, 2012.

——. *FDR.* New York: Random House, 2008.

Smith, Jordan Michael. "The Philosopher of the Post-9/11 Era." *Slate.* October 17, 2011. http://www.slate.com/articles/arts/books/2011/10/john_diggins_why_niebuhr_now_reviewed_how_did_he_become_the_phil.html.

Sorensen, Ted. *Counselor: A Life at the Edge of History.* New York: Harper, 2008.

Sorensen, Theodore C. Interview by Carl Kaysen. "Theodore C. Sorensen Oral History Interview—JFK #6, 5/20/1964." John F. Kennedy Presidential Library and Museum. https://www.jfklibrary.org/Asset-Viewer/Archives/JFKOH-TCS-06.aspx.

——. *Kennedy.* New York: Harper and Row, 1965.

Sparrow, James T., William J. Novak, and Stephen W. Sawyer, eds. *Boundaries of the State in U.S. History.* Chicago: University of Chicago Press, 2015.

Star, Alexander. "His Liberal Imagination." Q&A with Arthur M. Schlesinger. *New York Times.* Nov. 26, 2000. http://www.nytimes.com/books/00/11/26/reviews/001126.26int.html.

Steele, John L. "Two Books By and About Stevenson." Review of *The New America,* by Adlai E. Stevenson. *New Republic.* September 2, 1957.

Stegner, Wallace. *The Uneasy Chair: A Biography of Bernard DeVoto.* New York: Doubleday, 1974.

Stern, Sheldon M. *The Cuban Missile Crisis in American Memory: Myth versus Reality.* Stanford, CA: Stanford University Press, 2012.

Stoll, Ira. *JFK: Conservative.* Boston: Houghton Mifflin Harcourt, 2013.

Strand, William. "Senate Kills Dry Rider to 18 Year Draft." *Chicago Tribune.* October 23, 1942. http://archives.chicagotribune.com/1942/10/23/page/1/article/senate -kills-dry-rider-to-18-year-draft.

Sullivan, Patricia. "Gilbert Harrison, 92, Longtime Editor of New Republic." *Washington Post.* January 8, 2008. http://www.washingtonpost.com/wp-dyn/content/ article/2008/01/07/AR2008010703193.html.

Swaim, Barton. "Sifting the Wheat from the Chaff." Review of *Major Works on Religion and Politics,* by Reinhold Niebuhr. *Wall Street Journal.* June 26, 2015. http:// www.wsj.com/articles/SB11292601245819683363204581056111883885634.

Swisher, Carl Brent. Review of *The Age of Jackson,* by Arthur M. Schlesinger Jr. *The New England Quarterly* 19, no. 1 (1946): 122–123. http://www.jstor.org/ stable/361216. DOI:10.2307/361216.

Tanenhaus, Sam. *Whittaker Chambers.* New York: Random House, 1997.

Taylor, P. A. "Samuel Eliot Morison: Historian." *Journal of American Studies* 11, no. 1 (1977).

Thistlethwaite, Frank. Review of *The Crisis of the Old Order, 1919–1933,* by Arthur M. Schlesinger Jr. *The English Historical Review* 73 (1958): 329–331. http://www.jstor .org/stable/556989.

Thomas, Robert Jr. "Nixons Reported to Have Bought East Side House." *New York Times.* October 5, 1979. http://www.nytimes.com/1979/10/05/archives/nixons -reported-to-have-bought-east-side-house-drop-condominium.html.

Tinsley, James A. Review of *The Coming of the New Deal, 1933–1935,* by Arthur M. Schlesinger Jr. *The Journal of Southern History* 25, no. 3 (1959): 407–409. http:// www.jstor.org/stable/2954784. DOI:10.2307/2954784.

Troy, Tevi. *Intellectuals and the American Presidency: Philosophers, Jesters, or Technicians?* Lanham, MD: Rowman and Littlefield, 2002.

Turner, Frederick Jackson. *Rereading Frederick Jackson Turner: "The Significance of the Frontier in American History" and Other Essays.* New Haven, CT: Yale University Press, 1994.

"United States World War I Draft Registration Cards, 1917–1918." *FamilySearch.* Citing Columbus City no 4, Ohio, United States, NARA microfilm publication M1509. Washington, DC: National Archives and Records Administration; FHL microfilm 1,832,032. https://familysearch.org/ark:/61903/1:1:K6FN-D4N.

Vaughn, Stephen. *Reagan in Hollywood: Movies and Politics*. Cambridge: Cambridge University Press, 1994.

Walton, Calder. *Empire of Secrets: British Intelligence, the Cold War, and the Twilight of Empire*. New York: Overlook Press, 2013.

Ward, Timothy Jack. "Changes to Union Divide Harvard." *New York Times*. February 15, 1996. http://www.nytimes.com/1996/02/15/garden/changes-to-union-divide -harvard.html.

Warren, Sidney. Review of *The Imperial Presidency*, by Arthur M. Schlesinger Jr. *Journal of American History* 61, no. 4 (1975): 1156–1157. http://www.jstor.org/ stable/1890722.

Washburn, Wilcomb E. "Samuel Eliot Morison, Historian." *The William and Mary Quarterly* 36, no. 3 (July 1979).

"What Are the Outstanding Books of 1945?" *ALA Bulletin* 39, no. 12 (1945): 509–510. http://www.jstor.org/stable/25692238.

White, Theodore H. *In Search of History*. New York: Harper and Row, 1978.

———. *The Making of the President: 1960*. New York: Harper Perennial, 2009.

"White Paper on Cuba." *New York Times*. April 5, 1961.

Whitfield, Stephen J. *The Culture of the Cold War*. Baltimore: Johns Hopkins University Press, 1996.

Wilentz, Sean. *The Rise of American Democracy: Jefferson to Lincoln*. New York: W. W. Norton, 2005.

Wills, Garry. "Fierce in His Loyalties and Enmities." Review of *Robert Kennedy and His Times*, by Arthur M. Schlesinger Jr. *New York Times*. November 12, 1978. http://www.nytimes.com/books/00/11/26/specials/schlesinger-robert.html.

———. "A Pattern of Rising Power." Review of *The Imperial Presidency*, by Arthur M. Schlesinger Jr. *New York Times*. November 18, 1973. http://www.nytimes.com/ books/00/11/26/specials/schlesinger-imperial.html.

Wilmer, Ted, ed. *Listening In: The Secret White House Recordings of John. F. Kennedy*. New York: Hyperion, 2012.

Winkler, Allan M. *The Politics of Propaganda: The Office of War Information, 1942–1945*. New Haven, CT: Yale University Press, 1978.

Winks, Robin. *Cloak and Gown: Scholars in the Secret War, 1939–1961*. New Haven, CT: Yale University Press, 1987.

Wolfensberger, Donald R. "The Return of the Imperial Presidency?" *The Wilson Quarterly* 26, no. 2 (2002): 36–41. http://www.jstor.org/stable/40260602.

Wollons, Roberta. Review of *Before Head Start: The Iowa Station and America's Children*, by Hamilton Cravens. *Isis* 85, no. 4 (December 1994). http://www.jstor.org/ stable/235351.

Woods, Randall Bennett. *Fulbright.* Cambridge: Cambridge University Press, 1995.

Woolner, David, and Jack Thompson. *Progressivism in America: Past, Present, and Future.* Corby, UK: Oxford University Press, 2015.

"Woolworth Building." Cass Gilbert Society. http://www.cassgilbertsociety.org/works/nyc-woolworth-bldg.

Wreszin, Michael. "Arthur Schlesinger, Jr., Scholar-activist in Cold War America: 1946–1956." *Salmagundi* 63/64 (1984): 255–285. http://www.jstor.org/stable/40547663.

Wright, David McCord. Review of *The Vital Center,* by Arthur M. Schlesinger Jr. *The American Economic Review* 41, no. 1 (1951): 217–219. http://www.jstor.org/stable/1815990.

Wyatt, Wilson W. *Whistle Stops: Adventures in Public Life.* Lexington: University Press of Kentucky, 1985.

Zimmer, Louis B. *The Vietnam War Debate: Hans J. Morgenthau and the Attempt to Halt the Drift Into Disaster.* Lanham, MD: Lexington Books, 2011.

Zuckerman, Laurence. "How the C.I.A. Played Dirty Tricks with Culture." *New York Times.* March 18, 2000. http://www.nytimes.com/2000/03/18/books/how-the-cia-played-dirty-tricks-with-culture.html?pagewanted=all.

INDEX

Note: In the index, "AMS Jr." refers to Arthur M. Schlesinger, Jr.